George Sandys

Sandys Travels

Containing an history of the original and present state of the Turkish empire

George Sandys

Sandys Travels
Containing an history of the original and present state of the Turkish empire

ISBN/EAN: 9783337244576

Printed in Europe, USA, Canada, Australia, Japan

Cover: Foto ©Andreas Hilbeck / pixelio.de

More available books at **www.hansebooks.com**

Sandys Travels,

CONTAINING AN

HISTORY

OF THE

Original and present State of the *Turkish* EMPIRE:
Their Laws, Government, Policy, Military Force,
Courts of Justice, and Commerce.

The *MAHOMETAN* RELIGION and CEREMONIES.

A DESCRIPTION of *CONSTANTINOPLE*,
The Grand Signior's *seraglio*, and his manner of living:

ALSO,

Of *GREECE*, With the RELIGION and CUSTOM
of the *GRECIANS*.

Of *ÆGYPT*; the Antiquity, Hieroglyphicks, Rites, Customs
Discipline, and Religion of the *Ægyptians*.

A VOYAGE on the River *NYLUS*:

Of *Armenia*, *Grand Cairo*, *Rhodes*, the *Pyramides*, *Colossus*;
The former flourishing and present State of *ALEXANDRIA*.

A Description of the HOLY-LAND; of the Jews, and several
Sects of *Christians* living there; of *Jerusalem*, sepulchre of *Christ*,
Temple of *Solomon*; and what else either of Antiquity,
or worth observation.

LASTLY,

ITALY described, and the Islands adjoining; as *Cyprus*, *Crete*
Malta, *Sicilia*, the *Æolian* Islands; Of *Rome*, *Venice*, *Naples*, *Syracusa*,
Messena, *Ætna*, *Scylla*, and *Charybdis*; and other places of Note.

Illustrated with Fifty Graven Maps and Figures.

The Seventh Edition.

LONDON,
Printed for *John Williams Junior*, at the Crown in *Little-Britain*. 1673.

SIR,

THE *Eminence of the degree wherein God and Nature hath placed you, doth allure the eyes; and the hopefulness of your Virtues, win the love of all men. For virtue being in a private person an exemplary ornament; advanceth it self in a Prince to a publick blessing. And, as the Sun to the world, so bringeth it both light and life to a Kingdom; a light of direction by glorious example, and a life of joy through a gracious Government. From the just and serious consideration whereof, there springeth in minds not brutish, a thankful correspondence of affection and duty; still pressing to express themselves in endeavours of service. Which also hath caused me (most noble Prince) not furnished of better means, to offer in humble zeal to your Princely view these my doubled Travels; once with some toil and danger performed, and now recorded with sincerity and diligence. The parts I speak of are the most renowned Countries and Kingdoms: once the Seats of most glorious and triumphant Empires; the Theatres of valour and heroical actions; the soils enriched with all earthly felicities; the places where Nature hath produced her wonderful works; where Arts and Sciences have been invented and perfected; where wisdom, virtue, policy, and civility have been planted, have flourished: and lastly, where God himself did place his own Common-wealth, gave Laws and Oracles, inspired his Prophets, sent Angels to converse with men; above all, where the Son of God descended*

to become man; where he honoured the earth with his beautiful steps, wrought the work of our Redemption, triumphed over death, and ascended into glory. Which Countries, once so glorious and famous for their happy estate, are now through vice and ingratitude, become the most deplored spectacles of extream misery; the wild beasts of mankind having broken in upon them, and rooted out all civility, and the pride of a stern and barbarous Tyrant possessing the Thrones of ancient and just Dominion. Who aiming only at the height of greatness and sensuality, hath in tract of time reduced so great and goodly a part of the world, to that lamentable distress and servitude, under which (to the astonishment of the understanding beholders) it now faints and groaneth. Those rich lands at this present remain waste and overgrown with bushes, receptacles of wild beasts, of thieves and murderers, large Territories dispeopled, or thinly inhabited; good Cities made desolate; sumptuous buildings become ruines, glorious Temples either subverted, or prostituted to impiety; true Religion discountenanced and oppressed, all Nobility extinguished; no light of learning permitted, nor virtue cherished: violence and rapine insulting over all, and leaving no security save to an abject mind, and unlook'd on poverty. Which calamities of theirs, so great and deserved are to the rest of the world as threatning instructions. For assistance wherein, I have not only related what I saw of their present condition, but so far as conveniency might permit, presented a brief view of their former estates, and first antiquities of those people and countries: thence to draw a right image of the frailty of man, the mutability of whatsoever is worldly; and assurance that as there is nothing unchangeable saving God, so nothing stable but by his Grace and Protection. Accept, Great Prince, these weak endeavours of a strong desire: which shall be always devoted to do your Highness all acceptable service, and ever rejoice in your prosperity and happiness.

GEORGE SANDYS.

A
RELATION
OF A
JOURNEY;
CONTAINING

A Defcription of the *Turkifh* Empire of *Egypt*, of the *Holy Land*, of the remote Parts of *Italy*, and ISLANDS adjoyning.

THE FIRST BOOK.

Began my Journey through *France*, hard upon the time when that execrable Murther was committed upon the perfon of *Henry* the Fourth, by an obfcure Varlet, even in the ftreets of his principal City, by day, and then when Royally attended; to fhew that there is none fo contemptible, that contemneth his own life, but is the mafter of another mans. Triumphs were interrupted by Funerals, and mens minds did labour with fearful expectations. The Princes of the Blood difcontented, the Nobles factious: thofe of the Religion daily threatned, and nightly fearing a Maffacre. Mean-while a number of Souldiers are drawn by fmall numbers into the City to confront all outrages.

France I forbear to fpeak of, and the lefs remote parts of *Italy*, daily furveyed and exactly related. At *Venice* I will begin my Journal. From whence we departed on the 20. of *Augufti* 1610. in the little Defence of *London*. Two days after we touched at *Rovigno*, a Town of *Iftria*, and under the *Venetians*, high-mounted on a Hill, not unfruitful in Olives; the Haven convenient and guarded with a Caftle. Here thofe that are bound for *Venice*, do take a Pilot for their fecurer entrance at the Bars of *Malamocco*. The Town is poor (as are the reft thereabout) by reafon of the Neighbourhood of *Venice*, fome twenty leagues diftant, which doth draw unto it the general Commerce: they prohibiting all Traffick elfewhere throughout the whole Gulph. The Country adjoyning, mountainous and wide; yet celebrated for Quarries of excellent Marble, which do fo adorn the *Venetian* Palaces: one Mountain furmounting the reft, called *Monte majore*, firft difcovered by the Sailer, abounding with rare and far-fought Phyfical Simples. The *Iftrians* are faid to defcend of the *Colchians*, of thofe that were fent by *Oeta* in purfuit of the *Argonauts*. Their chief City is called *Cape d'Iftria*, heretofore *Juftinopolis* of *Juftinian* the Builder,

This

This Sea (now the Gulph of *Venice*) was formerly named *Adriaticum* of *Adria*, a famous City built by the *Thuscans* at the mouth of *Eridanus*.

Olim ingens decus Hesperiæ, lux addita terræ,
Eridani cujus proluit unda pedes :
Nunc vix nomen habet, lethoque informe cadaver,
Et famulis fordens Adria putret aquis.
Translatum est alio Imperium titulique vetusti :
Ecce novos ditat prisca ruina lares.
Dira tamen frustra facias fortuna superbos.
Discite quam valeant sceptra manere diu.
Nunc igitur melius mea res : secura timoris,
Cum vigeo, fortis lege soluta meæ.

J. C. Scaliger.

The pride of Italy, that did bestow
On Earth a beauty, washt by silver Po :
Scarce nam'd, a deform'd carcass, noysom steams
Now Adria vents, being foul in her own streams.
Empire, and title, both from thee are born :
And thy old ruines newer Lar's adorn.
Fortune thou falsly liftest up on high :
Of Scepters see the perpetuity !
In better state now stand I ; dispossest
Of fears : from my hard destinies releast.

Of this the there born Emperour *Adrian* received his name. The Gulph divideth *Italy* from *Illyria*, joyning East-ward with the *Mediterraneum*, about the Cape of *Otranto* : being seven hundred miles in length, and sevenscore in latitude. It affordeth few Harbors unto *Italy*, (*Ancona, Brundusium*, and *Otranto*, the principal, and almost only) but many to the opposite shore, with multitudes of Islands. A Sea tempestuous and unfaithful : at an instant incensed with sudden gusts ; but chiefly with the Southern winds.

Quo non arbiter Adriæ
Major, tollere seu ponere vult freta.
*Hor.*l. 1. *Ode* 3.

On Adria none more great than those :
Would they enrage, or scar compose.

But more dreadful are the Northern, beating upon the harbourless shore. The *Venetians* are Lords of this Sea ; but not without contention with the Papacy. On Ascension-day the Duke, accompanied with the *Clarissimo's* of that Signiory, is rowed thither in the *Bucentoro* , a triumphal Galley , richly and exquisitely guilded : above there is a room (beneath which they row) comprehending the whole length and breadth of that Galley, near the Poup a Throne ; the rest accommodated with seats, where he solemnly espouseth the Sea, confirmed by a Ring thrown therein : the Nuptial pledge and Symbole of subjection. This Ceremony received a beginning from that same Sea-battel fought and won by the *Venetians*, under the conduct of *Sebastiano Zani*, against the Forces of *Frederick Barbarossa*, in the quarrel of Pope *Alexander* the Third : who flying the Emperours fury, in the habit of a Cook, repaired to *Venice*, and there lived long disguised in the Monastery of *Charity*. *Zani* returning in Triumph with the Emperours Son, was met by the Pope, and saluted in this manner : Here take, Oh *Zani*, this Ring of Gold, and by giving it to the Sea, oblige it unto thee. A Ceremony that shall on this day be yearly observed, both by thee and thy Successors : that posterity may know how you have purchased the Dominion thereof by your valours, and made it subject unto you, as a Wife to her Husband. But the Pirates hereabout do now more than share with them in that Soveraignty, who gather such courage from the timerousness of divers , that a little Frigat will often not fear to venture on an *Argosie* : nay , some of them will not abide the encounter ; but run ashore before the pursuer : (as if a Whale should flye from a Dolphin) glad that with wrack of Ship, and loss of Goods they may prolong a despised life, or retain undeserved liberty.

We sailed all along in the sight of *Dalmatia*, which lyeth between *Istria* and *Epirus*, called anciently *Illyria*, of *Ilyrius* the Son of *Cadmus* , afterwards *Dalmatia*, of the City *Dalminium* ; and at this day *Sclavonia*, of the *Sclavi*, a people of *Sarmatia* : who leaving their own homes in the Reign of *Justinian*, were planted by him in *Thracia*, and afterward in the days of *Mauritius* and *Phocas*, became possessors of his Country. Patient they are of labour, and able of body. The meaner sort will tug lustily at an Oar; and are by their Soveraigns of *Venice* (such as remain under that State) imployed to that purpose. The Women married not till the age of 24. nor the men until 30. perhaps the cause of their strength, and so big proportions : or for that bred in a mountainous Country , who are generally observed to over-size those that dwell on low levels. Three thousand Horsmen of this Country, and the Islands hereabout are inrolled in the *Venetian Militia*. They dissent not from the *Greek* Church in their Religion,

LIB. I.   *Illyria. Corcyra. Leucadia.*   3

gion. Throughout the North part of the World their Language is understood and spoken: even from thence almost to the Confines of *Tartaria*. The men wear half-sleeved Gowns of Violet-cloth; with Bonnets of the same. They nourish only a lock of hair on the crown of their heads, the rest all shaven. The Women wear theirs not long, and dye them black for the most part. Their chief City is *Ragusa* (heretofore *Epidaurus*) a Common-wealth of it self: famous for Merchandise and plenty of Shipping. Many small Islands belong thereunto, but little of the Continent. They pay Tribute to the *Turk*, 14000 Zecchins yearly, and spend as much more upon them in gifts and entertainment: sending the Grand Signior every year a Ship loaden with Pitch for the use of his Gallies, whereby they purchase their peace, and a discharge of Duties throughout the *Ottoman* Empire.

Corfu, the first Island of note that we pass by, lyeth in the *Ionian* Sea; stretching East and West in form of a Bow: 54 miles long, 24 broad, and distant about 12 from the Main of *Epirus*. Called formerly *Cocyra*, of *Corcyra* the Daughter of *Æsopus* there buried: but more anciently *Phæacia*. Celebrated by *Homer* for the shipwrack of *Ulysses*, and Orchards of *Alcinous*.

These at no time do their rare fruits forego:
Still breathing Zephyrus makes some to grow
Others to ripen. Growing fruits supply
The gathered: and succeed so orderly.

Ex iis fructus nunquam perit, neque deficit,
Hyeme, neque æstate, toto anno durant, sed sane semper
Zephyrus spirans h.ec crescere facit aliaque maturescere.
Pirum post pirum senescit, pomum post pomum,
Porro post uvam uva, ficus post ficum.
Hom. Od. l. 1.

The South part thereof is mountainous, and defective in waters; where they sow little Corn, in that subject to be blasted by the Southern winds, at such times as it floweth: the North part level; the whole adorned with Groves of Oranges, Lemons, Pomegranates, Fig-trees, Olives, and the like; enriched with excellent Wines and abundance of Honey. Upon the North-side stands a City that takes the name of the Island, with a Castle strongly seated on a high Rock, which joyneth by an Isthmus to the Land, and impregnably fortified. The *Turks* have testified as much in their many repulses. It is the Chair of an Archbishop: inhabited for the most by *Cretians*, as is the whole Island, and subject to the *Venetians*.

St. *Maura* lyeth next unto this: once adjoyning to the Continent, and separated by the labour of the Inhabitants: yet no further removed than by a Bridge to be past into. Called it was formerly *Leucadia*, of a white Rock which lyeth before it, towards *Cephalenia*, on which stood the Temple of *Apollo*: from whence by leaping into the Sea, it is said, that such as unfortunately loved, were cured of that fury. To this the Poetress *Sappho* was thus advised.

Hic to Ambracia, since unequal fires
Consume thee. From a rock there that aspires:
Phœbus doth all the ample deep survey:
Men call't Actæum and Leucadia.
Deucalion mad for Pyrrha, grief to ease,
Leapt down from thence, and safely prest th' Seas.
Forthwith chang'd Love fled from the careless breast
Of drench't Deucalion, and his fury ceast.
That place retains this vertue: thither haste,
And fear not from on high thy self to cast.

———Quoniam non ignibus æquis
Uteris, Ambracia est terra petenda tibi.
Phœbus ab excelso, quantum patet, aspicit æquor,
Actæum populi, Leucadiumque vocent.
Hinc se Deucalion Pyrrhæ succensus amore
Misit & illæso corpore pressit aquas.
Nec mora, versus amor fugit lentissima mersi
Pectora: Deucalion igne levatus erat.
Hanc legem locus ille tenet: pete protinus altam
Leucada: nec saxo desiluisse time.

Ovid. Ep. 21.

And so she did, if we may credit *Menander*.

Who with ambitious glory flung
And scorn'd Loves fury, head-long flung
Her self from high cliff, after she,
Phœbus, had made her vows to thee.

Superbam nimium venata gloriam,
Furioso desiderio præcipitem dedit
Ab aerio sese scopulo, cum Rex tibi
(Phœbe) vota secisset.

Others more curious in the search of Antiquities, do attribute the first doing thereof unto *Cephalus* to: the Love of *Ptereela*. It is said, *Artemisia* after the death of *Mausolus*, contemned by *Dar Janus* a Youth of *Abydos*, in revenge there of pulled forth his eyes notwithstanding still desperately loving, repaired to this Rock for a remedy: who perished in the fall, and had here her sepulture. It was a custom amongst the *Leucadians* in their yearly solemnities, as a propitiatory Sacrifice to *Apollo*, to throw some one from the top, condemned before for his offences, stuck with all sorts of feathers, and birds tyed about him, that his fall by their flutterings might become the less violent: received below by a number in Boats, and so thrust out of their confines. In this Island they have a City inhabited for the most part by *Jews*: received from *Bajazet* the second, at such time as they were expulsed *Spain* by King *Ferdinand*.

Val de Compare, a little beyond presenteth her rocky Mountains, containing in circuit about fifty miles: now inhabited by Exiles and Pirates, once called *Ithaca*, so celebrated for the birth of *Ulysses*; who was not only Lord of that barren Island, but

At Ulysses ducebat Cephalenenses magnanimos,
Qui Ithacam tenebant & Neritum frondosam:
Et Crocylia habitabant & Ægilipam asperam,
Quique Zacynthum habitabant & qui Samum incolebant.
Quique Epirum habitabant & oppositam Continentem incolebant.
His quidem Ulysses imperabat Jovi consilio par.
Homer. Iliad. 2.

The valiant Cephalenians, and they Who Egilipa, Same, Ithaca, Woody Neritus, watry Crocatyl, Zacynthus and Epire possess: who still Th' opposed Continent, Ulysses led In counsel like to Jove.——

between this and the mouth of the Gulph of *Lepanto* (once named the Gulph of *Corinth*) lie certain little Islands, or rather great Rocks, now called *Curzolari*, heretofore *Echinades*: made famous by that memorable Sea-battel there obtained against the *Turk* by *Don John* of *Austria*, in the year 1571. and sung by a crowned Muse.

We sailed close by *Cephalenia*, retaining that ancient name of *Cephalus*, the Son of *Deioneus*; who banished *Athens* for the unfortunate slaughter of *Procris*, repaired to *Thebes*, and accompanying *Amphitryo* in his Wars, made his abode in this Island; which was called formerly *Teleboa* and *Melena*. It is triangular in form, and 160 miles in circumference: the Mountains intermixed with profitable Vallies, and the Woods with Champain. Unwatered with Rivers; and poor in Fountains, but abounding with Wheat, Honey, Currans, Manna, Cheese, Wool, Turkies, excellent Oyl, incomparable (though not long lasting) Muscadines, and Powder for the dying of Scarlet. This grows like a blister on the leaf of the holy Oak a little shrub, yet producing Acorns, being gathered, they rub out of it a certain red dust, that converteth after a while into worms, which they kill with Wine, when they begin to quicken. Amongst her many Harbours, *Argostoli* is the principal & capacious enough for a Navy. The Inhabitants of this Island are *Grecians*, and *Venetians* their Soveraigns. Having past through the Straights that divide this Island from the next (vulgarly called *Canale del Zant*) on the second of *September* we entred the Haven of *Zacinthus*, and saluted the Castle with our Ordnance.

This Island (900 miles distant from *Venice*) so called of *Zacinthus* the Son of *Dardanus*, and at this day *Zant*; containeth in circuit not past 60 miles. On the South and South-East sides rocky and mountainous, but plain in the midst, and unspeakably fruitful, producing the best Oyl of the World, and excellent strong Wines, both white and red, which they call *Ribolla*. But the chief Riches thereof consisteth in Currans, which draweth hither much Traffick (especially from *England* and *Holland*; for here they know not what to do with them) insomuch that whereas before they were scarce able to free themselves from importunate famine, they now (besides their private gettings, amounting to 150000 Zecchins) do yearly pay unto St. *Mark* 4800 Dollars for Customs and other Duties. It is impossible that so little a portion of Earth, so imployed, should be more beneficial; that mountainous part being barren, and the rest comprised within two or three not very ample Vallies, but those all over-husbanded like an entire Garden. They sow little Corn, as imploying their grounds to better advantages, for which they sometimes suffer, being ready to starve, when the weather continueth for a season tempestuous, and that they cannot fetch their provision, which they have as well of Flesh as of Corn, from *Morea*, being ten leagues distant. They have Salt-pits of their own, and store of fresh water, but little or no wood, though celebrated for the abundance thereof, by *Homer* and *Virgil*. Of which, his *Æneis* r together with the Islands before mentioned.

Woody

Woody Zacinthus, Sea-girt, we descrie,
Dulichium, Same, Neritus cliff hie.
From Ithacan rocks, Laertes land, we fled,
And cutst the soil that dire Ulysses bred.
Anon the Cloud topt Leucata appear'd:
And high Apollo by the sailor fear'd.

> Jam medio apparet fluctu nemorosa Zacynthos,
> Dulichiumque, Sameque, & Neritos ardua saxis.
> Effugimus scopulos Ithacæ, Laertia regna.
> Et terram altricem lævi execramur Ulyssis.
> Mox & Leucatæ nimbosa cacumina montis,
> Et formidatus nautis aperitur Apollo.
> *Virg. Æn. l. 3.*

About the Island there are many Roads, but one only Harbour (if I may so name it, being undefended from the North-East and North-West winds) lying on the North-East side thereof, and opening towards *Moreo*: safe, and of a convenient receipt for Ships, respect we either the number or burden: and much frequented from all parts; who here commonly touch in their going forth, and in their returns. So that you shall not long stay for a passage, be you either bound for *Venice, Constantinople, Tripoly, Alexandria*, the Islands of the Mid-land Sea, or divers places of the Ocean. It is here a custom strictly observed (as also elsewhere within the Straits belonging to the Christians) not to suffer any to traffick, or come ashore, before they have a *Prattick* from the Signiors of Health: which will not be granted until forty days after their arrival, especially if the Ship come from *Turkie*, and bring not a Certificate, that the place from whence they came is free from the infection: if so, perchance their restraint may be shortned: during which time they have a Guardian set over them. They will not suffer a Letter to be delivered, if sealed with thread, before it be opened and aired. If such as come to speak with them do but touch one of the Ships, or sometimes but a Rope, they shall be forced to ascend, and remain there for the time limited, it being death to him that shall come ashore without licence. Notwithstanding, they at request will carry you to the *Lazaretto* (which is in the nature of a Pest-house) there to abide until the date be expired. But if any fall sick amongst them in the mean-season, their *Prattick* is accordingly prolonged. A great inconvenience to the Merchants, but at *Venice* intolerable: where when they have a *Prattick*, they are inforced to unlade at the *Lazaretto*. So under pretence of airing, their Goods are opened; their quantity, quality and condition known; redounding much to their detriments. But for that we came from *Venice*, we were freed from this mischief, and presently suffered to land.

The Town taking or giving a name to the Island, stretcheth along between the West-side of the Haven, and the foot of the Mountain; perhaps a mile in length, in breadth but narrow. The streets unpaved, the building low, by reason of the often Earthquakes whereunto this Island is miserably subject.

When through Earth hollows, the collected wind
Throngs from some part, nor ready vent can find
The vast caves it assails with horrid might:
Earth-quakes percussed men with the affright.
Then eminent ruines those proud structures threat
That most aspire; more safe to be less great.

> Præterea ventus cum per loca subcava terræ
> Collectus parte ex una procumbit, & urget
> Obnixus magnis speluncas viribus altas,
> Incumbit tellus, quo venti prona premit vis.
> Tum supra terram quæ sunt extructa domorum,
> Ad cœlumque magis quanto sunt edita quæque,
> Inclinata minax in eandem prod.ta partem,
> Protractæque trabes impendent ire paratæ.
> *Lucret. l. 6.*

Two hapned during my short abode there, though of small importance. Although the seat of the Town be excessive hot, yet it is happily qualified by a North-East gale that bloweth from Sea most constantly about the midst of the day. Divers of their houses are shadowed with Vines that bear a certain great grape, which in regard of their shape were called *Bumastos* by the *Grecians*, the clusters being of a marvellous greatness. High above the Town, on the top of a steep round Mountain stands the Castle, which over-looketh the Sea, and commandeth the Harbour: a little City of it self, ascended unto by a difficult passage, strong, and well stored with munition. Here a Garrison is kept; supplied by the Towns-men upon each sudden summons. Upon the Wall a Watchman standeth continually, to discover the shipping that approacheth: who hangs out as many Flags as he descryeth Vessels; square if Ships, if Gallies pendants. Here the Governour of the Island hath his residence, whom they call the *Providore*, with two *Configlieri*, all Gentlemen of *Venice* (the consent of two prevailing against the third) together with the Chancellour (who are every third year removed) with other inferiour Officers, where all Causes are adjudged, both Criminal and judicial. Over the Court of Justice there is written this Distichon:

Hic locus odit, amat, punit, conservat, honorat,   *This place doth hate, love, punish, keep, requite,*
Nequitiam, pacem, crimina, jura, probos.   *Voluptuous Riot, Peace, Crimes, Laws, th'upright.*

    The Great *Turk* hath yearly a present of Falcons from the Governour (accompanied, as some say , with 1200 Zecchins) which he calleth a Tribute : it being in his power to distress them at his pleasure, by restraining the relief of Victuals which they have from *Morea*, and his adjoyning Dominions. Whilst we were here, the *Captain Bassa* past by with 60 Gallies : who yearly about this time saileth in circuit, to receive Tribute, suppress Pirates, and to do some Exploit upon the *Maltefes*, *Spaniards*, and *Florentines*, with whom they are only in Hostility. Divers of their Gallies putting into the Haven, were courteously entertained : for the *Venetians* endeavour, as much as in them lies , to keep good quarters with the *Turk* ; not only for the reason aforesaid (which perhaps might intend as far as their City: their Territories, though large and fruitful , too narrow to sustain so populous a State, if unrelieved from *Turkie*, and that their passage into the Mid-land Sea were interrupted) nor for the loss they should sustain by the cessation of Traffick with the *Mahometans* ; but knowing him by dear experience too powerful an Adversary for them by Land, and though they are perhaps strong enough by Sea , yet, should they lose a Navy, their loss were unrecoverable , whereas the *Turk* within the space of a year is able to set forth another.

    The Inhabitants of this Land are in general, *Græcians* (of whom we will speak no more than concerns the particular customs of the place , reserving the rest to our relation of that people) in habit they imitate the *Italians*, but transcend them in their revenges, and infinitely less civil. They will threaten to kill a Merchant that will not buy their Commodities : and make more conscience to break a Fast , than commit a Murther. One of them at our being here, pursued a poor Sailer (an *Englishman*) for offering but to carry a little Bag of Currans aboard uncustomed , and killed him running up a pair of stairs for succour. He is weary of his life that hath a difference with any of them, and will walk abroad after day-light. But cowardize is joyned with their cruely, who dare do nothing, but suddenly upon advantages, and are ever privately armed. Encouraged to villanies by the remissness of their Laws ; for none will lay hands upon an offender , until fourteen days after that he be called to the Scale (an eminent place where one doth stand and publickly cite the offender) who in the mean time hath leisure to make his own peace , or else to absent himself. If then he appear not , they banish him , and propound a reward according to the greatness of the offence , to him that shall either kill or take him alive : and if it be done by one that is banished, his own banishment (the least reward) is released. The Labourers do go into the fields with Swords and Partizans, as if in an Enemies Country, bringing home their Wines and Oyls in Hogs-skins , the insides turn'd outward. It is a custom amongst them to invite certain men unto their Marriages, whom they call Compeers. Every one of these do bestow a Ring, which the Priest doth put upon the Bride and Bridegrooms fingers, interchangeably shifting them ; and so he doth the Garlands of their heads. Of these they are never jealous (an abuse in that kind reputed as detestable a crime , as if committed by a natural Brother) so that they lightly chuse those for their Compeers, that have been formerly suspected too familiar. The Bridegroom entring the Church, sticks his Dagger in the door , held available against Inchantment. For here it is a common practice to bewitch them : made thereby impotent with their Wives, until the Charm be burnt , or otherwise consumed : insomuch that oftentimes (as they say) the Mothers of the betrothed , by way of prevention do bewitch themselves, and again unloose them as soon as the Marriage is consummated. A practice whereof former times have been guilty : some manner perhaps delivered by *Virgil* in these Verses.

Necte tribus nodis ternos Amarylli colores,   *Three knots knit on three threds of different dye,*
Necte Amarylli modo,& Veneris,dic,vincula,necto.   *Haste Amaryll, and say, Loves bonds I tye.*
Eclog. 8.

    And in another following, the Inchantress having made two images of her Beloved, the one of Clay, the other of Wax, and throwing them into the fire, saith :

As his clay, and this wax, the fire the same	Limus ut hic durescit, & hæc ut cera liquescit,
Hardens, and melts; so he, in our loves flame.	Uno eodemque igni; sic nostro Daphnis amore. *Idem.*

The Nuptial sheets (as in some cases commanded by the *Mosaical* Law) are publickly shown, and preserved by their presents as a testimony of their uncorrupted Virginities.

There be here two Bishops: one of the *Greeks*, and another of the *Latines*. The *Greeks* have divers Churches, the principal that of *St. Nicholas* (which giveth to the Haven a name, and not far removed) with a Monastery of *Colieros*; for so are their Monks called. On the other side of the Harbour, upon the top of the Promontory they have another far less, with a Chappel dedicated to the Virgin *Mary*, called *Madonna del Scopo*, reputed an Effectress of Miracles, and much invocated by Sea-faring men. As the Duke of *Venice* doth marry the Sea; so yearly doth this Bishop upon the Twelf-day baptize it: although with less state, yet with no less Ceremony. The *Venetians* here (as in *Candy*) do joyntly celebrate the *Greci an* Festivals, either to gratifie, or else to avoid occasions of tumult. As for the Roman Catholick Bishop, he hath his Cathedral Church, and residence within the Castle, where there is a Convent of *Franciscans*. And a mile and half off, in sight of the Town, on the side of a Mountain, they have another Monastery, called the *Anuneiata*, where the *Latines* have their Burials: built in the year 1550. when under the ground there were found two Urns; one full of ashes, and the other of water, in an ancient Sepulchre. Upon a square stone that covered the Tomb, was ingraven *M. TUL. CICERO. I AVE ET TU JEPTIA ANTONIA*, and under the Urn which containeth the ashes, *AVE MAR. TUL.* It being supposed that *Cicero* was there buried: peremptorily affirmed by a Traveller then present, reporting withal that he saw this Epitaph:

Of Orators the Prince of Speech the Pride,	Ille Oratorum Princeps, & gloria linguæ
Tully, with his wife in this urn abide:	Romanæ jacet hac cum conjuge Tullius urna,
Tully, that of himself, thus writ, O Rome	Tullius ille, inquam, de se qui scripserat olim,
Blest, in that I thy Consul am become.	O fortunatam natam me Consule Romam.
	Adamus Tesellenius in suo Irin.

The *Jews* have here a Synagogue (of whom there are not many) one having married an *English* Woman, and converted her to his Religion. They wear a blue Ribband about their Hats for a distinction. The forcign Merchants here resident are for the most part *English*, who by their frequent deaths do disprove the Air to be so salubrious as is reported, who have their purchased Interments in Gardens; neither suffered by *Greeks* nor *Latines* to be buried in Churches. If a stranger take here a fraught of a *Venetian*, and a *Venetian* Ship be in Port, the Master thereof, upon a protestation, will inforce the stranger to unlode, and serve his own turn therewith, it it be for his benefit. In this Island there are forty Villages.

On the 4. of *September* I imbarked in another *English* Ship, called the *Great Exchange*; first bound for *Chios*, and then for *Tripoli*. With a prosperous wind we compassed a part of *Morea*, more famous by the name of *Peloponesus*; shaped like a Plantane-leaf, and imbraced almost by the *Corinthian* and *Saronian* Arms of the Mediterranean. On the North it adjoyneth to the rest of *Greece* by a narrow Isthmos; where stood that renowed City of *Corinth*, in hearing of both Seas, and having a Port unto either. Divers great Princes (as *Demetrius, Julius Cæsar, Caligula,* and *Nero*) with successless labour, have attempted to make that rocky straight a navigable passage, both to strengthen the same, and that the Voyage into the *Ægean* Sea might thereby become more short, and less perilous. In succeeding time, a division was made by a strong Wall, thrown down by the *Turkish Amurath*, repaired in the year 1453. by the *Venetians*, in fifteen days space, by the hands of thirty thousand Pioneers, and again subverted by the *Mahometans*. This fruitful Country was divided into eight Provinces, *Corinthia, Argia, Laconia, Messenia, Elis, Achaia, Sicyonia,* and *Arcadia*, glorious throughout the World, for the Common-wealths of the *Mycenians, Argives, Lacedemonians, Sicyonians, Eliants, Arcadians, Pylians,* and *Messenians,* watered by the noble Rivers of *Alopus, Peneus, Alpheus* (which receiveth Tribute of an hundred and forty Springs) *Panisus, Eurotas,* and *Inachus,* so highly celebrated by the ancient Poets.

But

But now presenting nothing but ruines, in a great part desolate, it groaneth under the *Turkish* thraldom being governed by a *Sanzacke*, who is under the *Beglerbeg*, or *Græcia*; and is to serve him a thousand Horse whensoever he is called upon. The Inhabitants are for the most part *Grecians*.
On the left hand left we two little Islands.

———Strophades Graio stant nomine dictæ
Insulæ in Ionio magno, quos dira Celano,
Harpyæque colunt aliæ, Phineia postquam
Clausa domus, mensasque metu liquere priores.
Tristius haud illis monstrum, nec sævior ulla
Pestes, & ira Deum Stygiis sese extulit undis.
Virginei volucrum vultus, fœdissima ventris
Ingluvies, uncæque manus, & pallida semper
Ora fame.

Virg. Æn. l. 3.

*In Greek called Strophades; within the great
Ionian Sea: the dire Celænos seat,
Which th'other Harpyes since that chac'd they were
From Phineus house, and left his boord for fear.
More horrid monsters, nor worse plagues than those.
Or wrath of Gods, from Stygian flood ere rose.
Like fowls with Virgins faces, purging still
Their filthy paunches: arm'd with talons ill,
And ever pale with famine.*

This *Phineus* was King of *Arcadia*, who bereft his Sons of their eyes by the instigation of their step-mother: for which offence the offended gods (as the story goes) deprived him of his, and sent these ravenous *Harpyes* to afflict him. But the *Argonauts* being by him courteously entertained, sent *Zetes* and *Calais*, the winged issue of *Boreas* and *Orithia*, to chase them away. Who pursuing them to these Islands, were commanded by *Iris* to desist from doing further violence to the Dogs of *Jupiter*; of whose return the Islands were so named. And what were these *Harpyes*, but flatterers, delators, and the inexpleably covetous? who abuse, devour, and pollute the fame of miserable Princes, blinded in the understanding. *Zetes* and *Calais*, are said to have wings by some, in regard of the fashion of their garments, by others, for their long and beautiful hair. But I rather think, for their wholesom advice, and expedite execution in freeing the State of those Monsters, called the Dogs of *Jupiter*; that is, infernal Furies, and Ministers of his Vengeance. *Alphonsus* King of *Naples*, was wont to say merrily, that the *Harpyes* had let the *Strophades* to inhabit *Rome* : intimating thereby the avarice of the Clergy. These Rocks are at this day called the *Strivaly* : where only live a few *Greek Coliers*, that receive their sustenance of alms from the neighbouring Islands. There is in one a Spring of fresh water, supposed to have his original in *Peloponesus*, and so to pass under the Sea : in regard of a certain Tree over-shadowing a little Lake; the leaves thereof (or like unto those) being often found in this Fountain, there growing none of that kind in the Island.

We thrust between Cape *Malio* and *Cerigo*, about five miles distant : once called *Porphyris* of his excellent *Porphyr*; but better known by the name of *Cythera*. An Island consecrated unto *Venus*. In the Town, rising two furlongs up unto the Haven, stood her celebrated Temple (the most ancient that the *Grecians* had of that Goddess) and therein her Statue in compleat Armour. Out of this it is said, that *Paris* made a Rape of *Helena*, or rather here first enjoyed her in his return from *Sparta*. The ruines are now to be seen, together with that of *Urania*. The Island is sixty miles in compass : it hath divers Harbours; but those small and unsafe. And delightful soil : Inhabited by *Grecians*, and subject to the *Venetians*.

This is the first of the *Ægean* Sea : the largest arm of the *Mediterraneum*, extending to the *Hellespont*, and dividing *Greece* from the lesser *Asia*. So called of *Ægeus*, the Father of *Theseus*: who going to combate the *Minotaure*, was charged to turn the black Sails of his Ship into white, if he returned with Victory. Which forgetting to do, *Ægeus* thinking him slain, leapt into the Sea, from a Promontory where he expected his arrival. But *Pliny* saith, that it took that name of an Island , or rather a Rock, which lies between *Chios* and *Tenedos* : called *Æx*, in that formed like a Goat, now about to skip into the Surges : *Strabo* of *Ægæ* a City of *Euboa*, or of *Æga* a Promontory of *Bœotia*, now vulgarly called the *Arches*. A Sea dangerous and troublesom to sail through, in regard of the multitude of Rocks and Islands, every where dispersed. Insomuch, that a man is proverbially said to fail in the *Ægean* Sea, that is, incumbred with difficulties. The Islands of this Sea were anciently divided into the *Sporades* and *Cyclades*. The *Sporades* are those that lie scattered before *Crete*, and along the Coast of *Asia* : the *Cyclades*, so called, in that they lie in a Circle.

Amongst the rest of the last named, we sailed by *Delos* (now *Diles*) hem'd with sharp Rocks : even from the Reign of *Saturn* of special veneration. Once a floting Island.

Which kind Jove (shifting to and fro) did tie
To Gyaros and high-brow'd Myconie
For culture fixt; and bold winds to defie.

Quam pius Arcitenens, oras & littora circum
Errantem Mycone cella Giaroque revinxit;
Immotamq; coli dedit, & contemnere vento.
Virg. Æn. l. 3.

For the Fable goes, that when all the Earth at the intreaty of *Juno*, had abjured the Receipt of *Latona*, *Delos* at the same time under the water was erected aloft, and by *Jupiter* fixed to entertain her; then named *Delos*, which signifies apparent.

Nurse of Latona's brood: whom Jove while-ere
Bad in Ægean surges to appear.
I hold thee happy in Apollo's birth:
And that Diana calls thee her own earth.

Latonæ partus nutrix, quam Jupiter olim
In maris Ægæi sistere jussit aquis.
Te voco felicem quod Phœbum ceperis, & quod
Solam te patriam clara Diana vocat.
Alpheus.

But the truth is: it was said to be unstable, in that miserably shaken with Earth-quakes, until freed thereof by a Petition made to *Apollo*: who enjoyning certain Sacrifices, commanded, that thenceforth they should neither bury their dead there, nor suffer a Dog to enter the Island: (so that the *Delians* had their interments in *Rhena*, a little desart Island four furlongs distant) and called *Delos*; for that where in other places his Oracles were obscure and ambiguous, they here were manifest and certain. On a Plain within the environing Rocks, stood the City, so honoured for the Temples of *Apollo* and *Latona*, under the Mountain *Cynthus*: of which *Apollo* was called *Cynthius* and *Diana Cynthia*: as *Delius* and *Delia* of the Island, made more famous by the neighbouring *Cyclades*, that like a Ring did environ it: and yearly sent multitudes of men, and Troops of Virgins to celebrate his Solemnities with herds of Sacrifices; as thus in reputation, so increast in wealth through the subversion of *Corinth* by the *Romans*. The Merchants removing hither, invited by the immunities of the Temple and conveniency of the place, it lying in the passage between *Greece* and *Asia*, and frequented by so great a concourse of people.

Upon the re-edifying of *Corinth*, it was held by the *Athenians*, and flourished both in her Rites and Traffick, until laid waste by *Mithridates*. From that time continuing poor, and when Oracles ceased, utterly forsaken. Which doubtless was upon the passion of our Saviour. For *Plutarch* reports from the mouth of one *Epitherses*, who had been his School-master, that he imbarking for *Italy*, and one evening becalmed before the *Paxe* (two little Islands that lie between *Corcyra* and *Leucadia*) they suddenly heard a voice from the shore (most of the Passengers being yet awake) calling to one *Thamus* a Pilot, by birth an *Egyptian*, who till the third call would not answer. *Then* (quoth the voice) *when thou art come to the Palodes, proclaim it aloud, that the great Pan is dead*. All in the Ship that heard this, were amazed. When drawing near to the aforesaid place, *Thamus* standing on the poupe of the Ship, did utter what formerly commanded; forthwith there was heard a great lamentation, accompanied with groans and skreeches. This coming to the knowledge of *Tiberius Cæsar*, he sent for *Thamus*, who avouched the truth thereof. Which declared the death of Christ (the great Shepherd) and subjection of Satan, who now had no longer power to abuse the illuminated World with his impostures. The ruines of *Apollo*'s Temple are here yet to be seen, affording fair Pillars of Marble to such as will fetch them, and other stones of price, both in their nature and for their workmanship; the whole Island being now un-inhabited.

Three days after our imbarkment (as quick a passage as ever was heard of) we arrived at *Sio*, a famous Island formerly called *Chios*, which signifieth white, of *Chione* a Nymph,

—*Who rich in beauty*
A thousand suiters pleas'd—

——quæ ditissima forme
Mille procis placuit ——
Ovid. Metam. l. 3.

and therefore so named. Others say of the Snow, that sometimes covers those Mountains. Sixscore and five miles it containeth in circuit, extending from South unto North: the North and West quarters extraordinary hilly. In the midst of the Island is the Mountain *Arvis* (now *Amisia*) producing the best *Greek* Wines, so prised by the ancient.

But

Et multo in primis hilarans convivia Baccho,	Pleasant with plenteous Bacchus, when we feast
Ante focum, si frigus erit; si messis in umbra:	By th' fire, if cold: in shades, if heat molest:
Vina novum fundam calathis Arvisia nectar.	I Bowls will with Arvisian Nectar fill,
Virg. Eclog. 5.	

But the *Lentisk* Tree, which is well-nigh only proper to *Sio*, doth give it the greatest renown and endowment. They grow at the South-end of the Island, and on the leisurely ascending Hills that neighbour the shore. In height not much exceeding a man, leafed like a Cervice, and bearing a red berry, but changing into black as it ripeneth. Of this Tree thus writeth an old Poet;

Jam vero semper viridis, semperque gravata	*The Lentisk, ever green, and ever great,*
Lentiscus, triplici solita est grandescere fœtu:	*With grateful fruit, three difficult sorts doth bear,*
Ter fruges fundens, tria tempora monstrat arandi.	*Three harvests yields, is thrice drest in one year.*
Cic. de Divin. ex vet. Poet.	

And that with no less diligence than Vines; otherwise they will afford but a little Mastich, which yearly yields to the Inhabitants eighteen thousand Sultanies. In the beginning of *August* lanch they the rind, from whence the Mastich distilleth, until the end of *September*, at which time they gather it. None suffered to come amongst them during the *interim*, it being death to have but a pound of new Mastich found in their houses. The Wood thereof is excellent for Tooth-picks, so commended of old:

Of equal value with a Venice Zecchin.

Lentiscum melius; sed si tibi frondea cuspis	*Lentisk excels: if Tooth-picks of the Lentisk*
Defuerit dentes penna levare potest.	*Be wanting, of a Quill then make a Tooth-pick.*
Mart. l. 14. *Ep.* 22.	

By reason of these Trees they have the best Honey of the World, which intermingled with water, is not much inferiour in relish to the costly Sherbets of *Constantinople*: The Island produceth Corn and Oyl in indifferent plenty. Some Silk they make, and some Cottons here grow, but short in worth unto those of *Smyrna*. It hath also Quarries of excellent Marble: and a certain green Earth, like the rust of Brass, which the *Turks* call *Terra Chia*; but not that so reputed of by the ancient Physicians. The Coast, especially towards the South, is set with small Watch-towers, which with smoke by day, and fire by night, do give knowledge unto one another (and so to the Up-land) of suspected enemies. The environing Sea being free from concealed Rocks, and consequently from peril.

On the East-side of the Island, four leagues distant from the Main of *Asia*, from that part which was formerly called *Ionia*, stands the City of *Sio*: having a secure Haven (though daily decaying) yet with something a dangerous entrance, straightned on the North side by the Sea-ruined Wall of the Mole, incroaching near the *Diamond*; which stands on the other side of the mouth, (so called of the shape, rising out of the Sea, and supporting a Lanthorn, erected by the *Genoueses*) insomuch that Ships of the greatest size do anchor in the Chanel: but ours thrust in, when going ashore, I was friendly entertained of the *English* Consul. The Town stretcheth along the bottom of the Haven: back'd on the West with a rocky Mountain: the building mean, the streets no larger than Allies. Upon the Castle-hill there is a Bannia, which little declines from the state of a Temple; paved with fair Tables of Marble, and supported with Columns, containing several Rooms, one hotter than another, with Conduits of hot Water, and natural Fountains. On the North side of the City stands the Castle ample double walled, and environed with a deep Ditch: manned and inhabited by *Turks*, and well stored with munition. This not many years since was suddenly scaled in a night by the *Florentines*: who choaking the Artillery, and driving the *Turks* into a corner, were now almost Masters thereof: when a violent storm of wind, or rather of fear, enforced their Companions to Sea, and them to a composition; which was, to depart with Ensigns displayed. But the Governour having gotten them into his power, caused their heads to be struck off: and to be piled in Mortar on the Castle-wall; whereas yet they remain, but not un-revenged. For the Captain *Bassa* upon his coming strangled the perfidious Governour: either for dishonouring the *Turk* in his breach of promise, or for his negligence in being so surprised. Since when, a Watch-word every minute of the night goeth about the Walls, to testifie their vigilancy. Their Orchards are here enriched with excellent fruits: among the rest, with Oranges, Lemons, Citrons, Pomegranates, and Figs, so much esteemed by the *Romanes* for their tartness.

LIB. I.   *Chios. Smyrna.*   11

The Chian figs, which Setia to me sent,
Taste like old wine : they wine and salt present.

Chia seni similis Baccho, quàm Setia misit !
Ipsa merum secum portat, & ipsa salem.
Mart. l. 13. Epig. 23.

Upon these Fig-trees there hangs a kind of unsavoury fig : out of whose corruption certain small worms are ingendred, which by biting the other (as they say) procure them to ripen. Partridges here are an ordinary food, whereof they have an incredible number, greater than ours, and differing in hew : the beak and feet red, the Plume ash-colour. Many of them are kept tame, these feeding abroad all day, at night upon a call return unto their several owners.

The *Chiots* were first a free people, being a Common-wealth of themselves, and maintaining a Navy of fourscore Ships (not destitute of diversity of Harbors) whereby they became the Lords of the Seas. Their City is one of those that contended for the birth of *Homer* (stamping his figure on their Coin) although not mentioned in that Distichon.

Seven Cities strive for Homers birth, Smyrna, Chios,
Rhodes, Colophon, Salamis, Athens, and Argos.

Septem Urbes certant de stirpe insignis Homeri.
Syrmna, Rhodos, Colophon, Salamis, Chios, Argos, Athenæ.

They also boast of his Sepulchre about the *Phanæan* Promontory; not far from whence, in a Grove of *Palmes* stood the Temple of *Apollo*. They at this day shew a place not past a quarter of a mile from the Town, not far from the Sea, now by the Islanders called *Erithrea*, (I know not upon what ground) where they say, that *Sybil* prophesied. The Rock there riseth aloft, ascended by stairs on the West-side, cut plain on the top, and hallowed with benches about, like the seats of a Theatre. In the midst a ruined Chair, supported with defaced Lyons, all of the same stone, which yet declares the skill of the Workman. Here, they say, she sate, and gave Oracles. But the relique in my conceit doth disprove the report. For there are the shape of Legs annexed to the Chair : the remains of some Image, perhaps erected in her honour, though I never read of a *Chian Sybil*, nor of an *Erithrea* in this Island; yet stood there a Town so named on the opposite shore; why rather not some Idol of the *Pagans*? In times past they were for the most part served by Slaves. Insomuch that when *Philip* the Son of *Demetrius* besieged the City, he proclaimed freedom to such as would rebel, and their Mistresses to Wives, for reward of their Treasons. Which contrarily so provoked their loyal fury, and the Womens indignations, that they joyntly endeavoured with hands and encouragements, in such sort as repulsed the besiegers. At length they became Subjects to the *Romans*, and then to the *Greek* Emperour : *Andronicus Paleologus* bestowing, or rather selling the same to the *Justinians*, a Family of *Genoa*. After it grew tributary to the *Turk*; yet was it governed and possessed by the *Genoese*, who paid for their immunities the annual sum of fourteen thousand Ducats. But *Solyman* the Magnificent, picking a quarrel with the Governour, for a suspected correspondency with the great Master of *Malta*, during those Wars and discovery of his designs, having besides neglected accustomed presents with the payment of two years tribute, sent *Pial* the *Captain Bassa* to seize on the Island, who on *Easter*-day in the year 1566. presenting himself before *Sio* with fourscore Gallies, so terrified the Inhabitants, that before they were summoned, they quietly surrendred both it and themselves to his disposure. The Governour, together with the principal Families, intending to depart for *Italy*, he sent unto *Constantinople*, and suffered the common people to stay or remove at their liking. So that the whole Island is now governed by *Turks*, and defiled with their superstitions : yet have the Christians their Churches, and un-reproved exercise of Religion. Besides impositions upon the Land, and upon Commodities arising from thence, the great *Turk* receives yearly for every Christian above the age of sixteen, two hundred Aspers, but the Husbandmen are exempted until Marriage. The Inhabitants for the most part are *Turks* and *Grecians*; those living in command, and loosly, the other husbanding the Earth, and exceeding them infinitely in number. They are in a manner released of their thraldom, in that unsensible of it is : well meriting the name of merry *Greeks*, when their leisure will tolerate. Never Sunday, or Holy-day passes without some publick meeting, or other-where intermixed with Women, they dance out the day, and with full-crown'd cups enlengthen their jollity : not seldom passing into *Asia* and the adjoyning Islands, unto such Assemblies. The streets do almost all the night long partake of their Musick. And whereas those of *Zant* do go armed into the field to bring home their Vintage, these bring home theirs with Songs

120 *Aspers amount to a Sultanie.*

and

and Rejoycings. Most differ but little from the *Genouse* in habit, of whom there are many: and though they have corrupted one anothers language, yet retain they their Religion distinctly. The Women celebrated of old for their beauties, yet carry that fame: I will not say undeservedly. They have their head trickt with Tassels and Flowers. The bodies of their Gowns exceed not their Arm-pits: from whence the skirts flow loosly, fringed below; the upper shorter than the nearer; of Damasks or Stuffs less costly, according to their condition. The Merchants pay here for custom but three in the hundred; and in their return but one and an half, if they have paid custom at *Constantinople*.

Smyrna is not far distant from *Chios*: but by reason of the doubling of a certain Cape which stretcheth to the North, requiring two contrary winds, it is by Sea a longer and more troublesom journey. The Bay doth take the name of the City, at the end whereof it is seated. Overthrown by the *Lydians*, re-edified by *Antigonus*, and after by *Lysimachus*. The most beautiful part thereof possessed the Hill: but the greater the Plain, adjacent to the Sea. Amongst other goodly Temples they had one consecrated to *Homer*, (for the *Smyrnians* will have him a Citizen of theirs) containing his honourable Image. For less beholding was he to *Pythagoras*, who reports that he saw him hanging in Hell, for so fabling of the gods. A City not so reputable for her Schools of Learning and admirable Library, as in the title of one of the Primitive Churches of *Asia*. But now violated by the *Mahometans*, her beauty is turned to deformity, her knowledge into barbarism, her Religion into impiety. Frequented notwithstanding it is by foreign Merchants: *Natolia* affording great store of Chamolets and Grograms, made about *Angra*, and a part brought hither, before such time as the Goats (whose hair they pull, white, long, and soft) were destroyed by the late Rebels, consisting for the most part of the expulsed Inhabitants of burned Towns; who having lost all that they had, knew not better how to recover their losses, than by preying upon others, and so joyned with their undoers. Led by *Calender Ogly* and *Zid Arab*; and grown to so fearful a head, that the Great *Turk* (some say) had once a thought to have forsaken the Imperial City, they being fifty thousand, and destitute of Artillery. After foiled by *Morat Bassa* the great *Visier*, who for that service (but chiefly for the overthrow of *Jamballat* the Bassa of *Aleppo*, and natural Lord of the rich Valley of *Achilles*) was called by him his Father and Deliverer. They besieged this City, and were by certain *English* Ships, that lay in the Road, unfriendly saluted. In the end they burnt a part thereof, and took a ransom for sparing the rest. But the principal Commodity of *Syrmna* is Cotten-wool, which there groweth in great quantity. With the seeds thereof they do sow their field as we ours with Corn. The stalk no bigger than that of Wheat, but rough as the Beans: the head round and bearded, in size and shape of a Medlar, hard as a stone, which ripening breaks, and is delivered of a white soft Bombast intermixed with seeds, which they separate with an instrument. You would think it strange, that so small a shell should contain such a quantity; but admire, if you saw them stive it in their Ships, enforcing a Sack as big as a Wool-pack into a room at the first too narrow for your arm, when extended by their instruments; so that often they make the very Decks to stretch therewith.

Our Ship (ere to depart from *Tripolis*) being bound for this place, where her business would detain her for some fifteen days, my desire laid hold on the interim (informed, that although I came short of this passage, I should light upon another not long after) to see the City of *Constantinople*. Taking with me a *Greek* that could speak a little broken *English*, for my Interpreter, on the twentieth of *November* I did put my self into a Bark, *Armado* of *Simo*, a little Island hard by the *Rhodes* (the Patron a *Greek*, as the rest) being laden with Sponges. That night we came to an Anchor under the South-West side of *Mitylen*.

This Island, not past seven miles distant from the Continent of *Phrygia*, containeth eightscore and eight miles in circuit. The South and West parts mountainous and barren, the rest level and fruitful, producing excellent Corn,

Et Lesbia farina, nive candidior. *Horat*.   And Lesbian flour, more white than snow.

(whereof the *Turks* make their *Trachana* and *Bouhort*, a certain hodgepodge of sundry ingredients) and Wines, compared by *Athenæus* and *Ambrosia*, of principal request at *Constantinople*, yet not so ready as the ordinary.

Here

LIB. I.   *Lesbos.*   13

Here underneath some shady vine;
Full cups of hurtless Lesbian wine
Will we quaff freely: nor yet shall
Thyonian Liber with Mars brawl.

Hic innocentis pocula Lesbii
Ducis sub umbras, nec Semel ejus,
Cum Marte confundet Thyoneus
Prælia.
Hor. l. 3. Ode 17.

A vertue feigned to have been given it by *Bacchus*. The *Jews* have taught them how to help the colour (of it self but pallid) with Berries of *Ebulum*. Sheep and Cattel are here bred and sustained in great plenty: Horses, although low of stature, yet strong and couragious. This Country was first inhabited by the *Pelasgians* under the conduct of *Xanthus* the son of *Triopus*, after that by *Macarius*, who followed by certain *Ionians*, and people of sundry nations, here planted himself. Through the bounty of the soil he acquired much riches: and by his justice and humanity the Empery of the neighbouring Islands. Then *Lesbus* the son of *Sapithus*, (so advised by an Oracle) sailing hither with his family, espoused *Methymna* the daughter of *Macarius*. Of these the Island was called *Pelasgia*, *Macaria*, and *Lesbos*. As *Methymna* had a City which retained her name, so had her sister *Mitylene*: which gave, and doth at this day give a name to the Island; seated on a *Peninsula* which regardeth the main land, strong by nature, and fortified by Art, adorned heretofore with magnificent buildings, and numbred amongst the Paradises of the earth for temperate air and delightful situation.

Others will praise bright Rhodes, *fair* Mitylene,
Ephesus, *and* Corinth, *which two seas confine.*

Laudabunt alii claram Rhodon, aut Mitylenen,
Aut Ephesus, bimarisve Corinthi mœnia.
Hor. l. 1. Ode 7.

On either side it enjoyeth a Haven; that on the South convenient for Gallies; the other (inclosed with Rocks, and profound) for Ships of good burthen.
A number of celebrated wits have in their birth made this country happy, as *Pittacus*, one of the seven Sages, *Sappho*, and *Alcæus*;

Sad Sappho'*s Æolian strings*
Of harder hearted Virgins sings,
Alcæus *in a higher key*
On golden lyre, of ills at Sea
In flight sustain'd, and Wars stern ire;
The attentive ghosts do both admire,
Worthy of sacred silence ———

——— Æoliis fidibus querentem
Sappho, puellis de popularibus:
Et te sonantem plenius aureo
Alcæe plectro, dura navis,
Dura fugæ mala, dura belli.
Utrumque sacro digna silentio
Mirantur umbræ dicere———
Hor. l. 1. Ode 13.

succeeding *Orpheus* in the excellency of lyrical Poesie. Whereupon the fable is grounded, that when cut in pieces by the *Ciconean* women,

Hebrus *had head and harp. Whilst born along*
The harp sounds something sadly: the dead tongue
Sighs out sad ditties: the banks sympathize
That bound the River in their sad replies.
Now born to Sea, from countries stream they drive
And at Methymnian Lesbos *shore arrive.*

——— Caput Hebre, lyramque
Excipis: (& mirum) medio dum labitur amne,
Flebile nescio quid queritur lyra, flebile lingua
Murmurat exanimis, respondent flebile ripæ.
Jamq; mare invectæ, flumen populare relinqunt
Et Methymneæ potiuntur littore Lesbi.
Ovid. l. 11.

It is said also that the Nightingales of this country sing more sweetly than elsewhere. On their Coin they stamped the figure of *Sappho*. Nor less honoured they *Alcæus*: a bitter inveigher against the rage of Tyrants that then oppres'd this country: Amongst whom the forenamed *Pittacus* might seem one; but his purpose was contrary: who usurped the soveraignty of all, that by suppressing the inferior Tyrants he might restore the people to their liberty. From whence came also *Arion*, *Theophrastus*, and others. This Island was given by *Calo Joannes* the *Greek* Emperor, together with his sister, unto *Franciscus Gatalusius* a *Genoese*, in the year 1355. in recompense of his valour and service done him in the *Turkish* wars. In whose posterity it long continued, they governing the same with great justice: linkt in alliance with the Emperors of *Trapezond*, and other *Grecian* Princes. But when the *Turk* had possest himself of all the confining Nations, they became his tributaries: paying for the same the annual sum of 4000 Ducats. *Dominicus Catalusius*, having surprised his elder brother, and delivered him to *Baptista* a *Genoese*, partaker of the conspiracy, and after having murther'd him, invested himself in the soveraignty. The last and wicked Prince of that family;

C   For

For *Mahomet* the Great, in the year 1462. incensed against him, as well for harbouring the Pirats of *Italy* and *Spain*, who sold to him their slaves, and gave him part of their booty, as for the execrable murther of his Brother, passing into *Asia* with not above two thousand *Janizaries* (but followed by an hundred sail of Ships & Gallies) came by land to *Possidium*, over against *Lesbos*: whither transported he over-ran the whole Island, and besieged the Prince in the City of *Mitylen*, who after seven and twenty days siege surrendred the same, together with all the strong Forts of the Island, upon condition that he should give him some other Country equal unto it in value: whereupon by solemn oath he obliged himself. But the faithless *Turk* possest of his prey, commanded the Prince to remove to *Constantinople*; puts a strong Garrison into the City; and distinguished the Inhabitants according to their degrees, the better sort he leadeth away with him, giveth away those of the middle condition, (afterwards sold as they do Sheep in Markets) and leaveth behind the dregs of the people to their own arbitrement, as dangerless, and unprofitable: reserving to himself eight hundred boys and virgins, excelling the rest both in birth and beauty. But deserv'd vengeance would not so relinquish the fratricide; cast not long after into prison upon this occasion. A youth that had escaped out of the great *Turks Seraglio*, was by him entertained at *Mitylen*, whom he had converted to the Christian Religion, and after notwithstanding most wickedly contaminated. Un-mindful of him in this tempest of calamities, he had left him behind him: when after, being presented to the Emperour for his admirable beauty, he was known, and the Prince clapt up as his inveigler. Now every day expecting the Executioner, for his safety he abjured his Saviour: whereupon circumcised and vested by the Great *Turk*, he was set at liberty. Too dear a purchase for so short a breath: imprisoned again soon after, and finally strangled. This Island in such sort subjected to the *Turkish* obedience, at this day so continueth, inhabited for the most part by *Grecians*. All that is left of the City of *Mitylen*, which deserveth observation, is the Castle, exceeding strong, and manned by an able Garrison, and the Arsenal for Gallies: whereof divers are here kept continually to scour these Seas, infested greatly by Pirats.

On the one and twentieth of *September* the winds grew contrary: and Seas (though not rough) too rough to be brooked by so small a Vessel, no bigger, and like in proportion to a *Graves-end* Tilt-boat; yet rowing under the shelter of the land, we entred the Gulph of *Calonus*: they hoping to have found some purchase about a Ship cast there away but a litle before, divers of them leapt into the Sea, and diving unto the bottom stayed there so long, as if it had been their habitable element. And without question they exceed all others in that faculty; trained thereunto from their childhood: and he the excellentest amongst them that can best perform it: Insomuch, that although worth nothing, he shall be proffered in marriage the best endowed and most beautiful virgin of their Island. For they generally get their living by these sponges, gathered from the sides of Rocks about the bottom of the *Straights*; sometimes fifteen fathom under water. A happy people that live according to nature; and want not much, in that they covet but little. Their apparel no other than linen breeches; over that a smock close girt unto them with a towel; putting on sometimes when they go ashore, long sleeveless coats of home-spun cotton. Yet their backs need not envy their bellies: Bisket, Olives, Garlik, and Onions being their principal sustenance. Sometimes for change they will scale the Rocks for Sampier, and search the bottom of the less deep Seas for a certain little fish (if I may so call it) shaped like a burr and named by the *Italians*, *Riccio*. Their ordinary drink being water; yet once a day they will warm their bloods with a draught of wine, contented as well with this, as those that with the rarities of the earth do pamper their voracities.

Discite quam parvo liceat propucere vitam;
Et quantum natura petat: non erigit ægros
Nobilis ignoro diffusus Consule Bacchus.
Non auro myrrhaque bibunt; sed gurgite puro
Vita redit satis est populis fluviusque Ceresque.
Lucan. l. 3.

*Learn with how little, life may be sustain'd
And how much nature would. Not gen'rous wines
Of unknown age avail where health declines.
In Gold nor Myrrh drink they: but the pure flood
Preserves them, bread and it suffice for food.*

When they will they work, and sleep when they are weary: the bank that they row upon, their couches (as ours was the poup:) hardned by use against heat and cold, which day and night interchangeably inflicteth. So chearful in poverty, that they will dance whilest their legs will bear them, and sing till they grow hoarse: secured from the cares and fears that accompany riches.

O safe condition of mean estate! a good
Given by the Gods, as yet not understood.

——— O viræ tuta facultas
Pauperis, angustique laris! O munera nondum
Intellecta Deum! ——— *Lucan. l. 5.*

Upon the two and twentieth of *September*, the winds continuing contrary, we but a little shortned our journey, descrying a small Sail that made towards us, and thinking them to be Pirates, we rowed back by the shore with all possible speed. In the evening we returned to the place that we fled from; when going a-shore, one attired like a woman, lay groveling on the sand, whilst the rest skipt about him in a ring, muttering certain words, which they would make me believe were prevalent charms to alter the weather to their purpose. On the three and twentieth we continued weather-bound, removing after it grew dark to another anchorage; a custom they held, lest observed by day from Sea or shore, they might by night be surprized. We lay in a little Bay, and under a cliff, where not one of us but had his sleep interrupted by fearful dreams, he that watched affirming that he had seen the Devil; so that in a great dismay we put from shore about mid-night: But whether it proceeded from the nature of the vaporous place, or that infested by some spirit, I leave to decide. It is reported of a little rocky Island hard by, named formerly *Æx*, and sacred unto *Neptune* (whereof we have spoken something already) that none could sleep upon it for being disturbed with apparitions.

On the four and twentieth the Sea grew calm, and we proceeded on our voyage; towards evening we went ashore on the firm of *Asia* for fresh water, and came that night unto *Tenedos*.

In sight of Troy, *an Isle of wealth and fame*
Whilest Priam *in this state abode:*
Now but a Bay; for Ships a faithless road.

Est in conspectu Tenedos notissima fama
Insula, dives opum, Priami dum regna manebant;
Nunc tantum sinus, & statio malesida carinis.
Virg. Æn. l. 2.

And so it is at this day: to which adjoineth the Town so named, with a Castle of no great importance. This Island containeth in circuit not above ten miles, removed but five from the *Sigean* shore; rising into a round Mountain towards the North, the rest level, and producing exceeding strong wines, which declare the Inhabitants to be *Grecians*. First, it was called *Leucophryn*, then *Tenedos*, of *Tenes* the son of *Cyenus*, who reigned in *Colone* a City of *Troas*. It is said, that accused by his step-mother (in revenge of her repulses) for proffering that which she incestuously sought, his father put him into a Chest, and threw him into the Sea: being born by a tempest unto this Island, and so admirably delivered; where from that time forward he reigned. And because a Musician was of the conspiracy with his mother, he made a Law, that no Musician should enter the Temple which he had built, and consecrated to *Apollo Smintheus* then Protector of this Island, as appeareth by the invocation of *Chryses*.

O Smintheus, *thou that bear'st the silver bow;*
That Chrysa *guard'st, with* Cilla *most divine,*
And Tenedos, *to my dire curse incline.*

Audi me argenteum habens arcum qui Chrysen
undique tueris,
Cillamque valde divinam, Tenedoque fortiter
imperas
Smintheu——— *Hom. Il. l. 1.*

But certain it is, that *Tenes* came hither, and peopled it, being desolate before. In the wars of *Troy* he was slain by *Achilles*. And for that he was a just Prince, full of worth and magnanimity, they honoured him after his death with their sacrifices and a Temple; wherein it was not lawful so much as to mention *Achilles*.

With the morning they renewed their labour, rowing along the chalky shore of the lesser *Phrygia*. Now against Cape *Janizary* (desirous to see those celebrated fields where once stood *Ilium* the glory of *Asia*, that hath afforded to rarest wits so plentiful an argument) with much importunity and promise of reward) it being a matter of danger) I got them to set me ashore. When accompanied with two or three of them, we ascended the not high Promontory, level above, and crown'd with a ruinous City, whose imperfect walls do shew to the Sea their antiquity. Within are more spacious Vaults, and ample Cisterns for the receipt of water. The foundation hereof should seem to have been laid by *Constantine* the Great, who intending to remove the seat of his Empire, began here to build: which upon a new resolution he erected at *Byzantium*. This is that famous Promontory of *Sigeum* honoured with the Sepulchre of *Achilles*, which *Alexander* (visiting it in his *Asian* expedition) covered with flowers, and ran naked about it, as then the custom was in Funerals: sacrificing to the Ghost of his kinsman, whom he reputed most happy, that had such a Trumpet as *Homer* to re-sound his vertues.

The first that reigned in this Country was *Teucer*; begot (as they feign) by the River *Scamander* on the Nymph *Idea*. Him succeeded *Dardanus* the son of *Jupiter*, and *Electra* the daughter of *Atlas*, and wife to *Coritus* King of *Hetruria*; who flying *Italy* for the death of his brother *Jasius*, first planted in *Samothracia*, and afterward removing hither, espoused *Batea* the daughter of *Teucer*, and in her right possessed this Kingdom. Whose off-spring is thus related by *Æneas*.

Dardanum quidem primum genuit nubi cogus Jupiter, Condiditq; Dardaniam. Quoniam nondum Ilium sacrum In campo conditum erat oppidum diversarum linguarum ho-Sed adhuc loca sub montana habitabant fontosæ Idæ. (minū. Dardanus vero genuit Erichthonium Regem. Qui cum ditissimus erat mortalium omnium. Troem autem Erichthonius Trojanis Regem. Ex Troe vero tres filii inculpati nati sunt, Ilusque, Assaracusque, & divinus Ganymedes, Qui sane pulcherrimus fuit mortalium hominum. Ilus vero genuit filium præclarum Laomedonta. Laomedon vero Tithonum genuit Priamumque Lampumq; Clitiumq; Hicetaonemq; ramum Martis. Assaracus autem Capym genuit: hic Anchisem genuit filium, Sed me Anchises.—— *Hom. Il. l. 20.*	*Cloud chasing Jove did Dardanus beget, Who built Dardania: sacred Ilium yet Decks not the lower Plains possest by men Of differens tongues; they populated then The foot of fount-full Ida.* Joves *son begot King Erichthonius, richer liv'd there not. Rich Erichthonius, Tros the Trojan King. From Tros three un-impeached sons did Ilus, Assaricus, divine Ganymed, (spring. The fairest youth that ever mortal bred, Ilus begot far-fam'd Laomedon, He Tithon, Priam, brave Hicetaon, Lampus, and Clitius. Great Assaracus Got Carys, he Anchises, and he, us.*

Ilus was the first that after the Flood adventured to inhabit the Plains. For before men dwelt on the tops of Mountains: and by little and little descended as their terrors forsook them, changing their conditions with the places: and by how much nearer the Sea, by so much the more civil. In the Plain beyond us (for we durst not straggle farther from the shore) we beheld where once stood *Ilium* by him founded: called *Troy* promiscuously of *Tros*. Afterward fained to have been walled about by Neptune and *Phæbus* in the days of *Laomedon*. Who hath not heard of this glorious City, the former taking, the ten years war, and latter final subversion? which befell according to *Eusebius*, in the year of the world 2784, and second of *Abdons* government of *Israel*,

Scaliger refers unto the year of the world 2768.

——Si magna fuit censusque virisque Perque decem potuit tantum dare sanguinis annos, Nunc humiles veteres tantummodo Troja ruinas, Et pro divitiis tumulos ostendit avorum. *Ovid. Met. l. 5.*	*So rich, so powerful, that so proudly stood, That could for ten years space spend so much blood: Now prostrate, only her old ruins shows, And Tombs that famous Ancestors inclose.*

But those not at this day more than conjecturally extant. They that favour not the inventions of *Virgil*, report that *Æneas* removed not from hence: but succeeded in this Kingdom: which for a long time after remained in his posterity: highly honoured by the *Grecians* themselves for his wisdom, valour, and piety, (he not consenting to the rape of *Helena*) who forbare to damnifie both his person and fortunes. Whereupon suspected it was, that he betrayed the City. But the prophecy that *Homer* makes of him in the person of *Neptune*, then ready to be done to death by *Achilles*, in my opinion is a testimony for *Virgil:*

Sed cur hic nunc innocens dolores patitur In cassium ob alienas culpas? grata autem semper Munera diis exhibet, qui cœlum latum habitant. Sed agite, nos saltem ipsum a morte subducamus, Ne forte Saturnides irascatur si Achilles Hunc interimat: fatale enim ei est evitare. Ut ne sine prole genus & prorsus extinctum pereat Dardani, quem Saturnides præ omnibus dilexit liberis Qui in se nati sunt mulieribus mortalibus Jam enim Priami genus odit Saturnus, Nunc autem jam Æneæ vis Trojanis imperabit Et nati natorum qui deinceps nascentur. *Hom. Il. l. 20.*	*Why crimeless, suffers he for others crimes? Who gods with grateful gifts so many times Hath feasted. Come, now free we him from death: Lest if through wounds Achilles force his breath, Jove chance to storm. Fate doth his scape intend, For fear the stock of Dardanus should end: Whom Jove (who now doth Priams race detest) Of all begot on mortal dames lov'd best. Æneas, and his childrens children shall The Trojans rule, and re-erect their fall.*

there

LIB. I.   Troy.

there being no mention made of any of his Progeny that here reigned after him. North of this Promontory is that of *Rhæteum*, celebrated for the Sepulchre of *Ajax*, and his statue: by *Antonius* transported into *Egypt*, and restored unto the *Rhæteensi* by *Augustus*. *Pausanias* reports from the mouths of the *Æolians*, who re-peopled re-edified *Ilium*, how that the Armor of *Achilles* (the cause of his madness, and self-slaughter) was, after the shipwrack of *Ulysses*, thrown up by the Sea upon the basis of his monument.

Which given to Seas by Tempests Neptune caught; And juster, to the true deserver brought.	Justior arripuit Neptunus in equora jactum Naufragio, ut dominum possit adire suum. *A'ciat. Emb.*

'Twixt these two Capes there lyeth a spacious Valley. Near *Sigeum* was the station for the *Grecian* Navy: but nearer *Rhæteum* the River *Simois* (now called *Simores*) dischargeth it self into the *Hellespont*. This draweth his birth from the top of *Ida*, the highest mountain of *Phrygia*, lying Eastward from hence; and resembled, for that it hath many feet, unto a certain rough worm, which is called *Scolopendra*: approaching the Sea not far short of *Mitylen*, and stretching North-ward to the lesser *Mysia*. Famous for the judgement of *Paris*, and pregnancy in Fountains: from whence descend four Rivers of principal repute, *Æsopus* and *Granicus* (made memorable by *Alexander*'s victory,) these turn their streams to the North: *Simois*, and *Scamander*, that regard the *Ægeum*. Two not far disjoyning vallies there are that stretch to each other, and joyn in an ample plain (the theatre of those so renowned bickerments) where stood the antient *Ilium*, if not fortunate, not inglorious, nor un-revenged.

Old Troy by Greeks twice sackt: twice new Greece rued Her conquering Ancestors. First when subdued By Rome's bold Trojan progeny: and now When forc'd through Turkish insolence to bow.	Bis vetus eversum est Argivis Ilion armis, Bis nova victores Græcia luget avos. Maxima Trojanos retulit cum Roma nepotes: Atq; iterum imperium cum modo Turkus habet. *I. C. Scal.*

Through these fore-named vallies glide *Simois*, and divine *Scamander*: so named saith *Homer* by men; but *Xanthus* by celestials. *Xanthus*, in that the sheep that drunk thereof had their fleeces converted into yellow, according to *Aristotle*: *Scamander*, of *Scamander*, who therein drowned himself. Of this River they made a Deity, and honoured it with Sacrifices. It was an antient custom amongst the *Trojan* Virgins, for such as were forthwith to be marryed, to bathe themselves therein, and with these words to invocate the River:

Come, O Scamander, pluck my Virgin flower.	Sume, O Scamander, virginitatem meam.

So that on a time *Cimon* an *Athenean*, for the *Athenians* were mixed with the *Trojans*) being in love with *Callirrhoe* a Lady of principal parentage, now betrothed to another, crowned his head with Reeds, and hid himself in the Sedges adjoining: when upon her singing of that used verse, he leapt out of the covert, and replyed most willing, by constraint defloured her: upon which occasion, that solemnity was abrogated. Nearer the Sea it joineth with *Simois*: there it should seem where *Achilles* was so ingaged by the waters;

Nor shrunk Scamander, but inrag'd the more A climing billow high in air up-bore. And with an out-cry silver Simois thus Exhorteth: Come, dear brother, now let us Our forces join, &c.	Neque Scamander remisit suam vim, sed adhuc magis Succensuit Pelidæ: extulit autem undam aquæ, In altum sublatus, Simoentem ut hortabatur clamans : Chare frater, rubur viri ambo salteim Cohibeamus, &c. *Hom. Il. l. 21.*

and proceeding, do make certain Lakes and Marishes. These Rivers, though now poor in streams, are not yet so contemptible, as made by *Bellonius*, who perhaps mistaketh others for them, (there being sundry rivolets that descend from the mountains) as by a likelyhood he hath done the the site of the antient *Troy*. For the ruines that are now so perspicuous, and by him related, do stand four miles South-west from the fore-said place, described by the Poets, and determined of by the Geographers: seated on a hanging hill, and too near the naval station to afford a field for such disperfed encounters, such long pursuits, interception of scouts, (then when the *Trojans* had pitched nearer the Navy) and executed stratagems, as is declared to have hapned between the Sea and the City. These reliques do sufficiently declare the greatness of the latter, and not a little the excellency. The walls (as *Bellonius*, but more largely, describeth it) consisting of great square stone, hard, black, and spongy, in divers places yet standing; supported on the inside with pillars about two yards distant one from another, and garnished once with many now ruined Turrets: containing a confusion of thrown-down buildings, with ample Cisterns for the receipt of rain; it being seated on a sandy soyl, and altogether destitute of Fountains. Foundations here are of a Christian Temple; and two Towers of Marble, that have better resisted the fury of time: the one on the top of a hill, and the other nearer the Sea in the valley. From the wall of the City another extendeth (supported with Buttresses, partly standing, and partly thrown down) well-nigh unto *Ida*: and then turning is said to reach to the Gulph of *Satelia*, about twenty miles distant. Half a mile off, and West of these ruins, opposing *Tenedos*, are the hot-water-bathes, heretofore adorned, and nighboured with magnificent building: the way thither inclosed as it were with Sepulchres of Marble, many of the like being about the City, both of Greeks and Latins, as appeareth by the several characters. Two Baths there be; the one choaked with rubbige, the other yet in use, though under a simple coverture. But now the ruins bear not altogether that form, lessened daily by the *Turks*, who carryed the pillars and stones unto *Constantinople* to adorn the buildings of the great *Bassaes*; as they now do from *Cyzicus*. This notable remainder of so noble a City, was once a small Village of the *Ilians*. For the *Ilians*, after the destruction of that famous *Ilium*, often shifting the seat of the new, here fixt it at last, as is said, by the advice of an Oracle; containing one only contemptible Temple dedicated to *Minerva*, at such time as *Alexander* came thither: who then offered up his shield, and took down another (that which he used in his fights) enriching the Temple with gifts, and honouring the Town with his name; exempting it from tribute, and determining upon his return to erect in it a sumptuous Temple, to institute sacred games, and to make it a great City. But *Alexander* dying, *Lysimachus* took upon him that care: who immured it with a wall containing forty furlongs in circuit; yet suffered to retain the name of *Alexandria*. After it became a Colony, and an University of the *Romans*, of no mean reputation. *Fimbria* the Questor, having in a sedition slain the Consul *Valerius Faccus* in *Bithynia*, and making himself Captain of the *Roman* Army, the Citizens refusing to receive him, as a Robber and a Rebel, besieged this City, and in eleven days took it, who boasted that he in eleven days had done that, which *Agamemnon* with five hundred sail of Ships, and the whole *Greek* nation, could hardly accomplish in ten years. To whom an *Italian* answered, That they wanted an *Hector* to defend them. Pieces of ruines throughout these Plains lye every where scattered.

Returning again to our Barque, hard by, on the left hand left we *Imbrius*, now called *Lembro*, once sacred to *Mercury*, and not far beyond *Lemnos*; famous for the fabulous fall of *Vulcan*.

Me quoque de cœlo pede jecit Jupiter olim
Contra illum auxilium misero ut mihi ferre pararem.
Ast ego cum cœlo Phœboque cadente ferebar
In Lemnum ut cecidi, vix est vis ulla relicta.
Hom. Il. l. 1.

'Gainst Jove once making head, he caught me by
The foot, and flung me from the profound skie:
All day I was in falling: and at night
On Lemos fell: life had forsook me quite.

Whereupon, and no marvel, he ever after halted. The *Grecians* there now inhabiting do relate

——(Quid non Græcia mendax
Audet in historia?)——

——(*What dares not lying* Greece
In Histories insert?)——

that he brake his thigh with a fall from a Horse on the side of a hill, which at this day beareth his name. The earth in that place thereupon receiving those excellent vertues of curing of wounds, stopping of fluxes, expulsing poysons, &c. now called *Terra Sigillata*, in that sealed; and there only gathered. In regard of the quality of this earth which is hot, the Island was consecrated to *Vulcan*, who signifieth fire. For the Antient expresseth under these Fables, as well the nature of things, as manners of persons. And now, so heretofore in the digging thereof they used sundry ceremonies: ceremony which giveth repute unto things in themselves but trivial. It was wont to be gathered by the Priests of *Venus*, who amongst other rites, did mingle the earth with the blood of a Goat (printing the little pellets whereinto divided, with his form) which was sacrificed unto her. The neglect of this her honour by the women

LIB. I. Lemnos, Hellespont. 19

of the Island, was the cause, as they fable, of their goat-like favour: so that loathed by their husbands (who shortly after making wars upon the *Thracians*, had espoused their Captives) and burning with a womanly spleen, in one night they massacred them all, together with their Concubines; after murdering their own Children, lest they in time to come should revenge the blood of their Fathers: and so extinguished the whole generation. This Hill lyeth South of the ruins of that antient *Hephestia* which gave a name unto *Vulcan*, and about three flight-shots removed. Between which standeth *Sotica*, a little Chappel frequented by the *Greek Colieros* upon the sixth of *August*: where they begin their Orisons, and from thence ascend the Mountain to open the vein from whence they produce it, which they do with great preparations and solemnities, accompanied with the principal *Turks* of the Island. That which covereth it, being removed by the labour of well-nigh fifty Pioners; the Priests take out as much as the *Cady* doth think for that year sufficient, (lest the price should abate by reason of the abundance) to whom they deliver it: and then close it up in such sort, as the place where they dig'd, is not to be discerned. The vein discovered, this precious earth, as they say, doth arise like the casting up of worms: and that only during a part of that day: so that it is to be supposed rather, that they gather as much as the same will afford them. Certain bags thereof are sent to the great *Turk*: the rest they sell, (of which I have seen many cups at *Constantinople*: but that which is sold to the Merchants is made into little pellets, and sealed with the *Turkish* character. The ceremonies in the gathering hereof, were first inducted by the *Venetians*.

And now we entred the *Hellespont*,

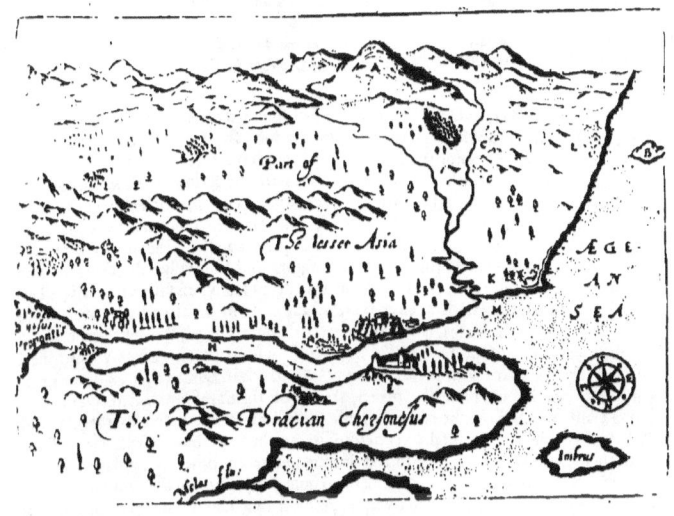

A. *Mount Ida*. D. *Abydos*. G. *Zembenit*. K. *Cape Janizary*.
B. *Tenedos*. E. *Sestos*. H. *Hellespont*. L. *Ruins of Alexandria*.
C. *Seat of old Troy*. F. *Mayto*. I. *Callipolis*. M. *Mouth of Simois and Scamander*.

so called of *Helle* the daughter of *Athamas* King of *Thebes*, and sister of *Phryxus*: who flying the stratagems of their Step-mother *Ino*, was drowned therein. Bounded on the left hand with the *Thracian Chersonesus* (vulgarly called St. *George's* arm) a peninsula pointed to the South-west: whereon stood the Sepulcher of *Hecuba*, called *Cynossema*, which signifieth a Dog: fained to have been metamorphosed into one, in regard of her impatiency. She in the division of the *Trojan* Captives, contemned, derided, and avoided of all, fell to the hated share of *Ulysses*: when to free her self from shame and captivity, she leapt into the *Hellespont*. But *Dictys Cretensis* faith, that distracted with her miseries, and execrating the enemy, she was slain by them, and buryed in the aforesaid Promontory. On the right hand the *Hellespont* is confined with the lesser *Phrygia*. It divideth *Europe* from *Asia*, in sundry places, not above a mile

broad,

broad, in length about forty, (now called the Chanel of *Constantinople*) and having a current that setteth into *Ægeum*: a trade-wind blowing either up or down, which when contrary to the stream, doth exceedingly incense it, the Mountains on each sides are clothed with Pines, from which much pitch is extracted.

Three Leagues above the entrance, and at the narrowest of this Straight stand *Sestos* and *Abydos*, opposite to each other: formerly famous for the unfortunate loves of *Hero* and *Leander*, drowned in the uncompassionate Surges, and sung by *Musæus*. Here *Xerxes*, whose populous Army drank Rivers dry, and made Mountains circum-navigable, is said to have past over into *Greece* upon a bridge of Boats. Whereof *Lucan*.

———*Fama canit tumidum super equora Xerxem*
Construxisse vias, multum cum pontibus ausus
Europamque Asiæ, Sestonque admovit Abydo:
Incessitque fretum rapidi super Hellesponti,
Non Eurum, Zephyrumque timens
Longæque tremuit super æquora turres.
 Lucan. l. 2.

Fame sings how Xerxes *upon* Neptune*'s Brine*
Erected ways: that by a Bridge durst join
Europe to Asia, Sestos *to* Abydos:
Who on the fretful Hellespontus *goes,*
Not dreading Zephyrus, *now* Eurus *raves;*
The high Towers tremble on the wrathful Waves.

Which when broken by Tempests, he caused the Sea to be beaten (as if sensible) with three hundred stripes, and fetters to be thrown therein; forbidding any to sacrifice unto *Neptune*. Nor sped the winds better.

In Corum atque Eurum solitus sævire flagellis
Barbarus, Æolio nunquam hoc in carcere pasios.
 Juv. Sat. 10.

Who scourg'd the East & North-east winds: till then
Never so serv'd, not in Æolian *den.*

O the dog-like rage and arrogant folly of Ideots advanced to Empire!

Sed qualis rediit? Nempe una cruentis
Fluctibus, & tarda per densa cadavera prora.
 Idem.

But how return'd? Dismaid, through blood stain'd
With one Boat, stopt by floating carcasses. [Seas

Abydos stands in *Asia*, which the *Milesians* first founded by the permission of *Gyges* King of *Lydia*, unto whom all the country was subject. Taken by the *Turks* in the reign of *Orchanes*, successor unto *Ottoman*, through the treason of the Governours daughter; who, like another *Scylla*, bewitched with the person of *Abdurachman*, and his valour, often seen from the towers of the Castle, as he approached near the wall, threw down a Letter tyed unto a stone, wherein she manifested her affections and promised the delivery of the Castle, if he would perswade the General to remove his siege, and return himself in the dead of the night, and follow her directions. The defendants over-joyd at the enemies departure, drink freely, and sleep soundly, when *Abdurachman* coming with a selected crew was let in by his attending Lover, who conducted him to the Gates, where he slew the drowsie Guard, and set them open to his followers, surprising the Captain in his bed, whom he carryed away prisoner, and fortified the place with *Mahometans*. *Sestos* stands in *Europe*, though never great yet strongly built, and once the principal City of the *Chersonesus*: afterward defaced, a Castle was built in the room thereof. *Abydos* is seated upon a low level: and *Sestos* on the side of a Mountain, yet descending to the Sea: both bordering the same with their Castles; whereof the former is four-square, the other triangular. Terrible towards the Sea in regard of the number and huge proportion of the Ordnance planted level with the water. Moreover, kept by strong Garrisons: yet nothing less than invincible, by reason of the over-peering Mountains that back the one, and slender fortification of the other to land-ward. These at this day are vulgarly called the Castles. All Ships are suffered to enter, that by their multitude and appointment do threaten no Invasion, but not to return without search and permission: of which we shall speak in the process of our Journal. A little beyond we past by the ruines of a Castle, which the *Turkish* Carmasals and Gallies still sailing by, salute with their Ordnance, it being the first Fort by them taken in *Europe*, who call it *Zembenick*. Surprised by *Solyman*, the eldest son of the foresaid *Orchanes*: who passing the *Hellespont* by night, conducted by a *Greek*, whom he had taken before, by means of a dung-hill which surmounted the wall, with facility entred it; the Inhabitants not dreaming that they could have past into *Europe*, (who had made upon the sudden certain little Boats for that purpose, yet more generally said to be transported by the *Genoeses* for a ducate a head,) being dispersed in their Vineyards, and treading their Corn, which they accustom to do by night in these Countries. The besotted *Grecians* (a presage

of

of their approaching ruine) being so far from endeavouring a recovery, that they jested at the loss, and said that they had but taken a Hogs-stie, alluding to the name, called *dochastron*. That night we came to *Callipolis*, some twenty miles distant: and thrust *Coiro* into a little Haven North of the Town; but only capable of small Vessels.

Callipolis is a City of *Cherfonesus*, seated at the bottom of a Bay: so shallow, that Ships do there usually anchor, as throughout the whole *Hellespont*. Some converting C into G, do conjecture that it was called *Gallipolis* of the *Gauls* that over-ran those Countries, under the conduct of *Brennus* a Britain (if our Chronicles err not) and brother to *Belinus*. But in that a *Greek* sirname, it seemeth to deny the receit thereof from a Foreigner. *Pausanius* maketh mention of one *Callirolis*, the younger son of *Calcothous*, who had sent *Echopolis* his elder brother to assist *Meleager* in chase of the Bore of *Calydon*. *Echopolis* there slain, and the news thereof coming to *Callipolis*, in a rage he ran into the Temple, and threw the wood from the Altar, his Father then sacrificing to *Apollo*: who thinking that it had been in contempt of his sacrifice, struck out his brains with a fire-brand, and so deprived himself of posterity. *Callipolis* maketh a fair shew afar off, but entred, is nothing less than it promised: a part thereof possessing the shore, and the rest the rising of the Mountain: unwalled, and without either Citadel or Fortress. Along the shore there are divers dry stations for Gallies. On the South-side of the City, in a little Plain, are sundry round Hills: the Sepulchres, as they say, of certain *Thracian* Kings; for such was the ancient custom of burial. The Country above, is champion and not barren; but rarely inhabited. The infinite number of *Turkish* Graves by the high-way sides, and adjoyning Hills, do shew it to have been plentifully inhabited by them, and of a long continuance; it being the first City that they took in *Europe*, under the leading of the aforesaid *Solyman*, in the year 1338. Here is a Ferry for Transportation into *Asia*. *Greeks* and *Jews*, together with the *Turks* do inhabit the Town, and are admitted their Churches and Synagogues. Here also is a Monastery of *Romish* Friers, of the Order of St. *Augustine*: one of them being at this time (but not dwelling in the Covent) the *Frank* Consul; whose office is to dispatch and discharge the dues of all Christian Ships, not Subject to the *Grand Signior*, and admitted free Trading, below at the Castles. To this house I repaired, with hope of some refreshment after my wearisom voyage: but he then from home, I was forced to return to my water-bed; there being no Inns for entertainment throughout in-hospital *Turkie*: yet is this Town well furnished with all sorts of provision. What is here sold by the *Greeks*, you may agree for a price: but the *Turks* will receive your mony, and give you a quantity for it, according to their own arbitrement; but truly enough, and rather exceeding, than short of your expectation. For two or three Aspers (whereof twenty are near upon a shilling) a Butcher will cut off as much Mutton (for they divide it not into joynts) as will well satisfie three though hungry: which they carry to the Cooks, who make no more ado, but slicing it into little gobbets, prick it on a prog of Iron, and hang it in a Furnace. Derided, and flouted at by divers of the baser people, at night we returned to our Bark. And departing the next morning, were forth-with met with a contrary wind, which drove us to the shelter of a Rock not far from the Town: where we abode all that day, and the night ensuing: they opening and washing part of their Sponges: which laid on the shore, by the bulk you would have thought to have been a fraught for a Pinnace, which stived into Sacks, when wet, were bestowed under the side benches and cross banks of their little Vessels.

On the seven and twentieth of *September*, before day, we left the shore, and after while entred the *Propontick* Sea: confined with *Thrace* on the one side, and with *Bythynia* on the other: joyning to the *Euxine* Sea by the Streights of *Bosphorus*, as it doth to the *Ægean* by the *Hellespont*. It is a hundred and fifty Furlongs in length, and almost of like Latitude; so that those which sail in the midst, may descry from all parts the environing land, called now *Mar de Marmore* by the *Italians* of *Marmora*, a little, but high Island, which standeth against the mouth of the *Hellespont*, and in light of *Callipolis*: at whose South side that night we arrived.

This Island was anciently called *Proconsus*, the Country of *Aristeus*, a famous Poet, that flourished in the days of *Cræsus*, and a notable Jugler: who dying (or so seeming to do) his body could be no where found by his friends that were assembled to bury him. It had two Cities of that name, the Old and the New: the former built by the builders of *Abydos*. Celebrated for excellent Quarries of white Marble; and therefore now called *Momora*: where a number of poor Christian slaves do hew stones daily for that magnificent *Mosque* which is now a building at *Constantinople* by

this

this *Sultan*. It hath a small Village towards the North, with a Haven peopled by *Greeks*. The soil apt for Vines, and not destitute of Corn: affording also pasturage for Goats, whereof they have plenty. Incredible numbers of Partridges, like to those of *Sio*, here run on the Rocks, and fly chiding about the Vineyards. Having climbed the Mountains, steep towards the Sea, we got to the Town, and bought us some victuals. At night we returned to our Boat which lay in an obscure Bay, where they spent the next day in washing the residue of their Sponges: whilst I and my Interpreter spent our time on the top of the Mountain in the Vineyards: not well pleased with this their delay, now more affecting their case than when without the *Hellespont*: being rid of that fear (for no Pirate dare venture to come within the Castles) which had quickned their expedition. In the evening we descended; where we found the Patron lying on his back upon a Rock, all dropping wet: speechless, and struggling with death to our seeming. The *Greeks* together by the ears, every one with his fellow; some in the Boat, and some upon the shore. Amongst the rest there was a blind man, who had married a young wife that would not let him lie with her, and thereupon had undertaken this journey to complain unto the Patriarch. He hearing his brother cry out at the receipt of a blow; guided to the place by the noise, and thinking with his staff to have struk the striker, laid it on with such a force, that meeting with nothing but air, and not able to recover himself, he fell into the Sea: and with much difficulty was preserved from drowning. The clamor increased with their contentions: and anon the Patron starting up, as if of a sudden restored to life; like a mad man skips into the Boat, and drawing a *Turkish* Cymiter, beginneth to lay about him (thinking that his Vessel had been surprised by Pirates,) when they all leapt into the Sea; and diving under the water like so many Dive-dappers, ascended without the reach of his fury. Leaping ashore, he pursues my *Greek*, whom fear had made too nimble for him; mounting a steep cliff, which at another time he could have hardly ascended. Then turning upon me only armed with stones, as God would have it, he stumbled by the way; and there lay like a stone for two hours together: that which had made them so quarrelsom being now the peace-maker; having cast the fetters of sleep upon their distemperatures. For it being proclaimed death to bring wine unto *Constantinople*, and they loth to pour such good liquor into the Sea, had made their bellies the overcharged vessels. When the Patron awaked, and was informed by my *Greek* how he had used me, and withal of my resolution (which was rather to retire unto the Town, and there expect a passage, than to commit my safety unto such people) he came unto me, and kissed me, as did the rest of his companions, (a testimony amongst them of good will and fidelity) and so inforced me aboard. The winds the next day blew fresh and favourable. That night we came to anchor a little below the seven Towers: and betimes in the morning arrived at the Custom-house. Then crossing the Haven, I landed a *Galata*, and so ascended the vines of *Pera*: where by Sir *Thomas Glover*, Lord Ambassador for the King, I was freely entertained: abiding in his house almost for the space of four months. Of whom without ingratitude and detraction, I cannot but make an honourable mention.

Pausanias King of *Sparta*, that is said to have built, did but re-edifie this City: then called *Byzantium* of *Byza* the founder, and taken by assault but a little before from the *Persians*. A while after he sendeth for *Cleonice* the daughter of an honourable *Byzantine*, with purpose to have abused her: who vainly wasting tears and entreaties, desires that for modesties sake the light might be extinguished. The time delayed by her lingring address, he falleth asleep: and suddenly awaked with her ominous stumbling, then coming unto him, starts up, misdoubting some treason, and strikes her to the heart with a dagger. Haunted by her ghost, or through the terrors of his guilt so perswaded, ever sounding in his ears this saying;

Tu cole justitiam, teque atque alios manet ultor.   *Be just, Revenge attends on thee and others:*
Plut. in Mar.

Zosimus.

he was forced to repair unto *Heraclea*, where the spirits of the deceased, by certain spels and infernal sacrifices were accustomed to be raised. Which performed, the ghost of *Cleonice* appeared, and told him that soon after his arrival at *Sparta* his trouble should end. Which did with his life, mewed up by the *Ephori* in the Temple of *Minerva*, (where he had taken sanctuary:) condemned by them for the intended betraying of his Country unto *Xerxes*. *Byzantium* from that time forward grew famous, and held an equal repute amongst the principal Cities; three years besieged e're taken by the Emperour *Severus*; and at last made Sovereign of the rest by the Emperour *Constan-*

Constantinople. Who detesting the ascent of the Capitol, the Senate, and people, amplified the same, called it *Constantinople*, and made it the seat of his Empire: enduing it with the priviledges of *Rome*, the Citizens of one being free of the other, and capable of the dignities of either. But the chief cause of his remove was, that by being near, and drawing into those parts his principal forces, the Empire towards the East might be the better defended, then greatly annoyed by the *Persians*. The divine determination having so appointed or permitted, that way may be given to the spiritual usurper, and to restore to the Western world their temporal freedom, by with-drawing of their Legions, in the absence of the Emperors, by the succeeding division, and consequent subversion of that Empire. He intended first to have built at *Chalcedon*, on the other side of the *Thracian Bosphorus*, in view of this, and a little below it, whereof the *Megarians* were the builders called blind by the Oracle, for that, first arriving at that place they made choice of the worse and less profitable site: the fish (especially the *Tunny*, bred in the Lake of *Mæotis*, which exceedingly enriched the *Byzantines*) that came out of the *Euxine* Sea, being driven to the contrary shore by the stream, and frighted by the whiteness of the Cliffs from the other. And even at this day fish of sundry kinds, at sundry times, in incredible multitudes, are forced by the aforesaid current into the Haven: when many entring far in, and meeting with the fresh, as if inebriated, turn up their bellies, and are taken. It was reported, that when the workmen began to lay the platform at *Chalcedon*, how certain Eagles conveighed their lines to the other side of the *Straight*, and let them fall right over *Byzantium*: whereupon the Emperour altered his determination, and built his City whereas now it standeth, as if appointed to do so by the D.ity. Finished it was in the eleventh of *May*, in the year 331. and consecrated to the Blessed Virgin. *Rome* he bereft of her ornaments to adorn it: fetching from thence in one year more antiquities, than twenty Emperours had brought thither before in an hundred. Amongst the rest that huge Obelisk of *Theban* Marble, called *Placaton* by the *Greeks*, (formerly brought out of *Egypt*) and erected it in the *Forum*, with a brazen Statue of antique and *Dedalian* work man-ship, set upon the top of a Column, and called by his name (but supposed to be the counterfeit of *Apollo* translated from *Ilium*) thrown down by a violent wind in the reign of *Alexis*. This place was also beautified with the *Trojan Palladium*; an Image of *Pallas* three Cubits high: in the right hand holding a Spear, in the left, a Spindle, and appearing as if it walked; which he gave, as they feign unto *Dardanus* in dowry with his daughter *Chryssa*. By *Ilus* removed unto *Ilium*, it was told them by an Oracle, that as long as it included the same, the City should remain in-expugnable. Whereupon it was placed in the most secret part of the Temple, and another made like it, exhibited to the view: stoln after from thence by *Ulysses* and *Diomedes*. But the true one (together with the *Trojan Penates*) was delivered by *Syeus* to *Æneas*, who carried it with him into *Italy*: removed from *Alba longa* to *Rome*, and placed in the Temple of *Vesta*. Which set accidentally on fire, *Lucius Metellus* being then High-priest, did rescue with the loss of his eyes.

This City by destiny appointed, and by nature seated for Soveraignty, was first the seat of the *Roman* Emperors, then of the *Greek*, as now it is of the *Turkish*: built by *Constantine* the son of *Helena*, and lost by *Constantine* the son of another *Helena* (a *Gregory* then Bishop, whose first Bishop was a *Gregory*) to *Mahomet* the second, in the year 1453. with the slaughter of her people, and destruction of her magnificent Structures. The like may be observed of the Roman Emperors; whose first was *Augustus*, and whose last was *Augustulus*. So have they a Prophecy that *Mahomet* shall lose it.

The Turks call it Stambol, as much as to say, the fair or large City.

Ludovicus Vives in Aug. de Civ. Dei. l. 1. c. 2. ex variis Autor Paulanias in Atticis reports of another daughter of hers by Æsculapius called Hygio.

To powerful Asia oppos'd, in Europe seated:
Of old the bound to both, and now the Head.
Fortune remov'd with the Imperial seat:
And with new fortunes this grew far more great.
Who forc'd, enlarg'd, what now Earths shoulders makes
The basis of her height: even proud Rome quakes.
Not old, a Strumpet whom new lusts defame:
That estimates it no crime not to shame.
Arise thou fiercest, strike, kill, thine's the day:
Laws only add to Arms: rule and obey.

Europæ imposita hæc Asiaque objecta potenti:
Limes utrique olim, nunc utriusque caput.
Translato imperio pariter fortuna recessit:
Crevit, & auspiciis maxima facta novis:
Auxit qui rapuit: sed nunc servicibus oris
Imminet: ipsa etiam Roma superba tremit.
Non vetus illa: novo, meretrix sed perdita luxu:
Quæ nullum crimen nolle pudere putat.
Surge ferox, quate, cæde: tua est victoria: tantum
Milce armis leges: accipe, daque jugum.

J. C. Scalig.

Constantinople.

It stands on a Cape of Land near the entrance of the *Bosphorus*. In form triangular: on the East-side washed with the same, and on the North-side with the Haven,

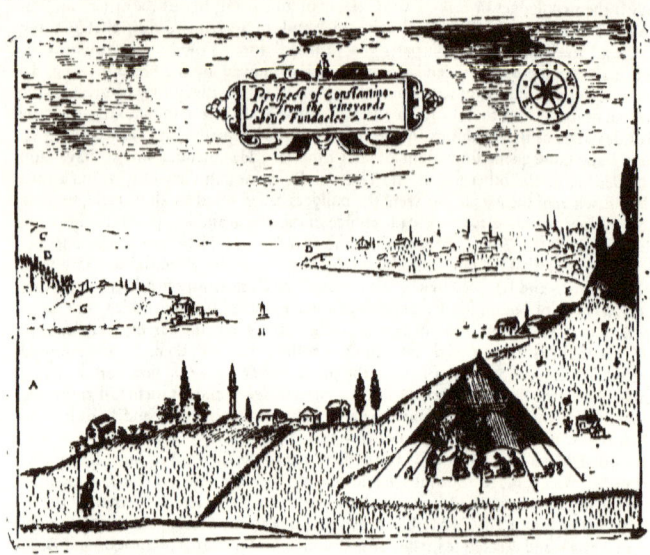

A. *The Thracian Bosphorus and way to the Black Sea.*
B. *The Bay of Ismit.*
C. *The high land over Bursia.*
D. *The entrance into Propontis.*
E. *The Haven of Constantinople.*
F. *Point of Foundaclee.*
G. *Point between Scutari and Chalcedon.*
H. *The Maiden-Tower.*

adjoyning on the West to the Continent. Walled with brick and stone, intermixed orderly: having four and twenty Gates and Posterns; whereof five do regard the Land, and nineteen the Water; being about thirteen miles in circumference. Than this there is hardly in nature a more delicate object, if beheld from the Sea or adjoyning Mountains: the lofty and beautiful Cypress Trees so intermixed with the buildings, that it seemeth to present a City in a Wood to the pleased beholders. Whose seven aspiring heads (for on so many hills and no more, they say it is seated) are most of them crowned with magnificent Mosques, all of white Marble, round in form, and coupled above; being finished on the top with guilded spires, that reflect the beams they receive with a marvellous splendor: some having two, some four, some six adjoyning Turrets, exceeding high, and exceeding slender: tarrass aloft on the out-side like the main top of a Ship and that in several places equally distant. From whence the *Talismanni* with elated voices (for they use no bells) do congregate the people, pronouncing the *Arabick* sentence, La Illa Illella Muhemet resul Allah: viz. *There is but one God, and* Mahomet *his Prophet.* No Mosque can have more than one of these Turrets, if not built by an Emperor. But that of *Sancta Sophia*, once a Christian Temple, (twice burnt, and happily, in that so sumptuously re-edified by the Emperor *Justinian*) exceedeth not only the rest, by whose pattern they were framed, but all other Fabricks whatsoever throughout the whole Universe. A long labour it were to describe it exactly: and having done, my eyes that have seen it would but condemn my defective relation. The principal part thereof riseth in an oval: surrounded with Pillars, admirable for their proportion, matter, and work-man-ship. Over those others; thorough which ample Galleries, curiously paved, and arched above, have their prospect into the Temple: dignified with the presence of Christian Emperors at the time of Divine Service; ascended by them on horf-back. The Roof compact and adorned with *Mosaick* painting. An antique kind of work, composed of little square pieces of Marble; guilded and coloured according to the place that they are to assume in the figure or ground: which set together, as if imbossed, present an unexpressible stateliness, and are of a marvellous durance: numbred by *Pancirollus* amongst
things

things that are lost: but divers in Italy at this day excel in that kind: yet make the particles of clay, gilt, and coloured before they be neiled by the fire. The rest of the Church, though of another proportion, doth joyn to this with a certain harmony. The sides and floor are all flagged with excellent Marble: vaulted underneath, and containing large Cisterns, replenished with water from an Aquæduct. Before the entrance there is a goodly Portico; where the Christians that visit it upon curiosity as well as the *Turks*, do leave their shooes before they do enter. Within on the left hand there is a Pillar covered with Copper, ever sweating, (I know not why, unless in being passed thorow by some Conduit) which the *Turks* wipe off with their handkerchers: through a vain superstition perswaded, that it is of sacred and soveraign vertue. The doors are curiously cut through, and plated: the Wood of one of them feigned to be of the Ark of *Noe*, and therefore left bare in some places to be kissed by the devouter people. *Evagrius*, that lived a thousand years since, affirmeth, this Temple to have been from East unto West, two hundred and threescore feet long, and in height one hundred and fourscore: and *Antonius Menavinus*, that in the days of *Bajazet*, it contained at once six and thirty thousand *Turks*. Perhaps the ancient Fabrick then standing entire; whereof this now remaining was little more than the Chancel. Better to be believed than *Bellonius*, a modern eye-witness, who reports that the doors thereof are in number equal to the days of the year: whereas if it hath five, it hath more by one than by me was discerned. *Mahomet* the Great, upon the taking of the City, threw down the Altars, defaced the Images, (of admirable Workmanship, and infinite in number) converting it into a Molque. To every one of these principal Mosques belong publick *Bagnios*, Hospitals, with Lodgings for *Santons* and Ecclesiastical persons, being endowed with competent Revenues. The inferiour Mosques are built for the most part square: many pent-hous'd with open Galleries, where they accustom to pray at times extraordinary: there being in all (comprehending *Pera*, *Scutari*, and the buildings that border the *Bosphorus*) about the number of eight thousand.

Suntque in eo Templo (si licet dicere) tot portæ quot in anno dies. *Observ. lib.*1. *cap* 76.

But this of *Sophia*, is almost every other *Friday* frequented by the *Sultan*: being near unto the fore-front of his *Seraglio*, which possesseth the extreamest point of the North-East Angle, where formerly stood the ancient *Byzantium*: divided from the rest of the City by a lofty Wall, containing three miles in circuit; and comprehending goodly Groves of Cypresses intermixed with Plains, delicate Gardens, artificial Fountains, all variety of Fruit-trees, and what not rare? Luxury being the steward, and the Treasure unexhaustible. The proud Palace of the Tyrant doth open to the South: having a lofty Gate-house without Lights on the outside, and engraven with Arabick Characters, set forth with Gold and Azure, all of white Marble. This leadeth into a spacious Court three hundred yards long, and above half as wide. On the left side thereof, stands the Round of an ancient Chappel, containing the Arms that were taken from the *Grecians* in the subversion of this City; and at the far end of his Court a second Gate, hung with Shields and Cymiters, doth lead into another full of tall Cypress-trees, less large, yet not by much than the former. The Cloisters about it leaded above, and paved with stone, the Roof supported with Columns of Marble, having Copper Chapiters and Bases. On the left hand the *Divano* is kept, where the *Bassas* of the Port do administer Justice; on that side confined with humble buildings. Beyond which Court on the right hand there is a street of Kitchins: and on the left is the Stable, large enough for five hundred Horse; where there is now to be seen a Mule so admirably streak'd, and dappled with white and black, and in such due proportion, as if a Painter had done it, not to imitate nature, but to please the eye, and express his curiosity. Out of this second Court there is a passage into the third, not by Christians ordinarily to be entred: surrounded with the Royal Buildings, which though perhaps they come short of the *Italian*, for contrivement and fineness of Workmanship; yet not in costly curiousness, matter, and amplitude. Between the East-wall (which also serveth for a Wall to the City) and the water, a sort of terrible Ordnance are planted, which threaten destruction to such as by Sea shall attempt a violent entry or prohibited passage. And without on the North-side stands the *Sultans* Cabinet in form of a sumptuous Summer-house; having a private message made for the time of waxed linen from his *Seraglio*: where he often solaceth himself, with the various objects of the Heaven; and from thence takes Barge to pass unto the delightful places of the adjoyning *Asia*. This Palace, howsoever enlarged by the *Ottomans*, was first erected by *Justinus*.

Qua resonante freto fluctus cava littora tundunt;
Et duplici Pontus nomine scindit humum,
Inclytus uxori celebranda palatia struxit
Rex Sophiæ, multus quam decoravit honos.
Quam bene (Roma potens) tua gloria constitit, unde
Europa atque Asiæ fertilis arva patent.
Agathius.

*Where flouds encountring hollow shores resound
And straightned Seas of two names cut the ground;
The King for his Sophia did erect
A stately Palace, sumptuously deckt.
How well (great Rome) did he thy glory raise,
Which Asia's, and Europe's Fields surveys!*

and named it *Sophia* of the Empress.

Now next to these *Ottoman Mansolia's* do require their regard, built all of white Marble, round in form, coupled on the top, and having stately Porches. Within each is the Tomb of a several *Sultan*, with the Tombs of his children, that either have died before him, or have after been strangled by their tyrannical brethren, according to the *Turkish* piety. The Tombs are not longer nor larger than fitting the included bodies, each of one stone higher at the head than feet, and compass'd above, without other ornaments than covers of green, and Turbants laid upon the upper ends. At the four corners of those of the *Sultans*, there stand four Tapers of Wax, as big as a thigh, but not lighted. The floors of the Monuments are spread with Carpets, and some there are that do continually live therein; performing such duties of prayers and lamentations as agreeth to their customs, at certain times besprinkled with the tears of their off-spring.

The South-east angle of this City is taken up by the seven Towers, called anciently *Janicula*; employed as the Tower of *London*, for a Store-house of the *Sultans* Treasure and Munition, being also a Prison for capital offenders. We omit to speak of the great mens *Seraglios*, that of the women belonging to the deceased Emperours; and that of the *Virgins*; the *Alberges* of *Janizaries*; the several Seminaries of *Spachies* and *Giamoglans*: the *Besestans* (where finer sorts of commodities are sold) Hospitals; Markets of men and women, &c. since hereafter we are to treat of most of their Orders; the buildings themselves not meriting a particular description, converting our discourse to those few remainders of many Antiquities, whereof the *Aquaduct* made by the Emperour *Valentinian*, and retaining his name, doth principally challenge remembrance: this hath his heads near to the black Sea, not far from a Village called *Domuz-dere*, of the abundance of wild Hogs thereabout, the place being woody and Mountainous; where many Springs are gathered together, and at sundry places do jointly fall into great round Cisterns, from thence conveyed to conjoin with others (amongst which, as supposed, is the Brook *Cydarius*) led sometimes under the earth, now along the level, then upon mighty Arches over profound Vallies, from hill to hill, for the space well-nigh of thirty miles, until arriving at the City, and surmounting the same, it falleth at length as from a head-long cataract, into an ample Cistern, supported with near two hundred pillars of Marble, and is from thence by Conduits conducted unto their publick uses. This was repaired by *Solyman* the Great, Grandfather of this now reigning *Achmet*, whose wishes and endeavours are said to have aimed at three things; which were, the re-edifying of *Ponte Picolo*, and *Ponte Grande* (which cross two arms of the Sea) and the restoring of this *Aquaduct*; these he accomplished, but the third which was the expugnation of *Vienna*, he could never accomplish. Not far from the Temple of *Sancta Sophia*, there is a spacious place surrounded with buildings, like to that of *Smith-field*, and anciently called the *Hippodrom*, for that there they exhibited their Horse-races.

Pulvereumque fugax Hippodromon ungula pulsat.
Mart. l. 12. Epig. 50.

The swift foot beats the dusty Hippodrom.

As now *Atmidan* by the *Turks*, a word of like signification, where the *Spachies* of the Court play every *Friday* at *Giocho di Canni*, which is no other than Prison-base upon horse-back, hitting one another with Darts, as the other do with their hands; which they never throw counter, but at the back of the flyer. Nor is it the least contentment to the Christian, to behold the terrible falls that they often get (not rarely costing their lives) whilst by the wreathing of their bodies, or a too hasty turn, they seek to avoid the pursuer; and sometimes the Darts not lighting in jest on their naked necks, and reversed faces. In this place there standeth a stately Hieroglyphical Obelisk of *Theban* Marble. On the one side of the Pedestal, this Epigram is engraven, which for that imperfect (as the rest) and of no import, I will forbear to interpret.

DIFFI-

LIB. I. Constantinople.

DIFFICILIS QUONDAM DOMINIS PARERE SERENIS
JUSSUS ET EXTINCTIS PALMAM PORTARE TYRANNIS
OMNIA THEODOSIO CEDUNT SOBOLIQUE PERENNI
TER DENIS SIC VICTUS CECOD... MITUSQUE DIEBUS
JUDICE SUB PROCLOSI......SELATUS AD AURAS.

And this on the other side.

ΚΙΟΝΑ ΤΕΤΡΑΠΛΕΥΡΟΝ ΑΕΙΣ ΘΟΝΙΚΕΙΜΕΝΟΝ ΑΧΘΟC
ΜΟΥΝΟC ΑΝΑCΤΕCΑΙ ΘΕΥΔΟCΙΟC ΒΑCΙΛΕΥΟC
ΤΟΛΜΗCΑC ΠΡΟΚΛΟC ΕΠΕΚΕΚΛΕΤΟ ΚΑΙ ΤΟCΟC ΕCΤΗ
ΚΙΩΝ ΗΕΛΙΟC ΕΝ ΤΡΙΑΚΟΝΤΑΔΥΩ.

A little removed there standeth a Column of wreathed Brass, with three infolded Serpents at the top, extended in a Triangle, looking severall ways. And beyond both these, another high Obelisk, termed by some a Colossus, built of sundry stones, now greatly ruined, covered heretofore with plates of guilded Brass; whose basis do ye retain this Inscription,

—ΤΟ ΤΕΤΡΑΠΛΕΥΡΟΝ ΘΑΥΜΑ ΤΩΝ ΜΕΤΑΡCΙΩΝ
ΧΡΟΝ ΩΦΘΑΡΕΝ ΝΥΝ ΚΩΕCΤΑΝΤ ΝΟC ΔΕCΠΟΥΗC
ΟΥ ΡΩΜΑΝΟCΗΑΙC ΔΟΖΑ ΤΗΣ CΚΗΠΤΟΥΧΙΑC
ΚΡΕΙΤΤΟΝ ΝΕΘΥΡΙΕΙ ΤΗΣ ΠΑΛΛΙΘΕΩΡΙΑC
Ο ΒΑΡ ΚΟΛΟCCΟCΘ ΑΜΒΟC ΗΝ ΤΗ ΡΟΛΩ
ΚΑΙ ΧΑΛΚΟC ΟΤΤΟC ΘΑΜΒΟC ΕCΤΙΝ ΕΝΘΑΛΕ.

And in *Aurathasar* (that is, the Market of women) there is an historicall Column to be ascended within, far surpassing both *Trajans*, and that of *Antonine*, which I have seen in *Rome*: the work-man having so proportioned the Figures, that the highest and lowest appear of one bigness.

And right against the Mansion of the *German* Emperors Ambassadour (who only is suffered to lodge within the City) stands the Column of *Constantine*: about the top whereof you may read this Distichon.

ΤΟ ΘΕΙΟΝ ΕΡΓΟΝ ΕΝΘΑΛΕ ΦΘΑΡΕΝ ΧΡΟΝΩ.
ΝΕΟΙ ΜΑΝΟΤΗΛ ΕΥΣΕΒΗΣ ΑΥΤΟΚΡΑΤΩΡ.

These are all the remains that are left, (or all that are by the Christians to be seen, besides the reliques of the Palace of *Constantine*, now made a stable for wild beasts) of so many goodly buildings, and from all parts congested antiquities, wherewith this sovereign City was in times past so adorned. And with them are their memories perished. For not a *Greek* can satisfie the Inquirer in the history of their own calamities. So supine negligent are they, or perhaps so wise, as of passed evils to endeavour a forgetfulness. But to say something of *Constantinople* in generall: I think there is not in the world an object that promiseth so much afar off to the beholders, and entred so deceiveth the expectation: the best of their private buildings, inferiour to the more contemptible sort of ours. For the *Turks* are nothing curious of their houses: not only for that their possessions are not hereditary; but esteeming it an egregious folly to erect such sumptuous habitations, as if here to live for ever, forgetful of their Graves, and humane vicissitude. Reproved likewise by the Poet,

Thou Marble hew'st, ere long to part with breath:	Tu secanda marmora
And H uses rear'st, unmindful of thy death.	Locas sub ipsum funus: & sepulchri
	Immemor, struis domos.
	Horat. l. 2. Od. 18.

None being above two stories high, some of rough Stone, some of Timber, some of Sun-dried Brick: their Roofs but rising a little, covered with such Tiles as are laid on the Ridges of ours, one contrary to another; Yet some part of some of them flat, (those belonging to men of principal degree) planted with Flowers and Trees of the rarest colours and productions. Many vacant places there are in the City, and many rows of buildings, consisting of Shops only, all belonging to the *Grand Signior*, who lets them out unto Trades-men; into which their Wives come not. Women being prohibited by *Mahomet* to buy or sell (though not now seldom doms they do, or shew themselves publickly. The streets for the most part are exceeding narrow; some raised on the sides for more cleanliness; many having steep ascents, in many places bounded with long dead walls, belonging to great mens *Scraglios*. So negligent are they of exteriour garnishings.

THE HISTORICALL COLVMNE IN AVRAT BASAR

All the Suburbs that this City hath, lie without the Gate of *Adrianople*; adjoining to the North west angle thereof, and stretching along the uppermost of the Haven. Where within a stately Monument, there standeth a Tomb of principal repute in the *Mahumetan* devotion; the Sepulchre of *Jupe Sultan a Sammor* of theirs, called vulgarly and ridiculously, the Sepulchre of *Job*. To which the *Captain Bassa* doth repair before he sets forth, and at his return; there performing appointed Oraisons and Ceremonies, and upon a victory obtained, is obliged to visit the same every morning and evening, for the space of three weeks. Before this in a Cypress Grove there standeth a Scaffold, where the new *Sultans* are girt with a Sword by the hands of the *Mufti*, their principal Prelate, with divers solemnities.

Now speak we of the Haven, rather devoured than increased by a little River called formerly *Barbyses*, now by the *Greeks*, *Chartaricon*, and *Chay* by the *Turks*; much frequented by Fowl, and rigorously preserved for the *Grand Signiors* pleasure, who ordinarily hawks thereon; insomuch that a servant of my Lord Ambassadors was so beaten for presuming to shoot there, that shortly after he died (as it is thought of) the blows. This falleth into the West extent of the Haven: throughout the world the fairest, the safest, the most profitable. So conveniently profound, that the greatest Ships may lay their sides to the sides thereof, for the more easie receipt, or discharge of their burthen. The mouth of it is land-lockt by the opposite *Asia*; opening Eastward into the *Thracian Bosphorus*, which by a long narrow Chanel stretching North and South, joins the black and white Seas: so call they the Seas North and South of the *Bosphorus*. So that no wind bloweth, which brings not in some Shipping or other to the furnishing of this City; (having as it hath been said before) on the left hand the *Euxine Sea*, with the Lake of *Maeotis*, inhabited about by multitudes of Nations, and entred into by many navigable Rivers, whereby whatsoever groweth, or is nourished in those far-distant Countries, is easily transported unto it: on the right hand *Propontis* and the Mid-land Sea, (bordered with *Natolia*, *Syria*, *Egypt*, *Africa*, *Spain*, *France*, *Italy*, *Greece*, and *Dalmatia*, with their fruitful Islands) and without the great Ocean. Insomuch as it seemeth by the opportunity of Navigation to participate with their several commodities, daily brought hither by Foreigners, seated of it self in a Country, though not altogether barren, yet not sufficient to sustain the Inhabitants. *Moldavia* and *Valachia* do serve them with Beeves and Muttons; and as for Fish, the adjoining Seas yield store and variety; as the concaves of the Rocks do Salt, white, pure, and solid; made only by the labour of the surges. But notwithstanding all this,

What place so wretched see we, so retired?
Worse than the fearful blaze f houses fired,
Their dayly falls, with thousand mischiefs more,
Of that dire City.

Quid tam miserum, tam solum vidimus, ut non
Dererius credas? horrere incendia, lapsus
Tectorum assiduos, ac mille pericula sævæ
Urbis.

Juven. Sat. 3.

For I know not by what fate or misfortune, subject it hath been to sundry horrible combustions. Unto that which befel in the days of *Leo*, and not long after in the reign of *Basilicus*, (when amongst other infinite losses that famous Library perished, containing 120000 volumes: where, in the inward skin of a Dragon the Odysses and Iliads of *Homer* were written:) and to divers others this last, though less, may be added, which hapned on the 14. of *October* in the year 1607. in which 3000 houses were burnt to their foundations. Nor is it to be marvelled at; the Citizens themselves not daring to quench the fire that burneth their own houses, or by pulling down some, to preserve the remainder. An office that belongeth to the *Aga* and his *Janizaries*, who nothing quick in their assistance, do often for spite or pillage beat down such buildings as are farther removed from danger. So that the mischief is not only wished for the booty, but prolonged. And not seldom they themselves set the *Jews* houses on fire, who made wary by the example, are now furnished of arched Vaults for the safeguard of their goods, which are not to be violated by the flame. The tall of houses heretofore by terrible and long-lasting earth-quakes, now by negligence in repairing, tempests, and the matter that they consist of, is here also most frequent, many (as hath been said) being built of Sun-dried Brick. And although it enjoys a delicate air, and serene skies even during the winter, when the East, the West, or South wind bloweth, yet the boisterous *Tramotana*, that so in the black Sea doth sweep its black substance, here most violently rages, bringing often with it such storms of Snow, that in *September* I have seen the then flourishing Trees so overcharged therewith, that their branches have broken,

accom-

accompanied with bitter frosts; which diffolving, refolve therewith the infirm matter that fuftains them. Laftly, the plague (either hapning through the vice of the Clime, or of thofe mif-believers, or hither brought by the many frequenting nations) for the moft part miferably infecteth this City: increafed by the fuperftition of the *Mahometans*, from whom it may be that fome one amongft us derived that damnable doctrine; which coft fo many lives in the time of our great infection. To thefe add the Scepter of a Tyrant, with the infolency of Slaves: and then, O new *Rome*, how are thy thus balanced profits and delights to be valued!

On the other fide of the Haven (continually croffed by multitudes of little Boats called *Permagins*, and rowed for the moft part by *Egyptians*) ftands the City of *Galata*, fo called (as fome write) of the *Gauls*, once the mafters thereof; or as others will have it, of *Galac*, which fignifieth Milk; for that there the *Greeks* kept their Cattle, as *Pera* (another name thereof,) which fignifieth beyond, in that on the other fide of the Haven, but more anciently *Cornu Bizantium*. Infirmly walled; yet great, if you comprehend the Suburbs therewith, extending from along the fhore to the upper tops of the Mountains; furpaffing *Conftantinople* in her lofty buildings. Built by the *Genoefi*, who bought it of the *Greek* Emperors, (in their declining eftate poffeft of little more than the regal City, and Title; for the moft part fuftained by foreign contributions:) and was by them furrendred unto *Mahomet* the Great, the day after the facking of *Conftantinople*. At the Weft end thereof the *Grand Signiors* Gallies have a dry ftation, and at the Eaft end, right againft the point of his *Seraglio*, called *Tophana*, and *Fundacle*, lies a number of great Ordnance un-planted; moft of them the fpoil of Chriftian Cities and Fortreffes, as may appear by their Infcriptions, and Impreffes: and many of them of an incredible greatnefs.

Now right againft the mouth of the Haven on the other fide of the *Bofphorus*, ftands *Scutari*, a Town of *Bithynia*, fo named of the Garrifon there kept: and formerly called *Chryfopolis*, for that there the *Perfians* received their tribute from other Cities of *Afia*. An ample Town, environed with goodly Orchards, and honoured with the neighbour-hood of a Royal *Seraglio*. Before it on a little Rock a good way off from the fhore a Tower is erected called the *Maiden*-Tower, whereof a fable they tell, not worth the relating: now ferving as well for a Fort as a watch-Tower, having in it twenty pieces of Ordnance. And although the Sea be fo deep between it and the fhore that a Ship may fail through, yet is it ferved with frefh water, fome fay, brought thither by art, I rather think from a natural Fountain. *Scutari* fometimes belonged to *Chalcedon*, once a free City, and feated a little below it: fo called of a Brook, now without a name, that runs into *Propontis*; called alfo, The City of the blind, becaufe of the foolifh *Megarians* that built it. Famous for the fourth general Council there holden: and now only fhewing a part of her ruines.

The black Sea is diftant fome fifteen miles from *Conftantinople*, fo named of its black effects, or for the thick mifts that ufually hang over it; or as fome fay, of a princely Bridegroom and Bride that therein perifhed. Firft, called *Axenus*, which fignifieth un-hofpital: by reafon of the coldnefs thereof, and humanity of the bordering Nations; who accuftomed to facrifice their guefts, to eat their flefh; and of their skulls to make drinking-bowls. But after the *Ionians* and *Greeks* had planted certain *Colonies* thereabout, and difplanted the barbarous, it was called *Euxinus*, which hath a contrary fignification. Of this the exiled *Ovid*.

Frigida me cohibent Euxini littora Ponti,
Dictus ab antiquis Axenus ille fuit.
Ovid Trift. l. 4. Eleg. 4.

Me the cold coafts of Euxine Pontus bold,
More fitly termed Axenus of old.

The form thereof is compared to a *Scythian* Bow when extended. On the South-fide from the *Bofphorus* it is bordered with *Pontus*, *Bithynia*, and *Cappadocia*, (wherein the Imperial City of *Trapezond*) *Colchis* it hath on the Eaft; on the North between it and *Caucafus* lies a part of *Sarmatia Afiatica*. Then the Fens of *Mæotis*,

Quam Scythiæ gentes circumdant undique ripis:
Et matrem Ponti perhibent Mæotidis undam.

Which favage Scythians inhabit round:
For Mother of the Pontick Sea renown'd.

and therefore called *Temerinda*: fed by the mighty River of *Tanais*, which divideth *Afia* from *Europe*. The reft of the North fide is bounded by the *European Sarmatia*. On the Weft is confined part of *Dacia*, and the hither *Mafia*, feparated by *Danubius*, and the remainder with *Thracia*. The Sea is lefs falt than others, and much annoyed with Ice in the Winter.

There

LIB. I.   *Euxine Sea. Thracian Bosphorus.*   31

There where stiff Winter which no Spring remits,   Et qua bruma rigens ac nescia vere remitti
With bonds of Ice the Scythian Pontus knits.   Astringit Scythicum glaciali frigore Pontum.
                                                                                                   Lucan. l. 1.

Here the *Turk* prohibiteth Foreigners to traffick, there being no other passage therein-to but by Rivers; neither this passage of *Bosphorus* as some conjecture, hath been

A. *Part of Thrace.*   B. *The Lanthorn.*   C. *Part of Bithynia.*   D. *Euxine Sea.*   E. *Bosphorus.*

always, but forced by the violence of streams that fell into the over-charged *Euxine.* Where it rusheth into the *Bosphorus*, there are two Rocks, that formerly bare the names of *Cyanee* and *Symplegades*: which for that so near, as many times appearing but as one, they were fained by the Poets un-stable, and at sundry times to justle each other. Here, upon the top of a Rock environed with the Sea, supposed by some to be one of these, if not too far removed from a fellow to be so, stands a pillar of white marble, called vulgarly the pillar of *Pompey.*

Upon the shore there is an high Lanthorn, large enough at the top to contain about three-score persons, which by night directeth the Sailer into the entrance of the *Bosphorus.*

The *Bosphorus* setteth with a strong current into *Propontis*, and is in length about twenty miles: where broadest, a mile, and in two places but half a mile over. So called, for that Oxen accustomed to swim from the one side to the other: or as the Poets will have it, from the passage of Metamorphosed *Io.*

Now day and winds invite: to Sea put they,   Jamque dies auræque vocant: rursusque capessunt
Where Bosphorus doth his rough floods display.   Æquora, qua rigidos eructat Bosphorus amnes.
Io, not then a Goddess, crost the same   Illos (Nile) tuis nondum Dea gentibus Io
(Nile) to thy soil: it therefore took that name.   Transierat fluctus: unde hæc data nomina Ponto;
                                                                                                   Val. Flac. Argen. l. 4.

A. *The Rock suppos'd one of the Symplegades.*
B. *The Black Sea.*
C. *The entrance of the Bosphorus towards Constantinople.*
D. *The Coast of Asia towards Trapesond.*
E. *Part of Thrace.*
F. *The foot of the Lanthorn Tower.*

The basis whereof did bear these now worn-out Characters.

DIVO. CÆSARI. AUGUSTO.
L. CLANNIDIUS.
L. F. CLA. PONTO.

One of those two fore-mentioned Straits lye before *Constantinople*, the othe five miles and above a half, where on *Europe* side there standeth a Castle called formerly *Damalis*, and now the *black Tower*: strongly fortified, and commanding that entry, with the help of the other on the opposite shore: environed with a wall two and twenty foot broad, and containing three great Towers; their walls exceeding ten yards in thickness. This is also a Prison for Captives of principal quality, at such time as the deservedly beloved Mr. *Barton* lay here Ambassador for our Nation, there was a certain *Hollander*, called *Hadrian Cant*, who being taken by a *Renegado*, then Captain of two Gallies, was by the *Grand Signiors* commandment shut up in this place; they expecting great matter for his ransom. Where after he had remained three years, arising one morning before day, and finding the doors open, he descended without the privity of his keepers into the Court of the Castle. When advising with himself of his escape, and casting his eyes about him, he found a Rope that was tied to a Tree, not far from the wall, which he ascending, by the benefit thereof without danger descended on the other side, and from thence conveyed into the house of our Ambassador; then (as now) a Sanctuary for escaped Captives, where for three days they hid him under a Wood-stack, and not long after shipt him for *Holland*. In the morning the Captain of the Castle having vainly sought for his Prisoner, filled forth with a Coffin with Clay, and caused it to be thrown into the *Bosphorus*; giving it out that he was dead, affrighted with the punishment of his predecessor being ganched for the escape of certain Noblemen of *Germany* committed to his custody. Five miles above this, the *Bosphorus* was passed over a Bridge of Boats by *Darius* the Father of *Xerxes*. The *European* side is bordered almost with continued buildings, the other with fruitful Hills and Orchards, not yielding (I suppose) in delights to that celebrated *Thessalian Tempe*, when kept by the more curious Christians, and adorned with their now prostrate Palaces.

A. *The black Tower.* C. *Thracian Bosphorus.* E. *Part of Bithynia.*
B. *The opposite Castle.* D. *Part of Thracia.*

Of *Novo Roma* (a name of *Constantine*) the adjoining Country is at this day called *Romania*: formerly *Thracia*, of *Thrax* the son of *Mars*, or of *Thracia* an enchatress, or rather of the fierce and savage disposition of the people (for so the name importeth) who sacrificed men to *Mars* and *Bellona*, when about to join battel. Of these thus *Sidonius* in his Panegyrick to *Antemius.*

Thrace stor'd with worthies thy dominions know,	Thracum terra tua est, heroum fertilis ora,
Here Infants lye on Ice, and Cymbrian snow,	Excipit hic natos glacies, & matris ab alvo
Their soft limbs harden, from the hour they are born	Artus infantum molles nix Cymbrica durat.
The brest doth nourish few; they from thence torn	Pectore vix aliter quisquam sed ab uhere tractus
Suck more from Horses wounds. milk leaving, so	Plus potat per vulnus equum; sic lacte relicto,
All gather courage. For while they grow,	Virtutum genus rota bibit, crevere parumper,
They sporting fight with Darts, whom strokes incite.	Mox pugnam ludunt jaculis; hos suggerit illis
Boys, apt for hunting, savage beasts delight	Nutrix plaga jocos, pueri venatibus apti
To rouse from Dens. The youth enricht with spoil	Lustra feris vacuant. Rapto ditata juventus,
Make Swords their Laws, esteeming spent age vile,	Jura colit gladiis consuumaramque senectam.
Which steel sends not to death. Even such a life	Non ferro finire pudet. Tali ordine vitæ
Lead Mars his brood. ——	Cives Martis agunt, ——

This Country is confined on the North with mount *Hæmus*, called *Catena mundi* by the *Italians*; on the East it hath the *Pontick* and *Propontick* Seas; on the South the *Ægean* joining on the West to *Macedonia* and the upper *Masia*. Her more famous mountains are that afore-said *Hæmus*, *Rhodope* still topt with Snow, and celebrated for the songs of *Orpheus*; *Pangeus* rich in Silver, and *Massapus* for high steep piked Rocks to be wondred at. The chief Rivers are, slow *Hebrus*, salubrious *Tranus*, and troubled *Nessus*. The chief Cities next unto this, *Nicopolis Philippi* yet boasting of her Amphitheater, *Philipolis*, *Hadrianopolis*, *Trajanopolis*, *Selymbria*, *Perinthus*, *Phinapolis*, and *Apollonia*. In length it containeth twenty days journey, in Latitude seven. Towards the Sea it is indifferent fruitful; producing Corn, and not contemptible Wines, but the farther removed, the less profitable; lying in a wild champion, made barren by the bitter cold of the Climate. It is under the government of the *Beglerbeg* of *Grecia*, who is also called the *Beglerbeg* of *Romania*.

The *Turks* now Lord of this Imperial City, (together with the goodliest portion on of the earth) arrived at this height of dominion from so secure an original, as the same is rather conjectured at, than positively delivered by any. But certain it is, they were a people of *Scythia*; who forsaking their own homes, in the year 844. constrained by famine, or expelled by their neighbours, entred through the Straights of the *Caspian* Mountains, and by strong hand possest themselves of *Armenia* the greater; called thereupon *Turcomania*, as it is at this day, multiplying by the daily accession of their Country-men; being in Religion Pagans, and living in wandring Troups, according to the *Scythian Nomades*. Now the *Saracen* Empire drawing nigh a period by the division of the *Mahometan* Princes, *Mahomet Sultan* of *Persia*, too weak for the *Caliph* of *Babylon*, intreated aid of the *Turks* who sent him three thousand Souldiers, under the leading of *Tangrolipix*, the chief of the *Selzuceian* family, by whose assistance he overthrew the *Caliph*. Yet would he compell the *Turk* to do him further service, whereupon a quarrel, and consequently a Battel was commenced between them; In which, *Mahomet* miscarrying, *Tangrolipix* by consent of both Armies was elected *Sultan*. To *Persia* he adjoyned the temporal jurisdiction of *Babylon*, having subdued the *Caliph*, but continued the spiritual to his successor, as successors unto their false Prophet; the *Turk* having then embraced the *Mahometan* superstition, which was two hundred and fourteen years after their eruption out of *Scythia*. *Axan* succeeded his Father *Tangrolipix*: who upon agreement with *Cutlu-Muses* and his kinsman (of him likewise unto him) then in Arms, assigned unto them the absolute sovereignty of whatsoever they could purchase with their swords from the *Grecian* Emperor: who by him aided, subdued *Media*, much of *Armenia*, *Cappadocia*, *Pontus*, *Bithynia*, and most of the lesser *Asia*: On the other side, the *Sultan* gave to *Ducas* and *Melech*, two other of his kinsmen, the Cities of *Damascus* and *Aleppo*, with their territories, to hold of him in chief, with whatsoever they could win from the *Saracens*, who shortly became masters of the greater part of *Syria*. But soon after beaten out of it (as for the most part out of *Asia* the less) by *Godfrey* of *Bullen*, and his Christian Forces, they were forced to retire into the more Easterly parts of their dominions; so that now their declining glories did seem to imitate, or rather exceed their swift ascension unto Empire. But they shortly after recovered their losses in the lesser *Asia*. For the warlike *Solyman* (the son of *Cutlu-Muses*) that so withstood the Western Christians, being now dead, *Mahomet* succeeded him. Between whom, and *Masut* then *Sultan* of *Iconium*, there besel a War, and forthwith an agreement. But *Masut* in fine possest of the whole *Turkish* Kingdom in that part of *Asia*, dying; did divide it amongst his three sons. To *Calizast Iban* he gave the regal City of *Iconium*, with the under-Provinces; to *Jagupasan*, *Amasta*, and *Ancyra*, with part of *Cappadocia*, and the territories adjacent: but to *Dadune* he gave the ample Cities of *Cesaria* and *Sebastia*; and all the spacious Countries adjoining: the whole being lately a parcel of the declining *Greek Empire*. But these ambitious brethren like the sons of the Earth, drew their swords on each other. The eldest dispossessing *Dadune* of his patrimony; and turning his Forces upon *Jacupasan*, (who died in the preparation of that War) seized also upon his. Then invading the adjoyning parts of the Empire, in a mortal Battel he overthrew *Emmanuel Comnenus* the valiant, but unfortunate Emperour; subduing after his death the Country of *Phrygia*, with divers frontier Cities and Castles. This aged *Sultan* dying, left behind him four sons, *Masut*, *Coppatine*, *Reneratine* and *Chaichosroes*. To *Masut* he bequeathed *Amasa*, *Ancyra*, *Doryleum*, with sundry other Cities of *Pontus*: to *Coppatine*, *Melitene*, *Cesarea*, *Taxara*: to *Reneratine*, *Aminsum*, *Docea*, with the Sea bordering Cities; but to *Chaichosroes* (besides the regal seat of *Iconium*) *Lycaonia*, *Pamphilia*, and the bordering Countries as far as *Cotyanium*, with the title of *Sultan*. But these fell also at discord; for *Coppatine* dying soon after, *Reneratine* and *Masut* contended in arms for his possessions. *Reneratine* prevailing, invadeth the *Sultan*, takes from him *Iconium*, expels him out of his dominions, and retaineth sole Sovereign. As these thus here prevailed; so the race of *Ducas* and *Melech* before spoken of, recovered all *Syria* from the contentious Christians, conducted by the glorious *Saladine*, having also joyned *Egypt* to that Empire who left nine sons behind; all murthered but one, by *Saphradine* their Uncle: and he escaping by the means of his fathers favourites, called also *Saphradine* and *Sultan* of *Aleppo*. Of that treacherous *Saphradine*, *Meleden Sultan* of *Egypt* descended, and *Coradin*, *Sultan* of *Damascus* & *Jerusalem*. The mighty Empire of *Saladine* again rent in pieces, yet was still possest in parts by the *Selzuceian* family until driven out of *Syria* by the Tartars and dispossest of *Egypt* by the *Mamuluchs*. But the *Turkish* Empire that was planted in *Persia* by *Tangrolipix*, and in those Eastern Countries, after it had continued an hundred

hundred three-score and ten years was utterly subverted by the *Tartars*. A fierce and barbarous people, dwelling on the North of the mountain *Caucasus*; who oppressed by Famine, at the perswasion of one *Zingis*, a Prophet of theirs, their Leader, and honoured by them with the stile of Great *Cham*, like a violent Inundation brake over those Mountains that had for many ages contain'd them, and over-spread all the East of *Asia*, even as far as the great Ocean. Heereat a his son built *Quinsay* in *China*, and *Cambalu* in *Catbata*, making the last named the seat of the Empire. Dividing his populous Army, some he sent into the South, some into the North, some into the West; who subdued the *Aracosians, Margians, Medes, Persians, Parthians, Assyrians, Mesopotamians, Armenians, Colchians* and *Iberians*; with whom the *Turks* not able to encounter, quitted those countries, and led by *Aladine* one of the *Selzuccian* family, joined themselves with the Country-men in the lesser *Asia*; who took *Cilicia* from the *Greeks*, with the places adjoining, then in wars with the *Latines*; first planting the seat of their new kingdom in *Sebastia*, and after at *Iconium*. *Aladine* left behind him two sons, *Azadin*, and *Jathatine*; they falling out for the sovereignty, the younger was driven by the elder into exile. But *Azadin* dying *Jathatine* returneth, and is received for *Sultan*: after slain in single combat by *Theodorus Lascaris* the Greek Emperor. Another of that name succeeded him; who, overthrown by the victorious *Tartars*, and forced out of *Iconium*, the *Turks* were at length constrained to pay them tribute, and to become their liege-men. *Jathatine* dying in exile, the Great *Cham* divideth his kingdom between *Masut* and *Cei-cubades* (descended both of the *Selzuceia* family) as to his tributary vassals. Thus this late mighty Empire, extinguisht in *Egypt* by the *Mammaluckes*, in the greater *Asia* by *Tartars*, as also in the less was for a time deprived of all principality. For not long continued they under the government of the aforesaid Princes, every one seizing on a part, according to the proportion of his power, and of the ruines of a Monarchy, erected an Anarchy. The baser sort possessing themselves of the straights of the Mountains, by their many incursions annoying the Christians; and having given the Emperors Lieutenant a bloody overthrow in *Paphlagonia*, over-ran all the Country unto the River *Sangarius*, subduing *Pontus* and *Galatia*; and South-ward unto the *Lycian* and *Carian* Seas, and to the River *Eurimedon*, which they divided into several Toparchies. Now of those two fore-named Princes, *Masut* died issue-less, but *Aladin* succeeded his father *Cei-cubades*, titular Lord of the whole, but tributary to the *Tartar*, the last of the *Selzneeian* family. He dying, *Sahib* the head *Vesir* usurped the Sovereignty, yet held it not long. The Great ones sharing amongst them (as they had done the rest) the remainder of that dis-membred Kingdom.

Ottoman among these possessed *Siguta*, a little Lordship in *Bithynia*. Not seized on by force, but given by *Aladin* the first, unto his father *Ertogriel* the son of *Solyman*, one of the *Oguzian* family, and once *Sultan* of *Machan*, who forsaking his Kingdom for fear of the *Tartars*, long led a wandring life with uncertain fortunes. But *Ertogriel* turning into the lesser *Asia*, requested of *Aladin* that he would allot some corner of his so large a Kingdom, for him, his distressed Country-man, and his family to rest in. Who mindful of what himself had suffered (having besides in a Battel almost lost against the *Tartar*, by his unexpected supply of four hundred Horse, recovered the Victory) assigned him this Village to winter in, and the Mountains adjoining for the summering of his Cattel, with some command upon the frontiers. Where he long lived a quiet life, beloved both of *Turks* and Christians continuing, for his peaceable nature and good offices done them. Dying in the fourscore and thirteenth year of his age, and in the year of our Lord 1289, he left three sons behind him, *Jundus, Sarugatin*, and this *Ottoman*, whom the *Ogusians* elected for their Governor. Now the Christians having done some outrages to his people, he thereupon surprized divers of their Castles, overthrew the *Greeks* in sundry conflicts, took from them the City of *Nice*, for which he made many honours proffered by the latter *Aladin*, which whilest he lived he forbore to accept; but dead, took upon him the title of *Sultan*, making *Neapolis* his regal seat, in the year 1300 to which is to be referred the beginning of the *Ottoman* government. Who in those seven and twenty years that he reigned, annexed *Bithynia, Cappadocia*, and most of those strong holds that border on the *Euxine* Sea to his Kingdom. Him his son *Orchanes* succeeded, who took the great City of *Prusa*, and honoured it with his residence. Having much enlarged his dominions, he dyed in the two and thirtieth year of his reign, resigning his State to *Amurath* his son. He upon the dissention of the *Greeks*, first passed over the Straights into *Europe*, took *Abydos* and *Calippolis* with the whole *Chersonesus*. Then entring further into *Thracia*, subdued *Philippolis* & *Adrianople*; and proceeding conquered *Servia* and *Bulgaria*, passeth

into

into the upper *Mysia*: and stabbed by a common Souldier, in the one and thirtieth year of his Reign, was succeeded by his Son *Bajazet*. He, possest of the greatest part of *Thrace*, subdued a large part of *Greece*, with the Country of *Phocis*; twice but vainly, besieging *Constantinople*. Taken at length by *Tamberlain*, and carried about in an Iron Cage, he desperately brained himself in the year 1399. his Son *Calepine* (some say) succeeded him, attributing unto him six years of Government: esteemed by others but a Fable; who give the succession to his youngest Son *Mahomet*: the cause of this diversity of opinions proceeding from the *Turkish* Kingdom thus again suppressed by the *Tartars*. The many Sons of *Bajazet*, and other *Mahometan* Princes, possest of several Provinces, and striving with one another for undivided Soveraignty : by *Mahomet* at length was obtained: who united again that dismembred Empire: enlarging the same with the accession of *Dacia*, *Walachia*, the greater part of *Sclavonia* and *Macedonia*, even unto the *Ionian* Sea. Who translated the seat of his Empire from *Prusa* unto *Adrianople*, where he died, having reigned seventeen years; if the same be accounted from the death of his Father. His Son by the name of *Amurath* the Second ruled in his stead: who conquered *Epirus*, *Ætolia*, *Attica*, *Bœotia*, *Achaia*, and *Thessalonica*. He left his State to *Mahomet* the Second (after he had reigned eight and twenty years) whose Conquests deservedly gave him the addition of Great: having utterly ruinated the *Greek* Empire, taken from them *Constantinople* the Imperial City, the Emperour *Constantine* being trod to death by the press of people in *Adrianople* Gate, and thereby gained the Title of Emperour. He subdued also the Empire of *Trapezond*, erected there by *Alexius Comnenus*, at such time as the *Greeks* did lose their *European* Empire to the *Latines*. Moreover, *Athens*, *Corinth*, all *Peloponnesus*, *Bosna*, *Lemnos*, *Eubœa*, *Mitylen*, &c. and died not without suspicion of poyson, in the one and thirtieth year of his Empire. *Bajazet* the Second, his Son, having ended his Wars with his Brother, conquered all *Cilicia*, a part of *Armenia*, with the rest of *Cappadocia*, which before belonged to the *Carmanian* Kingdom. He invaded *Syria*, but with worse success: and then converting his forces against the *Venetians*, took from them *Naupactus*, *Methona*, *Dyrrachium*, and almost depopulated *Dalmatia*. But in the six and thirtieth year of his Reign, he was poysoned by a *Jew*, at the procurement of *Selymus* his Son and Successor: (who, besides the civil Wars with his Father and Brethren) conquered all *Syria* and *Egypt* from the ruinated *Mammalucks*, and brought *Arabia* under his subjection. After, intending to invade the Christians, he died of a most loathsom disease, when he had reigned eight years. His Son *Solyman* taketh *Rhodes*, at several times over-runneth *Hungary*: possessing himself of *Buda*, *Strigonium*, *alba regalis*: dispossesseth the *Persians* of *Tauris*: and joyneth *Babylon*, with the Countries of *Media*, *Mesopotamia*, and *Assyria*, to his Empire. *Arabia* is not free from his Conquests; nor the *Portugals* in *India* enough removed from the reach of his ambition. He died in the six and fortieth year of his Reign. *Selymus* the Second succeeded, the only Son that he had left unmurthered: who won by his Lieutenants *Cyprus* from the *Venetians*. They also enlarged his bounds with *Valachia*, *Moldavia*, and the Kingdom of *Tunis*. He reigned eight years. Him *Amurath* the Third succeeded: who warred not in person, nor atchieved much by his Deputies, yet reigned he nineteen years. Neither was *Mahomet* the Third his Son a Souldier, being but once in the field, and thence terribly affrighted. Nor enlarged he his Dominions by the valour of others: his forces being chiefly imployed in suppressing of intestine Rebellions. He reigned eight years ingloriously, and left the now reigning *Achmet* to succeed him: the fourteenth *Sultan*, and the eighth Emperor of the Ottoman Family; who yet hath added nothing to his so vast an Empire; the greatest that is, or perhaps that ever was from the beginning. For first, the *European* part thereof extendeth West-wards unto the Archdukes of *Austria*'s Dominions, stretching to the *Adriatick* Sea, by the Confines of *Ragusa*, bounded on the South with the *Mediterraneum*, on the East with *Ægeum*, *Propontis* and *Pontus*, even to *Theodosia*, a City of the *Scythian Chersonesus*; and on the North almost to *Russia* and *Polonia*: containing *Romania*, *Bulgaria*, *Servia*, *Rascia*, the tributary Principalities of *Valachia* and *Moldavia*; the greater part of *Hungary*, *Bosna*, *Albania*, *Macedon*, *Epirus*, all *Grecia* and *Peloponnesus*; all the fruitful Islands of the *Ægean* Sea. *Ragusa* pays for her liberty: nor his *Candie*, *Zant*, or *Cephalonia* held without presents. But what is this compared to her ancient Territories? within which, all *Natolia* is comprised, on the three ages embraced with the *Ægean*, *Euxine*, and *Cilician* Seas: containing the Provinces of *Pontus*, *Galatia*, *Bithynia*, *Phrygia*, *Lycia*, *Pamphylia*, *Cilicia*, *Cappadocia*, and the lesser *Armenia*, beyond which also *Colchis* thence stretching North-ward to *Catai*, and bounded on the East with the

Coun-

The Turkish Policy.

Country of the Georgians, whereof the Turks possess not a little. A great part it also containeth of the greater Armenia: all Syria (in which Coelestria, Phoenicia, and Palestine Babylonia, and Mesopotamia, Arabia felix which stretcheth out into the South Sea, interposing the Persian and Arabian Gulphs, do bow to that Soveraignty: so do the Inhabitants of Petrea and Deserta; such I mean as have known Habitations: In Africa it extendeth all along the Coasts of the Mediterraneum; even from the Red Sea, to Aerath, a City of Mauritania (except some few places possest by the Spaniard) wherein is the Country of the Troglodytes, the miraculously fertile Kingdom of Egypt, Tripoly in Barbary, the Kingdom of Tunis, and City of Argiers with her Territories, with the Tributary Kingdoms of Fesse and Morocco. To this add Cyprus, Rhodes, and all the fertile Islands of the mid-land Sea, that lye East of Candy. Thus great at this day is the Ottoman Empire; but too great for it are their assumed Titles: as, God on Earth, shadow of God, sole Monarch of the World, King of Kings, Commander of all that can be commanded, Soveraign of the most Noble Families of Persia and Armenia, possessor of the holy Cities of Mecca and Jerusalem, Lord of the black and white Seas, Sultan of Babylon; and so proceeding with a repetition of their several Kingdoms. Like swelling Attributes gave this now reigning Sultan to our Soveraign in a Letter writ lately, which I will insert for the strangeness.

Unto the most glorious and most mighty King James, *one of the Great Lords of the creation of* Jesus, *and most laudable amongst all the Princes of the Nations of Messias, a Judge of all debates and differences of the people of* Nazareth, *Possessor of the great Majesty, riches, and glory, a Judge of the most great Kings of* England, &c. farcing his Letter with like sustain, calling his own Court, *Our most happy and shining Port, a Port of refuge for the world*: and subscribing, *From our Imperial Residence at* Constantinople, *most strongly and mightily guarded.* Yet in his own stile more modest, containing no more than *Sultan Achmet Chan: Son to Mahomet Chan most invincible.*

But the barbarous policy whereby this Tyranny is sustained, doth differ from all other: guided by the heads, and strengthened by the hands of his Slaves, who think it as great an honour to be so, as they do with us that serve the Courts of Princes: the natural *Turk* (to be so called a reproach) being rarely employed in command or service. Among these Slaves there is no nobility of blood, no known Parentage, Kindred, nor hereditary Possessions, but are as it were the *Sultans* Creation, depending upon him only for their sustenance and preferments, who disposeth, as well of their lives as their fortunes, by no other rule than that of his will; although sometimes for form he useth the assent of the never gainsaying *Mufti.* These are the Sons of Christians (and those the most compleatly furnished by Nature) taken in their Childhood from their miserable Parents, by a Leavy made every five years (or oftner or seldomer, as occasion requireth) throughout the whole Empire, (excepting certain priviledged places, amongst which are *Sio* and *Constantinople*) who are bestowed in several Seminaries, instructed in the *Mahometan* Religion (changing their Names upon their Circumcision) taught the use of their several Weapons, and made patient of hunger and labour, with inured abstinence, and continual exercise. These they call first *Jemoglans*, who have their Faces shaven (the token of servitude,) wearing long Coats and copped Caps, not unlike to our Ideots. The choicest of them for spirit and feature, and after a while received into the *Grand Signiors Seraglio*: distinguished by Chambers like to those in Hospitals, according to their Seniorities: where all are brought up in the discipline of War, and not a few acquainted with the secrets of State: such as by the excellency of their gifts do assure the expectation of a future eminency; those of the first Chamber are the first preferred; yet not in order, but according to the worth of the place, and worthiness of the person. Of these come the *Beglerbegs* (the name signifying a Lord of Lords) of whom there be only two: the one of *Greece*, and the other of *Natolia*: who command all the Horsmen in those Countries under the General: the great *Bassas*, (whereof some are Generals of Armies, some Viziers of the Port, the rest Vice-roys of the Provinces:) the *Sanziacks* Governours of Cities, for so the name signifieth, with their Territories and forces, and other Officers both of War and Peace, with those of the Court of principal place and attendance. Of the other *Jemoglans* some come to the Chiauses; who go on Embassies, execute Commandments; and are as Pursuivants, and Under-Sheriffs, attending the employment of the Emperour; (who mounted on Horseback carry *Dabuzes*, a weapon like a Mace before him) and on the Courts of Justice: sollicting also the causes of

their

their Clients. But the *Spachies* and *Janizaries* which are most made of these *Jemoglans* (the principal cause of their institution) are the Nerves and Supporters of the *Turkish* Monarchy. The *Spachies* are Horsemen, weaponed for the most part at once with Bow, Mace, Lance, Harquebush, and Cymitar, whereof they have the several uses: agreeing with their fights, their flights, or pursuements. For defence some wear Bucklers and Shirts of Male. The skirts of their Coats, when they ride, are gathered within long Stammel brogs that reach to their ankles, and there do join to their Buskins shod with Iron; and supply the want of Spurs with their large and sharp Stirrops. Their Saddles are plated behind and before, the seat deep and hard: and for caparison they use for most part the Skins of Leopards, Lyons, Tygers, Panthers, and the like. In Cities when on foot they wear Gowns of Stammel with long Hanging sleeves: and are distinguished from others by the folding up of their Shashes. Of these there be two sorts: the *Uleffgi*, which is to say, stipendiary, who are almost altogether made of these *Jemoglans*; and the *Timariots*, who consist of all sorts of people. The first as yet unpreferred, under the command of several Captains, do attend upon the immediate employment of the Emperour: who alloweth unto each the daily pension of ten Aspers, paid them every quarter. Of these there be two and thirty thousand. The one half of them are called *Spahcieglans*, who wear red Pendants on their Spears, and when in the Field, march on the right hand the *Sultan*, as the other on the left, who are called *Silihtarspaheis*, bearing yellow and white Pendants. The other dispersed throughout the whole Empire, do live upon their particular Tenements for term of life assigned them; and thereupon so called. It being the policy of his State to erect in the conquered Countries a number of *Timariots*, answerable to the greatness thereof: whereby the principal part of the Souldiery is provided for, and the Empire strengthened,

Some say there are a million. both against foreign invasions and revolts of the subdued. Of these, as they say, there are upward of seven hundred thousand, every one being to find as many Horse as his Farm doth double the yearly value of sixty *Sultanies*: ready to be commanded by their several *Zanziacks*; as they by their *Baffas*: these bear on their Lances white and red Pendants. But the *Janizaries* (a name that signifieth new Souldiery) at those that bear such great sway in *Constantinople*: insomuch that the *Sultans* themselves have been sometimes subject to their insolencies. They are divided into several Companies, under several Captains: but all commanded by their *Aga*, a place of high trust, and the third in repute through the Empire: howbeit, their too much love is to him an assured destruction. These are the flower of the *Turkish* Infantry, by whom such wonderful Victories have been atchieved. They call the Emperour Father (for none other is there for them to depend on) to whose valour and faith in the time of War he committeth his person: they having their stations about the Royal Pavillion. They serve with Harquebushes, armed besides with Cymitars and Hatchets. They wear on their heads a Bonnet of white Felt, with a lap hanging down behind to their shoulders; adorned about the brows with a wreath of metal, guilt, and set with stones of small value; having a kind of sheath or socket of the same erected before, wherein such are suffered to stick Plumes of Feathers as have behaved themselves extraordinary bravely. They tuck up the skirts of their Coats when they fight or march: and carry certain days provision of Victuals about with them. Nor is it a cumber: it being no more than a small portion of Rice, and a little Sugar and Honey. When the Emperour is not in the Field, the most of them reside with him in the City: ever at hand upon any occasion to secure his person, and are as were the *Pretorian* Cohorts with the *Romans*. They are in number about forty thousand: whereof the greater part (I mean of those that attend on the Court) have their being in three large *Seraglios*; where the Juniors do reverence their Seniors, and all obey their several Commanders (as they their *Aga*) with much silence and humility. Many of them that are married (a breach of their first institution) have their private dwellings: and those that are busied in foreign employments, are for the most part placed in such Garrison Towns as do greatly concern the safety of the Empire. Some are appointed to attend on Ambassadors: others to guard such particular Christians as will be at the charge, both about the City, and in their Travels, from incivilities and violences, to whom they are in themselves most faithful: wary and cruel in preventing and revenging their dangers and injuries: and so patient in bearing abuses, that one of them of late being strucken by an Englishman (whose humorous swaggering would permit him never to review his Country) as they travelled along

long through *Morea*, did not only not revenge it, nor abandon him to the pillage and outrages of others, in so unknown and savage a Country, but conducted him unto *Zant* in safety, saying, God forbid that the villany of another should make him betray the charge that was committed to his trust. They are all of one Trade or other. The pay that they have from the *Grand Signior* is but five Aspers a day: yet their elder Sons as soon as born are enrolled and received into pension; but his bounty extendeth no further unto his progeny, (the rest reputed as natural *Turks*): nor is a *Janizary* capable of other preferments than the command of ten, of twenty, or of an hundred. They have yearly given them two Gowns apiece, the one of Violet Cloth, and the other of Stammel; which they wear in the City: carrying in their hands a great tough Reed, some seven foot long, and tipped with Silver; the weight whereof is not seldom felt by such as displease them. Who are indeed so awful, that Justice dare not proceed publickly against them, (they being only to be judged by their *Aga*:) but being privately attached, are as privately thrown into the Sea in the night time. But then are they most tumultuous, (whereto they do give the name of affection) upon the dangerous Sicknesses of their Emperours: and upon their deaths commit many outrages. Which is the cause that the great *Baffas* as well as they can, do conceal it from them, until all things be provided for the presentment of the next for them to salute. Whereupon (besides the present largess) they have an Asper a day increase of pension: so that the longer they live, and the more Emperours they outlive the greater is their allowance.

But it is to be considered, that all these before-named, are not only of that tribute of Children. For not a few of them are Captives taken in their childhood; with divers Renegadoes, that have most wickedly quitted their Religion and Country, to fight against both: who are to the Christians the most terrible Adversaries. And withal they have of late infringed their ancient Customs, by the admitting of those into these orders, that are neither the Sons nor Grand-sons of Christians: a natural *Turk* born in *Constantinople*, before never known, being now a *Baffa* of the Port.

Over and above these, and besides the Auxiliary *Tartars*, whereof there are lightly threescore thousand (who live on Spoil, and serve without Pay) that are ever assistant; the *Grand Signior* hath other Forces whom they call *Achingi*, who have nothing but what they can get by forraging, being Hindes of the Country, and tied to serve on Horseback for certain priviledges that they hold, in number about thirty or forty thousand, but small in value: as are the *Azapi*, who serve on Foot (yet properly belonging to the Gallies) better acquainted with the Spade than Sword; thrust forward with purpose rather to weary, than to vanquish the Enemy; whose dead bodies do serve the *Janizaries* to fill up Ditches, and to mount the Walls of assaulted Fortresses: besides many Voluntaries, who follow the Army in hope to succeed the slain *Spaheis* and *Janizaries*: Now nothing curious at such a time to receive those that be not the Sons of Christians into the Order. Such are the *Turkish* Forces, both in quality and proportion: and he that shall see three hundred thousand of these in an Army (as he might have done this last Summer in *Bithynia*) so disciplined, so appointed, and so daringly resolute; whose only repute consists in their Valours; and whose defeats are punished in their Commanders as offences: furnished with such abundance of great Ordnance (much whereof they cast according to their occasions, carrying with them the metal upon the backs of Camels) will not only not wonder at their Victories, but rather how the rest of the yet unvanquished World hath withstood them. I have heard a Prince (and he of no small experience) impute the sundry overthrows given them by a small number of Christians to the paucity of Commanders, and their want of experience, some one *Sanziack* having under his Conduct five thousand *Timariots*, and he perhaps but newly crept out of the *Sultans Seraglio*, exercised only in speculative Conflicts. So that their numbers prove often but cumbers; and the advantage loss, encountred by the many expert Directors of few; who are also far better defensively armed. But he that hath bounded the Sea, hath also limited their furies. And surely it is to be hoped, that their greatness is not only at the height, but near an extream precipitation: the body being grown too monstrous for the head, the *Sultans* unwarlike and never accompanying their Armies in person; The Souldier corrupted with ease and liberty; drowned in prohibited Wine, enfeebled with the continual converse of Women; and generally lapsed from their former austerity of life, and simplicity of manners. Their Valours now meeting on

The Turkish Forces.   LIB. I.

all sides with opposition; having of late given no encrease to their Dominions: and Empire so got, when it ceaseth to increase, doth begin to diminish. Lastly, in that it hath exceeded the observed period of a Tyranny, for such is their Empire. Now when they march, the *Tartars* do scour the Country two days journey before: then follow the *Achingi*; after them the *Timariots*; next those few *Jemoglans* that be; next them the *Janizaries*; the *Chausis* follow on Horseback, (who carry Bows and Arrows besides their Maces and Cimyters:) then comes the *Sultan* with the Officers of his Court, and Archers of his Guard who are Footmen; the stipendary *Spaheis* marching on either side of him. An hundred Coaches covered with red, with four Horses a piece, are drawn after, which carry the *Hicoglans* (his Pages) and Eunuchs: about these the *Jemoglans* called *Baltagies* are placed. The Carriages of the Army ensue; followed by Voluntaries, who go in hope (as beforesaid) to be entertained in the rooms of the slain; with the Servants of the *Saphees* in the Court, and certain *Janizaries, At-toglans Lepzlers* and *Perygilers*. The *Janizaries* have Boots, Swords of Wood, and the like born before them for their Ensigns: and the royal Standard is no other than a Horse-tail tyed to the end of a Staff: which though seeming rude, and answerable to their original, doth retain, perhaps something of Antiquity. For *Homer* sticketh the like in the Crest of the gallantly-armed (though not so spirited) *Paris*.

Capiti autem forti galeam affabre factam imposuit,
Cristatam ex setis equinius: horribilis autem crista
desuper mutabat,   Il. l. 3.

*Then puts he on a Helm well wrought and brave,
Plum'd with Horse hairs that horribly did wave.*

As for their Forces at Sea, they are but small in comparison of what they have been, and compared to those of particular Christian Princes, but contemptible. Approved by the *Florentine*, who with six Ships only hath kept the bottom of the Straights for these three years past in despight of them: insomuch as they have not dared to hazard the Revenue of *Egypt* by Sea. But have sent it over Land with a Guard of Souldiers, to their no small trouble and expences: the whole Armado coming often in view, yet not so hardy as to adventure the onset. The Admiral having thought it a safer course to employ the Pirats of *Tunis* and *Algiers* in that service, who have many tall Ships (the spoil of Christian Merchants) and warlikely appointed: now grown expert in Navigation, and all kind of Sea-fights, by the wicked instruction of our fugitive Pirats, and other Renegadoes. But those Pirats have no heart to such an enterprise, where the Victory would prove so bloody, and the Booty so worthless. The Navy that is yearly set forth in the beginning of *May*, to annoy the Enemy, suppress Pirats, collect Tribute, and reform disorders in the Maritine Towns that belong to the Admiralty; consists of not above threescore Gallies: which are all that can be spared from their other places of employment. And that there be no more is said to proceed from the want of Captives, by reason of their general Peace with the Christians: for such, and such as are condemned for Offences, are only chained to the Oar, except the necessity be urgent. As for matter to build with, they want none: no more do they workmen: many excellent in that Art, and those Christians, being enticed from all parts with liberal pensions to work in their Arsenals. The Captain *Bassa* (for so is the Admiral called) when not in service, hath his Residence in *Constantinople* and *Galli-poli*. A man in regard of his place, of principal repute: and commanding the Commanders of *Gallipoli, Galata, Lemnos, Nicomedia, Lesbos, Chios, Naxus, Eubæa, Rhodes, Cavalla, Nauplia, Lepanto, Cyprus,* and *Alexandria*. In *October* he returneth from his annual circuit: as he did now during our abode in the City, and entred the Haven in triumph. The Gallies divided into sundry Squadrons, and tricked all in their gallantry, rowing at their sterns three or four little Vessels no bigger than Fisher-Boats. A ridiculous glory, and a prize to be ashamed of. But it was thought that the *Grand Signior* would have given him but a bad welcome, that durst not adventure with such ods of number on the becalmed *Florentines*. During the Winter the Armado is dispersed, and the Gallies are drawn into their dry stations. In which time the Pirats, both Christians and Mahometan, do rob on the *Ægean* and *Mediterranean* uncontrolled, but by the defensive strength of the assailed.

Thus

Thus is the Great *Turk* served by those whom he may advance without envy, and destroy without danger. The best of them living a wandring and unhappy life, removed from one Command to another; and to parts so far distant, that often more time is spent in their journey than in their abode. The greatest Commander, and in the strength of his Command, submitting his neck unto the Executioners Bow-string, when sent by the Tyrant with the fatal Box that includeth the Commission. Nor booteth it to resist in hope of partakers, when one mans preferment is built on the desired overthrow of another: being also, as is said before, without Kindred or Alliance: so that Rebellions do but rarely happen. And although these great Slaves attain to great Riches, yet are they (as it were) but the Collectors thereof for his treasure: whither at their deaths it returneth, all, save what it pleaseth him to bestow on their posterity: who never are advanced to eminent place, it being a cause of the greater neglect to have had excellent Parents, as to them of ruine to be beloved in their Governments. Nay, so much the continuance of honours in Families are avoided, that when a *Bassa* is given (for so I may term it) to the Sister or Daughter of a *Sultan* for an Husband, the Children begotten on them do most rarely rise above the degree of a private Captain. But more severe are these Tyrants to their own, who lop all the Branches from the Bole; the unnatural Brother solemnizing his Fathers Funerals with the slaughters of his Brothers. So fearful are they of rivalty, and so damnably politick; making all things lawful that they may secure the perpetuity of their Empire. Not now to seek in those precepts of *Photinus*,

Sceptres do lose their sway when Kings grow just:	Sceptorum vis tota petit, si pendere iusta
Respects of honesty, towres tomb in dust.	Incipit: evertitque arces respectus honesti.
Free villanies a hated Reign assure;	Libertas scelerum est quæ regna invisa tuetur.
And Swords still drawn: dire deeds do but secure	Sublatu'que modus gladiis, iacere omnia fæve,
The Doer whilst a doing. Courts shun they	Non impune licet nisi quum facis: exeat aula.
That would be good. Virtue and soveraign sway.	Qui vult esse pius: virtus & summa potestas
Still jar. Still fear be whom foul facts dismay.	Non coeunt, semper metuet quem sæva pudebunt.
	Lucan. l. 8.

Yet they mourn for those being dead, whom they murdered: honouring them with all dues of burial, and customary lamentations. Now if the *Ottoman* Line should fail, the *Crim Tartar* is to succeed (both being of one Family: and of one Religion:) as the *Turk*, the *Tartar*; who hath at this day the election of the *Tartarian* Emperours; but with this limitation, that he is to be of one of the Sons of the deceased.

Their Moral and Ecclesiastical Laws, the *Turks* do receive from *Mahomet* the *Saracen* Law-giver: a man of obscure parentage, born in *Itrarip* a Village of *Arabia*, in the year 551. His Father was a Pagan, his Mother a Jew both by birth and Religion. At the first he exercised merchandise; having by the marriage of his Mistress (not effected, as was thought, without witch-craft) attained to much riches: whereupon he became a Captain of certain voluntary *Arabians* that followed the Emperor *Heraclius* in his *Persian* Wars. Who falling into a mutiny, for that they were denyed the Military Garment; and incensing the rest of their Nation with the reproachful answer given them by the Treasurer, which was, That that ought not to be given unto Dogs, which was ordained for the Roman Souldiers; a part of them chose *Mahomet* for their Ring-leader, who had aggravated their discontents, and confirmed them in their Rebellion. But being disdained by the better sort for the baseness of his birth; to avoid ensuing contempt, he gave it out, that he attained not to that honour by military favour, but by divine appointment. That he was sent by God to give a new Law unto Mankind; and by force of Arms to reduce the world unto his obedience. That he was the last of the Prophets, being greater than Christ, as Christ was greater than *Moses*. Two years together he lived in a Cave, not far distant from *Mecca*; where he compiled his damnable Doctrine, by the help of one *Sergius* a *Nestorian* Monk, and *Abdalla* a Jew: (containing a hodge-podge of sundry Religions:) which he first communicated to his Wife, perswading her that it was delivered him by the Angel *Gabriel*, who had cut open his heart, and taken from thence the little black Core (which the *Turks* do affirm to be in the heart of every man) wherein the Devil doth plant his temptations: and shewed him withall the joys and mysteries of Paradise. His new Religion by little and little he divulged in *Mecca*; countenanced by the powerful alliance which he had by his sundry Wives: and followed by many of the Vulgar, allured with the liberty thereof, and delighted with the novelty.

But the Nobles of *Mecca* going about to apprehend him, he fled to *Medina*, not two days journey distant: whither followed by a number, wicked of life, and desperate of fortunes, he waged a successful War against the *Syrians*; planted his Religion amongst the vanquished: and after making himself Lord of *Mecca*, made that the place of his residence. Where he died in the great Climacterical year of his age; having made them believe, that the third day after he would ascend into Heaven: whereupon he was kept above ground till the air was infected with his favour, and then buried at *Medina*. Another promise he made concerning his return, which should have been a thousand years after, which the *Mahometans* excuse as mis-understood, by reason of his feeble voice, even then a dying; and that he did say two thousand: to which time they have prorogued their expectations. Mean of stature he was, and evil proportioned: having ever a scald head, which (as some say) made him wear a white Shash continually: now worn by his Sectaries. Being much subject to the Falling-sickness, he made them believe that it was a propheticall trance; and that then he conversed with the Angel *Gabriel*. Having also taught a Pigeon to feed at his ear, he affirmed it to be the Holy Ghost, which informed him in divine precepts. Not unlike to *Numa's* feigned familiarity with Ægeria and *Pythagoras* his Eagle; whose policy perhaps he imitated: whereby as they the *Romans* and *Crotonians*; so drew he the gross *Arabians* to a superstitious obedience. For he had a subtle wit, though viciously employed; being naturally inclined to all villanies. Amongst the rest, so insatiably leacherous, that he countenanced his incontinency with a Law: wherein he declared it, not only to be no crime to couple with whomsoever he liked, but an act of high honour to the party, and infusing sanctity. Thus planted he his irreligious Religion, being much assisted by the iniquities of those times: the Christian estate then miserably divided by multitudes of Heresies. So that the disunity of the Professors, made many to suspect the profession, and to embrace a Doctrine so indulgent to their affections. Which enlarging as the *Saracens* and *Turks* enlarged their Empires, doth at this day well-nigh over-run three parts of the earth; of that I mean that hath civil Inhabitants. Yet are the *Mahometans* divided into threescore and twelve Sects, sprung from the two fountains. Of that named *Imamia*, the *Persians* are drunk; of the other called *Lestare*, the *Syrians*, *Arabians*, *Turks*, and *Africans*.

The Alcoran, which containeth the sum of their Religion, is written in *Arabick* Rhime, without due proportion of numbers: and must neither be written nor read by them in any other Language. Besides the positive doctrine, (to it self contradictory) it is farced with Fables, Visions, Legends, and Relations. Nor is it at this day the same that was written by *Mahomet*, (although so credited to be by the Vulgar:) many things being secretly put in, and thrust out; and some of the repugnancies reconciled by the succeeding *Caliphs*. *Mahomet* the second is said to have altered it much, and added much to it. This Book is held by them in no less veneration, than the Old Testament by the Jews, and the New by the Christians. They never touch it with unwash'd hands: and a capital crime it is, in the reading thereof to mistake a Letter, or displace the Accent. They kiss it, embrace it, and swear by it: calling it, *The Book of Glory, and director unto Paradise*. To speak a little of much; they teach that God is only to be worshipped, only one, and the Creator of all: righteous, pitiful; in wisdom and power incomprehensible. How God made man of all sorts and colours of earth; and being formed, for thousands of years laid him a baking in the Sun, until he was pleased to breathe life into him. Then commanded he all his Angels to reverence him: which the Devil, at that time an Angel of light, refused to do; expostulating why he should so honour that Creature whom he knew would become so polluted with all manner of (by him particularized) vices. That God therefore condemned the Devil to Hell; who ever since hath continued an enemy to man. Idolatry they hold to be the most accursed of Crimes, and therefore they interdict all Images and Counterfeits whatsoever; reputing the Christians Idolaters, for that they have them in their Churches and Houses: imagining also that we worship three Gods, as not apprehending the mystery of the Trinity. They deny the Divinity of Christ, yet confess him to be the Son of a Virgin: *Mary* conceiving by the smell of a Rose which was presented her by the Angel *Gabriel*, and that she bare him at her Breasts. They hold him to be a greater Prophet than *Moses*; and the Gospel better than the Law: insomuch as no *Jew* can turn *Turk*, until he first turn Christian, they forcing him to eat Hogs-flesh, and calling him *Abdula*, which signifieth the Son of a Christian: who after two or three days, abjuring Christ, is made a *Mahometan*. They say, that the blessed Virgin was free from original sin and the temptations of the Devil.

LIB. I.   *The Mahometan Religion.*   43

Devil. Chrift is called in the Alcoran, the Breath and Word of God; faid to know the fecrets of hearts, to raife the dead to life, cure difeafes, reftore fight to the blind, and fpeech to the dumb: and that his Difciples wrought miracles by his virtue. Yet vifit they not his Sepulchre in their Pilgrimages (not thinking him to have dyed) as generally bruited. For being, as they fay, led toward the place of execution, God not permitting fo bafe a people to put to death fo holy a Prophet (for they confefs that he never finned) did affume him into Heaven: when mift, and fought by the Souldiers in the throng, they laid hold of one of the Judges that had condemned him, who refembled him much in favour and proportion, telling him that he fhould not efcape from them again; and fo not believing whatfoever he faid, did execute him in his room. They fharply punifh all fuch as blafpheme him; and fay that he fhall return to judgment about forty years before the worlds ending. The Holy Ghoft they acknowledge; yet not to be diftinct in perfon, but only as a power and operative virtue in the God-head, which infpireth good motions into the heart, the producer of good actions. They are commanded feven times a day to refort unto publick Prayers: the firft affembling is called *Tingil-namas*, which is two hours before day: the fecond *Sabah-namas*, at day break: the third *Vyle-namas* at Noon: the fourth *Kyndi-namas* at three of the Clock: the fifth *Akfham-namas*, after Sun-fet: the fixth *Chogie-namas*, two hours within night: and the feventh *Giumas-namas*, at ten of the Clock in the morning: the laft alfo on *Fridays* obferved by all, on the other days but by the more religious. Congregated they are, as aforefaid, by the chanting of the Prieft from the tops of Steeples: at which times lightly though they be in the fields, they will fpread their upper Garments on the earth, and fall to their devotions. Moreover, I have feen them conjointly pray in the corner of the Streets, before the opening ot their Shops in the morning. *Friday* is their Sabbath, and yet they fpend but a part thereof in their Devotion, and the reft in Recreations: but for that time they obferve it fo rigoroufly, that a *Turk* here lately had his ears nailed to his Shop-board for opening it too timely. Before they pray, they wafh all the organs of their fenfes; their legs to their knees, and their arms to their elbows: their privities after their purging of Nature; and fometimes all over from top to toe: for which there are Houfes of Office with Conduits belonging to every principal Mofque. Where water is wanting they do it with duft. At the door of the Mofque they put off their fhoos; and entring, fit crofs-legged upon rows of Mats one behind another, the poor and the rich promifcuoufly. The Prieft in a Pulpit before them, not otherwife diftinguifhed in Habit, but by the folding up of their Turbant. When they pray they turn their faces towards *Mecca*: firft ftanding upright, without any motions of their bodies, holding the Palms of their hands upward; fometimes they ftop their eyes and ears, and oft pull their hair on the fides of their faces: then thrice they bow, as in their falutations; and as often proftrating themfelves on the earth, do kifs it. Doing this fundry times, they will look back upon no occafion, until they come unto the falutation of *Mahomet*: at which time they reverfe their faces, firft over the right fhoulder, and then over the left, believing that his coming will be behind them when they are at their devotion. The Prieft doth fometimes read unto them fome part of the Alcoran (holding it, in reverence to the Book, as high as his chin,) fometimes fome of their fabulous Legends, intermixing expofitions and inftructions: which they hearken unto with heedy attention, and fuch fteddy poftures of body as if they were intranced. Their Service is mixed with Songs and Refponfes: and when all is done they ftroke down their Faces and Beards with looks of devout gravity. If they find a Paper in the Streets, they will thruft it in fome Crevice of the adjoining Wall, imagining that the Name of God may be contained therein, and then prophane to be trod under foot, or otherwife defiled. They number their often repetition of the Names of God and his Attributes (with other fhort ejaculations of prayer or praife) upon Beads: fome fhaking their heads inceffantly, until they turn giddy: perhaps in imitation of the fuppofed Trances (but natural infirmity) of their Prophet. And they have an Order of Monks, who are called *Dervifes*, whom I have often feen to dance in their Mofques on *Tuefdays* and *Fridays*; many together, to the found of Barbarous Mufick, Dances that confift of continual turnings, until at a certain ftroke they fall upon the Earth; and lying along like Beafts, are thought to be rapt in fpirit unto coeleftial converfations. Now the Women are not permitted to come into their Temples (yet have they fecret places to look in through Grates) partly for troubling their devotions, but efpecially for that they are not excited, as are the Women of *Perfia* and *Æthiopia*.

Nor

Nor circumcise they the Males until they be able to anſwer the Prieſt, and promiſe for themſelves: which is for the moſt part at the age of eight. They are circumciſed in the Houſes of their Parents, at a Feſtival meeting, and in the midſt of the Aſſembly; the Child holding up his fore-finger, in token that he is a *Mahometan*. As ſoon as cut, the Prieſt waſheth the wound in water and ſalt, and bindeth it in Linnen. Who changeth not his name, but is from thenceforth called a *Muſſelman*: which is a true Believer. This done, he is carried unto the *Banna*, where his hair (before that time worn at full length) is ſhaven, and ſo kept ever after: all ſaving a lock on the top of his crown, by which they dream that they ſhall be aſſumed by *Mahomet* into Paradiſe: then put they on him a white Turbant; and ſo returning with Drums and Hoboys, is with great ſolemnity conducted to the Moſque, and preſented with gifts according to his quality.

The *Turks* do faſt one Month in the year, which they call *Ramazan*: which changeth yearly, (ſo that in thirty years they faſt one) wherein, they ſay, that the Alcoran was delivered unto *Mahomet* by the Angel. Obſerved by all but the infirm and Travellers: who are to faſt for as long a time, when ſo they recover, or come to the end of their journey. But they faſt but during the day: in the night they feaſt; and then all their Steeples ſtuck round with Lamps, which burn till the morning: affording an object of great Solemnity. Such as inſtead of abſtaining from meats, do abſtain at that time from their Moſques, they carry about in ſcorn, and ſeverely chaſtiſe: but ſuch as then drink Wine, they puniſh with death. Upon the diſcovery of the New Moon (which they ſuperſtitiouſly gratulate, eſteeming him happy that diſcovereth it firſt, and by the courſe thereof do reckon their year;) falling out this year on the ſeventh of *December*, the Feaſt of the great *Byram* did begin; which doth continue for three days together: obſerved by them as *Eaſter* is with us. On the firſt day the *Grand Signior* rode to *Sancta Sophia* in all the pomp and glory of Empire: of which we ſhall ſpeak hereafter. Upon his return we ſaw a ſort of Chriſtians, ſome of them half-earth already, crooked with age, and trembling with Palſies; who by the throwing away of their Bonnets and lifting up of their Fore-fingers, did profeſs themſelves to become *Mahometans*. A ſight full of horrour and trouble, to ſee thoſe deſperate wretches that had profeſſed Chriſt all their life, and had ſuffered, no doubt, for his ſake much contumely and oppreſſion, now almoſt dying, to forſake their Redeemer, even then when they were to receive the reward of their patience. To theſe the Tyrant a little retired his Body: who before not ſo much as caſt his eye aſide, but ſate like the adored Statue of an Idol. For they hold it a great grace and an act of ſingular piety, to draw many to their Religion; preſenting them with money, change of raiments; and freeing them from all Tribute and Taxes. Inſomuch that if a Chriſtian have deſerved death by their Law, if he will convert, they will many times remit his puniſhment. But they compel no man. During this Feſtival they exerciſe themſelves with various paſtimes: but none more in uſe, and more barbarous, than the ſwinging up and down, as Boys do in Bell-Ropes, for which there be Gallowſes (for they bear that form) of an exceeding height, erected in ſundry places of the City: when by two joining Ropes, that are faſtned above, they will ſwing themſelves as high as the tranſom. Perhaps affected in that it ſtupifies the ſenſes for a ſeaſon: the cauſe that *Opium* is ſo much in requeſt, and of their toreſaid ſhaking of their heads, and continued turnings. In regard whereof they have ſuch as have loſt their wits, and natural Ideots, in high veneration; as men raviſhed in ſpirit, and taken from themſelves, as it were, to the fellowſhip of Angels. Theſe they honour with the title of Saints, and lodge them in their Temples: ſome of them going almoſt ſtark naked; others clothed in ſhreds of ſeveral colours; whoſe neceſſities are ſupplied by the peoples devotions: who kiſs their Garments as they paſs through the Streets, and bow to their benedictions. Yea, many by counterfeiting the Ideot, have avoided puniſhment for offences which they have unwittingly fallen into. Whilſt the *Byram* laſteth you cannot ſtir abroad but you ſhall be preſented by the *Dervices* and *Janizaries*, with Tulips and trifles, beſprinkling you with ſweet water; nor ceaſe ſo to do, till they have drawn reward from you.

The *Turks* are incouraged to Alms by their Alcoran, as acceptable to God, and meritorious in it ſelf, if given without vain-glory, and of goods well-gotten: alledging it to be a temptation of the Devils to abſtain from Alms for fear of impoveriſhment. Their more publick Alms conſiſt in Sacrifices (if not ſo wrongfully termed) upon their Feſtivals, or performance of Vows: when Sheep and Oxen are

ſlain

LIB. I. The Mahometan Religion.

slain by the Priest, and divided amongst the poor; the owners not so much as retaining a part thereof. They say, they give much in private: and in truth, I have seen but few Beggars amongst them. Yet sometimes shall you meet in the streets with couples chained together by the neck, who beg to satisfie their Creditors in part, and are at the years end released of their bonds; provided that they make satisfaction if they prove afterward able. At their deaths they usually give Legacies for the release of Prisoners, the freeing of Bond-slaves, repairing of Bridges, building of Hanes for the relief of Passengers: and the Great men, to the erecting of Mosques and Hospitals, which they bui'd not seldom in their life time. But *Mahomet* the Great, and *Solyman* the Magnificent, have in that kind exceeded all others: whose stately and sumptuous structures do give a principal ornament to the City; where the sick and impotent are provided for, and the stranger entertained, (for here be no Inns:) the revenue of that of *Mahomets* amounting to an hundred and fifty thousand *Sultanies*. To these there belong Physicians, Chirurgions, Apothecaries. The charge thereof is committed unto their Priests, who bring up a certain number of Youths in the *Mahometan* Law, and frequently pray for the departed Souls of the Founders in the Chappels, of their Sepulchres. They extend their charity to Christians and Jews, as well as to them of their own Religion: nay birds and beasts have a taste thereof. For many only, to let them loose, will buy Birds in Cages; and bread to give unto Dogs. These have in this City no particular owners; being reputed an unclean Creature, and therefore not suffered to come into their Houses: thinking it nevertheless a deed of piety, to feed, and provide them Kennels to litter in, most of them repairing to the Sea-side nightly, where they keep such a howling, that if the wind sit Southward, they may be easily heard to the upper side of the City of *Pera*.

With the *Stoicks* they attribute all accidents to destiny, and constellations at birth, and say with the *Tragedian*,

Fates guide us: unto Fates yield we,	Fatis agimur: cædite Fatis.
Care cannot alter their decree.	Non sollicitæ possunt curæ.
For what we suffer, what we do,	Mutare rati staminа fusi.
Cælestial Orbs, proceed from you.	Quicquid patimur mortale genus,
All go in a prefixed way.	Quicquid facimus, venit ex alto,
The first prescribeth the last day.	Omnia certo tramitæ vadunt,
	Primusque dies dedit extremum.
	Senec. in Oedi.

affirming that their ends were written in their foreheads:

——*Thereby freed from deaths affright,*	——Quos ille timorum
The worst of fears, thence take they heart to fight	Maximus haud urget lethi metus, inde ruendi
And rush on Steel——	In ferrum mens prona viris.
	Lucan.l.1.

since it can be neither hastened nor avoided: being withal perswaded that they dye bravely that dye fighting; and that they shall be rewarded with Paradise, that do spend their blood upon the enemies of their Religion, whom they call *Shahides*, which is Martyrs. For although they repute murder to be an execrable Crime, that crys to Heaven for vengeance, and is never forgiven: yet are they commanded by their law, to extend their profession by violence, and without compassion to slaughter their opposers. But they live with themselves in such exemplary concord, that during the time that I remained amongst them (it being above three quarters of a year) I never saw *Mahometan* offer violence to a *Mahometan*, nor break into ill language: but if so they chance to do, a third will reprove him, with Fye *Mussel-men*, fall out? and all is appeased; he that gives a blow, hath many gashes made in his flesh, and is led about for a terrour: but the man-slayer is delivered to the Kindred or Friends of the slain, to be by them put to death with all exquisite torture.

Now their opinion of the end of the World, of Paradise, and of Hell, exceed the vanity of dreams, and all old Wives Fables. They say that at the winding of a Horn, not only all flesh shall dye, but the Angels themselves: and that the earth with Earthquakes shall be kneaded together like a lump of dough, for forty days so continuing. Then shall another blast restore beauty to the world, and life unto all that ever lived. The good shall have shining and glorified faces; but the bad, the countenance of Dogs and Swine, and such like unclean Creatures. *Moses*, *Christ*, and *Mahomet* shall bring their several Followers to judgment, and intercede for them. *Cain* that did the first murder

murder shall be the Ring-leader of the damned; who are to pass over the Bridge of Justice, laden with their sins in Satchels; where the great sinner shall fall on the one side into Hell; where they shall consume in fire, and be renewed to new torments. Yet God will have pity upon them in the end, and receive them unto mercy: and the Devil shall cease to be, since his malice is such as he cannot be saved. I was told by a *Sicilian* Renegado, an Eunuch, and one greatly devoted to their Superstition, that the burning Globe of the Sun (for such was his Philosophy) was the Continent of the damned. Those that tumble from the other side of the Bridge are laden with less sins: and do but fall into Purgatory: from whence they shall shortly be released, and received into Paradise. But as for the Women, poor souls! be they never so good, they have the gates shut against them: yet are consigned to a mansion without, where they shall live happily; as another repleat with all misery for others. It is to be more than conjectured; that *Mahomet* grounded his devised Paradise, upon the Poets invention of *Elisium*. For thus *Tibullus* describeth the one:

Sed me, quod facilis tenero sum semper amori,
   Ipsa Venus campos ducet in Elysios.
Hic choreæ, cantusq; vigent: passimq; vagantes.
   Dulce sonant tenui gutture carmen aves.
Fert casiam non culta leges, totosque per agros
   Floret odoratis terra benigna Rosis.
Ad juvenum series teneris immista puellis
   Ludit: & assidue prælia miscet amor.
   Eleg.l.s.   Eleg.l.33.

For that my heart to love still easily yields,
   Love shall conduct me to the Elisian fields.
There Songs and Dances revel: choice birds flie
   From tree to tree, warbling sweet melody.
The wild Shrubs bring forth Cassia: every-where
   The bounteous soil doth fragrant Roses bear.
Youths intermixt with Maids disport at ease,
   Incountring still in loves sweet skirmishes.

And *Mahomet* promiseth to the possessors of the other, magnificent Palaces spread all over with Silk Carpets, flowry Fields, and crystalline Rivers; Trees of Gold still flourishing; pleasing the eye with other goodly forms, and the taste with their fruits;

———primo avulso non deficit alter
Aureus, & simili frondescit virga metallo.
   Virg. Æn.l.6.

Which being pluckt, to others place resign,
And still the rich twigs with like metal shine.

Under whose fragrant shades they shall spend the course of their happy time with amorous Virgins, who shall alone regard their particular Lovers: not such as have lived in this world; but created of purpose; with great black eyes, and beautiful as the Hyacinth. They daily shall have their lost Virginities restored: ever young, (continuing there, as here at fifteen, and the men as at thirty) and ever free from natural pollutions. Boys of divine feature shall minister unto them, and set before them all variety of delicate Viands. But *Avicen* that great Philosopher and Physician, who flourished about four hundred and fifty years since, when *Mahometanism* had not yet utterly extinguished all good literature; who was by linage an *Arabian* of a Royal House, in Religion a *Mahometan*, but by Country and Habitation a *Spaniard*, and Prince (as some write) of *Corduba*, teacheth a far different Doctrine. For although as a *Mahometan*, in his Books *De Anima* and *De Almahad*, addressed particularly to a *Mahometan* Prince, he extolleth *Mahomet* highly, as being the *seal* of divine Laws, and the *last of the Prophets*; excusing his sensual felicities in the life to come, as meerly Allegorical, and necessarily fitted to rude and vulgar capacities: (for saith he, it the points of Religion were taught in their true form to the ignorant dull *Jews*, or to the wild *Arabians*, employed altogether about their Camels; they would utterly fall off from all belief in God:) yet besides that this excuse is so favourable and large, that it may extend as well unto all Idolaters, and in brief to the justifying of the absurdest errours, it is a point of Doctrine so contrary to his own opinion, as nothing can be more. For *Avicen* himself, in the aforesaid Books, doth esteem so vilely of the body, that he pronounceth bodily pleasures to be false and base; and that the souls being in the body is contrary to true beatitude: whereupon he denieth also the Resurrection of the flesh. Yet in favour, as hath been said of *Mahomet*, (who by sensual Doctrine sought to have the rude world to follow him) he not only by his Allegorical construction approveth the Doctrine of the Resurrection of the body, wherein the *Jews* and *Mahometans* consent with the *Christians*; but withal the transmigration of souls from one body into another, (by which means *Mahomet* devised how a Camel might pass through the eye of a Needle; the soul of a sinner for purgation entring first into the body of a Camel, then of a lesser Beast, and finally, of a little Worm which should creep through the eye of a Needle; and so become

come perfect:) and lastly, not once reproveth that impious saying of *Mahomet, That God himself at the Resurrection should also have a body, no doubt, to enjoy those sweet sensual felicities, though all such opinions are disclaimed by him*: but contrariwise reproveth the Doctrine of the Christians touching Spiritual Happiness, and that saying of our Saviour, that, *The Saints in the world to come shall be as Angels* (yet professeth the same to be true) *as being weak and ill fitted to vulgar understanding*. So strangely may wise men be besotted with faction, to excuse and commend the teaching of absurd errours even by themselves condemned, and to lay an aspersion upon the purity of Divine Doctrine, in that unfit to be so communicated to the ignorant: as if Truth were to make her self to please bestial Ignorance, and Ignorance not rather to be enlightened by degrees, and drawn up to behold the Truth. But now this *Avicen*, laying down for a while his outward person of a *Mahometan*, and putting on the habit of a Philosopher; in his Metaphysicks seemeth to make a flat opposition between the truth of their Faith received from their Prophet, and the truth of understanding by demonstrative argument: And saith in effect, that this Law and Prophecy delivered by *Mahomet*, which taught that God himself at the Resurrection should have a body, placeth the happiness of the life to come in bodily delights. But wise Theologians, saith he, have with greater desire pursued spiritual pleasures proper to the soul: and for this corporal felicity, although it should be bestowed upon them, would not esteem it in comparison of the other, whereby the mind is conjoined to the first truth, which is God. And here he never mentioneth that strained excuse of an Allegory; but with just indignation and some acerbity of speech, detesteth that gross opinion broached in their Law, which placeth the predominance of everlasting felicity in the baseness of sensuality, and in that low voluptuousness: and saith that a prudent and understanding man, may not think that all delight is like the delight of an Ass; and that the Angels who are next to the *Lord of the worlds*, should live deprived of all pleasure and joy, and that he who is the highest in beauty and virtue, should consist in the last and lowest degree of swavity. And therefore concludeth, that neither in excellency, nor in perfection, nor yet in multitude, nor in any thing praise-worthy or to be desired in pleasure, there is any comparison between those felicities: and though base souls be addicted to that base felicity, yet the worthy desires of holy minds are far removed from that disposition; and contrariwise being joined to their perfection (which is God) are filled with all true and happy delights: and if that the contrary persuasion or affection should be remaining in them, it would hurt and with-hold them from attaining unto that height of happiness. This being his better advised and more sincere discourse, it utterly excludes his former excuse of an Allegory, whose right use, being by plain and sensible allusions to draw up the understanding to an apprehension of divine things, represented in those similitudes: the course held by *Mahomet* worketh a clean contrary effect; and drowneth their understanding part and affection in the hope and love of these corporal pleasures. Whereby it is true, that he greatly enlarged his own earthly Dominion; but by this judgment even of *Avicen*, with-held his Followers from the true felicity. And it is worthy observation, that in the judgment of *Avicen*, one thing is true in their faith, and the contrary in pure and demonstrative reason. Whereas (to the honour of Christian Religion be it spoken) is confessed by all, and enacted by a Council, that it is an errour to say, One thing is true in Theology, and in Philosophy the contrary. For the truths of Religion are many times above reason, but never against it. So that we may now conclude, that the *Mahometan* Religion being derived from a person in life so wicked, so worldly his projects, in his persecutions of them so disloyal, treacherous, and cruel, being grounded upon base and false revelations, repugnant to sound reason, and that wisdom which the divine hand hath imprinted in his Works; alluring men with those inchantments of fleshly pleasures, permitted in this life, and promised for the life ensuing; being also supported with tyranny and the Sword (for it is death to speak there against it,) and lastly, where it is planted rooting out all virtue, all wisdom and science, and in sum, all liberty and civility, and laying the earth to waste, dispeopled and un-inhabited; that neither it came from God (save as a scourge by permission) neither can bring them to God that follow it.

Ebbubecher, *Omar*, *Ozman*, and *Haly*, followed *Mahomet* in the Government; the great enlarger of their Religion and Dominions: but *Haly* was persecuted, and slain in the end by the other, for assuming the right of succession, in that he had married the Daughter of their Prophet. From him the *Persians* do challenge priority of Government in matters of Religion, the main cause of the hatred between them and the *Turks*) alledging moreover, that the former three, to confirm their authorities, did falsly add to the Alcoran, and put out what they listed; and in such sort falsified, left it to their Followers. Then succeeded the *Caliphs* of *Babylon*, who bore both the spiritual and temporal jurisdiction. After the *Egyptians* set up a *Caliph* of their own. But in process of time they were both suppressed; the one (as hath been said before) by the *Tartars*, and the other by the *Sultans*. The dignity amongst the *Turks* with much abatement, doth now remain in the *Mufties*,(which name doth signifie an Oracle, or answer of doubts) as successors to *Ebubecher*, *Omar*, and *Ozman*: The *Caliphs* having been both High-Priests, and Princes, these being Patriarchs, as it were, and Soveraigns of their Religion. Throughout the whole *Turkish* Territories there is but one; who ever recideth in the Royal City; or follows the person of the Emperour. He is equal to the ancient Popes; or rather greater both in repute and authority. The *Grand Signior* doth rise at his approach to salute him, and sets him by him, and gives him much reverence. His life is only free from the Sword; and his fortunes most rarely subject to the subversion. The Emperour undertaketh no high design without his approvement. He hath power to reverse both his sentence, and the sentence of the *Divan*, if they be not adjudged by him conformable to the Alcoran; but his own is irrevocable. In matters of difficulty they repair to him; and his Exposition standeth for a Law. To conclude, he is the supream Judge, and rectifier of all actions, as well Civil as Ecclesiastical; and an approver of the Justice of the military. The place is given by the *Grand Signior* to men profoundly learned in their Law, and of known integrity. He seldom stirs abroad, and never admits of impertinent Conversation. Grave is his look, grave is his behaviour,

Rarus sermo illis, & magno libido tacendi.

Juv. Sat. 1.

Highly affecting silence, and most spare Of speech.

For when any come to him for Judgment, they deliver him in Writing the state of the question; who in writing briefly returns his oraculous answer. He commonly weareth a Vest of green, and the greatest Turbant in the Empire: I should not speak much out of compass, should I say as large in compass as a Bushel. I oft have been in this mans *Seraglio*, which is neither great in receit nor beauty: yet answerable to his small dependency, and infrequency of Suters. He keepeth in his House a Seminary of Boys, who are instructed in the mysteries of their Law. He is not restrained, nor restraineth himself from the penalty of women. His Incomes are great, his disburflings little, and consequently his wealth infinite: yet he is a bad pay-master of his debts, though they be but trifles. He much delighteth in Clocks and Watches: whereof, as some say, he hath not so few as a thousand.

Next in place to the *Mufti* are the *Cadileschiers*, that are Judges of the Armies (but not to meddle with the *Janizaries*) and accompany the *Beglerbegs* when they go into the Field. Of these there are only two: one of the *European* part of the Empire, and another of the *Asian*: These are also elected by the *Grand Signior*, as the *Cadies* by them (yet to be allowed by the *Grand Signior*, and to kiss his Vest:) of whom there is one in every Town, who besides their spiritual functions, do administer Justice between party and party, and punish Offenders. Of inferiour Priests there be some particularly appointed to sing at the tops of their Steeples, and to congregate the people; some to look to the Ceremonies, and some to read and interpret the Alcoran. There are also other Religious Orders, which I omit to speak of being of others own taking up; neither commanded nor commended, and rather to be esteemed Vagabonds than Religious persons, consider we either their life, or their habits.

Amongst the *Turkish* Commandments, one is, that, drawn originally from our Saviour, *Thou shalt not do what thou wouldst not have done to thee*: Whereupon for the most part their Civil Justice is grounded; not disagreeing greatly from the Laws of *Moses*. All evictions there as elsewhere, depend upon Witnesses: yet will not the Oath of a Christian or a Jew be received against a *Turk*, as will a *Turks* against them, and theirs one against another. But the Kindred of *Mahomet* have their single testimonies in equal value with the testimony of two others. Notwithstanding, the Oath of a *Mahometan* will not be taken, if impeached for a drinker of Wine, or eater of Swines flesh. Every *Bassa* keeps a *Divan* (so they call the Court of Justice) within his

LIB. I. Of the Turkish Justice.

his Province: but the highest of all, and to which they may appeal from all other, is *They were* that which is kept four days of the week in the *Grand Signiors Seraglio*, from whence *formerly* no appeal is admitted but to the person of the *Muftie*. Here the *Vizier Bassa* of *but four, to whom Ma-* the Port, who are nine in number (or as many as then are not otherwise imployed) *homet the* do sit in Justice: where also they consult of matters of State, and that publickly, not *third add-* excepting against Embassadours Drogermen, lightly always present, so presume they *ed five.* of strong hand: assisted by the (*a*) Admiral, (*b*) Chancellor, the (*c*) Treasurer in the *a Captain* same room keeping his Court) where all Causes whatsoever that are heard, within *b Ruccli.* the space of three days are determined; the Grand *Vizier Bassa* being President *tab.* of the rest. But Bribery not known until lately amongst them, hath so corrupted their *cTeftedar,* integrity, that those Causes (if they bear such a colour of right) do seldom miscarry where gifts are the Advocates, yet this is the best of the worst, that they quickly know their successes. But many times when the oppressed subject can have no Justice, they will in Troops attend the coming forth of the Emperour, by burning straw on their heads or holding up Torches, provoke his regard: who brought unto him by his Mutes, doth receive their Petition, which oftentimes turns to the ruine of some of those great ones. For assurances of Purchases they have no Indentures, no Fines and Recoveries. The omitting of a word cannot frustrate their Estates, nor quirks of Law prevail against conscience. All that they have to shew, is a little Schedule, called a *Hodget* or *Sigil*, only manifesting the possession of the Seller, as his of whom he bought it, or from whom it descended unto him, which under-written by the *Cadi* of the place, doth frustrate all after-claims whatsoever. Now the punishments for offenders be either pecuniary or corporal. To impose the former, they will forge all the slanders that they can, to eat upon the less circumspect Christians: but the other are seldom unjustly inflicted. Their forms of putting to death, (besides such as are common elsewhere) and impaling upon stakes, ganching (which is to be let fall from on high upon Hooks, and there to hang until they die by the anguish of these wounds, or more miserable famine) and another invented (but now not here used) to the terrour of mankind by some devillish *Perillus*, who deserved to have first tasted of his own invention, *viz*. they twitch the offender about the waste with a Towel, inforcing him to draw up his breath by often pricking him in the body, until they have drawn him within the compass of a span, then tying it hard, they cut him off in the middle, and setting the body on a hot plate of Copper, which seareth the veins, they so up-prop him during their cruel pleasure: who not only retaineth his sense, but the faculties of discourse, until he be taking down, and then departeth in an instant. But little faults are chastised by blows, received on the soles of the feet with a Bastinado, by hundreds at a time, according to the quality of the misdemeanour. A terrible pain that extendeth to all the parts of the body: yet have I seen them taken for money. The Master also in this sort doth correct his Slaves; but Parents their Children with stripes on the belly. The *Subashie* is as the Constable of a City both to search out and punish offences.

It remaineth now that we speak of the persons of the *Turks*, their dispositions, manners, and fashions. They be generally well complectioned, of good statures, and full bodies, proportionably compacted. They nourish no hair about them, but a lock on the crown, and on their faces only; esteeming it more cleanly, and to be the better prepared for their superstitious washings. But their beards they wear at full length, the mark of affected gravity, and token of freedom, (for Slaves have theirs shaven) insomuch that they will scoff at such Christians as cut, or naturally want them, as if suffering themselves to be abused against nature. All of them wear on their heads white Shashes and Turbants, the badge of their Religion: as is the folding of the one, and size of the other, of their vocations and quality. Shashes are long Towels of Calico wond about their heads: Turbants are made like great Globes, of Calico 100, and thwarted with rouls of the same, having little copped Caps, on the top, of green or red Velvet, being only worn by persons of rank; and he the greatest, that weareth the greatest, the *Muftie* excepted, which over-sizeth the Emperors. And although many Orders have particular ornaments appointed for their heads, yet wear they these promiscuously. It is an especial favour in the *Turk*, to suffer the Christian tributary Princes, and their chiefest Nobles to wear white heads in the City, but in them, what better than an Apostolical insinuation? But to begin from the skin: the next they wear is a Smock of Calico, with ample sleeves, much longer than their arms: under this, a pair of Calsouns of the same, which reach to their ancles, the rest naked, and going in yellow or red slip-shooes, picked at the Toe, and plated

plated on the sole: over all they wear an half-sleeved Coat girt unto them with a Towel: their neck all bare: and this within doors is their Summer-accoutrement. Over all when they go abroad they wear Gowns, some with wide half-sleeves (which more particularly belong to the *Grecians*) others with long hanging sleeves, buttoned before: and a third sort worn by the meaner sort, reaching but a little below the knee, with hanging sleeves not much longer than the arm, and open before; but all of them ungathered in the shoulders. In the Winter they add to the former Calsodns of Cloth, which about the small of their leg are sewed to short sir ooth buskins of leather without soles, sit for the foot, as a Glove for the hand: lining their Gowns with Fur, as they do their Coats; having then the sleeves (or quilted Waste-coats under them) reaching close to their wrists. They wear no Gloves. At their Girdles they wear long Hankerchers, some of them admirable for value and workmanship. They never alter their fashions: not greatly differing in the great and vulgar more than in the richness. Cloth of Tissue, of Gold and Silver-velvet, Scarlet, Sattin, Damask, Chamolets, lined with Sables and other costly Furs, and with Martins, Squerrils, Foxes, and Coney-skins, are worn according to their several qualities. But the common wear is Violet-cloth: they retain the old Worlds custom in giving change of garments: which they may aptly do, when one Vest sitteth all men, and is of every mans fashion. The Clergy go much in green, it being *Mahomets* colour; and his Kinsmen in green Shashes, who are called *Emers*, which is, Lords: the Women also wear something of green on their heads to be known. There lives not a race of ill-favoureder people, branded perhaps by God for the sin of their seducing Ancestor, and their own wicked assuming of hereditary holiness. But if a Christian out of ignorance wear green, he shall have his cloaths torn from his back, and perhaps be well beaten. They carry no Weapons about them in the City; only they thrust under their Girdles great crooked Knives of a Dagger-like size, in sheathes of metal; the hafts and sheathes of many being set with stones, and some of them worth five hundred Sultanies. They bear their bodies upright, of a stately gate, and elated countenance. In their familiar salutations they lay their hands on their bosoms, and a little decline their bodies: but when they salute a person of great rank, they bow almost to the ground, and kiss the hem of his garment. The ornaments of their heads they never put off upon any occasion. Some of them perfume their beards with Amber and the insides of their Turbants: and all of them affect cleanliness so Religiously, that besides their customary lotions, and daily frequenting of the *Bannios*, they never so much as make water, but they wash both their hands and privities: at which business they sequester themselves, and couch to the earth; reviling the Christian whom they see pissing against a wall, and sometimes striking him. This they do, to prevent that any part of either excrement should touch their garments, esteeming it a pollution, and hindring the acceptation of prayer, who then are to be most pure both in heart and habit. So slothful they be, that they never walk up and down for recreation, nor use any other exercise but shooting: wherein they take as little pains as may be, sitting on Carpets in the shadow, and sending their Slaves for their Arrows. They also shoot against earthen walls, ever kept moist in Shops and private Houses for that purpose, standing not above six paces from the Mark, and that with such violence, that the Arrow passes not seldom thorow: nay, I have seen their Arrows shot by our Ambassadour thorough Targets of Steel, pieces of Brass of two inches thick, and thorough wood, with an Arrow headed with wood, of eight inches. Their Bows are for form and length, not unlike the Lath of a large Cros-bow, made of the Horns of Buffoloes, intermixed with sinews, of admirable workmanship, and some of them exquisitely gilded. Although there be Wrestlers among them, yet they be such as do it to delight the people, and do make it their profession, as do those that walk upon Ropes, wherein the *Turks* are most expert; going about when they have done, to every particular Spectator for his voluntary benevolence. Of Cards and Dice they are happily ignorant; but at Chess they will play all the day long, a sport that agreeth well with their sedentary vacancy; wherein notwithstanding they avoid the dishonest hazard of money. The better sort take great delight in their Horses, which are beautiful to the eye, and well ridden for service; but quickly jaded, it held to a good round trot (for amble they do not) in an indifferent journey. But the *Turks* do not lightly ride so fast as to put them unto either. Their Saddles be hard and deep, though not great, plated behind and before, and some of them with silver, as are their massie Stirrups, and the reins of their Bridles, suited unto their costly Caparisons.

When

LIB. I.   Of the Turks, their Manners, &c.

when they stand in the Stable they feed them for the most part, if not altogether, with Barley; being here of small value, and only serving for that purpose. They litter them in their own dung, first dryed in the Sun, and pulverated, which keeps their skins clean, smooth, and shining.

The Turks do greatly reverence their Parents, (so commanded to do by their Law) as the Inferiour his Superiour, and the young the aged, readily giving the Priority to whom it belongeth, the left hand as they go in the streets preferred before the right, in that made Masters thereby of the Sword of the other, and the chiefest place the farthest from the wall, who live together, as if all of a brother-hood. Yet give they no entertainment unto one another, nor come there any into their houses but upon special occasion, and those but into the publick parts thereof; their Women being never seen but by the Nurses and Eunuchs which attend on them. Yea so jealous they are, that their Sons, when they come to growth, are separated from them. As their Houses are mean, so are their Furnitures: having nothing on the inside but bare white walls, unless it be some special Room in the house of some of high Quality. But the Roofs of many of them are curiously seeled with inlaid Wood, adorned with Gold and Azure of an excessive costliness; the greater part of the floor, and that a little advanced, being covered with Turkie Carpets, whereon when they tread, they do put off their slip-shooes. Many of their rooms have great out-windows, where they lie on Cushions in the heat of the day. They lye upon Mattresses, some of silk, some stained linen, with Bolsters of the same, and Quilts that are suitable, but much in their Cloaths, the cause perhaps that they are so lousie. Nor shame they thereat: many you shall see sit publickly a lousing them in the Sun, and those no mean persons. They have neither Tables nor Stools in their Houses, but sit cross-leg'd on the floor at their Victuals, all in a Ring. Instead of a Cloth, they have a skin spread before them, but the better sort sit about a round Board, standing on a foot not past half a foot high, and brim'd like a Charger. The dishes have feet like standing Bowls, and are so set one upon another, that you may eat of each without removing of any. Their most ordinary food is Pillaw, that is, Rice which hath been sod with the fat of Mutton: Pottage they use of sundry kinds, Eggs fryed in Honey, Tanlies, (or something like them) Pasties of sundry ingredients: the little flesh which they eat is cut into gobbets, and either sod, or roasted in a Furnace. But I think there is more in London spent in one day than in this City in twenty. Fish they have in indifferent quantity. But the commons do commonly feed on Herbs, Fruits, Roots, Onions, Garlick, a beastly kind of unpressed Cheese that lieth in a lump; hodg-podges made of flowre Milk and Honey, &c. so that they live for little or nothing, considering their fare, and the plenty of all things. They are waited upon by their Slaves, given them, or purchased with their Swords or Money: of these to have many it is accounted for great riches. When one hath fed sufficiently he riseth, and another taketh his room, and so continue to do until all be satisfied. They eat three times a day: but when they feast they sit all the day long, unless they rise to exonerate nature, and forthwith return again. They abstain from Hogs-flesh, from Blood, and from wha hath dyed of it self, unless in cases of necessity. Their usual drink is pure water, yet have they sundry Sherbets, (so they call the Confections which they infuse into it) some made of Sugar and Lemmons, some of Violets, and the like, whereof some are mixed with Amber) which the richer sort dissolve thereinto. The Honey of Sio is excellent for that purpose: and they make another of the Juyce of Raisins, of little cost, and most usually drunk off. Wine is prohibited them by their Alcoran: they plant none, they buy none: but now to that liberty they are grown (the natural Turk excepted) they that will quaff freely when they come to a house of a Christian: insomuch as I have seen but few go away unled from the Embassadours Table. Yet the feared disorders that might ensue thereof, have been an occasion that divers times all the Wine in the City hath been stayed (except in Embassadours houses) and death hath been made the penalty unto such as presumed to bring any in. They prefer our Beer above all other Drinks. And considering that Wine is forbidden, that water is with the rawest (especially in this Clime) the dearness of Sherbets, and plenty of Barley (being here sold not for above nine pence a Bushel) no doubt but it would prove infinitely profitable to such as should bring in the use thereof amongst them. Although they be destitute of Taverns, yet have they their Coffa-houses, which something resemble them. There sit they chatting most of the day; and sip of a drink called Coffa (of the Berry that is made of) in little

F 2   China

China Dishes, as hot as they can suffer it: black as soot, and tasting not much unlike it (why not that black broth which was in use amongst the *Lacedemonians?*) which helpeth, as they say, digestion, and procureth alacrity: many of the Costa-men, keeping beautiful Boys, who serve as Stales to procure them Customers. The *Turks* are also incredible takers of Opium, whereof the lesser *Asia* affordeth them plenty, carrying it about them both in Peace and War; which, they say, expelleth all fear, and makes them couragious: but I rather think giddy-headed, and turbulent dreamers, by them, as should seem by what hath been said, religiously affected. And perhaps for the self same cause they also delight in Tobacco: which they take thorow Reeds that have joyned unto them great heads of wood to contain it. I doubt not but lately taught them, as brought them by the *English*: and were it not sometimes lookt into (for *Morat Bassa* not long since commanded a pipe to be thrust thorow the nose of a *Turk*, and so to be led in derision thorow the City) no question but it would prove a principal Commodity. Neverthelefs they will take it in corners, and are so ignorant therein, that that which in *England* is not salable, doth pass here amongst them for most excellent.

They are by their Law in general exhorted to marry, for the propagation of their Religion: and he ill-reputed of that forbeareth so to do, until the age of five and twenty. Every man is allowed four Wives, who are to be of his own Religion, and as many Concubine Slaves as he is able to keep of what Religion soever. For God (saith the Alcoran) that is good and gracious, exacteth not of us, what is harsh and burdensom, but permits us the nightly company of Women, well knowing that abstinency in that kind is both grievous and impossible. Yet are they to meddle with none but their own peculiars: the offending Women they drown, and the men they gansh. They buy their Wives of their Parents, and record the Contract before the *Cadi*, which they afterward solemnize in this manner: Many Women are invited by the Mother of the Bride to accompany her the night before the Marriage-day, whereof they spend a great part in feasting; then lead they her into a Bath, where they anoint and bathe her. So breaking company, they depart unto their several rests, and in the morning return to her Chamber; where they trick her in her richest Ornaments, tying on her silken Buskins with knots not easily unknit. The Bridegroom having feasted a number in like manner, in the morning they also repair to his house in their best Apparel, and gallantly mounted, from whence they set forward by two and two, to fetch home the Bride, accompanied with Musick; and conducted by the *Sagdich*, who is the nearest of his Kindred. Unto whom the Bride is delivered with her face close covered: who set a-stride on Horse-back, hath a Canopy carried over her; in such sort as no part of her is to be discerned. So the Troop returning in order as they came: after them are carried in Serpets (a kind of Baskets) their Presents and Apparel: then followeth she; and lastly her Slaves, if any have been given her. The Bridegroom standeth at his door to receive her, who is honoured by his Guests (yet go they not in) with sundry Presents before their departure. If she be of Quality, she is led to the Bride-chamber by an Eunuch, where Women stand prepared to undress her. But the Bridegroom himself must untye her Buskins (as among the *Romans* they did their Girdles) to which he is fain to apply his teeth. Now he is to entertain his Wives with an equal respect: alike is their Diet, alike is their Apparel, alike is his Benevolence (for such sweet stuff is contained in the Precepts of their Doctors) unless they consent to give or change turns, or else they may complain to the *Cadi*, and procure a Divorcement. But the Husband may put away his Wife at his pleasure: who may marry unto another within four months after, provided she prove not with Child, and then not until so long after her delivery. But if he will have her again, he must buy her: and if after the third Divorce, another is first to lie with her, as a punishment inflicted for his levity. They give him the reverence of a Master; they are at no time to deny him their embracements whom he toucheth not again, until they have been at the *Bannia*. They receive chastisement from him, and that they hold to be an argument of his affection. They feed apart, and inter-meddle not with Houshold-affairs. All that is required at their hands, is to content their Husbands, to nurse their own Children, and to live peaceably together: which they do (and which is strange) with no great jealousie or envy. No male accompanies them above twelve years old, except they be Eunuchs; and so strictly are they guarded, as seldom seen to look out at their doors. They be Women of elegant Beauties

Of the Turks, their Manners, &c.

for the most part ruddy, clear, and smooth, as the polished Ivory; being never ruffled by the weather, and daily frequenting the *Bannia*; but withal by the self-same means they suddenly wither. Great eyes they have in principal repute, affected both by the *Turks* and the *Grecians*, as it should seem from the beginning. For *Mahomet* doth promise Women with such, (nay as big as Eggs) in his imaginary Paradise: which *Homer* attributes, as an especial excellency, unto *Juno*:

——— *To whom replies* *Adoreth Juno with the Cows fair eyes.*	Huic respondit postea bovinos oculos habens Veneranda Juno. *Hom. l'iad. 1.*

And again,

The great ey'd Juno smil'd.	——— Risit autem magnis oculis veneranda Juno. *Iliad. 1.*

And of those the blacker they be, the more amiable: insomuch that they put between the eye-lids and the eye a certain black powder with a fine long Pencil, made of a Mineral brought from the Kingdom of *Fez*, and called *Alcohole*; which by the not disgraceful staining of the lids, do better set forth the whiteness of the eye, and though it trouble for a time, yet it comforteth the sight, and repelleth all humours. Into the same hue (but likely they naturally are so) do they die their eye-bries and eye-brows: (the latter by Art made high, half-circular, and to meet, if naturally they do not) so do they the hair of their head:

And led a more fair showing *In black hair loosly flowing.*	Leda fuit nigra conspicienda coma, *Ovid. Am. l. 2. Eleg. 4.*

as a foil that maketh the white seem whiter, and more becoming their other perfections. They part it before in the midst, and plate it behind, yet sometimes wearing it dishevelled. They paint their Nails with a yellowish red. They wear on the top of their heads a Cap not unlike the top of a Sugar-loaf, yet a little flat, of Paste-board, and covered with Cloth of Silver or Tissue. Their Under-garments (which within doors are their upper-most) do little differ from those that be worn by the men, which we have presented to the eye to avoid repetition.

The better sort about the upper part of their Arms and smalls of their Legs wear Bracelets, and are elsewhere adorned with Jewels. When they go abroad they wear over all long Gowns of Violet-cloth or Scarlet, tyed close before, the large Sleeves hanging over their hands; having Buskins on their Legs, and their Heads and Faces so mabled in fine Linen, that no more is to be seen of them than their Eyes: nor that of some, who look as through the sight of a Bever. For they are forbidden by the Alcoran to disclose their beauties unto any but unto their Fathers and Husbands. They never stir forth, but (and then always in Troops) to pray at the Graves, and to the publick *Bannia*, which for excellency of buildings are next to their Mosques. But having in part already described some of their forms, I will a little treat of their uses which have been in times past, and are at this present in such request with these Nations (as once with the *Romans*, as may appear by their regardable ruines) that few but frequent them twice in the week, as well for their health, as for delight and cleanliness. For the stomachs crudity proceeding from their usual eating of fruits and drinking of water, is thereby concocted; which also after exercise and travel restoreth to the wearied body a wonderful alacrity.

Pœna tamen præsens, cum tu deponis amictus
Turgidus, & crudum pavonem in balnea portas.
Hinc subitæ mortes, atque intestata senectus.
Juv. Sat. 1.

Ye punish straight, if you disrob'd, and full
To the Bath do undigested viands bring.
Hence sudden deaths, and age intestate spring.

The men take them up in the morning, and in the afternoon the Women. But both amongst the *Romans* did ordinarily frequent them together: a custom, as they say, continued in *Switzerland* at this day, and that among the most modest. The men are attended upon by men, and the Women by Women. In the outer-most room they put off their cloaths, then having Aprons of stained Linen tyed about their Wastes, they enter the Baths to what degree of heat they please: for several rooms, and several parts of them are of several temperatures, as is the water let in by Cocks to wash the sweat and filth of the body. The Servitors wash them, rub them, stretch out their joynts, and cleanse their skins with a piece of rough Grogoram: which done, they shave the heads and bodies of men, or take away the hair with a composition of Rusma (a Mineral of *Cyprus*) and unsleakt Lime: who returning to the place where they left their cloaths, are dryed with fresh linning, and for all this they pay not above three or four Aspers, so little, in that endued with Revenues by their Founders. But the Women do anoint their bodies with an Oyntment made of the Earth of *Chios*, which maketh the skin soft, white, and shining, extending that on the face, and freeing it from wrinkles. Much unnatural and filthy lust is said to be committed daily in the remote Closets of these darksom *Bannias*, yea Women with Women; a thing incredible, if former times had not given thereunto both detection and punishment. They have generally the sweetest Children that ever I saw, partly proceeding from their frequent bathings and affected cleanliness. As we bear ours, in our arm, so they do theirs astride on their shoulders.

Now next to their Wives, we may speak of their Slaves: for little difference is there made between them, who are Christians taken in the Wars, or purchased with their money. Of these there are weekly Markets in the City, where they are to be sold as Horses in Fairs; the men being rated according to their faculties or personal abilities, as the Women for their youths and beauties, who are set out in best becoming attires, and with their aspects of pity and affection endeavour to allure the Christians to buy them, expecting from them a more easie servitude and continuance of Religion: when being thrall to the *Turk*, they are often inforced to renounce it for their better entertainment. Of them there be many of excellent outward perfection: and when the buyer hath agreed of the price (but yet conditionally) they are carried aside into a Room. And as those,

Who Horses cheapen, search them, and make proof,
Lest a good shape, propt by a tender hoof,
Cheat him that should un-circumspectly buy
For that short-headed, broad-spread, crested high.

—Ubi equos mercantur apertos
Inspiciunt, ne si facies, ut sæpe, decora
Molli fulta pede est, emptorem inducat hiantem
Quod pulchræ clunes, breve quod caput, ardua cerviz.
Hor. Serm 1. *Sat.* 2.

So,

To assure you of deceitful wares they shew
All that they sell; nor boast they of the best,
Nord hide the bad, but both give to the test.

——quod mercem sine furis gestat aperte
Quod venale habet ostendit, nec si quid honesti est,
Jactat, habetque palam, quarit quo turpia celet.
Idem.

even to the search of her mouth, and assurance (if so she be said to be) of her Virginity. Their Masters may lie with them, chastise them, exchange and sell them at their pleasure. But a Christian will not lightly sell her whom he hath lyen with, but give her her liberty. If any of their Slaves will become *Mahometans*, they are discharged of their bondage; but if a Slave be a *Turk*, he only is the better intreated. The *Turks* do use their bond-men with little less respect than their Wives, and make no difference between the Children begotten of the one or the other: who live together without jealousie, it being allowed by their irreligious Religion: notwithstanding their Wives do only receive, as proper unto them, their Sabbaths benevolence. The old and the most deformed are put to the most drudgery. The men-slaves may compel their Masters before the *Cadie*, to limit the time of their bondage, or set a price of their redemption, or else to sell them unto another; but whether of the two, they lightly refer to the Slaves election. If they be only fit for labour, they will accept of the time, but if skilfull in any craft, of the price: which expired or paid, they may return into their Countries. But Gally-slaves are seldom released, in regard of their small number, and much imployment which they have for them: nor those that are Slaves unto great ones, to whom the *Cadies* authority extends not. Many of the Children that the *Turks* do buy (for their Markets do afford of all ages) they castrate, making all smooth as the back of the hand, (whereof divers do dye in the cutting) who supply the uses of nature with a silver Quill, which they wear in their Turbants. In times past, they only did but geld them; but being admitted to the free converse of their Women, it was observed by some, that they more than befittingly delighted in their Societies: For according to the Satyre.

With feeble Eunuchs some delighted are:
Kisses still soft, Chins that of beards despair:
Who need force no abortments.

Sunt quos Eunuchi imbelles & mollia semper
Oscula delectant, & desperatio barbæ,
Et quod abortivo non est opus.
Juv. Sat. 6.

But others say, that *Selymus* the Second, having seen a Gelding cover a Mare, brought in among them that inhumane custom. The first that ever made Eunuch, was *Semiramis*. They are here in great repute with their Masters, trusted with their states, the government of their women and houses in their absence, having for the most part been approved faithful, wise, and couragious; insomuch as not a few of them have come to sit at the stern of State, (the second *Visier* of the Port being now an Eunuch) and others to the government of Armies.

But now speak we of their Funerals. After their death, the men by the men, and the women by the women are laid out in the midst of the room. When divers of their Priests do assemble, and having performed certain idle Ceremonies, (as in wrapping their Beads about it, and in the often turning it, invoking God to have mercy on the departed) they wash it, shave it, and shrowd it in linen, which they have untied both at hand and feet. Then lay they the Corse on a Bier, placing a Turbant at the upper end, and carry it to the Grave, with the head forward: some of the *Dervises* going before with Tapers, the Priest singing after, and lastly his friends and acquaintance. But persons of principal quality have their horses led before them, with Ensigns trailed on the earth, and other Rites of that nature, divers of the Santons going before, naming of God, and shaking of their heads, and turning about until they fall down giddy. The sides and bottom of the grave are boarded, and a board laid over the Corse to keep the earth from it, leaving a sufficient compass to kneel in. For they are of opinion, that two terrible Angels called *Mongir* and *Gudaquir*, do presently repair unto the grave, and put the soul again into the body, as if (saith the Alcoran)

Alcoran) a man should put on a shirt, and raising him on his knees, with his head uncovered, (the winding-sheet being left unknit for that purpose) demand of him in particular how he hath behaved himself in this life: which if not well, the one strikes him on the head with a hammer nine fathoms into the earth, the other tearing him with an Iron hook; and so continue to torment him until the day of Judgment. A Purgatory so feared, that in their Matins they petition God to deliver them from the examinations of the Black Angels, the tortures of the grave, and their evil journey. But if he have satisfied them in his reply, they vanish away, and two white Angels come in their places, the one laying his arm under his head, the other sitting at his feet, and so protect him until Dooms day. The Emperours, and some of the great *Bassas* (whereof we have spoken sufficiently before) have their particular *Mausolæums*. Those of a second condition are buried in their Gardens in Sepulchres without covers, filled within above the cover with earth, and set with varieties of flowers, according to the custom of the *Pythagoreans*, and universal wishes of the *Ethnicks*,

Dii majorum umbris tenuem & sine pondere terram
Spirantesque crocos, & in urna perpetuum sui.
Persius.

Lie earth light on their bones, may their graves bear
Fresh fragrant flowers, let spring-tide still live there.

they being (as they thought) sensible of burdens, and delighted with favours, or with the honour therein done them. But the common sort are buried by the high-way sides, and fields of most frequency, adjoyning to the City, having a stone of white Marble more than a foot broad, four feet high, ingraven with *Turkish* Characters, erected at the head, and another at the feet; the grave between lying like a Trough. To these the Women flock every *Thursday* in multitudes, weeping over their Children, Husbands, Kinsfolks, and dead Progenitors; often kissing the stones, and praying for their delivery from the aforesaid black tortures: many times leaving bread and meat on their graves (a custom also of the *Pagans*) for Dogs and Birds to devour, as well as to relieve the poor, being held an available alms for the deceased. The better sort do mourn in white (as for black, I never saw it worn by a *Turk*) and but for a little season. And the Women are not to marry by their Law, until four months and ten days after the deaths of their Husbands.

To speak a word or two of their Sciences and Trades: some of them have some little knowledge in Philosophy. Necessity hath taught them Physick, rather had from experience than the grounds of Art. In Astronomy they have some insight, and many there are that undertake to tell Fortunes. These frequently sit in the streets of the City, resorted unto by such as are to take a journey, or go about any business of importance. They have a good gift in Poetry, wherein they chant their Amours in the *Persian* Tongue to vile Musick; yet are they forbidden so to do by their Law, Gitterns, Harps, and Recorders being their principal Instruments. But their loud Instruments do rather affright than delight the hearing. On a time the *Grand Signior* was perswaded to hear some choice *Italian* Musick; but the foolish Musicians (whose wit lay only in the ends of their fingers) spent so much time in unseasonable tuning, that he commanded them to avoid, belike esteeming the rest to be answerable. They study not Rhetorick, as sufficiently therein instructed by Nature; nor Logick, since it serves as well to delude as inform, and that wisdom (according to the opinion of the *Epicures*) may be comprehended in plain and direct expressions. Some there be amongst them that write Histories, but few read them, thinking that none can write of times past truly, since none dare write the truth of the present. Printing they reject, perhaps for fear lest the universality of learning should subvert their false grounded Religion and Policy, which is better preserved by an ignorant obedience: moreover, a number that live by writing, should be undone, who are, for the most part, of the Priesthood. The *Turkish* Tongue is lofty in sound, but poor of it self in substance: for being originally the *Tartarian*, who were needy ignorant Pastors, they were constrained to borrow their terms of State and Office from the *Persians*, (upon whose ruines they erected their greatness) of Religion (being formerly *Pagans*) from the *Arabians*, as they did of the Maritime names (together with their skill) from the *Greeks* and *Italians*. In *Natolia* it is most generally spoken. They use (as the *Persians*) the *Arabick* Character. In writing they leave out the Vowels, unless it be in the end of a word, so that much is contrived in a little room. They curiously sleek their Paper, which is thick, much of it being coloured and dappled like Chamblets, done by a trick they have

LIB. I.   Sultân Achmet.   57

have in dipping it in the water. They have Painters amongst them, exquisite in their kind, (for they are not to draw by their Law, nor to have the figure of any thing living) yet now many privately begin to infringe that Precept; and the *Grand Signior* himself hath a Fan, whereon the Battels of *Hungary* are painted. Colours also they have, no less fair than durable. Every one hath some Trade or other, not so much as the *Grand Signior* excepted. Their Trades are lightly such as serve for their own uses, neither much supplying foreign Marts, nor frequenting them. A lazy people that work but by fits, and more esteem of their ease, than their profit, yet are they excessive covetous. And although they have not the wit to deceive (for they be gross-headed) yet have they the will, breaking all compacts with the Christians that they find discommodious: so that they seldom will deal with them. But with one another they buy and sell only for ready money, wherein the most of their substance consisteth, the occasion that few Suits do happen amongst them. I have spoken sufficiently, at least what I can, of this Nation in general: now convert we to the Person and Court of this *Sultan*.

He is, in this year 1610. about the age of three and twenty, strongly limb'd, and of a just stature, yet greatly inclined to be fat: insomuch as sometimes he is ready to choke as he feeds, and some do purposely attend to free him from danger. His face is full and duly proportioned: only his eyes are extraordinary great, by them esteemed (as is said before) an excellency in beauty. Flegm hath the predominancy in his complexion. He hath a little hair on his upper lip, but less on his chin, of a darksom colour. His aspect is as haughty as his Empire is large. He beginneth already to abstain from exercise: yet are there Pillars with inscriptions in his *Seraglio*, between which he threw a great Iron Mace, that memorizeth both his strength and activity. Being on a time rebuked by his Father *Mahomet*, that he neglected so much his exercises and studies, he made this reply: that, now he was too old to begin to learn; intimating thereby, that his life was to determine with his Fathers, whereat the *Sultan* wept bitterly. For he then had two Elder Brothers, of whom the Eldest was strangled in the presence of his Father upon a false suspicion of Treason; and the other by a natural death did open his way to the Empire. Perhaps the consideration thereof that made him keep his younger Brother alive, contrary to their cruel custom, but strongly guarded, and kept within his *Seraglio*. For he is of no bloody disposition, nor otherwise notoriously vicious, considering the austerity of that Government, and immunities of their Religion. Yet he is an un-relenting punisher of offences, even in his own Houshold: having caused eight of his Pages, at my being there, to be thrown into the Sea for Sodomy (an ordinary crime, if esteemed a crime, in that Nation) in the night time; being let to know by the report of a Cannon, that his will was fulfilled. Amongst whom it was given out, that the Viceroy's natural Son of *Sicilia* was one (a Youth lately taken Prisoner, and presented unto him) yet but so said to be, to dishearten such as should practise his escape. His Valour rests yet untryed, having made no War but by disputation: nor is it thought that he greatly affects it, despairing of long life in regard of his corpulency. Whereupon he is now building a magnificent Mosque, for the health of his Soul, all of white Marble; at the East-end and South-side of the Hippodrom; where he first broke the earth, and wrought three hours in person. The like did the *Bassa*: bringing with them Presents of Money and Slaves to further the Building. His occupation (for they are all tyed to have one) is the making of Ivory Rings, which they wear on their Thumbs when they shoot, whereupon he works daily. His Turbant is like in shape to a Pompion, but thrice as great. His under and upper garments are lightly of white Sattin, or Cloth of Silver tissued with an eye of green, and wrought in great branches. He hath not so few as four thousand persons that feed and live within his *Seraglio*; besides *Capagies*, of whom there are five hundred attired like *Janizaries*, but only that they want the Socket in the front of the Bonnets, who wait by fifties at every Gate. The chief Officers of the Court are the Master (as we may term him) of the Requests, the Treasurer and Steward of his Houshold, his Cup-bearer, the *Aga* of the Women, the Controuller of the *Jemoglans*: who also steereth his Barge, and is the principal Gardiner. Divers of these *Jemoglans* marching before the *Grand Signior* at solemn Shows, in a vain ostentation of what they will undergo for their Lord, gathering up the skin of their Temples, do thrust quills through, and stick therein feathers for a greater bravery: so wear they them to their no small trouble, until the place putrifie, and some, when the old breaks out, make new holes

close

close to the broken. Yea the Standard-bearers of this crue, thrust the slaves sometimes of their Standards thorow the skin and fat of their bellies, resting the lower end on a Stirrup of Leather; and so bear them thorow the City. Fifty Mutes he hath born deaf and dumb, whereof some few be his daily Companions, the rest are his Pages. It is a wonderful thing to see how readily they can apprehend and relate by signs, even matters of great difficulty. Not to speak of the multitude of Eunuchs, the Foot-men of his Guard, Cooks, Sherbet-men (who make the foresaid Beverage) Gardeners, and Horse-keepers: we now will treat of his Women; wherein we will include those as well without as within his *Seraglio*.

And first begin we with his Virgins, of whom there are seldom so few as five hundred, kept in a *Seraglio* by themselves, and attended on only by Women, and Eunuchs. They all of them are his Slaves, either taken in the Wars, or from their Christian Parents, and are indeed the choicest Beauties of the Empire. They are not to be presented to the Emperour, until certain months be expired after their entrance, in which time they are purged and dieted, according to the custom of the ancient *Persians*. When it is his pleasure to have one, they stand ranckt in a Gallery, and she prepared for his Bed, to whom he giveth his Handkercher: who is delivered to the aforesaid *Aga* of the Women (a Negro Eunuch) and conducted by him into the *Sultan's Seraglio*. She that beareth him the first Son, is honoured with the title of *Sultana*. But for all his multitude of Women, he hath yet begotten but two Sons and three Daughters, though he be that way unsatiably given, (perhaps the cause that he hath so few) and useth all sorts of food that may enable performance. He cannot make a free Woman his Concubine, nor have to do with her whom he hath freed, unless he do marry her. This was well known to the wickedly witted *Roxolana*: who pretending devotion, and desirous for the health, forsooth, of her Soul to erect a Temple, with an Hospital; imparting her mind to the *Mufti*, was told by him, that it would not be acceptable to God, if built by a Bond-woman. Whereupon she put off a habit of a counterfeit sorrow; which possest the doting *Solyman* with such a compassion, that he forthwith gave her her freedom, that she might pursue her intention. But having after a while sent for her by an Eunuch, she cunningly excused her not coming, as touched in conscience with the unlawfulness of the fact, now being free; and therefore not to consent unto his pleasure. So he, whose soul did abide in her, and not able to live without her, was constrained to marry her. The only mark that she aimed at, and whereon she grounded her succeeding Tragedies. This also hath married his Concubine, the Mother of her younger Son, (she being dead by whom he had the eldest) who with all the practices of a politick Step-dame, endeavours to settle the succession on her own: adding, as it is thought, the power of Withcraft to that of her beauty, she being passionately beloved of the *Sultan*. Yet is she called *Caseek Cadoun*, which is, the Lady without hair: By Nature her self, both graced and shamed. Now when the *Sultan* dyeth, all his Women are carried into another *Seraglio*; where those remain that were his Predecessors, being there both strictly lookt unto, and liberally provided for. The *Grand Signior* not seldom bestowing some of them (as of his Virgins, and the Women of his own *Seraglio*) upon his great *Bassas* and others, which is accounted a principal honour. But for his Daughters, Sisters, and Aunts, they have the *Bassa* given them for their Husbands, the *Sultan* saying thus, *Here, Sister, I give thee this man to thy slave, together with this Dagger, that if he please thee not thou mayst kill him.* Their Husbands come not unto them until they be called: if but for speech only, their shooes which they put off at the door, are there suffered to remain: but if to lye with them, they are laid over the bed by an Eunuch, a sign for them to approach; who creep in unto them at the Beds feet. Mustapha and Hadir (two of the *Visiers* of the Port) have married this *Sultans* Sister and Niece, and *Mahomet Bassa* of *Cairo*, his Daughter: a Child of six years old, and he about fifty, having had Presents sent him according to the *Turkish* Solemnities, who give two hundred thousand *Sultanies* in Dowry. Not much in habit do the Women of the *Seraglio* differ from other, but that the Favourite wears the ornament of her head more high, and of a particular fashion, of beaten gold, and inchased with Gems, from the top whereof there hangeth a Veil that reacheth to her Ankles: the rest have their Bonnets more depressed, yet rich, with their hair disheveled.

When the *Sultan* entertaineth Embassadours, he sitteth in a Room of white Marble, glittering with Gold and Stones, upon a low Throne, spread with curious

Carpets,

LIB. I.   *Sultan Achmet.*   59

Carpets, and accommodated with Cushions of admirable workmanship; the *Bassa* of the Bench being by, who stand like so many Statues without speech or motion. It is now a custom that none do come into his presence without presents: first sallied upon his *Bassa*, as they say, by a *Persian* Embassadour; who thereupon sent word to the *Sophy* his Master, that had conquered *Turkie*. The stranger that approacheth him is led between two: a custom observed ever since the first *Amurath* was slain by the *Servian Cobelitz*, a common Souldier, who in the overthrow of *Cossoes*, rising from amongst the dead bodies, and reeling with his wounds, made towards the *Sultan*, then taking a view of the slain, as if he had something to say: by whom admitted to speech, he forthwith stab'd him with a Dagger hid under his Cassock for that purpose. They go backward from him, and never pull off their hats, the shewing of the head being held by the *Turk* to be an opprobrious indecency. Now when he goeth abroad, which is lightly every other *Friday* (besides at other times, upon other occasions) unto the Mosque; and when in state, there is not in the World to be seen a greater spectacle of humane glory, and if (so I may speak) of sublimated manhood. For although, as hath been said, the Temple of *Sancta Sophia*, which he most usually frequenteth, is not above a stones cast from the out-most Gate of the *Seraglio*, yet hath he not so few as a thousand Horse (besides the Archers of his Guard and other Footmen) in that short procession: the way on each side inclosed as well within as without, with *Capagies* and *Janizaries*, in their Scarlet Gowns and particular Head-ornaments. The *Chiauses* ride foremost with their gilded Maces, then the Captains of the *Janizaries* with their *Aga*, next the Chieftains of the *Spachies*, after them the *Sanziaks*: those of the Souldiery wearing in the fronts of their Bonnets the feathers of the Bird of Paradise, brought out of *Arabia*, and by some esteemed the Phœnix. Then follow the *Bassa* and *Beglerbegs*, after them the Prætorian Footmen, called the *Solacchi*, whereof there be in number three hundred. These are attired in Calsouns and Smocks of Calico, wearing no more over them than half-sleeved Coats of Crimson Damask, their Skirts tuckt under their Girdles, having Plumes of Feathers in the top of their copped Bonnets, bearing Quivers at their backs, with Bows ready bent in their left hands, and Arrows in their right, gliding along with a marvellous celerity. After them seven or nine goodly Horses are led, having Caparisons and Trappings of inestimable value, followed by the idolized *Sultan* gallantly mounted. About whom they run forty *Peichi*, (so called, in that they are natural *Persians*) in high-crowned brimless Caps of beaten gold, with Coats of Cloth of gold girt to them with a Girdle called *Chochiab*: the Pages following in the Rear, and other Officers of the Houshold. But what most deserveth admiration amongst so great a concourse of people, is their general silence: insomuch as had you but only ears, you might suppose (except when they salute him with a short and soft murmur) that men were then folded in sleep, and the World in midnight. He that brings him good news (as unto others of inferiour condition) receiveth his reward, which they call *Mustolooke*. But this *Sultan*, to avoid abuses in that kind, doth forthwith commit them to Prison, until their reports be found true or false, and then rewards or punisheth accordingly. Although he spends most of his time with his Women, yet sometimes he recreates himself in Hawking,: who for that purpose hath (I dare not name) how many thousand Faulkners in pension, dispersed thoroughout his Dominions, and many of them ever attendant. Their long-winged Hawks they whistle not off as we do; but putting a bridle about their necks, they make them couch to their fists, and so galloping to the Brook, sling them off at the Fowl, being reared suddenly by the noise of a Drum that hangs at their Pummels, by use made cunning in that kind of preying. They carry them on the right hand. A hardy Hawk is highly esteemed; and they have a kind of them called *Spahans*, much less than a Faulcon, yet so strangely couragious, that nothing flyeth in the Air that they will not bind with. They also hawk at the field, for I have seen them carry Spaniels with them, yet those in beauty not like unto ours, but of a bastard generation. They feed their Hawks with hard Eggs when flesh is wanting, and seldom bellow of them the mewing. The old World, as is thought, was ignorant of this sport: being rarely, if mentioned, by any ancient Author; so that said by some to have been invented by *Frederick Barbarossa*, during the time that he beleaguered *Rome* with his Army. But this Distich of *Martial* doth confute that opinion.

The

Prædo fuit volucrum, famulus nunc aucupis idem
Decipit, & captas non fibi mœret aves.

The thief of fowl, the fowlers thief, now makes
Her mone, that she fowl for another takes.

Although he affects not Hunting, yet he entertains a number of Huntsmen. Their Dogs they let go out of Ships in pursuit of the Wolf, the Stag, the Bore, the Leopard, &c. Those that serve for that purpose are slickle haired, and not unlike the *Irish* Gray-hounds.

Now the yearly Revenue which he hath to defray his excessive disbursements, such a world of people depending upon him, amounts not to above fifteen millions of *Sultanies*, (besides the entertainment for his *Timariots*) which is no great matter, considering the amplitude of his Dominions, being possest of two Empires, above twenty Kingdoms, besides divers rich and populous Cities; together with the Red, most of the Mid-land, the *Ægean, Euxine,* and *Propontick* Seas. But it may be imputed to the barbarous wasts of the *Turkish* Conquests, who depopulate whole Countries, and never re-edifie what they ruine. So that a great part of his Empire is but thinly inhabited, (I except the Cities) and that for the most part by Christians, whose poverty is their only safety and protectress. But his casual incomes do give a main accession to his Treasury; as Taxes, Customs, Spoils, and Extortions. For as in the Sea the greater fishes do feed on the less, so do the Great ones here on their inferiours, and he on them all: being, as aforesaid, the Commander of their lives, and general Heir of their substances. He hath divers Mines of Gold and Silver within his Dominion: that of *Siderocapsa* in *Macedon* having been as beneficial unto him as the largest City of his Empire, called anciently *Chrysites*: and not unknown to *Philip* the Father of *Alexander*, who had the gold from thence wherewith he coyned his *Philips,* as also from those of *Cranider,* from whence he yearly extracted a thousand Talents. He hath only two sorts of Coyn, the *Sultanie* and *Asper.* The *Sultanie* is equal in value to the *Venice Zecceene,* and sixscore *Aspers* amount to a *Sultanie,* called rather *Aspro,* of the whiteness thereof, in that consisting of silver.

Constantinople is said to contain seven hundred thousand persons: half of them *Turks*, and the other half *Jews* and *Christians*, and those for the general, *Grecians.* But *Pera* hath three *Christians* for one *Mahometan* : for no *Jew* dwells in *Pera,* though they have their shops there. We omit to speak of the *Jews,* until we come into *Jewry,* and now will bend our discourse to the *Grecians*: a Nation no less scattered than they, but infinitely more populous. For not only three parts of the Inhabitants of all *Greece* and *Romania* are *Grecians*, but almost all that dwell in the Islands of the Mid-land Sea, *Propontis* and *Ægeum.* Infinite numbers there are of them both in the Less and the Greater *Asia,* and in *Africa* not a few. For (besides divers *Colonies* by them formerly planted) when *Antipater, Perdicas, Seleucus, Lysimachus, Antigonus, Ptolomy,* and the rest of the Successors of *Alexander* had shared his Empire among them, they endeavoured as much as they could to plant his new-got Kingdoms with their Country-men, whose posterity in that part remaineth to this day, (though vassaled to the often changes of foreign Governours:) supplied by the extention of the latter *Greek* Empire who yet retain wheresoever they live, their Name, their Religion, and particular Language. A Nation once so excellent, that their precepts and examples do still remain as approved Canons to direct the mind that endeavoureth virtue. Admirable in Arts, and glorious in Arms; famous for Government, affecters of freedom, every way noble: and to whom the rest of the World were reputed *Barbarians.* But now their knowledge is converted, as I may say, into affected ignorance, (for they have no Schools of Learning amongst them) their liberty into contented slavery, having lost their minds with their Empire. For so base they are, as thought it is, that they had rather remain as they be, than endure a temporary trouble by prevailing succours, and would with the *Israelites* repine at their deliverers. Long after the loss of their other virtues they retained their industry:

Ingenium velox, audacia perdita, sermo
Promptus, & Isæo torrentior: ede quid illum
Esse putes, quemvis hominum secum attulit ad nos :
Grammaticus, Rhetor, Geometres, Pictor, Aliptes,
Augur Schœnobates, Medicus, Magus; omnia novit
Græculus efuriens; in cœlum jusseris, ibet.

Juv. Sat 3.

Quick-witted, wondrous bold, well spoken, than
Ijæus fluenter; tell, who all men
Brought with himself: Sooth-sayer, a Physician,
Magician, Rhetorician, Geometrician,
Grammarian, Painter, Rope-walker. All knows
The needy Greek: bid go to heaven, he goes.

But

LIB. I.   *Of the Grecians.*   61

But now they delight in ease, in shades, in dancing and drinking; and no further for the most part endeavour their profit, than their bellies compell them. They are generally taxed by the stranger Christians of perfidiousness, insomuch as it is grown into a Proverb, *Chi fida in Greco, sara intrigo*, in them more anciently noted.

> *By others heads the Grecians were*   ——— Nondum Græcis jurare pararis
> *Less prone themselves than to forswear.*   Per caput alterius, *Juv. Sat.* 6.

An Oath in use at this day, as it is with the *Turk* when he most desireth to be believed. Nor will they themselves trust any; whereof comes that other Proverb,

> *To trade with Grecian trust.*   Mercari Græca fide.

which is not to part with their wares without money. There be divers rich men of them in *Pera*, but those I think were descended of the *Genoefi*, who were, as hath been said, the owners of that City. Many of them exercise merchandize in Vessels called Carmasals, and have of late gotten the use of the Compass, yet dare they not adventure into the Ocean. They are of divers Trades in Cities, and in the Country do till the earth (for the *European Turks* do little meddle with Husbandry) and dress their Vines, by them only planted. They have a ceremony of baptizing of their Wines, which is the reason that the *Jews* will not drink thereof, performed in the memory, and on that day wherein Christ converted Water into Wine: the Priest in the midst of his orisons pouring thereinto a small quantity of water. Their ancient habits may be conceived by that description of *Homer*,

> *He putteth on a coat, fine, fair, and new,*   ——— mollem autem induit tunicam,
> *When over that an ample Cloak he threw,*   Pulchram, novam, circa autem magnum jecit pallium.
> *And ties to his feet gay shoes.*   Pedibus autem sub teneris ligavit pulchra calcemaenta.
>   *Il. lib.*

Wearing their hair long, being frequently called by him

> *The long hair'd Greeks.*   Achivi comati.

But now both in cut and attire they do in most things agree with the people whom they live under, like the *Venetians* in the *Venetian* territories, and like *Turks* in *Turkie*, as also in their manners. The half sleeved Gown of Violet cloth, with Bonnets of the same, or divers coloured Slashes, is here most appropriate unto them: The *Greek Genoefes* in *Pera* wear their Gowns black, and of richer stuffs, with Velvet Caps, not unlike unto those that were in fashion amongst us. The antique *Grecians* used to lie along at their meals, from whom the *Romans* received that custom, as they from the effeminate *Asians*, upon Beds that circled three parts of the Table, which was round and low, (the waiters standing in the vacant part and behind them) leaning on their elbows raised with Pillows, in their feastings crowned with chaplets of Flowers, and garlands of Lawrel: but the women did sit when admitted, which was rarely amongst them, for them to lie along, esteemed too provokingly lascivious. The number of the convivals at private entertainments exceeded not nine, nor were under three, proportionating themselves unto the *Graces* and *Muses*. And as it should seem, they drank in that manner,

> ——— *To three or nine*   ——— tribus aut novem
> *Fill bouls befitting full of Wine.*   Miscentur cyathis pocula commodis.
> *Let ravisht Poets drink thrice three,*   Qui Musas amat impares,
> *Of whom the un-even Muses be*   Ternos tres cyathos attonitus petit
> *Belov'd. The Grace mis-doubting jarrs,*   Vates, tres prohibet supra
> *Link to her naked Sisters, barrs*   Rixarum metuens tangere Gratia.
> *Draughts that exceed their number.*   Nudis juncta sororibus.
>   *Horat. l. 3. Od. 19.*

To which add that Greek Proverb,

> *Drink thrice, or three thrice told,*   Ter bibe, vel toties ternos, sic mystica lex est.
> *A mystick law of old.*

Together with their song,

Aut quinque bibe, aut tres, aut non quatuor.

*Three drink, if more;
Five, but not four.*

Of their first cups they shed a little on the Table, as an offering to some of the gods, whom they desired to be propitious, as they did of the rest in the honour of their friends particular named; drinking small draughts at the beginning, until they arrived at the height of intemperancy; and sometimes as many together, as there were letters contained in the names of their Mistresses,

Nævia sex cyathis, septem Justina bibatur,
Quinque Lycas Lyde quatuor, Ida tribus.
Mart. Epig. l. 1. ep. 27.

*Six healths to Nævia drink, seven to Justina,
To Lycas five, to Lyde four, and three to Ida.*

insomuch that those were proverbially said to Greek it, that quaft in that fashion. At these, but more temperate drinkings, wherein they consumed most of the night, the chiefest sort consulted of matters of State; as appeareth by *Nestors* advice to *Agamemnon*,

Præbe convivium senibus, decet te, nec indicens est:
Plena tibi vino tentoria, quod naves Achivorum
Quotidianæ ex Thracia per latum pontum advehunt.
Omnis tibi est commoditas excipiendi multisq; imperas.
Multis autem congregatis, illi obedies qui optimum
Consilium consuluerit.
Il. I.

*Least thou the Ancient, if it befits thy place:
With Wine by Greek Ships daily brought from
Thy Tents abound. Provision at hand (Throce,
Of all sorts hast thou, and men at command
Many assembled so, amongst the rest,
His counsel follow that adviseth best:*

and the grave discoursed of Philosophy; but of such as was pleasant as well as profitable and delightful unto the hearers, as may appear by *Plato's convivium*, and *Plutarch's Symposiacks*: the first named dying at such a Banquet, in the four-score and one year of his age, and on the seventh of *November*, which was also his birth day. And although the *Greeks* do now for the most part imitate the *Turks*, (I mean here in *Turkie*) in sitting at their meat, yet retain they still that vice of immoderate drinking. They pledge one another in order, and he that calls for Wine out of his turn, is reputed uncivil. Their Glasses are little, but at every draught emptied, and when they have once drunk hard, they observe no rule, but provoke one another to excess. Never silent, and ever and anon kissing those that sit next them on the cheek and fore-head; and so likewise they do in their salutations after a long absence, and to those to whom they would give an assurance of their good will. Used of long, as appeareth by the Scriptures amongst these Eastern Nations. But to kiss their women is an unsufferable wrong, unless it be between the Resurrection and Ascension; using also this greeting, that, *Our Saviour is risen*. The women for the most part are brown of complexion, but exceedingly well favoured and excessively amorous. Their garments differ little from theirs amongst whom they live; yet have they in *Pera* this particular fashion. * They cover not their faces (the Virgins excepted) unless it be with painting, using all the supplement of a sophisticate beauty, and not without cause; for when they grow old, they grow most contemptible, being put to do the drudgery of the house, and many times to wait on their Children. They are costly in their attire, and will complain to the Patriarch, if their husbands maintain them not according to their substances. The *Greeks*, as the *Turks*, do use little houshould-stuff, and lye upon Mattresses.

* See the next page.

I need not to speak of the excellency of their Primitive language, excellent in regard of the Philosophy & liberal Sciences, together with the Divinity delivered therein, and excellent in it self, for the lofty sound, significant expressions, and genuine suavity, for which it grew in so much request amongst the *Roman* Dames, that they generally used it in their Court-ships, made thereby (as they thought) more graceful and aimable, whereof the Satyre thus exclaimeth,

Nam quid rancidius, quam quod se non putet ulla
Formosam, nisi quæ de Thusca Græcula facta est:
Hoc sermone pavent: hoc iram, gaudia, curas,
Hoc cuncta effundunt animi secreta, Quid ultra?

*None be with their own beauties well apaid,
If of a Thuscan not a Grecian made.
O gross! in Greek they fear, fret, joy deplore:
In Greek all their souls secrets vent, What more?*

LIB. I. *Of the Grecians.* 63

In Greek they couple. This to girls allow.
Greek yet use you, whom eighty six years bow,
Even unto death? In th'old 'tis impudence,
As oft as that light speech incites the sense;
My life, my soul.

Concumbunt Græce. Dones tamen illa puellis
Tunc etiam, quam sextus & octogesimus annuus
Pulsat adhuc Græce? Non est hic sermo pudicus
In vetula, quoties lasciviam intervenit illud,
Ζωὴ ϗ ψυχή. *Juv. Sat. 6.*

This figure belongeth to the former page line 45. but could not be there placed.

But now the *Grecians* themselves (except some few) are ignorant therein, it being called the *Latine Greek*, and is a language peculiar to the learned. Yet the vulgar *Greek* doth not differ so far from the same, as the *Italian* from the *Latine*; corrupted not so much by the mixture of other tongues, as through a supine retchlesnesse. In some places they speak it more purely than in others. For the boys of *Pera* will laugh, when they hear the more barbarous dialect of other Maritime *Grecians*. And there be yet of the *Laconians* that speak so good *Greek*, (though not grammatically) that they understand the learned, and understand not the vulgar. Their Liturgy is read in the ancient *Greek*, with not much more profit perhaps to the rude people, than the *Latine* Service of the Romish Church to the illiterate Papists.

They have four Patriarchs, one of *Constantinople*, another of *Alexandria*, the third of *Jerusalem*, and the fourth of *Antioch*. He of *Constantinople* hath under his jurisdiction all *Peloponnesus*, *Grecia*, *Thracia*, *Dacia*, *Mæsia*, *Macedonia*, *Epirus*, *Albania*, *Dalmatia*, *Illyria*, a great part of *Polonia*, *Russia*, the Islands of the *Adriatick* Sea, and of the *Archipelagus*, with *Candy*, *Rhodes*, *Coos*, almost all the lesser *Asia*, *Colchis*, not a few that inhabit about the Fenns of *Mæotis*, and Northern shore of *Euxinus*, as *Sicilia* and *Calabria* were, until they turned to the See of *Rome*. Under the Patriarch of *Alexandria* are those of *Egypt* and *Arabia*. The *Greeks* of *Palestine*, and of the Countries thereabout, do obey the Patriarch of *Jerusalem*. And he of *Antioch*, who hath his seat in *Damascus* (for *Antiochia* is now desolate) hath subject unto him the *Grecians* of the lesser *Armenia*, *Cilicia*, *Berius*, *Tripoly*, *Aleppo*, and other places of the greater *Asia*. In all these parts they have the free exercise of their Religion, with publick Temples, and numbers of strong Monasteries. If a Patriarch dye, another is elected by a Synod of Bishops. But the Patriarch of *Constantinople* hath the supremacy of the rest assigned him by the Council of *Chalcedon*, as Metropolitan of the Imperial City, whose Diocess exceedeth the other so much, in that most of those Northern Nations were won to Christianity by the industry of his predecessors, and reduced to their government. So if we do consider it, the *Grecian* Religion both in extent and number exceedeth the *Romain*. And as the Papists attribute an extraordinary holinesse to *Rome*, so do the *Greeks* unto *Athos*, a Mountain of *Macedonia*; so named of *Athon* the son of *Neptune*,

G 2 deckt

decked with still flourishing Trees, and abounding with Fountains; called also, The Holy Mountain by the Christians. A place from the beginning dedicated to Religion: lying directly West from *Lemnos*, and so high, that though it be seven hundred furlongs distant, yet it is said a little before the setting of the Sun to cast a shadow on that Island. Whereupon the proverb:

Athos celat latera Lemniæ bovis.   *Aspiring Athos hides*
The Lemnian Heifers sides.

This stretcheth out into the Sea, and joins unto the Continent by an *Isthmos* about a mile and half broad: which was cut thorow by *Xerxes* (as hath been intimated before) and made circum-navigable. But time hath left now no impressions of his barbarous labour. It is well nigh three days journey in length, considering the difficulty of the way, and a half day over. The top thereof resembleth the form of a man, stretched on his back from West unto East; and formed (according to *Strabo*) to the similitude of *Alexander*. This Mountain is only inhabited by *Grecian* Monks, whom they call *Coloieros*, un-intermixed with the Laity; of whom there are there residing not so few as six thousand, that live in Monasteries strongly munited against the incursions of Robbers and Pirats. Of these there be in number twenty four. The *Coloieros* wear Gowns of black, of a homely stuff, with Hoods of the same; and the hair at full length. They never marry, abstain from flesh, and often (especially during their Lents) from Fish that hath blood in it. They live hardly, feeding on Bisket, Onions, Olives, Herbs, and such Fish as they take in the adjoining Seas. For they all of them labour for their sustenance, leaving their Monasteries betimes in the morning; and imploying the day, some in Tillage, some in the Vineyards, some in making of Boats, some in fishing; others at home, Spin, Weave, Sew, and do all the offices that belong unto women; so that none but are busied about one thing or another, to the behoof of their particular Covents. And men they be that are only meet for such drudgeries. For amongst so many, not past three or four can write or read throughout a whole Monastery: insomuch that at their Liturgies, that is read to them first, which they are to sing after. In these Monasteries many excellent manuscripts have been preserved; but those that now are, be only of Divinity, all other learning (as amongst the *Turks*) is at this day detested by the Religious. The *Coloieros* of this place have a repute above all others; and for their strictness of life; and observancy of ceremonies, are in their several Monasteries relieved from several Nations. The Patriarch of *Constantinople* is said to pay yearly to the *Grand Signior*, for the Priests and *Coloieros* that are under his jurisdiction, within the *Turkish* dominions, twelve thousand Sultanies.

The Patriarchs of *Constantinople* were heretofore men of singular gravity and learning, but now nothing less; rather chosen for temporal respects, than either for their knowledge or devotion: admitted not seldom to the place at the age of forty, though prohibited if under threescore, by an ancient Canon. Although elected by their own Bishops, yet are they often appointed, and ever to be allowed by the *Grand Signior*; frequently displanted, and banished unto *Rhodes* by the bribery of their successors. Some few of their Priests are learned. For them it is lawful to marry: but bigamy is forbidden them, and trigamy detested in the Laity. There are no other Orders amongst them, besides the aforesaid *Coloieros*, and certain Nunns, whom they call *Coloitros*. Yet of the last, but a few, who are for the most part poor old Widows, that exercise themselves in sweeping of the Churches, attending on the sick, and actions of like nature: Their Churches are many of them well set forth and painted with the represents of Saints; but they have no carved nor imbossed Images. Lamps they have continually burning. Their ordinary Liturgy is Saint *Chrysostom*'s, but on festival days they do read Saint *Basil*'s, and then are attired in their Pontificals. Their behaviour therein expresseth, to my understanding, no great either decency or devotion. They administer the Eucharist in both kinds: if the bread be not leavened, they think it not available, and they drink of the Cup very liberally. One Article they hold against the Catholick Creed; which is, that the Holy Ghost proceedeth only from the Father. Four Lents they have in the year, and then a damnable sin it is to eat flesh, or fish that hath blood in it (except in the Lent before Easter, when all sorts of fish may be eaten by the Laity;) but shell-fish they eat, and the Cuttle, whose blood, if I may so term it, is like Ink; a delicate food, and in great request. They fall on Wednesdays,

Of the Grecians.

nesdays, Fridays, and on holy eves, but on Saturdays they feast, in regard that it was the old Sabbath. They compute the year as we do. They yield no supremacy to the Roman Papacy, but hold that Church for schismatical. And although many times out of the necessity of their affairs, and to purchase relief, they have treated of a reconciliation: and sometimes it hath been by their Agents concluded: yet what they have done, hath been generally rejected upon their return, both by the *Greeks*, and those other Nations that professe their Religion. Of their marriages I have elsewhere spoken, and now conclude we will with their Funerals; wherein they retain not a few of their ancient and heathen ceremonies. Of old the nearest in love or kindred laid their mouths unto theirs, to receive their last breath, and closed the eyes of the dying.

His body (hers) she imbrac'd: and dismaid,	―― sociosque amplectiplectitur artus,
Between his lips, her cleaving soul convaid	Hærentemque animam non tristis in ora mariti
And with her dear hand clos'd his sightless eyes.	Transtulit, & chara pressit sua lumina dextra.
	Stat. Silv. l. 5.

Being dead, they washed their bodies with sweet Oyls, crowned them with garlands of Flowers, and clothed them (as they now do) in their richest apparel; for fear, saith the scoffer *Lucian*, that they should take cold by the way, or be seen naked by *Cerberus*; decking their houses with branches of Cypress; a Tree destinated to the dead; in that once being cut, it never reflourisheth. So laying them upon their backs on beds, they conveyed them unto the funeral pile (as now unto the Grave) on Biers: but their lamentations are the same that they were, and beyond all civility. The women betimes in the morning do meet at appointed places, and then cry out mainly; beating of their brests, tearing their hair, their faces and garments: And that the clamour may be the greater, they hire certain *Jewish* women

Who Grecian woes wail with fain'd piety,	―― fictâ pietate dolores
And at (not their own) funerals do cry.	Mygdoniosque colunt, & non sua funera plorant.
	Statius.

that have lowdest voices, joining therewith the praises of the dead, from the hour of his Nativity, unto the hour of his dissolution; and keeping time with the melancholick musick. The manner of their lamentings of old may appear by this ironical personating of the Father following the exequies of his Son, introduced by *Lucian*: *O my sweet Son! thou art lost, thou art dead; dead before thy day, and hast left me behind, of men the most miserable. Not experienced in the pleasures of a Wife, the comfort of Children, Warfare, Husbandry; not attained to maturity. Henceforth, O my Son, thou shalt not eat, nor love, nor be drunk amongst thy equals.* And although these Ethnick lamentations reproved in the Scripture were prohibited by the *Athenian* Law-giver, the Civil Law, and lastly by the *Venetians* within their *Greek* jurisdiction; yet still the *Grecians* do use them. Nor want they store of spectators; partly drawn hither to delight their eyes, and partly by jealousie. For then the choice and prime women of the City (if the deceased were of note) do assist their obsequies, with bosoms displaid, and their hair disheveled; glad that they have the occasion to manifest their beauties, which at other times is secluded from admirers. The ancient *Greeks* wont to cut their locks, and cover the coarse therewith before they committed it to the fire: as in the Funeral of *Patroclus*.

His corps with curls they covered,	Capillis autem totum mortuum tegebant quos injiciebant
Shorn from each mourning Princes head.	Tondentes.―― *Hom. Il. 23.*

When *Achilles*,

A part the pile cuts his long yellow hair,	Stans seorsum a pyra flavam abscidit comam,
To Spergius vowed upon his home repair.	Quam Sperchio fluvio nutriebat florescentem.
Quoth he for that I never shall return	Dixit, quoniam non rediho amplius dilectam in patriam
To my lov'd soil, I give these to be born	Patroclo heroi præbeo asportandum.
By dear Patroclus to the dead. This said,	Sic fatus comam in manibus dilecti socii
In his friends hand he his fair tresses laid.	Posuit. ――
	Idem.

And *Lycurgus* in that of his sons,

His locks cropt he, and therewith did bespread	Cæsariem ferro minuit, sectisque jaciente
There as he lay, the pale face of the dead.	Obnubuit tenuis ora comis.
	Statius Theb. l. 6.

They burnt with the body, if of principal regard, rich odours, Apparel, herds of Cattel, flocks of Sheep, Horses, Hounds, and sometimes the Concubines and Slaves whom they most respected, to supply their wants, to serve their delights, and attend upon them in the lower shades. And *Achilles*;

Duodecim etiam Trojanorū magnanimorū filios fortes
Ferro mactavit; mala autem mente meditabatur opera;
Is que ignis robur projecit ferreum, ut depascantur.
Hom. Il. l. 23.

Twelve Trojan youths of hopeful fortitude;
All high-born, flue; with savage thought endu'd:
And gave for food to the Iron force of Fire.

But to end with *Papinius* his description of that funeral fire, wherein the body of *Archemorus* was consumed, and appertaining solemnities.

――――― Non unquam opulentior illo
Ante cinis; crepitant gemmæ atque immane liquescit
Argentum & pictis exudat vestibus aurum.
Nec non Assyriis pinguescunt robora succis,
Pallentique croco stridunt ardentia mella,
Spumantesque mero pateræ verguntur, & atri
Sanguinis & rapti gratissima cymbia lactis.
Tunc septem numero turmas (centenus ubique
Surgit eques) versis ducunt insignibus ipsi
Grajugena Reges, lustranteque ex more sinistro.
Orbe togum, & flantes inclinant pulvere flammas;
Ter curvos egere sinus, illisaque telis
Tela sonant, quater horrendum pepulere fragore
Arma, quater mollem famularū brachia planctum;
Semianimis alter pecudes, spirantia & ignis
Accipit armenta, &c.

Stat. Theb. l. 6.

Never were ashes with more wealth repleat;
Gems crackle, Silver melts, Gold drops with heat,
Embroidered Robes consume. Okes fatned by
The juice of sweet Assyrian Gums, flame high.
Fir'd Honey and pale Saffron hiss, full bowls
Of Wine pour'd on; and goblets (gladding souls)
Of black blood, and snatcht milk. The Greek Kings then
With guidous trail'd on earth, led forth their men
In seven Bands; an hundred in each Band,
Who girt the pile, and move to the left hand;
Choking the flame with dust. Thrice it they round,
Their weapons clash: four times a horrid sound
Struck armours rais'd; as oft the Servants beat
Their bare breasts with out-cries. Herds of Neat,
And Beasts half slain, another wastful fire
Devours, &c.

The reason why the *Grecians* did burn their dead, was because that part which was divine in them, should as it were in a fiery Chariot, again re-ascend to the celestial habitations; as unto earth the earthly returned. They used to quench the fire with red Wine, and gathering the bones together to include them in Urns, as the Urns in Sepulchres, (which had no title, unless they were slain in fighting for their Country) exhibiting Games, and prizes for the Victors in honour of the deceased. Notwithstanding all were not burnt, but some buried in their apparel, as now being Christians they are; who use extreme unction, as inducted by Saint *James*, yet not only deny the Roman opinion of purgatory; but furthermore, many amongst them erroneously maintain, that neither the souls of the blessed nor damned do suffer either joy or torment, or shall till the general Judgment. But enough of the *Grecians*.

The *German* Emperour, the Kings of *England*, and of *France*, have here their Leiger Ambassadours; as the *Venetians* their Baily, and divers tributary Princes their Agents. Some meerly employed about State-affairs; others together therewith, about the traffick of their Nations. But the *English* only negotiates for the Merchants, having two in the hundred upon every Ship, besides a large pension, with the name of a great proportion of provision from the *Grand Signior*. The *English* Consulship of *Chios* is in his disposing, and accountable to him; and out of that of *Alexandria* he hath no small share, though served by a *French* man. There hath been some contention between him and the *French*, about the protection of the *Dutch* Merchants; but now they do divide the profits. The *English* Consul of *Aleppo* is absolute of himself, yet hath from hence his redresses of injuries, whose chief employment is to protect the persons and goods of our Nation, to labour a revenge of wrongs, and a restitution of losses. And to give This no more than his due, for his place no man can be more sufficient; expert in their language, and by a long experience in their natures and practices, being moreover of such a spirit, as not to be daunted. And surely his chiefest fault hath been his mis-fortune; in the too violent, chargeable, and successless soliciting of the restitution of the Prince of *Moldavia*, (whom adversity hath rather made crafty than honest;) whose house doth harbour both him and his dependants, being open also to all of our Nation. A Sanctuary for poor Christian slaves that secretly fly hither; whom he causeth to be conveyed into their Countries, and redeemeth not a few with his money. The
Western

LIB. I.   *Of the Franks.*

Western Christians are called *Franks*, that are admitted to trade here; either of the name which signifieth free, or for that the *French* men were the first that had amity and traffick with the Infidels. They live freely, and plentifully, and many of them will not lie alone where women are so easily come by. For besides the aforesaid markets, it is a use, not prohibited but only by our Religion, to purchase for their Concubines the beautiful daughters of the *Grecians*, wherewith the adjoining Islands are plentifully stored, sold by their parents at a rate; whereof they have half in hand, and the rest when they put them away, recording the contract in the *Cadies* book. These are to their Lovers exceeding obsequious; well knowing that at the second hand they shall be prized but as a worn garment. But death it is for a Christian to meddle with a *Mahometan* woman. And many times the treacherous *Turks* will practise to bring them into suspition, that they may with their purses redeem the calumny. Practised of late between the *Subassee* of *Galata* an *Italian* Frier; whom the Lord Ambassadour had received into his house upon the Consuls of *Chios* commendation, where I before had seen him. A man ignorant in learning, yet learned in the art of villany and dissimulation. Expulsed, as they say, at *Constantinople* from amongst their fraternity; coming down into *Chios*, he had insinuated himself into the knowledge of the Consul; professing how God in his mercy had opened his eyes, to behold the vanity and deceit of their Religion; and that now he would endeavour both with tongue and pen, as much as in him lay, to reduce the seduced from their errors. Who easily perswaded to believe, (a fault incident to the best natures) sent him up unto *Constantinople*, unto the Ambassadors, by (whom casting off the weeds of his Order) he was clothed anew, set at his Table, and supplied with mony by a general contribution; where he preached every *Sunday*, at the least wittily: and so contested with the *Franciscans* that came to reconcile him, that the Ambassador, much contented therewith, sent intelligence of the same into *England*, with purpose to have sent him hither shortly after. But he whose only religion (as himself after confessed) was eating, drinking, and whoring; who thought he had exchanged for the greater liberty, finding the contrary, and that he was to go into a Country where his imposture would not only be discovered, but severely chastised, cast about for himself, and conspired with the *Subassee*, to bring certain Gentlemen that lay in the Ambassadors house, into a Garden, where divers women should have been placed of purpose; and so to have been taken amongst them. But failing in that project, he failed not in another. For in the house there was a *Spaniard*, of whom he informed the *Subassee* that he was a Spy, and secretly practised the escape of the *Vice-roys* natural son of *Silicia*, agreeing for a certain reward to betray him. So having inticed him to walk amongst the Graves, upon a sign given, the *Turks* rusht in, and apprehended him, clogging him with chains, and intended to torture out of him a confession; whereof the Ambassador hearing, and expostulating the matter, the *Subassee* told him that he was a Spy, and discovered the Intelligencer: wherein being satisfied, and perhaps not unbribed, he granted his release. But a heavy reckoning befel the Frier, that suspected no such matter; being thrown into prison, and after brought to a publick hearing before our whole nations; who shewed how much a man could say for himself in so bad a cause. In the end he was sent unto the *Venetians* Baylics, and that in the night, (lest he should have cryed out that he would have turned Mussel-man, and have been taken from them) who made sure to have him, and sent him (as they say) to row in the Gallies at *Candy*. The principal commodities that our Merchants fetch from hence, are *Turkie* Carpets, Chamolets, and Grogerams. They take in here also some quantity of raw Silk, and Carpets of *Persia*, brought over-land from thence by the *Armenian* Merchants. But the *Sultanies*, and especially the Royals of eight, wherewith this City is well stored, and which in no place lose of their value, is that they most seek for by the sale of their Ware which they bring hither. For although they lose by their broad Cloths and Kersies, yet amends is made by the plentiful returns of the Silks that are sent from *Aleppo* to *Tripoly*, and other other commodities of the *Levant* purchased with that money. The main of our commodities brought hither, is Cloth and Kersies, but Tin is the most profitable: here exceedingly used, and exceedingly wasted; for they tin the in-sides of their Vessels, and monthly renew it. The Mosses teeth, all kind of Furrs, and wrought Iron, do here sell to much profit, with other Wares, which I forbear to mention, since it is no part of my skill or profession.

FINIS LIBRI PRIMI.

THE SECOND BOOK.

Anuary being now well spent, we departed from *Constantinople* in the Trinity of *London*, a Ship of better defence than Sail. By the way we made some stay before *Callipoly*, sending a shore for the Consul, (an old Frier, and a boon companion) who sick of his last nights surfeits, sent his Drogerman with a *Janizary* along with us, to clear our Ship below at the Castles. For these two Forts comand this passage of the *Hellespont*; permitting no Christians Ships to pass out, untill there they have remained for three days, (whereas the *Turkish* Ships are discharged in one) that if so be any thing hath been done above un-justifiable, intelligence may be given: and there are also searched for concealed Slaves, and goods contrabanded; which found, import no less than loss both of Ship and liberty.

A. *Abydos.*   B. *Sestos.*   C. *Tenedos*
D. *Cape Janizary appearing afar off like two Islands.*

Like these are those on the Straights of *Bosphorus*, by which the *Turk*, as it were chaineth up the *Propontick* Sea, so that none pass in or out, without his allowance, and discharge of duties. A little short of these we came to an anchor.

Right against where we lay, and on *Europes* side, stands *Mayto*, called formerly *Macidos*, and *Maditos*, a large Town, almost altogether inhabited by *Grecians*. On the top of a round hill there are the remains of an edifice, whose ruine would perswade

swade that it flourished in the old worlds child-hood. The Inhabitants call it the Virgin Tower, and that is all they can say thereof. A Wedding here in the forenoon, entertained our time in the after-noon. They dance in rings about the Musician, a man, and then a woman, taking hands a-cross, and using variety of not uncomly action; the Country wenches cloathed in Damask and Sattin, their hair and bosoms set forth with Pearl and Stones; rich, if not counterfeit. Of these the day following we met with divers carrying Pitchers on their heads, and stuck with Rags, below the condition of poverty. The marriage day they consume in dancing, and the night in feasting; the Bride not breaking company until the break of day, and (as they say) not known by her husband until the third night following. The night out-watched, made us make a night of the morning, until rowz'd from our groundbeds by the report of the Canon. When from the shore, between the Castles, you might behold a Gally passing, and that so leisurely, as if empty, and purposely suffered to drive with the current, rather to exercise the Artillery, than manned by men, endeavouring satety, and so beset with destruction. At length the Sea entred at her many breaches; and by little and little devoured the spectacle. The men, some slain, some drown'd, others by Boats from each side cruelly saved, out-lived to envy their dead companions. These were Christian-slaves, that hewed stones in the Quarries at Marmora, who, to compass their liberty, had slain their Guardians, and stoln away with the Gally. Hither they came too late, nor durst they linger unto the evening, to proceed or return was now grown equally desperate. Approaching near, a warning-piece was given them to come to an anchor; when they, leaving their Oars, lay down, all saving he that steered, and committed themselves to the wind, that then blew fresh and favourably; but like an hollow friend, shrunk from their sails in their greatest necessity. More happy success not long before had a Gally for the most part manned by *English*, who passed by, and that by day, in despite of them. Cheaper wines than here are hardly elsewhere to be had, or in greater plenty; insomuch as most Christian ships returning from *Constantinople*, do at this place take in their provision. Dispatched at length, not without some gifts and much sufferance, we hoised sails, and the night ensuing we tossed to and fro, on the West of *Mitylen*. The next day we laboured to get in between *Chios* and the Continent, but failed; when sailing on the other side of the Island, the wind came about, whereof we took the benefit for *Alexandria*.

Hard by, and on the left hand, left we *Samos*, now *Samo*, in which it was said that *Juno* was born under a white Willow, close by the River *Imbrasius*: and for that she *Of the Ri-* was there brought up, whilst yet a Virgin, it was called *Parthenia*. Allegorically she *ver Par-* is taken for the element of the Air; and famed for that cause to have been born in *Sa-* *thenium.* *mos*; for that the Air is here so pure, and so excellent. *Samos* doth also challenge one of the *Sibyls*, whose name was *Pytho*, and *Heriphile*; and flourished in the days of *Numa Pompilius*, of Christ thus prophecying.

Thy God, thou foolish Juda knew'st not; known	Tu enim stulta Judæa Deum tuum non cognovisti
Not unto earthly minds: but crowned hast	Lydentem mortalium mentibus.
His brows with Thorns, and given him Gall to taste.	Sed spinis coronasti, horridumque fel miscuisti.

But in nothing more famous than in the birth of *Pythagoras*.

From Heaven though far remov'd, he with his mind	——iisque licet cœli regione remotus
Drew near the Gods: what natures power denies	Mente Deos adiit: & quæ natura negabat
To humane sights, he saw with his souls eyes.	Visibus humanis, oculis ea pectoris hausit.
	Ovid. Met. l. 15.

The first that brought Philosophy into *Greece*, and from thence into *Italy*. This Island is not above a quarter of a mile distant from the Continent of *Asia*, fruitful in all things but Vines, which is the rather to be noted, in that the Countries round about produce such store, and so excellent. At the South end stood the City of *Samia*, with a goodly harbour adjoining; now (as the rest) by reason of the Pirats that infest their Seas, almost altogether desolate. Of the earth thereof were those Vessels made of such great esteem; sovereign also for divers uses both in Physick and Chirurgery. The North-west of the Isle is high land, environed with unaccessible cliffs, full of tall wood within, and most commodious for building of Ships.

On the right hand, and near, lyeth *Niceria*, heretofore *Icaria*, taking that name, as doth the adjacent Sea, as the Poets sain, from the fall of *Icarus*.

When.

Oraque cærulea patrium clamantia nomen
Excipiuntur aqua, quæ nomen traxit ab illo.
Ovid. Met. l. 8.

When crying, Help, O Father! his exclame
The blue Seas stops, which took from him their name.

And in this Island he

Devovitque suas artes, corpusque sepulchro
Condidit, & tellus a nomine dicta sepulti est
Ibid.

Cursing his arts, interr'd the corps, that gave
The land a name, which had given it a grave.

called *Pergamum* before. Who were said to flie in regard of their sails, by *Dædalus* then first invented to out-strip the pursuit of *Minos*; when *Icarus* in another vessel, by bearing too great a sail, suffered ship-wrack hereabout. It is now rarely inhabited, yet abounding with good pasturage: Corn it also produceth plentifully. It hath no Haven, but divers Roads, sufficiently commodious. Between these two Islands lye those sharp Rocks, in times past called *Melanthii*, and now the *Fornoli*; well known, and in the night much feared by Mariners.

South of these we sailed by *Palmosa* formerly *Patmos*; a little Island consisting only of three or four rocky Mountains. On one of them stands a Town, and on the very top thereof a Monastery of *Greek Coloieros*, having large exhibitions from sundry places of Christendom. Men ignorant in letters, studious for their bellies, and ignominiously lazy, unless some few that give themselves to Navigation, and become indifferent good Pilots. About this Isle there are variety of excellent Harbours, and not so few as forty sail of Ships belonging to the Town, by the trading whereof they bring in that sustenance which the soil affordeth not, being so barren that nothing grows, as I have heard, especially near unto the Town, except on such earth as is brought thither from other places. And therefore inflicted as a punishment unto St. *John*, hither banished by the Emperor *Trajan*, or as some write, by *Domitian*; for so the *Romans* accustomed to confine offenders.

Aude aliquid brevibus Gyaris aut carcere dignum,
Si vis esse aliquid; probitas laudatur & alget.
Juv. Sat. 1.

If thou intend'st to thrive, do what deserves
Short Gyaros, or Gyves; prais'd Vertue sterves.

On the North-side of this hill, we saw the house wherein (they say) he writ his Revelation; and a little above, the Cave in which it was revealed: both held in great devotion by those Christians. After the death of the Emperor, he removed unto *Ephesus*, and being a hundred and twenty years old, causing a Grave to be made, is said to have entred it alive, in the presence of divers, to whom seeming dead, they covered him with earth, which, if we may believe St. *Augustine*, * bubleth like water, to testifie his breathing, and that he is not dead, but sleepeth. In that Monastery is reserved a dead mans hand, which they affirm to be his, and that the nails thereof being cut, do grow again.

Aug. in Job. Tract. 124.

Amongst divers other Islands we passed by *Coos*, now called *Longo*, a delicate Country to behold, lying for the most part level, only towards the East not un-profitably mountainous; from whence fall many Springs, which water the Plains below, and make them extraordinary fruitful, where grow those Wines so celebrated: Cypress-trees, and Turpentine, with divers others, as well delightful as profitable. In this was *Hippocrates* born, who revived Physick then almost lost, and the ancient practice of *Æsculapius*, unto whom this Island was consecrated. In the Suburbs he had his Temple, famous, and rich with offerings. Those that had been sick, upon recovery there registred their cures, and the experiments whereby they were effected: of these *Hippocrates* made an abridgement, and committed them to posterity. In this Temple stood that rare picture of *Venus*, naked, as if newly rising from the Sea, made by *Apelles*, who was also this Country-man; after removed unto *Rome* by *Octavius Cæsar*, and dedicated unto *Julius*, she being reputed the mother of his family. It is said, that at the drawing thereof, he assembled together the most beautiful women in the Island, comprehending in that his own work their divided perfections. For this picture the *Coans* had a hundred Talents remitted of their tribute. The Town and Citadel are now only inhabited by *Turks*; the Villages by *Grecians*; whereof in all are but two.

Next unto this stands *Rhodes*, of all the rest the most famous and beautiful; once covered with the Sea, or at least an unhabitable Marish, as they feign, beloved of the Sun, and erected above the Waves by his powerful influence. For no day
passeth

LIB. II.   Rhodes.

passeth wherein the Sun here shines not clearly: perhaps the occasion of that Fable,

Others will praise bright Rhodes.   Laudabunt alii claram Rhodon. *Hor. l. od. 7.*

obtaining thereby that title as a peculiar Epithite. Some write that it took this name of *Rhoda* a Nymph of the Sea; and there compressed by *Apollo*: others that there he lay with *Venus*, and of her begat *Rhoda*.

Rhodes was begot by Solon Cyprides   Insula dicta Rhodos de Sole & Cypride nata est
*Of whose three sons descended are * three Cities.*   De tribus & natis horum tres sunt simul urbes.
Then when the God approacht the Goddess, showers   Cuique Deam Deus accessit guttis pluit auri.
Of Gold pour'd down, with Roses, and white Flowers. Purpureaque rosæ lutre, ac lillia flores.
                                                  * *Lindus, Camirus, Jalysus.*

For *Rhodes* in the *Greek* tongue signifieth a Rose; and by likelihood so called of the abundance of Roses, which this soil produceth. This Island therefore was to the Sun held sacred, to whom they erected that huge *Colossus* of Brass, worthily reputed amongst the Worlds seven wonders; made by *Charetes* of *Lindus*, the Servant of *Lysippus*; and whereof, as some affirm, they were called *Colossians*. In height it was three-score and ten cubits, every finger as great as an ordinary Statue, and the thumb too great to be fathomed. Twelve years it was a making, and about three-score and six years after thrown down by an Earth-quake, which terribly shook the whole Island, prophesied of by *Sibyl*. The pieces thereof made wonderful ruptures in the earth; and another wonder it was to see the mass of stones contained therein, whereby the work-men had confirmed it against the violence of weather. With the Brass thereof nine hundred Camels were laden. No place in times past was held superiour unto this for conveniency of harbour, magnificent buildings, and other excellencies. Famous it was for government, and men so expert in Navigation, that they became Lords, and for many years held the sovereignty of the Seas. The air is here most temperate, producing fruits abundantly; rich pastures sprinkled with Flowers, and Trees still flourishing. The felicity of the place affording an argument to that Fable of the golden showers that fell thereon. Their Wines thus *Virgil* celebrateth,

Receiv'd by gods, and last crown'd cups, will I   Non ego te Diis & mensis accepta secundis,
Thee Rhodia, nor thy long big Grapes, go buy   Transferim Rhodia, & tumidis bumasta racemis.
                                                  Georg. l. 2.

where also it is said, that the Vine was first found out and planted. After that the Knights of Saint *John de Acre* had lost the City of *Acre*, the last that they held in the Holy Land; they had this place consigned them by *Emanuel* the *Greek* Emperour, in the year 1308. which they took from the *Turk*, and maintained to his terror. Having then one City only, but that well fortified, seated towards the morning Sun, on the ascending hill, a part on the level shore, embracing, as it were, a most safe and admirable Haven; treble walled, adorned with Towers, and fortified with five strong Fortresses; often invaded, and to little purpose: at length it was taken by *Solyman* the Magnificent (*Villerius* being the Great Master) with six months siege, a world of people, and the loss of most of them, in the year 1522. after it had been by them defended against the Infidels two hundred and fourteen years; and then honourably surrendred, although to the general dishonour of the Christian Princes in their tardy succours.

Bright Rhodes, bright in times past, now black with clouds: Clara Rhodos, sed clara olim, nunc horride
Thy shining fore-head a dire tempest shrouds.   nimbis:
O grief! O death! O what than grief is worse,   Obnubunt nitidum dira procella caput.
And death! than that! if there be such a curse,   Ah dolor, ah mors, ah aliquid morte atq; do-
Sleep? and the fell wolf seizeth the spoil?   Durius aut etiam tertius esse potest? (lore!
O shame to have ta'n a voluntary fall!   Stertitis! & ferus armenti lupus optima capit?
                                                               O jam sit jam aliquis velle perire pudor.

Unto this lamentable subversion (though meant perhaps by a former) may that prophecy of *Sibyl* be unwrestedly applyed.

Daughter of Phœbus. Rhodes, long shalt thou reign: Tuque diu nulli Rhode subdita, filia Solis:
Abound in wealth, and rule of Seas obtain.   Durabis, multaque olim pollebis opum vi,
                                                       Imperioque matris primas eris —

> Præda tamen studio tandem rapieris amantum
> Cerviceæque jugo, dives formosaque subdes.
> *Orat. Sib. 3.*
>
> *Yet forc'd by those that covet thee, at last
> Yok'd shalt thou be, rich, fair, for glory past.*

Such as would, according to composition were suffered to depart, who from hence removed unto *Malta*; so that now it is inhabited by *Turks* & *Jews*, those Christians that be, being *Greeks*, and not suffered after Sun-set to abide in the City, the Suburbs whereof are utterly razed. I have heard that all the Monuments, Statues, and Inscriptions belonging to the Knights of the Order, are by the *Turks* preserved entire, excepting such as the Wars had demolished. Here the *Grand Signior* maintaineth five Gallies, about this Island we expected to have met with Pirats, but we were happily deceived.

Now having lost the sight of *Rhodes*, we saw no land until the third day after; in the evening doubtfully discovering the Coast of *Egypt*; fearing the Lee-shore, all night we bore out to Sea, the Lightning ministring uncomfortable light, intermixed with Thunder and Tempest. The next day we entred the Haven of *Alexandria* newly defamed with a number of wracks, which scattered here and there, did miserably testifie the unsafe protection of that Harbour. For not past two nights before, the Northern winds beating full upon the mouth of the Haven, with violent Seas drove the foremost Ships from their Anchors, who falling foul on the rest, sunk all for company, even two and twenty in number, amongst the rest, that great and warlike Ship called the Red Lion, taken but the year before from the Knights of *Malta*.

But before we proceed any farther in particulars, meet it is that something be said of *Egypt* in general. *Egyptus* the son of *Belus*, for his greater glory so named this * kingdom, called *Misraim* by the *Hebrews*, of *Misraim* the son of *Chus*, *Mesre* by the *Arabians*, and *Chibith* by the Inhabitants, of *Chibith* the first Lord of this Land, and who first began to build houses. On the East it is confined with the *Arabian* Desarts, those of *Bara*, *Libia*, and *Numidia* lying on the West; on the South divided from *Æthiopia* by the great Cataract, and bounded Northward by the *Egyptian* Sea, being a part of the *Mediterranean*. A Coast dangerous and unhospitable, full of Flats, and having no Haven save that of *Alexandria*, which is by a Desart divided from the rest of the habitable Country, so that it is neither by Sea nor Land to be invaded, but with much difficulty. It is said to extend from North to South, five hundred and threescore miles, (for a long tract contracted between barren Mountains, in many places scarce four, in few above eight miles broad, until not far above *Cairo*, it beginneth by degrees to inlarge, and so continueth to do, even to the Sea: being between *Rosetta* and *Damiata*, which stand upon the West and East confines of that which is overflowed by the natural course of the River an hundred and forty miles; and from *Rosetta* to *Alexandria* thirty, all low ground, and lying in a Champion level.

Or of Nilus, called formerly Egypt.

> Terra suis contenta bonis, non indiga mercis,
> Aut Jovis; in solo tanta est fiducia Nilo.
> *Lucan. l. 8.*
>
> *That needs nor merchandize, nor Jove, a soil
> Pleas'd with it self, so confident in Nile.*

By means whereof, saith *Isocrates*, they have both drought and moisture in their own disposition, which is elsewhere bestowed by *Jupiter*. The wonderful fertility of the soil is rather to be admired than expressed: in times past reputed the Granary of the World, insomuch that it was not thought possible for the *Roman* Empire to subsist, if not assisted by the affluence of *Egypt*. The occasion of that saying of *Selimus*, when he had conquered the Country, that, Now he had taken a Farm that would feed his *Jemoglans*. Amongst other commodities which this earth doth yield, and are fetcht from hence by Foreigners, Sugar, Flax, Rice, all manner of Grain, Linen-Cloth, Hides, Salt, Butargo, and Cassia, being now the principal.

Whatsoever here is estimable, proceedeth from the munificency of this River; for progress and property of all other the most excellent: unto former ages, though often attempted, (and that of great * Potentates) of an un-discovered original.

Sesostris, Cambyses, Alexander, Philadelphus, Nero, &c.

> Cum videant primi, quærunt tamen hi quoq; Seres,
> Æthiopumq; se satis alieno gurgite campus:
> Et te terrarum nescit cui debeat orbis.
> Arcanum natura caput non prodidit ulli:
> Nec licuit populis parvum te, Nile, videre,
> Amovitque sinus, & gentes maluit ortus
> Mirari quam nosse tuos ——
>
> *Lucan. l. 10.*
>
> *When first they Seres see, yet seek, who bears
> Through Ethiopian fields streams none of theirs.
> Nor knows the wondring world, in who world bred:
> So Nature, Nile, conceals thy sacred head;
> None seeing thee not great. The Fountains she
> Hath set apart, and would that they should be
> Rather admir'd than known:*

Yet

LIB. II.   Nilus.

Yet *Nero* with his best success sent two Centurions, who assisted by the King of *Ethiopia*, and by him commended to the neighbouring Princes, after a long and troublesome journey, came at length unto certain great Marishes, of whose extents the Inhabitants themselves were ignorant, nor possible to be discovered by them; for were the Weeds infolded with the water, not to be waded, nor by Boat to be past thorow. There saw they two Rocks, from whence a Current gusht with excessive violence. But whether this was the Fountain, or only an augmentation; whether then beginning, or before received into the earth, and there re-ascending, was uncertain. But our more presuming Geographers do raise his concealed head from the Lake of *Zembre*, (in which, they say, are Syrens and Tritons) eleven degrees beyond the *Æquator*, seated amongst high and unaccessible Mountains, and so great, as deserving rather the title of a Sea. From whence it passeth, wandring thorow spacious Desarts, and multitudes of Kingdoms, not seldom seeming to affect his forsaken Fountains, now dispersed into ample Lakes, and again re-collecting his extravagant Waters, which often divide to make fortunate Islands, (amongst which *Meroe* the fairest and most famous) appearing ever more great than violent.

But when rough crags and head-long Cataracts	——*Sed cum lapsus abrupta viarum*
Receive his falls, mad that each rock distracts	*Excepere cios, & præcipites cataractæ,*
His former un-impeached source, he laves	*Ac nusquam vetitis ullas obsistere cautes*
The stars with spume, all tremble with his waves:	*Indignaris aquis; spuma nunc astra lacessis;*
The mountain roars, and fuming with high spite,	*Cuncta tremunt undis, & multo murmure montis*
Immantleth his unvanquisht waves in white.	*Spumeus invictis albescit fluctibus amnis.*
	Lucan. l. 1o.

For unlike himself, like a raving Torrent, struggling amongst the broken Rocks, and less free passages, at length he spouts down from a wonderful height into the Valley below; and that with such a roaring of waters, that a Colony there planted by the *Persians*, made almost deaf with the noise, were glad to abandon their habitations: otherwise for all uses of life sufficiently commodious. Amongst the rest, the incredible boldness of these people was not the least to be wondred at, daring to commit themselves in little Boats, but capable of two only (the one steering, and the other rowing) unto the raging Current and impetuous Eddies, passing the Straights of the Rocks by little Chanels, and at length rush down with the stream to the amazement of the beholders, who giving them lost, behold them after a while, as if shot out of an Engine, far from the place of their fall, and rowing safely in the asswaged waters. Not far below, and a little above, where once stood the City *Elephantis, Schrophi* and *Mophi*, two piked Rocks, lift up their eminent heads, which do make the lesser Cataract, and are called, The Vines of *Nilus*: where, as *Herodotus* reports from an *Egyptian* Priest, are Fountains of an unsearchable profundity, into which rich gifts were thrown in their annual Solemnities. Increased, as is supposed, by this accession in deeper streams and stricter limits, kept in on both sides with not far distant Mountains, after a long procession: *Seneca l.4. Nat. quæst.*

First, Memphis gives thee scope, and free release	*Prima tibi campos permittit, apertaque Memphis*
From bounders that might limit thy increase.	*Rura, modumque vetat crescendi pouere ripas.*
	Lucan. l. 10.

Four miles below *Cairo* it divideth into two main and navigable branches: that, next the East running into the Mid-land Sea by *Damiata* (heretofore *Pelusium*:) the other inclining unto the West, and formerly called *Canopus*, falleth into the self same Sea, a little below *Rosetta*, making of the richest portion of the Land a triangular Island named *Delta*, in that it beareth the form of that Letter: the fresh water keeping together, and changing the colour of the salt, far further into the Sea, than the shore from thence can be discerned. Two other branches there be that run between these, but poor in waters; besides divers Chanels cut by the labour of man, for conveyances in the time of inundation; which also are no small strengthening to the Country. Of these seven mentioned by *Herodotus*, and those nine by *Ptolomy*, these are all that I either saw or could hear of. Nor is it a thing extraordinary for Rivers to lose their Chanels, either choaked by themselves, or by the adverse Seas, with beds of Sand, and turned-up Gravel resisting their passages. But amongst the hidden Mysteries of Nature, there is none more

                   H   wonderful

wonderful, than is the overflowing of this River, making of a meer Desart (for such is *Egypt* unwatered by *Nilus*) the most fruitful part of the habitable World; little when others are great, and in their decrease, increasing.

The Image of Nilus brought by Vespasian out of Egypt and now to be seene at Rome in the Vatican.

LIB. II.   *Nilus.*   75

Not ty'd to Laws of other streams; the Sun
When farthest off, thy streams then poorest run.
Intemperate heaven to temper, midst of heat,
Under the burning Zone, bid to grow great.
Then Nile assists the world; lest fire should quell
The earth, and make his high-born waters swell
Against the Lions flaming jaws———

Inde etiam leges aliarum nescit aquarum,
Nec umet Hybernus, quum longe sole remoto
Officiis caret undis suis, dare justus iniquo
Temperiem cœlo, mediis æstatibus exit
Sub torrente plaga, ne terras dissipet ignis,
Nilus adest mundo, contraque accensa Leonis
Ora tumet ———

Lucan. l. 10.

The earth then burnt with the violent fervour, never refreshed with Rain, (which here falls rarely, and then only in the Winter) hath help from *Nilus*, most constantly observing his accustomed seasons, beginning to arise with the rising Sun on the seventeenth of *June*: swelling by degrees, until it mount sometimes four and twenty cubits, but that the uttermost. Heretofore sixteen was the most that it attained to; presented by that Image of *Nilus*, having sixteen Children playing about it; brought from thence, and dedicated by *Vespasian* in his Temple of Peace: now in this form to be seen in *Rome* in the *Vatican*.

This year at *Cairo* it rose three and twenty. About two miles above the City, at the end of old *Cairo*, in the beginning of *Augusti* they cut the banks, then when ascended unto his principal height: before kept in, lest that the too timely Deluge should destroy the fruits of the earth, ere fit to be reaped. At which the *Bassa* is himself in person (who giveth the first stroke) accompanied with a world of people, rowed in Gallies and Barges of Triumph, and for divers days feasting: the *Bassa* in the Castle of *Michias*, an Island surrounded with *Nile* (so called, in that there the Pillar doth stand, by which they observe the increase of the River) others under Pavillions pitched by the shore, with barbarous Solemnities and general Rejoycings. Of their night-triumphs this following Picture representeth the form

They cut it again in the half way between Cairo and Roseta.

A, *The Castle in the Island where the Bassa at the cutting of the Banks of the Caliz (for so is that Trench called that watereth the East of Egypt) keeps his three days and three nights feast with his Women, (yet separated from men) accompanied with the principal Persons of the Land.*

B, *The Pillar, standing in a Vault within the Castle, entred by the Nile, by which they measure his increase, whereof Boys with yellow Banners in their hands, inform the Citizens daily, and for their news receive gifts of divers.*

C, *Two great Jerbies, whereon buildings are raised an huge height, with Masts and Rafters for those three nights, stuck all with burning lamps, which afford a glorious spectacle. They report here, that in the time of Paganism, the Egyptians accustomed to sacrifice a maid and a young man to Isis and Osiris, at the yearly solemnity. But that inhumane custom abolished, that these lights were offered to those Idols in their room: being observed since both by Christians and Mahometans, though not as a Sacrifice.*

H 2   At

D. *The Plain lying between old Caird and Nile, where (the admirable Fire-works ending with the night) they play at Giocho di cani: shewing other Exercises on Horse-back, and entertaining the time with sundry devices. Mean while the Fire-works are for the next nights triumphs a renewing. Every Sanjack and Turk of great account hath a gallant Boat, furnished with Chambers and lesser shot, adorned with all variety of Streamers and Pendants each Boat assuming a several colour. So making Sea fights by day, in the night they set them forth with lamps of all colours, which giveth a brave addition to the other; the light being so ingeniously placed, that they present the forms of Gallies, Ships, Jerbies, Horses, Castles, and the like.*

At their return they are met by those of the City, who bestrew their heads with Flowers, as the welcome fore-runners of that they long wished. The turned in water followeth them at the heels; Boats now rowed, where but now they trampled; filling the dusty Trenches and long emptied Cisterns: and a while after covering in many places the superficies of the Land, which there then appeareth as a troubled lake. Answerable to the increase of the River, is the plenty or scarcity of the year succeeding; bringing with it both earth and water into a sandy and thirsty soil, of it self unprofitable: so that it as well manures as moistens with the fat and pregnant slime which it leaveth behind it. Unto which they own not their riches only, but themselves. For the Plague, which here oft miserably rageth, upon the first of the flood doth instantly cease: insomuch as when five hundred dye at *Cairo* the day before, which is nothing rare, (for the sound keep company with the sick, holding death fatal, and to avoid them irreligion) not one doth dye the day following. Wherefore no marvel though ignorant and superstitious Antiquity under the name of *Osiris* adored this River, which afforded them so many benefits, and such as not apprehended, were thought supernatural. Thus where covered with water, it is no unpleasant sight to behold the Towns appearing like little lands; The people passing and re-passing by Boat, and not seldom swimming: who, the less they see of their Country, the more is their comfort. About the midst of *September* it ceaseth to augment; and retiring a month after within his proper bounds, giveth way unto Husbandry, (the earth untilled, by throwing the grain on the Mud and Rice into the water, affording her first increase) until *May* decreasing, and then in a marvellous penury of water. Of the cause of this Inundation divers have conjectured diversly. The *Egyptians* by three Pitchers deciphered the same in their Hieroglypicks, proceeding (as they thought) from a threefold cause. First, from the earth, by nature apt to breed of it self, and bring forth water abundantly. Next, from the South Ocean, from whence they imagined that it had his Original: and lastly, from the rain which fell in the upper *Æthiopia* about the time of the overflow. The most ancient opinion was, that it proceeded from the Snow dissolving in those Mountains: of which *Anaxagoras* and *Æschylus*: thus also expressed by *Euripides*.

Aquam pulchram defcernes
Fluminis Nili, quæ ex terra destluit
Nigrorum hominum, & tunc tumefacit undas
Quum Æthiopicæ nives liquunrur.

The goodly streams of Nilus leaving,
Which from the land of Negroes flow:
Their inundations receiving
From thaws of Æthiopian snow.

But the excessive heat of those Climates, the stones there burning hot, and earth not by day to be trod upon, confute sufficiently that errour. But to answer him by one of his own profession;

Vana fides veterum, Nilo quod crescat in arva
Æthiopum prodesse nives, Non arctos in illis
Montibus, aut Loreas, testis ubi sole perusti
Ipse color populi, calidisque vaporibus Austri.
Adde quod omne caput fluvii quodcunque soluta
Præcipitat glacies, ingresso vere tumescit
Prima tabe nivis——

Lucan. l. 10.

Vain th' old belief, that Æthiopian snow
Availeth Nile's increase; No weak winds blow,
Nor frosts benum those mountains. This aver
The sultry South-winds and black Climater.
Add, that all streams which from dissolv'd snow draw
Their heady torrents, swell with the first thaw
In flow'ry Spring-tide——

Nor snoweth it ever in *Egypt*, a Country more temperate by many degrees:

Memphin carentem Scythoria nive.
Hor. lib. 3. Od. 25.

Scorcht Memphis knows
No Scythian snows.

being here in the depth of Winter as hot as with us in *July. Thales* attributes it unto the Northern Winds, which then blowing up the River, resists the Current, and

and force the reverberated Streams to retire: so that not increased, but prohibited, at length it descendeth with such a multitude of waters. Which opinion is rather alledged, than confirmed, by *Lucretius*.

Or that the North winds do his mouths oppose,
Then yearly when the Etesia firmly blows,
Wh[o]se long encountring blasts resist his way,
Beat back his streams, enforcing him to stay.

Aut quia sunt æstate Aquilones ostia contra
Anni tempore eo, quo Etesia flabra feruntur,
Et contra fluvium flantes memorantur, & undas
Cogentes sursum replent, coguntque manere.
Lucr. l. 6.

For if so, all other Rivers whatsoever, running the same way, would have the same property. Besides, how could it then increase and decrease so leisurely? or how becometh it so troubled and slimy?

Or rolling sands, which adverse floods provoke
To raise in shelves, his yawning mouths up-choke,
When seas throng in amain, enrag'd by winds,
So that the stream a less free passage finds,
His force curb'd with their waters.

Est quoque uti possit magnus congestus arenæ
Fluctibus adversis oppilare ostia contra,
Cum mare permotum ventis ruit inter arenam,
Quo fit uti pacto liber minus exitus amni,
Et proclivis idem fiat minus impetus undis.
Ibid.

But the *Etesie* blows mildly, and the increase well known to begin far above the *Cataracts*. *Herodotus* in dislike of these, preferreth his own. How that the Sun performing his course in the Winter Tropick, and exhaling much moisture from *Nilus*, diminisheth him contrary to his nature; when again inclining to the North, the River recovers his greatness: seeming in the Summer to increase, when it so but seems to do by his decreasing in the Winter. But this is also reproved by *Diodorus Siculus*, who imputes the cause thereof unto abundance of rain falling on the *Æthiopian* Mountains for forty days together, at such time as the Sun approacheth to the sign of *Cancer*: which by the Inhabitants is likewise affirmed to be true; as being received from strangers frequenting *Cairo* from sundry parts of *Æthiopia* and *Lybia*, who come down with the flood, and bring with them Slaves, Monkies, Parrots, and such like Commodities. And not unlikely; those Mountains being of an incredible height, where the air removed so far from the reflecting heat, must be much more cool, the Sun then being in the contrary Tropick. Moreover, some months before, for divers days you shall here see the troubled air full of black and ponderous Clouds, and hear a continual rumbling, threatning, as it were, to drown the whole Country, yet seldom so much as dropping, but are carried South-ward by the Northern winds which constantly blow at that season. Some have written, that by certain Kings inhabiting above, the *Nilus* should there be stopped; and at a time prefixed, let loose upon a certain Tribute paid them by the *Ægyptians*. The errour springing perhaps from a truth (as all wandring reports for the most part do) in that the *Sultan* doth pay a certain annual sum to the *Abissin* Emperour for not diverting the course of the River, which they say he may, or impoverish it at the least. Otherwise what Dam can contain such a confluence of waters? how continueth it so long? or where doth it gather that slime that so inricheth the Country? To prove that it proceedeth from a natural cause; this one, though strange, yet true experiment will suffice. Take of the earth of *Egypt*, adjoyning to the River, and preserve it carefully, that it neither come to be wet nor walked: weigh it daily, and you shall find it neither more nor less heavy until the seven tenth of *June*; at which day it beginneth to grow more ponderous, and augmenteth with the augmentation of the River: whereby they have an infallible knowledge of the state of the Deluge, proceeding without doubt from the humidity of the Air, which having a recourse through all passable places, and mixing therewith, increaseth the same as it increaseth in moisture. In the tenth and eleventh year of *Cleopatra*, it is by Writers of those times for a certainty affirmed, that the *Nilus* increased not, which two years defect, prognosticated the fall of two great Potentates, *Cleopatra* and *Anthony*. Many Ages before *Callimachus* reports, that it did the like for nine years together. For the same cause, no question, but that seven years dearth proceeded in the time of *Pharaoh*.

A vulgar experiment generally affirmed, as by Alpinus inMed Æ-gypt. l. 4. c. 8. who long lived here upon the testimonies of Paulus Marcinus the French Consul, Baptista Elianus a Jesuit, and John Vaslot an English man.

Slow Nile with low-sunk streams shall keep his brays,
Nor bring-down bead, nor fruitful slime up-raise,
Dry fields, dry Solstice, all dryed up, nor shall
Fat floods from high skie-kissing mountains fall.

Ipse inter ripas demisso flumine Nilus
Curret iners, supraque caput limuumque terracem
Non tolit: sicca arebunt arva, omnia sicca
Solstitia, nulli descendent montibus amnes.

From this River there afcend no vapours, the humour being rarified by fo long a progrefs; fo that although exhaled, it affumed no vifible body, but undiftinguifh-ably mixed with the purer Air, agreeing with the fame in tenuity. Than the waters whereof there is none more fweet, being not unpleafantly cold, and of all others the moft wholefom. Confirmed by that anfwer of *Pefcentius Niger* unto his murmuring Souldiers, *What? crave you wine, and have Nilus to drink of?* Such is it in being fo concocted by the Sun, at all times in fome part directly over it, and by length of courfe, running from South to North (befides in ambages) above one and forty degrees. So much it nourifheth, as that the Inhabitants think that it forthwith converteth into blood, retaining that property ever fince thereinto metamorphofed by *Mofes*. For which caufe the Priefts of *Ifis* would not permit their *Apis* to drink of the fame; becaufe they would neither have him nor themfelves too fat and corpulent, that the foul might the better exercife her faculties, being cloathed in a light and delicate body. Befides, it procureth liberal urine, cureth the dolour of the reins, and is moft foveraign againft that windy melancholy arifing from the fhorter ribs, which fo faddeth the mind of the difeafed. Out of the River, they put the water into large Jars of ftone, ftirring it about with a few ftampt Almonds, wherewith alfo they befmear the mouth of the veffel; and for three or four hours do fuffer it to clarifi.

Alpinus de Med. Ægypt l. 1. cap. 12.

It alfo produceth abundance of fifh, in fhape and quality much differing from ours; but by reafon of the muddy Chanel, not altogether favoury nor wholefom. Moreover, divers ftrange and monftrous Creatures; as Bulls, of the River, (fo they write) not much unlike to thofe of the Land, but no bigger than a Calf of half a year old, and which will live for a long time out of the water. River-horfes, called *Hippotami*, having great heads, wide jaws, being armed with tusks as white as the Ivory, of body as big as a Cow, and proportioned like a Swine, of a brownifh bay, fmooth-skinned, and fo hard, as hardly to be pierced by a Weapon: yet (otherwife and contrary to each other, defcribed by *Herodotus*, *Diodorus*, and *Pliny*, though the firft had feen of them here, and the laft at *Rome* in a Triumph:) hufiful they be, ravenous, and revengeful. It is reported in the *Spanifh* Navigations, how that two of them being found afhore by a few *Portugals*, and having gotten from them into the water, affailed the Boat with great fury, into which they faw them afcend, undaunted with their fhot, biting the fides of the Veffel, and departing rather out of defpair of hurting, than otherwife terrified. In another Voyage, others endeavoured to overturn a Boat, that they might have devoured the men that were in her.

But thefe (if of thefe there be now any) are rare to the Crocodile, in fhape not unlike a Lizard, and fome of them of an uncredible greatnefs. So great from fo fmall a beginning is more than wonderful, fome of them being above thirty foot long, hatcheth of Eggs no bigger than thofe that are laid by a Turkie. His tail is equal to his body in length, wherewith he infoldeth his prey, and draws it into the River. His feet are armed with claws, and his back and fides with fcales fcarce penetrable; his belly tender, foft, and is eafily pierced; his teeth indented within one another; having no tongue, and moving of his upper jaw only; his mouth fo wide, when extended, as fome of them are able to fwallow an entire Heifer. Four months of the year he eateth nothing, and thofe be during the Winter: on the Land thick-fighted, not fo in the Water, to whom both Elements are equally ufeful. The Female lays an hundred Eggs, as many days they are in hatching; and as many years they live that do live the longeft, continually growing. Where fhe layeth, there is (as they write) the uttermoft limit of the fucceeding overflow: Nature having endued them with that wonderful prefcience, to avoid the inconveniencies, and yet to enjoy the benefit of the River. By the figure therefore of a Crocodile, Providence was by the *Egyptians* Hieroglyphically expreffed. Between the Dolphins and thefe there is a deadly Antipathy. *Babillus*, a man highly commended by *Seneca*, obtaining the Government of *Egypt*, reported that he faw at the mouth of *Nilus*, then called *Heracliotieum*, a fhole of Dolphins rufhing up the River, and encountred by a fort of Crocodiles, fighting, as it were for Soveraignty; vanquifhed at length by thofe mild and harmlefs Creatures, who fwimming under, did cut their bellies with their fpiny fins, and deftroying many, made the reft to flye, as overthrown in battel. A Creature fearful of the bold, and bold upon the fearful. Neither did the *Tentyritæ* mafter them in regard of their blood or favour, (as fome have conjectured) but being fierce and couragious. A people dwelling far above, in an Ifland environed by *Nilus*,

The Dolphin and his Porpus allore called Sus marinus of his vomiture is a Swine.

only

only hardy against those, and the only men that durst assail them before, out of an innate hatred greedily pursuing the encounter. But now few keep so low as *Cairo* by three days journey. They will devour whom they catch in the River; which makes the Country-people to shunne in those places where they fetch their water: By day for the most part he liveth on the land, when between sleeping and waking, they write, that a little bird called *Trochilus*, doth feed her self by the picking of his teeth, wherewith delighted, and gaping wider, the *Ichneumon* his mortal enemy spying his advantage, whips into his mouth, and gliding down his throat, like an arrow, gnaweth a way through his belly, and destroys him. This, though now little spoken of, in times past was delivered for a truth, even by the *Egyptians* themselves, who gave Divine honour unto the *Ichneumon* for the benefit he did them in the destroying of that Serpent. And true, perhaps it is, though not observed by the barbarous. The bird is at this day known, described to be about the bigness of a Thrush, of colour white, the points of his feathers sharp, which he sets up on end like bristles, when he sits, and so pricketh the mouth of the Crocodile, if he but offer to close it. As for the *Ichneumon*, he hath but only changed his named, now called the Rat of *Nilus*. A beast particular to *Egypt*, about the bigness of a Cat, and as cleanly, snouted like a Ferret, but that black, and without long hair, sharp tooth'd, round ear'd, short leg'd, long tail'd (being thick where it joynts to the body, and spiny at the end) his hair sharp, hard, and branded, bristling it up when angry, and then will flye upon a Mastiff. They are thought (for they have an appearance of both) to be of both genders. Their young ones are brought to Markets by the Country-people, and greedily bought by the Towns-men for the destroying of Mice and Rats, which they will notably hunt after, strong, nimble, and subtil withal. They will rest themselves upon their hinder feet, and rising from the earth, jump upon their prey with a violent celerity. They prey also upon Frogs, Lizards, Chamelions, and all sorts of lesser Serpents : being a deadly enemy to the Asp, and do destroy the Eggs of the Crocodile wheresoever they can find them. They will strangle all the Cats they meet with; for their mouths are so little, that they can bite nothing that is thick. They love nothing better than Poultry, and hate nothing more than the wind. But to return to the Crocodiles, the Country-people do often take them in Pit-falls, and grapling their chaps together with an Iron, bring them alive unto *Cairo*. They take them also with Hooks, baited with Sheep or Goats, and tyed with a rope to the trunk of a tree. The flesh of them they eat, all saving the head and tail, and sell their skins unto Merchants, who convey them into Christendom for the rarity. It is written in the *Arabian* Records, how *Hameth Aben Thaulon* (being Governour of *Egypt* for *Gisar Mutanichi Caliph* of *Babylon*) in the 270 year of their *Hegir*, caused the leaden Image of a Crocodile, found amongst the ruines of an ancient Temple, to be molten; since when the Inhabitants have complained, that those Serpents have been more noysom unto them than before; affirming, that it was made, and there buried by the ancient Magicians to restrain their endamagings.

Throughout this Country there are no Wines, yet want they none, in that they desire them not. Neither are here any Trees to speak of, but such as are planted, and those in Orchards only, excepting Palms, which delight in Desarts; and being naturally theirs, do grow without limits. Of these they have plenty, pleasing the eye with their goodly forms, and with diversity of benefits enriching their owners. Of body streight, high, round, and slender, (yet unfit for buildings) erected about, and by means thereof with facility ascended. The branches like Sedges, sit on the neather side, and ever green; growing only on the uppermost height, resemble fair Plumes of Feathers, which they yearly prune, by lopping off the lowest, and at the top of all by baring a little of the bole. Of these there be male and female : both thrust forth Cods (which are full of seeds like knotted strings) at the root of their branches, but the female is only fruitful: and not so, unless growing by the male, (towards whose upright growth she inclines her crown) and have of his seeds commixed with hers, which in the beginning of *March* they no more fail to do, and to sow the earth at accustomed seasons. Their Dates do grow like fingers, and are thereof named : not ripe until the time of *December* : which begin to cod about the beginning of *February*. They open the tops of such as are fruitless, or otherwise perisht; and take from thence the white pith, of old called the brain, which they fell up and down : an excellent Sallad, not much unlike in taste, but far better than an Artichoke. Of the branches they make Bed steads,

Lattices,

Lattices, &c. of the Web of the Leaves, Baskets, Mats, Fans, &c. of the outward Husk of the Cod, good Cordage, of the inward, Brushes, &c. such and such like afford they yearly without impair to themselves. This Tree they held to be the perfect image of a man, and by the same represented him. First, for that it doth not fructifie, but by coiture: next, as having a brain, as it were, in the uppermost part, which once corrupted, as man, even so it perisheth: and lastly, in regard that on the top thereof grow certain strings which resemble the hair, the great end of the branches appearing like hands stretcht forth, and the Dates as fingers. And because the Palm is never to be suppressed, but shooteth up against all opposition, the boughs thereof have been proposed as rewards for such as were either victorious in Arms or Exercises,

—— Palmaque nobilis
Terrarum dominos evehit ad Deos.
Hor. l. 1. Od 1.

—— *And noble Palms advance
Earths Potentates to Gods* ——

which they bare in their hands at their return from Victory. A custom first instituted by *Theseus* in the Island of *Delos*. Wood then is here but scarce, in regard of the quantity; and yet enough, if their uses for the same be considered. For they eat but little flesh, (fresh Cheese, sowre Milk made solid, Roots, Fruits, and Herbs, especially *Colucasia*, anciently called the *Ægyptian* Bean, though bearing no Bean, but like the leaf of a Colewort, being their principal sustenance, baking their bread in Cakes on the Hearth, and mingling therewith the seeds of Coriander.) As for cold, they know it not, having sufficient of the refuse of Palms, Sugar-canes, and the like, to furnish them with fuel answerable to their necessities. But Foreigners that feed as in colder Countries, do buy their wood by weight, which is brought in hither by shipping. The Gallions also of *Constantinople* always go into the Black Sea for Timber, before they take their Voyage for *Cairo*. Omit I must not the sedgie Reeds that grow in the Marishes of *Egypt*, called formerly *Papyri*, of which they make Paper, and whereof ours made of Rags, assumeth that name. They divided it into thin flakes, whereinto it naturally parteth: then laying them on a Table, and moistning them with the glutinous water of the River, they prest them together, and so dried them in the Sun. By this means *Philadelphus* erected his Library. But *Eumenes* King of *Pergamus* striving to exceed him in that kind, *Philadelphus* commanded that no Paper should be transported out of his Kingdom; whereupon *Eumenes* invented the making and writing upon Parchment, so called of *Pergamus*.

The *Ægyptians* were said to have esteemed themselves the prime Nation of the World, in regard of their unknown beginning, the nature of the soil, and excellent faculties attained unto through a long continuance. But certain it is, that most of, or all *Egypt* was a See when other parts of the World were inhabited, made manifest by the shells and bones of fishes found in the intrails of the earth, and Wells which yield but salt and bitter waters: amongst so many, one only (and that reported to have sprung by a Miracle) to be drunk of. So that by the operation of the River, this Country hath this (being properly called, (*The gift of Nilus*) bringing down earth with his Deluges, and extruding the Sea by little and little. Insomuch as the Isle of *Pharus* thus described by *Homer*,

Insula deinde quondam est valde undoso in ponto
Ægyptum ante (Pharum vero ipsam vocant)
Tantum sumora quantum tota die cava navis
Conficit, cui stridulus ventus spirat à puppi.
Odyss. l. 4.

*An Isle there is by surging seas embrac't
Which men call Pharus, before Egypt plac't,
So far removed, as a swift ship may
Before the whistling winds sail in a day.*

doth now adjoyn to the Haven of *Alexandria*.

Busiris, as the fairest seat of the earth, made choice of this Country to reign in: selecting the people unto several callings, and caused them to intend those only, whereby they became most excellent in their particular faculties. He possessed them first with the adoration of the Gods, emboldening and awing their minds with a being after death happy or unhappy, according to the good or bad committed in the present: and instituted the honouring of contemptible things; or for some benefit they did, or to appease them for such hurt as they had the power to inflict. Of these thus *Juvenal*, who then lived amongst them.

What honour brain-sick Ægypt to things vile
Affordeth, who not knows? a Crocodile
This part adores, that I his serpent fed.
Monkie of gold they there divinely dred,
Where Memnons half form yields a magick sound;
And old Thebes flood, for hundred gates renown'd,
Here fishes of the Sea, there of the River:
Whole Towns a dog; none but that bears the Quiver.
Onions and Leeks to eat, height of impieties.
O sacred Nation sure, wh have these Deities
Grow in your gardens! all from sheep abstain:
'Tis sin to kill a Kid: yet humanes slain,
Inhumanely they feed on ——

Quis nescit Volusi Bithynice, qualia demens
Ægyptus portenta colat? Crocodilon adorat
Pars hæc : illa pavet saturam serpentibus Ibin.
Effigies sacri nitet aurea Cercopitheci,
Dimidio magicæ resonant ubi Memnone chordæ.
Atque vetus Thebe centum jacet obruta portis.
Illic cæruleos, hic piscem fluminis : Ibic
Oppida tota canem venerantur : nemo Dianam
Porrum & cœpe nefas violare ac frangere morsu.
O sanctus gentes quibus hæc nascuntur in hortis
Numina lanatis animalibus abstinet omnis
Mensa : nefas illic fœtum jugulare capellæ,
Carnibus humanis vetci licet.

Juven. Sat. 15.

For the *Tentcrites* bearing an inveterate hatred to the *Combos* their Neighbours, for adoring the Crocodile, which they hated, fell upon them unawares in their civil janglings at the Celebration of their Festival; and putting them to flight, cut the hindermost in pieces, whom reeking hot, with heart yet panting, they greedily devoured : The Poet himself an eye-witness of the fact. Such Jars proceeded from their fertility of Gods, differing in each several Jurisdiction, and instituted by their politick crafty Kings, that busied with particular malice, they should not concur in a general Insurrection. Above all they honoured *Isis* and *Osiris* : which Fable (too tedious for our professed brevity) contained sundry Allegories. Amongst others, by *Osiris* they prefigured *Nilus*, by *Isis* the Earth made pregnant by the River, and by *Typhon* the Sea. They said, that *Typhon* was vanquished by *Osiris*, in that the River had so repulsed the Sea; and by *Typhon* afterward murdered, because at length the Sea doth as it were devour it. Their Priests were next in dignity to the King, and of his Council in all businesses of importance. From amongst them he was chosen; or if of the Souldiery, he forthwith was invested in the High-Priesthood, and instructed by them in the Mysteries of their Philosophy; delivered under Fables and Ænigmatical expressions. They drank no Wine, until the time of *Psametichus* the last of the *Pharaohs*, esteeming it to have sprung from the blood of the Giants, in that it provoked the mind to lust, impatience, cruelty, and all the disordered affections that those contemners of the gods were endued with. Of all the Heathen they were the first that taught the Immortality of the Soul, and the Transmigration thereof into another body, either of man or beast, clean or unclean, as it had behaved it self in the former. From whom *Pythagoras* received that opinion, and divulged it to the *Grecians*, who, the better to perswade, affirmed himself to have been once *Æthalides* the Son of *Mercury*, and commanded by his Father to ask what he would, immortality excepted, did desire after death to know what had passed in his life, and to have his memory entirely preserved, which by not drinking of *Lethe* befell him accordingly. After the death of *Æthalides*, he became *Euphorbus* :

I (remember) at the Wars of Troy,
Euphorbus was, Pantheus son, and fell
By Menelaus lance. I knew right well
The shield which our left arm us'd to sustain,
At Argos lately seen in Juno's Fane.

Ipse ego (nam memini) Trojani tempore belli,
Panthoides Euphorbus eram, cui pectore quondam.
Hæsit in adverso gravis hasta minoris Atridæ.
Cognovit clypeum lævæ gestamina nostræ.
Nuper Abanteis templo Junonis in Argis.
Ovid. Met. l. 15.

and then *Hermotymus*, then *Delius*, then *Pyrrhus* a Fisherman, and last of all *Pythagoras*. By means whereof he withdrew the *Grecians* from luxury, and possest their minds with the terrour of ill-doing.

The *Egyptians* first invented Arithmetick, Musick, and Geometry; and by reason of the perpetual serenity of the air, found out the course of the Sun and the Stars, their Constellations, Risings, Aspects, and Influences; dividing by the same the year into months, and grounding their divinations upon their hidden properties. Moreover, from the *Egyptians*, *Orpheus*, *Musæus*, and *Homer*, have fetcht their Hymns and Fables of the Gods : *Pythagoras*, *Eudoxus*, and *Democritus*, their Philosophy, *Lycurgus*, *Solon*, and *Plato*, the form of their Governments, by which they all in their several kinds have eternized their memories. Their Letters were invented by *Mercury*, who writ from
the

the right hand to the left, as do all the *Africans*. But in holy things especially they expressed their conceits by Hieroglyphicks, which consist of significant figures: whereof there are yet many to be seen, though hardly to be interpreted. One I will produce for example, said to be pourtraicted within the Porch of *Minerva*'s Temple in the City of *Sai*:

In this Hieroglyphiam the Cutter chose rather to follow, than reform an errour.

The Infant signifieth those that enter into the World, and the Old man those that go out of it; the Falcon, God; the Fish, hatred, because they hated fish that bred in the Sea, which symbolized *Typhon*; and by the River-horse, murder, impudence, and injustice: for they say that he killeth his Sire, and ravisheth his own Dam, which put together importeth, *O you that enter the World, and go out of it; God hateth injustice.*

The word signifies a King.

At the first they were governed by *Pharaohs* of their own; of whom *Sesostris* was the most famous and puissant, who entred the Red Sea in Gallies, which he first invented: subdued *Arabia*, and the greater part of *Æthiopia* and *Lybia*. Elated with these beginnings, he affected the Empire of the World: over-running not only those Countries of the greater *Asia*, long after overcome by *Alexander*; but to the uttermost Confines of the South and East Continent, extending his Conquests. Then inclining West-ward, he vanquished the *Scythians*, and those Nations that border on the *Exine* Sea: passing over into *Europe*, he subdued the *Thracians*. When oppressed by famine, by reason of those more barren Countries, and the multitude of his people, he was constrained to give over his enterprise; and returning by the River *Phasis* overcame the *Getes*, where he left his most tired Souldiers, and supplied his Army with the people of that Country. Whereof *Flaccus*, describing the doors of the Temple of *Colchis*, figured with the Original of the *Colchians*.

Nec minus hic varia dux lætus imagine Templi,
Ad geminas fert ora fores; cunabula gentis
Colchidos hic, ortusque tuens: ut prima Sesostris
Intulerit Rex bella Getis; ut clade suorum
Territus; hos Thebas, patriumq; reducat ad amnem:
Phasidis hos imponat agris, Colchosque vocari
Imperet: Arsinoen illi, trepidaque requirunt
Otia læta Phari, pinguemque sine imbribus annum,

Val. Flac. Arg'n. l. 5.

*Delighted with the various imagery,
Upon the two-leav'd doors he throws his eye,
And views the Colchians stem: how first on Getes
Sesostris warr'd; how freighted with defeats,
Those he transports to Thebes, and famed Nile,
These plants in fields of Phasis, and doth stile
It Cholchos: they led to Arsinoes towers.
Pharus delights, and earth rich without showers.*

In the vanquished Countries he erected Pillars, whereon were engraven (besides the acts that he had done, the figures of men, and on divers the privities of a Woman, to testifie

LIB. II. The Hiſtory of Egypt.

teſtifie the valour of cowardize or the conquered. At his return into Egypt on ſolemn days, he was drawn by tributary Kings unto the Temples of the gods, which he had adorned with their ſpoils. He cauſed many Trenches to be cut thorow the land, and ſome of them navigable. Whereby unprofitable Mariſhes were drained, the Country ſtrengthned, Traffick made eaſie, and ſuch places relieved as laboured with the penury of waters. He attempted to have made a navigable Chanel between the Red Sea and the River, afterwards ſeconded by Darius; but both deſiſted upon the like ſuſpicions. For that Sea was found to lie higher than Egypt: which made them miſdoubt, that it would either drown the Country, or elſe by mixing with the Nilus, diſſeaſon his waters. The marks of their proud endeavours are at this day extant: neverthelſs, in ſome ſort long after effected by Philadelphus. Cambyſes was the firſt that made them ſtoop to a foreign yoke, who overthrew their Temples, and maſſacred their Prieſts, after that with his own hands he had wounded their Apis, deriding their ſubverted and bleeding gods, of them and of themſelves ſuch infirm protectors. For which they reported, that he became from thenceforth mad, and had ſuch ill ſucceſs in his ſucceeding expedition.

* *The Ethiopians, who are ſaid ordinarily to live unto 120 years.*

*Furious Cambyſes to the * long liv'd went:
Fed with the ſlaughter of his own half ſpent,
Returned into the Eaſt ———*

———Verſanus in ortus
Cambyſes longi populos pervenit ad ævi:
Defectuſque epulis, & paſtus cæde ſuorum
———redit ———
Lucan. l. 10.

In the time of Darius that was called Nothus, they expulſed the Perſians, and again were governed by Kings of their own. But Ochus reduced them unto their former obedience: continuing ſo, until Alexander the Great with the reſt of the world ſubdued that Country. After whoſe death, in the diviſion of his Empire, Egypt fell to Ptolomæus the Son of Lagus, and continued in his Family for the ſpace of two hundred and four years, ten Kings, and all of that ſirname, ſucceeding each other. Philadelphus being the ſecond in deſcent, but firſt in glory; then Evergetes, Philopater, Epiphanes, Phylometer, Phyſcon, (ſo called for his deformity) Lathures and Auletes: who left his Son Dionyſius, together with Cleopatra, the Co-heirs of his Scepter. But her, her Brother baniſhed.

*Left of the Lagi, worſt: now to leave State
To thy inceſtuous ſiſter, life to Fate.*

Ultima Lageæ ſtirpis, perituráque prole
Degener inceſtæ ſceptris ceſſure ſorores.
Lucan l 8.

Who truſt up in a Mattreſs, and conveyed by night into a little Boat, unto the Lodging of Cæſar lately purſuing Pompey, and then his Murtherers, with her bewitching blandiſhments prevailed ſo well, that ſhe conquered the Conquerour. A fatal Monſter unto Rome, and like Sejanus his Horſe unto her wretched Lovers: yet made ſhe an end unto her life ſo unanſwerable.

*Who ſeeking nobly how to dye
Not like a woman, timorouſly
Avoids the ſword: nor with ſwift oars
Sought Nilus abſtruſe and untrac'd ſhores,
That with a clear brow durſt behold
Her down-caſt ſtate: and uncontrol'd
By horror, office her firm breſt
To touch of Aſps, and deaths arreſt.
More brave in her deliberate end,
Great ſoul, diſdaining to deſcend
To thraldom, and a vaſſal go
To grace the triumph of her foe.*

——— Quæ generoſius
Perire quærens, non mulieriter
Expavit enſem, nec latentes
Claſſe cita reparavit oras.
Auſa & jacentem viſere regiam
Vultu ſereno frontis, & aſperas
Tractare ſerpentes: ut atrum
Corpori combiberit venenum.
Deliberata morte ferocior.
Sævis Liburnis ſcilicet invidens
Privata deduci ſuperbo
Non humilis mulier triumpho.

Hor. l. 1. Od. 37.

Her Tragedy acted, Octavius Cæſar reduced Egypt into the form of a Province. Under the Roman bondage they received the Chriſtian liberty, by the Miniſtry of St. Mark th' Evangeliſt. In the diviſion of that Empire they became ſubject to the Conſtantinopolitan Emperours. But the Egyptians ſoon weary of their oppreſſions, (not long after the impoſtury of Mahomet) as ſome ſay, called in the Saracens to aſſiſt them in the expulſion of the Greeks: But howſoever they were expulſed by Homro General to Omar the ſecond Mahometan high Prieſt, in the year 635. Who only impoſing a Tribute, afforded unto all the liberty of Religion. So Egypt became ſubject unto the
Caliphs

Caliphs of *Babylon*, until they set up a *Caliph* of their own; yet reputed for Schismaticas. Three hundred and two years the *Egyptian Caliphs* continued, until the time of *Almerieus* the sixth King of *Jerusalem*. By him invaded, the *Caliph* intreated aid of the *Sultan* of *Syria*, who sent him *Saraeco*, that repelled the Christians, and by murdering the assisted, usurped his Soveraignty. To him succeeded *Saladine*, the utter subverter of the Holy-land. Who dying, forbade all Funeral pomp, save only a shirt to be carried about on the point of a Spear, with this Proclamation:

> *Great Saladine the Conquerour of the East,*
> *Of all the state and glory he possest,*
> *(O frail and transitory good!) no more*
> *Hath born away, but that poor shirt he wore.*

Seventy and six years that Kingdom continued with the *Turks*, until the Reign of *Melee-sala*, who often foiled by the Christians, having lost most of his men, and distrusting the *Egyptians*, bought a multitude of *Circassian* Slaves (a people bordering on the *Euxine* Sea, heretofore called *Getes*) of the *Tartars* which then had overrun that Nation. These he armed, and by their valour not only freed his Country, but gave the *French*-men a fearful overthrow, taking King *Lewis* Prisoner hard by *Damiata*. But these Slaves a while after murdered *Melee sala*, and elected a *Sultan* of their own, tyrannizing over the natural Inhabitants, and still maintaining their power by the yearly purchase of *Circassian* Children, brought unto *Alexander* by Rovers and Merchants. These they instructed in the *Mahometan* Law, and exercise of Arms, the Son not succeeding the Father neither in Empire nor Military profession, no not so much as in the name of a *Mammaluke*. Dreadful in power, and abounding in riches, for two hundred and seventy years they upheld that Government. Overthrown at length by *Selymus*, the first *Turkish* Emperour, and after sundry doubtful and mortal conflicts, utterly extinguished; together with their lives, they lost their Dominion to the Conquerour. In whose posterity it remaineth at this day, and is now governed by a *Bassa*, who hath his residence in *Cairo*, and commandeth as an absolute Soveraign. Under whom are sixteen *Sanziacks*, and an hundred thousand *Spachies*. The Revenues of this little Country amounting to three millions of Shariffs. The Great *Turk* having one (viz. four hundred thousand disbursed yearly in Sugar and Rice, and sent to *Constantinople*, the residue sent over-land with a Guard of six hundred Souldiers for fear of the *Florentine*) another million is spent in pays, and in setting forth the *Caravan* unto *Mecha* : the third hath the *Bassa* for the support of his own estate, and entertainment of his dependants. But this is little in regard of that which was raised thereof in the Reign of *Auletes*, who received seven millions and a half of Crowns, much more supposed to have yielded to the more provident *Romans*.

Having the same stamp with the Sultanic, the name of Cairo added where it is coyned, of better value, in that of finer gold by two or three Aspers.

The *Bassa* now being, and called *Mahomet*, is a man well stricken in years, of a sowre and inflexible nature. At his first entrance he cut off the heads of four thousand *Spachies*, that had born themselves too insolently, and committed many outrages and extortions. He sent the great men that bore over-much sway, unto *Constantinople*: those that refused to go, he caused to be strangled, using the aid of the *Arabians* (who justly hated the other) in all his executions. If a robbery be committed, and the Thieves escape, such as are appointed to guard those Quarters, do suffer in their stead; insomuch as often as they attach poor innocents, when they cannot apprehend the guilty, to deliver themselves from punishment. They bore holes thorow the condemned's arms, stretcht wide on Staves, in which are Candles stuck, that burn down into the flesh, and are led in that manner thorow the City, unto the place of execution. Others are stript of their skins, yet live in horrible torment so long as the executioners steel offends not the navel. Drunkenness is punished with death, and all disorders so severely lookt into, that I think if in no other place you shall see so few among such a multitude of people. The malice his rigour procured, had caused himself to confine himself to the Castle for a twelve month before our coming to *Cairo*: but his Government is so well approved of by the *Grand Signior*, that to do him the more honour, he hath given him his Daughter in Marriage, a Child of four years old, which hath been solemnized with all possible Ceremonies. One thing more is in him praise-worthy, that he will hardly suffer a Christian to turn *Mahometan*, either out of the dislike of his own Religion, or knowing well that they do it only for commodity and preferment.

Egypt

made the midst of the Land the Seat of their Empire, both the better to keep the whole in subjection, and for fear of the Christians invading the maritime places. The *Egyptians* of the middle times, were a people degenerating from the worth of their Ancestors; prone to invocations, devoted to luxury, cowardly, cruel; naturally addicted to scoff and to cavil, detracting from whatsoever was gracious and eminent. Those that now inhabit the Country, are for the most part *Moors*. *Turks* there are many, and *Jews*, which reside only in Cities, store of *Arabians*, and not a few *Negroes*. Of Christians the native *Copties* are the most in number: some *Greeks* there be, and a few *Armenians*.

The Egyptian *Moors* (descended of the *Arabians*, and understanding each other) are men of a mean stature, tawny of complexion, and spare of body, shrill-tongued, and nimble footed; naturally industrious, affecting more their profit than their ease, yet know they how to live of a little, as in nothing, riotous. Rather crafty are they than wise, more observant than faithful; and by much more devout than the *Turks* in the *Mahometan* Religion. In Learning they are utterly ignorant. Amongst them none are Noble: few admitted to the Souldiery, (nor suffered in Towns to wear Weapons) not any to Magistracy. In Cities the best of them exercise Merchandise: rich by means of their traffick with the *Indians*; yet that decayed since our *East-Indian* Voyages; insomuch as Spices brought out of the *Levant* heretofore, are now with profit brought thither by our Merchants. In habit they differ little from the *Turks*, excepting some of the younger sort, who wear side Coats of Linen (the ancient Habit of that Country) girt to their wastes, and Towels thrown about the necks of the same. (Divers of the *Negroes* wear Vests like Surplices.) The poorer people wear long Garments of hair, streak'd black and white; in the Winter, side Coats of Cotton. The Beggars by singing, both get relief, and comfort their poverty; playing withall upon Drums which are fashioned like Sieves. A number here be afflicted with sore eyes, either by the reflecting heat, the salt dust of the soil, or excessive venery: for the Pox is uncredibly frequent amongst them. The Women, when out of their Houses, are wrapt from the crown of the head to the foot in ample Robes of Linen, spreading their arms underneath to appear more corpulent. For they think it a special excellency to be fat; and most of them are so: so in frequenting the *Bannias*, for certain days together, wherein they use such diet and frictions, as daily use confirmeth for effectual. They cover their faces with black Cypress bespotted with red. Their under Garments are of lighter Stuffs than the *Turkish*, but not differing in fashion. The better sort wear hoops of Gold and Silver about their Arms, and above their Ancles: others of Copper; with pieces of Coin half covering their foreheads; and Plates hung about their necks, &c. Both men and Women do brand their arms for the love of each other. Divers of the women I have seen with their Chins distained into knots and flowers of blue, made by pricking of the skin with Needles, and rubbing it over with Ink and the juice of an Herb, which will never wear out again. They have quick and easie labour, bearing heretofore often two, and sometimes three at a burthen; though also born in the eighth Month living; rarely, if elsewhere heard of. In the adjoining Desarts of Saint *Macario*, a Plant there is, low, leaf-less, brown of colour, branched like Coral, and cloth'd at the top: this, in the time of the labour of women, they set in water, in some corner of the room, which strangely displayeth; procuring (as they generally conjecture) easie deliveries. The Country people do follow Husbandry. They are not long in dressing themselves, being only wrapt in a Russet Mantle: nor have the women any better coverture: hiding their faces with beastly Clouts, having holes for their eyes; which little is too much to see, and abstain from loathing. Over their Shashes the men wear rounds of stiffened Russet: to defend their brains from the piercing fervour. A people breathes not more savage and nasty, crusted with dirt, and stinking of smoke, by reason of the * fuel, and their Houses which have no Chimneys. Some of them dwell under beggarly Tents, and those esteemed of the old Inhabitants.

Stercus hominum.

But

doing it rather, in that an ancient Custom of their Nation (mentioned by *Herodotus*) than out of Religion. They were infected with that Heresie of one Nature in Christ, long before *Jacobus* (of whom now named, and of whom we shall speak hereafter) divulged it in *Syria*. At this day they profess him to be perfect God and perfect man; yet dare not distinguish his Natures, for fear of dividing his person. They baptize not their Children until forty days old. On Saturday presently after midnight, they repair to their Churches, where they remain well-nigh until Sunday at Noon; during which time, they neither sit nor kneel, but support themselves upon Crutches. The Priest is veiled, and vested in Linen, having two or three Boys apparelled alike, and sequestred from the rest of the people, to assist him; for they confer inferiour Orders upon Children. They sing over most part of the Psalms of *David* at every meeting, with divers parcels of the Old and New Testaments; the latter as written by *Nicomedes*: some in the *Coptick* Language, understood but by few, most in the *Moresco*. Often both Priest and People conjoin in savage noises, to our judgments not articulate. The Priest not seldom elevateth a red Cloth (under which, I suppose, is the Sacrament) which they administer in both kinds, and give it to Infants presently after Baptism. In the Churches they have the Picture of our Saviour, and the blessed Virgin, but not over their Altars; nor for any thing I could perceive do they reverence them. In certain Chests they preserve the bones and ashes of such as have turned *Mahometans*, and afterwards recanted, for which they have suffered Martyrdom. At their entrance they kiss their hands, and lay them upon one another; the Women in grated Galleries separated from the men. Extreme Unction, Prayer for the dead, and Purgatory, they admit not of. The *Roman* Church they hold for heretical, and reject all general Councils after that of *Ephesus*. Yet a multitude of late have been drawn to receive the Popish Religion (especially in *Cairo*) by the industry of Fryars: having had the Roman Liturgy sent them from *Rome*, together with the Bible in the *Arabick* Language. Of *Alexandria* hath the Patriarch his name; but his aboad is in *Cairo*. Six days journey above *Cairo*, up the River, they have a great City called *Saiet*; where Christ and his Mother, was said to have made their aboad until the death of *Herod*: unto which, growing old and sickly, they repair, as desirous to dye there: where there is a goodly Church, though something ruinous: built by *Hellen* the Mother of *Constantine*, and consecrated to the blessed Virgin. They never eat in the day time during the Lent, but on Saturdays and Sundays. They wear round Caps, Towels about their necks, and Gowns with wide Sleeves, of Cloth, and Stuffs less ponderous. These live in more subjection than the *Moors*, by reason of their Religion: and pay yearly a certain sum for their heads to to the *Bassa*; ignorant they are in the excellencies of their Ancestors, but retaining their vices. Some of them profess some knowledge in Magick, being but juglers, compared with the former, by whom such miracles were effected.

20000 according to Pliny *l*.5. *c*.6.
An incredible number of Cities are reported by Authors to have been in this Country: of whom the most famous were *Syene*, (now *Asna*) seated under the Tropick of Cancer (in which was a well of marvellous depth, enlightned throughout by the Sun, in the Summer Solstice:) the Regal *Thebes* destroyed by *Cambyses*; eighty furlongs long, and built all upon Vaults:

Qua centum portarum sunt: ducenti autem per unamquamque.
Viri egrediantur cum equis & curribus.
——Ubi multæ in domibus opes reconditæ jacent.
Hom.Il.l.9.

With hundred Gates: through each two hundred may On Chariots mounted pass in fair array; Whose houses much hid treasure hold——

Called by the Turks Scandaria.
(called after, the City of *Jupiter*, now shewing some few foundations and reliques of old glories:) *Memphis*, *Babylon*, and *Alexandria*: whither it is high time that we return. After *Alexander* had subdued *Egypt*, determining to build a City, that might preserve his memory, and to plant it with *Grecians*, he made election of his Promontory; advised

LIB. II.   *Alexandria when it flourished. Pharus.*   87

advised (as is said) thereunto by *Homer* in a dream, who seemed to pronounce these Verses.

An Isle there is by surging Seas embrac'd
Which men call Pharus, before Egypt plac'd.

Insula deinde quædam est valde undoso in Ponto
Ægyptum ante (Pharum vero ipsam vocant.)
Odyss l.4.

The Platform for want of Chalk, was laid out with Meal; prognosticating thereby her ensuing felicity: drawn in the figure of a *Macedonian* Cloak; and afterward walled by *Ptolomy*. The sides stretching out in length, contained in diameter three thousand seven hundred paces; those in the latitude, a thousand contracted at the ends by narrow Isthmuses; here bounded with the Lake, and there with the Sea. The Contriver and Overseer of the work was *Dinocrates*. From the Gate of the Sun, unto that of the Moon, on each side of the way stood ranks of Pillars; in the midst a spacious Court, let into by a number of Streets; insomuch as the people that passed throughout, in some sort did seem to have undertaken a Journey. On the left hand of this stood that part of the City which was named of *Alexander*; being as it were a City of it self, whose beauty did herein differ: for look how far those Columns directly extended in the former, so did they here, but obliquely placed. So that the sight dispersed through multitudes of ways, and ravished with the magnificence thereof, could hardly be satisfied. A wonderful adorning thereunto were the Fans and regal Palaces possessing well nigh a fourth part of the City; for every one did strive to add some Ornament as well to the Houses of their Kings, as to the Temples of their Gods; which stood on the East side of the City, adjoining and participating one with another. Amongst the which was that famous *Musæum*, founded by *Philadelphus*, and endowed with ample Revenues: planted with such as were eminent in liberal Sciences, drawn thither by rewards, and cherished with favours. He caused the Philosophy of the *Egyptians* (before all one peculiar to the Priests) to be divulged in Greek for the benefit of Students. He procured seventy of the principal learned amongst the Jews to translate the Bible, called at this day the *Septuagint*: And erected that renowned Library furnished with seven hundred thousand Volumes, burnt long after by mishap, that time when *Cæsar* was driven into a narrow exigent by the unlookt for assault of *Achilles*. Renewed and augmented by the *Roman* Emperours, it flourished until the *Mahometans* subdued *Egypt*, and subverted all excellencies with their barbarism. Within a *Seraglio* called *Somia*, belonging to the Palaces, the *Ptolomies* had their Sepultures, together with *Alexander* the Great,

Of Macedon, in sacred Vault possest,
And under high Piles Royal Ashes rest.

Cum tibi sacrato Macedon servatur in antro,
Et regum cineres extructo monte quiescunt.
Lucan.l.8.

For *Ptolomy* the Son of *Sadus* took his Corps from *Perdiccas*: who bringing it from *Babylon*, and making for *Egypt*, with intention to have seized on that Kingdom, upon his approach was glad to betake himself into a desart Island, where he fell (thrust through with Javelins) by the hands of his Souldiers: who brought the body unto *Alexandria*, and buried it in the place aforesaid; then inclosed in a Sepulchre of Gold: But *Cybiosactes* the *Cyprian*, espousing the eldest Daughter of *Auletes*, and in her right possest of the Kingdom, (she being elected Queen) despoiled the body of that precious Coverture: when forthwith strangled by *Cleopatra*, he lived not to enjoy the fruits of his covetousness. After that it was covered with Glass; and so remained until the time of the *Saracens*. There is yet here to be seen a little Chappel; within, a Tomb, much honoured and visited by the *Mahometans*, where they bestow their Alms; supposing his body to lye in that place: Himself reputed a great Prophet, they being so informed by their *Alcoran*.

Against the City stands the Isle of *Pharus*, which was joined to the Continent by a Bridge (that also served to support an Aquaduct) through which Boats passed from one Haven into another, both made by the benefit of the Island. In a Promontory thereof, on a Rock environed by the Sea, *Philadelphus* caused a Tower to be built of a wonderful height, ascending by degrees, and having many Lanthorns at the top, wherein Lights burned nightly for a direction to such as sailed by Sea. For the Coasts upon both sides being rocky, low, and harbourless, could not otherwise be approached without eminent danger. Yet divers times the multitude of Lights appearing afar off as one, and mistaken for a Star, procured contrary effects,

Now called *Mag-rah*.

Acrolae chiar Prom.

to the promised safety. This had the repute of the Worlds seventh Wonder, named after the name of the Island. At this day a general name for such as serve to that purpose. *Sostratus* of *Gnydos*, the ambitious Architect, ingraved thereupon this Inscription: SOSTRATUS OF GNIDOS THE SON OF DEXIPHANES, TO THE GODS PROTECTORS FOR THE SAFEGUARD OF SAILERS; which he covereth with Plaister, inscribing the same with the Name and Title of the King: that that soon wasting, his own written in Marble might be celebrated to eternity. This Promontory stretching near unto that of the opposed Continent, doth make a narrow entrance into a dangerous Haven, called the Port of the Tower; before and within there being many Rocks, some covered, and others eminent, which continually trouble the repulsed waters. That on the other side, called the chained up Port, more secure than convenient, is now only reserved for the *Turkish* Gallies.

On the South-side of the City, and not far removed, is the Lake *Mareotis*, in time past resembling a Sea both in greatness and profundity. Made by the labour of man, as *Herodotus* conjectures by the two Pyramides in the middle: being as far under the water as above: that above surmounting it fifty paces. On each there stood a Colossus of stone, adding as much more to the height of the visible building. These were the Sepulchres of King *Maris* and his Wife, who is said to have digged that Lake, which naturally produces no water; having a dry and sandy bottom, but replenished yearly by the inundations of *Nilus*, let in by sundry Chanels, at whose mouths were flood-gates, to moderate the excess of ebbs and over-flows: increasing for six Months together, and for as long diminishing. A work of excessive charge, and incredible performance. To this not much interiour, adjoineth a Labyrinth; in the midst whereof were thirty seven Palaces, belonging to the thirty seven Jurisdictions of *Egypt*, (whereof ten were in *Thebais*, ten in *Delta*, and seventeen in the middle *Region*) unto which resorted the several Presidents to celebrate the Festivals of their gods (who had therein their particular Temples; moreover fifteen Chappels, containing in each a *Nemisis*) and also to advise of matters of importance concerning the general welfare. The passages thereunto were thorow Caves of a marvellous length; full of winding paths,as dark as Hell, and Rooms within one another; having many doors to confound the memory, and distract the intention; leading into inexplicable errour: now mounting aloft, and again re-descending, not seldom turning about walls infolded within one another, in the form of intricate mazes, not possible to thread, or ever to get out without a Conductor. The Building more under the earth than above, being all of massie stone, and laid with that art, that neither Cement nor Wood was employed throughout the universal Fabrick. The end at length attained to, a pair of stairs of ninety steps conducted into a stately Portico supported with Pillars of *Theban* stone: the entrance into a spacious Hall (a place for their general Conventions) all of polished Marble, adorned with the Statues of gods and men; with others of monstrous resemblances. The Chambers were so disposed, that upon their opening, the doors did give reports no less terrible than Thunder. The first entrance was of white Marble, within throughout adorned with Marble Columns, and diversity of Figures. By this disfigured they the perplexed life of man, combred and intangled with manifold mischiefs, one succeeding another: through which impossible to pass without the conduct of wisdom, and exercise of unfainting fortitude. *Dedalus* was said to have imitated this,in that which he built in *Crete*: yet expressing hereof scarce the hundredth part. Whoso mounted the top, should see as it were a large plain of stone: and withall those seven and thirty Palaces, environed with solid Pillars, and Walls consisting of stone of a mighty proportion. At the end of this Labyrinth there stood a square Pyramis of a marvellous breadth, and answerable altitude: the Sepulchre of King *Ismandes*, that built it. About this Lake grew excellent Wines,and long lasting.

———Gemmæque capaces
Excepere merum sed non Mareotidos uvæ
Nobile,sed paucis senium cui contulit annis.
*Lucan.l.*8.

———*And ample goblets swell,*
Not with the generous juice of Grapes that grow
By Mareotis, nor that lasteth so.

This Lake affordeth another Haven unto the City, than that of the Sea more profitable by reason of the Commodities of *India*, the *Arabian* Gulph, and up-land parts of *Egypt*, brought down by the conveniency of that passage by Chanels now
utterly

utterly ruined. And the same by a narrow cut was joined unto another Lake, far less and nearer the Sea: which at this day too plentifully furnisheth all *Turkie* with Salt-Petre. Between the less Lake and the City, there passeth an artificial Chanel, which serveth them with water (for they have no wells) in the time of the deluge: conveyed by Conduits into ample Cisterns (now most of them Fenny for want of use: and occasion of much sickness in the Summer) and so preserved until the succeeding overflow. For *Alexandria* was all built upon Vaults, supported with carved Pillars one above another, and lined with stone; insomuch as no small proportion thereof lay concealed in earth, consider we either the cost or quantity.

Such was this Queen of Cities and *Metropolis* of *Africa*: but

Ah how much different is	Heu quantum Niobe, Niobe diftabat ab illâ
That Niobe from this	*Ovid. Met. l. 6.*

who now hath nothing left her but ruines, and those ill witnesses of her perished beauties: declaring rather that Towns as well as men, have their ages and destinies. Only those Walls remain which were founded (as some say) by *Ptolomy*, one within another, embattelled and garnished with threescore and eight Turrets; rather stately than strong, if compared with the modern. Yet these, by the former descriptions, and ruines without, appear to have immured but a part of the City. After that destroyed by the *Saracens*, it lay for a long time waste; until a *Mahometan* Priest, pronouncing (as he said, out of *Mahomets* Prophecies) indulgences to such as should re-edifie, inhabit, or contribute money thereunto within certain days, did in a short season re-people it. But a latter destruction it received by the *Cypriots*, *French*, and *Venetians*, about the time that *Lewis* the Fourth was enlarged by the *Sultan*, who surprised the City with a marvellous slaughter. But hearing of the approach of the *Sultan*, (who had raised a great Army for their relief) despairing to maintain it, they set it on fire, and departed. The *Sultan* repairing the Walls as well as he could, built this Castle that now stands on the *Pharos*, for the defence of the Haven, and brought it to that state wherein it remaineth. Sundry Mountains are raised of the ruines, by Christians not to be mounted; left they should take too exact a survey of the City: in which are often found (especially after a shower) rich Stones, and medals engraven with the Figures of their Gods, and men, with such perfection of art, as these now cut, seem lame to those, and unlively counterfeits. On the top of one of them stands a Watch-Tower, where continual sentinel is kept, to give notice of approaching sails. Of Antiquities there are few remainders: only an Hieroglyphical Obelisk of *Theban* Marble, as hard well-nigh as *Porphyrie*, but of a deeper red, and speckled alike, called *Pharaohs Needle*, standing where once stood the Palace of *Alexander*: and another lying by, and like it, half buried in Rubbish. Without the Walls, on the South-west side of the City, on a little Hill stands a Column of the same, all of Stone: eighty six Palms high, and thirty six in compass, of the Palm consisting of nine Inches and a quarter, according to the measure *Genoa*, as measured for *Zigal Bassa* by a *Genoese*: set upon a square Cube (and which is to be wondred at) not half so large as the foot of the Pillar: called by the *Arabians Hemadstaeor*, which is, the Column of the *Arabians*. They tell a Fable, how that one of the *Ptolomies* erected the same in the farthest extent of the Haven, to defend the City from Naval incursions, having placed a Magical Glass of Steel on the top; of virtue (if uncovered) to set on fire such Ships as sailed by. But subverted by Enemies, the Glass lost that power; who in this place re-erected the Column. But by the Western Christians it is called, The Pillar of *Pompey*: and it is said to have been reared by *Caesar*, as a memorial of his *Pompeian* Victory. The Patriarch of *Alexandria* hath here a house adjoining to a Church; which stands (as they say) in the place where Saint *Mark* was buried, their first Bishop and Martyr: who in the days of *Trajan*, haled with a Rope tyed about his neck, unto the place called *Augeles*, was there burned for the testimony of Christ, by the Idolatrous Pagans. Afterward his bones were removed to *Venice* by the *Venetians*, he being the Saint and Patron of that City. There be at this day two Patriarchs, one of the *Greeks*, another of the *Circumcised*, the universal Patriarch of the *Cofties* and *Abyssines*. The name of the Greek Patriarch now being, is *Cyril*, a man of approved virtue and learning, a friend to the Reformed Religion; and opposing the contrary: saying, That the differences between us and the *Greeks*, be but shells; but that those are kernels between them and the other. Of him something more shall be spoken hereafter. The buildings now being, are mean and few, erected on the ruines of the former: that part that lieth along the shore inhabited only, the rest desolate: the walls almost quadrangular; on each side a Gate; one opening towards *Nilus*, another regards *Mariotis*, the third the Desart of *Barcha*, and the fourth the Haven. Inhabited by *Moors*, *Turks*, *Jews*, *Costies*, and *Grecians*, more in regard of Merchandize (for *Alexandria* is a free Port, both for friend and enemy) than for the conveniency of the place: seated in a Desart, where they have neither tillage nor pasturage, except what borders on the Lake; that little, and unhusbanded; yet kept they good store of Goats, that have ears hanging down to the ground, which feed amongst the ruines. On the Isle of *Pharus*, now a part of the Continent, there stands a Castle, defending the entrance of the Haven; which hath no water but what is brought upon Camels from the Cisterns of the City: this, at our coming in, as is the use, we saluted with our Ordnance. As many of us as came ashore were brought to the Custom-house, to have our selves and our Valeisas searched: where ten in the hundred is to be paid for whatsoever we have, and that in kind, only money pays but one and a half; whereof they take an exact account, that thereby they may aim at the value of returned Commodities; then paying eleven in the hundred more, even for such goods as are in property unaltered; at so high a rate is this free Traffick purchased: the *Mahometan* here paying as much as the Christian. The Customs are farmed by the *Jews*, paying for the same unto the *Bassa* twenty thousand Madeins a day, thirty of them amounting to a Royal of eight. We lodged in the house of the *French* Consul, unto whose protection all Strangers commit themselves. The Cane lockt up by the *Turks* at noons and nights, for fear that the *Franks* should suffer or offer any outrage. The Vice-Consul keeps a Table for Merchants: the Consul himself a *Magnifico*, less liberal of his Presence, than industrious to pleasure; yet rather stately than proud, expecting respect, and meriting good will: that was a Priest, and would be a Cardinal; with the hopes whereof, they say, that he feasteth his ambition. By him we were provided of a *Janizary* for our guard unto *Cairo*; his hire five pieces of Gold, beside his own diet and his mans; with provision of Powder. For our Asses (not inferiour in this Country unto Horses for travel) half a shariff a piece, for our Camels a whole one. At the Gate they took a Madein a head, for our selves and our Asses, so indifferently do they prize us; through which we could not pass without a *Tescaria* from the *Cadee*, the principal Officer of this City.

On the second of *February* in the Afternoon we undertook our journey; passing throw a desart producing here and there a few unhusbanded Palms, Capers, and a weed called *Kall* by the *Arabs*. This they use for fuel, and then collect the ashes, which crusht together like a Stone, they sell in great quantity to the *Venetians*; who equally mixing the same with the Stones that are brought them from *Pavia*, by the River of *Ticinum*, make thereof their crystalline Glasses. On the left hand we left divers ruinous Buildings, once said to have been the Royal Mansion of *Cleopatra*. Beyond which stands *Bucharis*; once a little, but ancient City; now only shewing her Foundations: where grow many Palms which sustain the wretched people that live thereabouts in beggarly Cottages. There on a Rock a Tower affordeth light by night to the Sailer, the place being full of danger. Anon we passed by a Guard of Souldiers, there placed for the securing of that passage, paying a Madein for every head. Seven or eight miles beyond we ferried over a Creek of the Sea. On the other side stands a handsome Cane, not long since built by a *Moor* of *Cairo*, for the relief of Travellers, containing a quadrangle within, and arched underneath. Under one of these Arches we reposed; the Stones our Beds, our Fardels the Bolsters. In such like places they unload their Merchandize, refreshing themselves and their Camels with provision brought with them, secured from Thieves and violence. Giving a trifle for Oil, about midnight we departed, having here met with good store of company; such as were allowed travelling with their Matches light, and prepared to receive all on-sets. The *Moors* to keep themselves awake, would tell one tale an hundred times over. By the way again we should have paid *Caphar*, but the benefit of the night excused us. Travelling along the Sea-shore, and at length inclining a little on the right hand, before day we entred *Rosetta*, repairing to a Cane belonging to the *Franks*. Our best entertainment an under-room, musty, without light, and the unwholsome floor to lie upon.

This City stands upon the principal branch of the *Nile*, (called heretofore *Canopus*,) which about some three miles beneath dischargeth it self into the Sea. Having here (as at *Damiata*) his entrance crossed with a bar of Sand, changing according

to

LIB. II. Canopus. Our Voyage up the Nile.

to the changes of the Winds, and beating of the Surges; insomuch that the Jerbies that pass over, are made without Keels, having flat and round bottoms: a Pilot of the Town there sounding all the day long, by whose directions they enter, and that so close unto him, that one leaps out of that Boat into the other to receive Pilotage, and returneth swimming. The Jerbies that can pass over this Bar, may, if well directed, proceed unto *Cairo*. *Rosetta* (called *Rasid* by the *Egyptians*) perhaps derived of *Ros*: which signifieth *Rice*, and so named for the abundance that it uttereth; (they here stealing Monthly three hundred quarters) was built by the Slave of an *Egyptian Caliph*. The Houses are all of Brick, not old, yet seeming ancient: flat-rooft, as generally all be in these hotter Countries, (for the *Moors* use much to lie on the tops of their Houses) jetting over aloft like the Poops of Ships, to shadow the Streets that are but narrow, from the Suns reflections. Not small, yet of small defence; being destitute of Walls, and other Fortifications. I think no place under Heaven is better furnished with Grain, Flesh, Fish, Sugar, Fruits, Roots, &c. Raw Hides are here a principal commodity, from hence transported into *Italy*.

In this place, or not much below it, stood that infamous City of *Canopus*: so called of *Canobus Menelaus* his Pilot, there buried by his Master, who on these Coasts had suffered ship-wrack. For of all the Princes of *Greece* that survived the *Trojan* Wars, not one but mis-carried: either by incensed Seas, or domestical Treasons. As they feign through the rage of *Minerva* their late Protectress, for the Rape of *Cassandra*, committed in her Temple; and angry gods, the bootless favourers of subverted *Ilium*;

――*This know*
Euboean Rocks, Minerva's adverse Star
And vengeful Caphareus. From Troys War
Toss'd unto sundry shores, to that far land
Stray'd Menelou, where Proteus Columns stand.

――Sic triste Minervæ
Sidus & Eboicæ cautes, ultorque Caphareus
Militia ex illa diversum ad litus abacti.
Atrides Protei Menelaus ad usque columnas,
Exulat, &c.
Virg. Æn. l. 11.

For *Proteus* then was King of *Egypt*: by whom friendly entertained, after eight years wandring, he returned into his Country. Of this place thus speaketh that Prince of Poets;

Happy Inhabiters of Greek Canopus
Where Nile all over spreads with his high flow,
Who o're their fields in painted frigots row.

Nam qua Pellæi gens fortunata Canopi
Accolit effuso, stagantem flumine Nilum
Et circum pictus vehitur sua rura phaselis.
Virg. Georg. l 4.

Throughout the world notorious for luxury, and practised variety of effeminacy, and beastliness. Whereof the Satyre then, dwelling in the Province of *Thebais*.

The barbarous crew of defam'd Canopus
Mate not the luxury here seen by us.

――Luxuria quantum ipse notavi
Barbara famoso non cedit turba Canopo.
Juv. Sat. 25.

For within *Canopus* stood the Temple of *Serapis*: to whose often Festivals resorted a world of people from *Alexandria* down the artificial Chanels. Which day and night were well-nigh covered with painted Boats, fraught with men and women: chanting amours, and dedicating their behaviours to the excess of liberty. Of which *Pampinius* excusing himself that he;

Nor, trading did in loud delights delight
Of Pharian Barges, nor Boys exquisite
In infamies of Nile, whose tongues consent
Unto their gestures; both like impudent.

Non ego mercatus Pharia de puppe loquaces
Delicias, doctumve sui convitia Nili
Infantem, linguaque simul salibusque protervum
Dilexi.
Statius. l. 5.

The City it self containing divers Lakes in which were Bowers and places of solace, agreeable to their vanities. Amongst whom (saith *Seneca*) who so avoided vice avoided not infamy: the very place administring a suspicion.

The next day but one that followed, we imbarqued for *Cairo*, in a Jerbie unto which seven water-men belonged; which we hired for twelve Dollars. This arm of the *Nile* is as broad at *Rosetta*, as *Thames* at *Tilbury*; straitning by little and little, and then in many places so shallow, that oft we had much ado to free our selves from the flats that had ingaged us: the water being ever thick, as if lately
troubled

troubled, and paſſing along with a mute and unſpeedy current. Ten miles above *Roſetta* is that cut of the River which runs to *Alexandria*. By the way we often bought as much Fiſh for ſix pence, as would have ſatisfied twenty. On each ſide of the River ſtand many Towns, but of no great eſteem, for the moſt part oppoſite: but partly of Brick and partly of Mud; many of the poorer houſes appearing like Bee-Hives: ſeated on little Hills thrown up by the labour of man: to preſerve them and their Cattel in the time of the Overflow. Upon the Banks all along are infinite numbers of deep and ſpacious Vaults, into which they do let the River; drawing up the Water into higher Ciſterns, with Wheels ſet round with Pitchers, and turned about by *Buffoloes*. From whence it runs along in little trenches made upon the ridges of Banks, and ſo is conveyed into their ſeveral grounds, the Country lying all in a level. The winds blew ſeldom favourable: inſomuch as the poor *Moors* for moſt part of the way were enforced to hale up the Boat; often wading above their middles to deliver it from the ſhallows. At every enforcing of themſelves (as in all their labours) crying *Elough*: perſwaded that God is near them when they name him, the Devil far off, and all impediments leſſened. Of theſe it is ſtrange to ſee ſuch a number of broken perſons; ſo being by reaſon of their ſtrong labour and weak food. The pleaſant Walks which we had on the ſhore, made our lingring paſſage leſs tedious. The fruitful ſoil poſſeſſing us with wonder; and early maturity of things, there then as forward as with us in *June*; who begin to reap in the ending of *March*. The Sugar Canes ſerved our hands for ſtaves, and feaſted our taſtes with their Liquor. By the way we met with Troops of Horſemen: appointed to clear thoſe paſſages from Thieves, whereof there are many, who alſo rob by Water in little Frigots. Which made our careful *Janizary* (for ſo are moſt in their undertaken charges) aſſiſted by two other (to whom we gave their paſſage, who otherwiſe would have taken it) nightly to keep watch by turns: diſcharging their Harquebuſhes in the evening, and hanging out kindled Matches to terrifie the Thieves, and teſtifie their vigilancy. Five days now almoſt ſpent ſince we firſt embarqued, an hour before Sun-ſet we ſailed by the Southern angle of *Delta*, where the River divideth into another Branch, not much inferiour unto this, the Eaſt bounds of that Iſland (which whether of *Aſia* or *Africa*, is yet to be decided) entring the Sea, (as hath been ſaid) before below *Damiata*. Proceeding up the River, about twilight we arrived at *Balac*, the Port Town to *Cairo*, and not two miles diſtant: where every Frank at his landing is to pay a Dollar. Leaving our Carriages in the Boat, within night we hired ſix Aſſes, with their Drivers, for the value of ſix pence to conduct us unto *Cairo*; where by an Engliſh Merchant we were kindly entertained, who fed and houſed us gratis.

Huchs Hibnu Nafiſh the *Arabian*, invading a part of *Africa*, and making himſelf Lord of the ſame, built a City in the Deſarts, as fearing the treachery of the *Africans*, ſome hundred and twenty miles from the ruines of *Carthage*, which he called *Cairo*: the name ſignifieth in the *Arabick* tongue, a place of Convention: or rather *Elchahira*, which ſignifieth a Compeller. From that time the *Arabians* began to mix with the *Moors*, from whence this affinity in their ſpeech doth proceed; yet accuſtomed they in their Songs to mention their Genealogies, and to join with their own names the name of their Nation. This Kingdom for certain years continued in his Family, and grew ſo great in the days of *Elcan Caliph*, who entred on that Principality and Prieſthood in the year of our Lord 996. that he ſent out *Gehor*, by birth a *Dalmatian* (whom of a Slave he had made of his Council) with a mighty Army; who ſubdued all *Numidia* and *Barbary*; and in a ſecond expedition conquered both *Egypt* and *Syria*. But miſtruſting the Forces of *Eluir Caliph* of *Babylon*, (to whom the *Vice-Caliph* of *Egypt* was fled) he built for a refuge this great, and then ſtrong City, which he named *Elchairo* in memorial of the other. *Scaliger* the elder writes, that *Gehor* built it to fortifie himſelf againſt his Maſter, having rebelled: but *Leo* the *African*, that he ſent for the *Caliph* into *Barbary*, and inveſted him in his Conqueſts. This City is ſeated on the Eaſt-ſide of the River, at the foot of the Rocky Mountain *Muccat*: winding therewith, and repreſenting the form of a Creſcent: ſtretching South and North with the adjoining Suburbs, five *Italian* miles; in breadth ſcarce one and a half where it is at the broadeſt. The Walls (if it be walled) rather ſeem to belong unto private houſes than otherwiſe: yet is the City of a marvellous ſtrength: as appeared by that three days Battel carried through it by *Selymus*, and maintained by a
poor

poor remainder of the *Mamalucks*. For the Streets are narrow, and the Houses high-built, all of Stone, well-nigh to the top: at the end almost of each a Gate; which shut (as nightly they are) make every Street as defensive as a Castle. The Houses more beautiful without, than commodious within: being ill contrived with comberfom passages. Yet are the roofs high pitcht: and the uppermost lightly open in the midst, to let in the comfortable air: flat and plaistered above; the walls surmounting their Roofs, commonly of single Bricks, (as are many of the Walls of the uppermost Stories) which ruined on the top, to such as stand aloft afford a confused spectacle: and may be compared to a Grove of flourishing Trees, that have only seer and perished Crowns. Their Locks and Keys be of Wood, even unto Doors that are plated with Iron. But the private Buildings are not worth the mentioning, if compared to the publick: Of which the Mosques exceed in magnificency: the Stones of many being curiously carved without, supported with Pillars of Marble, adorned with what Art can devise, and their Religion tolerate. Yet differ they in form from those of *Constantinople*; some being square with open Roofs in the middle of a huge proportion, the covered circle tarrast above: others stretching out in length; and many fitted unto the place where they stand. One built (and that the greatest) by *Gihor* called *Gemith sharè*: He being named *Hashare* by the *Caliph*, which signifieth Noble. Of these in this City there is reported to be such a number as passes belief; so that I list not name it. Adjoining unto them are Lodgings for *Santons* (which are Fools and mad men) of whom we have spoken already. When one of them dye, they carry his body about in Procession, with great rejoycings: whose soul they suppose to be wrapt into Paradise. Here be also divers goodly Hospitals, both for Building, Revenue, and Attendance: amongst which, that built by *Pisor* the first Sultan of the *Mamalucks*, is most remarkable; endowed by him with the yearly Revenue of two hundred thousand *Shariffs*. Next to these in beauty are the great inens *Seraglio's*: by which if a Christian ride, they will pull him from his Ass (for they prohibite us Horses, as not worthy to bestride them) with indignation and contumely. The Streets are unpaved, and exceeding dirty after a shower (for here it raineth sometimes in the Winter, contrary to the received opinion, and then most subject to Plagues) over which many beams are laid athwart on the tops of Houses, and covered with Mats, to shelter them from the Sun. The like coverture there is between two high Mosques in the principal Street of the City: under which, when the *Bassa* passeth, or others of Quality, they shoot up Arrows, which stick above in abundance. The occasion of that Custom I know not. During our abode in the City, fell out the Feast of their little *Byram*, when in their private Houses they slaughter a number of Sheep; which cut in gobbets, they distribute unto their Slaves and to the poorer sort of people, besmearing the doors with their blood: perhaps in imitation of the Passover. The *Nyle* (a mile distant) in the time of the inundation, by sundry Chanels flows into the City. When these Chanels grow empty, or the water corrupted, they have it brought them thenceforth from the River, by Camels. For although they have many Wells, yet is the water bad, and good for no other use than to cool the Streets, or to cleanse their Houses. In the heart of the Town stands a spacious Cane, which they call the *Besestan*, in which (as in those at *Constantinople*) are sold all kind of Wares of the finer sort: selling old things by the call of, *Who gives more*? imitating therein the *Venetians*, or imitated by them. Three principal Gates thereby to this City: *Beb. Naufree*, or the Gate of Victory, opening towards the Red Sea; *Beb. Zuelia*, leading to *Nilus* and the old Town (between these the chief Street of the City doth extend) and *Bebel Futuli*, or the Port of Triumph, on the North of the City, and opening to the Lake called *Esbikie*. Three sides thereof are inclosed with goodly Buildings, having Galleries of pleasure which jet over sustained upon Pillars. On the other side (now a heap of ruines) stood the stately Palace of *Dultibie*, Wife to the *Sultan Caitheus*: in which were doors and jaumes of Ivory; the Walls and Pavements checquered with discoloured Marble: Columns of Porphyry, Alabaster, and Serpentine: the Cielings flourished with Gold and Azure, and in-laid with Indian Ebony, a Wood affirmed to be only proper to that Country.

India only doth enjoy	——Sola India nigrum
The growing sable Ebony.	Fert Ebenum ——
	Virg. Georg. l. 2.

Yet manifest it is, that there grew thereof by the Lake *Mareotis*,

Nor

―Hebenus Mareotica vastos
Non operit postes.
  Lucan. 10.

―nigris Meroen fecunda colonis,
Lɛta comis hebeni.―
  Ibid.

――*Nor are the mighty Pillars wrought,*
With Ebony from Mareotis brought.

And in the Island of *Meroes,*

Black peopl'd Meroes (hemm'd with Rocks,)
Exulting in her Ebon locks.

a Tree, which being cut down, almost equals a Stone in hardness. In a word, the magnificency was such as could be devised or effected by a Womans curiosity, and the Purse of a Monarch. Levelled with the ground by *Selymus,* the Stones and Ornaments thereof were conveyed unto *Constantinople.* The Lake both square and large, is but only a Lake when the River over-floweth; being joined thereunto by a Chanel; where the *Moors,* (rowed up and down in Barges, shaded with Damasks and Stuffs of *India*) accustom to solace themselves in the Evening. The water fallen, yet the place rather changeth than loseth its delightfulness: affording the profit of five Harvests in a year, together with the pleasure; frequented much in the cool of the day. I cannot forget the injury received in this place, and withall the Justice. Abused by a beggarly *Moor* (for such only will) who then but seemed to begin his Knavery, we were glad to fly unto another for succour, seeming a man of good sort; and by kissing of his Garment, insinuated into his favour; who rebuked him for the wrong he did us. When crossing us again, e're we had gone far, he used us far worse than before. We offered to return to the other, which he hearing, interposed: doing us much villany, to the merriment of the beholders, esteeming of Christians as of Dogs and Infidels. At length we got by, and again complained; He in a marvellous rage made his Slaves to pursue him; who caught him, stript him, and beat him with rods all along the level; calling us to be lookers on, and so conveyed him to the place of correction; where, by all likelihood, he had an hundred blows on the feet to season his pastimes. Beyond this, are a number of straggling Houses extending well-nigh to *Bolac,* which is the Key unto *Cairo*: a large Town, and stretching alongst the River, in fashion of building, in some part not much inferiour to the other. Within and without the City are a number of delicate Orchards, watered as they do their Fields, in which grow variety of excellent Fruits: as Oranges, Lemmons, Pomegranates, Apples of Paradise, Sicamore Figs, and others (whose Barks they bore full of holes, the Trees being as great as the greatest Oaks, the Fruit not growing amongst the Leaves, but out of the Bole and Branches) Dates, Almonds, Cassia fistula, (leaved like an Ash, the Fruit hanging down like Sausages; Locust, flat, and the form of a Cycle) Galls growing upon Tamarix, Apples no bigger than Berries, Plantains, that have a broad flaggy leaf growing in Clusters, and shapen like Cucumers, the rind like a Pescod, solid within, without Stones or Kernels, to the taste exceeding delicious, (this the *Mahometans* say was the forbidden Fruit; which being eaten by our first Parents, and their nakedness discovered unto them, they made them Aprons of the leaves thereof) all the year, and many more not known by name, nor seen by me elsewhere: some bearing Fruit all the year, and almost all of them their leaves. To these add those whole Fields of Palms; (and yet no prejudice to the under-growing Corn) of all others most delightful.

In the aforesaid Orchards are great numbers of Camelions; yet not easily found, in that near to the colour of that whereon they sit. A creature about the bigness of an ordinary Lizard. His head unproportionably big, his eyes great and moving, without the writhing of his neck which is inflexible: his back crooked, his skin spotted with little tumours, less eminent as nearer the belly; his tail slender and long: on each foot he hath five fingers, three on the outside, and two on the inside: slow of pace, but swiftly intending his tongue, of a marvellous length for proportion of his body, wherewith he preys upon flyes, the top whereof being hollowed by Nature for that purpose. So that deceived they be, who think that they eat nothing, but only live upon air; though surely air is their principal sustenance. For those that have kept them for a whole year together, could never perceive that they fed upon any thing else; and might observe their bellies to swell after they had drawn in the air, and closed their jaws, which they expanse against the Rays of the Sun. Green they be of colour, and of a dusky yellow; brighter and whiter towards the belly; yet spotted with blue, white, and red. They change not into all colours as

reported:

reported; laid upon green, the green predominates; upon yellow the yellow: but laid upon blue, or red, or white, the green retaineth his hue notwithstanding, only the other spots receive a more orient lustre: laid upon black, they look black, yet not without a mixture of green. All of them in all places are not coloured alike. They are said to bear a deadly hatred to the Serpent: insomuch as when they espy them basking in the Sun, or in the shade, they will climb to the over-hanging branches, and let down from their mouths a thread, like to that of a Spinster, having at the end a little round drop which shineth like Quick-silver, that falling on their heads doth destroy them: and what is more to be admired, if the boughs hang not so over, that the thread may perpendicularly descend, with their former feet they will so direct it, that it shall fall directly. Aloft, and near the top of the Mountain, against the South end of the City, stands the Castle, (once the stately Mansion of the *Mamaluck Sultans*, and destroyed by *Selymus*) ascended unto by one way only, and that hewn out of the Rock, which rising leisurely with easie steps and spacious distances, (though of a great height) may be on Horseback without difficulty mounted. From the top, the City by reason of the Palms dispersed throughout, appeareth most beautiful; the whole Country below lying open to the view. The Castle so great, that it seemeth a City of it self, immured with high Walls, divided into partitions, and entred by doors of Iron; wherein are many spacious Courts, in times past the places of exercise. The ancient Buildings all ruinated, do only shew that they have been sumptuous; there being many Pillars of solid Marble yet standing, and of so huge a proportion, that how they came thither is not least to be wondred at. Here hath the *Bassa* his residence, wherein the *Divan* is kept on Sundays, Mondays, and Tuesdays: the *Chauses* as Advocates, preferring the suits of their Clients. Forty *Janizaries* he hath of his Guard, attired like those at *Constantinople*: the rest employed about the Country, for the most part are not the Sons of Christians; yet faithful unto such as are under their charges; whom, should they betray, they not only lose their lives, but also the pay which is due to their posterity. Such is this City, the fairest in *Turkie*, yet differing from what it was, as from a body being young and healthful, doth the same grown old and wasted with diseases.

Hither, the sacred thirst of gain, and fear of poverty, allureth the adventurous Merchant from far removed Nations: by reason of the Trade with *India*, and neighhood of the Red Sea; being from hence not past two days journey: so called of *Erythra* an *Egyptian* King, which signifieth *Red* in that language. Yet little is the *Turk* advantaged thereby: slothful, of a gross conceit to devise new ways unto profit; and unexpert in Navigation; which to an industrious and knowing people would afford an unspeakable benefit. Neverthelefs they have here a Haven called *Sues*, heretofore *Arsinoes*, flourishing and abounding with Merchandise in the time of the *Ptolomies*. Built by *Philadelphus*, and so named in honour of his Sister, a Lady of surpassing beauty, given in marriage to *Lysimachus* King of *Macedon*. The Sea there being at a low water, no broader than a River: and every where dangerous to sail through, by reason of the multitude of shelves and un-discoverable Rocks. Speaking of this Sea, I cannot but remember the wonderful project of *Cleopatra*, who flying from the Battel of *Actium*, and gathering together all her portable riches, attempted to have hoist her shipping out of the Mid-land-sea, and to have haled them into this; with purpose to have planted in another Country, removed far from the danger and bondage threatned by that War: but the coming of *Anthony* altered her purpose. Now it is a place of small Commerce, and inhabited by a few in regard of the scarcity of all manner of provision, and penury of waters. Yet is there a station for Gallies, being in number about five and twenty. These are brought from *Constantinople* unto *Cairo*; and taken in pieces, are carried unto *Sues* upon Camels, and there put together. But the main of Commodities which come to *Cairo*, are brought over land by *Caravan* from *Mecha*; as precious Stones, Spices, Stuffs of *India*, Indico, Gums, Amber, all sorts of Perfumes, &c. But the *English* have so ill utterance for their warm Clothes in these hot Countries, that I believe they will rather suffer their Ships to rot in the River, than continue that Trade any longer.

Now *Cairo* this great City is inhabited by *Moors*, *Turks*, *Negroes*, *Jews*, *Copties*, *Greeks*, and *Armenians*; who are here the poorest, and every where the honestest: labouring painfully, and living soberly. Those that are not subject to the *Turk*, if taken in Wars, are freed from bondage: who are, live freely, and pay no tribute of Children as do other Christians. This priviledge enjoy they, for that a

certain

Laonicus Chal. l.

certain *Armenian* foretold of the greatness and glory of *Mahomet*. They once were under the Patriarch of *Constantinople*: but about the Heresie of *Eutiches*, they fell from his Government and Communion with the *Grecians*, whom they detest above all other: re-baptizing such as convert to their Sect. They believe that there is but one Nature in Christ, not by a commixion of the Divine with the Humane, as *Eutyches* taught, but by a conjunction: even as the soul is joined to the body. They deny the real presence in the Sacrament, and administer it as the *Coptics* do: with whom they agree also, concerning Purgatory, and not praying for the dead: as with the *Greeks*, that the Holy Ghost proceedeth only from the Father, and that the dead neither do, nor shall feel joy or torment until the day of Doom. Their Patriarch hath his being at *Tyberis* in *Persia*: in which Country they live wealthily, and in good estimation. There are three hundred Bishops of that Nation. Priests marry not twice; eat flesh but five times a year; and then, lest the people should think it a sin to eat in regard of their abstinence. They err that write, that the people abstain from all meats prohibited by the Mosaical Law; for Hogs flesh they eat where they can without offence to the *Mahometans*. They observe the Lent most strictly: yet eat flesh upon *Fridays* between *Easter* and *Whitsuntide*. As for Images they adore them not. Here they have their Assemblies in obscure Chambers. Coming in (which was on a Sunday in the Afternoon) we found one sitting in the midst of the Congregation, in habit not differing from the rest, reading on a Bible in the *Chaldean* Tongue. Anon the Bishop entred in a Hood and Vest of black, with a Staff in his hand; to which they attributed much holiness. First, he prayed, and then sung certain Psalms, assisted by two or three; after all sung jointly, at interims praying to themselves; resembling the *Turks* in the posture of their bodies, and after prostrations: the Bishop excepted; who erecting his hands, stood all the while with his face to the Altar. The Service ended, one after another do kiss his hand, and bestow their Alms, he laying the other on their heads, and blessing them. Lastly, he prescribeth succeeding Fasts and Festivals. Where is to be noted, that they fast upon the day of the Nativity of our Saviour.

Here also is a Monastry of Greek *Coloieros*, belonging unto the Capital Monastry of Saint *Katherine* of Mount *Sinai*, from *Cairo* some eight days journey over the Deserts. She is said to be the Daughter of King *Costa*, a King of *Cyprus*, who in the time of *Maxentius* converted many unto Christ. Tortured on a Wheel, and finally beheaded at *Alexandria* (where two goodly Pillars of *Theban* Marble (though half swallowed with ruines,) reserve the memory of the place) she was conveyed (as they affirm) by an Angel, and buried in this Mountain. It hath three tops of a marvellous height: that on the West side, of old called Mount *Horeb*, where God appeared to *Moses* in a Bush; fruitful in Pasturage, far lower, and shadowed when the Sun ariseth to the middlemost: which is that whereon God gave the Law unto *Moses*. The Monastry stands at the foot of the Mountain, resembling a Castle, with an Iron door; wherein they shew the Tomb of the Saint much visited by Pilgrims, from whence the top by fourteen thousand steps of Stone is ascended, where stands a ruined Chappel. A plentiful Spring descendeth from thence, and watering the Valley below, is again drunk up by the thirsty sand. This strong Monastry is to entertain all Pilgrims, (for there is no other place of entertainment) having an annual revenue of 60000 Dollars from Christian Princes. Of which foundation six ... twenty other depend, dispersed through divers Countries. They give also daily a... to the *Arabs*, to be the better secured from outrage. Yet they will not suffer them to enter, but let it down from the Battlements. Their Orchard aboundeth with excellent Fruits: amongst which are Apples rare in these Countries, transferred from *Damasco*. They are neither subject to Pope nor Patriarch; but have a Superintendent of their own, at this present in *Cairo*. These here made us a Collation, where I could not but observe their gulling in of Wine with a dear felicity; whereof they have their provision from *Candy*.

Four Sects of *Mahometans* there were in the time of *Leo Africanus*, in this City: sprung in times past from four several Interpreters of the *Alcoran*; who will not easily relinquish their opinions. Yet do they not traduce one another, although they repute each other for heretical. That called *Chenefsia* is the principal; whose Priests do feed on Horse-flesh. Such Horses as are unfit for service their Caterers do buy, and fat for their Palats. Each Sectary is punished for transgressions against the rules of their Religion by the Judge of that Order.

During

During our aboad here, a *Caravan* went forth with much solemnity, to meet and relieve the great Caravan in their return from *Mecha*, which consisteth of many thousands of Pilgrims that travel yearly thither in devotion and for merchandize; every one with his ban-roll in his hand: and their Camels gallantly trickt, (the *Alcoran* carried upon one in a precious case covered over with Needle-work, and laid on a rich Pillow, environed with a number of their chanting Priests) guarded by divers Companies of Souldiers, and certain Field-pieces. Forty calme days journey it is distant from hence: divided by a Wildernefs of Sand, that lyeth in drifts, and dangerously moveth with the wind: through which they are guided in many places by Stars, as Ships in the Ocean. Now within three days journey they ascend a Mountain (the same, they say, where *Abraham* would have sacrificed *Isaac*.) Here sacrifice they a number of Sheep: and stripping themselves, wrapt only in a Mantle without knot or hem, proceed unto *Mecha*. Where is a little Chappel (within a goodly Mosque) about eight yards square: the cause of this devotion, (towards which, when they pray, wheresoever they be, they do return their faces) built, as they affirm, by *Abraham*: within, it is hung with Crimson Sattin, and vested about with a richer stuff, sent thither yearly by the Emperour, (as to that of *Medina*, *Talnaby*,) provided at *Cairo*; the * *Emer* of *Mecha* having the old for his fee. The Camels that bring them, are from thenceforth freed from Burthens. But a sight it is no lefs strange than ridiculous, to behold the honour they do unto the Camel at his return unto *Constantinople*, that supported their *Alcoran*, (as at *Cairo* in some sort to that that carried the vestures) crowding about him, as led through the Streets: some pulling off his hairs, and preserving them as Reliques, some kissing, others with his sweat besmearing their eyes and faces: and cutting him at length into little Gobbets, give thereof to eat unto their Friends and Familiars. Many of the Pilgrims by poaring on hot Bricks, do voluntarily perish their sights, as desiring to see nothing profane, after so sacred a spectacle. He that at his return giveth over the World, and himself to contemplation, is esteemed as a Saint; all are called * *Hadges*; and so call they their Camels; hanging as many little Chains about their fore-legs, as they have been times there. In that City of *Mecha*, some say, their false Prophet was born; but erroneously. Seated it is in a pleasant soil, but environed with desarts and hills; having no water but what proceedeth from one Spring, which they say was shewed by an Angel unto *Hagar*, and almost miraculous it is that it should suffice such a multitude of people and cattel. A place of principal traffick; not only by the means of the *Indian* Caravans, which thither yearly repair with their Commodities; but of the Country adjoining, whose precious productions have instiled it happy.

* *A Giver, none or Lord.*

* *A word importing holinefs.*

——— In *Costus, Amomum,*
And * *Cinnamon, rich let Panchaia be:*
Bear't incenfe and rare flowers; fo it bear thee,
O Myrrhe ———

——— sit dives Amomo,
Cinnamaque costuinque suam, su lataque ligno
Thura ferat florefque alios Panchaia tellus:
Dum foret & myrtham. *Ovid. Met. l. 10.*
* Now no Cinnamon grows in Arabia.

Into which the Poets feign that the incestuous Lady was converted.

Who though she lost sense with her form, yet she
Weeps still, and warm drops fall from the sad tree;
Tears of high value, which retain as yet
Their Mistris name whom no Age shall forget.

Et quanquam amisit veteres cum corpore sensus
Flet tamen, & tepidæ manant ex arbore guttæ.
Est honor in lachrymis, stilla atque cortice Myrrha
Nomen herile tenet, nulloque tacebitur ævo.
Idem.

The Christian dyeth that approacheth this place within five miles compafs. After fourteen days they return unto the aforesaid Mountain; a part of them parting from the rest, going out of the way to *Medina Talnabi*, which is by interpretation, The City of the Prophet; famous for concourse of people; though in a barren Country; scarce two days journey from *Mecha*. Where in a little Chappel lightned with three thousand Lamps that there burn perpetually, lie *Mahomet, Omer*, and *Halys*; in simple Tombs of the ancient fashion, cut out like Lozenges. That of *Mahomet* (not hanging in the air, as reported) is covered with green, having on the top a Carbuncle as big as an Egg, which yields a marvellous lustre. These meet again with the rest of the Caravan at the place appointed.

But to digress no farther. Than *Cairo* no City can be more populous, nor better served with all sorts of provision. Here hatch they Eggs by artificial heat in infinite

infinite numbers; the manner as seen thus briefly. In a narrow entry on each side stood two rows of Ovens, one over another. On the Floors of the lower, they lay the offels of Flax; over those Mats, and upon them Eggs; at least six thousand in an Oven. The floors of the upper Ovens were as roofs to the under: grated over like Kilns, only having Tunnels in the middle, with Covers unto them. These gratings are covered with Mats, on them, three Inches thick, lyeth the dry and pulverated dung of Camels, Buffaloes, &c. At the higher and farther sides of those upper Ovens, are Trenches of Lome; a handful deep, and two handfuls broad. In these they burn of the forelaid dung, which giveth a smothering heat, without visible Fire. Under the mouths of the upper Ovens are Conveyances for smoak: having round roofs, and vents at the top to shut and to open. Thus lie the Eggs in the lower Ovens for the space of eight days: turned daily, and carefully lookt to, that the heat be but moderate. Then cull they the bad from the good, by that time distinguishable (holding them between a lamp and the eye) which are two parts of the three for the most part. Two days after they put out the fire, and convey by the passage in the middle, the one half into the upper Ovens: then shutting all close, they let them alone for ten days longer; at which time they become disclosed in an instant. This they practise from the beginning of *January* until the midst of *June*, the Eggs being then most fit for that purpose, neither are they (as reported) prejudiced by Thunder: yet these declare that intimated Nature will never be equalled; all of them being in some part defective or monstrous.

Most of the Inhabitants of *Cairo* consists of Merchants and Artificers: yet the Merchants frequent no foreign Marts. All of a Trade keep their Shops in one place, which they shut about the hour of five, and solace themselves for the rest of the day, Cooks excepted, who keep theirs open till late in the evening. For few but such as have great Families dress meat in their Houses, which the men do buy ready drest, the women too fine fingered to meddle with Housewifry, who ride abroad upon pleasure on easie going Asses, and tye their Husbands to the benevolence that is due; which, if neglected they will complain to the Magistrate, and procure a divorcement. Many Practitioners here are in Physick, invited thereunto by the store of Simples brought hither, and here growing: an art wherein the *Egyptians* have excelled from the beginning.

Talia Jovis filia habebat pharmaca utilia	Such *Helens* potion was; a friend to life:
Bona, quæ illi *Polydamna* præbuit *Theonis* uxor	Egyptian *Polydamne's* gift, *Theons* Wife.
Ægyptica, quæ plurima producit fertilia terra	That fruitful soil doth many Drugs produce,
Pharmaca, plurima quidem salubria mixta, multa lethalia.	Hurtful and healthful fit for every use;
Medicus vero unusquisque peritus supra omnes	All are Physicians, expert above all:
Homines: sane enim Pæionis sunt ex generatione.	And fetch from *Pæion* their original.
Hom. Odyff l.4.	

A kind of Rue is here, much in request, wherewith they perfume themselves in the mornings; not only a preservative against infection, but esteeming it prevalent against hurtful spirits. So the Barbarians of old accustomed to do with the roots of wild Galingal. There are in this City, and have been of long, a sort of people that do get their livings by shewing of feats with Birds and Beasts, exceeding therein all such as have been famous amongst us: I have heard a Raven speak so perfectly, as hath amazed me. They use both their throats and tongues in uttering of sounds, which other Birds do not: and therefore more fit for that purpose. *Scaliger* the Father, reports of one that was kept in a Monastry hard by him; which when hungry, would call upon *Comrade* the Cook so plainly, as often mistaken for a man. I have seen them make both Dogs and Goats, to set their four feet on a little turned Pillar of wood about a foot high, and no broader at the end than a palm of a hand: climing from one to two, set on the top of one another, and so to the third and fourth; and there turn about as often as their Masters would bid them. They carry also dancing Camels about, taught when young, by setting them on the hot hearth, and playing all the while on an Instrument, the poor beast through the extremity of heat, lifting up his feet one after another. This practise they for certain Months together: so that at length whensoever he heareth the Fiddle, he will fall a dancing. Asses they will teach to do such tricks, as it possest with reason: to whom *Banks* his Horse would have proved but a *Zany*.

The time of our departure prorogued, we rode to *Mataræa*; five Miles North-east of the City. By the way we saw sand fall upon the Earth, to moderate the fertility.

Here

LIB. II.   *Matarea.*   *The Pyramides.*   99

Here they say, that our Saviour and the blessed Virgin, with *Joseph*, reposed themselves, as they sled from the fury of *Herod*; when oppressed with thirst, a Fountain forthwith burst forth at their feet to refresh them. We saw a well environed with a poor Mud wall, the Water drawn up by *Buffolo's* into a little Cistern, from whence it ran into a Laver of Marble within a small Chappel, by the *Moors* (in contempt of Christians) spitefully defiled. In the wall there is a little concave lined with sweet Wood (diminished by affectors of Reliques) and smoaked with Incense: in the sole, a Stone of Porphyry, whereon (they say) she did set our Saviour. Of so many thousand Wells (a thing most miraculous) this only affordeth gustable Waters: and that so excellent, that the *Bassa* refuseth the River to drink thereof, and drinks of no other; and when they cease for any time to exhaust it, it sendeth forth of it self so plentiful a stream, as is able to turn an Over-fall Mill. Passing through the Chappel, it watereth a pleasant Orchard; in a corner whereof there standeth an over-grown Fig-tree, which opened (as they report) to receive our Saviour and his Mother, then hardly escaping the pursuers; closing again till the pursuit was past; then again dividing, as now it remaineth. A large hole there is through one of the sides of the leaning bulk; this (they say) no bastard can thread, but shall stick fast by the middle. The Tree is all to be hackt for the Wood thereof, reputed of soveraign virtue. But I abuse my time, and provoke my Reader. In an inclosure adjoining, they shewed us a Plant of Balm; the whole remainder of that store which this Orchard produced; destroyed by the *Turks*, or envy of the *Jews*, as by the other reported; being transported out of *Jury*, in the days of *Herod* the Great, by the commandment of *Antonius*, at the suit of *Cleopatra*; but others say, brought hither out of *Arabia Felix*, at the cost of a *Saracen Sultan*.

Salim-cus ivit. 10 c. 6. dares tore port Cair: saith himself seeing it) that from Sunday at noon until Munday morning they will not labour in the drawing up of water, though urged with stripes.

A day or two after, we crossed the *Nilus*. Three miles beyond on the left hand left we the place, where upon *Good Friday*, the Arms and Legs of a number of men appear stretched forth of the earth, to the astonishment of the multitude. This I have heard confirmed by *Christians*, *Mahometans*, and *Jews*, as seen upon their several Faiths. An imposture perhaps contrived by the Water-men, who fetching them from the Mummies (whereof there are an un-consumable number) and keeping the mystery in their Families, do stick them over-night in the sand; obtaining thereby the yearly Ferrying over of many thousands of Passengers. Three or four miles farther, on the right hand, and in sight, athwart the Plain, there extendeth a Causey supported with Arches, five Furlongs long, ten paces high, and five in breadth, of smooth and figured Stone; built by the Builder of the Piramides, for a passage over the soft and unsupporting earth with weighty Carriages. Now having ridden over a goodly Plain, some twelve miles over, (in that place the whole breadth of *Egypt*) we came to the foot of the *Lybian Desarts*.

Full West of the City, close upon those Desarts, aloft on a rocky level adjoining to the Valley, stand those three Pyramides (the barbarous Monuments of prodigality and vain-glory) so universally celebrated. The name is derived from a flame of fire in regard of their shape, broad below, and sharp above, like a pointed Diamond. By such the Ancient did express the original of things; and that formless form-taking substance. For as a Pyramis beginning at a point, and the principal height by little and little dilateth into all parts: so Nature proceeding from one undivideable Fountain (even God the Soveraign Essence) receiveth diversity of Forms; effused into several kinds and multitudes of Figures; uniting all in the Supreme head, from whence all excellencies issue. The labours of the *Jews*, as themselves report, and is alledged by *Josephus*, were employed in these; which deserveth little better credit (for what they built was of Brick) than that absurd opinion of *Nazianzenus*; who, out of the consonancy of the names, affirmeth, that they were built by *Joseph* for Granaries, against the seven years of Famine; when as one was thrice seven years, saving one, in erecting. But by the testimony of all that have writ, amongst whom *Lucan*,

When high Pyramides do grace   Quum Ptolomæorum manes seriemq; pudendam
The Ghosts of Ptolomies lewd race: Pyramides claudant.   *l.8.*

and by what shall be said hereafter, most manifest it is that these, as the rest, were the regal Sepulchres of the *Egyptians*. The greatest of the three, and chief of the worlds seven wonders, being square at the bottom, is supposed to take up eight Acres of ground. Every square being 300 single paces in length, the square at the top,

K 2   consisting

The Pyramides. LIB. II.

confisting of three Stones only, yet large enough for threescore to stand upon, ascended by two hundred fifty five steps, each step above three feet high, of a breadth proportionable. No Stone so little throughout the whole, as to be drawn by our Carriages: yet were these hewn out of the *Trojan* Mountains far off in *Arabia*; so called of Captive *Trojans* brought by *Menalaus* unto *Egypt*, and there afterward planted. A wonder how conveyed hither: how so mounted, a greater. Twenty

years was it building; by three hundred threescore and six thousand men continually wrought upon: who only in Radishes, Garlick, and Onions, are said to have consumed one thousand and eight hundred Talents. By these and the like inventions exhausted they their Treasure, and employed the people; for fear left such infinite wealth should corrupt their Successors, and dangerous idleness beget in the Subject a desire of innovation. Besides, they considering the frailty of man, that in an instant buds, blows, and withereth; did endeavour by such sumptuous and magnificent Structures, in spite of death to give unto their fames eternity. But vainly:

Nam neque Pyramidum sumptus ad Sydera ducti,	*Not sumptuous Pyramids to Skies up-rear'd,*
Nec Jovis Elæi cœlum imitata domus,	*Nor Elean Joves proud Fane, which Heaven competr'd,*
Nec Mausolæi dives fortuna sepulchri,	*Nor the right fortune of Mausolus Tomb,*
Mortis ab extrema conditione vacant:	*Are priviledg'd from deaths extremest doom:*
Aut illis flamma, aut imber subducet honores,	*Or fire, or worms, their glories do abate,*
Annorum aut ictu pondere victa ruent.	*Or they, age-shaken, fall with their own weight.*
Propert.l.3.Eleg 3.	

Yet this hath been too great a morsel for time to devour; having stood, as may be probably conjectured, about three thousand and two hundred years: and now rather old than ruinous: yet the North-side is most worn, by reason of the humidity of the Northern wind, which is here the moistest. The top at length we ascended, with many pauses and much difficulty; from whence, with delighted eyes, we beheld that Soveraign of Streams, and most excellent of Countries. South-ward and near hand the *Mummes*: afar off divers huge Pyramides; each of which, were this away, might supply the repute of a wonder. During a great part of the day, it casteth no shadow on the earth, but is at once illuminated on all sides. Descending again, on the East-side below, from each corner equally distant, we approached the entrance, seeming heretofore to have been closed up, or so intended, both by the place it self, as appeareth by the following Picture and conveyances within. Into this our *Janizaries* discharged their Harquebushes, lest some should have skulkt within

to

LIB. II.   *The Pyramides.*   181

The entrance in to the Great Pyramis

to have done us a mischief, and guarded the mouth whilst we entred, for fear of the wild *Arabs*. To take the better footing, we put off our shoes, and most of our apparel; fore-told of the heat within not inferiour to a Stove. Our guide (a *Moor*:) went foremost: every one of us with our lights in our hands. A most dreadful passage, and no less cumbersom; not above a yard in breadth, and four feet in height, each stone containing that measure. So that always stooping, and sometimes creeping, by reason of the rubbidge, we descended (not by stairs, but as down the steep of a hill) a hundred feet, where the place for a little circuit enlarged, and the fearful descend continued, which they say none ever durst attempt any farther, save that a *Bassa* of *Cairo*, curious to search into the secrets thereof, caused divers condemned persons to undertake the performance, well stored with lights, and other provision; and that some of them ascended again well-nigh thirty miles off in the Desarts. A Fable devised only to beget wonder. But others have written, that at the bottom there is a spacious Pit, eighty and six Cubits deep, filled at the over-flow by concealed Conduits: in the midst a little Island, and on that a Tomb containing the body of *Cheops*, a King of *Egypt*, and the builder of this *Pyramis*: which with the truth hath a greater affinity. For since I have been told by one out of his own experience, that in the uppermost depth there is a large square place, (though without water) into which he was led by another entry opening to the South, known but unto few (that now open, being shut by some order) and entred at this place where we feared to descend. A turning on the right hand leadeth into a little room: which by reason of the noysom savour and uneasie passage, we refused to enter. Clambering over the mouth of the aforesaid dungeon, we ascended as upon the bow of an arch, the way no larger than the former, about an hundred and twenty feet.

K 3   Here

The Pyramides. The Colossus. LIB. II.

Here we passed thorow a long entry, which led directly forward; so low, that it took even from us that uneasie benefit of stooping. Which brought us into a little Room with a compact Roof, more long than broad, of polished Marble; whose Grave-like smell, half full of Rubbidge, forced our quick return. Climing also over this entrance, we ascended as before, about an hundred and twenty feet higher. This entry was of an exceeding height, yet no broader from side to side than a man may fathom; benched on each side, and closed above with admirable Architecture: the Marble so great, and so cunningly joined, as it had been hewn through the living Rock. At the top we entred into a goodly Chamber, twenty foot wide, and forty in length: the Roof of a marvellous height, and the Stones so great, that eight floors it, eight roofs it, eight flag the ends, and sixteen the sides, all of well-wrought *Theban* Marble. A'thwart the Room at the upper end there standeth a Tomb, uncovered, empty, and all of one stone, brest high, seven feet in length, not four in breadth, and sounding like a Bell. In this (no doubt) lay the body of the builder. They erecting such costly Monuments, not only out of a vain ostentation, but being of opinion, that after the dissolution of the flesh the soul should survive; and when thirty six thousand years were expired, again be joined unto the self-same body restored unto his former condition, gathered in their conceipts from Astronomical demonstrations. Against one end of the Tomb, and close to the wall, there openeth a Pit with a long and narrow mouth, which leadeth into an under Chamber. In the walls on each side of the upper Room there are two holes, one opposite to another; their ends not discernable, nor big enough to be crept into; sooty within, and made as they say, by a flame of fire which darted thorow it. This is all that this huge mass containeth within his darksom entrails, all, at least to be discovered. *Herodotus* reports that King *Cheops* became so poor by the building thereof, that he was compelled to prostitute his daughters; charging her to take whatsoever she could get, who affecting her particular glory, of her several customers demanded several stones, with which she erected the second *Pyramis*, far less than the former, smooth without, and not to be entred. The third which standeth on the higher ground, is very small, if compared with the other, yet saith both *Herodotus* and *Strabo*, greater in beauty, and of no less cost, being all built of Touch-stone; difficult to be wrought, and brought from the farthest *Æthiopian* Mountains. But surely not so, yet intended they to have covered it with *Theban* Marble, whereof a great quantity lieth by it. Made it was by *Mycerinus* the son of *Cheops*, some say by a Curtizan of *Naucretis*, called *Dorica* by *Sappho* the Poetress, and beloved of her brother *Caraxus*, who fraught with Wines, oft sailed hither from *Lesbos*. Others name *Rhodope* another of that Trade; at the first, fellow-slave with *Æsop* the writer of the Fables, who obtaining her liberty dwelt in this City, where rich in some sort were reputed noble. But that she should get by whoring such a mass of treasure, is incredible. Some tell a story, how that one day washing her self, an Eagle snatcht away her shooe, and bearing it to *Memphis*, let it fall from on high into the lap of the King. Who astonished with the accident, and admiring the form, forthwith made a search for the owner thereof throughout all his Kingdom. Found in *Naucretis*, and brought unto him, he made her his Queen, and after her death inclosed her in this Monument. She lived in the days of *Amasis*.

Not far off from these the *Colossus* doth stand, unto the mouth consisting of the natural Rock, as if for such a purpose advanced by Nature, the rest of huge flat stones laid thereon, wrought all together into the form of an *Æthiopian* woman, and adored heretofore by the country people as a rural Deity. Under this, they say, lieth buried the body of *Amasis*. Of shape less monstrous than is *Plinies* report, who affirmeth the head to be an hundred and two feet in compass, when the whole is but sixty feet high. The face is something disfigured by time, or indignation of the *Moors* detesting Images. The aforesaid Author (together with others) do call it a *Sphinx*. The upper part of a *Sphinx* resembled a Maid, and the lower a Lion; whereby the *Egyptians* defigured the increase of the River, (and consequently of their riches) then rising when the Sun is in *Leo* and *Virgo*. This but from the shoulders upward surmounteth the ground, though *Pliny* give it a belly; which I know not how to reconcile unto the truth, unless the Sand do cover the remainder. By a *Sphinx* the *Egyptians* in their hieroglyphicks presented an Harlot; having an amiable, and alluringface, but withal the tyranny, and rapacity of a Lion, exercised over the poor heart-broken, and voluntarily perishing Lover. The Images of these they also erected beforethe entrances of their Temples, declaring that secrets of Philosophy, and sacred mysteries.

mysteries, should be folded in ænigmatical expressions, separated from the understanding of the prophane multitude.

Five miles South-east of these, and two West of the River, towards which inclineth this brow of the Mountain, stood the Regal City of *Memphis*, the strength and glory of old *Egypt*; built by *Ogdoo*, and called *Memphis*, by the name of his daughter, compressed (as they feign) by *Nilus* in the likeness of a Bull. In this was the Temple of *Apis* (which is the same with *Osiris*) as *Osiris* with *Nilus*, *Bacchus*, *Apollo*, &c. For under several names and figures they expressed the divers operations of one Deity, according to that of the Poet:

Pluto, Persephone, Ceres, Venus, Love,
Tritons, Nereus, Thetis, Neptune, Jove,
Pan, Juno, Vulcan, he with th' aweful rod,
Phœbe, and archer Phœbus; all one God.

Pluto, Persephone, Ceres, & Venus alma,& Amores,
Tritones, Nereus, Thetis, Neptunus & ipse
Mercurius, Juno, Vulcanus, Jupiter, & Pan,
Diana, & Phœbus jaculator sunt Deus unus.
Hermesianax.

Here they kept their *Apis*, (whom also they adored) as containing the soul of *Osiris*. A black Bull with a white fore-head; and something differing in shape from the ordinary. By which marks they sought a successor, the old being dead, and mourned till they found him. Unto this adjoined the sumptuous Temple of *Vulcan*, who is said to have been King of *Egypt*, and the first that found out the commodity of fire.

Egyptian Vulcan in the days of Noe,
(Call'd also Noe, Osyris, Dionyse,)
First found out fire, and arts that thence arise.

Vulcanus quidē Ægyptius temporibus Noe,
Qui Noe, & Dionysius & Osiris vocatur,
Invenit ignem, & artes ex igne quæ sunt.
Zezes.

For in the winter season, drawing nigh a Tree set on fire by Lightning, and feeling the comfort of the heat, when almost extinct, he threw on more fuel, and so apprehending the nature and use did teach it unto others. Here also stood the Fane of *Venus*, and that of *Serapis*, beset with *Sphinxes*, adjoining to the Desart, a City great and populous, adorned with a world of Antiquities. But why spend I time about that that is not, the very ruines now almost ruinated? yet some few impressions are left, and divers thrown down, Statues of monstrous resemblances, a scarce sufficient testimony to shew unto the curious seeker, that there it had been. Why then deplore we our humane frailty?

When stones, as well as breath,
And names, do suffer death.

Mors etiam saxis, neminibusque venit.
Auson.

This hath made some erroneously affirm old *Memphis* to have been the same with new *Cairo*, new in respect of the other. But those that have both seen and writ of the former, report it to have stood three Schœnes above the South angle of *Delta*, (each Schœne containing five miles at the least, and sometimes seven and a half, differing according to their several customs) which South angle is distant but barely four miles from *Cairo*. Besides the Pyramides appertaining unto *Memphis*, recorded by *Martial*.

Of her Pyramides let Memphis boast
No more the barbarous wonders of vain cost:

Barbara Pyramidum sileat miracula Memphis.
Spell.

are affirmed to have stood five miles North-west of that City, standing directly West, and full twelve miles from *Cairo*. But the most pregnant proof hereof are the *Mummies*, (lying in a place where many generations have had their Sepultures) not far above *Memphis*, near the brow of the *Lybian* Desart, and straightning of the Mountains, from *Cairo* well-nigh twenty miles. Nor like it is that they would so far carry their dead, having as convenient a place adjoining to the City.

These we had purposed to have seen, but the chargeable guard, and fear of the *Arabs* there then solemnizing their festival; being beside, to have lain out all night, made us content our selves with what we had heard, having before seen divers of the embalmed bodies, and some broken up to be bought for Dollars a piece at the City. In that place are some indifferent great, and a number of little Pyramides, with Tombs of several fashions: many ruinated, as many violated by the *Moors*,

Of the Mummes.   LIB. II.

Moors, and *Arabians*, who make a profit of the dead, and infringe the priviledge of Sepulchres. There were the graves of the ancient *Egyptians*, from the first inhabiting of that Country: coveting to be there interred, as the place supposed to contain the body of *Osyris*. Under every one, or wheresoever lye stones not natural to the place, by removing the same, descents are discovered like the narrow mouths of Wells, (having holes in each side of the walls to descend by, yet so troublesom, that many refuse to go down, that come thither of purpose) some well-nigh ten fathoms deep, leading into long Vaults (belonging as should seem, to particular families) hewn out of the Rock, with pillars of the same. Between every Arch the Corses lye rankt one by another, shrouded in a number of folds of Linen, swathled with bands of the same: the brests of divers being stained with Hieroglyphical characters. Within their bellies are painted papers, and their Gods inclosed in little models of stone or metal: some of the shapes of Men, in Coat-armors, with the heads of Sheep, Hawks, Dogs, &c. others of Cats, Beetles, Monkies, and such like. Of these I brought away divers with me, such in similitude.

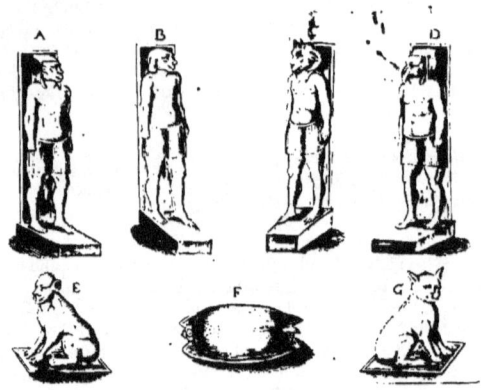

A. *This with the head of a Monkie or Baboon, should seem by what is said before, pag. 81. to have been worshipped by those of Thebais.*
B. *Anubis, whereof Virgil.*

Omnigenumque deum monstra, & latrator Anubis :   *The monster-Gods, Anubis barking, buckle*
Contra Neptunum & Venerem, contraque Minervam,   *With Neptune, Venus, Pallas.*
Tela tenent: Æn. l. 8.

Some say he was the eldest son of Osiris, being figured with the head of a Dog, in that he gave a Dog for his ensign. Others, that under this shape they adored Mercury, in regard of the sagacity of that creature. The Dog throughout Egypt was universally worshipped, but especially by the Cynopolites.
C. *Those of Sait did principally worship the Sheep, it should seem, in this form.*
D. *This I conjecture (however unlike) hath the head of a Hawk, being generally worshipped by the Egyptians; see page 82. under which form they presented Osiris.*
E. *I know not what to make of it: (for the original is greatly defaced) unless it be a Lion, under which shape they adored Isis.*
F. *Not so much as the Beetle but received divine honors : and why? see Plutarch in Isis and Osiris, near the end.*
G. *The Cat all generally adored : they honouring such creatures, for that their vanquisht and run-away Gods took on them such shapes to escape the fury of pursuing Typhon.*

The Linen pulled off (in colour, and like in substance to the inward film between the bark and the bole; long dryed and brittle) the body appeareth solid, uncorrupt and perfect in all his dimensions: whereof the musculous parts are brown of colour, some black, hard as stone-pitch; and have in Physick an operation not unlike, though more soveraign. In the preparing of these, to keep them from putrefaction, they drew out the brains at the nostrils with an Instrument of Iron, replenishing the same with preservative spices. Then cutting up the belly with an *Æthiopian* stone, and extracting the bowels, they cleansed the inside with wine, and stuffing the same with a composition of Cassia, Myrrh, and other odours, closed it again. The like the poorer sort of people effected with Bitumen (as the inside

of

LIB. II.   Of the Mummies. Egyptian Babylon.

of their skulls and bellies yet testifie) fetcht from the Lake of *Asphalites* in *Jury*. So did they with the juice of Cedars; which by the extream bitternels, and siccative faculty, not only forthwith subdued the cause of interior corruption, but hath to this day (a continuance of above three thousand years) preserved them uncorrupted. Such is the differing nature of that Tree, procuring life as it were to the dead, and death to the living. This done, they wrapt the body with Linen in multitudes of folds, besmeared with Gum, in manner of Sear-cloth. Their Ceremonies (which were many) performed, they laid the Corps in a Boat, to be wafted over *Acherusia*, a Lake on the South of the City, by one only whom they called *Charon*: which gave to *Orpheus* the invention of his infernal Ferry-man: an ill-favoured slovenly Fellow, as should seem by *Virgil*:

Charon, grim Ferriman, these streams doth guard,	Portitor has horrendus aquas & flumina servat,
Uglily nasty: his huge boary beard	Terribili squallore Charon, cui plurima mento
Knit up in elf locks, staring-fiery ey'd:	Canities inculta jacet, stant lumina flamma,
With robe on beastly shoulders hung, knot-ty'd.	Sordidus ex humeris nodo dependet amictus.
	Æn.l.6.

About this Lake stood the shady Temple of *Hecate*, with the Ports of *Cocytus*, an Oblivion, separated by Bars of Brass: the original of like Fables. When landed on the other side, the body was brought before certain Judges; to whom, if convinced of an evil life, they deprived it of burial; if otherwise, they suffered it to be interred as aforesaid. So sumptuous were they in their houses of death, so careful to preserve their Carcasses, for so much as the soul, knowing it selt by divine instinct immortal, doth desire that the body (her beloved Companion) might enjoy (as far forth as may be) the like felicity: giving, by erecting such lofty Pyramides, and those dues of Funeral, all possible eternity. Neither was the loss of this less feared, than the obtaining coveted: insomuch that the Kings of *Egypt*, accustomed to awe their Subjects (to them a most powerful curb, and a strong provokement) by threatning to deprive them of sepulture. The terrour of this made *Hector* to flie; the only fear and care of the dying *Mezentius*.

Not ills in death, not so came I to fight;	Nullum in cæde nefas, nec sic ad prælia veni;
Nor made my Lausus such a match. One rite	Nec tecum meus hæc pepigit mihi fœdera Lausus.
Afford (if pity stoop to a vanquisht Foe)	Unum hoc pet, si qua est victis venia hostibus oro,
Inter my Corps. Much hate of mine I know	Corpus humo patrare regi: scio acerba meorum
Infolds me. From their rage my body save:	Circumstare odia; hunc oro defende furorum
And lay me with my Son, both in one grave.	Et me consortem nati concede sepulchro.
	Virg.Æn.l.10.

Returning by the way that we came, and having re-pass'd the *Nilus*, we inclined on the right hand to see the ruines of the old City adjoining to the South of *Cairo*, called formerly *Babylon*, of certain *Babylonians* there suffered to inhabit by the ancient *Egyptian* Kings, who built a Castle in the self same place where that now standeth, described before: which was long after the Garrison Town of one of the three Legions, set to defend this Country in the time of the *Romans*. It anciently gave the name of *Babylon* to this City below; now called *Misrulhetick* by the *Arabians*: said to have been built by *Omar* the successor unto *Mahomet*; but surely rather re-edified by him than founded; having had in it such store of Christian Churches, as is testified by their ruines. We pass'd by a mighty Cistern closed within a Tower, and standing upon an inlet of the River: built, as they here say, at the charge of the *Jews*, to appease the anger of the King, incensed by them against the innocent Christians; who by the removing of a Mountain, (the task imposed upon their Faith) converted him unto their Religion, and his displeasure upon their Accusers. This serveth the Castle with water; running along an Aquaduct born upon 300 Arches. The ruines of the City are great; so were the Buildings: amongst which, many of Christian Monasteries and Temples; one lately (the last that stood) thrown down by this *Bassa* (as they say) for that it hindred his prospect; if so, he surely would not have given leave unto the Patriarch to re-build it: for which he was spitefully spoken of by the *Moors*, as a suspected favourer of the Christian Religion; who subverted forthwith what he had begun. Whereupon the worthy *Cyril* made a Voyage unto *Constantinople*, to procure the Grand Signiors Commandement for the support of his purpose: when by the *Greeks* there, not altogether with his will, he was chosen their Patriarch: but within a short space displanted (as the manner is) by the bribery devotions, and enriching it with their gifts; amounting to an hundred thousand *Shariffs* one year with another: diftributed amongst the poor Kindred of *Mahomet*, and amongst the Priests that had the charge of the Sepulchre; who by divulging forged miracles, increased the number of her Votaries. But *Selymus* fubduing *Egypt*, the Tomb was defaced and ranfackt by his *Janizaries*: who befides the Ornaments of Gold and Silver, took from thence in *Shariffs* above five millions. But the Chriftians fay, that this *Nafiffa* was an unfatiable Harlot; who out of colour (and that for *Mahomets* fake) to convert the unnatural lufts of the people, did proftitute her felf to all comers. The few Inhabitants that here be are *Greeks* and *Armenians*. Here we faw certain great *Siraglio's*, exceeding high, and propt up by buttreffes. Thefe they call the Granaries of *Jofeph*: wherein he hoarded Corn in the years of plenty againft the fucceeding Famine. In all there be feven, three ftanding and employed to the very fame ufe: the other ruined. From thence up the River for twenty miles fpace there is nothing but ruines. Thus with the day we ended our progrefs.

Upon the fourth of *March* we departed from *Cairo*, in the habit of Pilgrims; four of us Englifh, comforted with three Italians: of whom one was a Prieft, and another a Phyfician. For our felves we hired three Camels, with their Keepers; two to carry us, and the third for our provifion. The prize we fhall know at *Gaza*, upon the dividing of the great *Caravan*, anfwerable to the fuccefs of the Journey. We alfo hired a Copty for half a Dollar a day, to be our Interpreter, and to attend on us. Our provifion for fo long a Voyage we bore along with us, viz. Bisket, Rice, Raifins, Figs, Dates, Almonds, Olives, Oil, Sherbets, &c. buying Pewter, Brafs, and fuch like implements, as if to fet up Houfe-keeping. Our Water we carried in Goat-skins. We rid in fhallow Cradles (which we bought alfo) two on a Camel: harboured above, and covered with Linen: to us exceeding uneafie; not fo to the people of thefe Countries, who fit crofs-legg'd with a natural facility. That night we pitched by *Hangia*, fome fourteen miles from the City. In the evening came the Captain: a *Turk* well mounted, and attended on. Here we ftayed the next day following, for the gathering together of the *Caravan*; paying four Madeins a Camel unto them of the Village. Thefe (as thofe elfewhere) do nightly guard, as making good whatfoever is ftoln. Ever and anon one crying *Vafhed*, is anfwered *Elough* by another (jointly fignifying one only God:) which paffing about the *Caravan*, doth affure them that all is in fafety. Among us were divers *Jewifh* Women; in the extremity of their age undertaking fo wearifom a journey, only to dye at *Jerufalem*: bearing along with them the bones of their Parents, Husbands, Children, and Kinsfolk; as they do from all other parts where they can conveniently. The Merchants brought with them many *Negroes*; not the worft of their merchandizes. Thefe they buy of their Parents, fome thirty days journey above, and on the Weft fide of the River. As the wealth of others confifts in multitudes of Cattel; fo theirs in the inultitude of their Children: whom they part from with as little paffion; never after to be feen or heard of: regarding more the price than the condition of their flavery, who are defcended of *Chus*, Son of curfed *Cham*, as are all of that complexion. Not fo by reafon of their feed, nor heat of the Climate: the one confuted by *Ariftotle*, the other by experience, in that Countries, as hot, produce of a different colour, and colder by thirty degrees have done of the fame; (for *Alexander* in his Expedition into the Eaft, encountred Black-men: and fuch was *Memnon* the Son of the *Morning*,

——Nigri non illa parentem
nonis in rofeis fobria vidit equis.
Ovid. Am. l. c. El. 8.

*Black Memnons Mother fhe ne're fober faw
When rofie Steeds her day bright Chariot draw.*

fo feigned to be in that he reigned in the Eaft; who came to the Wars of *Troy* from *Sufis* a City of *Perfia*:) Nor of the foil, as fome have fuppofed; for neither haply will other faces in that foil prove black, nor that race in other foils grow to better complexion: but rather from the curfe of *Noe* upon *Cham* in the pofterity of *Chus*: who inhabited a part of *Mefopotamia*, watered by *Gihon* a River of Paradife, and one of
the

LIB. II.   Bilbesh. Catara. Salhia. Bayrena.

the branches of *Euphrates*. Driven from thence, they planted themselves in *Æthiopia* thereupon called also *Chus*. Perhaps the occasion of that errour in the Translations of *Genesis*; which interpret *Chus* for *Æthiopia*, and *Gihon* for *Nilus*; distant above a thousand times from *Eden*. A circuit without question too spacious for a Garden.

About ten of the Clock in the night the Caravan dislodged: and at seven the next morning pitched at *Bilbesh*, which is in the land of *Goshen*. Paying two Madeins for a Camel, at midnight we departed from thence. Our Companions had their Cradles struck down through the negligence of the Camellers: which accident cast us behind the Caravan. In danger to have been surprised by the Pesants, we were by a *Spahie* that followed, delivered from that mischief. About nine in the Forenoon we pitched by *Catara*: where we payed four Madeins for a Camel. Hereabout, but nearer the *Nile*, there is a certain tree called *Alchan* by the *Arabs*: the leaves thereof being dried, and reduced into powder, do dye reddish yellow. There is yearly spent of this thorow the *Turkish* Empire, to the value of fourscore thousand *Sultanies*. The Women with it do dye their hair and nails: some of them their hands and feet; and not a few, the most of their bodies, tempered only with Gum, and laid on in the *Bannia*, that it may penetrate the deeper. The Christians of *Bosnia*, *Valachia*, and *Russia*; do use it as well as the *Mahometans*. Trees also here be that do bring forth Cottons. The next morning before day we removed, and came by nine of the Clock to *Salhia*, where we overtook the rest of the Caravan: all Christians of those Countries riding upon Mules and Asses. They had procured leave to set forward a day before; desirous to arrive by *Palm-Sunday* at *Jerusalem*; (this Caravan staying ten days longer than accustomed, because of certain principal Merchants) but they durst not by themselves venture over the main Desarts: which all this while we had trented along, and now were to pass through.

A little beneath is the Lake *Sirbonis*, called by the old *Egyptians*, The place of *Typhons* expiration, now *Bayrena*, dividing *Egypt* from *Syria*. A place to such as knew it not, in those times full of unexpected danger. Then two hundred furlongs long being but narrow, and bordered on each side with Hills of Sand, which born into the water by the winds so thickned the same, as not by the eye to be distinguished from a part of the Continent: by means whereof whole Armies have been devoured. For the sands neer hand seeming firm, a good way entred slid farther off, and left no way of returning, but with a lingring cruelty swallowed the ingaged: whereupon it was called *Barathrum*. Now but a little Lake, and waxing less daily: the passage long since choaked up which it had into the Sea. Close to this standeth the Mountain *Cassius*, (no other than a huge mole of sand) famous for the Temple of *Jupiter*, and Sepulchre of *Pompey*: there obscurely buried by the piety of a private Souldier: upon whom he is made by *Lucan* to bellow this Epitaph.

Great Pompey here doth lie ; so Fortune pleas'd	Hic situs est magnus, placet hoc fortuna sepulchrum
To instile this stone; whom Cæsars self would have	Dicere Pompei : quo condit maluit illum
Interr'd before he should have mist a Grave.	Quam terra caruisse Socer.

Who lost his head not far from thence by the treachery and commandment of the ungrateful *Ptolomy*. His Tomb was sumptuously re-edified by the Emperour *Adrian*. North hereof lies *Idumea*, between *Arabia* and the mid-land Sea, extending to *Judæa*: called *Edom* in the Scriptures, of *Esau*; a name which was given him in regard of his colour, which signifieth Red in the Hebrew. Afterward called *Idumea* of the *Idumeans*: a people of *Arabia* the *Happy*; who in a mutiny quitting their Country: did plant themselves here; incorporating with the *Hebrews* (of whom originally descended) and observing their Ceremonies,

| *Idume rich in Palms.* | — A arbusto Palmarum dives Idumea, |
| | Lucan. |

as heretofore with Balsamum, and indifferent fruitful towards the Sea. Difficult to be subdued, by reason of the bordering Desarts and penury of Waters, yet have they many Wells, but hid, and only known to the Inhabitants: who are now subject to the *Turks*; and differ in life and customs not much from the *Arabians*.

The *Subassee* of *Salhia* invited himself to our Tent; who feeding on such provision as we had, would in conclusion have fed upon us; had not our commandment (which stood us in sour Shariffs) from the *Bassa* of *Cairo*, and the favour of
the

the Captain by means of our Physician protected us; otherwise right or wrong had been but a silly plea to barbarous covetousness armed with power. We seven were all the Franks that were in the company; we heard how he had served others, and rejoiced not a little in being thus fortified against him. The whole Caravan being now assembled, consists of a thousand Horses, Mules, and Asses; and of five hundred Camels. These are the Ships of *Arabia*; their Seas are the deserts. A creature created for burthen. Six hundred weight is his ordinary load; yet will he carry a thousand. When in lading or unlading he lies on his belly; and will rise (as it is said) when laden proportionably to his strength, nor suffer more to be laid on him. Four days together he will well travel without water; for a necessity fourteen; in his often belching thrusting up a Bladder, wherewith he moistneth his mouth and throat. When they travel, they cram them with Barly dough. They are, as some say, the only that ingender backward. Their pace is slow, and intolerable hard, being withal unsure of foot, were it never so little slippery or uneven. They are not made to amend their paces when weary. A Beast gentle and tractable, but in the time of his Venery: then, as if remembring his former hard usage, he will bite his Keeper, throw him down, and kick him: forty days continuing in that fury, and then returning to his former meekness. About their necks they hang certain Charms inclused in Leather, and writ by their *Dervises*; to defend them from mischance, and the poison of ill eyes. Here we paid five Madeins for a Camel.

Having with two days rest refreshed them, now to begin the worst of their journey, on the tenth of *March* we entred the main Deserts: a part of *Arabia Petræa*; so called of *Petra* the principal City, now *Rathalalah*. On the North and West it borders on *Syria* and *Egypt*; Southwards on *Arabia Felix*, and the Red Sea; and on the East it hath *Arabia* the Desart. A barren and desolate Country, bearing neither Grass nor Trees, saving only here and there a few Palms, which will not forsake these forsaken places. That little that grows on the earth, is wild Hysop, whereupon they do pasture their Camels, a Creature content with little, whose milk and flesh is their principal sustenance. They have no water that is sweet; all being a meer wilderness of sand: the winds having raised high mountains, which lye in drifts, according to the Quarters from whence they blow. About midnight (the Souldiers being in the head of the Caravan) these *Arabs* assailed our rear. The clamour was great; and the passengers, together with their Leaders, fled from their Camels. I and my Companion imagining the noise to be only an encouragement unto one another, were left alone; yet preserved from violence. They carried away with them divers Mules and Asses laden with Drugs, and abandoned by their Owners, not daring to stay too long, nor cumber themselves with too much luggage, for fear of the Souldiers. These are descended of *Ishmael*; called also *Saracen* of *Sara*, which signifieth a Desart, and *saken*, to inhabit. And not only of the place, but of the manner of their lives; for *Sarack* imports as much as a Thief: as now, being given from the beginning unto these and rapine. They dwell in tents which they remove like walking Cities, for opportunity of prey, and benefit of pasturage. They acknowledge no Soveraign: not worth the conquering, nor can they be conquered; retiring to places impassable for Armies, by reason of the rolling Sands, and penury of all things. A Nation from the beginning unmixed with others: boasting of their Nobility, and at this day hating all mechanical science. They hang about the skirts of the habitable Countries, and having robbed, retire with a marvellous celerity. Those that are not detested persons, frequent the neighbouring Villages for provision: and traffick without molestation; they not daring to intreat them evilly. They are of mean statures, raw-bone, tawny, having feminine voices: of a swift and noise-less pace; behind you, e're aware of them. Their Religion is Mahometanism; glorying in that the Impostor was their Country-man; their Language extending as far as that Religion extendeth. They ride on swift Horses (not misshapen) though lean, and patient of labour. They feed them twice a day with the milk of Camels; nor are they esteemed of, if not of sufficient speed to overtake an Ostridge. Of those there are store in the Deserts. They keep in Flocks, and oft affright the Stranger Passenger with their fearful skreeches, appearing a far off like a Troop of Horsmen. Their bodies are too heavy to be supported with their Wings, which useless for flight, do serve them only to run the more speedily. They are the simplest of Fowls, and symbols of folly, what they find they swallow, though without delight, even Stones and Iron. When they have laid their Eggs, not less great than the Bullet of a Culverin (whereof there are great numbers to be sold

in

in *Cairo*) they leave them, and unmindful where, fit on those they next meet with. The *Arabs* catch the young ones, running apace as foon as difclofed; and when fatted, do eat them: fo do they fome part of the old, and fell their skins with the feathers upon them. They ride alfo on Dromedaries; like in fhape, but lefs than a Camel, of a Jumping-gate, and incredible fpeed. They will carry a man (yet unfit for burthen) an hundred miles a day, living without water, and with little food fatisfied. If one of thefe *Arabians* undertake your conduct, he will perform it faithfully: neither will any of the Nation moleft you. They will lead you by unknown nearer ways; and farther in four days, than you can travel by Caravan in fourteen. Their Weapons are Bows, Darts, Slings, and long Javelings, headed like Partifans. As the *Turks* fit crofs-leg'd, fo do they on their heels: differing little in habit from the ruftick *Egyptians*.

About break of day we pitched by two Wells of brackifh water, called, The Wells of *Pueder*. Hither followed the *Subaffee* of *Salbia*, with the *Jews* which we left behind: who would not travel the day before, in that it was their Sabbath. Their fuperftition had put them to much trouble and charges: as of late at *Tunis* it did to fome pain. For a fort of them being to imbark for *Salonica*; the wind coming fair on the *Sunday*, and the Mafter then hoifting Sails; loth to infringe their Law, and as loth to lofe the benefit of that paffage: to cozen their confciences, they hired certain *Janizaries* to force them aboard; who took their money, and made a jeft of beating them in earneft. At three of the clock we departed from thence, and an hour before midnight pitched by the Caftle of *Catie*, about which there is nothing vegetive, but a few folitary Palms. The water here is bad, infomuch that that which the Captain drinks, is brought from *Tina*, a Sea-bordering Town, and twelve miles diftant. Threefcore Souldiers lie here in Garrifon. We paid a piece of Gold for every Camel, and half a Dollar apiece for Horfes, Mules, and Affes, to the Captain, befides five Madeins a Camel to the *Arabs*. It feemeth ftrange to me, how thefe Merchants can get by their Wares fo far-fetcht, and travelling thorough fuch a number of expences. The thirteenth fpent in paying of *Caphar*, on the fourteenth of *March* by five of the clock we departed, and refted about noon by the Wells of Slaves. Hither followed the Governour of *Catie*, accompanied with twenty Horfe, and pitched his Tent befide us. The reafon why he came with fo flight a conduct, thorough a paffage fo dangerous, (for there, not long before, a *Caravan* of three hundred Camels had been born away by the *Arabs*) was for that he was in fee with the chief of them: who upon the payment of a certain Tax, fecured both Goods and Paffengers. Of thefe there were divers in the Company. Before midnight we diflodged, and by fix the next morning we pitched by another Well of brackifh water, called, The Well of the Mother *Affan*. In the afternoon we departed. As we went, one would have thought the Sea to have been hard by, and to have removed upon his approaches, by reafon of the glittering Nitre. And no doubt, but much of thefe Defarts have in times paft been Sea; manifefted by the faltnefs of the foil, and fhells that lie on the fand in infinite numbers. The next morning by five of the clock we came to *Ariffa*; a Caftle environed with a few houfes, the Garrifon confifting of a hundred Souldiers. This place is fomething better than defart; two miles removed from the Sea, and bleft with good water. Here we paid two Madeins for a Camel, and half as much for our Affes; two of them for the moft part rated unto one of the other. On the feventeenth of *March* we diflodged betimes in the morning, refting about noon by the Wells of Fear; the earth here looking green, yet wafte and unhusbanded. In the evening we departed. Having paffed in the night by the Caftle *Haniaues*, by break of day they followed us to gather their *Caphar*; being three Madeins upon every Camel. The Country from that place pleafant, and indifferent fruitful. By feven of the clock we pitched clofe under the City of *Caza*.

FINIS LIBRI SECUNDI.

THE
THIRD BOOK.

NOW are we in the Holy Land, confined on the North with the Mountains of *Libanus*, and a part of *Phænicia*: on the East it hath *Cælosyria* and *Arabia Petræa*: on the South the same together with *Idumea*, the West is bounded, a part with *Phænicia*, and the rest with the Mid-land Sea. Distant from the Line one and thirty degrees; extending unto thirty three, and something upward. So that in length from *Dan* (the same with *Cæsarea Philippi*) unto *Beerſheba* (now *Gibelin*) it containeth not more than 140 miles: where broadest, not fifty. A Land that floweth with milk and honey: in the midst as it were, of the habitable World, and under a temperate Clime: adorned with beautiful Mountains and luxurious Vallies; the Rocks producing excellent waters, and no part empty of delight or profit. Having at once sustained of her own thirteen hundred thousand fighting men, (when then in all, proportioned with these?) and that with abundance. Divided it was into three Regions; *Judæa*, which lieth to the South, *Samaria* in the midst, and *Galilee*, extending unto *Libanus*: of which the Upper and the Neather watered by many Springs and Torrents, but not many Rivers: *Jordan* the Prince of the rest; seeming to arise from *Jor* and *Dan*, two not far distant Fountains. But he fetched his birth from *Phiala*, a round deep Well an hundred and twenty furlongs off; and passing under the earth, ascendeth at the places aforesaid: running from North to South, not navigably deep, nor above eight fathoms broad, nor (except by accident) heady: shadowed on both sides with Poplars, Alders, Tamarix, and Reeds of sundry kinds. Of some the *Arabians* make Darts and Javelins, of others Arrows of principal esteem; others they select to write with: more used than Quills by the people of these Countries. Passing along it maketh two Lakes: the one in the Upper *Galilee*, named *Samachonitis* (now *Houle*) in the Summer for the most part dry, over-grown with Shrubs and Reeds, which afford a shelter for Boars and Leopards: the other in the Inferiour, called the Sea of *Galilee*, the Lake of *Genezareth*, and of *Tyberias*, taking that name from a City so called, built there by *Herod*, in honour of *Tyberius Cæſar*, in length an hundred furlongs, and forty in breadth; the water exceeding sweet, and better to drink of than that of the River: abounding with sundry sorts of fishes, unto it peculiar. The soil about is of so admirable a nature, that fruits which are only proper to cold, to hot, and to temperate Countries, there joyntly thrive with a like felicity: the Plains about are now well-nigh over-grown with bushes and unhusbanded. Running a great way farther, with many windings, as it were to delay his ill-destiny; gliding through the Plains of *Jericho* not far below where that City stood, it is at length devoured by that cursed Lake *Asphaltides*: so named of the Bitumen which it vomiteth. Called also the Dead Sea, perhaps in that it nourisheth no living Creature; or for his heavy waters, hardly to be moved by the winds. So extreme salt, that whatsoever is thrown thereinto not easily sinketh. *Vespasian* for a tryal, caused divers to be cast in, bound hand and foot, who floted, as if supported by some Spirit. They say that birds flying over, fall in, as if enchanted. Nor unlikely, since other Lakes, as that of *Avernus*, have effected the like.

2 Sam.24. 9.

LIB. III.   *The dead Sea. History of the Holy Land.*   111

―――― *A name of right*
Impos'd, in that to all birds opposite,
Which when those airs swift passengers o're-fly,
Forgetful of their wings they fall from high
With out-stretcht necks on earth, where earth partakes
That killing property; where lakes, on lakes:

―――― Nomen id ab re
Impositum est, quia sunt avibus contraria cunctis
E regione ea, quod loca cum advenere volantes
Remigii obliræ pennarum vela remittunt,
Præcipitesque cadunt molli cervice profusa
In terram, si forte ita fert natura locorum :
Aut in aquam, si forte lacus substratus Averno est.
    Lucr. l. 6.

suffocated with the poyson of the ascending vapours. The whole Country have from hence their provision of Salt. Seventy miles it is in length, and sixteen over; having no egrets unless under the earth, nor yet increasing with the access of the River, and those multitude of Torrents. Once a fruitful Valley, compared for delight unto Paradise, and called *Pentapolis*, of her five Cities: destroyed with fire from Heaven, and converted then into this filthy Lake, and barren desolation that environs it. A fearful Monument of Divine vengeance. *Josephus* (and he that Country-man) reports, that about it are fruits, and flowers, most delectable to the eye, which touched, fall into ashes. An Historian perhaps not always to be credited. Yet not far off there grows a fruit like a green Walnut. This I have seen, which they say never ripeneth. At the foot of the bordering Mountains, there are certain black stones, which burn like coals (whereof the Pilgrims make fires) yet diminish not therewith, but only become lighter and whiter. Beyond *Jordan* are the warm Baths of *Callirhoe*, which discharge themselves into this Lake: exceeding soveraign for sundry diseases.

This famous Country, the Stage of Wonders,

Loved of God; planted by first Colonies:
Nurse of blest Saints, and Kingly Families;
Fruitful in Worthies; glorious in the birth
Of Christ: who here descending from the skies
Did with his Blood purge the polluted earth.

―――― Cara Deo, primis habitata colonis,
Tetra domus regum, sedes clarissima divum :
Nobilium antiqua serie fœcunda virorum
―――― Natale solum, quo lapsus ab astris
Detersit Christus mortales sanguine culpa.

was first inhabited by *Canaan* the Son of *Cham*, and called by his name : he dying, left it to his eleven Sons, the Authors of as many Nations. *Abraham* the tenth from *Noe*, the sixth from *Heber* (of whom the *Hebrews*, retaining in the confusion of Tongues their primitive Language) * departing from *Chaldea* by divine appointment dwelt in this Country, promised him by God in a vision : and thereupon called, The Land of Promise : as of *Jacob*, *Israel*, so named for struggling with the Angel. His posterity two hundred and eighteen years after descending into *Egypt*, were there for two hundred and seventeen years retained in bondage. Brought from thence by *Moses*; forty years after, under the conduct of *Josua* they entred *Canaan*, expulsed the *Canaanites*, and unto every Tribe they allotted a portion. At the first for three hundred and eighty six years they were governed by Captains and Judges: after that for four hundred and eighteen, by Kings, *Juda* the Scepter-bearer; the Regal City *Jerusalem*. From *Rehoboam* ten Tribes revolted, who chose the fugitive *Jeroboam* for their King : his Successors stiled Kings of *Israel* ; the seat of that Kingdom *Samaria*. Two hundred fifty and nine years that Kingdom had endured ; when in the ninth year of the Reign of *Hoshea* they were led into Captivity by the King of *Assyria* : and planted, as some say, beyond the *Caspian* Mountains; from whence they never returned. The *Assyrians* possest of their Land, were from thenceforth called *Samaritans* : who devoured by Lions for sacrificing to the Gods of their Country, revoked certain of the *Israelitish* Priests, to instruct them in their Law and Religion ; but no otherwise observed, then as leaving it free to worship what God each man best liked. To *Juda* only continued *Benjamin* with the best of the *Levites*. Oft oppressed by Tyrants, as oft wonderfully delivered ; at length in the Reign of *Zedechias* they were carried captive by *Nebuchadnezzar* into *Babylon*; Fifty nine years after set at liberty by *Cyrus*, with gifts and immunities they returned under the conduct of *Zerubbabel*. After this they were called *Jews* of *Juda*, the Patriarch, and the Country *Jury*. From which time until the *Maccabees*, a tract of three hundred sixty and four years, they were governed by an *Aristocracy*: tryed with many calamities, and subject to the insolencies of over-powerful neighbours. Of whom *Antiochus Epiphanes*, who, assisted by the factious, massacred the people, not sparing the Conspirators : interdicting, and by torture enforcing whatsoever by their Law they were

*Irreconcileable are the computations of Chronologers, I fol- low Christ. Helvicus, the last and reputed best. *A. M. 20. 23.*

How this may be reconciled to those 70. Jer. 25. Dan. 9. see Helvicus.

L 2   com-

commanded or prohibited. The *Samaritans* would be no more of kin to the *Jews*, but professed themselves to be descended of the *Sidonians*, and re-dedicated their Temple (before dedicated to God) on Mount *Garazin* unto *Jupiter*. To oppose this tempest, up stood *Mathias*, a Priest of the race of *Asmones*, with his five sons; all men of incomparable valour. Of whom *Judas Machabeus* did (if not restore) uphold their State from a further declination. *Judas* slain, *John* succeeded him; *Jonathan*, *John*; and *Simon*. *Jonathan*, the last of the Brethren, (for *Eleazar* was slain before by the fall of the Elephant which he slew, supposing it to have born the person of *Antiochus*:) all dying nobly in their Countries defence; a glorious and to be emulated Destiny. After *Simon*, *Hircanus* his son obtained the Priesthood, together with the Principality. A man more fortunate than the rest: who not only defended his own, but made many prosperous invasions. *Aristobulus* his son translated the Principality into a Kingdom: the first that wore a Crown: in worth degenerating; stained with the blood of his Mother and Brother. His Brother *Alexander* reigned in his stead; not inferiour in cruelty, ever in Wars, either foreign or civil; acquainted with variable fortunes. He left his Kingdom to *Alexandra* his Wife, for restraint of his cruelty, well beloved of the people. By him she had two Sons, *Hircanus* and *Aristobulus*, conferring upon the eldest the Priesthood and Kingdom. Out of her overmuch zeal mis-led by the *Pharisees*, the offended incense *Aristobulus* (a man of an aspiring spirit, and viciously daring) who upon the sickness and death of his Mother affected the Kingdom. *Hircanus* resigns: *Antipater* the *Idumean* procureth him to revoke his resignation: who after many bickerings, is at length restored by *Pompey*, who conquereth *Judæa*, and leadeth *Aristobulus* to *Rome*, with his Children, *Scaurus* here governing for the *Romans*. *Alexander*, his eldest Son, getteth loose, pursueth *Hircanus*, is suppressed by *Gabinius*, who succeeded *Scaurus* in the Government of *Syria*, and restored *Hircanus* to the Priesthood, alters the Government, divides *Judæa* into five Provinces, and commits them to several Governours. *Aristobulus* escapeth from *Rome*, attempteth the Kingdom: is overthrown, taken, and sent back again. *Crassus* succeeds *Gabinius*, him *Cassius*. *Aristobulus* set free by *Cæsar*, and furnished with an Army, is poysoned by *Pompey*'s Favourites: his Son *Alexander* beheaded before by *Scipio* at *Antioch*. *Antipater* for his manifold deserts is by *Cæsar* made Governour of *Judæa*, and the Priesthood for his sake confirmed to *Hircanus*, who unfit for rule, enjoying only the Title of a King, is directed by the other. *Antipater* soon after poysoned (a man of high valour and wisdom) leaveth four Sons behind him, *Phasælus*, *Joseph*, *Herod*, and *Pharora*. *Herod* by his Victories becometh famous: who with his Brother *Phasælus*, are made Tetrarchs by *Anthony*. *Antigonus* the second Son to *Aristobulus*, raiseth new tumults, assisted by the *Parthians*: by whom *Hircanus* and *Phasælus*, contrary to promise, are treacherously surprised, and delivered to *Antigonus*, who making *Hircanus*, by biting off his ears, uncapable of the Priesthood, assumeth unto himself the Soveraignty. *Herod* in distress repaireth to *Rome*, is aided, and created King of *Judæa* by *Augustus* and *Anthony*. The Wars after many conflicts, do end with the death of *Antigonus*: the last of the Race of the *Maccabees*, who held that Government one hundred thirty and one years. *Herod* reigned thirty four years; a man full of admirable virtues, and execrable vices; his acts had deservedly given him the addition of Great:, fortunate abroad, unfortunate in his Family; having put three of his Sons to death, and the Wife that he loved: his life tragical, his death desperate. His Crown he bequeathed to *Archelaus*, his Son by *Malthace* the *Samaritan*. But expulsed by the *Jews* for his cruelty, the matter was debated before *Augustus*, who gave him half of the Kingdom with the Title of an *Ethnarh*. The other half divided into two Tetrarchies, were bestowed on two of his Brethren, *Philip* (to whom *Agrippa* succeeded, the Son of *Aristobulus*, slain by his Father *Herod*, with the title of a King, given him by *Claudius Cæsar*) and *Antipas*, called also *Herod*. *Archelaus* banished soon after for his cruelty, did die in exile. His *Ethnarchy* reduced into a *Roman* Province, and the Government thereof committed unto *Pontius Pilate* by *Tiberius Cæsar*, under whom the Son of God did die for the offences of man, foretold by Heathen Oracles.

Sed manibus passis cum mensus cuncta coronam
De spiniis tulerit, necnon latus ejus arundo
Fixerit arcta manu, cujus causa tribus horis
Nox tenebrosa die medio monstrosaque fiet:

But when with hands out-stretch'd & head thorn bound,
A cursed spear his blessed side shall wound:
For which abortive night for three hours space
Shall mid-day mask: To mans affrighted race,

LIB. III. *The History of the Holy Land.*

The Temple then shall yield a dire osient:
He shall to profound Hell make his descent,
And shew the dead a way to life——

His name thus covertly expressed,

Explained *Four Vowels hath it, and two that are none,*
by the nu- *Of Angels two: The sum of all thus shone.*
meral *Eight Monades, Decades eight, Hecatons*
Greek *Declare his name to earths unfruitful sons.*
Letters, ΙΗΣΟΥΣ
10 8.200.70.
400.200.
8. 8.800.

Tunc hominum generi maximum
Templa dabunt. Ditis cum sera
Nunciet in vitam reditum quo morte;
Siby. Orac. l. 1.

——vocales quatuor autem
Peti, non vocalesque duas, binum geniorum:
Sed quæ sit numeri totius summa docebo.
Namque octo monadas; totidem decadas super istud
Atque hecatontadas octo, infidis significabat
Humanis nomen. *Siby. Orac. l. 3.*

Petronius succeeded *Pilate, Felix Petronius,* and then *Festus, Albinus,* and *Florus. Florus* his cruelty and bad government provoked the *Jews* to rebellion. But the calamities of that War inflicted by *Gallus, Vespasian,* and *Titus,* exceed both example and description, *His blood be upon us and ours*: a wish then granted, was now effected with all fulness of terrour. *Judea* deprived of her fertility, together with her Cities and people, is governed by *Lucius Bassus,* who by *Vespasians* appointment made sale of the Land, and on every head imposed an annual Tribute. So continued it until the Reign of *Adrian*: when the *Jews* impatient, that foreigners should possess their Country, raised a new commotion, to whom the dispersed resorted from all parts, *Barochab* the Ring-leader their counterfeit *Messias.* And because his name doth signifie the Son of a Star, he applied unto himself that Prophecy: *Out of Jacob shall a star arise*; But when slain, and discovered for an Impostor, they called him *Bencozban,* which is, Son of Lying. *Julius Severus* Lieutenant unto *Adrian,* (notwithstanding many of their desperate attempts) razed fifty of their strong Holds, nine hundred eighty five Towns, and slew of them five hundred and fourscore thousand. Insomuch that the Country lay waste, and the ruined Cities became an habitation for Foxes and Leopards. The Captives by the Emperours commandment were transported into *Spain,* and thence again exiled in the year 1500. by *Ferdinand* and *Emmanuel.* *Jury* now without *Jews,* imbraced the Christian Religion in the days of *Constantine,* whose Mother *Helena* is said to have built therein no less than two hundred Temples and Monasteries, in places made famous by the Miracles of Christ; or such as were the known habitations of his Disciples. The next change befell in the Reign of *Phocas,* when the *Persian* over-ran all *Palestine*, inflicting unheard of tortures on the patient Christians. No sooner freed from that yoke, but made to sustain a greater by the execrable S▓▓ens, under the conduct of *Omar,* Successor unto *Mahomet*; who were long aft▓▓pulsed by the *Turks,* then newly planted in *Persia* by *Tangrolipix.* When the Christians of the West, for the recovery of the Holy Land (so by them stiled) set forth an Army of three hundred thousand, *Godfrey* of *Bullein* the General, who made thereof an absolute Conquest, and was elected King of *Jerusalem.* Less than a year gave a period to his Reign. Him his Brother *Baldwin* succeeded, then *Baldwin* the second his Kinsman; him, *Fulk* his Son-in-law. *Fulk* left two Sons behind him; *Baldwin* the third, and *Almericus,* who succeeded his Brother; him, his Son *Baldwin* the fourth. Then *Baldwin* the fifth, his Sisters Son: a Child by his Mother poisoned within seven months of his Coronation, out of her cruel ambition to gain unto her self the Soveraignty, by conferring the same upon her Husband *Guy,* the ninth and last King of *Jerusalem.* Their troublesom Reigns, high Valours, the alternate changes of Foils and Victories (their Foes at hand, their succours afar off) and finally, their final overthrow procured by home-bred Treason, require a peculiar History. In the 89. year of that Kingdom, and during the Reign of *Guy,* the Christians were utterly dispossessed of *Judea,* by *Saladine* the *Egyptian* Sultan. A Country it seemeth anathematized for the death of Christ, and slaughter of so many Saints, as may be conceived by view of the place it self, and ill success of the Christian Armies: which in attempting to recover it, have endured there so often such fatal overthrows; or else, in reputing it a meritorious War, they have provoked the Divine vengeance. The airy Title our *Richard* the First did purchase of *Guy,* with the real and flourishing Kingdom of *Cyprus*; which now is assumed by the Kings of *Spain,* with as little profit, and the like ambition. But the possession remained with the *Egyptians*: until *Selymus,* by extinguishing of the *Mamalucks* did joyn the same to the *Ottoman* Empire. So it remaineth at this day; and now is governed by several *Sanziacks,* being under the Bassa of *Damasco.*

It is for the most part now inhabited by *Moors* and *Arabians*: those possessing the Vallies, and these the Mountains. *Turks* there be few: but many *Greeks*, with other Christians, of all Sects and Nations, such as impute to the place an adherent Holiness. Here be also some *Jews*, yet inherit they no part of the Land, but in their own Country do live as Aliens. A people scattered throughout the whole World, and hated by those amongst whom they live; yet suffered as a necessary mischief: subject to all wrongs and contumelies, which they support with an invincible patience. Many of them have I seen abused, some of them beaten; yet never saw I *Jew* with an angry countenance. They can subject themselves unto times, and to whatsoever may advance their profit. In general, they are worldly wise, and thrive wheresoever they set footing. The *Turk* imploys them in the receipt of Customs, which they by their policies have inhanced, and in buying and selling with the Christian, being himself in that kind a Fool, and easily couzened. They are men of indifferent statures, and the best complexions. These as well in Christendom, as in *Turkie*, are the remains only of the Tribes of *Juda* and *Benjamin*, with some *Levites* which returned from *Babylon* with *Zerubbabel*. Some say, that the other ten are utterly lost: but they themselves that they are in *India*, a mighty Nation, incompassed with Rivers of stone, which only cease to run on their Sabbath, when prohibited to travel. From whence they expect their *Messia*: who with fire and sword shall subdue the World, and restore their temporal Kingdom; and therefore whatsoever befalls them, they record it in their Annals. Amongst them there are three Sects. One only allow of the Books of *Moses*. These be Samaritan *Jews*, (not *Jews* by descent, as before-said) that dwell in *Damasco*: who yearly repair to *Sichem* (now *Neapolis*) and there do at this day worship a Calf, as I was informed by a Merchant dwelling in that Country. Another allow of all the Books of the Old Testament. The third sort mingle the same with Traditions and fantastical Fables devised by their *Rabbins*, and inserted in their *Talmud*. Throughout the *Turks* Dominions they are allowed their Synagogues; so are they at *Rome*, and elsewhere in *Italy*, whose receipt they justifie as a retained Testimony of the verity of Scriptures, and as being a means of their more speedy Conversions: whereas the offence that they receive from Images, and the loss of goods upon their Conversions, oppugn all persuasions whatsoever. Their Synagogues (for as many as I have seen) are neither fair without, nor adorned within; more than with a Curtain at the upper end, and certain Lamps (so far as I could perceive) not lighted by day-light. In the midst stands a Scaffold, like those belonging to Queristers, in some of our Cathedral Churches, where he stands that reads their Law, and sings their Liturgy: an Office not belonging unto any in particular, but unto him (so he be free from deformities) that shall at that time purchase it with most money, which redounds to their publick Treasury. They read in savage Tones, and sing in Tunes that have no affinity with Musick, joyning voices at the several closes. But their fantastical gestures exceed all Barbarism; continually weaving with their bodies, and often jumping upright (as is the manner in Dances) by them esteemed an action of Zeal, and figure of spiritual elevation. They pray silently, with ridiculous and continual noddings of their heads, not to be seen and not laught at. During the time of Service, their heads are veiled in Linen, fringed with knots, in number answerable to the number of their Laws, which they carry about with them in Procession, and rather boast of than observe. They have it stuck in the Jaums of their doors, and covered with glass, written by their *Cacams*, and signed with the Name of God, which they kiss next their hearts in their goings forth, and in their returns. They may print it, but it is to be written on Parchment, prepared of purpose (the Ink of a prescribed composition) not with a Quill, but a Cane. They do great reverence to all the Names of God, but especially to *Jehovah*, insomuch that they never use it in their speech. And whereas they handle with great respect the other Books of the Old Testament, the Book of *Esther* (that part that is Canonical, for the other they allow not of) writ in a long scroll, they let fall on the ground as they read it, because the Name of God is not once mentioned therein, which they attribute to the wisdom of the Writer, in that it might be perused by the Heathen. Their other Books are in the *Spanish* Tongue and Hebrew Character. They confess our Saviour to have been the most learned of their Nation, and have this Fable dispersed amongst them concerning him; How that yet a Boy, attending upon a great *Cacam*, at such a time as the Heavens accustomed to open, and whatsoever he prayed for was granted, the *Cacam* oppressed

Doctors of their Law.

LIB III. *Of the Jews.*

oppressed with sleep, charged the Boy, when the time was come, to awaken him. But he provoked with a frantick desire of peculiar glory (such is their devilish invention) made for himself this ambitious request; that like a God he might be adored amongst men. Which the *Cacam* over-hearing, added thereunto (since what was craved could not be revoked) that it might not be till after his death. Whereupon he lived contemptibly, but dead, was, is, and shall be honoured unto all posterity. They say withal, that he got into the *Sanctum Sanctorum*, and taking from thence the powerful names of God, did sew them in his Thigh. By virtue whereof he went invisible, rid on the Sun-beams, raised the dead to life, and effected like wonders. That being often amongst them, they could never lay hands on him, until he voluntarily tendered himself to their fury, not willing to defer his future glory any longer. That being dead, they buried him privately in a Dunghil, lest his body should have been found, and worshipped by his followers: when a Woman of great Nobility, seduced by his doctrine, so prevailed with the *Roman* Governour, that he threatned to put them forthwith to the sword, unless they produced the body. Which they digging up, found uncorrupted, and retaining that self-same amiable favour, which he had when he lived, only the hair was fallen from his crown; imitated, as they say, by the *Romish* Fryars. Such, and more horrible blasphemies invent they, which I fear to utter. But they be generally notorious lyars. Although they agree with the *Turk* in Circumcision, detestation of Images, abstinency from Swines flesh, and divers other Ceremonies; nevertheless the *Turks* will not suffer a *Jew* to turn *Mahometan*, unless he first turn a kind of *Christian*. As in Religion they differ from others, so they do in habit, in Christendom enforcedly, here in *Turkie* voluntarily. Their under-garments differing little from the *Turks* in fashion, are of Purple cloth; over that they wear Gowns of the same colour, with large wide sleeves, and clasped beneath the chin, without band or collar, on their heads high brimless Caps of Purple, which they move at no time in their salutations. They shave their heads all over, not in imitation of the *Turk*: it being their ancient fashion, before the other was a Nation, as appeareth by *Cherillus* (together with their Language and Bonnets then used) relating of the sundry people which followed *Xerxes* in his *Grecian* Expedition.

These wars a people rarely featur'd, follow;
Who unknown, the Phœnicean language spake.
On hills of Solyman by a vast lake
Have they their seat. Their heads they shave and guard
With Helms of horse-skin in the fire made hard.

Hujus miranda specie gens castra secuta
Phœnissam ignota linguam mittebat ab ore,
Sedes huic Solymi montes stagnum prope vastum,
Toma caput circum; squallenti vertice equini,
Exuvias capitis duratas igne gerebat.

Their familiar speech is *Spanish*: yet few of them are ignorant in the *Hebrew*, *Turkish*, *Moresco*, vulgar *Greek*, and *Italian* Languages. Their only Studies are Divinity and Physick: their occupations Brokage and Usury; yet take they no Interest of one another; nor lend but upon Pawns, which once forfeited, are un-redeemable. The poorer sort have been noted for Fortune-tellers, and by that deceit to have purchased their sustinance.

What dream soever you will buy
The Jews will sell you readily.

Qualiacunque Judæi somnia vendunt.
Juven. Sat.

They marry their Daughters at the age of twelve: not affecting the single life, as repugnant to Society and the Law of Creation. The Sabbath (their devotions ended) they chiefly imploy in nuptial benevolences, as an act of charity befitting well the sanctity of that day. Although no City is without them throughout the *Grand Signiors* Dominions; yet live they with the greatest liberty in *Salonica*, which is almost altogether inhabited by them. Every male above a certain age, doth pay for his head an annual Tribute. Although they be governed by the *Turkish* Justice; nevertheless, if a *Jew* deserve to dye by their Law, they will either privately make him away, or falsely accuse him of a crime that is answerable to the fact in quality, and deserving like punishment. It is no ill turn for the *Franks*, that they will not feed at their Tables. For they eat no flesh, but of their own killing, in regard of the entrails, which being dislocated or corrupted, is an abomination unto them. When so it falls out, though exceeding good (for they kill of the best) they will sell it for a trifle. And as for their Wines, being for the most part planted and
gathered

gathered by *Grecians*, they dare not drink of them for fear they be baptized; a Ceremony whereof we have spoken already. They sit at their meat as the *Turks* do. They bury in the fields by themselves, having only a stone set upright on their graves, which once a year they frequent, burning of incense, and tearing of their garments, for certain days they fast and mourn for the dead, yea, even for such as have been executed for offences. As did the whole Nation at our being at *Constantinople*, for two of good account that were impaled upon stakes, being taken with a *Turkish* Woman, and that on their Sabbath. It was credibly reported, that a *Jew*, not long before, did poyson his son whom he knew to be unrestrainably lascivious, to prevent the ignominy of a publick punishment, or loss by a chargeable redemption. The flesh consumed, they dig up the bones of those that are of their Families; whereof whole Bark-fulls not seldom arrive at *Joppa*, to be conveyed, and again interred at *Jerusalem*, imagining that it doth add delight unto the souls that did owe them, and that they shall have a quicker dispatch in the general Judgment. To speak a word or two of their Women: The elder mabble their heads in linen, with the knots hanging down behind. Others wear high Caps of plate, whereof some I have seen of beaten gold. They wear long quilted Waste-coats, with Breeches underneath; in Winter of Cloth, in Summer of Linen, and over all when they stir abroad, Loose-gowns of Purple, flowing from the shoulders. They are generally fat, and rank of the favours which attend upon sluttish corpulency. For the most part they are goggle-ey'd. They neither shun conversation, nor are too watchfully guarded by their Husbands. They are good Work-women, and can and will do any thing for profit, that is to be done by the Art of a Woman, and which suits with the fashion of these Countries. Upon injuries received, or violence done to any of their Nation, they will cry out mainly at their Windows, beating their cheeks, and tearing of their garments. Of late they have been blest with another *Hester*; who by her favour with the *Sultan*, prevented their intended Massacre, and turned his fury upon their accusers. They are so well skilled in lamentations, that the *Greeks* do hire them to cry at their Funerals.

———— plorat
Ubetibus semper lachrymis, semperque paratis
In statione sua, atque expectantibus illam
Quo jubeat manare modo ————
Juv. Sat. 6.

*Fruitful in tears! tears that still ready stand
To sally forth, and but expect command.*

But now return we unto *Gaza*, one of the five Cities, and that the principal that belonged to the *Palestines*, (called *Philistins* in the Scriptures) a warlike and powerful people, of whom afterwards the whole Land of Promise took the name of *Palestine*. *Gaza* or *Aza* signifieth Strong. In the *Persian* Language a Treasury: so said to be called by *Cambyses*, who invading *Egypt*, sent thither the Riches purchased in that War. It was called *Constantia* by the Emperour *Constantine*, *Gaza* again by *Julian*, and now *Gazra*. First, famous for the acts of *Sampson*, who lived in the time of the *Trojan* Wars: (an Age that produced Worthies) whose force and fortunes, are said to have given to the Poets their inventions of *Hercules*, who lived not long before him. And afterward famous for the two wounds there received by *Alexander* the Great, then counted the principal City of *Syria*. It stands upon a Hill, environed with Vallies, and those again well-nigh closed with Hills; most of them planted with all sorts of delicate fruits. The building mean, both for form and matter. The best but low, of rough stone, arched within, and flat on the top, including a Quadrangle: the Walls surmounting their Roofs, wrought thorow with Pot-sherds, to catch and strike down the refreshing winds; having Spouts of the same, in colour, shape, and site, resembling great Ordnance. Others are covered with Mats and Hurdles; some built of Mud; amongst all, not any comely or convenient. Yet there are some reliques left, and some impressions that testifie a better condition. For divers simple Roofs are supported with goodly Pillars of *Parian* Marble; some plain, some curiously carved. A number broken in pieces, do serve for Threshods, Jaums of doors, and sides of Windows, almost unto every beggarly Cottage. On the North-East corner, and summity of the Hill, are the ruines of huge Arches sunk low in the earth, and other foundations of a stately Building. From whence the last *Sanziack* conveyed Marble Pillars of an incredible bigness, inforced to saw them asunder ere they could be removed, which he imployed in adorning a certain Mosque below in the Valley. The *Jews* do fable this place to have been the Theatre of *Sampsom*, pulled down on the head of the *Philistins*. Perhaps some Palace there built by *Ptolomy* or *Pompey*, who re-edified the City: or Christian

stian Temple erected by *Constantine*, or else that Castle founded by *Baldwin* the third, in the year 1148. The Castle now being, not worthy that name, is of no importance: wherein lyeth the *Sanziack* (by some termed a *Bassa*) a sickly young man, and of no experience, who governs his Province by the advice of a *More*. His Territories begin at *Arissa*, on the West-side of the City, out of sight, and yet within hearing, is the Sea, seven furlongs off; where they have a decayed and unsafe Port, of small avail at this day to the Inhabitants. In the Valley on the East-side of the City, are many straggling Buildings, Beyond which there is a Hill more eminent than the rest, on the North-side of the way that leadeth to *Babylon*, said to be that (and no question the same described in Scriptures) to which *Sampson* carr'ed the Gates of the City, upon whose top there standeth a Mosque, environed with the Graves and Sepulchres of *Mahumetans*. In the Plain between that and the Town, there stand two high Pillars of Marble, their tops much worn by the weather; the cause of their erecting unknown, but of great antiquity. South of this, and by the way of *Egypt*, there is a mighty Cistern, filled only with the fall of rain, and descended into by large stairs of stone, where they wash their Cloaths, and water their Cattel.

The same day that we came, we left the Caravan, and lodged in the City under an Arch in a little Court, together with our Asses. The door exceeding low; as are all that belong unto Christians, to withstand the sudden entrance of the insolent *Turks*. For they here do live in a subjection to be pitied, not so much as daring to have handsom houses, or to imploy their grounds to the most benefit. So dangerous it is to be esteemed wealthy. During our abode here, there came a Captain with two hundred *Saphcis*, sent by *Morat Bassa*, to raise thirty thousand Dollars of the poor and few Inhabitants of this City. The *Grecians* have certain small Vineyards, but that they have Wine they dare not be known, which they secretly press in their houses. They bury their Corn under ground, and keep what they are to spend, in long Vessels of Clay, in that it is subject to be eaten with worms (as throughout *Egypt*) and will not last, if not so preserved. In the principal part of the City, they have an ancient Church, frequented also by the *Coptics*. The *Greekish* Women (a thing elsewhere unseen) here cover their faces, dying their hands black, and are apparelled like the *Moors* of *Cairo*. Every *Saturday* in this Church-yard, upon the graves of the dead, they keep a miserable howling, crying of custom, without tears or sorrow. The *Subassee* would have extorted from us well-nigh as much money as we are masters of; which we had hardly avoided, had not the sick *Zinziack* (in that administred unto by our Phylician) quitted us of all payments. So that there is no travelling this way for a *Frank* without special favour.

Thrust out of our Lodging (as we were about to leave it) by the uncivil *Sapheis*, who seized on divers of our necessaries; on the ninteenth of *March* we returned to the Caravan. We paid half a Dollar apiece to the place for our Camels; and for their hire from *Cairo*, for those of burthen six *Sultanies*; for such as carried Passengers eight. We gave them two *Sultanies* more apiece to proceed unto *Jerusalem*. Here the Caravan divided, nor a small part thereof taking the way that leadeth unto *Babylon*. The next day we also dislodged, leaving the *Jews* behind us, who were there to celebrate their Festival. The Captain of the Caravan departed the night before, taking his way through the mountainous Country by *Hebron*, out of his devotion to visit the Graves of the Patriarchs; a place of high esteem amongst them, and much frequented in their Pilgrimages. The ancient City (the seat of *David* before he took *Sion* from the *Jebusites*) is utterly ruinated. Hard by there is a little Village, seated in the field of *Machpelah*, where standeth a goodly Temple, erected over the Cave of their Burial, by *Helena* the Mother of *Constantine*, converted now into a Mosque. We past this day through the most pregnant and pleasant Valley that ever eye beheld; On the right hand a ridge of high Mountains, (whereon stands *Hebron*;) on the left hand the *Mediterranean* Sea, bordered with continued Hills, beset with variety of fruits, as they are for the most part of this days Journey. The Champion between about twenty miles over; full of flowry Hills ascending leisurely, and not much surmounting their ranker Vallies; with Groves of Olives, and other fruits dispersedly adorned. Yet is this wealthy bottom (as are all the rest) for the most part un-inhabited, but only for a few small and contemptible Villages, possessed by barbarous *Moors*, who till no more than will serve to feed them; the grass waste-high, unmowed, uneaten, and uselesly withering. Perhaps so desolate, in that infested by the often recourse of Armies, or masterful *Saphcis*, who before they go into the field (which is seldom until the

latter

latter end of harvest, left they should starve themselves by destroying of the Corn, are billitted in these rich Pastures, for the benfit of their Horses, lying in Tents: besides them, committing many outrages on the adjoyning Towns and distressed Passengers.

Ten miles from *Gaza*, and near unto the Sea, stands *Ascalon*, now a place of no note: more than that the *Turk* doth keep there a Garrison. Venerable heretofore amongst those Heathen, for the Temple of *Dagon*, and Birth of *Semiramis*, begotten of their Goddess *Decreta*. Who inflamed with the love of a certain Youth that sacrificed unto her, and having by him a Daughter; ashamed of her incontinency, did put him away, exposed the Child to the Desarts, and confounded with sorrow, threw her self into a Lake replenished with fish, adjoyning to the City, and is feigned to have been converted into one of them.

——— Narres
Decreti, quam versâ squamis velantibus artus
Stagna Palæstini credunt coluisse figura.
Ovid. Met. l. 6.

——— Or of *Decreta* tell,
That did (as Palestine believe) forsake
Her form: and cloath'd with scales liv'd in a lake.

Whereupon the *Syrians* abstained from the fish thereof, as reputed Deities. This *Decreta* is said to be that *Dagon* the Idol of the *Askaloniter*, (but with what congruity I know not) mentioned in the Scripture, which signifieth the fish of sorrow: who had her Temple close by that Lake, with her image in the figure of a fish, all excepting the face, which resembled a Woman. But the Infant nourished by Doves, which brought her Milk from the Pails of the Pastors, after became the Wife of *Ninus*, and Queen of *Assyria*; whereupon she was called *Semiramis*, which signifieth a Dove in the *Syrian* Tongue. Now when she could no longer detain the Empire from her Son, not enduring to survive her glory, she vanisht out of sight; and was said by them to have been translated to the Gods, according to the answer of the Oracle. Others feign with like truth, that she was turned into a Dove;

——— Ut sumptis illius filia pennis
Extremos altis in turribus egerit annos.
Ovid. Met. l. 6.

Who with assumed wings made her ascent
To high-top't Towers, and there her old age spent.

in memorial whereof the *Babylonians* did bear a Dove in their Ensigns: confirmed by the Prophesie of *Jeremiah*, who foretelling of the devastation of *Judea*, adviseth them to flye from the Sword of the Dove. Ten miles North of *Ascalon* along the shore stands *Azotus*: and eight miles beyond that *Acharon*, now places of no reckoning.

About two of the clock we pitched by *Cane Sedoe*; a ruinous thing, hard by a small Village, and not a quarter of a mile from the Sea, the Caravan lying in deep Pastures without controulment of the Villages. The next day we departed two hours before Sun-rise; descending into an ample Valley, and from that into another, having divers Orchards towards the Sea. The Country such (but that without Trees) as we past thorow before: no part so barren, but would prove most profitable, if planted with Vines and Fruits, made more than probable by those that grow about *Gaza*. Passing thorow a spacious field of Olives, about noon we pitched on a little Hill lying East, and within a furlong of *Rama*: called *Ramula* by the *Moors*, which signifieth sandy. It is seated on a Plain, on a little rising of the earth, stretching North and South, built of free stone, the streets narrow, the houses contemptible. Yet are there many goodly ruines, which testifie far better building, especially those of the Christian Churches. Here is a Monastery, much of it standing, founded by *Philip* the good, Duke of *Burgundy*; in that place where sometimes stood the House of *Nicodemus*: built for the relief and safety of Pilgrims in their passage to *Jerusalem*. And although quitted by the Fryars, yet at this day it serveth to that purpose: called *Sion*-house, and belongeth to the Monastery of Mount *Sion*.

Though out of my way, it will not be far from my purpose, to say something of *Joppa*, which is a Haven, and was a Town ten miles West of this place, and said to have been before the general Deluge. Others write that it was built by *Japhet*. It stood upon, and under a Hill, from whence, as *Strabo* reports (but impossible to be true) *Jerusalem* might be discerned. Having an ill Haven, defended from the South and West, with eminent Rocks, but open to the fury of the North: which driving the waves against the ragged cliffs, do make them more turbulent, and the place less safe than the open Sea incensed with tempests. Here reigned *Cepheus* (who repaired the same, and called it *Joppa*) the Son of *Phœnix*, and Father of *Andromeda*. Who is feigned to have been chained unto a Rock hard by, for the pride of her Mother *Cassiope*, there to be devoured by the Monster.

For Mothers tongue unjust Jove charg'd that she
Should suffer here, who from all fault was free.
Whose arms when Perseus saw to hard rocks chain'd,
But that warm tears from her full eye springs rain'd,
And light winds gently fann'd her fluent hair,
He would have thought her marble: t're aware
Hid fire be assumeth, and astonish'd by
Her beauty, had almost forgot to fly.

—— Hic immeritam maternæ pendere linguæ
Andromedam pœnas injustus justerat Ammon
Quam simul ad duras religatam brachia cautes
Vidit Abantiades; nisi quod levis aura capillos
Moverat & tepido manabant lumina fletu.
Marmoreum ratus esset opus: trahit inscius ignes
Et stupet eximiæ correptus imagine formæ,
Pene suas quatere est oblitus in aere pennas.
Ovid. Met. l. 4.

Who by overcoming the Monster, received her as the reward of his Victory: whom thus *Scaliger* personates.

My mother err'd: I suffer; yet content
For guilty here to dye, though innocent.
Thy form (O mother) bound me here, but mine
Unbound me: therefore fairer it than thine.
Fairer; nor Nymphs provoke I with my pride.
Most fair, and best, that well the tongue can guide.

Erravit genitrix: plector cur filia? quanquam
Pro sonte in sontem matre petîre juvat.
O mater, tua me facies huc perdidit æqui
Hinc mea me solvit: Pulchrior ergo mea est.
Pulchrior ergo mea est: nec Nymphas provoco longè.
Pulchrius & melius sit bene scire loqui.
J. C. Scal.

This is said to have hapned (though intermixed with fiction) about the time that the Judges began to govern in *Israel*. The Inhabitants many years after religiously preserved sundry old Alters, inscribed with the Titles of *Cepheus* and his Brother *Phineus*. *Ovid* makes *Æthiopia* the Scene of this Story; but is contradicted by S. *Jerom*; back with the credits of *Pliny* and *Mela*. *Marcus Scaurus* in his Ædilship, brought from hence, and produced the bones of this Monster, being by forty foot longer than the Ribs of an Elephant, and the Back-bone half a foot thicker. This City was destroyed by *Cestius*: and again (becoming a Receptacle for Pirates) by *Vespasian*, who here built a Castle to prohibit the like outrages. It was called the Port of *Jury*, the only one that it had. Then more convenient than now; much of it choaked with sand, and much of it worn with the continual assault of the waters. Of the City there is no part standing more than two little Towers, wherein are certain Harquebushes, a crock for the safeguard of the Harbour. Under the cliff, and opening to the Haven, are certain spacious Caves hewn into the Rock: some used for Ware-houses, and others for shelter. The Merchandizes here imbarqued for Christendom are only Cottons: gathered by certain *French-men*, who reside at *Rama* in the House of *Sion*. The Western Pilgrims do for the most part arrive at this place, and are from hence conducted to *Jerusalem* by *Attala*, a *Greek* of *Rama*, and Drugardman to the *Pater-Guardian*, paying seven *Sultanies* apiece for his Mules, his labour and discharge of *Caphor*. The like rate he hath for bringing them back again: a great expence to poor Pilgrims for so small a Journey; which must be paid, although they accept not of his conduct. Yet by this means they do pass securely, he being in Fee with the *Arabians* that possess the Mountains.

Now the *Caravan* did again divide: the *Moors* keeping on the way that leadeth to *Damascus*. Here we should have paid two Dollars apiece for our heads to a Sheck of the *Arabs*; but the *Zanziack* of *Gaza* had sent unto him that it should be remitted. He came unto our Tent, and greedily fed on such Viands as we had set before him. A man of tall stature, cloathed in a Gambalock of Scarlet, buttoned under the chin with a Boss of Gold. He had not the patience to expect a present, but demanded one. We gave him a piece of Sugar, and a pair of Shooes, which he earnestly inquired for, and chearfully accepted. On the two and twentieth of *March*, with the rising Sun, we departed from *Gaza*. A small remainder of that great *Caravan*; the *Nostrains* (so name they the Christians of the East) that ride upon Mules and Asses being gone before: amongst whom were two *Armenian* Bishops, who footed it most of the way; but when (alighting themselves) they were mounted by some of their Nation. Before we were gone far, we were stayed by the *Arabs*, until they had taken *Caphar* of the rest. The *Subassee* of *Rama* besides had two

So call they their Leaders for the most part. *Santos*. A kind of Riding-Rayne town.

Madines

Madeins upon every Camel. The day thus wasted, did make us misdoubt that we should not get that night unto *Jerusalem*, but the missing of our way (for the *Arabs* had left us contrary to the custom) turned our fear to despair. Some six miles beyond *Rama* the Hills grew bigger and bigger, mixed with fruitful Vallies. About two miles farther we ascended the higher Mountains, paying by the way two Madeins a head, but at several places. A passage exceeding difficult; straightned with Wood, and as it were paved with broken Rocks: which by reason of the rain then falling, became no less dangerous to our Camels. At length we came to a small Village where we first discovered our erring. Some counselled to stay, others to proceed; both dangerous alike: the way unknown, unsafe, the Inhabitants Thieves, as are all the *Arabians*. Whilst we thus debated, the night stole upon us, and bereft us of the election. The much rain enforced us to flie for shelter unto a ruinous Chappel, where distrust set the watch, which we carefully kept till the morning. Betimes we forsook the Village, descending the way we had ascended, guided by the chief of the Town, who for a sum of money had undertaken our conduct to the top of the Mountains: having hired Asses for our more expedition. Yet others crossing us as we returned along the Valley; with shews of violence, would have extorted more money. Our passage for five hours together lay thorow a narrow straight of the Mountains; much of our way, no other than such as seemed to have been worn by the Winters Torrent. We past by a ruinous Fort, seated near a Fountain; sufficient, when it stood, to have made good that passage. In the way we sprang a number of Partridges; others on each side running on the Rocks, like in colour to those of *Chios*. Ascending by little and little, at length we attained to the top; which over-topt and surveyed all the Mountains that we had left behind us. From hence to *Jerusalem* the way is indifferent even. On each side are round Hills, with ruines on their top; and Vallies such as are figured in the most beautiful Landskips. The soil, though stony, not altogether barren, producing both Corn and Olives about inhabited places. Approaching the North-gate of the City, called in the times past, The Gate of *Ephraim*, and now of *Damascus*; we only of all the rest were not permitted to enter. When compassing the Wall unto that of the West, commanded by the Castle, we were met by two *Franciscan* Fryars, who saluted and conveyed us to their Covent.

Although divers both upon inquisition and view, have with much labour related the site and state of this City, with the places adjoyning, (though not to my knowledge in our Language) insomuch as I may seem unto some, but to write what hath been written already: yet notwithstanding, as well to continue the course of this discourse, as to deliver the Reader from many erring reports of the too credulous devote, and too too vain glorious: the one,

Seminat in vulgus nugas ——   *Do toys divulge* ——

The other charactred in the remainder carried in that Distick:

—— auditaque lingua   —— *Still add to what they hear,*
Auget, & ex humili tumulo producit Olympum.   *And of a mole-hill do a mountain rear :*
Bapt. Mant. l. 3.

I will declare what I have observed, unswayed with either of their vices.

Herein I follow the computation of Adrichomius much versst in this argument.

This City, once sacred and glorious, elected by God for his seat, and seated in the midst of Nations; like a Diadem crowning the head of the Mountains; the Theatre of Mysteries and Miracles; was founded by *Melchisedech* (who is said to be *Sem* the son of *Noe*, and that not improbably) about the year of the World 2023. and called *Salem* (by the Gentiles, *Solyma*, as they write, of the Mountains adjoyning, but rather the Mountains of the City) which signifieth Peace: who reigned here fifty years. After possessed by the *Jebusites*, by them it was named *Jebus*; who held it wholly or in part eight hundred and four and twenty years: when Sion the Fort still remaining in their hands, being assaulted by *David*; they placed the blind, the lame, and other ways impotent, upon the Walls, in contempt of his power, as sufficient to repulse such an enemy. But in fine, he took Mount *Sion* by force, expulsed the *Jebusites*, re-edified and adorned it and the City with goodly buildings: and removing from *Hebron*, made it the seat of his Kingdom. From thenceforth it was called *Jerusalem*, which is to say, *Jebusalem*; converting *b* into *r*, for the better harmony. His Son *Solomon* and the succeeding Kings of *Juda* much enlarged

LIB. III.   *Jerusalem.*

enlarged the City, then containing in circuit about fifty furlongs: fortified it with stronger Walls and deeper Trenches, hewn out of the living Rock, and added thereunto an absolute perfection by the structure of that magnificent Temple, their sumptuous Palaces, and other stately Edifices. In this excellency it continued for four hundred threescore and seventeen years. When destroyed by *Nebuchadnezzar*, for threescore and ten years it lay waste, until the *Jews* returning from that Captivity began to re-edifie the same; which it was un-immured for threescore and three years after: and then effected by *Nehemias* in the space of two and fifty days. It contained at that time in circuit three and thirty furlongs: and was after enlarged unto threescore. Adorned by the *Maccabees*; but especially by the many and admirable Buildings erected by *Herod*, it seemed not much to decline from her former beauty and amplitude. This re-built City flourished for the space of five hundred threescore and two years: and then was destroyed by the wrath of God, and fury of *Titus*: wherein eleven hundred thousand by Famine, Pestilence, the Enemies Sword, and civil butcheries most desperately perished. Only three Towers, *Hippicum, Phaseolum* and *Mariamne* (built by *Herod* and adjoining to his Palace) he left un-razed, exceeding the rest in greatness and beauty; and a part of the Wall which environed the West of the City: both to be a defence to the *Romans*, and to declare unto posterity the strength of the place, and valour of the Vanquishers. But threescore and five years after, *Ælius Adrianus* inflicting on the rebelling *Jews* a wonderful slaughter, subverted those remainders, and sprinkled Salt upon the foundation. Where not long after he built a City, but less in circuit: taking in Mount *Calvary*, and a part of Mount *Gihon*, with a Valley between; which lay on the West-side, and were excluded in the former City; setting over the Gate that openeth towards *Bethlehem* the Portraicture of a Swine: prohibiting the *Jews* for ever to enter, or so much as to look upon it from any more eminent Mountain: and after his own name named it *Ælia Capitolia*. But not long after inhabited by Christians, and dignified with a Patriarchal See, it recovered the ancient name of *Jerusalem*; and remained for five hundred years in the possession of the Christians, but not without sundry persecutions. Then taken by the *Saracens* in the year of our Lord 636, won by *Godfrey Bullein* in the year 1099, and taken by *Saladine* in 1187, it was finally conquered by *Selymus* in the year 1517, and is now called the *Cuds* of the *Mahometans*, which signifieth Holy. So that from the first foundation to this present 1611. three thousand five hundred and six and forty years are expired.

This City is seated upon a rocky Mountain: every way to be ascended (except a little on the North) with steep descents, and deep Valleys naturally fortified: for the most part environed with other not far removed Mountains, as if placed in the midst of an Amphitheater. For on the East is Mount *Olivet*, separated from the City by the Valley of *Jehosaphat* (which also circleth a part of the North) on the South the Mountain of *Offence*, interposed with the Valley of *Gehinnon*: and on the West it was formerly fenced with the Valley of *Gihon*, and Mountain adjoining. To speak something thereof as it flourished in the days of our Saviour; it was divided then into four parts, separated by several Walls, stretching East and West, as if so many several Cities. The next the South over-looking the rest, and including Mount *Sihon*, was then called, The upper City, but before, The City of *David*. In the midst whereof he erected a strong and magnificent Castle; the Seat of the succeeding Kings. In the West corner and upon the wall stood his Tower, of which we shall speak hereafter, as of his Sepulchre, the *Cænaculum*, the house of *Annas*, and that of *Caiaphas*. Here King *Herod* built a sumptuous Palace, containing two Houses in one, which he named by the names of *Cæsar* and *Agrippa*: adorned with Marble, and shining with Gold: in cost and state superiour to the Temple. The walls of this part of the City broken down by *Antiochus* were strongly repaired by the *Maccabees*; which adjoining every way with the downfall of the Rock did make it impregnable. But *Sion* raised in that general subversion, is now for the most part left out of the City. From the upper City they descended into the nether, over a deep Trench, which was called *Tyrœon*, and plentifully inhabited; now fill'd with rubbidge, and hardly distinguishable. This part, as some deliver, was named the daughter of *Sion*; in greatness by far exceeding the Mount. On the East side of this *Sion*, upon Mount *Maria* stood that glorious Temple of *Solomon*: and between it and the Mount *Sion*, his Throne, his Palace (which by a high Bridge had a passage into the Temple) the Palace of the Queen, and the house of the Grove of *Libanus*: now all without the walls of the City.

M   West

West of the Temple, and on a high Rock, the place of the *Maccabees* was seated, which surveyed the whole City, after re-edified, and dwelt in by King *Agrippa*, near unto which stood the Theatre built by King *Herod*, adorned with exquisite Pictures; expressing the Conquests, Trophies, and Triumph of *Augustus*. Against the South corner of the Temple stood the Hippodrom, made also by *Herod*; wherein he instituted divers Exercises, of five years continuance; in honour of the Emperour. And when he grew old, and unrecoverably sick, knowing how acceptable his death would be to the *Jews*, he caused the chief of them to be assembled together, and to be there shut up: that his death accompanied with their slaughter, might at that time in despite of their hatred, procure a general lamentation. Within the West Wall of the City, and near it, was Mount *Acra*, steep and rocky, where once stood a Citadel erected by *Antiochus*, and raised by *Simon*, who abated the extraordinary height thereof, that it might not surmount the Temple: whereon *Helena* Queen of the *Adiabenes* (a Nation beyond *Euphrates*) built her Palace; who converting from Paganism to Judaism, forsook her Country, and dwelt in *Jerusalem*. Afterward embracing Christian Religion. She much relieved the distressed Christians in that Famine prophecied of by *Agabus* (which hapned in the Reign of *Claudius Cæsar*) with the Corn she bought, and caused to be brought out of *Egypt*. Without the City she had her Sepulchre not far from the Gate of *Ephraim*; adorned with three Pyramides, and undemolished in the days of *Eusebius*. On the North side of *Acra* stood *Herod's* Amphitheater, spacious enough to contain fourscore thousand people, imitating in the shews there exhibited, the barbarous cruelty of the *Romans*. Near unto the North Wall of this second part stood the Common Hall, and Courts of Justice. And adjoining well-nigh to the North side of the Temple, upon a steep Rock fifty Cubits high, stood the Tower of *Baris*, belonging to the Priest of the Race of *Asmones*. But *Herod* obtaining the Kingdom, and considering how convenient a place it was to command the City; built thereon a stately strong Castle, having at every corner a Tower, two of them being fifty Cubits in height, and the other two threescore and ten; which, to insinuate with *Antonius*, he called *Antonia*. In this the *Romans* did keep a Garrison, suspiciously over-eying the Temple; lest the *Jews* being animated with the strength thereof, should attempt some innovation: unto which it was joined by a Bridge of marvellous height, which passed over the artificial Valley of *Cedron*. On the North side of *Antonia*, a Gallery crossed the Street (whereof we shall speak hereafter) unto the Palace of the *Roman* President. Now for the third City, which was but narrow; and whose length did equal the breadth of the other: the West end thereof as the circuit then ran, was wholly possessed by the Royal Mansion of King *Herod*; confining on the three Walls: for cost excessive, and for strength impregnable; containing Groves, Gardens, Fish-ponds, and other places of delight, and for exercise. On the South-east corner of the wall stood *Mariannes* Tower, fifty Cubits high, besides the natural height of the place, of excellent workmanship: built in the memory, and retaining the name of his too wellbeloved Wife by him rashly murdered. On the South-west corner stood that of *Phaseolus*; threescore and ten Cubits high: called after the name of his Brother, (who dasht out his own brains; being contrary to the Law of Nations, surprised and imprisoned by the *Parthians*) exceeding strong, and in form resembling the Tower of *Pharus*. And in the North wall on a lofty hill stood the Tower of *Hippie*, eighty four Cubits high, foursquare, and having two spires at the top: in memorial of the *Hippici* his two friends, and both of them slain in his Wars. In this third City were the Houses of many of the Prophets: and that of *Mary* the Mother of *John*, *Mark*, frequented by the Primitive Christians. The fourth part of *Jerusalem* lay North of this, and was called the New City: once but a Suburb to the other, and inhabited by the baser Tradesmen. The out-wall of which was re-edified by King *Agrippa*, and made of a wonderful strength, (the whole City only on that side assailable) in the height twenty five Cubits, and fortified with ninety Towers, two hundred Cubits distant from each other. The soil where the New City stood, and a part of the next, is now left out of the walls of *Jerusalem*.

Thus little of much have I spoken, and yet by these few imperfect lineaments the perfection thereof may be in some sort conjectured. More will be said when we speak of the Modern exactly represented in the following Figure, with the site of she remarkable places; whereof mention is made in the process of our Journal.

Hic genua, hic animum, hic lachrymas, hic carmina pono : *My knees, affections, tears, verse, here place I;*
Menique mea ad partium subvolat aucta polum. *My enlarged soul to her heavenly home doth flie.*

O promis'd

LIB III.   Jerusalem.

O promis'd to the Old World, to the New;
That gav'st blest laws of freedom to ensue:
Why lies a widow! O what scars disgrace
Thy looks! who thus hath backt thy sacred face!
Earth, how shall I thee praise! a fair heaven made.
We made of heaven; are in base earth array'd.
Thou need'st no praise, nor can our Muse thee adorn
Tet glorious twice that us for thee hast born.

O promissa novo, populo promissa vetusto:
Quæ libertatis jura beata dabas,
Cur vidua, orba, jaces? sancti quæ vulnera vultus?
Quis suit ætherias qui scidit ille genas?
Quam te terra canam? cœlum que facta serenum es;
Nos facti è cœlo sordida terra sumus.
Tu nec laudis eges; nec nostro augebere cantu:
At me abs te dici, gloria utrinque tua est.

J. C. Scal.

1. The Gate of Joppa.
2. The Castle of the Pisans.
3. The Monastery of the Franciscans.
4. The Temple of the Sepulchre.
5. A Mosque, once a Collegiate Church, where stood the house of Zebedeus.
6. The Iron Gate.
7. The Church of St. Mark, where his house stood.
8. A Chappel, where once stood the house of S. Thomas.
9. The Church of St. James.
10. The Church of the Angels, where once stood the Palace of Annas the High Priest.
11. The Port of David.
12. The Church of St. Saviour, where stood the Palace of Caiaphas.
13. A Mosque, once a goodly Temple there standing where stood the Cœnaculum.
14. Where the Jews would have taken away the body of the Blessed Virgin.
15. Where Peter wept.
16. The Fountain Siloe.
17. The Fountain of the Blessed Virgin.
18. Port Sterquiline.
19. The Church of the Purification of the Blessed Virgin, now converted into a Mosque.
20. The Court of Solomons Temple.
21. A Mosque, where stood the Temple of Solomon.
22. The golden Gate.
23. The Gate of St. Steven.
24. The Church of Anna, now a Mosque.
25. The Pool Bethesda.
26. Where the Palace of Pilate stood.
27. Where stood, as they say, the Palace of Herod.
28. Pilates Arch.
29. The Church of the Blessed Virgins swouning.
30. Where they met Simon of Cyrene.
31. Where the rich Glutton dwelt.
32. Where the Pharisee dwelt.
33. Where Veronica dwelt.
34. The Gate of Justice.
35. Port of Ephraim.
36. The Bazar.
A. The Circuit of part of the old City.

We entred as aforesaid, at the West gate, called the Gate of Joppa. On the right hand, and adjoining to the wall, there standeth a small ill-fortified Castle; yet the only Fort that belongeth to the City, weakly guarded, and not over-well stored with Munition, built by the Pisans at such time as the Christians inhabited this City. Turning on the left hand, and ascending a part of Mount Gibon, we came to the Monastery of the Franciscans (now being in number between thirty and forty) who in the year 1561. thrust out of that which they had on Mount Sion, had this place assigned them. But of the Founders name I am ignorant: nor is he much wronged by being forgotten, since so mean a building can give no fame to the builder.

The Pater-guardian with due complement entertained us; a reverend old man of a voluble tongue, and winning behaviour. His Name Gaudentius, his Nation Italy, every

Franciscans. *Knights of the Sepulchre.* LIB. III.

third year they are removed, and a successor elected by the Pope, from whom they have a part of their exhibition; the rest from the *Spaniard*, and *Florentine*. Nor is it a little that they get by the resort of the Pilgrims of Christendom. For all that come must repair to their Covent, otherwise they shall be accused for spies, and suffer much trouble; the *Roman* Catholicks rewarding them out of devotion, and the rest out of courtesie; which, if short of their expectations, they will repine at as losers. We four, for eight days entertainment, bestowed little less among them than 100 Dollars; and yet they told us that we had hardly paid for what we had eaten. A costly rate for a Monastical diet. But the *Turk* is much more fierce upon them; awaiting all advantages that may give a colour to extortion. A little before our coming, a *Turk* being denied by a Frier of some trifle that he requested, gave himself such a blow upon the nose, that the blood gushed forth; and presently exclaiming as if beaten by the other, complained to the *Sanziack*; for which *Avania* they were compelled to part with eight hundred Dollars. Brought much behind-hand, as they alledge, with such losses; they use oft to rehearse them as motives unto charity.

The Covent had also another in-come by the Knights of the Sepulchre, who pay thirty *Sultanies* a piece to the *Pater-guardian*, who by the virtue of his Patent doth give them that dignity. The Kings of *France* were Sovereigns of that Order; by whom it was instituted in the year 1099, who granted them divers immunities. They bare five crofs gules, in form of that which is at this day called,The *Jerusalem* Crofs; representing thereby the five wounds that violated the body of our Saviour. None were to be admitted, if of a defamed life, or not of the Catholick Religion. They are to be Gentlemen of Blood, and to have sufficient means to maintain a port agreeable to that Calling, without the exercise of mechanical Sciences. But now they will except against none that bring money; insomuch, that at our being there they admitted of a *Roman*, by trade an Apothecary, late dwelling in *Aleppo*. They take the Sacrament to hear every day a Mass, if they may conveniently: If Wars be commenced against the Infidels, to serve there in person, or to send others in their stead no less serviceable: To oppugn the persecutors of the Church; to shun unjust Wars, dishonest gain, and private Duels. Lastly, to be reconcilers of dissention, to advance the common good, to defend the Widow and Orphane, to refrain from swearing, perjury, blasphemy, rapine, usury, sacriledge, murder, and drunkenness; to avoid suspected places, the company of infamous persons, to live chastly, irreprovably, and in word and deed to shew themselves worthy of such a dignity. This Oath taken, the *Pater-guardian* layeth his hand upon his head, as he kneeleth before the entrance of the Tomb, bidding him to be loyal, valiant, virtuous, and an undaunted Souldier of Christ, and that holy Sepulchre. Then gives he him the Spurs, which he puts on his heels, and after that a Sword (the same, as they say, which was *Godfreys* of *Bulloign*) and bids him use it in defence of the Church, and himself, and to the confusion of Infidels; sheathing it again, he girts himself therewith. Who then arising, and forthwith kneeling close to the Sepulchre, inclining his head upon the same, he is created by receiving three strokes on the shoulder, and by saying thrice, *I ordain thee a Knight of the Holy Sepulchre of our Lord Jesus Christ, in the Name of the Father, the Son, and the Holy Ghost*. Then kisses he him, and puts about his neck a Chain of Gold, whereat hangeth a *Jerusalem* Crofs; who arising, kisses the Sepulchre, and restoring the aforesaid Ornaments, departeth. From the top of this Monastery you may survey the most part of this City, whereof much lies waste; the old buildings (except some few) all ruined, the new contemptible, none exceed two stories; the under no better than Vaults; the upper arched above, and standing upon Arches, being well confirmed against fire, as having throughout no combustible matter; the Roofs flat, and covered with plaister. Inhabited it is by Christians out of their devotion; and by *Turks*, for the benefit received by Christians: otherwise perhaps it would be generally abandoned.

After a little refreshment, the same day we came (which was upon *Maundy Thursday*) we went into the Temple of the Sepulchre; every one carrying with him his Pillow and Carpet. The way from the Monastery continues in a long descent, the East-side of *Gihon*) and then a little ascendeth to *Mount Calvary*. *Mount Calvary*, a rocky Hill, neither high nor ample, was once a place of publick execution; then without, but now well-nigh within the heart of the City; whereupon the Emperor *Adrian* erected a Fane unto *Venus*. But the virtuous *Helena* (of whom our Country may justly glory) overthrew that receptacle of Paganism, and built in the room thereof this magnificent Temple; which not only possesseth the *Mount*, but the Garden below, together with a part of the Valley of *Carcasses* (so called, in

that

LIB. III.   *The Temple of Christs Sepulchre, &c.*   125

that they threw thereinto the bodies of the executed) which lay between Mount *Cal-vary* and the Wall of the old City.   The Frontispiece opposing the South, of an excellent Structure;

A *The Chappel of the Immolation of Isaac.*   B. *The ascent thereunto.*

having two joyning doors, the one now walled up, supported with Columns of Marble, over which a Transom engraven with historical Figures; the Walls and Arches crusted and garnished with Floritry.   On the left hand there standeth a Tower, now something ruined (once, as some say, a Steeple, and deprived by *Saladine* of Bells, insufferable to the *Mahometans*:) on the right hand, by certain steps, a little Chappel is ascended; coupled above, and sustained at the corners with Pillars of Marble. Below, thorow a Wall, which bounds the East-side of the Court, a pair of stairs do mount to the top of the Rock (yet no Rock evident:) where is a little Chappel built (as they say) in the place where *Abraham* would have sacrificed *Isaac*; of much devotion, and kept by the Priest of the *Abissines*.   This joyneth to the top of the Temple, level, and (it I forget not) floored with Plaister.   Out of the Temple there arise two ample Cupaloes: that next the East (covering the East-end and lies of the Chappel to be ascended by steps on the outside: the other over the Church of the Sepulchre, being open in the middle.   O!, who can without sorrow, without indignation, behold the enemies of Christ to be the Lords of his Sepulchre ! who at festival times sit mounted under a Canopy, to gather money of such as do enter: the profits arising thereof, being farmed at the yearly Rent of eight thousand *Saltanies*.   Each *Frank* pays fourteen (except he be of some Religious Order, who then, of what Sect soever, is exempted from payments) wherein is included the Impost due at the Gate of the City; but the Christians that be subject to the *Turk* do pay but a trifle in respect thereof. At other times the door is sealed with the Seal of the *Sanziack*, and not opened without his direction: whereat there hang seven Cords, which by the Bells that they ring give notice to the seven several Sects of Christians (who live within the Temple continually) of such as would speak with them; which they do thorow a little Wicket, and thereat receive the Provision that is brought them.   Now to make the Foundation even in a place so uneven, much of the Rock hath been hewn away, and parts too low supplied with mighty Arches: so that those natural forms are utterly deformed, which would have better satisfied the beholders; and too much regard hath made them less regardable. For, as the Satyr speaketh of the Fountain of *Ægera*.

The Roof of the Temple is of a high pitch, curiously arched, and supported with great Pillars of Marble; the out-Iles gallery'd above: the universal Fabrick stately and sumptuous. But before I descend unto a particular Description, I will present you with the Platform, that the intricacies thereof may be the better apprehended.

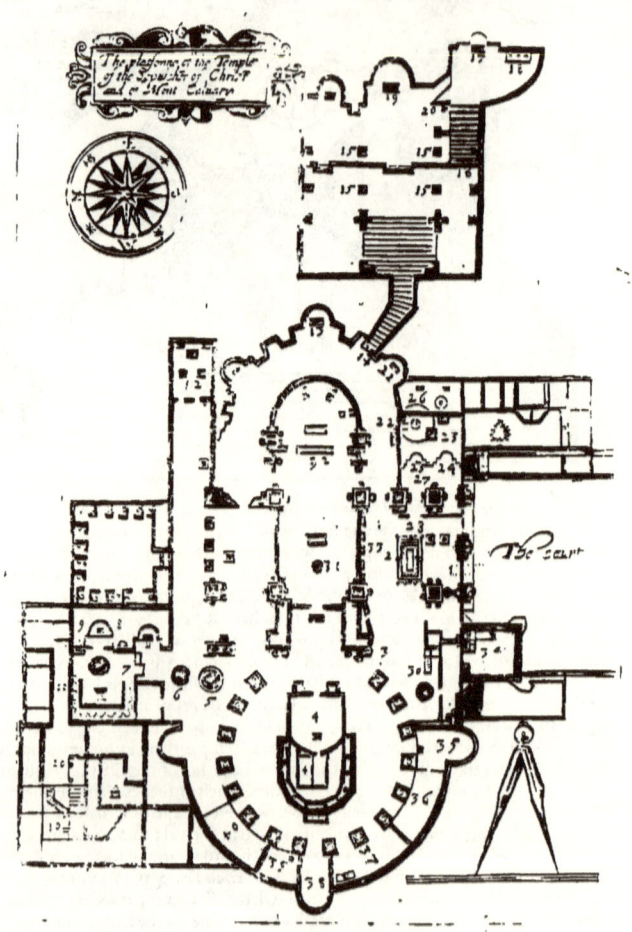

1. *The Entrance.*
2. *The Stone of the Anointing.*
3. *The passage to the Sepulchre.*
4. *The Sepulchre.*
5. *Where Christ appeared to Mary Magdalene.*
6. *Where Mary Magdalene stood.*
7. *The Chappel of the Apparition.*
8. *The Altar of the Scourging.*
9. *The Altar of the holy Cross.*
10. *The Rooms belonging to the Latines.*
11. *The Chappel of the Angels.*
12. *The Prison of Christ.*
13. *The Cappel of the division of his Garments.*
14. *The descent into the Chappel of S. Helena.*
15. *The sweating Pillars.*
16. *The descent into the place of the invention of the Cross.*
17. *Where the Cross of Christ was found.*
18. *Where the two others were found.*
19. *The Chappel of S. Helena.*
20. *Her Seat.*
21. *The Chappel of the Derision.*
22. *The ascent to the Mount Calvary.*
23. *The Chappel of the Immolation of Isaac.*
24. *Where Christ was nailed to the Cross.*
25. *Where Crucified.*
26. *Where they kept the Altar of Melchisedech.*
27. *The Rent of the Rock.*

28. *The*

LIB. II.   *The Temple of Chrifts Sepulchre, &c.*   127

28. *The Chappel of St.* John.
30. *Where the Virgin* Mary *and* St. John *ſt:od at the time of the Paſſion.*
31. *The pitch which they call the Navel of the World.*
32. *The Quire of the Church.*
33. *Sepulchre.*
34. *The Foundation of the Tower.*
35. *The Chappel of the* Abiſſines, *over which the Chappel of the Armenians.*
36. *The Chappel of the* Jacobites.
37. *The Chappel of the* Copties.
38. *The Sepulchre of* Joſeph *of* Arimathea *under ground.*
39. *The Chappel of the* Georgians.
40. *The Chappel of the* Marionites.

After we had difpofed of our Luggage in part of the North-gallery belonging to the *Latines*, the Confeſſor offered to ſhew us the holy and obſervable places of the Temple, which we gladly accepted of; he demanding firſt, if Devotion and Curioſity had poſſeſt us with that defire. So that for omitting *Pater Noſters* and *Ave Maries*, we loſt many years indulgences, which every place doth plentifully afford to ſuch as affect them; and contented our ſelves with an hiſtorical Relation. Which I will not declare in order as ſhewn, but take them as they lie from the firſt entrance of the Temple. Right againſt the door, in the midſt of the South Ile, and level with the Pavement, there lyeth a white Marble, in form of a Graves-ſtone, environed with a Rale of Braſs about a foot high : the place (as they ſay) where *Joſeph* of *Arimathea* and *Nicodemus* anointed the body of our Saviour with ſweet Oyntments. This they kiſs and kneel to, rubbing thereupon their Crucifixes, Beads, and Handkerchiefs; yea, whole Webs of Linen, which they carry into far Countries, and preſerve the ſame for their ſhrowding ſheets. Over this there hang ſeven Lamps, which burn continually. Againſt the Eaſt end of the ſtone there is a little Chappel. Near the entrance, on the right hand, ſtands the Sepulchre of *Godfrey* of *Bulloign*; with a Latine Epitaph, thus Engliſhed.

Here lieth the renowned Godfry of Bulloign,who won all this Land to the worſhip of Chriſt.Reſt my ſoul in peace, Amen.

Hic jacet inclytus Godefridus de Buglion, qui totam iſtam terram acquiſivit cultuiChriſtiano cujus anima requieſcat in pacem. Amen.

On the left hand his Brother *Baldwins*, with this Inſcription:

Baldwin, the King, another Machabee,
The Churches,Countries,ſtrength,hope,both their glory,
Whom Cæſar, Egypts Dan, Damaſcus fraught
With homicides, both fear'd, and tribute brought;
O grief! within this little Tomb doth lie.

Rex Baldwinus, Judas alter Machabeus,
Spes patriæ, vigor Eccleſiæ, virtus utriuſque :
Quam formidabant qui dona tributa ferebant,
Cæſar, Ægypti Dan, ac homicida Damaſcus,
Proh dolor ! in modico clauditur hoc tumulo.

The firſt and ſecond King of *Jeruſalem*. The farther end of this Chappel, called the Chappel of St. *John* (and of the Anointing, by reaſon of the ſtone which it neighboureth) is confined with the foot of *Calvary*, where on the left ſide of the Altar there is a Cleft in the Rock, in which, they ſay, that the head of *Adam* was found, as they will have it, there buried; others ſay in *Hebron*, that his bones might be ſprinkled with the real blood of our Saviour, which he knew ſhould be ſhed in that place by Prophetical fore-knowledg. Over this are the Chappels of Mount *Calvary*, aſcended on the North-ſide thereof by twenty ſteps; the higheſt hewn out of the Rock, as is a part of the paſſage, obſcure and extraordinary narrow. The floor of the firſt Chappel is checker'd with divers coloured Marbles, not to be trod upon by feet that are ſhod. At the Eaſt-end,under a large arched concave of the Wall, is the place whereon our Saviour did ſuffer, which may aſſuredly be thought the ſame : and if one place be more holy than another, reputed in the World the moſt venerable. He is void of ſenſe, that ſees, believes, and is not then confounded with his paſſion. The Rock there riſeth half a yard higher than the Pavement, level above, in form of an Altar, ten foot long, and ſix foot broad; flagged with white Marble, as is the Arch and Wall that adjoyneth. In the midſt is the place wherein the Croſs did ſtand, lined with Silver, gilt, and imboſſed. This they creep to, proſtrate themſelves thereunto, kiſs, ſalute; and ſuch as uſe them, ſanctifie therein their Beads and Crucifixes. On either ſide there ſtandeth a Croſs : that on the right ſide, in the place where the good Thief was crucified; and on the left, where the bad; divided from Chriſt by the rent of the Rock (a figure of his Spiritual ſeparation) which clove aſunder in the hour of his paſſion. The inſides do teſtifie that Art had no hand therein; each ſide to other being anſwerably rugged, and there were unacceſſible to the Work-man. That before ſpoken of, in the Chappel below, is a part of this, which reacheth (as they ſay) to the Center. This place belongeth to the *Georgians*: whoſe Prieſts are poor, and accept of alms. No other Nation ſay Maſs on that Altar, over which there hang forty ſix Lamps, which burn continually; On the ſelf-ſame floor, of the ſelf-ſame form in that other Chappel belonging to the *Latines*, divided

only

A. *The first Chappel of Mount Calvary.*
B. *The second Chappel.*
C. *The Cleft of the Rock.*
D. *The cleft continuing in the Chappel below, where they say, the head of Adam was found.*
E. *The Sepulchre of* Godfrey of Bulloign.
F. *The Sepulchre of King* Baldwin.
G. *The Stone of the Anointing.*
H. *The descent to Mount Calvary.*
I. *The descent into the place of the invention of the Cross.*
K. *The Door that enters into the Temple.*

only by a Curtain, and entred thorow the former. In the midst of the Pavement is a Square, inchased with stones of different colours, where Christ, as they say, was nailed upon the Cross. This place is too holy to be trod upon. They wear the hard stones with their soft knees, and heat them with their fervent kisses: prostrating themselves, and tumbling up and down with such an over-active Zeal, that a fair Greek Virgin, ere aware, one morning shewed more than she intended: whom the Fryar that helpt the Priest to say Mass, so took at the bound, that it ecchoed again, and disturbed the mournful Sacrifice with a mirthful clamour; the poor Maid departing with great indignation. Over the Altar, which is finely set forth, three and thirty Lamps are maintained. These two Chappels looking into the Temple, are all that possess the summit of the Rock: excepting that of the Immolation of *Isaac*, without, and spoken of before; and where they keep the Altar of *Melchisedech*. Opposite to the door of the Temple, adjoyning to the side of the Chancel, are certain Marble Sepulchres without Titles or Epitaphs. Some twenty paces directly West from Mount *Calvary*, and on that side that adjoyneth to the Tower, a round white Marble, level with the Pavement, retaineth the memory (as they say) of that place where the Blessed Virgin stood, and the Disciple whom Christ loved, when from the Cross he commended each to other, over which there burneth a Lamp. A little on the right hand of this, and towards the West, you pass between certain Pillars into that part of the Church which is called, The Temple of the Resurrection, and of the holy Sepulchre. A stately Round, cloistered below and above, supported with great square Pillars, flagged heretofore with white Marble; but now in many places deprived thereof by the sacrilegious Infidels. Much of the neather Cloister is divided into sundry Chappels belonging unto several Nations and Sects, where they exercise the Rites of their several Religions. The first, on the left hand, to the *Abissins*, the next to the *Jacobites*, the third to the *Copties* (close to which, on the left side of another, there is a Cave hewn out of the Rock, with a narrow entrance, the Sepulchre of *Joseph* of *Arimathea*) the fourth to the *Georgians*, and the fifth to the *Maronites*. The Chappel of the *Armenians* possesseth a great part of the Gallery above; and the rest, lying towards the North, belongeth to the *Latines*, though not imployed to Religious uses. Now between the top of the upper Gallery, and extreme of the upright Wall, in several Concaves, are the Pictures of divers of the

Saints

LIB. III. *The Temple of Christs Sepulchre, &c.*

Saints in Mosaique work, full-fac'd, and unheightned with shadows, according to the *Greek* painting; but much defaced by malice, or continuance. In the midst, on the South-side, is the Emperor *Constantine*'s, opposite to his mothers, the memorable Foundress. This Round is covered with a *Cupolo* sustained with Rafters of *Cedar*, each of one piece, being open in the midst like the *Pantheon* at *Rome*, whereat it receiveth the light that it hath, and that as much as sufficeth. Just in the midst, and in view of Heaven stands the glorified Sepulchre, a hundred and eight feet distant from *Mount Calvary*; the natural Rock surmounting the sole of the Temple, abated by Art, and hewn in the form of a Chappel,

A. *The Cupolo.*
B. *The Sepulchre.*
C. *The Portico.*
D. *The Altar within.*
E. *The inside of the Portico.*
F. *The entrance of the Portico.*
G. *The entrance of the Sepulchre.*
H. *The stone, whereon they erroneously say, that the Angel sate.*

more

more long than broad, and ending in a semi-circle, all flagged over with white Marble. The hinder part being something more eminent than the other, is environed with ten small Pillars adjoining to the wall, and sustaining the Cornish. On the top (which is flat) and in the midst thereof, a little Cupolo covered with Lead is erected upon six double, but small *Corinthian* Columns, of polished Porphyry. The other part, being lower than this by the height of the Cornish, smooth above, and not so garnished on the sides (serving as a Lobby or Portico to the former) is entred at the East end; (having before the door a long pavement, erected something above the floor of the Church included between two white Marble walls, not past two foot high) and consisting of the self-same Rock, doth contain therein a Concave about three yards square, the Roof hewn compass, and flagged thorowout with white Marble. In the midst of the floor there is a stone about a foot high, and a foot and half square, whereon, they say, that the Angel sate, who told the two *Maries* that our Saviour was risen. But St. *Matthew* saith, he sate upon the great stone which he had rolled from the mouth of the Sepulchre; which, as it is said, the Empress caused to be conveyed to the Church of *Saint Saviour*, standing where once stood the Palace of *Caiaphas*. Out of this a passage thorow the midst of the Rock, exceeding not three feet in height, and two in breadth, having a Door of grey stone with hinges of the same, un-divided from the natural, affordeth a way to creep thorow into a second Concave, about eight foot square, and as much in height, with a compact Roof of the solid Rock, but lined, for the most part with white Marble. On the North-side there is a Tomb of the same, which possesseth one half of the Room; a yard in height, and made in the form of an Altar, insomuch that not above three can abide there at once; the place no larger than affordeth a liberty for kneeling. It is said, that long after the Resurrection, the Tomb remained in that form wherein it was when our Saviour lay there; when at length, by reason of the devouter Pilgrims, who continually bore away little pieces thereof (reliques, whereunto they attributed miraculous effects) it was inclosed within a grate of Iron. But a second inconveniency, which proceeded from the Tapers, hair, and other offerings thrown in by Votaries, which defiled the Monument, procured the pious *Helena* to enclose the same within this Marble Altar, which now belongeth to the *Latines*, whereon they only say Mass, yet free for other Christians to exercise their private devotions; being well set forth, and having on the far side an antique and excellent Picture demonstrating the Resurrection. Over it perpetually burneth a number of Lamps, which have sullyed the Roof like the in-side of a Chimny, and yields unto the Room an immoderate fervour. Thousands of Christians perform their vows, and offer their tears yearly, with all the expressions of sorrow, humility, affection and penitence. It is a frozen zeal that will not be warmed with the sight thereof. And, Oh that I could retain the effects that it wrought, with an unfainting perseverance! who then did dedicate this hymn to my Redeemer.

> *Saviour of mankind, Man, Emanuel:*
> *Who sinless died for sin, who vanquisht Hell:*
> *The first-fruits of the Grave; whose life did give*
> *Light to our darkness; in whose death we live:*
> *O strengthen thou my faith, correct my will,*
> *That mine may thine obey; protect me still,*
> *So that the latter death may not devour*
> *My soul seal'd with thy seal. So in the hour*
> *When thou, whose body sanctifi'd this Tomb,*
> *Unjustly judg'd, a glorious Judge shalt come*
> *To judge the world with justice; by that sign*
> *I may be known, and entertain'd for thine.*

Without, and to the West end of this Chappel, another very small one adjoineth, used in common by the *Egyptians* and *Æthyopians*. Now on the left hand, as you pass unto the Chappel of the Apparitions, there are two round stones of white Marble in the floor: that next the Sepulchre covering the place where our Saviour, and the other where *Mary Magdalen* stood (as they say) when he appeared unto her. On the North-side, and without the limits of the Temple, stands the Chappel of the Apparition; so called (as they say) for that Christ in that place

did

did shew himself to his sorrowful Mother, and comforted her, pierced with anguish for his cruel death, and ignominious sufferings. This belongeth to the *Latines*, which serveth them also for a Vestry; from whence they proceed unto their pompous Processions. On the East side there stand three Altars: that in the midst in a Closet by it self, dedicated to God and our Lady. That on the right hand is called The Altar of the Holy Cross, whereof a great part was there (as they say) reserved. But when *Sultan Solyman* imprisoned the Fryars of Mount *Sion*, (whom he kept in durance for the space of four years) the *Armenians* stole it from thence, and carried it to *Sebastia* their principal City. That on the left hand in the corner, and near unto the entrance, is called the Altar of the *Scourgins*; behind which there is a piece of a Pillar, of that as they say) whereunto our Saviour was bound when they scourged him. This stood on Mount *Sion*, and there supported the Portico to a Church in the days of Saint *Jerome*, when broken by the *Saracens*, the pieces were re-collected, and this part here placed by Christians. The rest was distributed by *Paul* the Fourth unto the Emperour *Ferdinand*, *Philip* King of *Spain*, and the Signory of *Venice*; in honour whereof they celebrate the sixth of *April*. It is (as I remember) about three foot high, of a dusky black vein'd Marble, spotted here and there with red; which they affirm to be the marks of his blood wherewith it was besprinkled. Before it there is a Grate of Iron, insomuch as not to be toucht but by the mediation of a stick prepared for the purpose; being buttoned at the end with Leather, in manner of a foil, by which they convey their kisses, and bless their lips with the touch of that which hath touched the Relique. Through the aforesaid Vestry, a passage leads into certain Rooms, heretofore a part of the Colledge of the Knight-Templars: an Order erected by the Princes of *France* (of whom the chief were *Hugo de Pagonis* and *Godfredus à Sancto Audamaro*) about the year of our Lord 1119, in the days of *Baldwin* the Second, who assigned them this place adjoining to the Temple, and whereupon they were called Templars. It is said, that they received their institutions from St. *Bernard*, together with their white Habit: and after that, the red Cross from *Eugenius* the Third Pope of that Name: The one a symbol of innocency, the other of not to be refused Martyrdom; and of the blood which they were profusely to shed in defence of this Country. At first they grew glorious in Arms; then rich in Revenues: which corrupted their virtues, and betrayed them to the most detested kinds of lasciviousness: Insomuch as by a general Council held in *Vienna*, in the year 1312. the Order was extinguisht, and their Lands for the most part conferred upon the Knight-Hospitallers of Saint *Johns* of *Jerusalem*, of whom we shall speak when we come unto *Malta*. The Temples in *London* belonged unto them: where in the Church (built round in imitation of this) divers of their Statues are to be seen, and the posture used in their burials. Here the *Francisans* entertained us during our abode in the Temple. Returning again through the Chappel of the Apparition, a little on the left hand there is a concave in the Wall, no bigger than to contain two persons besides the Altar; which is called the Chappel of the Angels: belonging also to the *Latines*, but lent by them to the despised *Nestorians* during the celebration of *Easter*. Winding with the Wall along the outward North-Alley of the Chancel, at the far end thereof there is a Grot hewn out of the Rock, where, they say, that the *Jews* imprisoned our Saviour, during the time that they were providing things necessary for his crucifying. This is kept by the *Georgians*, without other ornament than an ungarnished Altar: over which hangeth one only Lamp, which rendreth a dim light to the Prison. Untreading a good part of the aforesaid Alley, we entred the Ile (there but distinguished by Pillars) which borders on the North of the Chancel: and turning on the left hand, where it begins to compass with the East end thereof, we passed by a Chappel containing an Altar, but of no regard, wherein they say, the Title was preserved which was hung over the head of our Saviour: now shown at *Rome* in the Church of the Holy Cross of *Jerusalem*. Next to this in the same Wall, and midst of the semi-circle there is another, the place (where they say) the Souldiers did cast lots for his Garments: of which the *Armenians* have the custody. A little beyond you are to descend a pair of large Stairs of thirty Steps, part of the passage hewn out of the Rock of *Calvary*, which leadeth into a Lobby: the Roof supported with four massie Pillars of white Marble, which is ever moist through the dampness of the place (being under-ground) and sometimes dropping, are said to weep for the sorrowful passion and death of Christ. At the far end, containing more than half of the Room, is the Chappel of Saint *Helena*: having two great Altars erected by Christian

ſtian Princes in her honour; On the South-ſide there is a ſeat of Stone, over-looking a pair of Stairs which deſcend into the place of the invention of the Croſs: where they ſay, that ſhe ſate whilſt the Souldiers removed the rubbidge that had covered it. Theſe Stairs (eleven in number) conduct into an obſcure Vault, a part of the Valley of *Carcaſſes.* There threw they our Saviours Croſs, and covered it with the filth of the City: when after three hundred years, the Empreſs *Helena* travelling unto *Jeruſalem* in the extremity of her age, to behold thoſe places which Chriſt had ſanctified with his corporal preſence, threatned torture and death to certain of the principal *Jews*, if they would not reveal where their Anceſtors had hid it. At laſt forſooth they wreſted the truth from an old *Jew*, one *Judas*, firſt almoſt famiſhed: who brought them to this place. Where, after he had petitioned Heaven for the diſcovery, the earth trembled, and breathed from her cranies Aromatick odours. By which miracle confirmed, the Emperour cauſed the rubbidge to be removed, where they found three Croſſes, and hard by the Superſcription. But when not able to diſtinguiſh the right from the other, they ſay that *Macarius*, then Biſhop of *Jeruſalem*, repairing together with the Empreſs unto the Houſe of a Noble woman of this City, uncurably diſeaſed, did with the touch of the true Croſs reſtore her to health. At ſight whereof the *Jew* became a Chriſtian, and was called thereupon *Quiriscus.* Being after Biſhop of *Jeruſalem*, in the Reign of *Julian* the Apoſtate, he was crowned with Martyrdom. At which time it was decreed, that no Malefactor ſhould thenceforth ſuffer on the Croſs; and that the third of *May* ſhould be for ever celebrated in the memorial of that Invention. In this Vault are two Altars, the one where the Croſs of Chriſt was found, and the other where the other. Aſcending again by the aforeſaid ſtair into the Temple; on the left hand between the entrance and Mount *Calvary*, there is a little Room which is called the Chappel of the Deriſion. Where under the Altar is reſerved a part (as they ſay) of that Pillar to which Chriſt was bound, when *Pilats* Servants crowned him with Thorns, being cloathed in an old Purple Robe, and placed a Reed in his hand, inſtead of a Scepter, crying, *Hail, King of the Jews*: with other opprobrious taunts and revilings. This is kept by the *Abyſſens.* Now nothing remaineth to ſpeak of, but the Quire, not differing from thoſe in our Cathedral Churches. The Weſt end openeth upon the Sepulchre: the Eaſt ending in a ſemicircle, together with the Iles, is covered with a high Cupolo: on each ſide ſtand oppoſite doors which open into the North and South Alleys; all jointly called the Temple of *Golgatha.* A partition at the upper end excludeth the half round (behind which is their high Altar) which riſeth in a manner of a lofty Screen, all richly guilded (as moſt of the Chancel) and adorned with the Pictures of the Saints Antique Habits: flat and full-faced, according to the manner of the *Grecians,* to whom this place is aſſigned. Towards the Weſt end from each ſide equally diſtant, there is a little pit in the pavement, (which they ſay) is the Navel of the World, and endeavour to confirm it with that ſaying of the Scripture, *God wrought his ſalvation in the midſt of the earth,* which they fill with holy water. The univerſal Fabrick, maintained by the *Greek* Emperours during their Soveraignty, and then by the Chriſtian Kings of *Jeruſalem*, hath ſince been repaired in the ſeveral parts by their particular owners. The whole of ſo ſtrong a conſtitution, has rather decayed in beauty than ſubſtance.

Having viſited theſe places which beſtow their ſeveral Indulgences, (and are honoured with particular Oriſons) after Even-ſong, and Proceſſion, the *Pater-guardian* putting off his pontifical Habit, and cloathed in a long Veſt of Linen girt cloſe unto him, firſt waſhed the feet of his fellow Fryars, and then of the Pilgrims: which dryed by others, he kiſſed with all outward ſhew of humility. The next day being *Good Friday*, amongſt other Solemnities, they carried the Image of Chriſt on a ſheet, ſupported by the four corners, in proceſſion, with Banners of the Paſſion: firſt to the place where he was impriſoned, then in order to the other; performing at each their appointed Devotions. Laying it where they ſay he was fixed on the Croſs, the Fryar-Preacher made over it a ſhort and paſſionate Oration; who acted his part ſo well, that he begot tears in others with his own, and taught them how to be ſorrowful. At length they brought it to the place, where, they ſay, he was embalmed: where the *Pater-guardian* anointed the Image with ſweet Oyls, and ſtrewed it with Aromatick Powders, and from thence conveyed it to the Sepulchre. At night the lights put out, and company removed, they whipped themſelves in their Chappel of Mount *Calvary.* On Sunday their other Solemnities performed, they carried the Croſs in proceſſion, with the Banners of the burial, to the aforeſaid

LIB III.   Sects of Christians here celebrating Easter.   133

said Chappel, creeping to it, kissing, and lying groveling over it. On Easter day they said solemn Service before the door of the Sepulchre. The whole Chappel covered on the out-side with cloth of Tissue; the gift (as appeareth by the Arms imbroydered thereon) of the *Florentine*. In this they shewed the variety of their Wardrobes, and conclude with a triumphant procession, bearing about the Banners of the Resurrection. Those ceremonies that are not local, I willingly omit. At noon we departed to the Monastery, having lain on the hard stones for three nights together, and fared as hardly.

The other Christians (excepting such as inhabit, within of each sort a few, and those of the Clergy) entred not until Good-friday, being *Greeians, Armenians, Copties, Abiſſens, Jacobites, Georgians, Maronites,* and *Neſtorians*. Of the *Greeians, Copties,* and *Armenians* no more shall be said (since we have spoken of them already) than concerns the celebration of this Festival.

The *Abiſſens* or *Æthiopians* be descended of the cursed generation of *Chus*. But their Emperours do derive themselves from *Solomon*, of one begotten by him on the Queen of *Saba*, in regard whereof they have ever favoured that Nation. They received the Doctrine of Christ from the *Eunuch* instructed by *Philip*: which in the Year of our Lord 470. did generally propagate thorowout all *Æthiopia*, under the Reign of *Abraham* and *Atba*, two brethren: who thereupon were stiled the Propagators and Defenders of the Christian Religion; *Abraham* out-living his Brother, (and after his own death canonized by their Clergy) to avoid dissention in his posterity, (so advised, as they say, by a Vision) was he that first confined the Royal progeny within high and un-ascendable Mountains, having only one entrance, and that impregnably fortified. A custom observed to this day, wherein they enjoy whatsoever is fit for Delight, or Princely Education. Out of these, if the Emperour die son-less, a Successor is chosen, of such a Spirit as their present affairs do require. There have they the goodliest Library in the World, where many Books that are lost with us, or but meerly mentioned, are kept intire, as hath been lately reported by a *Spanish* Frier that hath seen them, if we may believe him; amongst which, they say, are the Oracles of *Enoch* (with other mysteries that escaped the Flood, engraven by him upon Pillars) and written in their Vulgar Language. The Priests do marry but once, they labour for their livings, and have their preferments given them by the King. They shave their heads, and foster their beards, contrary to the Laity. The chief of them are Judges in causes, as well Civil as Ecclesiastical. They acknowledge the Patriarch of *Alexandria* for their Primate, I mean the Patriarch of the Circumcised. Pictures they have in their Churches, but no carved Images; neither bestow they upon them any undue reverence. They admit of no Crucifixes. The Cross they use as a badge of their profession, and according to the first Institution. Men and Women are both circumcised, not as a matter of Religion, but as the *Copties* do, out of an ancient custom of their Nation: their Priests say, that they now do it in imitation of our Saviour. They baptize not the Male until forty, nor the Female until threescore days old; and if it die in the mean time, they say, that the Eucharist received by the Mother when it was in her Womb, is sufficient to save. Upon the twelfth day, they Baptise yearly, and have certain Ponds and Lakes reserved for that purpose: Which they do not Sacramentally, but in memorial that Christ was at this day baptized by *John* in *Jordan*; a custom introduced not past an hundred years since, by a King of *Æthiopia*. They receive the Eucharist in both kinds, but with Unleavened Bread, nor spit they all the day after. Incense they use and Holy-water. Confess they do, but not greatly in private. The Lent is most strictly observed by them, wherein they eat little but Herbs and Fruits, and that not until Sun-set. During which time, not a few of their Priests do flie the concourse of men, lying in Caves and Desarts, and inflicting on themselves excessive Penance. They abstain from such meats as were prohibited to the Jews, and celebrate the Saturday as well as the Sunday. All the Passion-week they forbear to say Mass, putting on mourning Garments, and countenances suitable. They use no extream-Unction, but carry the Dead to the Grave with the Cross, the Censer and Holy-water, and say Service over them. To conclude, they join with the *Copties* for the most part in subsance of Religion, and in Ceremony, one Priest here serving both: an *Æthiopian*, poor, and accompanied with few of his Nation; who fantastically clad, doth dance in their processions with a skipping motion, and distortion of his body, not unlike to our Antiques. To which their Musick is answerable, the Instruments no other than Snappers, Gin-

N   gles,

gles, and round bottom'd Drums, born upon the back of one, and beaten upon by the followers.

The *Jacobites* are so called of *Jacobus* the *Syrian*, an obscure Fellow, and of no reputation, who for his poverty was named *Zanzalus*. He infected these Countries with divers heretical opinions, amongst the rest, that the God-head of Christ was passible, and confused with his Manhood. They mark their Children before Baptism with the sign of the Cross. They use not auricular confession; pray not for the dead; reject the opinion of Purgatory; believe that the Soul doth rest in the Grave with the Body, and shall so do till Christs second coming. The Priests do marry, and they in both kinds communicate in the Sacrament. They reject the fourth Synod, and authority of the Fathers. This Sect began in the days of the Emperour *Mauritius*, dispersing through the Cities of *Syria*, *Mesopotamia*, and *Chaldea*; yet under other names their Religion extendeth far further, the *Copties* and *Abyssins* being in a manner no other than *Jacobites*. They had two Patriarchs; one resident in the Mountain *Tur*, the other in the Monastery of *Giftan*, near unto the City *Modin*, (they say) on so high a Mountain, that no Bird flieth over it. But now they have but one Patriarch, and that he of *Giftan*, always a Monk of the Order of St. *Anthony*, and named *Ignatius*, stiling himself the Patriarch of *Antioch*, who for the more conveniency is removed to *Carmit*. They have a Bishop still residing in *Jerusalem*, the Patriarch whereof is also a *Jacobite*.

The *Georgians* differ not much from the *Grecians* in their opinions; not called (as some write) of Saint *George* their selected Patron, but of their Country, so named long before the time wherein he is supposed to have lived; lying between *Colchos*, *Caucasus*, the *Caspian* Sea, and *Armenia*, heretofore *Iberia* and *Albania*. A warlike people, infested on both sides with the *Turkish* and *Persian* insolencies. They have a Metropolitan of their own; some say, the same that is resident in Mount *Sinai*. They say that they marry within prohibited degrees: they are divided into eighteen Bishopricks, and are not here to be distinguished from the *Syrians*, nor they from them, being almost of one Religion, and called *Melchites* heretofore of their Adversaries, which signifieth a King in the *Syrian* tongue, for that they would not imbrace the Heresies of *Eutyches* and *Dioscorus*, but obeyed the Edict of the Emperour, and Council of *Chalcedon*. Their Patriarch is the true Patriarch of *Antioch*; who abides in *Damasco*, for that *Antioch* lies now well nigh desolate. The Bishop is here poor, so are his Ornaments; in their processions, for state, or in regard of his age, supported on both sides. Their musick-less Instruments are fans of Brass, hung about with Rings, which they gingle in stops according to their marchings.

The *Maronites* are Christians inhabiting Mount *Libanus*, so called of *Marona* a Village adjoining, or of *Maro* their Abbot: they use the *Chaldean* tongue, and *Syrian* character, in holy matters. A limb they were of the *Jacobites*, and once subject to the Patriarch of *Antioch*, but won to the Papacy by *John Baptist* a Jesuite, in the days of *Gregory* the thirteenth, who sent them a Catechism Printed at *Rome* in the *Arabian* language, so that now they do join with the *Latines*; an ignorant people, easily drawn to any Religion, that could not give a reason for their own: poor in substance, and few in number.

But the *Greeks* do here surpass all the rest in multitudes; and the *Armenians* in bravery, who instead of Musical Instruments, have Sawcers of Brass (which they strike against one another) set about with gingles. All differ in habit, and most in rites; yet all conjoin (the *Latines* excepted) in celebration of that imposture of fetching fire from the Sepulchre upon Easter-Eve. The *Turks* deride, yet throng to behold it, the Galleries of the round Temple being pestered with spectators. All the Lamps within the Church are at that time extinguished; when they often compassing the Sepulchre in a joint procession, are fore-run and followed by the people with savage clamours (the women whistling) and frantick behaviours, befitting better the solemnities of *Bacchus*, extending their bare arms with unlighted Tapers. At length the chief Bishops approach the door of the Sepulchre, but the *Æthiopian* Priest first enters, (without whom, they say, the miracle will not sadge) who after a long stay (mean while the people hurrying about like mad men) returns with the sacred flame, supposed at his prayers to burst out of the Sepulchre; whereat confusedly they fire their lights, and snatching them one from another, strive who should convey it to their particular Chappels, thrusting the flame amongst their cloaths, and into their bosoms, (but swiftly withdrawing it) perswading strangers that it will not burn

them:

them: kindling therewith all their Lamps, unlighted with other fire until that day twelve-month.

But I had almost forgot the *Nestorians*, so called of *Nestorius*, by birth a *German*, who lived in the days of *Theodosius*, and was by him made Bishop of *Constantinople*. These hated of the rest, in an obscure corner, without Ceremonies or Pontificial habit, full of seeming zeal and humility, do read the Scriptures, and in both kinds administer the Sacrament, denying the real presence: the Priest (not distinguished from the rest in habit) breaking the bread, and laying it In the palm of the Communicants hand, they supping of the Cup which is held between his hands. They kiss the Cross, but pray not before it, nor reverence they Images. They will not have *Mary* to be called the Mother of God. Their chiefest Heretic is, that they divide the Divinity of Christ from his Humanity. Their Doctrine dispersech it self throughout all the East, by means of *Cosro* the *Persian* King, who inforced all the Christians within his Dominion (out of a mortal hatred that he bare to the Emperour *Heraclius*) either to forsake his Empire, or to become *Nestorians*: as thorow a great part of *Cataia*. It is now embraced but by few, most of that Sect inhabiting about *Babylon*. Their Patriarchal Seat is *Musal* in *Mesopotamia*, seated on the Bank of *Tygris*: their Patriarch not elect, but the dignity descending from the Father to the Son. For Marriage, it is generally allowed in their Clergy; and when Widowers, to marry again at their pleasure. They have the Scriptures, and execute the Ministery in the *Chaldean* Tongue. They allow not of the Council of *Ephesus*, nor any that succeeded it.

All this while there was no less than a thousand Christians, Men, Women, and Children, who fed and lodged upon the Pavement of the Temple. On *Easter*-day about one of the clock in the morning, the Nations and Sects above-mentioned with joyful clamors, according to their several Customs, circled the Church; and visited the holy places in a solemn Procession; and so for that time concluding that Ceremony, departed.

Upon *Easter*-Monday we hired certain Asses to ride to *Emaus*, accompanied with a Guard, and certain of the Fryars. About the mid-way, at the foot of a Hill, there are the ruines of a Monastery, built by St. *Helena*, they say, in that place where Jesus appeared to the two Disciples. Here the *Latines* performed certain devotions, and took of the stones (as generally they did from all such like places) preserved as precious. *Emaus* stands seven miles off, and West of *Jerusalem*. The way thither mountainous; and in many places as if paved with a continual Rock; yet where there is earth, sufficiently fruitful. It was seated (for now it is not) upon the South-side of a Hill, overlooking a little Valley, fruitful in Fountains. Honoured with the presence of our Saviour, who was there known by the breaking of bread, in the house of *Cleophas* his Cou-in-german, and afterward the second Bishop of *Jerusalem*. In the self-same place a Temple was erected by *Paula* (a *Roman* Lady, of whom we shall speak hereafter) whose ruines are yet extant, near the top of the Mountain; unto which the *Arabians* would not suffer us to ascend, who inhabit below in a few poor Cottages, until we had payed the *Caphar* they demanded. This City was burnt in the *Jewish* Wars, by the commandment of *Varus*: and upon the destruction of *Jerusalem*, re-edified by the *Romans*, who, in regard of their Victory, called it *Nicopolis*. In the year 131. thrown down by an Earth-quake, it was fourscore and twelve years after restored by the Emperour *Marcus Aurelius*: and afterward dignified, during the Government of the Christians, with an Episcopal See, being under the Metropolitan of *Cæsarea*. *Nicephorus*, and the *Tripartite* History report of a miraculous Fountain by the highway side, where Christ would have departed from the two Disciples: who, when he was conversant upon earth, and wearied with a long journey, there washed his feet; the water from thenceforth retaining a curable virtue against all Diseases. But relations of that kind have credit only in places far distant. In our return, we inclined a little to the left hand, and after a while ascended to the top of a Mountain, (whose Western Valley was the field, they say, of that Battel, when the Sun and Moon stood still at the commandment of *Joshua*.) Out of the ruines of an ancient Building a smallMosque is advanced, where they would that the Prophet *Samuel* was buried, who had his Sepulchre in *Ramah* on Mount *Ephraim*, though divers other Towns so seated, are so called; which signifieth *high* in their Language. But our Guides were well practised in that precept;

Atque aliqua ex illis dom regum nomina quærunt,   *Of streams, Kings, fashions, Kingdoms ask, there shewn;*
Quæ loca, qui mores, quæve feruntur aquæ :   *Answer to all : th' unknown relate as known.*
Omnia responde; nec tantum si qua rogabit,
Et quæ nescires, ut bene nota refer.   *Ovid.*

who

who endeavour to bring all remarkable places within the compass of their Processions. The *Mahometans*, either deceived with this Tradition, or maintaining the report for their profit, would not suffer us to enter but at an excessive rate; which we refused to part with. The next Mountain unto this doth wear on his Crown the ruines of a Castle that belonged to the *Maccabees*. Another more humble, and nearer the City, presenteth a pile of stones, square, flat, and solid: the Sepulchre, they say, of the seven Brethren who were tortured to death by *Antiochus*. Whom I rather judge to have been buried at *Modin*, the ancient seat of that Family; which stands on the uttermost confines of the Mountains of *Judæa*, where were to be seen seven Sepulchres of white Marble, each bearing a Pyramis on his square; said by *Josephus* to have served, in his time, for Sea-marks. From hence we approached the North-West side of the City, where, in the Vineyards, are sundry places of Burial hewn out of the main Rock: amongst the rest, one called the Sepulchre of the Prophets. The first entrance large, and like the Mantle-tree of a Chimney; cut curiously on the outside: thorow which we crept into a little square room, (every one carrying a Light in his hand) the sides cut full of holes (in manner of a Dove-house:) two yards deep, and three quarters square. Out of that Room we descended by two straight passages into two other Rooms, likewise under ground: yet more spacious, and of better workmanship, but surrounded with the Sepulchres as the former: neighboured with a Vault, which serves for a Cistern, and is filled with a living Fountain. A little beyond, upon the West-side of a large square Court, hewn into the Rock some three fathoms deep, and entred under the Arch of the same, there is another mansion for the dead, having a Porch like to that of the Prophets, and garnished without (amongst other Figures) with two great Clusters of Grapes, in memorial of those, as they say, which were brought by the Spies into the Host of the *Hebrews*. On the left hand you creep thorow a difficult descent, which leadeth into fair Rooms under the ground, and one within another; benched about with Coffins of stone bereft of their Covers, there being some bones yet remaining in some of them. This is famed to be the houshold Monument of certain of the Kings of *Judah*. In which there is nothing more admirable, than is the artificial contriving of the doors, the hinges and all, of the self-same stone, unseparated from the Rock without other suppliment. Hitherto (if no further) by all likelihood the City extended. From hence we returned to the Covent.

The day following we rid towards *Bethlehem*; which stands about six miles South from *Jerusalem*. Going out of the Gate of *Joppa*, and turning on the left

The way to Bethlehem:

A The ruines of David's Tower.
B Bethsha's Fountain.
C The Turpentine Tree.
D The Tower of Simeon.
E The Cistern of the Sages.
F The Church of Habakkuk.
G The Monastry of Elias.
H Elias his Image.
I Jacob's house.
K The field where the Inhabitants gather little stones like pease, and sell them to Pilgrims who keep them in honour of the blessed Virgin.
L The Sepulchre of Rachel.
M Ramah.
N The Cistern of David.
O The Monastry of Bethlehem.
P The house of Joseph.
Q The Village of the Shepherds.
R Where they kept their sheep.
S The Mountains of Bethulia.
T The Mountains of Arabia.
V The Monastry of the holy Crofs.

hand by the foot of Mount Sion. Aloft on whose uttermost angle stood the Tower of David (whose ruines are yet extant) of a wonderful strength and admirable beauty, adorned with Shields and the Arms of the Mighty. Below on the right hand of the way in our passage, they shewed us a Fountain at the South side of a square Seraglio, delivered to be that wherein Bethsheba bathed. North of which, the Valley is crossed with a ruinous Aquæduct, which conveyed water unto the Temple of Solomon. Ascending the opposite Mountain, we passed through a Country, hilly, and stony; yet not utterly forsaken of the Vine, though only planted by Christians, in many places producing Corn, here shadowed with the Figtree, and there with the Olive. Sundry small Turrets are dispersed about, which serve for solace, as well as for safe-guard. Some two miles from the City, on the left hand, and by the Highway side, there groweth a Turpentine Tree, yet flourishing, which is said to have afforded a shelter to the Virgin Mary, as she passed between Bethlehem and Jerusalem. This Tradition however absurd, is generally believed by those Christians, a place of high repute in their Devotions. Towards the West, above two miles off, on a little Hill stands an ancient Tower, which is said to have been the Habitation of Simeon. A mile beyond the foresaid Tree, in the midst of the way, there is a Cistern, vast within, and square at the mouth, which is called the Cistern of the Star. For that (as they say) the Wise-men of the East, there first again did see that conducting Star, which went before them to the place of our Saviours Nativity. A little on the right hand, there are the small remains of an ancient Monastry, built, they affirm, in that place where the Angel took up *Habakkuk* by the Hair of the Head, and conveyed him to *Babylon*. Half a mile further, on the left-side of the way, there is another Religious House, but in good repair, in form of a Fortress, and environed with high Walls, to withstand the insolencies of the Infidels; possessed by the *Greek Coloieros*, and dedicated to *Elias*. Hard by, there is a flat Rock, whereon they told us that the Prophet accustomed to sleep, and that it bears as yet, the impression of his body. Indeed there are certain hollows in the same, but not by mine eyes apprehended to retain any manly proportion. As far beyond, are the decays of a Church, which stood (as they say) in the place where the Patriarch *Jacob* inhabited. About a mile further West of the way, and a little off, stands the Sepulchre of *Rachel*, (by the Scripture affirmed to have been buried hereabout) if the entireness thereof do not confute the imputed antiquity, yet kept perhaps in repair by her off-spring as a monument of venerable memory. The Tomb it self resembleth a great Trunck, covered with a Cupolo, mounted on a square, which hath on each side an ample Arch sustained only by the corners. This is invironed with a four-square Wall, within which stand two other Sepulchres, little, but of the same proportion; kept, and used for a place of prayer by the *Mahometans*. Below it on the side of a Mountain, stands the ruines of that *Rama*, whereof the Prophet: *A voice was heard in Rama, Rachel weeping for her Children, &c.* From this ridge of the Hills, the Dead Sea doth appear as if near at hand, but not so found by the Traveller; for that those high declining Mountains are not to be directly descended. Within half a mile of *Bethlehem*, separated from the same by a Valley, and a little on the left hand of the way, are the Cisterns of *David*, whereof he so much desired to drink, and when they brought him of the water, he refused it: A large deep Vault, now out of use, having only two small Tunnels at the top, by which they draw up the water.

And now we are come to *Bethlehem*, first called *Ephrat* of *Ephrata*, the Wife of *Caleb*. A City of *David*, the long possession of his Ancestors, and not the least amongst the Princes of *Juda*; seated on the utmost of the Ridge of a Hill, stretching East and West; in a happy soil, and most delicate prospect.

For

Bethlehem.

O sola magnarum urbium,	*Of Cities greater than the Great*
Major Bethlehem, cui contigit	*O Bethlehem, in the happy birth*
Ducem salutis cœlitus,	*Of God and man, from Heavens high seat*
Incorporatum gignere	*Come to incorporate with Earth,*
Quam Stella quæ Solis rotam	*Lost, Mans Redeemer, frail, divine;*
Vincit decore ac lumine,	*When born declar'd by that fair Star*
Venisse terris nunciat	*To wandring eyes; which did outshine*
Dum carne terrestri Deum.	*The radiant Saints flame bearing carr.*
Prudentius in Hymno.	

For when *Augustus Cæsar* had apointed that all the World should be taxed, every one repaired unto the City of his Family; and *Joseph* with *Mary* came up to *Bethlehem*, where in a Grot at the East-side of a City, employed for a Stable (the Inn being pestred with strangers) she fell in Travel, and produced unto the World a Saviour. In this Cave from the time of *Adrian*, unto the Reign of *Constantine*, they celebrated the impious lamentation of *Adonis* (much honoured by the *Syrians*) who above had his Statue shadowed with a Grove of Myrtles. Which the virtuous *Helena* subverted, and erected thereupon this goodly Temple (yet entire, and possest by the *Franciscans* of *Jerusalem*, of whom some few are here continually resident) and called it Saint *Maries* of *Bethlehem*: In form it representeth

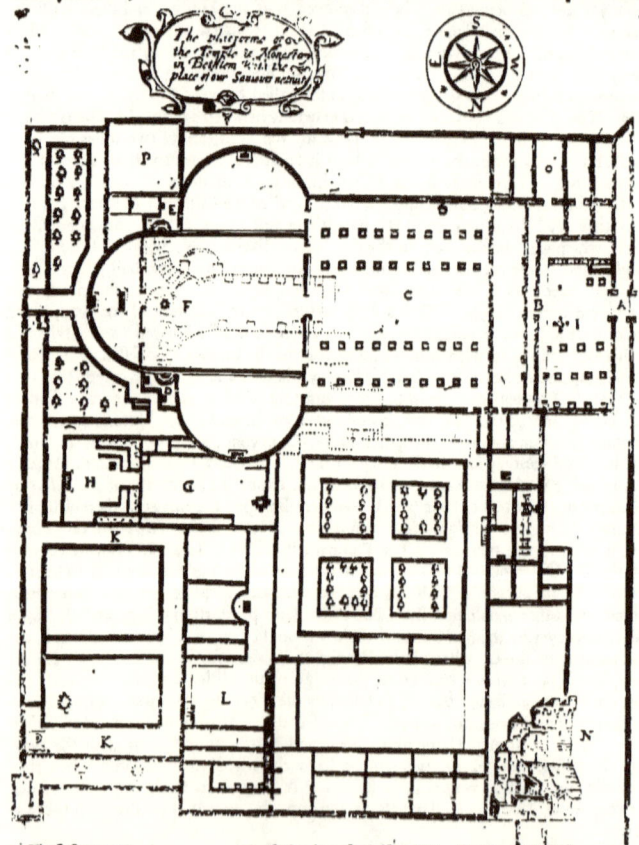

A. *The first entrance.*
B. *The second.*
C. *The body of the Church.*
D. *The Chappel of the Grecians.*
E. *The Altar of the Circumcision.*
F. *The Chancel, with the delineati-*
ons *of the place of Christs Nativity, &c. under ground.*
G. *The Chappel of S. Katherine.*
H. *The Vestry.*
I. *The Portico.*
K. *The Garden.*
L. *The old Vestry.*
M. *The dividing room.*
N. *The ruined tower.*
O. *The lodging of the Armenians.*
P. *The lodging of the Grecians.*

✠ *a Cross*

LIB. III.   Bethlehem.

a Cross; the stalk whereof comprifeth the body, and is entred at the lower end through a portico fuftained with fixteen pillars. The Roof, in the midft, is lofty, flat, and (if I forget not) of Cedar; the fides of the fame Fabrick (but much more humble) are upheld with four ranks of Pillars, ten in a row, each of one entire Marble, white, and in many places beautifully speckled; the largest, and fairest that ever I saw; whose upper ends do declare, that they have in part been exquisitely gilded. The Walls are flagged with large Tables of white Marble, well-nigh to the top; the rest adorned with Mofaick painting, although now greatly defaced. It is both here Reported and Recorded by History, that a *Sultan* of *Egypt* allured with their beauty, set certain Mafons on work to take down thofe Tables, with intent to have transported them unto his Caftle of *Cairo*; when a dreadful Serpent iffued out of the Wall, and brake in pieces fuch as were removed, fo that terrified therewith, he defifted from his enterprife. The three upper ends of the Crofs do end in three Semicircles, having in each an Altar. In the midft ftands a Chancel, roofed with a ftately Cupulo, covered without with Lead, garniflhed within with Mofaick Figures. This Church is left for the moft part defolate, the Altar naked, no Lamps maintained, no Service celebrated, except at times extraordinary: yet are there a few poor *Greeks* and *Arminians*, who inhabit within on the right hand of the entrance, and in the oppofite corners. Adjoining on the left hand ftands the Monaftry of the *Francifcans*, entred through the Church, fufficiently fpacious, but of no commendable building, accommodated with divers Gardens, and environed with defencible walls; at whofe North-weft corner, a tottered Tower doth challenge regard for the wafte received in that places protection. They brought us into their Chappel, not flightly fet forth and dedicated to S. *Katherine*, having Indulgencies conferred thereupon from Mount *Sinai*. From which we defcended with Lights in our hands, and then were led

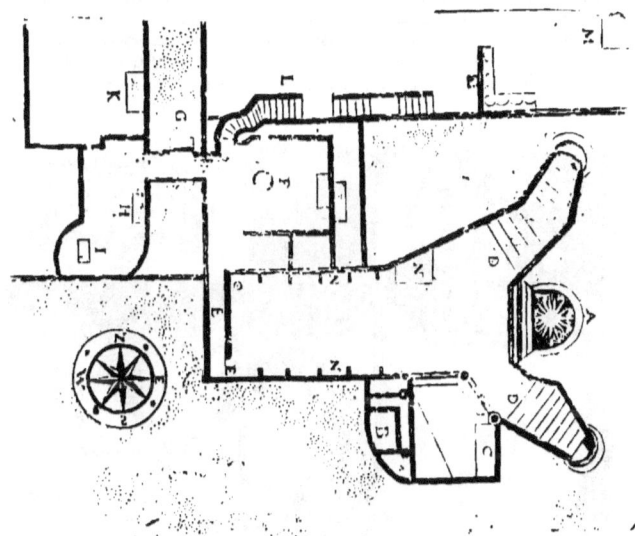

A. *The Altar of Nativity.*
B. *The Manger.*
C. *The Altar of the Magi.*
D. *The ftairs that afcend into the Temple above.*
E. *The entry.*
F. *The Chappel of the Innocents.*
G. *The Sepulchre of Eufebius.*
H. *The Sepulchre of Saint Jerom.*
I. *The Sepulchre of Paula and Euftochius.*
K. *S. Jeroms ftudy.*
L. *The afcent into the Chappel of S. Katherine.*
M. *The Chappel of S. Katherine.*
N. *The Oratories.*

by a narrow long Entry, into a little fquare Cave, fupported in the midft with a Pillar of the Rock. On the left hand ftands an Altar, and under that is a paffage into a Vault, wherein they fay, that the Infants flain by the bloody Edict of *Herod*, were buried. Out of this Cave or Chappel, there are two other Entries; in that on the right hand, ftands the Sepulchre of *Eufebius* the Confeffor, and Difciple unto S. *Jerome*. This directeth into another Grot, wherein are two Tombs, in form not unlike unto Altars; the

farther

Bethlehem. LIB. III.

farther contained the body of *Paula* a Roman Lady, descended of the ancient Families of *Gracchi* and *Cornelii*, who stands indebted to S. *Jerom* for this Epitaph:

Scipio quam genuit Paulæ sudere parentes,
Gracchorum soboles Agamemnonis inclyta proles,
Hoc jacet in tumulo; Paulam dixere priores.
Eustochii generis : Romani prima Senatus,
Pauperem Christi Bethlemitica rura sequuta.

Scipio begot who Paula bore. Th' off-spring
Of Gracchus, of the fam'd Micenian King,
Here lies; earst Paula called: Mother to
Eustochius, chief of Romes grave Senate; who
To Christ and Bethlem vow'd, bade pomp adieu.

ingraving also on the Front of the Entrance,

Aspicis angustum precisa rupe sepulchrum?
Hospitium Paulæ est, cœlestia regna tenentis,
Fratrem, cognatos, Romam, Patriamque relinquens,
Divitias, sobolem, Bethlemita conditur antro.
Hic presepe tuum, Christæ, atque hic mystica Magi
Munera portantes hominique Deoque dedere,

Seest thou this Tomb hewn in the growing Stone?
'Tis Paula's Inn, possest of Heavenly throne,
Who leaving Brother, Kindred, Rome, what gave
Her birth, wealth, children, lies in Bethlems Cave.
Christ, here's thy Cratch: the Wise did hither bring
Mysterious gifts, to God, a Man, a King.

Her Son *Eustochius* lies with her in the self same Monument. She built four Monasteries near adjoining to this Temple (whose ruines do yet give testimony of her Piety, one she planted with men, the three other with Virgins, who never past the bounds of their Convents but on Sundays only) and then attending on their several Governesses, to perform their Oraisons in the Church, and Cave of the Nativity: her self the Abbess of one of them, and so for the space of twenty years did continue. She likewise built an adjoining Hospital for Pilgrims, whose ruines declare it to have been no mean Fabrick. The other Tomb did cover the body of S. *Jerome*, who lived in her time, and in the Monastry which she had founded: his bones, together with the bones of *Eusebius*, were translated to *Rome*, and shrined in the Church of *Santa Maria Maggiore*, over which Pope *Sixtus Quintus* hath erected a sumptuous Chappel. Out of this we past into another Grot, which they call his Cell, wherein he lay (as they say) full fifty years, and six months, and there twice translated the Bible. Returning into the aforesaid Chappel of the Innocents, by the other entry we passed into a Vault or Chappel,

A. *The Altar of the Nativity.*
B. *The Manger.*
C. *The Altar of the Magi.*
D. *The Stairs that ascend into the Temple above.*
E. *The picture of the imaginary figure of Saint Jerom.*

twelve

LIB. III. Bethlehem.

twelve foot wide, forty long, and fifteen in height, the sides and floor all lined with fair white Marble: the compassed roof adorned with Mosework, and Mosaick gilding, though now much perished. At the upper end, in an arched Concave, stands an Altar garnished with a Table of the Nativity. Under this is a semicircle; the sole set forth with stones of several colours, in the form of a Star; and in the midst a Serpentine, there set to preserve the memory of that place where our Saviour was born. The credit whereof I will neither impeach nor inforce. In this City it was, and in a Stable; nor is the report by the site refuted, though under ground, hewn out of the living Rock, as is the rest before spoken of. For he that travels through these Countries, will not wonder to see such Caves imployed to like uses. Neither is it likely, that they that succeeded those times so nearly, should erre in that place so celebrated in their devotions, and beautified with such cost. On either side of this Altar, in the corners, there are two equal ascents, which land on the opposite outsides of the Chancel, closed with doors of brass cut thorow: thorow which they pass in their solemn Procession. Now on the South-side, and near unto the foot of the stairs, you descend by three steps into a lesser Grot; separated only from the former by three fine Columns of divers coloured Marble, which seem to support the over-hanging Rock. On the West-side there is a Manger hewn out in a Concave, about two foot high from the floor, and a little way hollowed within: wherein, they say, that our new-born Saviour was laid by the Virgin; now flagged about with white Marble, as the Rock that roofs it; at the left end sustained with a short Serpentine Pillar. In the bottom of this manger, and just in the middle, a round Serpentine is set, to denote the place where he lay, which retaineth, as they would make us believe, the Effigies of S. *Jerom*; miraculously framed by the natural veins of the stone, in reward of his often and affectionate kisses. But surely, they be the eyes of faith that must apprehend it: yet present they it in picture, as it is set forth in the former Table. On the opposite side of this Grot there is a Bench in the Rock, not unlike to an Altar, where the *Magi* of the East, that were conducted hither by the Star, disposed, as they say, of their Presents. Whom they of *Colen* will have to be Kings, and three in number: and moreover, that they returned no more into their Countries, but came and dwelt in their City; where, in their principal Church, these Verses are extant:

Three Kings, the King of Kings, three gifts did bring;	Tres Reges, Regi Regum, tria dona ferebant;
Myrrh, Incense, Gold, as to Man, God, a King.	Myrrham homini, unctò aurum, thura dedere Deo;
Three holy gifts be likewise given by thee	Tu tria facultatem dones pia munera Christo;
To Christ, even such an acceptable be,	Muneribus gratus si cupis esse ruis.
For Myrrha, tears; for Frankincense, impart	Pro Myrrha lachrymas, auro cor porrige purum;
Submissive prayers: for pure Gold, a pure heart.	Pro thure, ex humili pectore funde preces.

These places be in the keeping of the *Franciscans*: and not less reverenced than *Calvary*, or the Sepulchre: visited also by the *Mahometan* Pilgrims. Where Lamps still burning, do expel the natural darkness; and give a greater state thereunto than the light of the day could afford it. *Baldwin* the Second did honour this place with an Episcopal See (being before but a Priory) annexing thereunto, together with the Church of *Ascalon*, many Towns and Villages. In the place where this City stood, there are now but a few poor Cottages standing. Most of the few Inhabitants *Greeks* and *Armenians*: who get a beggarly living by selling unto Strangers the Models of the Sepulchre, and of the Grot of the Nativity; cut in Wood, or cast in Stone, with Crosses, and such like Merchandize; and in being serviceable unto Pilgrims.

After dinner we descended afoot into the Valley which lyeth East of the City; fruitful in Pasturage: where *Jacob* fed his flock (at this day called his field) near the Tower of *Ader*. But more famous for the Apparition of the Angels, who there brought to the Shepherds the glad tidings of our Salvation. In the midst of the field, on the self-same place, as is supposed, and two miles distant from *Bethlehem*; Saint *Helena* erected a Church, and dedicated it to the Angels; now, nothing but ruines. Returning from thence, and turning a little on the left hand, we came to the Village where those Shepherds dwelt, as yet so called. In the midst whereof there standeth a Well; the same, as the rumour goeth, that the Blessed Virgin desired to drink of, when the churlish Villagers refusing to draw her up water, it forthwith miraculously flowed to the brim, greedy to pass thorow her blessed lips, and satisfie

fie her longing. Of this the *Arabs* would not suffer us to drink before we had given them money. Nearer to *Bethlehem*, and at the foot of the Hill, are the ruines of a Chappel, where *Joseph* (as they say) had his dwelling at such time as the Angel commanded him to flye into *Egypt*. Near the top, and not far from the back of the Monastery, there is a Cave containing two Rooms, one within another, descended into by a narrow entrance, and in some places supported by Pillars. In this, it is said, that *Joseph* hid our Saviour and his Mother, whilst he prepared things necessary for his journey. The stone thereof pulveriz'd and often washed, of much a little will remain, not unlike to refined Chalk ; which taken in drink, is said to have a soveraign virtue in restoring milk both to Women and Cattel ; much used by the *Moors* themselves for that purpose. Over this stood one of the Nunneries built by *Paula*, not only shewing the foundation, and wherein she died. These places seen, we re-entred the Monastery, and there reposed our selves the night following.

Each of us bestowing a piece of Gold on the Vicar, betimes in the morning we departed ; bending our course to the Mountains of *Judea*, lying West from *Bethlehem*. Near to which, on the side of the opposite Hill, we pass by a little Village called, as I take it, *Bezee* (inhabited only by Christians :) mortal (as they say) to the *Mahometans* that attempted to dwell therein. About two miles further we passed by *Bethsur*, seated in a bottom between two rocky Mountains ; once a strong Fort : first built by *Rehoboam*, and after repaired by the *Maccabees* ; famous for sundry Sieges ; being in the upper way between *Jerusalem* and *Gaza*. Where we saw the ruines of an ample Church : below that a Fountain, not unbeholding to Art ; whose pleasant Waters are forthwith drunk up by the earth that produced them. Here, they say, that *Philip* baptized the Eunuch ; whereupon it retaineth the name of the *Æthiopian* Fountain. And no question but the adjoyning Temple was erected out of devotion to the honour of the place, and memory of the fact. Yet seemeth it strange to me, that a Chariot should be able to pass those rocky and declining Mountains, where almost a Horse can hardly keep footing. Having travelled about a mile and a half further, we came to the Cave

A *The Desart*.
B *The Cave of S. John Baptist*.
C *The Fountain*.
D *The Ruines of the Monastery*.

where *John Baptist* is said to have lived from the age of seven, until such time as he went unto the Wilderness by *Jordan* ; sequestred from the abode of men, and feeding on such wild nourishment as these un-inhabited places afforded. This Cave is seated

on

LIB. III.   *Mountains of Juda.*

on the Northern-side of a Desart Mountain (only beholding to the Locust Tree) hewn out of the precipitating Rock; so as difficultly to be ascended or descended to: entred at the East corner, and receiving light from a Window in the side. At the upper end there is a Bench of the self same Rock, whereon (as they say) he accustomed to sleep; of which whoso breaks a piece off, stands forth-with excommunicate. Over this, on a little flat, stand the ruines of a Monastery, on the South-side, naturally walled with the steep of a Mountain, from whence there gusheth a living Spring which entreth the Rock, and again bursteth forth beneath the mouth of the Cave; a place that would make solitariness delightful, and stand in comparison with the turbulent pomp of Cities. This over-looketh a profound Valley, on the far side hem'd with aspiring Mountains, whereof some are cut (or naturally so) in degrees like Allies, which would be else un-accessibly fruitless; whose levels yet bear the stumps of decayed Vines, shadowed not rarely with Olives and Locusts. And surely, I think that all or most of those Mountains have been so husbanded, else could this little Country have never sustained such a multitude of people. After we had fed of such provision as was brought us from the City, by other of the Fraternity that there met us, we turned towards *Jerusalem*, leaving the way of *Bethlehem* on the right hand, and that of *Emaus* on the left. The first place of note that we met with was there where once stood the dwelling of *Zachary*; seated on the side of a fruitful

A. *The Church of John Baptist.*   B. *The Fountain.*   C. *The house of Elizabeth.*

Hill, well stored with Olives and Vineyards. Hither came the blessed Virgin to visit her Cousen *Elizabeth*. Here died *Elizabeth*, and here in a Grot on the side of a Vault or Chappel, lies buried; over which a goodly Church was erected, together with a Monastery, whereof now little standeth but a part of the Walls, which offer to the view some fragments of painting, which shew that the rest have been exquisite. Beyond, and lower, is our Ladies Fountain, (so called of the Inhabitants) which maintaineth a little current through the neighbouring Valley. Near this, in a bottom, and uttermost extent thereof, there standeth a Temple, once sumptuous, now desolate: built by *Helena*, and dedicated to S. *John Baptist*, in the place where *Zachary* had another house, where the Prophet was born in a Room hewn out of the Rock, of principal devotion with those Christians; possest, as the rest, by the beastly *Arabians*, who defile it with their Cattel, and employ it to the basest of uses. Transcending the less steep Hills, and passing through Vallies of their Roses voluntarily plentiful, after awhile we came to a Monastery, seated in a Straight between two Rocky Mountains rains, environed with high Walls, and entred by a door of Iron, where a Bishop of the *Georgians* hath his residence, who courteously entertained us. Within they have a handsom Chappel, at the upper end an Altar, and under that a Pit, in which they say, that the Palm did grow (but rather, if any, the Olive, whereof that place hath store) of which a part of the Cross was made. For it was framed (as they report) of four several woods; the foot of Cedar, the bole of Cypress, the transom of Palm, and the title of Olive. This is called thereupon, The Monastery of the holy Cross. Where, in stead of Bells, they strike on a hollow beam (as the *Grecians* do in the Temple of *Golgotha*) to summon their Assemblies. Between this and *Jerusalem*, we saw nothing worth noting, that hath not been spoken of already.

The day following, we went to review the remarkable places about the City, passing by the Castle of the *Pisans*, on the left hand entring at a little square passage, we were shewed a small Chappel, the Door and Windows rammed up; for that (as they say) the *Mahometans* became mortally sick, that, though but by chance, did come into it: standing, where stood the Temple of St. *Thomas*. From hence we were brought to the Palace of *Annas*, destroyed by the Seditious in the time of the Siege, where now standeth a Church dedicated to the blessed Angels, and belonging to the *Armenians*, who have their dwellings about it. Within the Court there is an old Olive-tree, environed with a low Wall, unto which, it is said, that they bound our Saviour. Turning on the right hand, we went out at the Port of *Sion*. South, and not far from thence,

A. *A Mosque, where once stood the Cœnaculum.*
B. *The Church of S. Saviour, where stood the house of Caiaphas.*
C. *Where the Jews would have taken away the body of the Virgin Mary from the Apostles.*
D. *Where Peter wept.*
E. *Port Esquiline.*
F. *The Pool and Fountain of Siloe.*
G. *Where the Oak Rogel stood.*
H. *The Church of the purification of the blessed Virgin.*
I. *The Fountain of the blessed Virgin.*
K. *The Bridge that passeth over Cedron, with the Rock that bears the impression, as they say, of Christs footsteps.*
L. *The Field of Blood.*
M. *Where certain of the Apostles hid themselves.*
N. *The Mountain of offence.*
O. *Where the house of Annas the High Priest stood.*
P. *Where the Franks are buried.*
Q. *Port Sion.*

on the midst of the Mount, is the place, as they say, where Christ did eat his last Supper; where also, after his Resurrection, the doors being shut, he appeared to his Apostles, where they received the Holy Ghost; where *Peter* converted three thousand; and where, as they say also, they held the first Council, in which the Apostles Creed was decreed. Here *Helena* built a most sumptuous Temple, including therein the Cœnaculum; where that Marble Pillar was preserved that stood
before

LIB. III. *Mount Sion. The Valley of Gehinnon.*

before in the Palace of Pilate, to which they tied our Saviour when they whipped him. This Church subverted by the *Saracens*, in the self-same place, the *Franciscans* had a Monastery erected, who in the year 1551. were removed by the *Turks*: they building here a Mosque of their own, into which no Christian is permitted to enter. Yet not in the respects aforesaid, so reverenced by the Infidels, but in that it is delivered by Tradition, (and not unlike) that *David* had there his Sepulchre. His Monument was enriched with a mass of Treasure, out of which *Hircanus*, 830 years after, took three thousand Talents, to divert the War which was threatned by *Antiochus*. *Herod*, with unlike success, attempted the like. For having already taken out a great sum, and persisting in his sacriledge, a flame of Fire brake out of the Tomb, and consumed divers of his Instruments. In expiation whereof, he adorned the same with a stately Monument, which stood intire for a long time after. Between this and the walls of the City, the *Franks* have their burial; where lie six *English* men, (sent, as may be suspected) unto their long-homes not many years since, though coloured by the *Franciscans*, in whose Monastery they lay, with pretence of Divine vengeance, for the supposed murder of their *Drogarman*. Seven they were in all, all alive, and well in one day, six dead in the other; the out-diver, becoming a Convert to their Religion. Turning a little on the left hand we came to a small Church, enclosed within a square wall, arched within with a wall on the top, in manner of a Cave; the habitation of their *Armenians*, who have of this Church the custody. Here flourished the proud Palace of *Caisphas*, in which our Saviour was buffeted, spit upon, and so spitefully reviled. Here *Helena* built a fair Church to Saint *Peter*; but that destroyed, in the room thereof, this lest was erected, and dedicated to Saint *Saviour*. On the right hand, in the Court, they undertook to shew where the Fire was made, by which *Peter* stood, when he denied his Master: and at the side of the Church door, the Chapiter of a Pillar, whereon the Cock crowing, did move him to contrition. At the upper end of the Church, upon a large Altar, lieth a stone, that (as they say) which was rolled against the mouth of the Sepulchre. From hence we descended into the Valley of *Gehinnon*, which divideth Mount *Sion*, from the Mountain of *Offence*; so called, for that *Solomon*, by the perswasion of his Wives, here sacrificed to *Chamoch*, and *Molech*; but now by these Christians, called, The Mountain of *Ill-counsel*, where, they say, the Pharisees took counsel against Jesus; whose height yet shews the reliques of no mean buildings. This Valley is but straight, now serving for little use; heretofore most delightful, planted with Groves, and watered with Fountains; wherein the *Hebrews* sacrificed their Children to *Molech*; an Idol of Brass, having the head of a Calf, the rest of a Kingly Figure, with arms extended to receive the miserable sacrifice, seared to death with his burning embracements. For the Idol was hollow within, and filled with fire. And lest their lamentable shrieks, should sad the hearts of their Parents, the Priests of *Molech*, did deaf their ears with the continual clangs of Trumpets and Timbrels; whereupon it was called the Valley of *Tophet*. But the good *Josias* brake the Idol in pieces, hewed down the Groves, and ordained that that place (before a Paradise) should be, for ever, a receptacle for dead carkasses, and the filth of the City. *Gehenna*, for the impiety committed therein, is used for Hell, by our Saviour. On the South-side of this Valley, near where it meeteth the Valley of *Jehosaphat*, mounted a good height, on the side of the Mountain, is *Aceldama*, or Field of Blood, purchased with the restored reward of Treason, for a Burial place for Strangers. In the midst whereof, a large square Room was made by the Mother of *Constantine*; the South-side walled with the natural Rock; flat at the top, and equal with the upper level, out of which arise certain little Cupoloes, open in the midst, to let down the dead bodies. Through these we might see the bottom all covered with Bones, and certain Coarses but newly let down, it being now the Sepulchre of the *Armenians*. A greedy Grave, and great enough to devour the dead of a whole Nation. For, they say (and I believe it) that the earth thereof, within the space of eight and forty hours, will consume the flesh that is laid thereon. The like is said of St. *Innocents* Church-yard in *Paris*; and he that sees the multitude of bones that are there piled about it, the daily burials (it being a general receptacle for Strangers) and smalness of the circuit; may be easily induced to credit it. And why might not the earth be transported from hence, as well as that at *Rome*, in *Campo Sancto*, brought thither in 270 Ships, by the commandment of the aforesaid Empress? which, though changing soyls, retaineth her virtues it being also a place of burial for Foraigners. In the Rock about there are divers Sepulchres,

O and

A. The place of the Cœnaculum.
B. Of the Oak Roguel.
C. Where the Apostles did hide themselves.
D. The Field of Blood.

E. The Mountain of offence.
F. Part of the Valley of Jehosaphat.
G. Part of the Valley of Gehinnon.

and some in use at this day, having great stones rolled against their mouths, according to the ancient custom. Beyond, on the point of the Hill, a Cave hewn out of the Rock, consisting of several Rooms, is said to have hidden six of the Apostles in the time of Christs Passion. First, made without doubt for a Sepulchre, and after serving for an Hermitage; the Roof of the larger Room retaining some shew of guilding. Below, where the Valley of Gehinnon and Jehosaphat, like conjoining streams, do tend to the South, there is a dry Pit, where the Priests are said to have hid the sacred Fire, when the Jews were carried captive into Babylon; and seeking it after their return, did find it converted into Water. But Nehemiah caused it to be sprinkled on the Altar; when forth-with, with the beams of the Sun, it miraculously flamed. This Valley of Jehosaphat (so called of that good King) from hence extendeth full North, and then inclineth a little to the West, first presenting (though Natural) no other than a large dry Ditch to the East of the City, contracted between it and the over-pearing Hills of the opposite Olivet. It is said to be about two miles long, and if so but short ones; where broadest fruitful: watered by the Torrent Cedron, which runneth no longer than fed with showers, losing his intermitted streams in the Lake of Asphaltis. It was also called the Valley of Cedron, and of the King; where the general Judgment shall be, if the Jews or Latines may be believed, who ground their opinions upon the Prophecy of Joel; which I will not gain-say, since some of our Divines, have of late, so laboured to approve it. Of the same opinion are the Mahometans. In the Wall about it there is a Window, not far from the Golden Gate, where they say that Mahomet shall sit whilst Christ doth execute Justice. Passing to the City-side of the Valley, at the foot of the Hill, and East of the South-East corner, is the place where the Prophet Isaiah was sawn asunder, by the commandment of Manasses his Grand-child by the Mother, and there buried; where there is a little pavement used for a place of prayer by the Mahometans. Close below this stood the Oak Roguel, where now a white Mulberry is cherished. North of it, in a gut of the Hill (above which, in the wall, stood the Tower) was the Fish-pool of Siloe, containing not above half an Acre of Ground, now dry in the bottom; and beyond the Fountain that fed it, now no other than a little Trench walled in on the sides, full of filthy water, whose upper part is obscured by a building (as I take

LIB. III.   Sepulchre of Zachary, Abſaloms Pillar.   147

take it, a Moſque) where once flouriſhed a Chriſtian Church, there built by Saint *Helena*. Though deprived of thoſe her ſalubrious ſtreams, yet is ſhe held in honour for their former virtues. Paſſing along, we came to our Ladies Fountain (upon what occaſion they ſo call it, is not worth the relating) in a deep Cave of the Rock, deſcended into by a large pair of ſtairs, and repleniſhed with pleaſant waters. Here the Valley ſtreightneth, and a little beyond is no broader than ſerves for a Chanel to the Torrent. On the other ſide ſtands the Sepulchre of *Zachary*, who was ſlain between the Temple and the Altar; all of the natural Rock, eighteen foot high, four ſquare, and beautified with Dorick Columns of the ſame unſeparated ſtone ſuſtain-

A   *A part of the Pillar of Alſalom.*
B   *The Cave of S. James.*
C   *The Sepulchre of Zachary.*
D   *The Torrent Cedron.*

ing the Corniſh, and topt like a pointed Diamond. Cloſe to this there is another in the upright Rock; the front like the ſide of an open Gallery, ſupported with Marble Pillars, now between rammed up with ſtones. Within is a Grot, whither *James* retired (as they ſay) after the Paſſion of our Saviour, with purpoſe never to have received ſuſtenance, until he had ſeen him, who in that place appeared unto him after his Reſurrection. In memorial whereof, the Chriſtians erected a Church hard by, whoſe ruines are now ruined. A little farther, there is a ſtone Bridge of one Arch, which paſſeth the Torrent. In a Rock, at the foot thereof, there are certain impreſſions, made (as they ſay) by our Saviours feet, when they led him thorow the water. At the Eaſt-end of this Bridge, and a little on the North, ſtands the Pillar of *Alſalom*, which he here erected in his life-time, to retein the memory of his name, in that his iſſue male failed (but he was not buried therein) being yet intire, and of a good Fabrick, riſing in a lofty ſquare; below adorned with half Columns, wrought out of the ſides and corners of the Dorick form; and then changing into a round, a good height higher doth grow to a point in faſhion of a Bell, all framed of the growing ſtone. Againſt this there lieth a great heap of ſtones, which increaſeth daily. For both *Jews* and *Mahometans* paſſing by, do throw ſtones againſt it, yet execrating *Abſalom* for his rebellion againſt *David*. Adjoyning there is a large ſquare, but lower by far, which hath an entrance like the Frontiſpiece of a Porch, cut curiouſly without, the earth almoſt reaching to the top of the entrance, having a Grot within hewn out of the Rock: ſome ſay, a Kingly Sepulchre, perhaps appertaining to the former. A little more North, and up the Torrent, at the foot of *Olivet*, once ſtood the Village *Gethſemane*; the place yet fruitful in Olives: and hard by the delightful

O 2   Garden

148 *Garden of Gethsem. The B. Vir. Sepulchre.* L I B. III.

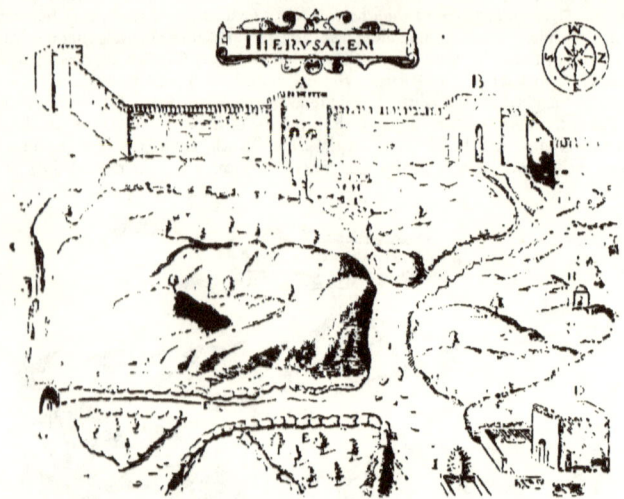

A *The golden Gate of the Temple.*
B *The Gate of S. Steven.*
C *Where S Steven was stoned to death.*
D *The Sepulchre of the Bleſſed Virgin.*
E *The Garden of Mount Olivet.*

F *The Torrent of Cedron.*
G *The Bridge of the Torrent.*
H *Sepulchres of the Mahometans.*
I *Where Thomas ſtood, as they will have it, when the Bleſſed Virgin let fall her Girdle.*

Garden wherein our Saviour was betrayed. They point at the place where he left two of his Diſciples, and a little higher the third, when he went to pray; and withal the place where he was taken. In this Garden there is alſo a ſtone, whereon they ſay that our Lady ſate, and beheld the Martyrdom of S. *Steven*, who ſuffered on the ſide of the oppoſite Hill. Without the ſaid Garden, in the joyning of two ways, they ſhewed us the place, as they will have it, where S. *Thomas* ſtood, when incredulous, forſooth, of our Ladies Aſſumption, ſhe let fall her Girdle to inform his belief.

And now are we come to the Sepulchre of the Bleſſed Virgin, made thus, as it is, by the Mother of *Conſtantine*. Before it a Court; the building above ground a ſquare Pile only, flat at the top, and neatly wrought, like the largeſt Portico to a Temple. You enter at the South-ſide, and forthwith deſcend by a goodly pair of ſtairs of fifty ſteps. About the midſt of the deſcent are two ſmall oppoſite Chappels; in that on the right hand, are the Sepulchres of *Joacim* and *Anna*; in that on the left, of *Joſeph*, the Parent and Spouſe of the Mother of Jeſus. The ſtairs do lead you into a ſpacious Church, ſtretching Eaſt and Weſt, walled on each ſide, and arched above with the natural Rock. Upon the right hand, in the midſt, there is a little ſquare Chappel, framed of the eminent Rock, but flagged both within and without with white Marble, and entred at two doors. At the far ſide thereof ſtands her Tomb, which taketh up more than the third part of the Room; now in form of an Altar, under which (they ſay) that ſhe was decently buried by the Apoſtles, and the third day after aſſumed into Heaven by the Angels. In this there burn eighteen Lamps continually; partly maintained by the Chriſtians, and partly by the *Mahometans:* who have this Palace in an eſpecial veneration. Near the Eaſt ſemicircle of the Church, there ſtandeth a great Altar (over which the little Light that this dark place hath, doth deſcend by a Cupolo: near the Weſt another, but both unfurniſhed: and by the former, a Well of an excellent water. In a canton of the Wall, right againſt the North-end of the Sepulchre, there is a clift in the Rock, where the *Turks* do affirm that our Lady did hide her ſelf, when ſhe was perſecuted by the *Jews*; into which I have ſeen their Women to creep, and give the cold Rock affectionate kiſſes. The oppoſite Canton is alſo uſed for an Oratory, by the *Mahometans*, who have the keeping of the whole, and will not ſuffer us to enter of free cult. Remounting the ſame ſtairs, not far off on the left hand, towards the Eaſt, and not above a ſtones caſt from the Garden of *Gethſemane*, a ſtraight paſſage deſcendeth

into

LIB. III. *The B. Virgins Sepulchre. Chrift's Oratory.*

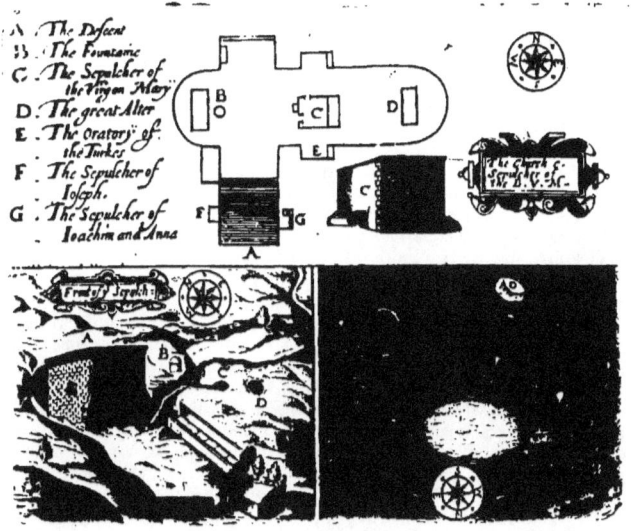

A *The entrance and building above ground of the Church of the Sepulchre of the bleſſed Virgin.*
E *The place from whence it receiveth light.*
C *The entrance of the Oratory of Chriſt.*

D *The place from whence it receiveth light.*
AA *Where Chriſt prayed.*
EB *Where the Angel ſtood.*

into a vaſt round Cave; all of the natural Rock, the Roof confirmed with Arches of the ſame, receiving a dim light from a little hole in the top, which was, in times paſt, all over curiouſly painted; The place (they ſay) where Chriſt did pray, when in that bloody agony he was comforted by the Angels. From hence we bent our courſe to the City. High on the Hill, where three ways meet, and upon the flat of a Rock, is the place where S. *Stephen* (who bore the firſt Palm of Martyrdom) was ſtoned to death. The Stones thereabout have a red ruſt on them, which, they ſay, give teſtimony of his blood-ſhed. A little above, we entred the City at the Gate of S. *Stephen* (where on each ſide a Lyon retrograde doth ſtand) called in times paſt, The port of the Valley, and of the Flock; for that the Cattel came in at this Gate, which were to be ſacrificed in the Temple, and were ſold in the Market place adjoining. On the left hand there is a Stone Bridge, which paſſeth at the Eaſt end of the North wall into the Court of the Temple of *Solomon*: the head to the Pool *Betheſda* (underneath which it had a conveyance) called alſo *Probaticum*, for that the Sacrifices were therein waſhed ere delivered to the Prieſts. It had five Ports built thereto by *Solomon*; in which continually lay a number of diſeaſed perſons. For an Angel, at certain ſeaſons troubled the water; and he that could next deſcend thereinto, was perfectly cured. Now it is a great ſquare profundity, green, and uneven at the bottom; into which a barren Spring doth drill, from between the Stones of the North-ward wall, and ſtealeth away almoſt undiſcerned. The place is for a good depth hewn out of the Rock; confined above, on the North-ſide, with a ſteep Wall; on the Weſt, with high buildings (perhaps a part of the Caſtle of *Antonia*, where are two doors to deſcend by, now all, that are half choked with rubbidge) and on the South, with the wall of the Court of the Temple. Whereof it is fit that ſomething be ſpoken by us, although not ſuffered to enter without the forfeiture of our lives, or renouncing of our Religion.

I will not ſpeak of the former form and magnificency thereof, by ſacred Pens ſo exactly deſcribed. Firſt, built by *Solomon*, deſtroyed by *Nebuchadnezzar*, re-edified by *Zerubbabel*, (yet ſo far ſhort of the firſt in glory, that thoſe wept to behold it, who had beheld the former:) new built, or rather ſumptuouſly repaired by *Herod* the Great; and laſtly, utterly ſubverted by *Titus*. The *Jews* aſſayed to re-

Solomons Temple. Palace of Pilate. LIB. III.

edifie it in the Reign of *Adrian*: of whom he flew an infinite number, levelled it with the floor, and threw the rubbidge into the Valley of *Jehosaphat*, to make it less deep, and the place less defensible; planting in the room thereof a Grove which he consecrated unto *Jupiter*. Afterward *Julian* the Apostata, to disprove the Prophesie of our Saviour, did licence the *Jews* to rebuild it, furnishing them with money out of his Treasury: when lo, a terrible Earth-quake shook down what they had begun, and a flame bursting forth devoured the Workmen; reported by *Amianus Marcellinus* a Pagan, and living in those times. But who built this that now standeth, is doubtful. Some do attribute it to the Christians, others to a Prince of the *Arabians* (which is confirmed by the Christians of those Countrys) and he the *Saracen Omer*, next Successor unto *Mahomet*. Seated it is upon Mount *Moriah*, in the South-east corner of the City, without doubt, in the very place where *Solomon* stood; the more eminent building consisting of an eight square round, of a blewish stone, adorned with adjoining Pillars, and tarrased above. In the midst of the shelving Roof, another upright aspireth; though less by far, yet the same in form and substance with the former; being covered over with a Cupulo of Lead. To the West of this, a long building adjoineth, like the body of a Church, compast above, and no higher than the under tarras of the other, but like it in colour. Now the Court (the same with that of the old Temple) is just foursquare every way, about a slights shoot over. In the East-wall, which is also a wall to the City, stands the golden Gate, so called, in that it was gilded, which belonged only to the Temple, through which our Saviour passed in triumph. It is said, that the Emperour *Heraclius* returning from his *Persian* Victory, attempted to have entred thereat in all his glory; but was miraculously prohibited, until he had put off all his Princely Ornaments, in a simple habit bearing that part of the Cross of Christ on his shoulders which he had recovered from the *Persians*. This Gate is now rammed up by the *Turks*, to prevent, as some say, a prophetic, which is, that the City should be there entred by the Christians. A part of the South-side is also inclosed with the Wall of the City. The rest, not inferiour in strength, is environed with a deep Trench hewn into the Rock, (though now much choaked) heretofore inhabited in the bottom like a Street. In the midst of this out-Court, there is another, wherein the aforesaid Mosque doth stand, raised some two yards above the out-Court, and garnished on the sides with little Turrets, thorow which it is ascended; all paved with white Marble (the spoil of Christian Churches) where the *Mahometans*, as well as within, do perform their particular Orisons. Sundry low Buildings there are, adjoining to the wall of the out-Court; as I suppose, the habitation of their *Santons*. In the South-east corner, and a little in the out-wall, there is a handsome Temple covered with Lead, by the Christians called, The Church of the Purification of the Virgin; now also a Mosque, *Godfrey* of *Bulloign*, with the rest of the City took this place by assault, and slew within the Circuit thereof ten thousand *Saracens*. By him then was it made a Cathedral Church; who erected Lodgings about it for the Patriarch, and his Canons. Into this there are now but two entrances; that on the West, and this Gate over the head of the Pool *Bethesda*, (called of old, the Horse-Gate, for that here they left their Horses, it being not lawful to ride any further) resembling the Gate of a City. One thing by the way may be noted, that whereas our Churches turn to the East, the Temple of *Solomon* regarded the West; perhaps in respect of Mount *Calvary*.

Re-passing the aforesaid Bridge (seeing we might proceed no farther) on the North-side of the Street, that stretcheth to the West, now in a remote corner, stood the House of *Joachim*; where the goodly Church was built to the honour of S. *Anna*, with a Monastry adjoining, of which some part yet remaineth, but polluted with the *Mahometan* Superstition. Turning back, we took up the said Street to the West: not far onward, at the left hand, stood the Palace of *Pilate*, without all question the Castle of *Antonia*, near adjoining to the wall of the Temple, where now the *Sanziack* hath his Residence; deprived of those lofty Towers, and scarce appearing above the Walls that confine it. On the right hand, at the far end of a Street that pointeth to the North, stood the stately Mansion of *Herod*; of which some signs there are left, that witness a perished excellency. Now at the West-corner of that of *Pilates*, where the Wall for a space doth turn to the South, there are a pair of high Stairs, which lead to the place of Justice, and Throne of the *Roman* President, where the Saviour of the World was by the World condemned. The Stairs that, they say, then were called *Scala Sancta*, I have seen

at

LIB. III.   *Scala Sancta. The Dolorous way.*

at *Rome*, near St. *Johns*, in the *Lateran*; tranſlated thither by *Conſtantine*. Three pair there are in one front, divided but by walls: the middlemoſt thoſe; being of white Marble, and eighteen in number, aſcended and worn by the knees of the ſuppliants, who deſcend by the other. At the top there is a little Chappel called *Sanctum Sanctorum*, where they never ſay Maſs: And upon this occaſion, a holy Father, in the Room adjoining, having conſumed moſt part of the night in his devotions, is ſaid, an hour before the dawning, to have ſeen a Proceſſion of Angels paſs by him, ſome ſinging, and others (perhaps that had worſe voices) bearing Torches, amongſt whom was St. *Peter* with the Euchariſt; who executed there his Pontificial function; and that done, returned. This rumoured the day following about the City, numbers of people flock'd thither, who found the Room all to be dropt with Torches, in confirmation of this relation. Whereupon it was decreed, that not any (as not worthy) ſhould ſay Maſs on that Altar. Now the way between the place of thoſe Stairs and Mount *Calvary*, is called the dolorous way; along which our Saviour was led to his Paſſion: in which, they ſay, (and ſhew where) that he thrice fell under the weight of his Croſs. And a little beyond

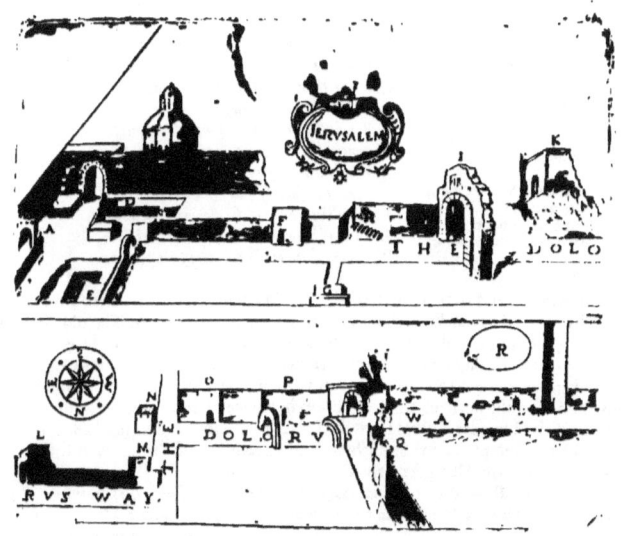

A *The Gate of Saint Stephen.*
B *The Gate that opens into the Court of the Temple.*
C *The Moſque, where once ſtood the Temple of Solomon.*
D *The Pool Betheſda.*
E *The Church of St. Anna.*
F *Where the Palace of Pilate ſtood.*
G *Where the Court of Herod.*
H *Where the holy Stairs.*
I *Pilates Arch.*

K *The Church of the ſwouning of the bleſſed Virgin.*
L *Where they met with Simon of Cyrene.*
M *Where Chriſt ſaid, weep not for me, you Daughters of Jeruſalem.*
N *Where the houſe of the rich glutton ſtood.*
O *Where the houſe of the Phariſee.*
P *Where the houſe of Veronica.*
Q *The Gate of Juſtice.*
R *Mount Calvary.*

there is an ancient Arch that croſſeth the Street, and ſupporteth a ruined Gallery: in the Eaſt ſide a two-arched Window, where *Pilate* preſented Chriſt to the people. An hundred paces farther, and on the left hand, there are the reliques of a Church, where, they ſay, that the bleſſed Virgin ſtood when her Son paſſed by, and fell into a Trance at the ſight of that killing ſpectacle. Sixty ſix paces beyond (where this Street doth meet with that other which leadeth to Port *Ephraim*, now called the Gate of *Damaſcus*) they ſay, that they met with *Simon* of *Cyrene*, and compelled him to aſſiſt our Saviour in the bearing of his burthen. Turning a little on the left hand, they ſhewed us where the women wept, and he replyed; *Weep not for me you Daughters of Jeruſalem, &c.* Then turning again on the right, we paſſed under a little Arch,

near

near which a house ascended by certain steps; the place where *Veronica* dwelt, who gave our Saviour, as they say, a Napkin as he passed by the door, to cleanse his face from the blood which trickled from his thorn-pierc'd brows, and spittle wherewith they had despightfully defiled him: who returned it again enriched with his lively counterfeit; now to be seen at *Rome* upon Festival days, in St. *Peter*'s Church in the *Vatican*. To which this Hymn was made, and published by Pope *John* the two and twentieth, with a grant of seven years indulgency to him that should devoutly utter it to that Picture.

Salve sancta facies nostri Redemptoris,
In qua nitet species divini splendoris,
Impressa Panniculo nivei candoris;
Dataque Veronicæ signum ob amoris.

Salve decus seculi, speculum sanctorum;
Quod videre cupiunt spiritus cœlorum:
Nos ab omni macula purga vitiorum,
Atque nos consortio junge beatorum.

Salve vultus Domini, imago beata,
Ex æterno munere mire decorata:
Lumen funde cordibus ex vi tibi data,
Et à nostris sensibus tolle colligata.

Salve robur fidei nostræ Christianæ,
Destruens hæreticos qui sunt mentis vanæ,
Horum auge meritum qui te credunt sanæ,
Illius effigie qui Rex sit ex pane.

Salve nostrum gaudium in hac vita dura,
Labili, & fragili; cito peritura,
Nos deduc ad propria ô fœlix figura,
Ad videndam faciem quæ est Christi pura.

Of our Redeemer, hail, O Face divine,
Wherein the beams of heav'nly beauty shine:
Fix'd in a Napkin, white as snow new driven;
And to Veronica (thy loves pledge) given.

Hail worlds renown, of Saints the mirrour bright,
Whose desir'd view would heaven thron'd spirit delight,
Purge us from stains which sinning souls infect,
And join to blest communion of th' elect.

Hail our Lords visage, happy counterfeit,
By gift etern' made wondrously compleat;
Our hearts illuminate with grace assign'd:
And our thrall'd senses by thy power unbind.

Of Christians faith, hail force, and fortress sure,
Destroying Hereticks, of minds impure:
Augment their merits that in thee do trust,
By his dear image made a God of crust.

Hail comfort of sad life, the only one,
Life tedious, brittle, fickle, and soon gone,
Lead to thine own, O happy Portraicture,
To see the face of Christ, the face so pure.

Fronting the far end of this Street, an ancient Gate which stood in the West wall of the old City, yet resists the subversions of time; called by *Nehemiah*, The old Gate; by the *Jebusites*, the Port of *Jebus*, and the Gate of Judgment; for that the Elders there sate in Justice: through which the condemned were led to execution unto *Mount Calvary*; then two hundred and twenty paces without, and a little on the left hand; though now almost in the heart of the City. From hence we ascended the East-side of *Mount Calvary* (eight hundred paces from the Palace of *Pilate*) and so descended into the Court of the Temple of the Sepulchre. Right against it are the ruines of lofty buildings, heretofore the Alberges of the Knight Hospitallers of St. *Johns*. Turning to the South, we were shewed where once stood the dwelling of *Zebedeus*, in which *James* and *John* were born, heretofore a Collegiate Church, but now a Mosque. A little higher we came to the Iron-Gate, a passage in times past between the upper City and the neather (which gave way unto *Peter* conducted by the Angel) built by *Alexander* the Great. Who having taken *Tyrus*, and the Sea-bordering Cities of *Phœnicia* and *Palestine*, begirt *Jerusalem* with his Army; when on a sudden the Gates were set open, *Jaddus* the High Priest issuing forth, clothed in his Pontifical Habit, and followed with a long train in white Rayments; whom *Alexander* espying, advanced before the rest of the company; and when he drew near, fell prostrate before him. For it came unto his remembrance, how once in *Dio* a City of *Macedon*, consulting with himself about his *Asian* enterprize, he had seen in a Vision one so apparelled, who bid him boldly proceed, and told him, that the God whom he served would protect his Army, and make him Lord of the *Persian* Monarchy. Then hand in hand they entred the City, the High Priest conducting him unto the Temple, where he sacrificed unto God according to the manner of the *Hebrews*: *Jaddus* expounding unto him the Prophecies of *Daniel*, which foretold of his Victories. From thence we proceeded unto the House of Saint *Mark*; of which an obscure Church in the custody of the *Sorians*, doth retain the memory. And beyond we came to the Church of Saint *James*, standing in the place where he was beheaded; erected by the *Spaniards*, together with an Hospital, and now possest by the *Armenians*. This seen, we returned to the Covent.

The day following, we went out (as before) at the Port of *Sion*. Turning on the left

LIB. III.   *Bethania. Bethphage.*   153

left hand along the Wall, we were shewed the place where *Peter* wept, when he had denied our Saviour; dignified once with a Church, and whereof there now remaineth some part of the foundation. Right against it, there is a Postern in the Wall, formerly called Port *Esquiline*; at which they bore forth the filth of the City. The foundation of this part of the Wall is much more ancient, and much more strong than the rest; consisting of black stones of a mighty size. Not far beyond we crossed the Valley of *Jehosaphat*, and mounted the South-end of Mount *Olivet*, by the way of *Bethania*. Having ascended a good height, on the right hand they shewed us where *Judas* hanged himself (the stump of the Sycamore, as they say, not long since extant) being buried in a Grot that adjoyneth; nearer the top where Christ cursed the Fig-tree, many there growing at this present. Descending the East side of the Mountain, a little on the left hand, we came to a desolate Chappel,

A *Mount Olivet*.
B *Bethphage*.
C *The Fountain of the Apostles*.
D *Where the House of Martha stood*.
E *The Stone whereon Christ sate*.
F *Where the House of Mary stood*.
G *The Sepulchre of Lazarus*.
H *The House of Lazarus*.
I *The House of Simon the Leper*.
K *The Valley of the cursed Fig tree*.
L *The way of Jerusalem*.
M *Quarantania*.

about which were divers ruines, the house heretofore of *Simon* the Leper. From thence we descended into the Castle of *Lazarus* (whereof yet there is something extant) the Brother to *Mary* and *Martha*. Close under which lies *Bethania* (two miles from *Jerusalem*) now a tottered Village, inhabited by *Arabians*. In it the Vault where Christ raised *Lazarus* from death; square and deep, descended into by certain steps. Above are two little Chappels, which have in either of them an Altar, where stood a stately Church erected by Saint *Helena*: and after that an Abbey; Queen *Millisent* the Foundress. A little North of *Bethania*, we came to the ruines of a Monastery, now level with the floor, seated in the place unto which the penitent *Mary* retired from the corrupting vanities of the City. Southward of this, and not far off, stood the house of *Martha*, honoured likewise with a Temple, and ruinated; alike equally distant from both, there is a stone, whereon, they say, that our Saviour sate, when the two Sisters intreated him to restore life to their Brother, now four days buried. The Pilgrim that breaks off a piece thereof stands excommunicated. A little above there is a Fountain of excellent water, deep sunk into the Rock, (by which we refreshed our selves with provision brought with us) called the Fountain of the Apostles. Now we ascended Mount *Olivet* again, by another way more inclining to the North. Upon the right hand, and not far from the top, stood *Bethphage*; whose

whose very foundations are now confounded; from whence Christ past unto *Jerusalem* in Triumph upon an Asses Colt; every Palm-Sunday by the *Pater-guardian* superstitiously imitated.

Here we look back, and for a while survey the high Mountain *Quarantania*, the low Plains of *Jericho*, *Jordan*, and the Dead-Sea; which we could not go to, by reason of our tardy arrival, the Pilgrims returning on the self-same day that we came unto *Jerusalem*. A Journey undertaken but once a year, in regard of the charge; the Passengers being then guarded by a *Sheck* of the *Arabians*, to resist the wild *Arabs*, who almost famished on those barren Mountains (which they dare not husband for fear of surprisal) rob all that pass, it inferiour in strength. Yet paid we towards that conduct, two Dollars apiece to the *Sanziak*. I have spoken before of the River and Lake that devoureth it, as much as here heard, and what I have read, that dissenteth not: the rest being such like stuff as the former, wherewith I have already tired my self, and afflicted my Reader. I will therefore forbear to deliver a particular report of that three days Pilgrimage, only thus much in general. *Jordan* runneth well-nigh thirty miles from *Jerusalem*, the way thither by *Bethania*, made long and troublesom by the steep descents and labyrinthian windings; being, to the judgment of the eye, not the fourth part of that distance. In this the Pilgrims wash themselves, and bring from thence of the water, sovereign (as they say) for sundry Diseases. A great way on this side the River, there stands a ruined Temple upon the winding of a crooked Chanel, forsaken by the stream, (or then not filled but by inundations) where Christ (as they say) was baptized by *John*. On the right hand stood *Jericho*, (a City of fame) and in the time of the Christians an Episco-

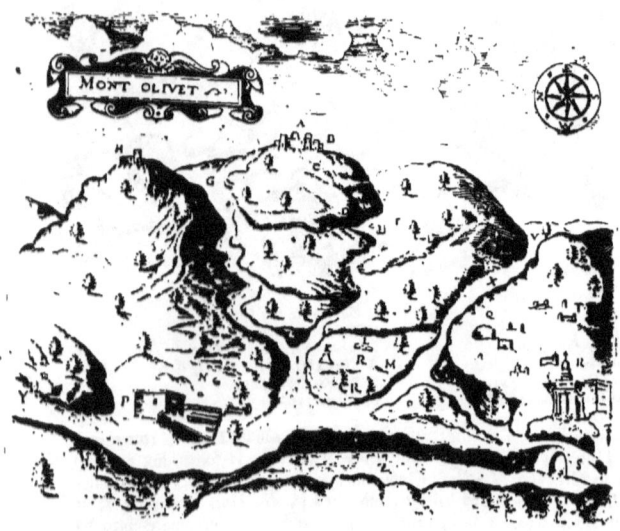

A *Where Christ ascended into Heaven.*
B *The Cell of Pelagia.*
C *Where Christ spake of the general Judgment.*
D *Where, they say, he taught the Lords Prayer.*
E *Where the Apostles made the Creed.*
F *Where Christ wept over the City.*
G *Where the Blessed Virgin reposed.*
H *Where the Angel said, You men of Galilee, &c.*
I *Where St. Thomas, as they say, took up the Blessed Virgins Girdle.*
K *Where the Blessed Virgin sate, and beheld the Martyrdom of St. Steven.*
L *Where Christ left the three Disciples.*
M *Where he was taken.*
N *The Coverture of Christs Oratory.*
O *Gethsemane.*
P *The Sepulchre of the Virgin Mary.*
Q *Where Judas hanged himself.*
R *The Pillar of Absalom.*
S *The Bridge that passeth over Cedron.*
T *Sepulchres.*
V *The Valley of the cursed Fig-tree.*
X *The way to Bethania.*
Y *The way to Jerusalem.*
Z *The Torrent Cedron.*
R *The Garden of Gethsemane.*

LIB. III.   *Quarantania. Mount Olivet.*   155

palSee) beautiful in her Palms, but chiefly proud of her *Balsamum*: a Plant then only thought particular unto *Jury*, which grew most plentifully in this Valley, and on the sides of the Western Mountains which confine it, being about two cubits high, growing upright, and yearly pruned of her superfluous branches. In the Summer they lanced the rind with a stone, (not to be touched with steel) but not deeper than the inward film; for otherwise it forthwith perished: from whence those fragrant and precious tears did distill, which now are only brought us from *India*; but they far worse, and generally sophisticated. The bole of this Shrub is of the least esteem, the rind of greater, the seed exceeding that, but the liquor of greatest, known to be right in the curdling of milk, and not staining of garments. Here remained two Orchards thereof in the days of *Vespasian*; in defence of which, a battel was fought with the Jews, that endeavoured to destroy them. Of such repute with the *Romans*, that *Pompey* first, and afterwards *Titus*, did present it in their triumphs as an especial glory; now utterly lost through the barbarous waste, and neglect of the *Mahometans*. Where *Jericho* stood, there stand a few poor Cottages inhabited by the *Arabians*. The Valley, about ten miles over, now producing but a spiny grass, is bordered on the East with the high *Arabian* Mountains, on the West with those of *Jury*.   Amongst which, *Quarantania* is the most eminent, being in that Wildernefs where Christ for forty days was tempted by the Devil: so high, that few dare attempt to ascend to the top, from whence the Tempter shewed him the Kingdoms of the Earth, now crowned with a Chappel, which is yet unruined.   There is, besides, in the side an Hermitage, with a Cistern to receive Rain-water; and another Grot, wherein the Hermits were buried. Here St.*Jerom* (as they say) fulfilled his four years penance.

But now return we to the summit of *Mount Olivet*, which over-toppeth the neighbouring Mountains; whose West-side doth give you a full survey of each particular part of the City, bedeck'd with Olives, Almonds, Fig-trees, and heretofore with Palms, pleasantly rich when husbanded, and now upbraiding the barbarous with his neglected pregnancy.   So famous in sacred Histories, and so often blest with the presence of Christ, and apparition of Angels. It is not much less than a mile in height, stretching from North to South, and having three heads. On the middlemost (and that the highest) there standeth a little Chappel, of an eight-square round, at every corner a Pillar, mounted on three degrees; being all of white Marble, and of an elegant

structure: Within it is not above twelve foot over; paved with the natural Rock, which beareth the Impression of a foot-step, they say, of our Saviours; the last that he set upon earth, when from thence he ascended into Heaven. A place in honour inferior unto none; frequented by Christians, possest by *Mahometans*, yet free to both their devotions. Built it was by the Mother of *Constantine*, and covered like the Sepulchre, with a sumptuous Temple (whose ruines yet look aloft) together with a Monastery, on the South side of which, they shewed us the Cell of *Pelagia*; a famous, rich, and beautiful Curtizan of *Antioch*; who converted by the Bishop of *Damiata*, retired hither unknown; and here, long lived in the habit and penury of an Hermit, being not, till dead, discovered for a woman. Descending, we were shewed by the way, where our Saviour taught them the *Pater Noster*, where he foretold of the destruction of *Jerusalem*, where the Apostles made the Creed, where he wept over the City, (a paved square, now a *Mahometan* Oratory) and such like traditions, not much worthy the mentioning. So crossing the Valley by the Sepulchre of the Blessed Virgin, we entred the City at the Gate of St. *Stephen*, returning the same way (as the day before) to the Monastery.

Much of the day, and all the night following we spent in the Church of the Sepulchre, they then concluding the ceremonies and solemnities of that Festival. The next day we prepared for our departure. We agreed with certain *Muccermen* (so call they their Muliters) of *Aleppo* (who had brought a *Portugal* hither, with his Janizary, and Interpreter, then newly come from *India*) to carry us unto *Tripoly*, and defray all charges (our diet excepted) for twenty six Dollars a man, and for half so much if we went but to *Acre*; greatly to the displeasure of *Atala* the *Drogarman*, that would not undertake our convoy under a great sum; who found a time to ask his malice; yet his little pains we rewarded with four Dollars. Caphar and Ass-hire about the Country had cost us six Sultanies. We gave money to the Frier-servants, and that not niggardly, considering our light purses, and long journy; whereof the *Pater-guardian* particularly inquired, lest their vow of poverty they should covetously infringe (or rather, perhaps, defraud his desire) by retaining what was given to their private uses. A crime with excommunication punished; yet that less feared, I suppose, than detection. They use to mark the Arms of Pilgrims with the names of *Jesus, Maria, Jerusalem, Bethlehem*, the *Jerusalem* Cross, and sundry other characters, done in such manner as hath been declared before. The *Pater-guardian* would needs thrust upon us several

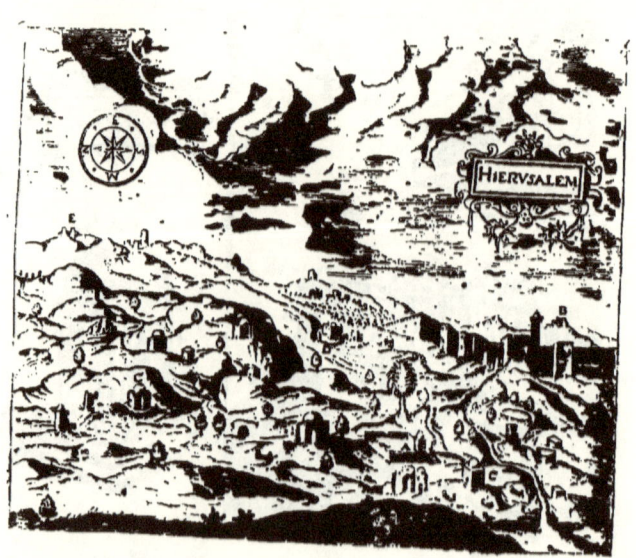

A. *A Fountain.*   B. *Mount Olivet.*   C. *Sepulchre.*   D. *A Mosque.*   E. *Sion.*

LIB. III.   *Silo. Rama Sophim. Valley of Teberinth.*   157

Certificates, which returned him as many *Zechines*. He defired that he would make their poverty known, with the dignity of thofe fanctified places, as a motive to relief, and more frequent Pilgrimages.

Leaving behind thofe friendly *Italians* that accompanied us from *Cairo*, (being now alfo upon their return) on the firft of *April* we departed from *Jerufalem*, in the company of that Apothecary (now Knight of the Sepulchre) and the *Portugal* before-mentioned, together with an *Alman* and a *French*-man, all bound for *Tripoly*. We returned by the way which we ftrayed from in our coming, lefs difficult to pafs; the Mountains more pleafant and fruitful. Near the City there are many Sepulchres and places of ruines, here and there difperfed. On the right hand, and in fight, is *Silo*, of a long time a ftation for the Ark of the Covenant, the higheft Mountain of *Jury*, which beareth on the top fome fragments of a City; North of it, on another, were the remains of that *Rama Sophim* (with more likelihood of truth than the other) which was the habitation of *Samuel*; whofe bones are faid to have been tranflated unto *Conftantinople*, by the Emperour *Arcadius*. After four miles riding, we defcended into the Valley of *Teberinth*, famous, though little, for the flaughter of *Goliah*. A Bridge here croffeth the Torrent, near which are the ruines of an ancient Monaftery; more worthy the obferving for the greatnefs of the ftones, than finenefs of the workmanfhip. Having rid four miles further, they fhewed us *Modin*, the ancient Seat of the *Maccabees*; towards the North, and feated on the top of an afpiring Hill, which yet fupporteth the reliques of a City, whereof there hath fomething been fpoken already. Beyond, by the highway fide there is another Monaftery, not altogether fubverted : of late inhabited by fome of the *Francifcans*; who befet one night by the *Arabs*, and not able to mafter their terrour, quitted it the day following. About a ftones caft off, there ftandeth a Church now defolate; yet retaining the name of the Prophet *Jeremy*. But whether here ftood that *Anathoth*, or no, that challengeth his birth, I am ignorant. About three miles further, we paffed by a place called *Sereth*; where, by certain ruines, there ftandeth a Pile like a broken Tower, engraven with *Turkifh* Characters, upon that fide which regardeth the way; erected, as they fay, by an *Ottoman* Emperour. Now, having for a while defcended thofe Mountains that neighbour the Champion, we came to the ruines of an ancient Building, over-looking the level, yet no lefs excelling in commodious fituation, than delicacy of profpect. They call it, The houfe of the Good Thief. Perhaps fome Abbey erected in that place, or Caftle here built to defend this paffage. Upon the right hand there ftandeth a handfom Mofque, every way open, and fupported with Pillars, the Roof flat, and charged on the Eaft-end with a Cupolo, heretofore a Chriftian Chappel. This is ten miles from *Rama*, whither we came that night; and wet as we were, took up our Lodgings on the ground in the houfe of *Sion*, nothing that day befalling, fave the violence done us by certain *Saphies*, who took our Wine from us, and payments of Head-money in fundry places, which was unto us neither chargeable nor troublefom.

Not until noon next day departed we from *Rama*; travelling through a moft fruitful Valley. The firft place we paffed by was *Lydda*, made famous by St. *Peter*; called after *Diofpolis*, that is, the City of *Jupiter*, and deftroyed by *Ceftius*. Here yet ftandeth a Chriftian Temple, built, as they fay, by a King of *England*, to the honour of St. *George*, a *Cappadocian* by birth, advanced in the Wars to the Dignity of a *Tribune*; who after became a Souldier of Chrift, and here is faid to have fuffered Martyrdom under *Dioclefian*. Others fay, that there never was fuch a man, and that the ftory is no other than an Allegory. The *Greeks* have the cuftody of this Church, who fhew a Skull, which they affirm to be Saint *Georges*. In the time of the Chriftians it was the feat of a Suffragan, now hardly a Village. Eight miles from *Rama* ftands the Caftle *Angia*, built like a Cane, and kept by a fmall Garrifon. A little beyond, the *Muccermen* would have ftayed (which we would not fuffer; being then the beft time of the day for travel) that they might by night have avoided the next Village, with the payments there due ; where we were hardly intreated by the procurement of *Attalo*, who holds correfpondency with the *Moors* of thofe Quarters. They would not take lefs than four Dollars a man (when perhaps as many Madenies were but due) and that with much jangling. They fought occafion, how to trouble us, beating us off our Mules, becaufe, forfooth, we did not light to do Homage to a fort of half-clad Rafcals, pulling the white Shaith from the head of the *Portugal* (whereby he well hoped to have paft for a *Turk*) his *Janizary* looking

P   on on. Here they detained us until two of the clock the next morning, without meat, without sleep, couched on the wet earth, and washed with rain, yet expecting worse, and then suffered us to depart. After a while we entred a goodly Forest, full of tall and delightsom Trees, intermixed with fruitful and flowry Lawns. Perhaps the earth affordeth not the like, it cannot a more pleasant. Having passed this part of the Wood (the rest inclining to the West, and then again extending to the North) we might discover a number of stragling Tents; some just in our way, and near to the skirts of the Forest. These were *Saphies* belonging to the Host of *Murat Bassa*, then in the Confines of *Persia*. They will take (especially from a Christian) whatsoever they like; and kindly they use him, if he pass without blows: nor are their Commanders at all times free from their insolencies. To avoid them, we struck out of the way, and crossed the pregnant Champaign to the foot of the Mountains, where, for that day, we reposed our selves. When it grew dark we arose, inclining on the left hand, and mingling after it a while with a small Caravan of *Moors*, we were injoyned to silence, and to ride without our Hats, lest we should be discovered for Christians. The Clouds fell down in streams, and the pitchy night had bereft us of the conduct of our eyes, had not the Lightning afforded a terrible light. And when the rain intermitted, the Air appeared as if full of sparkles of fire, born to and fro with the wind; by reason of the infinite swarms of Flies that do shine like Glow-worms; to a Stranger a strange spectacle. In the next Wood we out-stript that Caravan, where the thievish *Arabs* had made sundry fires, to which our Foot-men drew near to listen, that we might pass more securely. An hour after midnight, the Sky began to clear; when, on the other side of the Wood, we fell amongst certain Tents of *Spahees*; by whom we past with as little noise as we could, secured by their sounder sleepings. Not far beyond, through a large Glade, between two Hills we leisurely descended for the space of two hours (a Torrent rushing down on the left hand of us:) when not able longer to keep the backs of our Mules; we laid us down in the bottom, under a plump of Trees on the far-side of a Torrent. With the Sun we arose, and found our selves at the East-end and North-side of Mount *Carmel*.

Mount *Carmel* stretcheth from East to West, and hath his uttermost Basis washed with the Sea, steepest towards the North, and of an indifferent altitude; rich in Olives and Vines when husbanded; and abounding with several sorts of Fruits and Herbs, both medicinable and fragrant, though now much over-grown with Woods and Shrubs of sweet savour. Celebrated it was for the habitation of *Elias*; whose house was after his death converted into a Synagogue; where Oracles, it is said, were given by God; called by *Suetonius*, The God *Carmelius*; whose words are these, intreating of *Vespasian*; *In Judea, consulting with the Oracle of the God Carmelius, the Oracle assured him, that whatsoever he undertook should be successful*. Where then was nothing more to be seen than an Altar. From hence proceeded the Order of the Fryar *Carmelites*, as Successor to the Children of the Prophets there left by *Elias*. Who had their beginning in the Desart of *Syria*, in the year 1180. instituted by *Almericus* Bishop of *Antioch*; and said to have received their white habit from our Lady; whom *Albertus* the Patriarch of *Jerusalem* transported first into *Europe*. There is yet to be seen the remains of their Monastery, with a Temple dedicated to the Blessed Virgin; under which a little Chappel or Cave, the ancient Dwelling of *Elias*. This is inherited by *Achmet*, an *Emer* of the *Arabians*, who, after the ancient custom of that Nation, doth live in Tents, even during the Winter, although possest of sundry convenient houses; whose Signiory stretcheth to the South, and along the Shore. Within his Precinct stands the Castle of the *Peregrines*, upon a Cape almost environed with the Sea, now called *Tortora*; built by *Raimond* Earl of *Polisa*, for their better security; and after fortified by the *Templars*. Ten miles South of this stood that famous *Cæsarea* (more anciently called, The Tower of *Strato*, of a King of *Aradus*, the Builder, so named; who lived in the days of *Alexander*) in such sort re-edified by *Herod*, that it little declined in Magnificency from the principal Cities of *Asia*; now level with the floor, the Haven lost, and Situation abandoned.

We passed the Torrent *Chison*, which floweth from the Mountains of *Tabor* and *Hermon*; and gliding by the North skirts of *Carmel*, dischargeth it self into the Sea. *Carmel* is the South bound to the ample Valley of *Acre*; bounded on the North by those of *Saron*, on the West it hath the Sea, and is inclosed on the East with the Mountains of *Galilee*. In length about fourteen miles, in breadth about half

LIB. III. The Valley of Acre. Acre.

half as much; the nearer the Sea, the more barren. In it there arose two Rivulets of living, but pestilent waters drilling from several Marishes. The first is the River of *Belus*, called by *Pliny*, *Pagida* and *Palus*, and *Badas* by *Simonides*; whose sand affordeth matter for glass, becoming fusible with the heat of the Furnace. *Strabo* reports the like of divers places thereabout. And *Josephus*, speaking of this, declareth, that adjoyning thereunto, there is a Pit an hundred cubits in circuit, covered with sand like glass, and when carried away (for therewith they accustomed to ballance their Ships) it forthwith filled again; born thither by winds from places adjacent: and moreover, that whatsoever Mineral was contained therein converted into glass; and glass there laid, again into sand. Near to this Pit stood the Sepulchre of *Memnon* the Son of *Tythonus* (who was Brother unto *Priamus*, and reigned in *Susa*, a City of *Persia*, by him founded) his Mother was called *Cissa*, (though feigned to have been begotten on *Aurora*, in regard that he reigned in the East; and perhaps a custom then in use to reward the most excellent, with repute of immortal Parentage : so *Sarpedon* was said to be the Son of *Jupiter*, *Æneas* of *Venus*, and *Achilles* of *Thetis*) who had extended his Conquests to the uttermost parts of *Æthiopia*, before he came to the Wars of *Troy*; where slain by *Achilles*, *Aurora* is feigned to have made this intercession for him unto *Jupiter*.

Rob'd of my Memnon, who brave Arms in vain	Memnonis orba mei venio : qui fortia frustra
Bore for his Uncle, by Achilles slain	Pro patruo tulit arma suo : primisque sub annis
In his youths flow'r (so would you Gods) came I,	Occidit à forti (sic dii voluistis) Achille.
O chief of Powers, a mothers anguish, by	Da precor huic aliquem solatia mortis honorem,
Some honour given him lessen, death with same	Summe Deûm rector, matremque vulnera leni.
Re-comfort; Jove assents, when greedy flame	Jupiter annuerat ; cum Memnonis arduus alto
Devour'd the funeral pile, and curled fumes	Corruit igne rogus : nigrique volumina fumi
Day over-cast : as when bright Sol assumes.	Infecere diem, veluti cum flumina natas
From streams thick vapours, nor is seen below,	Exhalant nebulas, nec Sol admittitur infra.
The flying dying sparkles joyntly grow	Atra favilla volat; glomerataque corpus in unum
Into one body : Colour, form, life spring	Densatur, faciemque capit, sumitque colorem
To it, from fire, which levity doth wing.	Atque animum ex igni : levitas sua præbuit alas.
	Ovid. Met. l. 13.

A fiction invented by flatterers, to insinuate into the favour of greatness, strengthning that opinion in the vulgar, by some illusion or other.

Having rid seven or eight miles along the skirts of the Hills, we crossed the Valley; and anon that other Rivulet a little above where it falleth into the Road of *Acre*; where, to our comfort, we espy'd the Ship that brought us to *Alexandria*, with another of *London*, called the *Elizabeth Consort*. When entring the Town, we were kindly entertained by our Country-men. Here we staid, the rest of our Company proceeded unto *Tripoly*, this being the mid-way between it and *Jerusalem*. But our *Muccerman* would not rest satisfied with half of his hire, according to our compact, whom we were glad to be rid of for twenty Dollars a man : our oaths being bootless against a True Believer; for so they do term themselves.

This City was called *Ace* at the first; a refuge for the *Persians* in their Ægyptian Wars : then *Ptolomais*, of *Ptolomy* King of *Ægypt*, *Colonia Claudii*, of *Claudius Cæsar*, who here planted a Colony, afterward *Acon*, and now *Acre*. Seated on a level, in form of a triangular Shield, on two sides washed with the Sea, the third regarding the Champaign. The carkass shews that the body hath been strong, double immured, fortified with Bulwarks and Towers, to each Wall a Ditch, lined with stone, and under those divers secret Posterns. You would think by the ruines, that the City rather consisted wholly of divers conjoyning Castles, than any way mixed with private dwellings; which witness a notable defence, and an unequal assault; or that the rage of the Conquerours extended beyond Conquest : the huge Walls and Arches turned topsie-turvy, and lying like Rocks upon the foundation. On the South-side lies the Haven, no better than a Bay; open to the West, North-West and South-West winds, the bottom stony, and ill for their Cables. When possest by the Christians, it was an Episcopal See, and under the Metropolitan of *Tyrus*. It was taken from them by *Omer* the *Saracen*; and recovered by *Baldwin* at the first, assisted by the *Gennoese* with threescore and ten Gallies; who had for their labour the third part of the revenue arising out of the Haven; with dwellings and other immunities assigned them : *Saladine* made it stoop again to the *Mahometan* yoke : again delivered in the third years siege, by our *Richard* the First, and Philip

Philip the *French* King. There are the ruines of a place, which yet doth acknowledge King *Richard* for the Founder; confirmed likewise by the paſſant Lion. An hundred years after it remained with the Chriſtians; and was the laſt receptacle in the Holy Land, for the Knights *Hoſpitallers* of St. *John* of *Jeruſalem*, called thereupon St. *John de Acre*; to whom a goodly Temple near the South-ſide of the City was conſecrated, which now over-toppeth the reſt of the ruines. In a Vault thereof a maſs of Treaſure was hid by the Knights of the Order, which being made known from time to time unto their Succeſſors, was fetch'd from hence about forty years ſince by the Gallies of *Malta*; the Inhabitants abandoning the Town upon their landing. In the year 1291. beſieged by an hundred and fifty thouſand *Mahometans*, *Acre* received an utter ſubverſion, which the *Mamalucks* after in ſome ſort repaired, and loſt it at laſt, with the name and the Empire, unto the *Turkiſh Selymus*. It is now under the *Sanziack* of *Saphet*, and uſurped with the reſt of that Province, by the *Emer* of *Sidon*. In the Town there are not above two or three hundred Inhabitants, who dwell here and there in the patch'd-up ruines; only a new Moſque they have, and a ſtrong ſquare Cave (built where once was the Arſenal for Gallies) in which the Franck Merchants ſecurely diſpoſe of themſelves and their Commodities. Who; for the moſt part, bring hither ready Monies, (*Dutch* Dollars being as generally, throughout *Jury* and *Phœnicia*, equivalent with Royals of eight, elſewhere leſs by ten Aſpers) fraughting their Ships with Cottons that grow abundantly in the Country adjoyning. Here have they a *Cadee*, the principal Officer. The *Engliſh* are much reſpected by the principal *Moors*; inſomuch, as I have ſeen the ſtriker ſtricken by his fellow: a rare example amongſt the *Mahometans*. Which I rather attribute to their policy than humanity; left, by their quitting of the place, they ſhould be deprived of their profit, they being the only men that do maintain their Trading. Here they wraſtle in Breeches of oyled Leather, cloſe to their Thighs; their bodies naked, and anointed according to the ancient uſe, derived, as it ſhould ſeem by *Virgil*, from the *Trojans*:

Exercent patrias oleo labente paleſtras
Nudati ſocii————
Virg. Æn.

*Diſrob'd they wraſtle in their Countries guiſe
With gliding oyl————*

who rather fall by conſent than by ſleight or violence. The Inhabitants do nightly houſe their Goats and Sheep, for fear of the *Jaccals* (in my opinion no other than Foxes) whereof an infinite number do lurk in the obſcure Vaults, and reedy Mariſhes adjoyning to the Brook; the Brook it ſelf abounding with Tortoiſſes.

Four days we ſtayed at *Acre*; in which time we vainly expected the leiſure of the Merchants to have accompanied us to *Nazareth*, diſtant from hence about fifteen miles; who go by one way, and return by another, for fear of the *Arabs*; now a ſmall Village of *Galilee*; ſeated in a little Vale between two Hills; where are the remains of a goodly Temple (once the Chair of an Archbiſhop) erected over the houſe of the Bleſſed Virgin; whereof there is yet one room to be ſeen, partly hewn out of the living Rock, amongſt the Chriſtians of great veneration. But the *Romaniſts* relate, that the room wherein ſhe was born, was born by the Angels (at ſuch time as the Country was univerſally poſſeſſed by the Infidels) over Seas and Shores to a City of *Illyria*. But when thoſe people grew niggardly in their offerings, it was wrap'd from thence, and ſet in the Woods of *Picenum*, within the poſſeſſions of a noble Lady named *Lauretta*; frequented by infinite numbers of Pilgrims: Where many miſcarrying by the ambuſhment of Thieves, who lurked in the Woods adjoyning, the Bleſſed Virgin commanded the Angels to remove it unto a certain Mountain belonging unto two Brethren, where ſhe got much riches and ſumptuous apparel, by the benevolence of her Votaries, and her charitable Miracles. By which means the two Brethren grew alſo rich, and withal diſſentious about the diviſion of their purchaſes. Whereupon it was once more tranſported by thoſe winged Porters, and ſet in the place where as now it ſtandeth, near to the *Adriatick* Sea, and not far from *Ancona*; yet retaining the name of *Lauretta*. Who can but wonder at the fautors of theſe wonders? amongſt whom *Muretus*, none of the leaſt learned.

O cœli dilecta domus, poſteſque beati,
V oſne per æthereas, Judææ à finibus, oras
Aligerum, mandante Deo, vexere manipli!
H e virgo, genitura Deum, genitricis ab alvo
Prodiit, & blandis mollit vagitibus auras!

*O houſe belov'd of heaven! O happy poſts!
By winged Miniſters, thorow skies from coaſts
Of Juda brought, Jehova bidding! Here
Was that bleſt Virgin born that God did bear!*

Here

Here, a maid pure, in truth and prais'd repute;
Her holy womb swell'd with that saving fruit.
He who all mind, th' etern and only Son,
To Father equal; who to man undone
Brought hope and life from heaven, here (little)play'd,
And kist his mother, in time happy made.

Hic quoque virginei servata laude pudoris
Sancta salutifero tumuerunt viscera foetu.
Ille opifex cunctorum, illa æterno unica proles,
Æqua patri ille homini primæva ab origine lapso
Spem cœlo vitamque ferens hac lusit in aula
Parvulus, & lanctæ blande obtulit oscula matri.

In which in her Image (made, as they say, by St. *Luke*) of the hue (though a *Jew*) of a *Black-a-more*. This Conclave hath a Cover of Marble; yet not touched by the same; included within a magnificent Temple, adorned with Armors and Trophies, and beset with Statues and Tables, representing her miraculous Cures and Protections, whereof the aforesaid Votary.

Lo, all the Church with tables hung, confess
Thy saving aid to wretched mans distress.
This is from bowel-torturing fever rid,
Beholding thee in soul. The setting Kid,
Sad Hyads, he safe sees; when deaf Seas roar
Storm-beat, by thee set on the long'd-for shore.
He upon whom a wrongful doom hath past,
Now death expecting in dark dungeon cast,
The wrong by thee reveal'd, reviews his wife,
His sons and parents, with a new-given life.

Certe equidem tota pendentes æde tabellas
Aspicio, quæ te miseris præsto esse loquuntur;
Hic te animo spectans torrentem viscera febrem
Depulit; ille Hyadas tristes Hœdumque cadentem
Spectavit tutus; vertentibus æquora ventis,
Et duce te patrias enavit salvus ad oras.
Criminis ille reus falsi, sub judice duro.
Dum mortem expectat, tenebroso in carcere clausus,
Munere Diva tuo, detecta fraude revisit,
Uxorem & natos, exoptatumque parentem.

And well hath she been paid for her labour; her Territories large, her Jewels inestimable; her Apparel much more than Princely, both in cost and variety; her Coffers full: of whom, though the Pope be a yearly Borrower, yet are they doubly replenished by the first and later spring tides of devotion. Now at *Nazareth* no Christian is suffered to dwell by the *Moors* that inhabit it. Most of the old City seemeth to have stood upon the Hill that adjoyneth; which bears the decays of divers other Churches. *Nazareth* gave the name of *Nazaretans* unto Christians, called here corruptly *Nostranes* at this present.

Upon the eighth of *April* we went aboard the *Trinity*, and hoised sails for *Sidon*; the winds favourable, and the Seas composed; but anon they began to wrangle, and we to suffer. Spouts of water were seen to fall against the Promontory of *Carmel*. The tempest increased with the night, and did what it could to make a night of the day that ensued. I then thought, with application, of that description of the Poet,

The bitter storm augments; the wild winds wage
War from all parts, and joyn with the Seas rage.
The sad clouds sink in showers; you would have thought
That high-swoln Seas even unto heaven had wrought,
And heaven to Sea descended. No Star shewn;
Blind night in darkness, tempests, and her own
Dread terrours lost; yet these dire lightning turns
To more fear'd light, the Sea with lightning burns.

Aspera crescit hyems, oraniaque à parte feroces
Bella gerunt venti, fretaque indignantia miscent.
Ecce cadunt largi resoluris nubibus imbres,
Inque fretum credas totum descendere cœlum,
Inque plagas cœli tumefactum scandere pontum:
——Caret ignibus æther.
Cæcaque nox premitur tenebris hyemisq; suisq;:
Discutiunt tamen has, præbentq; micantia lumen
Fulmina, fulmineis ardescunt ignibus undæ.
Ovid. Met. l. 11.

But the distemperature and horrour is more than the danger, where Mariners be *English*, who are the absolutest under heaven in their profession, and are by Forreigners compared unto fishes. About four of the clock we came before *Sidon*; the Ship not able to attain to the harborage of the Rock, which is environed by the Sea, and the only protection of that Road for Ships of good burthen. But some of us were so sick, that we desired to be set ashore in the Skiff, a long mile distant (which was performed, but not without peril.)

Phænicia is a Province of *Syria*, interposing the Sea and *Galilee*, stretching North and South from the River *Valanus*, to the Castle of the *Peregrines*, which is on the far-side of the Mount *Carmel*.

Phænix did give the Land a lasting name.

Et qui longa dedit terris cognomina Phœnix.
Sil. Ital. l. 1.

Brother unto *Cadmus*, and the fifth from *Jupiter*. His great Grand-father was *Epaphus*, his Grand-father *Belus Priscus*, (reputed a God, and honoured with Temples; called *Bel* by the *Assyrians*, and *Baal* by the *Hebrews*) his Father *Agenor*. *Belus* the less, called also *Methres*, was son unto *Phœnix*, King of *Phœnicia* by descent, and of *Cyprus* by Conquest. He had issue, *Pygmalion* and *Dido*, who well revenged of her Brother for the death of her Husband, fled unto the Confines of *Lybia*, and there erected the City of *Carthage*. The *Carthaginians* names, as *Hannibal*, *Asdrubal*, *Anna*, &c. did shew that they had their Original from hence. But the coming thither of *Æneas*, and cause of her death, is held by divers no other than a fiction. For *Appian* (if his credit may ballance with *Virgil*) reports that *Carthage* was built full fifty years before *Troy* was destroyed. And *Ausonius* upon her Picture:

Illa ego sum Dido vultu, quam conspicis hospes,	*I Dido, whom this table doth impart,*
Assimulata modis, pulchraque mirificis.	*Of passing beauty drawn by happy art;*
Talis eram; sed non Maro quam mihi finxit erat mens:	*Such was when living; not of such a mind*
Vita nec incestis læta cupidinibus.	*As Maro feign'd, to furious lusts inclin'd.*
Namque nec Æneas vidit me Troius unquam,	*Me Troys Æneas never saw; nor bore*
Nec Lybiam advenit classibus Iliacis.	*The Ilian ships unto the Lybian shore,*
Sed furias fugiens, atque arma procacis Iarbæ,	*But flying outrage, and Jarbas, I*
Servavi, fateor, morte pudicitiam.	*By death secur'd my besieg'd chastity. (brest*
Pectore transfixo castos quod pertulit enses;	*That struck the chaste steel through my constant*
Non furor aut læso crudus amore dolor.	*Nor rage, nor injur'd Love, with grief opprest.*
Sic cecidisse juvat, vixi sine vulnere famæ,	*So, pleas'd, I fell: liv'd undefam'd, (bely'd)*
Ulta virum, positis mœnibus oppetii.	*Reveng'd my husband, built a City, dy'd.*

Phœnicia is said by others to be named of a Date, which is called *Phœnix* in the *Ægyptian* Tongue; the abundance growing in that part of *Ægypt* having given a name to this people, who were formerly *Ægyptians*.

———Hi rubro gurgite quondam	*These earst from the red Gulph remov'd; who durst*
Mutavere domum, primique per æquora vecti,	*On Seas by new-found ways adventure first :*
Lustravere salum, primi docuere carinis	*First, taught to fraught ships with chang'd merchandize:*
Ferre cavis orbis commercia; sydera primi,	*First, stars observ'd in the character'd skies.*
Servavere poli———	
Dionys.	

together with Arithmetick and Letters,

Phœnices primi (famæ si creditur) ausi	*Phœnicians first imprest (if fame be true)*
Mansuram rudibus vocem signare figuris.	*The fixt voice in rude figures. Memphis knew*
Nondum flumineas Memphis contexere Byblos	*Not yet how stream-lov'd Byblus to prepare;*
Noverat; & saxis tantum volucresque feræque,	*But birds and beasts, carv'd out in stone, declare*
Sculptaque servabant magicas animalia lingua.	*Their Hieroglyphick wisdoms:*
Lucan. l. 3.	

which Letters *Cadmus*, banished by his Father (the Builder of *Thebes* in *Bœtia*, by him perhaps so called of the *Ægyptian Thebes*) did communicate to the *Grecians*. To them also some attribute the invention of Poetry; an Art by Art not to be attained; which giveth admirable fame and memory to the deserver, and inflameth the noble mind with a vertuous emulation. The chief Sea-bordering Cities of *Phœnicia* are *Tripolis*, *Byblis*, *Berytus*, *Sidon*, *Tyrus*, and *Ptolomais* now called *Acre*.

Tripolis is so called, because it was joyntly built by *Tyrus*, *Sidon*, and *Aradus*. It is seated under *Libanus*, and commanded by a well-furnished Citadel, manned with two hundred *Janizaries*. Before it there is an ill-neighbouring Bank of Sand, which groweth daily both in greatness and nearness; of which they have a Prophesie, that it shall in process of time be devoured. The Town and Territories are governed by a *Bassa*. Two miles off, and West from it, is the Haven; made by a round piece of Land adjoyning to the Main by an Isthmus; the mouth thereof regarding the North. On each side there is a Bulwark, kept by an hundred *Janizaries*, and planted with Ordnance to defend the entrance. Hither of late the *Grand Signior* hath removed the Seal, which was before at *Alexandretta*; a Town in the furthest extents of the *Streights*, beyond the River *Orontes*; most contagiously seated by reason of the Marishes and lofty bordering Mountains (towards the North, being a part of *Taurus*) which deprive it the rarifying Sun for no small

part

LIB. III.   *Byblis. Beritus. Sidon.*

part of the day; insomuch, that not many Foreigners escape, that there linger any season, who get not ashore before the Sun be high-mounted, and return again ere too low-declining. Notwithstanding the Merchants do offer great sums of Money, to have it restored unto that place, as more convenient for their Traffick with *Aleppo* (the principal Mart of that place of *Asia*, for Silks, and sundry other Commodities) from thence, but three days journey, being eight from *Tripoly*; which the *Turk* will not yet assent to, for that divers Ships have been taken out of that Road by Pirates, there being no Forts for protection, nor no fit place to erect them on. A thing usual it is between *Tripoly* and *Aleppo*, as between *Aleppo* and *Babylon*, to make tame Doves the speedy transporters of their Letters; which they wrap about their legs like Jesses, trained thereunto at such times as they have young ones, by bearing them from them in open Cages. A Fowl of notable memory. Nor is it a modern invention: For we read that *Thourosthones*, by a Pigeon stained with Purple, gave notice of his Victory at the *Olympian* Games, the self-same day to his Father in *Ægina*. By which means also the Consul *Hircius* held intelligence with *Decimus Brutus* besieged in *Mutina*. The like perhaps is meant by the Poet, when he saith,

As if from ports removed far, from some   ———Tanquam è diversis partibus orbis
A woful Letter swiftly wing'd should come.   Anxia præcipiti venisset Epistola penna.
                                               Juv. Sat. 4.

When the Christians besieged *Acre*, *Saladine* sent out one of these winged Scouts, to confirm the courages of the besieged, with promise of a speedy relief; when, I know not by what chance or policy, intercepted, and furnished with a contrary message, it occasioned a sudden surrender.

Byblis was the Royal seat of *Cyneras* (who was also King of *Cyprus*) the Father of *Adonis*, slain by a Boar; deified, and yearly deplored by the *Syrian*, in the month of *June*, they then whipping themselves, with universal lamentation. Which done, upon one day they sacrificed unto his Soul, as if dead; affirming on the next, that he lived, and was ascended into Heaven. For feigned it is, that *Venus* made an agreement with *Proserpina*, that for six months of the year, he should be present with her; alluding unto Corn, which for so long is buried under the Earth, and for the rest of the year embraced by the temperate Air, which is *Venus*. But in the general Allegory, *Adonis* is said to be the Sun, the Boar the Winter, whereby his heat is extinguished; when desolate *Venus* (the Earth) doth mourn for his absence, re-created again by his approach, and pro-creative vertue. Aloft, and not far from the Sea, stood his celebrated Temple: The City was first called *Hevæa*, of *Hevæus* sixth son unto *Canaan*. In the time of the Christians, it was an Episcopal See, now a place of no reputation. Three miles on this side runs the River of *Adonis*, which is said by *Lucian*, to have streamed blood upon that solemnized day of his Obsequies. At this day it is called *Canis*, as they there report; of a Dog of stone (that now lies with his heels upwards, in the bottom of the Chanel) which by strange Magical motions and sounds, fore-shewed the alternate Fate of that Country. This was the Northern Confines of the Kingdom and Patriarchy of *Jerusalem*.

Beritus was so called of the Idol *Berith*, but originally *Geris* of *Gergasus*, fifth son unto *Canaan*. It was subverted by *Tryphon*, and re-edified by the *Romans* that there planted a Colony, and called it *Julia Fælix*; who, by the bounty of *Augustus*, were endued with the Priviledges of Citizens of *Rome*. *Agrippa* there placed two Legions, by whom, and his Predecessor *Herod*, it was greatly adorned; as after with Christian Churches and the See of a Bishop, being under the Metropolitan of *Tyrus*. With the rest, it hath lost his beauty, but not his being; now stored with Merchandize, and much frequented by Foreigners.

But now return we to *Sidon*, the most ancient City of *Phænicia*, built, as some write, by *Sida* the Daughter of *Belus*; according to others, by *Sidon* the first-born of *Canaan*. Some do attribute the building thereof to the *Phænicians*, who called it *Sidon*, in regard of the plenty of Fish, which frequented those Coasts; for *Sidon* signifieth Fish, in their language. In same it contendeth with *Tyrus*, but exceedeth it in antiquity, and is more celebrated by the Ancients. The seat thereof is healthful, pleasant, and profitable; on the one side walled with the Sea, on the other side with the fruitful Mountains that lie before *Libanus*; from whence fall many Springs, wherewith they overflow their delicate Orchards, (which abound with all variety

of

of excellent fruits) and when they list, exclude them. The making of Cryſtal glaſſes was here firſt invented, made of the foreſaid ſand, brought hither before it would become fuſible. Amongſt others right famous, *Sidon* is honoured with the birth of *Boetius*, and was an Epiſcopal See, depending on the Archbiſhoprick of *Tyrus*. But this once ample City ſtill ſuffering, when the often changes of thoſe Countries, is at this day contracted into narrow limits; and only ſhews the foundations of her greatneſs, lying Eaſt-ward of this that ſtandeth, and overſhadowed with Olives. There is nothing left of antiquity, but the ſuppoſed Sepulchre of the Patriarch *Zebulon*, included within a Chappel amongſt thoſe ruines, and held (eſpecially by the *Jews*) in great veneration. The Town now being is not worth our deſcription; the Walls neither fair, nor of force; the Haven decayed, when at beſt but ſerving for Gallies. At the end of the Peir ſtands a paltry Block-houſe, furniſhed with ſuitable Artillery. The Moſque, the Bannia, and Cane for Merchants, the only Buildings of Note.

The Inhabitants are of ſundry Nations and Religions, governed by a ſucceſſion of Princes, whom they call *Emers*; deſcended, as they ſay, from the *Druſes*; the remainder of thoſe *French*-men which were brought into theſe parts by *Godfrey* of *Bulloign*, who driven into the Mountains above, and defending themſelves by the advantage of the place, could never be utterly deſtroyed by the *Saracens*. At length, they afforded them peace and liberty of Religion; conditionally, that they wore the white Turbants, and paid ſuch Duties as the natural Subject. But in tract of time, they fell from the knowledge of Chriſt, nor throughly embracing the other, are indeed of neither. As for this *Emer*, he was never known to pray, nor ever ſeen in a Moſque. His name is *Faccardine*, ſmall of ſtature, but great in courage and atchievments; about the age of forty, ſubtil as a Fox, and not a little inclining to the Tyrant. He never commenceth Battel, nor executeth any notable Deſign, without the conſent of his Mother.

Illa magas artes Æmaque carmina novit,
Inque caput liquidas arte recurvat aquas.
Scit bene quid gramen, quid torto confita rombo
Licia, quid valeat virtus amantis equæ.
Cum voluit toro glomerantur nubila cœlo:
Cum voluit puro fulget in orbe dies,
Sanguine, ſi qua fides, ſtillantia ſydera vidi,
Purpureus Lunæ ſanguine vultus erat.
Hanc ego nocturnas vivam volitare per umbras
Suſpicor, & pluma corpus anile regi.
Evocat antiquis proavos, atavoſque ſepulchris,
Et ſolidam longo carmine findit humum.
Ovid. Am l. 1. E. 8.

*Skil'd in black Arts, ſhe makes ſtreams backward run
The vertues knows of weeds; of laces ſpun
On wheels; and poyſon of luſt-ſtung Mare,
Fair days make cloudy, and the cloudy fair:
Stars to drop blood, the Moon look bloodily,
And plum'd (alive) doth through nights ſhadows fly.
The dead call for their graves to further harms,
And cleave the ſolid earth with her long charms.*

To this Town he hath added a Kingly Signiory; what by his Sword, and what by his Stratagems. When *Morat Baſſa* (now principal *Vizier*) came firſt to his Government of *Damaſco*, he made him his by his free entertainment and bounty., which hath converted to his no ſmall advantage; of whom he made uſe in his contention with *Freeke*, the *Emer* of *Balbec*, by his authority ſtrangled. After that he pickt a quarrel with *Joſeph Emer* of *Tripoly*, and diſpoſſeſt him of *Barut*, with the Territories belonging thereunto; together with *Gazar*, about twelve miles beyond it, a place by ſituation invincible. This *Joſeph* hated of his people, for his exceſſive Tyranny, got to be made *Sediar* of *Damaſco*, (which is, General of the Souldiery) and by that power intended a revenge. But in the mean ſeaſon, *Faccardine* ſackt *Tripoly* it ſelf, and forced th. *Emer* to fly in a *Venetian* Ship unto *Cyprus*, where again he imbarked in a *French*-man, and landed at the Caſtle of *Peregrines*; and there by *Achmet* the *Arabian* (formerly mentioned) entertained, he repaired to *Damaſco*, entred on his charge, converting his whole ſtrength upon the *Sidonian*, now in the field, and joyn'd with *Ali Baſſa* his confederate. In a Plain, ſome eight miles ſhort of *Damaſco*, the Armies met, the *Damaſceens* are foiled, and purſued to the gates of the City; the Conquerors lodge in the Suburbs, who are removed by the force of an hundred and fifty thouſand *Sultanies*. This Battel was fought about the midſt of *November*, in the year of our Lord 1606. Three months after a Peace is concluded amongſt them. But the Summer following, *Morat* the great *Vizier* having overthrown *Ali Baſſa* of *Aleppo*, that valiant Rebel (who in three main Battels withſtood his whole Forces; having ſet up an order of *Sedgmen* in oppoſition of the *Janizaries*) they ſought by manifold complaints, to incenſe him againſt the *Emer* of *Sidon*, as confederate with the Traitor; which they urged with gifts, received and loſt; for the old *Baſſa*, mindful of the friendly offices done him by the

LIB. III. *The Emier of Sidon.*

the *Emer*, (corrupted also, as is thought, with great sums of money) not only not molesteth, but declareth him a good Subject. Having, till of late, held good correspondency with the City and Garrison of *Damasco*, they had made him *Sanziack* of *Saphet*. Now, when according to the Government of *Turkie*, which once in two or three years doth use to remove the Governours of Cities and Provinces, and that another was sent by the *Damaseens*, to succeed him, he refused to resign it; notwithstanding tending to the *Teftadar* or Treasurer, the Revenue of that *Sanziakry*. This was the first occasion of their quarrel. He got from the improvident Peasants the Castle of *Elkiffe*, which he hath strongly fortified, and made the Receptacle of his Treasure, and the Castle of *Banias* from the *Sheck*, that ought it, by a wile; which standeth on a Hill by it self, and is indeed by nature invincible. For the *Emer*, in peaceable manner, pitching his Tents not far from the Wall, was kindly visited, and entertained by the *Sheck*; when desirous to see it, he conducted him up, having not above twenty or thirty in his company, but those privately armed, leaving order that the rest should ascend by two's and by three's, and so surprised it without blood-shed, planting the Inhabitants in other places within his Dominions, and strengthening this with a Garrison. Out of the Rock whereon it is mounted ariseth one of the two heads of *Jordan*. His Signiory stretching from the River of *Canis* (which they call *Celp*) to the foot of Mount *Carmel*. In which the places of principal note are *Gazir*, *Barut*, *Sidon*, *Tyrus*, *Acre*, *Saffet* (which was *Tyberias*) *Diar*, *Camar*, *Elkiffe*, *Banuias*, the two heads of *Jordan*, the Lake *Semochontis* (now called *Houle*) and Sea of *Tyberias*: with the hot bath adjoyning; *Nazareth*, *Cana*, and Mount *Tabor*. *Saffet* is the principal City, in which there abide a number of *Jews*, who affect the place, in that *Jacob* had his being thereabout, before his going down into *Ægypt*. The *Grand Signior* doth often threaten his subversion, which he puts off with a jest, that he knows that he will not this year trouble him; whose displeasure is not so much provoked by his incroaching, as by the revealed intelligence which he holds with the *Florentine*; whom he suffers to harbour within his Haven of *Tyrus*,(yet excusing it as a place lying waste, and not to be defended) to come ashore for fresh water, buys of him under-hand his Prizes, and furnisheth him with necessaries. But designs of a higher nature have been treated of between them, as is well known to certain Merchants imployed in that business. And I am verily perswaded, that if the occasion were laid hold of, and freely pursued by the Christians, it would terribly shake, if not utterly confound the *Ottoman* Empire. It is said of a certainty, that the *Turk* will turn his whole Forces upon him the next Summer; and therefore more willingly condescends to a Peace with the *Persian*. But the *Emer* is not much terrified with the rumour (although he seeks to divert the tempest by continuance of gifts, the favour of his Friends, and professed integrity:) for he not a little presumeth of his invincible Forts, well stored for a long War, and advantage of the Mountains; having besides forty thousand expert Souldiers in continual pay, part of them *Mores*, and part of them Christians; and if the worst should fall out, hath the Sea to friend, and the *Florentine*. And in such an exigent, intendeth, as is thought, to make for Christendom, and there to purchase some Signory: For the opinion is, that he hath a mass of Treasure, gathered by Wiles and Extortions, as well from the Subject, as from the Forreigner. He hath coyned, of large a number of counterfeit *Dutch* Dollars, which he thrusteth away in payments, and offers in exchange to the Merchants, so that no new *Dutch* Dollars, though never so good, will now go current in *Sidon*. He hath the fifth part of the increase of all things. The Christians, if *Jews*, do pay for their heads two Dollars apiece yearly; and head-money he hath for all the Cattel within his Dominions. A severe justicer; re-edifies ruinous, and replants depopulated places; too strong for his Neighbours, and able to maintain a defensive War with the *Turk*; but that it is to be suspected, that his people would fall from him in regard of his Tyranny. Now as for the Merchants, who are for the most part *English*, they are entertained with all Courtesie and Freedom, they may travel without danger, with their Purses in their hands, paying for Custom but three in the hundred. Yet these are but trains to allure them, and disguise his voracity; for if a Factor die, as if the Owner, and he his Heir, he will seize on the Goods belonging to his Principals, and seem to do them a favour, in admitting of a Redemption under the value; so that they do but labour for his harvest, and reap for his Garners: For such and such like things, they generally intend to forsake his Country. The Merchandize appropriate to this place are Cottons, and Silks, which here are

are made in the Mulberry-Groves, in indifferent quantity. Other Commodities (which are many, and not coorse) they fetch from *Damascus*, two days journey from hence; interpoled with the snow-topt Mountains of *Antelibanus*; so exceeding cold, that a *Moor*, at our being here, returning from thence in the company of an *English* Merchant, perished by the way; the heat then excessive great in the Vallies on both sides. *Damascus* is seated in a Plain, environed with Hills, and watered with the River *Chrysoras*, which descendeth with a great murmur from the Mountains; but after a while having entred the Plain, becometh more gentle; serving the City so abundantly, that few houses are without their Fountains, and by little Rivulets is let into their Orchards; than which the habitable Earth affordeth not more delicate for excellency of Fruits, and their varieties. Yet is this City subject to both the extremes of Weather; rich in Trades, and celebrated for excellent Artisans. We were desirous to have seen it, but were advised not to adventure, because of the lawless *Spahies*, there then residing in great numbers. The people about *Sidon* are greatly given to the nourishing of Cattel, (having notwithstanding not many) insomuch as Beef and Veal are seldom here to be had, but when by chance they do break their legs, or otherwise miscarry. They fodder them in the Winter (for they cut no Grass) with Straw and the Leaves of Trees, whereof many do flourish continually.

Our Ship returning to *Alexandria*, and carrying with her two of our fellow Pilgrims; on the five and twentieth of *April*, we returned also towards *Acre* by Land, in the company of divers *English* Merchants: the Champaign between the Sea and the Mountains, fruitful, though narrow, and crossed with many little Rivulets. After five miles riding, we came to a small solitary Mosque, not far from the Sea, erected, as they say, over the Widows house that entertained *Elias*. Close by it are the foundations of *Sarepta*, commended for her Wines,

Vina mihi non sunt Gazetica, Chia, Falerna :
Quæque Sareptano palmite missa bibas.
    Sidonius.

Gazetick, Chian, nor Falernian Wine
Have I: drink then of the Sareptan Vine.

It was the Seat of a Bishop, and subject unto *Tyrus*. Right against it, and high mounted on a Mountain, there is a handsom new Town, now called *Sarapanta*. Beyond, on the left hand of the way, are a number of Caves cut out of the Rock; the habitations, as I suppose, of men in the Golden Age, and before the Foundation of Cities.

——— Cum frigida parvas
Præberet spelunca domos, ignemque laremque,
Et pecus, & dominos communi clauderet umbra :
Sylvestrem montana thorum cum sterneret uxor
Frondibus & culmo, vicinarumque ferarum
Pellibus.   *Juv. Sat.* 6.

When cool caves humble dwellings did afford,
The fire, lar, cattel, with their owner plac't
All under one shed : when the wife then chast
(For then uncourtly) made her sylvan bed
Of straw and leaves, with skins of wild beasts spread.

These are mentioned in the Book of *Joshuah*, and called *Mearah* (which is, the Caves of the *Sidonians*) and were afterward called the Caves of *Tyrus*. A place then inexpugnable, and maintained by the Christians; until, in the year 1167. it was by the corrupted Souldiers delivered to the *Saracens*.

We crossed a little Valley divided by the River *Elutherus* (now called *Casmeir*) which derives its Original from *Libanus*, and goeth along with a speedy course thorow a strangely intricate Chanel; guilty of the death of the Emperour *Frederick Barbarossa*, who falling from his Horse as he pursued the Infidels, and oppressed with the weight of his Armour, was drowned therein, and buried at *Tyrus*. On the other side of the Valley stands an ancient Cane, whose port doth bear the portraicture of a Chalice. Five miles beyond, we came to a Village seated on a little Hill in the midst of a Plain; the same by all likelihood that was formerly called *Palætyrus*, or old *Tyrus*. Forget I must not the custom observed by the Inhabitants hereabout, who retain the old Worlds Hospitality. Be the Passenger Christian, or whatsoever, they will house him, prepare him extraordinary fare, and look to his Mule, without taking of one Asper. But these precise *Mahometans* will neither eat nor drink with a Christian, only minister to his wants; and when he hath done, break the earthen dishes wherein he was fed, as defiled. Now, thorow this Town there passes a ruinous Aquæduct, extending a great way towards the South, and thorow the Champaign, seeming oft to climb above his beginning, and from hence proceedeth directly West unto *Tyrus*, which standeth about two miles and a half below it.

Tyrus.

Tyrus was said to be built by *Tyras*, the seventh Son of *Japhet*; re-edified by *Phænix*, made a Colony of the *Sidonians*, and afterward the *Metropolis* of *Phœnicia*. The City was consecrated to *Hercules*, whose Priest was *Sichens*. The Citizens famous for sundry Excellencies and foreign Plantations. *Carthage*, æmulous of *Rome*, (who yearly sent hither their Embassadours) *Lettis* and *Utica*, do acknowledge them for their Founders, together with *Gades*. For, thinking those streights to be the uttermost bounds of the earth, on *Europe* side they placed that City, and a Temple unto *Hercules*, on the opposite shore, called thereupon the Pillars of *Hercules*.

——— *A people fierce in War.*   ——— Genus intractabile bello.
Nor were their Women unexpert in their Weapons.   *Virg. Æn. l. 1.*

The Tyrian Virgins Quivers use to bear,   Virginibus Tyriis mos est gestare pharetram,
And Purple buskins ty'd with ribands, wear.   Purpureoque alte suras vincire cothurno.
                                                      Ibid.

Yet branded with a twofold imputation :

Inconstant Tyrians ———   Et Tyrios instabiles ———
——— *Tyrians double-tongu'd.*   *Lucan. l. 3.*
                                     ———Tyriosque bilingues.
                                             Virg. Æn l. 4.

And no marvel, since their principal profession was Merchandize; having elected the site thereof for that purpose. For it stood upon a rocky Island, removed seven hundred paces from the Continent ; the shape thereof circular, the building lofty by Nature, and impregnably fortified : Soveraign of the Seas, and chief for Commerce thorowout the whole Universe, whose glory is described by *Ezekiel*, and destruction foretold ; inflicted by *Nebuchadnezzar*, who is said to have joyned it first to the Continent ; but that passage was soon after demolished by assaulting Seas and industry of the *Tyrians*. Yet seventy years the City lay waste, and then re-edified, was overthrown again 200 years after, by *Alexander*; whose undefatigable perseverance made all things possible. For when the rest of *Phœnicia* had resigned their freedoms to his service, the *Tyrians* rather accepted of amity, than subjection ; who sent him a Crown of Gold, with plenty of provision ; which he thankfully received, and made known withal, that he purposed to sacrifice unto *Hercules*, the Patron of their City, and his Ancestor. The Embassadour told him, that he might so do in his Temple in *Palætyrus*. Whereat enraged, *You contemn* (quoth he) *my Army of Foot, for that you inhabit an Island, but I ere long, will make it appear you are of the Continent*. They are dismissed, and he provides for the assault. *Palætyrus* affords him stones, and *Libanus* timber. The South-West winds, to which it lay open, the profundity thereof, and little shew of much labour, makes the Souldier desperate. But revenge re-inflamed their courages, by the refusal of Peace (being proffered), lest so long a Siege should prove an impediment to their Victories) and slaughter of their Heralds, aggravated with scoffs : *That they so glorious in Arms, should now bear burden like Asses; and demanding if Alexander were greater than Neptune*. But when, contrary to their expectations, they saw the pile mount above the superficies of the Sea, and fortified with Towers of Wood, to defend from all annoyances, they fired one of their greatest Ships, being full of combustible matter ; which driving against it, not only caught hold of the Towers, but of as much of the pile that surmounted the Water ; the fury of the Sea, subverting the remainder. His second attempt, they again made frustrate, whereupon he thought to have desisted; but lest he should impeach his Fame, which subdued more than his Sword, and that this City might witness to the World, that he was not to be withstood ; once more he renewed his enterprize, which by the arrival of his Navy was effected. After seven months siege, the City was taken and defaced, two thousand of the Citizens crucified all along the shore, the rest being put to the Sword ; save those that were under-hand saved by the *Sidonians*, then serving *Alexander*, and mindful that both were once but one people. But *Tyrus*, shortly after, overcame these calamities, and recovered both her former riches and beauty. That part which joyned to the forced Isthmus (which is not much more than a stones cast over) being fortified with four strong Walls, five and twenty foot thick, entred thorow a Bulwark, on each side whereof stood six high Towers, almost conjoyning to each other. On the South-side upon a Rock and adherent, stood the Castle, as invincible as stately ; the rest environed with a double Wall, well adorned with Turrets equally distant. On the North-side lay the Haven, entred between two Towers, and affording a most safe station. This City did justly boast of her Purples, the best of all other, and taken hereabout. A kind of shell-fish, having in the midst of his jaws, a certain white vein, which contained that precious liquor, a dye of soveraign estimation. The invention thereof is ascribed unto *Hercules*; who walking along the shore with a Damosel, whom he loved, by chance his Dog had seized on one thrown up by the Sea, and smerched his lips with the tincture; which she admiring, refused to be his, until he had brought her a Garment of that colour, who not long after accomplished it. This blood, together with the opened veins, were stilled in a Vessel of Lead, drawn thorow a Limbeck, with the vapour of a little boiling water. The tongue of a Purple is about the length of a finger, so sharp and hard, that he can open therewith the shell of an Oyster; which was the cause of their taking. For the Fisher-men did bait their Weels therewith, which they suffered to sink into the bottom of the Sea; when the Purples repairing thereunto, did thrust their tongues between the Osiers, and pricking the gaping Oysters (kept, for that purpose, long out of the water) were by the sudden closings of their shells, retained; who could neither draw them unto them, nor approach so near as to open them. They gathered together in the first of the Spring, and were no where to be found at the rising of the Dog-star. The Fisher-men strove to take them alive; for with their lives they cast up that tincture. The colour did differ according to the Coasts which they frequented: On the Coasts of *Africa*, resembling a Violet, or the Sea when enraged. Near *Tyrus*, a Rose, or rather our Scarlet, which name doth seem to be derived from them; for *Tyrus* was called *Sar*, in that it is built upon a Rock, which gave a name unto *Syria* (as the one at this day *Sur*, and the other *Suris*) by the *Arabians* (they pronouncing *sean* for *san*, and *sear* for *sar*) and the fish was likewise named *Sar*, or *Sear* rather in their Language:

Hic petit excidiis urbem, miserosque penates,
Ut gemma bibat, & Sarrhano dormiat ostro.
Virg. Georg. l. 2.

He Cities sacks, and houses fills with groans,
To lie in Scarlet, drink in precious stones.

A colour destinated from the beginning, to Courts and Magistracy; so that sometimes it is used for Magistracy it self, as by *Martial* unto *Janus*:

Purpura te fœlix, te colat omnis honos.
Lib. 8. Epist. 8.

The happy Purple, thee all honours honour.

The Murex, though differing from the Purple, are promiscuously used:

―――― Tyrioque ardebat murice lana. ――――The wool with Tyrian Murex shin'd.

The excellency of the double die, being light upon through defect of the former. But the Purple is now no more to be had, either extinct in kind, or because the places of their frequenting are now possest by the barbarous *Mahometans*. After the aforesaid restauration, *Tyrus* preserved her dignity for the space of nine hundred years, remaining, for six hundred thereof, in the Christians possession; a Confederate with the *Romans*, and for her faith unto them endued with the immunities of the City. When the Christian Religion grew powerful in these parts, it was the Seat of an Archbishop, next in precedency unto the Patriarch of *Jerusalem*; fourteen Bishopricks being under her Primacy, viz. *Porphyra, Acon, Sarepta, Sidon, Cæsarea Philippi, Beritus, Byblis, Betrus, Tripoly, Orthosia, Achin, Aradus, Tortosa*, and *Matades*. In the year of our Lord 636. it became enthrall'd to the *Saracens*. *Baldwin* the second, four hundred forty four years after, delivered it from that yoke, assisted by the *Venetian* Navy. It was then divided into three portions: two allotted to the King of *Jerusalem*, and the third to the *Venetians*, and was restored to her Archiepiscopal See, but not unto all her inferiour Bishopricks; those on the North of the River of *Casm* being then subject to the Patriarch of *Antioch*. After this, with admirable valour, they repulsed the assaults of *Saladine*, then Lord of *Jury*. But in the year 1280. it was subdued by the *Egyptian Mahometans*, and from them by the *Ottoman Selymus*. But this once famous *Tyrus*, is now no other than an heap of ruines; yet have they a reverent respect, and do instruct the pensive beholder with their exemplary frailty. It hath two Harbours, one on the North-side, the fairest, and best throughout all the Levant, (which the Curfours enter at their pleasure) the other choaked with the decays of the City. The *Emer* of *Sidon* hath given it, with the adjacent Territories, to his Brother for a possession, comprehending six miles

LIB. III.   *Solomons Cisterns. Mountain of Saron.*

breath, and in some places three. A level naturally fertil, but now neglected; watered with pleasant Springs; heretofore abounding with Sugar Canes, and all variety of Fruit-Trees.

We passed by certain Cisterns, some a mile and better distant from the City; which are called *Solomons* by the Christians of this Country. I know not why, unless these were they which he mentions in the *Canticles*. Square they are, and large, replenished with living water, which was in times past conveyed by the Aquæduct into the aforesaid Orchards; but now useless and ruined, they shed their waters into the Valley below, making it plashy in sundry places, where the air doth suffer with the continual croaking of Frogs, not unaptly feigned to have their beginning from those bauling *Peasants*,

—————— *Who still*
Do rudely wrangle, and of all shame void,
Though under water, under water chide.

——— *nunc quoque turpes*
Litibus exercent linguas, pulsoque pudore
Quamvis sunt sub aqua, sub aqua male dicere tentant.
Ovid. Met. l. 6.

Within night we came unto certain Tents that were pitched in those Marishes belonging to the *Emers* Brothers Servants, who there pastured their Horses; where, by a *Muletto*, the Master of his Horse (whose Sister he had married) we were courteously entertained. The next morning, after two or three hours riding, we ascended the high and woody Mountains of *Saron*, which stretch with intermitted Valleys unto the Sea of *Galilee*; and here have their white Cliffs wash'd with the surges; (called *Capo Banico* by the Mariner) frequented (though forsaken by men) with Leopards, Bores, Jaccals, and such like savage Inhabitants. This passage is both dangerous and difficult, neighboured by the precipitating Cliff, and made by the labour of man; yet recompencing the trouble with fragrant savours; Bays, Rosemary, Marjoran, Hysop, and the like, there growing in abundance. They say, that of late a Thief, pursued on all sides, and desperate of his safety, (for rarely are offences here pardoned) leap'd from the top into the Sea, and swam unto *Tyrus*, which is seven miles distant; who, for the strangeness of the fact, was forgiven by the *Emer*. A little beyond we passed by a ruinous Fort, called *Scandarone* of *Alexander* the Builder; here built to defend this passage: much of the Foundation overgrown with Oliers and Weeds, being nourished by a Spring that falleth from thence into the Sea. A *Moor* not long since was here assailed by a Leopard that sculk'd in the aforesaid Thicket; and jumping upon him, overthrew him from his Ass: but the Beast having wet his feet, and mist of his hold, retired as ashamed without further violence. Within a day or two after he drew company together to have hunted him; but found him dead of a Wound received from a Bore. The higher Mountains now coming short of the Sea, do leave a narrow level between. Upon the left hand, on a high round Hill, we saw two solitary Pillars, to which some of us rid, in hope to have seen something of antiquity; where we found divers others laid along, with the half buried Foundation of an ample Building. A mile beyond we came to a Fort maintained by a small Garrison of *Moors*, to prohibit that passage if need should require, and to secure the Traveller from Thieves; a place heretofore unpassable, by reason of their outrages. The Souldiers acquainted with our Merchants, freely entertained us, and made us good chear, according to their manner of diet; which was requited with the present of a little Tobacco, by them greedily affected. They also remitted our Caphar; using to take four Dollars apiece of the stranger Christians. From hence ascending the more eminent part of the rocky and naked Mountains, which here again thrust into the Sea (called in times past the *Tyrian* Ladder) by a long and steep descent we descended into the Valley of *Acre*. Divers little Hills being here and there dispersed, crown'd with ruines, (the coverts for Thieves) and many Villages on the skirts of the bordering Mountains. E're yet night, we re-entred *Acre*.

FINIS LIBRI TERTII.

THE FOURTH BOOK.

NOW shape we our course for *England.* Beloved soil; as in scite,

...Penitus
toto divi-
sos orbe
Britannos.
Virg.Eccl.

————*Wholly from all the World disjoined*;

so in thy felicities. The Summer burns thee not, nor the Winter benums thee; defended by the Sea from wastful incursions, and by the valour of thy Sons from hostile invasions. All other Countrys are in some things defective; when thou, a provident Parent, dost minister unto thine whatsoever is useful: foreign additions but only tending to vanity and luxury. Virtue in thee at the least is praised, and Vices are branded with their names, if not pursued with punishments. That *Ulysses*

Qui mores hominum multorum vidit & Urbes.
Hom. Odyss. l.1.

Who knew many mens manners, and saw many Cities:

if as found in judgment as ripe in experience, will confess thee to be the Land that floweth with Milk and Honey.

Our Sails now swelling with the first breath of *May*, on the right hand we left *Cyprus*, sacred of old unto *Venus*, who (as they feign) was here first exhibited to mortals.

Venerandam auream coronam habentem pulchram
  Venerem
Canam, quæ Cypri munimenta sortita est
Maritimæ, ubi illam Zephyri vis molliter spirantis
Suscitavit per undam multisoni maris
Spuma in molli. *Hom. in Hymnis.*

I sing of Venus crown'd with Gold, renown'd
For fair; that Cyprus guards, by Neptune bound:
Her in soft some mild-breathing Zephyre bore
On murmuring waves unto that fruitful shore.

Thither

LIB. IV. *Cyprus.*

Thither said to be driven in regard of the fertility of the soil, or beastly lusts of the people, who to purchase portions for their Daughters, accustomed to prostitute them on the shore unto Strangers; an Offering besides held acceptable to their Goddess of Viciousness. Some write that *Cyprus* was so named of the Cypress-trees that grew therein. Others of *Cyrus*, who built in it the ancient City of *Aphrodisia*, but grosly; for *Cyrus* lived six hundred years after *Homer*, who had used that name; but more probably of *Crypus*, the more ancient name, in that often concealed by the surges. It stretcheth from East unto West in form of a Fleece, and thrusteth forth a number of Promontories; whereupon it was called *Cerastis*, which signifieth horned; so terming Promontories: as in *Phillis* to *Demophoon*,

A Bay there is like to a bow when bend,
Steep horns advancing on the shores extend.

Est sinus adductos modicè falcatus in arcus,
Ultima prærupta cornua mole rigent.
Ovid. Epist. 2.

the occasion of that Fable of *Venus* her metamorphosing the cruel Sacrificers of that Island into Oxen, or else called so of the tumours that grew in many of their foreheads: It is in circuit according unto *Strabo* 427 miles, 60 miles distant from the rocky shore of *Cilicia*; and from the main of *Syria* an hundred: from whence it is said to have been divided by an Earth-quake. Divided it was into four Provinces, *Salamina, Amathusia, Lapethia,* and *Paphia,* so named of their principal Cities. *Salamina* was built by *Teucer* in memorial of that from whence he was banished by his Father *Telamon,* for not revenging the death of his Brother.

When Teucer fled from fire, and Salamine,
Crown'd with a wreath of Poplar dip'd in Wine.
He thus his sad friends chears; Go we lov'd-mates
Which way soever Fortune leads, the Fates
Are kinder than my Father; nor despair
When Teucer guides you. He whose answers are
Most sure, Apollo, in another land,
Did say another Salamine should stand.

———Teucer Salamina patremque
Quum fugeret, tamen uva Lyæo
Tempora populea fertur vincisse corona,
Sic tristes affatus amicos.
Quo nos cunque feret melior fortuna parente
Ibimus ô socii comitesque:
Nil desperandum Teucro duce & aspice Teucro.
Certus enim promisit Apollo,
Ambiguam tellurem nova Salamine futuram.
Hor. l 1. Od. 7.

The Island being assigned unto him by *Belus,* if *Didoes* relation may be believed.

Teucer, exiled Greece, to Sidon came:
Who a new Kingdom sought by Belus aid.
My Father Belus then did Cyprus tame:
And that rich Country tributary made.

Atque equidem Teucrum memini idona venire,
Finibus expulsum patriis nova regna petentem
Auxilio Beli; genitor tunc Belus opimam
Vastabat Cyprum, & victor ditione tenebat.
Virg. Æn. l. 1.

This City was afterwards called *Constantia*; but destroyed by the *Jews* in the days of the Emperor *Trajan*; and finally by the *Saracens,* in the Reign of *Heraclius* upon the ruines thereof, the famous *Famagosta* was erected by King *Costa,* as they say, the Father of St. *Katharine.* Eternized in fame by the unfortunate valour of the *Venetians,* and their auxiliary Forces under the command of *Signior Bragadine*; who with incredible fortitude withstood the furious assaults made by the populous Army of *Selymus* the Second, conducted by *Mustapha*; and after surrendred it upon honourable conditions, infringed by the perjured and execrable *Bassa.* Who entertaining at his Tent with counterfeit kindness the principal of them, suddenly picking a quarrel, caused them all to be murdered, the Governour excepted, whom he reserved for more exquisite torments. For having cut off his ears, and exhibited him by carrying of earth on his back to the derision of the Infidels, he, finally fley'd him alive; and stuffing his skin with Chaff, commanded it to be hung at the main-yard of his Galley. *Famagosta* is seated in a Plain, between two Promontories; in form well-nigh quadrangular, whereof two parts are washed with the Sea, indifferent strong, and containing two miles in circumference. It standeth almost

oppo-

opposite unto *Tripoly*, having a Haven which openeth South-East; the mouth thereof being freightned with two Rocks which defend it from the weather. There was Saint *Barnaby* born, there suffered Martyrdom under *Nero*, and there buried; to whom the Cathedral Church was dedicated. This greatly ruined City is yet the strongest in the Island, the seat of the *Zanziack*; who was lately put into an affright upon the approach of the *Florentine* Ships, that he fully purposed, as is credibly reported, to have surrendred it upon their landing. But they (perhaps possest with a mutual terrour) forbear to attempt it. The aforesaid region of *Salamina* (which lyeth on the East of the Island) contained also the celebrated Cities of *Aphrodisium*, *Tamassus* abounding with Vitriol and Verdigrease, *Arsinoe*, *Idalium* and the neighbouring Groves so chanted of, the Olympian Promontory (where *Venus* had her Temple, into which it was not lawful for any Woman to enter) with the Hill on the opposite *Pedasium*, square on the top like a Table, and cried unto her, as all the afore-named. In the territory of *Lapathus* comprehending the North-part, where once stood *Tremitus* ; in the heart almost of the Island, and midst of a goodly Plain stands the late regal City of *Nicosia*; circular in form, and five miles in circumference; not yielding in beauty (before defaced by the *Turk*) unto the principal Cities of *Italy*; taken by the aforesaid *Mustapha* on the ninth of *September*, in the year 1570. with an uncredible slaughter, and death of *Dandalus* the un-warlike Governour. The chief of the Prisoners, and richest spoils, he caused to be imbarqued in two tall Ships, and a great Gallion, for a present to send unto *Selymus*: when a noble and beautiful Lady, preferring an honourable death before a life which would prove so replete with slavery, and hated prostitutions; set fire on certain Barrels of Powder, which not only tore in pieces the Vessels that carried her, but burnt the other so low, that the Sea devoured their Reliques. The *Franks* have their Factors resident in *Nicosia*; partly inhabited by the ancient *Greek Cypriots*, and partly by *Turks* and *Moors*. The Buildings are low, flat-roof'd, the entrances little, for the most part ascended by Stairs for the more difficult entry. North of this, and upon the Sea, stood *Cerevina*, erected by *Cyprus*, now of great strength, and called *Cerines*; (yet surrendred to the *Turk* before it was besieged) and at the West end of that Province, the City of the Sun, with the Temples of *Venus*, and *Isis*, built by *Phalerus* and *Achamus* the *Athenians*. The Mountain of *Olympus* lies on the South of *Lapathia*, high, and taking up fifty miles with his basis; now called, The Mountain of the Holy Cross; clothed with Trees of all sorts, and stored with Fountains, whereon are a number of Monasteries possest by the *Greek Coloieros* of the Order of Saint *Basil*. South of the which, even to the Sea, extendeth *Amathusa*.

——*gravidamque Amathunta metallis.*
  Ovid. *Met.* l.10.   ——*heavy with Mines of Brass:*

so called of the City *Amathus*, now scarcely shewing her foundation, sacred unto *Venus*, and wherein the Rites of her *Adonis* were annually celebrated. Built perhaps unto *Amasis* (for I do but conjecture by the name, and in that it lieth opposite unto *Egypt*) who was the first that conquered *Cyprus*. East thereof are the *Saline*, so named of the abundance of Salt that is made there; where the *Turk* did first land his Army; the shore thereabout being fit for that purpose. On the West-side of *Amathus* there is a Promontory, in form of a Peninsula, called formerly *Curias* (of the not far distant City built by the *Argives*, at this day named *Episcopia*, where *Appollo* had a Grove hard by a Promontory, from whence they were thrown that but presumed to touch his Altar) now called the *Cape of Cats*: whereon are the ruines of a Monastry of *Greek Coloieros*, fair when it flourished, with a sumptuous Temple dedicated to St. *Nicholas*. The Monks, as they say, being obliged to foster a number of Cats for the destruction of the abundance of Serpents that infested those quarters; accustoming to return to the Covent at the sound of a Bell when they had sufficiently hunted. *Paphia* comprehendeth the West of *Cyprus*; so called of the maritime City, built by the Son of *Pigmalion* by his Ivory Statue, such said to be in regard of her beauty; of whom having long lived a single life (in detestation of those lustful women) he became inamoured,

Illa Paphum genuit, de quo tenet insula nomen.   *She Paphus bare, whose name that Island bears.*
  Ovid. *Met.* l.10.

But *Paphus*, according to others, was built by *Cyneras* (both Father and Grand-father to
                                                                    Adonis)

LIB. IV. *Cyprus.* 173

Adonis) who called it so in remembrance of *Paphus* his Father. This *Cyneras* having sworn to assist *Menelaus* with fifty Ships, sent him only one, with the models of the other in Clay to colour his perjury. No place there was through the whole earth where *Venus* was more honoured.

An hundred fires Sabean gums consume
There in her fane, which fragrant wreaths perfume.

— *Ubi templum illi, centumque Sabæo*
Thure calent — , sertisque recentibus halent.
Virg. Æn. l. 1.

Five miles from thence stands the City of *Baffa*, called New *Papho* heretofore, and built by *Agapenor*, frequented from all parts both by men and women; who went from thence in a solemn Procession unto the Old, to pay their Vows, and celebrate her Solemnities. But her Temples both in the one and in the other (as throughout the whole Island) were rased to the ground by the procurement of Saint *Barnaby*. Well of this food *Cythera*, a little Village, at this day called *Conucba*; sacred also unto *Venus*, and which once did give a name unto *Cyprus*. That, and not the Island that lies before

Mine Amathus, high Paphos, Cythera,
Idalia Groves ———

Est Amathus est celsa mihi Paphos atque Cythera,
Idaliæque domus ———
Virg. Æn. 10.

The uttermost Promontory that stretcheth to the West, with the super-eminent Mountain, now called *Capho*, Saint *Pisano*; bore formerly the name of the *Athenian Acamus*: East of which stood the City of *Arsinoe* (at this day *Leseare*) renowned for the Groves of *Jupiter*. This Island boasts of the births of *Asclapiades*, *Solon*, *Zeno* the Stoick, and Author of that Sect, *Apollonius*, and *Xenophon*. At the first it was so overgrown with wood, that besides the infinite waste made thereof in the melting of metals: it was decreed that every man should inherit as much as he could make Champain. A Country abounding with all things necessary for life; and therefore called *Macaria*. Whose wealth allured the *Romans* to make a Conquest thereof: a prey that more plentifully furnished their Coffers, than the rest of their Triumphs. It affordeth matter to build a Ship from the bottom of the Keel to the top of her Top-gallant, and to furnish her with Tackle and munition. It produceth Oyl and Grain of several sorts; Wine that lasteth unto the eighth year, Grapes whereof they make Raisins of the Sun; Citrons, Oranges, Pomegranates, Almonds, Figs, Saffron, Coriander, Sugar-canes: sundry Herbs as well Physical as for food, Turpentine, Rubarb, Colloquintida, Scammony, &c. But the staple Commodities are Cotton-wools; the best of the Orient) Chamolets, Salt, and Sope-Ashes. They have plentiful Mines of Brass, some small store of Gold and Silver, green Soder, Vitriol, Alome, Orpiment, White and Red Lead, Iron, and divers kinds of precious Stones of inferiour value; amongst which the Emerald, and the Turky. But it is in the Summer exceeding hot, and unhealthy, and annoyed with Serpents. The Brooks (for Rivers it hath none) rather merit the name of Torrents, being often exhausted by the Sun: insomuch, as in the time of *Constantine* the Great, the Island was for six and thirty years together almost utterly abandoned; Rain never falling during that season. It was first possessed by the Sons of *Japhet*; payed tribute first by the *Egyptian Amasis*; then conquered by *Belus*, and governed by the posterity of *Teucer*, until *Cyrus* expulsed the nine Kings that there ruled. But after the *Grecians* repossest the Soveraignty, and kept it until the death of *Nicocles*; and then it continued under the Government of the *Ptolomees*, till the *Romans* took it from the last of that name: restored it was again to *Cleopatra*, and her Sister *Arsinoe*, by *Antonius*. But he overthrown, it was made a Province of *Rome*; and with the translmigration of the Empire, submitted to the *Bizantine* Emperours; being ruled by a succession of Dukes for the space of eight hundred years, when conquered by our *Richard* the first, and given in exchange for the titular Kingdom of *Jerusalem* unto *Guy* of *Lusignan*, it continued in his Family, until in the year 1473. it was by *Catharina Cornelia* a *Venetian* Lady, the Widow to King *James* the Bastard, who had taken the same by strong hand from his Sister *Carlotte*, resigned to the *Venetians*; who ninety seven years after did lose it to the Infidels, under whose yoke it now groaneth. But it is for the most part inhabited by *Grecians*, who have not long since attempted an unfortunate insurrection. Their Ecclesiastical estate is governed by one Arch-Bishop, and three Bishops; The Metropolitan of *Nicosa*, the Bishop of *Famagosta*, *Paphus*, and *Amathus*, who live upon stipends.

Much

Much becalmed, and not seldom crossed by contrary winds, for divers days we saw Sea and Air only (yet once within ken of a Promontory of *Licia*, called the seven Capes) until we approached the South-east of *Candy*, called formerly *Creta*,

Creta Jovis magni nutrix veneranda feraxque *Crete sacred Nurse to Jove, a fruitful ground*
Et frugum & pecoris——   *With Corn and Cattel stor'd*——
  Dionys.

and to make up the Distich with that of *Homers*,

——*pulchra, pinguis, circumflua.*   ——*fair, fat, sea-bound;*
  Hom. Odys. l. 19.

It lieth an hundred miles South-west from the lesser *Asia*, as many South-east from *Peloponesus*, and North of *Africa*, an hundred and fifty: wherefore aptly saith *Homer*,

Creta quidem terra medio est in nigro ponto.   *Crete in the midst of the dark Sea doth stand.*
 Idem.

imitated by *Virgil*,

Creta Jovis magni medio jacet insula ponto.   *Crete seated in the midst of Seas, Joves land.*
  Vir. Æn. l. 3.

lying neither in the *Adriatick*, Ægean, *Carpathian*, nor *Libian* Seas; which on each side environ it. It stretcheth two hundred and fifteen miles from East to West; containing forty five in breadth, and in circuit five hundred and twenty. Full of Mountains, yet those not unprofitable, affording excellent pasturage; the highest is *Ida*.

Ida frequens piceis & quercubus optima mater.   *In pitch rich above other,*
  Dionys.   *Of Oaks the pregnant mother:*

seated almost in the midst of the Island, now called *Psilorriti*; from whose lofty and spiny top both Seas may be discerned. Where standeth a little Chappel; compact of great square stones without lime, in form of an Arch; being there so exceeding cold in the heat of the Summer (at which time Goats and Sheep can only graze there) that the Shepherds are glad to descend before night into the Valley. From thence issue many Springs. Some part of it is a plain descent, some precipitate, some clothed with Trees of several kinds, but by the Cypress especially graced. It fostreth nothing that is wild, but Hares, Red Deer, and Fallow; and is the inheritance of the *Calargy*: a Family, that for this thousand years, have retained a prime repute in this Island. Two other Mountains of fame there be, the one at the West end, called anciently *Leucaore*, now *la Spachia*; another at the East end, now called *Sethia*, and anciently *Dicta*, which receiveth that name from *Diana*, to whom this Island was greatly devoted; it signifying Nets: she being an Huntress and Patroness of Hunters:

Ades en comita Diva Virago   *Virage, thou that Soveraign art*
Cujus regna pars terrarum   *Of woods, and wastes; the Cretan Hart*
Secreta vacat.——
——*tua Creteas*   *Thy hand pursues, and with quick cunning*
Dextra——   *Strikes through the swifter Fallow running.*
Sequitur cervas: nunc veloces
Figis Damas leviore manu.   *Senec. in Hipp.*

The story goes, how one *Britomart*, a Nymph of this Island, eagerly following the Chase, and overthrown ere aware in a toil, not able to free her self, the beast now rushing upon her; she vowed a Temple to *Diana*, if so be she escaped that danger; who forthwith set her on her feet; and of those Nets was called *Dictinna*: *Diana* also assuming that name for the love which she bare her. The ancient Geographers do jointly affirm, with *Virgil*, that the *Cretians*

Centum urbes habitant magnas.   *Did in an hundred ample Cities dwell:*
  Virg. Æn. l. 3.

which were not so many in the days of *Homer*:

——*in hâc nonaginta civitates,*   *With ninety Cities crowned. Of these most great*
Inter has Gnossas magna civitas ubi Minos   *High Gnossus; for nine years the royal seat*
Per novem annos regnavit Jovis magno con-   *Of Minos, he that talks with Jove.*
fabulator,   *Odys. l. 19.*

This

LIB. IV. Crete. 175

This City long held the Regality; seated in a Plain, not far from the East, extent of the Island, and from the North shore not above six Furlongs, where it had a convenient Haven: long since, having nothing left but a sound of the name; a little Village there standing, called *Cinosus*. The next in dignity was

Gortina strongly wall'd——   Gortina bene cincta mœnibus.
                                      Hom. Od. l. 19.

seated not far from the Southern basis of *Ida*: who sheweth what she was by her ruines; there yet remaining an Aquæduct entire, supported by a number of Arches, certain stragling Houses possessing the place, now named *Mataria*. The third *Cydonia*, now next to the greatest, and called *Canea*: seated towards the West, and on the North-shore; enjoying a large and safe Harbour. These three were all of those hundred that remained (or at least retained their repute) in the days of *Strabo*, who was of this Country. For only it hath at this day *Candy* and *Canea*, fortified by Art, *Rhetimo* and *Sitia* by Nature. *Candy*, that now giveth a name to the Island, standing upon the North-shore (as do all the rest) is a strong and well inhabited City, accommodated with an excellent Harbour; of which the elder *Scaliger*:

An hundred Cities finely wall'd (if true   Centum clim cinctas operosis mœnibus urbes
Fame sings) Times waste hath now reduc'd to few. Reddidit ad paucas imperiosa dies.
Small Towns I judge they were. Yet what destroy'd Oppida parva tamen reor illa fuisse, sed aucta
In all; alone by Candy is supply'd.   Quod deest ex reliquis Candia sola refert.
                                                     J. C. Scal.

The whole Island is divided into the Provinces of *Canea*, *Rhetimo*, *Candis*, and *Sitia*, lying further Eastward: strengthened both by the shore, in few places approachable, and by the many Fortresses. It hath no navigable Rivers. It aboundeth with Grain, Oyl, and Fruits of all kinds: among the rest, with the Apples of *Adam*, the juice whereof they tun up and send into *Turkie*, much used by them in their meats. The mountains afford diversity of Physical Herbs: as *Cistus* (and that in great quantity) from whence they do gather their Ladanum, Halimus, that resisteth Famine, and Dictamnus, so soveraign for wounds; whose virtue was first found out by Stags, and Bucks, that by eating thereof, ejected the Arrows wherewith they were wounded. Used by *Venus*, in the cure of her *Æneas*.

With her white hand she crops from Cretian Ide   Ipsa manu genetrix Cretea carpit ab Ida
The fresh-leav'd stalk, with flower in purple di'd, Pulveribus caulem foliis, & flore comantem
A soveraign Hearb well known to fearful Deer,   Purpureo, non illa feris incognita capris
Whose trembling sides the winged Arrows bear.   Gramina cum tergo voluere hæsere sagittæ.
                                                     Virg. Æn. l.12.

But that which principally enricheth this Country, is their Muscadines and Malmsies, those kind of Grapes brought first hither from *Arvisia*, a Mountain of *Chios*. Wines that seldom come unto us uncuted, but excellent where not, (as within the Streights) and compared unto *Nectar*.

Crete I confess, Joves Fortress to be: Vera quidem fateor Jovis incunabula magni:
For Nectar only is transferr'd from thee: Nam liquor haud alibi Nectatis ille venit.
                                                     J. C. S. al.

The ancient Inhabitants of this Island are related by *Homers Ulysses*:

Infinite people of mixt speech here dwell: ——In hac autem homines
Achaians, Eteocretans who excel   Multi infiniti——
In valour, Cidons, Dorians, Trichaites,   Alia alio non lingua mixta, in ipsa quidem Achivi,
Divine Pelasgians.   Ibi autem Eteocretes magnanimi ibique Cidones.
                                                     Dorencesque, Trichaites, divinique Pelasgi.
                                                     Hom. Odyss. l. 19.

But the natural people hereof were the *Cidonians*, and *Eteocretans*, or *Curetes*, so ancient, that they are feigned even in this place to have their creation. The last named inhabited *Ida*, *Cretas* their first King, of whom the Island was so named. They lived in Caves, (for Houses then were not) and used no other coverture than Nature afforded them. They found out many things useful for life, as the taming of certain Beasts, whom they gathered first into Flocks and Herds; and brought civility amongst men, by instituting Laws, and observing of Discipline. They taught how to direct the voice
                                                                                                 unto

unto harmony, possessing the mind with the awe of Religion, initiating with Orders and Ceremonies. They found out the use of Brass and Iron, with the Sword and Head-piece: the first inventers of shooting, hunting, and dancing in Armour. Being called *Idæi Dactili*, either in regard of their numbers, or observed measures: but according to *Diodorus*, of their ten *Ephori*. The Progeny of the *Painim* gods were born in this Island, to whom divine honours were ascribed: to some for their beneficial inventions, to others for introducing Justice amongst men, repulsing of injuries and violence, cherishing the good, deterring the bad, suppressing by force of Arms the Tyrants of the earth, and relieving the oppressed. But that they were no other than mortals, the *Cretians* themselves do testifie, who affirm that *Jupiter* was not only born and bred in their Country, but buried, and did shew his Sepulchre (though reproved by *Callimachus*)

Cretes mendaces semper Rexa hne sepulchrum
Erexere tuum; tu vivis semper & usque es.

Still lying Cretians, sacred King, dare rear
Thee a Tomb: thou ever liv'st, and art each where.

on the Mountain *Lassa*: and that he was fostered by the *Curetes* in *Æginus*, which lyeth on the South of *Ida*; concealed and delivered unto them by his Mother, to prevent his slaughter. For *Saturn* resolved to destroy his male children: either having so compacted with his Brother *Titan*, or to prevent the Prophecy, which was that his Son should depose him. A cruelty used amongst the *Grecians* it was (and therefore this not to be held for a Fable) to expose the Infants whom they would not foster, unto the mercy of the Deserts. Long after the death of these reputed Gods, lived *Minos*, and *Rhadamant*: who for their justice upon earth, were feigned after to have been Judges in Hell. Notorious is the adultry of *Pasiphae*, with the General *Taurus*; which gave unto the Poets the invention of their *Minotaur* (so called they the Bastard)

Destinat hunc Minos thalami removere pudorem,
Multiplicique domo cæcis includere tectis.
Dædalus ingenio fabræ celeberrimus artis
Ponit opus, turbatque notas & lumina flexu.
Ducit in errorem variarum ambage viarum.
Ovid. Met. l. 8.

To hide his marriage shame, him Minos dooms
To durance in un-explicable Rooms.
The work of witty Dedalus; confounding
Th' direct by resemblance: abounding
With winding ways, the Maze of errour rounding.

made an imitation of that in *Egypt*, as aforesaid. But no tract thereof remained in the days of *Pliny*, although at this day, the Inhabitants undertook to shew it unto strangers. For between where once stood *Gortina* and *Gnossus*, at the foot of *Ida*, under the ground are many Meanders hewn out of the Rock, now turning this way, and now that way; insomuch that it is not without a conductor to be entred, which you are to hire at the adjoining Village. I have heard an English Merchant say (who hath seen it) that it was so intricate, and vast, that a Guide which used to shew it unto others for twenty years together, lost himself therein, and was never more heard of. Within are little Turrets which over-look the walls that make the divisions, in many places not reaching to the top. But by most this is thought to have been but a Quarry, where they had the Stone that built both *Gnossus* and *Gortina*, being forced to leave such Walls for the support of the Roof, and by following of the veins to make it so intricate. *Metellus* first made the *Cretians* stoop to the *Romans*. After they were under the *Greek* Emperours, until *Baldwin* the *Latine* Emperour of *Constantinople* bestowed the Island upon *Boniface*, Marquess of *Monteferrato*, who sold it to the *Venetians* in the year 1194. But in the time of Duke *Dandalus*, they rebelled, and were again in the year 1343, reduced to their obedience. So remain they at this day, the *Greeks* being permitted the free exercise of their Religion, by whom it is for the most part inhabited. And although in many things they imitate the *Venetians*, yet still retain they their old vices; *Lyers, evil Beasts, slow Bellies*, whereof formerly upbraided by Saint *Paul*, out of their Poet *Epimenides*. They still exercise shooting; wherein throughout all Ages they have excelled,

———Gnossasque agitare pharetras
Doctis, nec Eois pejor Gortina sagittis.
Lucan. l.3.

Gnossians good Archers are, the use of Bows,
Not Parthia better than Gortina knows:

using the *Scythian* Bow, but much better than the *Scythians*. The Country people do dance with their Bows ready bent on their arms, their Quivers hanging on their

LIB. IV. *Malta.* 177

their backs, and their Swords by their sides, imitating therein their Ancestors, (a custom also amongst the *Lacedæmonians*) called by them *Pyrricha*: and as of old, so use they to sing in their dancings, and reply to one another. The better sort of men are apparelled like the *Venetians*, and so are the women, who seldom stir abroad, except it be to the Church, but in the night time. The common people are clothed like the *Greeks* of *Sio*, of whom we have spoken; the Women only wearing loose Veils on their heads, the breasts and shoulders perpetually naked, and died by the Sun into a loathsom tawny.

Now out of sight of *Candie*, the Winds both slack and Contrary, we were forced to bear Northward of our course, until we came within view of *Zant*; where our Master purposed to put in (since we could not shorten our way) to furnish the Ship with fresh Water and other Provisions. But anon, we discover five Sails making towards us, and imagining them to be men of War, made all things ready for defence: When to our better comfort, they proved all *English*, and bound for *England*, with whom we conforted; they having supplyed our necessities. Their names were the *Alithia* (Admiral) the *Centaure* (Vice-Admiral) the *Delight*, the *Blessing*, and a Ship of *Plimmouth*, called (if I forget not) the *Jonathan*. Two days after (the Winds now something more friendly) the Admiral gave chase to a little Ship, which we supposed a Pirat, who left her course, and fled before the Wind; so that without too much expence of time he could not approach her. We past by the South side of *Sicilia*, and left *Malta* on the left hand; when out of hope to be set a shoar (for it was the purpose of our Merchant before he met with these conforts, to have touched at *Messina*) and sadded with the apprehension of so tedious a Voyage; on the sudden the Wind came about, and blowing fiercely West and by North, did all the night following exercise his fury. Whereby our Ships rather losing than gaining of their way, and exceedingly tossed, the weather not likely to alter, they resolved to put into *Malta*. So on the second of *June* being Sunday, we entred the Haven that lies on the East-side of the City of *Valetta*; which we saluted with eighteen pieces of Ordnance. But we were not suffered to come into the City, (though every Ship had a neat Patent to shew, that those places from whence they came were free from Infection) nor suffered to depart when the Wind blew fair; which was within a day or two after. For the Galleys of the Religion were then setting forth, to make some attempt upon *Barbary*, and the reason of the restraint was, lest being taken by the Pyrats, or touching upon occasion at *Tripoly*, *Tunis*, or *Argire*, their designs might be by compulsion or voluntarily revealed: nor would they suffer any Frigot of their own for fear of surprisal, to go out of the Haven, until many days after that the Gallies were departed. But because the *English* were so strong (a great Ship of *Holland* putting also in to seek company)and that they intended to make no more Ports; on the sixth of *June*, they were licensed to set sail, the Masters having the night before in their several Long-Boats, attended the return of the Great Master (who had been abroad in his Galley, to view a Fort that then was building) and welcomed him home with one and twenty pieces of Ordnance.

But no intreaty could get me aboard; chusing rather to undergo all hazards and hardness whatsoever, than so long a Voyage by Sea, to my nature so irksome. And so was I left alone on a naked Promontory right against the City, remote from the concourse of people, without provision, and not knowing how to dispose of my self. At length a little Boat made towards me, rowed by an Officer appointed to attend on Strangers that had no Prattick, lest others by coming into their company should receive the infection; who carried me to the hollow hanging of a Rock, where I was for the night to take up my Lodging; and the day following to be conveyed by him unto the *Lazaretta*, there to remain for thirty or forty days, before I could be admitted into the City. But, behold, an accident, which I rather thought at first to have been a Vision, than (as I found it) real. My Guardian being departed to fetch me some Victuals, laid along, and musing on my present condition, a *Phaluceo* arrived at the place. Out of which there stept two old Women; the one made me doubt whether she were so or no, she drew her face into so many forms, and with such antick gestures, stared upon me. These two did spread a *Turkie* Carpet on the Rock, and on that a table-cloth, which they furnished with variety of the choicest Viands. Another arrived, which set a Gallant ashore with his two *Amorosaes*, attired like Nymphs, with Lutes in their hands, full of disport and sorcery. For little would they suffer him to eat, but what

he

he received with his mouth from their fingers. Sometimes the one would play on the Lute, whilst the other sung, and laid his head in her lap; their false eyes looking upon him, as if their hearts were troubled with passions. The attending Hags had no small part in the Comedy, administring matter of mirth, with their ridiculous moppings. Who indeed (as I after heard) were their Mothers, born in *Greece*, and by them brought hither to trade amongst the unmarried Fraternity. At length, the *French* Captain (for such he was, and of much regard) came and intreated me to take a part of their Banquet, which my stomach perswaded me to accept of. He willed them to make much of the *Forestier*; but they were not to be taught enterment, and grew so familiar, as was not much to his liking. But both he and they, in pity of my hard Lodging, did offer to bring me into the City by night (an offence, that if known, is punished by death) and back again in the morning. Whilst they were urging me thereunto, my Guardian returned, and with him a *Maltese*, whose Father was an English-man; he made acquainted therewith, did by all means dehort them. At length (the Captain having promised to labour my admittance into the City) they departed. When a good way from shoar, the Curtizans stript themselves, and leapt into the Sea; where they violated all the prescriptions of modesty. But the Captain the next morning, was not unmindful of his promise, solliciting the Great Master in my behalf, as he sate in Council; who with the assent of the Great Crosses, granted me Prattick. So I came into the City, and was kindly entertained in the house of the aforesaid *Maltese*: where for three weeks space, with much contentment I remained.

Malta doth lie in the *Libian* Sea, right between *Tripolis* of *Barbary*, and the South-East angle of *Sicilia*; distant an hundred fourscore and ten miles from the one, and threescore from the other. It containeth threescore miles in circuit: and was called formerly *Melita*, of the abundance of honey. A Country altogether champaign, being no other than a Rock covered with earth, but two feet deep where the deepest, having few trees but such as bear fruit, whereof of all sorts plentifully furnished. So that their wood they have from *Sicilia*; yet there is a kind of great Thistle, which together with Cow-dung, serves the Country people for fuel; who need not much in a Climate so exceeding hot, hotter by much than any other which is seated in that same Parallel: yet sometimes temperate by the comfortable winds, to which it lies open. Rivers there are none, but sundry Fountains. The soil produceth no Grain but Barley. Bread made of it, and Olives, is the Villagers ordinary diet; and with the straw they sustain their Cattel. Commin-seed, Annis-seed, and Honey, they have here in abundance, whereof they make Merchandize; and an indifferent quantity of Cotton-wooll, but that the best of all other. The Inhabitants die more with age than others, and heretofore were reputed fortunate for their excellency in Arts, and curious Weavings. They were at first a Colony of the *Phœnicians*, who exercising Merchandize as far as the great Ocean, betook themselves to this Island; and by the commodity of the Haven, attained to much riches and honour: (who yet retain some print of the *Punick* language, yet so, that they now differ not much from the *Moresco*) and built in the midst thereof the City of *Melita* (now called *Malta*) giving or taking a name from the Island. Now whether it came into the hands of *Spain*, with the Kingdom of *Sicilia*, or won from the *Moors* by their Swords, (probable both by their Language, and that it belongeth to *Africa*) I am ignorant: but by *Charles* the Fifth, it was given to the Knights of *Rhodes*, as appeareth by *Maninus* of *Utina*, exhorting *Philip* the Second to relieve them.

Est Melite patris munus: nam Carolus olim
Hanc dedit ejectis longo post tempore bello
Turcarum Rhodiis ducibus, magnoque Magistro.
Nunc quoq; sit Melite munus Rex magne Philippe,
Sit munus Rex magne ruum florentibus armis
Militibus nostri, tua quos nos vivida virtus
Servet ab exitio minitantis dira tyranni.
  Octav. Mavinus.

Malta's thy Fathers gift: which *Charles* did give
Th' expulsed Knights of *Rhodes*, that did out-live
That long war and sad fate, by *Turks* impos'd;
Be't now great *Philip* thine, new when inclos'd
By a dire Tyrant. Shield them from the foe:
And in strong arms thy lively virtue show.

This Order of Knight-hood received their denomination from *John*, the charitable Patriarch of *Alexandria*; though vowed to Saint *John Baptist*, as their Patron. Their first Seat was the Hospital of St. *John* in *Jerusalem* (whereupon they were called Knight-Hospitallers) built by one *Gerrard*, at such time as the Holy Land became famous, by the successful Expeditions of the Christians; who drew divers worthy

thy persons into that Society; approved by the Pope *Gelasius* the Second. They by the allowance of *Honorius* the Second, wore Garments of black, signed with a white Cross. *Raymond*, the first Master of the Order, did amplifie their Canons; intitling himself, *The poor Servant of Christ, and Guardian of the Hospital in Jerusalem*. In every Country throughout Christendom they had Hospitals, and Revenues assigned them; with Contributions procured by Pope *Innocent* the Second. They were tyed by their Vows to entertain all Pilgrims with singular humanity; to safe-guard their passages from Thieves and Incursions, and valiantly to sacrifice their lives in defence of that Country. But the Christians being driven out of *Syria*, the Knights had the *Rhodes* assigned them by the *Greek* Emperour, (others say by *Clement* the Fifth) which they won from the *Turk*, and lost again as aforesaid; retiring from thence unto *Malta*. There are of them here seven Alberges, or Seminaries: One of *France* in general, one of *Avergne*, one of *Province*, one of *Castile*, one of *Aragon*, one of *Italy*, one of *Almany*; and an eighth there was of *England*, until by *Henry* the Eighth dissolved, with what justice I know not. Yet is there one that supplies the place, in the election of the Great Master. Of every one there is a Grand Prior, who lives in great reputation in his Country, and orders the affairs of their Order. Saint *Johns* without *Smithfield* was in times past the Mansion of the Grand Prior of *England*. An *Irish* man living in *Naples*, and receiving a large Pension from the King of *Spain*, now beareth that Title; those that come for the Order, are to bring a testimony of their Gentry for six descents, which is to be examined, and approved by the Knights of their Nation; and is first to remain here a year for a probation. Nor are Women exempted from that dignity, admitted by a Statute made in the Master-ship of *Hugo Revelus*. Perhaps for that one *Agnis*, a noble Lady, was the Author, as they affirm, of their Order; but that there be any now of it, is more than I could be informed. The Ceremonies used in Knighting, are these: First, carrying in his hand a Taper of White Wax, he kneeleth before the Altar, clothed in a long loose Garment, and desireth the Order of the Ordinary. Then in the Name of the Father, the Son, and the Holy Ghost, he receiveth a Sword, therewith to defend the Catholick Church; to repulse and vanquish the Enemy, to relieve the Oppressed, if need should be to expose himself unto death for the Faith, and all by the power of the Cross, which by the Cross Hilt is defigured. Then is he girt with a Belt, and thrice strook on the shoulders with his Sword, to put him in mind, that for the honour of Christ he is cheerfully to suffer whatsoever is grievous: who taking it of him, thrice flourisheth it aloft as a provokement to the Adversary, and so sheaths it again, having wiped it first on his arm, to testifie that henceforth he will live undefiledly. Then he that gives him Knighthood, laying his hand on his shoulder, doth exhort him to be vigilant in the Faith, and to aspire unto true honour, by couragious and laudable actions, &c. Which done, two Knights do put on his Spurs, gilt, to signifie that he should spurn Gold as dirt, not to do what were ignoble for reward. And so goes he to Mass with the Taper in his hand; the works of Piety, Hospitality, and redemption of Captives, being commended unto him, told also of what he was to perform in regard of his Order. Then is asked if he be a Free-man, if not joined in Matrimony, if unvowed to another Order, or not of any Profession; and if he be resolved to live among them, to revenge their injuries, and quit the authority of secular Magistracy? Having answered thereunto, upon the receipt of the Sacrament, he vows in this order: *I vow to the Almighty God, to the Virgin Mary, his immaculate Mother, and to Saint John Baptist, perpetually, by the help of God, to be truly obedient to all my Superiours, appointed by God and this Order, to live without any thing of mine own, and withall to live chastly.* Whereupon he is made a partaker of their priviledges and indulgencies granted unto them by the See of *Rome*. Besides other Prayers, they are commanded to say an hundred and fifty Pater-nosters daily for such as have been slain in their Wars. They wear Ribands about their necks with brouches of the Cross; and Cloaks of black, with large white Crosses set thereinto on the shoulder, of fine Linen: but in the time of War, they wear Crimson Mandilions, behind and before so crossed, over their Armour. They come hither exceeding young, that they may the sooner attain to a *commendum* at home, (whereof many be of great value) not got by favour, but seigniority; and are to live here for the space of five years (but not necessarily together) and to go on four expeditions. If one of them be convicted of a capital crime, he is first publickly degraded in the Church of Saint *John*, where he received his Knight-hood; then

strangled

strangled, and thrown after into the Sea in the night time. Every Nation do feed by themselves in their several Alberges, and sit at the Table like Friars: but such as upon suit, do get leave to eat apart, have sixty Crowns allowed them by the Religious yearly; as all have five and twenty apiece for Apparel. There are here resident about five hundred, being not to depart without leave, and as many more disperfed through Christendom; who hither repair upon every Summons, or notice of Invasion. The Religion is their general Heir, wheresoever they dye; only each Knight may dispose of a fifth part of his substance. There be sixteen of them Counsellors of State, and of principal Authority, called Great Crosses; who wear Tippets, and Coats also under their Cloaks, that be signed therewith. Of these are the Marshal, the Master of the Hospital, the Admiral, the Chancellour, &c. When one doth die, another is Elected by the Great Master and his Knights, who give their voices (if I forget not) by Bullets, as do the *Venetians*, whereby both envy and faction is avoided. Now if the Great Master fall sick, they will suffer no Vessel to go out of the Haven until he be either recovered or dead, and another Elected, lest the Pope should intrude into Election, which they challenge to be theirs, and is in this manner performed. The several Nations Elect two Knights apiece of their own, and two are Elected for the English from amongst themselves; these sixteen chuse eight, and those eight do nominate a Knight, a Priest, and a Friar-Servant (who also wears Arms) and they three chuse the Great Master, out of the sixteen Great Crosses. This man is a *Pickard* born, about the age of sixty, and hath governed eight years. His Name and Title, *The Illustrious and most Reverend Prince, my Lord Friar Alofius of Wignian Court, Great Master of the Hospital of Saint Johns of Jerusalem; Prince of Malta, and Goza.* For albeit a Friar (as the rest of the Knights) yet is he an absolute Soveraign, and is bravely attended on by a number of gallant young Gentlemen. The Clergy do wear the cognizance of the Order; who are subject to like Laws, except in Military matters.

There are sixty Villages in the Island, under the command of ten Captains; and four Cities. Old *Malta* is seated (as hath been said before) in the midst of the Island

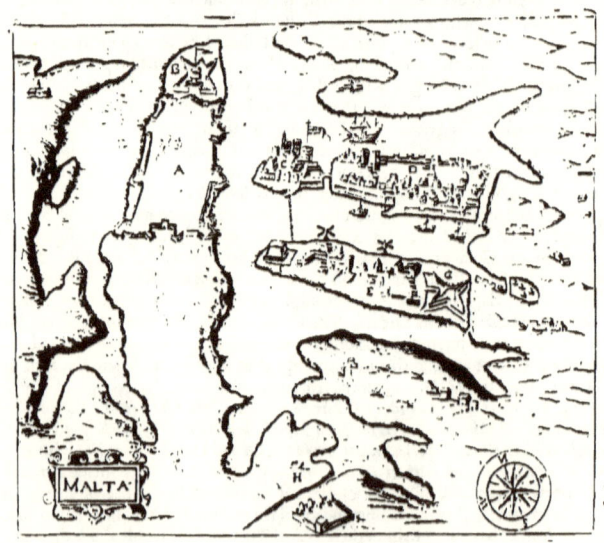

A *The City of Valetta.*
B *The Castle of S. Hermes.*
C *The Castle of S. Anglo.*
D *Burgo.*
E *La Insula.*
F *The Platform.*
G *The Fort of S. Michael.*
H *The Fountain.*

upon a Hill, and formed like a Scutcheon, held of no great importance, yet kept by a Garrison. In it there is a Grot, where they say Saint *Paul* lay when he suffered shipwrack, of great devotion amongst them. The refined stone thereof they

they cast into little Medals, with the Effigies of Saint *Paul* on the one side, and a Viper on the other, *Agnus Dei*, and the like; of which they vent store to the Foreigners. They say, that being drunk in Wine, it doth cure the venom of Serpents; and withal, though there be many Serpents in the Island, that they have not the power of hurting, although handled, and angered, bereft of their venom ever since the being here of the Apostle. The other three Cities (if they may all be so termed) are about eight miles distant, and not much without a Musket-shot each of other, near the East-end, and on the North side of the Island, where there is a double Haven divided by a tongue of Rock, which extendeth no further than the conveniently large entrance. The East Haven resembleth the horn of a Stag, the first branch (as the Palm) affording an excellent Harbour for the greatest Ships, and the second for Gallies; the rest are shallow. Close to the uppermost top there is a Fountain of fresh water, which plentifully furnisheth all Vessels that do enter. On the tip of the aforesaid tongue stood the strong Castle of St. *Hermes*, the first that the *Turk* besieged: which after many furious assaults, twenty thousand Cannon shot (whose horrible roarings were heard to *Messina*) and the loss of ten thousand lives, they took in the year 1565. in the month of *June*; but to the greater glory of the vanquished, that loss rather inraging than disheartning the remainder.

Worthy of heaven (brave souls) from whence you came,	Cœlo alto dem sæ animæ dignissima cœlo,
Lustre of men of honour, live your fame,	Lux invicta virtu m, lux nobilitatis, ab armis
That Malta can from Turkish powers defend:	Turcarum Meliten quæ fortiter ausa rueris:
Nor thousand ships, nor horrid conflicts, bend	Territa non acie horrenti, non mille carinis,
Your thoughts to fear, nor Scythian cruelty.	Sævitia aut dira Scythræa impieraris ab alto
Angels admire your valour from on high,	Mirantur superi fortissima Pectora ab alto
Angels shall send (slight threats and barbarous strength)	Demittunt (çoe'ne mi nas & barbara tela)
Merit might succour. Victory at length	Speratum merito auxilium. Victoria tandem
Will crown your toils, and y n to Olympus rear,	Excipiet fessos, claroque reponet Olympo
'Mongst Heroes old, whom better times did bear:	Heroas inter, meliorioues protulit ætas;
But if Fates would that you your best blood spend	Quod si ita reliquit patriæ pro mœnibus acres
In bold defence, and so great labours end:	Pugnando tar rosissimum finire labores:
O valiant hearts! what better than to die	Quid melius quàm pro patria procumbere si
For Country, Churches, Altars? Greater glory	Pro Fanis Arisque sacris? cui gloria major
Never befell to man, nor ever shall:	Contingit? aut ullo potis est contingere se
Vanquished you shall live vanquishers to all	Victores victi semper vivetis in omne
Eternity: your honours, and renown'd	Temporis æterni spatium; perque ora virorum
Exploits, shall ever in mens mouths be found.	Semper honos, semper clarissima gesta sonabunt.
	Octav. Manin.

Now upon the point of the Promontory, which lies between these two Branches of the Haven, where the Ships and Gallies have their stations, on a steep Rock stands the Castle of Saint *Angelo*, whose strength appeared in frustrating those violent Batteries, (being next besieged by the *Turk*) whereof it yet beareth the scars. At the foot of the Rock are certain Cannons planted, that front the mouth of the Haven. This Castle is not only divided by a Trench cut thorough the Rock, from the *Burgo*, a little City which possesseth the rest of that Promontory; being all a Rock, hewn hollow within for their better defence, and disjoyned by a great deep Ditch from the Land. South of this, and on the next Promontory, stands another Town, which is called *La Isola*: on the point thereof there is a Platform, and at the other end the strong Fort of St. *Michael*, yet interiour in strength to that of St. *Angelo*. Here remember we the piety of a *Mahometan*, descended, no doubt, of Christian Parentage, and favouring our Religion: who in the time of the thickest siege, and smallest comfort to the besieged, leap'd into the Sea, and maugre all the shot that was made at him, swam to this Fort; where first requiring and receiving Baptism, he made known unto them the secrets of the Enemy, advised how to frustrate their purposes, and bravely thrust himself forward in every extremity. But the Knights of the Order assisting one another, by their proper valour, so nobly behaved themselves, that the *Turk* began to despair of success; and upon the rumored approach of the Christian succours (which in the ball construction by the over-circumspect Viceroy of *Sicilia* had been dangerously protracted) imbarked themselves, and departed. But all, saving *Burgo* and Saint *Angelo*, reduced into powder, and the return of the *Turk* distrusted, it was propounded amongst the

R Knights,

Knights, to abandon the Island, rather than vainly to repair, and endeavour to defend those lamentable ruines; the adverſaries unequal power, and backward aid of the Chriſtian Princes conſidered. But it too much concerned the ſtate of Chriſtendom, (eſpecially of the Countries confining) it being as it were both the Key and Bulwark thereof, to have it ſo forſaken: Inſomuch, that the Pope, the *Florentine*, and the reſt of the Princes of *Italy*, encouraged them to ſtay; aſſiſting them with money, and all neceſſary proviſion. But eſpecially the King of *Spain*; who over and above, did ſend them theſe three thouſand Pioners, and levied in the Kingdom of *Naples* and *Sicilia*, to repair their old Fortreſſes, and begin a new City upon that tongue of Land which divideth the two Havens; now almoſt abſolutely finiſhed.

This is called the City of *Valetta* in the honour of *John de Valetta*, who then was Great Maſter. Not great, but fair, exactly contrived, and ſtrong above all other; mounted aloft, and no where aſſailable by Land, but at the South-end. The Walls of the reſt do joyn to the upright Rock, as if one piece, and are beaten upon by the Sea. That toward the Land is but a narrow Iſthmus, where the Rock doth naturally riſe: the Ditch without hewn down exceeding broad, and of an incredible profundity, ſtrongly flank'd, and not wanting what fortification can do. This way openeth the only gate of the City; (the other two, whereof one leadeth to Saint *Hermes*, and the other to the Eaſt Haven, being but ſmall Poſterns; and hard within are two great Bulwarks, planted on the top with Ordnance. At the other end (but without the Wall) ſtands the Caſtle of Saint *Hermes*, now ſtronger than ever; whereof (as that of Saint *Angelo*) no *French* man can be Governour. Almoſt every where there are Platforms on the Walls, well ſtored with Ordnance. The Walls on the inſide are not above ſix foot high, un-imbattell'd, and ſhelving on the outſide; the Buildings throughout a good diſtance off, both to leave room for the Souldier, and to ſecure them from battery. Near the South-end, and on the Weſt-ſide, there is a great Pit hewn into the Rock, out of which there is a Port cut under the Wall into the Weſt Haven, intended (for yet unfiniſhed) to have been made an Arſenal for their Gallies; that Harbour being too ſhallow for Ships: a work of a great difficulty. The Market-place is ſpacious, out of which the ſtreets do point on the Round. The Buildings are for the moſt part uniform; all free-ſtone, two ſtories high, and flat at the top: the upper Rooms of moſt having Out-terraſſes. The Great Maſters Palace is a Princely Structure, having a Tower which over-looketh the whole Iſland. The Chamber where they ſit in Council is curiouſly painted with their fights by Sea and by Land, both foreign and defenſive. The ſeven *Alberges* of the Knights be of no mean building, amongſt whom the City is quartered. Magnificent is the Church of St. *Paul*, and that of St. *Johns*; the one the Seat of a Biſhop, and the other of a Prior. And St. *Johns* Hoſpital doth merit regard, not only for the building, but for the entertainment there given; for all that fall ſick are admitted thereunto. The Knights themſelves there lodge, when hurt or diſeaſed; where they have Phyſick for the body, and for the ſoul alſo (ſuch as they give.) The Attendants many, the Beds over-ſpread with fair Canopies; every fortning it having change of Linen. Served they are by the junior Knights in ſilver; and every *Friday* by the Great Maſter, accompanied with the great Croſſes. A ſervice obliged unto from the firſt inſtitution; and thereupon called Knight-Hoſpitallers. The Jeſuits have of late crept into the City, who now have a Colledge a building. Here be alſo three Nunneries, the one for Virgins, another for penitent Whores, (of impenitent here are ſtore) and the third for their Baſtards.

The barrenneſs of this Iſle is ſupplied with the fertility of *Sicilia*, from whence they have their proviſion. The City is victualled for three years; kept under the ground, and ſupplied with new, as they ſpend of the old. They have ſome freſh water-fountains; and the rain that falleth they reſerve in Ciſterns. Beſides, the Knights and their dependants, the Citizens and Iſlanders be within the muſter of their Forces, in which there are not of living ſouls above twenty thouſand. They keep a Court of Guard nightly, and almoſt every minute of the night the Watch of one Fort gives two or three knolls with a Bell, which is anſwered by the other in order. The Religion hath only five Gallies; and ſtinted they are; as I have heard, to that number, (if more, they belong unto private men) and but one Ship. The cuſtom is, or hath been, having hung out a Flag, to lend money to all comers that would dice it; if they win, to repay it with advantage; if loſe, to ſerve until their entertainment amounted to that ſum. Now the expeditions that they make are little better than for booty; ſometimes landing in the night time on the Main of *Africa*, and ſurprizing

LIB. IV.   *Malta. Sicilia.*   183

zing some Village; or scouring along the Coasts, they take certain small Barks, which disburdened of their lading and people, they suffer to hull with the weather. For they make good profit of their Slaves, either imploying them in their drudgeries, (they having at this instant above fifteen hundred of them) or by putting them to ransom: for ever and anon you shall have a little Boat, with a Flag of Treaty, come hither from *Tripoly*, *Tunis*, and *Algiers*, to agree for the redemption of Captives; as from the *Maltises* to those places, who are served with the same measure. During my abode here, there arrived a Bark, brought in by eight *English* men, who had for a long time served the *Turkish* Pirates of *Tunis*: they bound for *Algiers*, took Weapons in hand, and drove the distrustless *Turks* (being twice as many) into the Stern, kept there by two, whilst the other dressed the Sails for *Malta*. Amongst them there was one, who saying he would never be Slave to a Christian, strip'd himself secretly, and propping up his Gown, and laying his Turbant upon it, as if still there, he drop'd into the Sea. But the deceiver was deceived by the high Land, which seemed nearer than it was; and so wearied with swimming, sunk in their sights. The Inquisition would have seized both on their persons and purchase, because they had served the Infidels: but they were protected by the Great Master (being desirous to serve him) who will not suffer their cruel authority to enter the new City; so that they are fain to reside in *Burgo*.

The *Maltises* are little less tawny than the *Moors*, especially those of the Country, who go half clad, and are indeed a miserable people: but the Citizens are altogether Frenchified; the Great Master, and major part of the Knights being *French* men. The Women wear long black Stoles, wherewith they cover their faces (for it is a great reproach to be seen otherwise) who converse not with men, and are guarded according to the manner of *Italy*. But the jealous are better secured, by the number of allowed Curtizans (for the most part *Grecians*) who sit playing at their doors on Instruments, and with the art of their eyes inveigle these continent by vow, but contrary by practice, as if chastity were only violated by marriage. They here stir early and late, in regard of the immoderate heat and sleep at noon day. Their Markets they keep on *Sundays*.

Now were the Gallies returned with indifferent success; and yet my stay was prorogued by the approaching Festival of their Patron; for until that was past, no Boat would stir out of the Harbour. The Palace, Temples, Alberges, and other principal Houses were stuck round on the outside with Lamps the evening before: and amongst other Solemnities they honoured the day with the discharge of all their Artillery. The Forts put forth their Banners, and every Alberg the Ensign of his Nation, at night having Bonfires before them. Five great ones were made in the Court of the Palace; whereof the first was kindled by the Great Master, the second by the Bishop, the third by the Prior, the fourth and fifth by the Mareshal and Admiral. On the four and twentieth of *June* I departed from *Malta* in a Falucco of *Naples*, rowed by five, and not twice so big as a Wherry; yet will she for a space keep way with a Galley. They use to set forth in such Boats as these, two hours before Set-set; and if they discover a suspected Sail between that and night (for the *Turks* continually lye there in wait) do return again; if not, they proceed, and by the next morning (as now did we) reach the Coasts of *Sicilia*.

Sicilia, the Queen of the *Mediterranean* Island, so said to be, not only for her greatness (containing 700 and fourscore miles in circumference) but for her other celebrated excellencies. It beareth the form of a Triangle, and was first called *Trinacria* of her three Promontories, *Pachinus*, *Pelorus*, and *Lilybæus*; after *Sicilia*, not (saith Scaliger) of the *Ligurian Siculi*, who expulsing the *Sicani*, inhabited in their rooms, as is for the most part believed; but so called of *Sicilex*, which signifieth cut and selected (as *Silex* signifieth a stone that is hewn and chosen) in that violently divided from *Italy*,

Or Seas the earth with sudden waters o're-laid,	Qua mare tellurem subitis aut obruit undis.
Or cut; and new shores of the midland made.	Aut scidit, & medias fecir tibi littora terras.
Where struggling streams still toil with might and main;	Vis illic ingens pelagi semperque laborant
Lest flood torn mountains should unite again:	Æquora, ne rupti repetant confinia montes.
	Lucan. l. 3.

Sacred of old unto *Ceres* and *Proserpina*; for that

The glebe with crooked plough first Ceres rent;	Prima Ceres unco glebas dimovit aratro:
First gave us corn, a milder nourishment:	Prima dedit fruges alimentaque mitia terris:
First Laws prescribed: ——	Prima dedit leges
	Ovid. Met. l. 15.

who

who are said here first to have inhabited, in regard of the admirable fertility of the soil: the Mountains themselves (whereof it hath many) even to their tops extraordinarily fruitful. Called by *Cato* the Granary and Nurse of the people of *Rome*; by *Cicero*, the treasury and life of the City: and *Lucan* speaking of it, and *Sardinia*,

Utraque frugiferis est insula nobilis arvis,	Both Islands famous for Corn-bearing fields,
Nec plus Hesperiam longinquis messibus ullæ,	No foreign soil to Italy more yields,
Nec Romana magis complerunt horrea terræ.	Nor so the Romans Granaries doth fill;
Libere vix glebæ superat cessantibus Austris,	Nor Libya when the Southern winds are still;
Cum medium nubes Horea cogente sub axem,	When clouds by Boreas chas'd, near scorching Zone
Effusis magnum Libyæ tulit imbribus annum.	Turn to fat showers, more plentiful is known.
Lucan. l. 3.	

Vines, Sugar-canes, Honey, Saffron, and Fruits of all kinds it produceth: Mulberry-trees to nourish their Silk-worms, whereof they make a great income: Quarries of Porphyrie and Serpentine: hot Baths, Rivers, and Lakes, replenished with fish; amongst which there is one called *Lago de Goridan*, formerly the Navel of *Sicilia*, for that in the midst of the Island, but more anciently *Pergus*: famous for the fabulous Rape of *Proserpina*.

——— non illo plura Cayster	*Caysters slowly gliding waters bear*
Carmina cygnorum labentibus audit in undis.	*Far fewer singing Swans then are heard here.*
Sylva coronat aquas cingens latus omne, suisque	*Wood crowns the lake, and cloath the banks about*
Frondibus, ut velo Phœbeos summovet ignes,	*With leafie veils, which Phœbus fires keep out.*
Frigora dant rami, varios humus humida flores;	*The boughs cool shade, the moist earth yields rare flowers:*
Perpetuum ver est ———	*Here heat, nor cold, the lasting spring devours.*
Ovid. Met. l. 5.	

In this Island is the far-seen Mountain of *Ætna*; the shady *Eryx* sacred to *Venus*, that gave unto her the name of *Erycina*: *Hibla* clothed with Thyme, and so praised for Honey. In the Sea that washeth the South-West Angle there is a Cordial found at this day. A soft Shrub, green when under the water, and bearing a white Berry,

Duritiem tacto capiant ut ab aere, quodque	*Hardness assuming from touch'd air alone;*
Vimen in æquore erat, fiat super æquora saxum.	*Under the Sea a sprig, above a stone.*
Ovid. Met. l. 15.	

and changeth into red.

We shall have occasion to treat of the more celebrated Cities in the process of our Journal: now a word or two of the changes it hath suffered in the divers Inhabitants and Governours, and of their present condition. It is said to have been first inhabited by the *Cyclopes*,

——— propago:	*High Heavens contemners, courteous of blood,*
Contemptrix superûm, sævæque avidissima cædis	*Most violent* ———
Et violenta fuit ——— *Ovid. Met. l. 1.*	

savage, and exercised in all kinds of impiety, whereupon they were said to war against Heaven; receiving that name from the form of their Beavers, the light being round, and therefore feigned to have had but one eye, and that in the Forehead. Their bones in sundry places digged up, and at this day to be seen, do give a sufficient testimony of their Giant-like proportions. They have yet an annual Feast at *Messena*, where they carry about the Statue of two Giants of both Sexes in procession. This Race extinguished, the *Sicani* succeeded, a people of *Spain*, so named of the River *Sicoris* in *Catalonia*; now *Agna naval.*

Hesperios inter Sicoris non ultimus amnis.	*Not least of the Hesperian streams.*
Lucan. l. 5.	

who were expulsed by the *Siculi*, a people of *Lyguria*, and both descended from one Original. After which the *Grecians* sent hither their Colonies; building sundry Maritime Cities, and incorporated themselves with the Inhabitants. To omit their several Wars and celebrated Tyrants; at length *Sicilia* having relinquished the *Roman* amity, to take part with *Hannibal*, was by *Marcellus* reduced into the form of a Province; and so held ever after (though not without sundry defections, by the

Roman

LIB. IV. *The History of Sicilia.*

Roman and *Greek* Emperours, until it became a prey unto the *Goths* in the year 485. together with *Italy*: who, about seven years after, were expulsed out of both by *Bellisarius* and *Narsetes*, Lieutenants to the Emperour *Justinian*. Long after it fell into the hands of the *Saracens*, by the Treason of *Euphemius*, a Prince of the people, who having stollen away a certain beautiful Nun, and being pursued by Justice, fled into *Africa* to the *Saracen Amiras*, promising to deliver him the Island, so that he would make him King of the same, and to pay a great Tribute yearly; which by his assistance, he effected. But vengeance did swiftly follow; for passing thorow *Sicilia* in state, and approaching near unto *Syracusa*, two Brethren of that City upon a sudden motion conspiring his death, and going out with the rest to meet him, as the insinuating Tyrant, bowed his body to every private Saluter, the one of them caught him by the hair, whilst the other struck his head from his shoulders. So got the *Saracens* the Soveraignty, and for two hundred years kept it. At the end of which time they were expulsed by the *Normans*, conducted by Count *Roger*. Him *Simon* succeeded, who not long out-living his Father, left his State to his Brother, a second *Roger*; whom Pope *Innocent* the Second by force of Arms would have dispossest; alledging it to be the Patrimony of St. *Peter*. But he took both him and his Cardinal Prisoners. Mean while a new Pope was elected at *Rome*, who to win Count *Roger* to his Faction, gave him the Title of King (as he had the possession) of both the *Sicilia's*. *William* succeeded *Roger* the Second; whom *Adrian* the Fourth excommunicated, for with-holding the Goods of the Church, and discharged his Subjects of their Fealty; who reconciled, received the Crown as from him, and from that time forward *Sicilia* was called St. *Peter's* Patrimony. Him succeeded *William* the Second, who left behind him one only Daughter called *Constantia*, and she a Nun. Whereupon, *Clement* the Third attempted by Arms to have seized the Island; but *Tancred* the base Son of King *Roger* (elected King by the Nobles) repulsed him. What force could not, his Successor *Celestine*, thought to compass by a wile; who getting *Constantia* out of the Nunnery, and dispensing with her Vow, did marry her unto the Emperour *Henry* the Fourth, upon condition that he should pay a yearly Pention for the same, and hold it in chief of the Papacy, who shortly after became Lord of the whole. It were tedious to relate how oft (and in what short time) they gave it from one to another; like the Ball of Discord, taken up with much Christian blood-shed. At length *Clement* the Fourth did give it from *Conradine*, unto *Charles* of *Anjou*, the *French* Kings Brother, betraying *Conradine* to the slaughter, who was overcome near *Naples* in a mortal Battel, and his head stricken off by *Clements* appointment. So fell the *Germans*, and so rise the *French*-men to the Kingdom of *Naples*, and both the *Sicilia's*: But here some seventeen years after they were bid to a bitter Banquet; all slain at the Tole of a Bell throughout the whole Island, which is called to this day the *Sicilian* Even-song. A just reward (if Justice will countenance so bloody a design) for their intolerable insolencies. The Author of this Massacre was *John de Procida*, sometime Servant to *Manfroy*, their late slain King. Don *Pedro* King of *Aragon*, had married *Constantia*, the only Daughter of *Manfroy*; In whose Right (although *Manfroy* was a Bastard, a Parricide and Usurper) he entred *Sicilia* in this Tumult, whereunto he was privily crowned King by the general consent of the *Sicilians*, it continuing in the House of *Aragon*, until united to *Castile*. So it remaineth subject unto *Spain*, and is govern'd by a Viceroy under the *Spanish* Council for *Italy*; which consisteth of three *Spaniards* and three *Italians*, the Constable of *Castile* being President. Who, by the Kings allowance, do institute Governours, Judges, Commanders, and dispose of Titles and Dignities. *Sicilia* yields to the Coffers of *Spain* yearly six hundred thousand Ducats, some say, a million: but that and more drawn back again in rewards and payments. There is in it, by computation; about a million of souls. We may conjecture of their force by the Army of *Don Garzia* of *Toledo*, consisting of three thousand Horse and ten thousand Foot (and that raised but out of the South Angle of the Island) to defend the large and unfortified Haven of *Augusta*, if the *Turk* should have there attempted to land, when he passed by to the invasion of *Malta*. But what was this, compared with that which we read of *Dionysius* the elder, being but Lord of *Syracusa* only, and the adjoyning Territories? who kept continually ten thousand Foot-men of his Guard, as many Horse-men, and four hundred Gallies. But now there are but eight maintained about the whole Island. The summit of the lesser Hills are crowned with Towns, and the Coasts beset with Watch-towers throughout; the Seas being seldom free from the *Turkish* Pirates of *Africa*.

The *Sicilians* are quick-witted and pleasant; *Epicharmus* of that Nation being the first Inventer of Comedies, and *Theocritus* of Pastoral Eclogues:

Ille ubi septena modulatus arundine carmen
Mulcebat sylvas, non unquam tempore eodem
Siflen affueros effundit in æquora cantus.
Scyllæi tacuere canes, stetit atra Charybdis,
Et lætus scopulis audivit jubila Cyclops.
Silius Italicus. l. 4.

*When he with Verse to pipe apply'd, did please
Even rude Woods, thus no Syren sung to Seas:
Scilla's dogs bark'd not, black Charybdis staid:
The joyful Cyclop listned whilst he play'd.*

Empedocles doth shew their excellency in Philosophy; *Euclide* and *Archimedes* in the Mathematicks. A people greedy of honour, yet given to ease and delight; talkative, meddlesom, dissentious, jealous, and revengeful. They have their Commodities fetch'd from them by Foreigners, with all the profit: who traffick little abroad, and are (though seated in the midst of the Sea) unexpert Navigators. So supinely idle, that they sell their Sugar as it is extracted from the Cane, to the *Venetians*; and buy what they spend of them again, when they have refined it. The Duke of *Osuna* is now Viceroy, who keeps his Court at *Palermo*, the ancient Seat of the *Sicilian* Kings styled the happy, for the delightful situation, now adorned with goodly Buildings: and frequented by Students. It is seated on the North-side of the Island, having naturally no Port, yet one lately made by a mighty Peer: a work of great expence, and no small admiration. This Viceroy hath well purged the Country of Banditties, by pardoning of one for the bringing in or death of another; who did exceedingly, and yet do two much infest it. Besides, the upland Inhabitants are so inhospitable to strangers, that between them both, there is no travelling by Land without a strong guard; who rob and murder whomsoever they can conveniently lay hold on. Their Religion is Romish (yet are they not so few as ten thousand who are of the tolerated *Greek* Church.) *Palermo*, *Messina*, and *Mont-royal*, have their Archbishops. The Bishops of *Agrigentine*, *Mazara*, and *Malta*, being under the first; the second hath *Pati*, *Cefaledi*, and *Lipari*; the third *Syracufa*. The Bishop of *Catania* is under none of them. There be in this Island seven Princes, four Dukes, thirteen Marquesses, fourteen Earls, one Viscount, and eight and forty Barons. The chief of the ancient *Sicilian* Nobility attend in the Court of *Spain*; a course of life rather politickly commanded than elected.

June 25. having compassed Cape *Passaro*, defended by a strong Fortress not long since erected, we rowed close under the Cliff called *Muro del Porco*, (in that those flat Rocks do resemble the snouts of Swine) where store of Tunny is taken. A fish that is bred, (as hath been said before) in the Lake of *Maoth*, but groweth unto his greatness in the Ocean, when about the midst of *May* they return again into these Seas. They cut them in pieces, salt them, barrel them up, and so vend them unto most places of *Europe*; esteemed heretofore a vile food.

Quod vocis pretium? ficcus pera funculus, & vas
Pelamidum, aut veteres Afrorum Epimenia bulbi.
Juv. Sat. 7.

*What's thy tongues fee? Dry Gammons, a base dish
Of Tunny, monthly presents of stale fish.*

and so is my judgment, in taste something resembling flesh, as in colour and solidity. I have read or heard how certain Merchants being bound to serve the *French* Army at the siege of *Naples*, with so many Tun of Tunny, and not able to perform it; hearing of a late fought Battel in *Barbary*, repaired to the place, and supplied the quantity with mans flesh drest in the same manner; which proved so over-high a feeding (most easily converting into the like) that their bodies brake forth into loathsom Ulcers: and from that infection the disease that taketh from them the name (not known before in our parts of the World) was introduced amongst us. And *Scaliger* in his 181 Exercise upon *Cardan*, and the 19. Section, doth also affirm, that it proceeded not originally from the impurity of Women, but from contaction; and that the *Spaniards* did first transport these rare Wares from the *Indians*; as common amongst them as the Meazles amongst us, and equally contagious. Which seemeth to affirm the former assertion; they having been Man-eaters for the most part. No Tunny is suffered to be sold at *Venice*, unless first discask'd, and search'd to the bottom. The story goes, how the *Genoa's* having seized on a part of *Venice*, and driven the *Venetians* into their houses; a Woman running to a Window to behold the Tumult, by chance threw down a Mortar of Brass, which lightning upon the head of their General, struck him dead on the earth. Whereupon, discomforted, the *Genoeses* retired in such haste, that they left a number

of

of their men behind them; who saved themselves for a time by mingling with the *Venetians*, being not to be distinguished by Habit, Language, Favour, nor Behaviour. At length all generally were commanded to ascend an high Tower, where (not unlike as the *Gileadites* served the *Ephraimites*) a sheep being set before them, they were compelled to name it. So being distinguished (the name differing in their Dialect) they were thrown down headlong. The *Genoäes* having after taken certain of their Gallies, wherein were the prime of their Gentry, in revenge of that cruelty, caused them to be cut in pieces, and drest like Tunny; nailing their hands to the bottom with Scedules of Tin containing their names, and so sent it thither to be sold, who bought, and almost had devoured it all, before it was discovered. But I have this only by relation. Still winding with the shore, we entred at length the Haven of *Syracusa*; and together with the Sun, made an end of that days Journey.

Archias not daring to return unto *Corinth*, having unnaturally abused a Youth of honest behaviour, imbarked himself with certain *Corinthians* and *Dorians*, and came, together with *Myscellus*, unto *Delphos*, to consult with the Oracle. Demanded by *Apollo*, whether it were Riches or Sanity, that they affected; *Myscellus* said, Sanity and *Archias* Riches. Whereupon he commanded the one to erect *Crotona*, and the other *Syracusa*; which he did in the second year of the second Olympiad. Where they in short time grew so wealthy by the fertility of the soil, and benefit of the Haven, that it became a Proverbial scoff unto the too sumptuous, that they were not worth the Riches of *Syracusa*. *Archias* slain by *Telephus*, whom he had formerly defiled; the Citizens converted the Government into an Aristocracy. But the Nobles, by a Law that they had made, as jealous that some of them should have affected the Tyranny, exiled one another; so that the Commons assumed the Government. After, to accord a dangerous Sedition, they chose *Gelon* for their Tyrant, in the year of our Lord 3474. *Hiron* succeeded *Gelon* the good; his cruelty tempered by the instructions of *Pindarus* and *Simonides*. *Thrasibulus* his Successor was expulsed by the *Syracusians* for his oppression; and the State again reduced into a Democracy; until threescore years after, it was usurped by *Dionysius*, a man admirably valiant. *Dionysius* his Son succeeded as execrably vicious, (although both the Hearers of *Plato*) who overthrown by *Dion* and *Temelion*, was sent unto *Corinth*, where he lived in great poverty. So recovered the *Syracusians* their liberty; but had not enjoyed it above twenty years, when *Agathocles* (a man of a base Original) did make them stoop to a cruel subjection. He dead, and after much civil dissention, they make choice of *Hieron*, the second of that name; most beautiful in body, and as beautiful in mind; whose prosperous Government lasted fifty years, being a friend to the *Romans*. *Hieronymus* his Son, within fifteen months after the death of his Father, was slain by his Guard. Now as for the *Syracusians*, although subject themselves to these Tyrants, yet were they the masters of others; and when free, delivered many from the servitude of the Barbarous. Memorable are the fights which they had with the *Athenians* and *Carthaginians*; and glorious their Victories.

> Portus æquoreis fueca insignire trophæis.
> *Sil. Ital.*

Still maintaining their own, until the fore-named *Hieronymus* sided with the *Carthaginians*; and they after him, against the *Romans*: who under the Conduct of *Marcellus*, sacked their City; defended for three years by the special labour and miraculous Engines of *Archimedes*, that excellent Mathematician, Inventer of the Sphere.

When Jove within a little glass survey'd	Jupiter in parvo cum cerneret æthere vitro
The heavens, he smil'd; and to the Gods thus said:	Risit, & ad superos talia dicta dedit:
Can strength of mortal wit proceed thus far?	Huccine mortalis progressa potentia curæ?
In a frail Orb my works presented are,	Jam meus in fragili luditur orbe labor.
Hither the Syracusians art translates	Jura poli, rerumque fidem, legemque virorum
Heavens form, the course of things, and humane feats	Ecce Syracusius transtulit arte senex.
Th' included spirit serv'd by star-deckt signs,	Inclusus variis famulatur spiritus astris,
The living work incessant motion winds.	Et vivum certis motibus urget opus.
Th' adulterate Zodiack runs a natural year,	Percurrit proprium, mentitur signifer annum;
And Cynthia forg'd horns monthly new light bear.	Et simulata novo Cynthia mense redit.

Jamque suum volvens audax industria mundum,	Viewing her own world, now bold industry
Gaudet, & humana sidera mente regit.	Triumphs, and rules with humane power the skie,
Quid falso insontem tonitru Salmonea mirot?	Salmoneus thunder why do I wonder at,
Æmula Naturæ parva reperta manus.	When a weak hand can Nature emulate.
C'aud. in Eplg.	

When the City was taken, a Souldier found him in his Study, busie about certain Geometrical peoportions; who ready to strike, was desired by him a little to stay until he had perfected his demonstration. Who forthwith slew him, offended with his answer, to the much grief of *Marcellus*; who not only spared his Kinsfolks for his sake, but had them in great honour.

Syracusa, in times past, contained four conjoyning Cities, environed with a Wall of two and twenty miles in circuit; *Ortygia*, *Neapolis*, *Acradina*, and *Tyche*; besides, a strong Fort called *Hexaple*, high mounted, and over-looking the whole. Seated it is on a rocky point of Land, which divides the two Havens. *Ortygia* stands at the uttermost extent; an Island joyned by a Bridge to the rest. Wherein is the so chanted Fountain of *Arethusa*, once a Nymph of *Arcadia*, (as they fable) beloved of the River *Alpheus*, and turned into a Spring by *Diana*, for safeguard of her chastity; being conducted by her under Seas and Earth, and re-ascending in this Island. Followed notwithstanding by the Lover.

Sicanio prætenta sinu jacet insula contra	Against Plemmyrium in Sicanian Bay,
Plemmyrium undosum: nomen dixere priores	There lies an Isle, carst call'd Ortygia.
Ortygiam, Alphæum fama est huc Elidis amnem	Hither Alpheus under-seas (fame goes)
Occultas egisse vias subter mare, qui nunc	From Elis straid; and at thy mouth arose
Ore Arethusa tuo Sicubis confunditur undis.	Lov'd Arethuse: from whence to Seas he flows.
Æn. l. 3.	

They so conjecturing, for that this Fountain was said to grow thick, and savour of Garbidge, at such time as they celebrated the Olympiads, and defiled the River with the blood and entrails of the Sacrifices. But *Strabo* derides the conceit, though (besides divers more ancient Authors) it be affirmed by *Seneca* and others. The Fountain is ample, and sendeth to the adjoyning Sea a plentiful tribute. Before, and even in the days of *Diodorus* the *Sicilian*, a number of sacred fishes were nourished herein; so said to be, for that whosoever did eat of them (though in time of War) were afflicted with sundry calamities. Now the North-side of the rest of the City was *Neapolis*, the South-side *Acradina*, and the West-end *Tyche*, which stretcheth far into the Land, so named of the Temple of *Fortune*. As for the Castle *Hexaple*, it stood further off upon the summit of a Rock; which *Cicero* doth call the great and magnificent labour of Tyrants: consisting of solid stone, and raised of a wonderful height, more strong than which there could be nothing made, or almost imagined. All being defaced by *Marcellus*, and suffering a further destruction by *Pompey*. *Saracusa* may yet say,

Illa ego sum Romæ laboraique injuria Pœni:	Of Rome th' excessive toil, the scourge of Carthage
Pro me etiam uragis Græcia sensit onus:	Am I: for me Greece also felt Wars rage,
Figere quæ voluere alios in sedibus atua:	Th' Ensigns they would in foreign seats have shewn,
Exturbata jacent sedibus orba suis.	Now hurl'd out, lie deprived of their own.
J. C. Scal.	

But *Augustus Cæsar* sent hither a Colony, and rebuilt a great part of that which lies next to *Ortygia*, with the Isle it self; whereon now there standeth a strong Castle possessing the whole compass of the Island, divided by a deep Trench (but not by the Sea) from the rest of the City. The City it self is strongly walled, (that which heretofore there was nothing more goodly) not far removed on both sides from the Sea: the point whereon it doth stand being but narrow towards the West, and so maketh by Land a difficult approach; without which are the ruines of the old City. The principal Gate is on the South-side, and near the West-end, over which is written,

SYRACUSA CIVITAS INVICTISSIMA,

DEO ET REGI FIDELISSIMA.

the City being styled, *Syracusa* the Faithful. The Garrison consists of two hundred *Spaniards*, and three hundred Town-smen; besides certain Horsemen

men of the Country adjoyning, who serve by turns, and are nightly sent forth to scour and guard the Sea-coast. The Buildings of the City are ancient, the Inhabitants grave, and their Women hid under long black Stoles, not unlike the *Maltesses*. The Winter is here most temperate, no day so tempestuous as affordeth not some Sun-shine; but again they are afflicted with the insalubrious heat of the Summer. Yet in the hottest season cool Springs gush out of the Rock (not to speak again of *Arethusa*) both within the Walls of the City and without: and that so near unto the Sea, that the salt doth mingle with the fresh upon every motion. Notwithstanding, there is a long ancient Aqueduct, which conveyeth waters from the nearer Mountains (yet reaching short of the City) wherewith the City is principally furnished. The two Havens that wash the South and North-sides of the City, (which by the inclining of the two opposite Promontories towards *Ortygia*, are defended from all weathers) do resemble in form a figure of 8. The greatest lies towards the South, the most goodly and most famous, that ever Nature or Art had a hand in; into which the little and gentle *Anapis* doth discharge it self, joyning not far above with the Fountain *Cyane*, whose conjunction hath given invention to their celebrated Loves and Nuptials.

Having stayed a day at *Syracusa*, we put again to Sea, and arrived before night at *Catania* the Renowned. A City more ancient than beautiful; seated on the North-side of a great, but shallow Bay, and therefore not to be approached by Ships; the cause perhaps that it is not kept by a Garrison. Once it was a Colony of the *Naxians*. But *Hieron* the first displanted the old Inhabitants, and peopled it with other; changing also the name thereof into *Ætna*. He is said to have built it anew; but after the death of the Tyrant, the *Catanians* recovered their City, overthrew his Monument, defaced his Titles, and again did call it *Catania*. Little is here note-worthy, more than that it is an University, and seated on a soil that aboundeth with all things. They have little Trading, and therefore the more inhabited by Gentlemen. Of late, not far from the City, and Image of our Lady was under earth (as they say) accidentally found; whose imputed Miracles have got her already much fame, but not yet a Temple: contented, until enriched by the tribute of their zeal, with a Canvas Pavillion. This City doth well-nigh joyn to the skirts of *Ætna*, whereby it receiveth both loss, and (if *Strabo* may be believed) advantage. For the ejected flames have heretofore committed horrible wastes, which gave *Amphinomus* and *Anapius*, two Brethren, an occasion to become famous for their piety; who rescued their Parents ingaged by the fire, and bare them away on their shoulders; whereof *Silius Italicus*,

Catania too near Ætna; honoured,
In that it two such pious brethren bred.

——*Catine nimium ardenti vicina Typheo,*
Et generasse pios quondam celeberrima fratres.
Lib. 13.

and *Ausonius*,

Who will forget Catania? of high fame
For piety of brothers sindg'd in flame.

Quis Catinam sileat? ——
Hanc ambustorum fratrum pietate celebrem.
Clar. Urb. 10.

And even at this day, once in three or four years, it falleth in great flakes on the Country below, to the terrour of the Inhabitants, and destruction of their Vintage. But on the contrary side (according to that Author) the ashes thereof doth so enrich the soil, that both Vines and Corn there prosper above admiration. Who reports besides, that the Grass so manured kills the Sheep that do feed thereon, unless within forty or fifty days they be let blood in the Ear. Howbeit, at this day much ground about it lies waste, by means of the ejected Pumice. Greatly desirous I was to have ascended this Mountain, but it required much time; besides, the Country hereabout is daily forraged by Thieves, who lurk in a Wood of eight miles compass, their neighbours the City. So the next morning we departed, and sailed for the space of thirty miles about the East skirts of that Mountain; whereof we now will make a Description.

Ætna, called by *Pindarus* the Celestial Column, is the highest Mountain of *Sicilia*, for a great space leisurely rising; insomuch as the top is ten miles distant from the uttermost Basis. It appeareth this way with shoulders, having an
eminent

. eminent head in the middle. The lower parts are luxuriously fruitful, the middle woody, and the upper rocky, steep, and almost covered with snow; yet smoaking in the midst like many conjoyning Chimnies, and vomiting intermitted flames, though not but by night to be discerned, as if heat and cold had left their contention, and imbraced one another. This burning Beacon doth shew her fire by night: and her smoak by day, in a wonderful way off; yet heretofore discerned far further, in that the matter perhaps is diminished by so long an expence. My self have seen both plainly unto *Malta*: and the Mountain it self is to be discovered an hundred and fifty miles off by the Sailer. Those that have been at the top do report, that there is there a large Plain of Cinders and Ashes, environed with a brow of the same; and in the midst a Hill of like substance, out of which bursted a continual wind hangs about it like a great long cloud; and often hurling forth stones and cinders. Wherefore the story of *Empedocles* the *Sicilian* Philosopher, then whom

———— N I hoc habuisse viro præclarius in se,
Nec sanctum magis, & mirum carumqs videtur,
Carmina quin etiam divini pectoris ejus
Vociferantur & exponunt præclara reperta;
Ut vix humana videtur stirpe creatus.
Lucr. l. 1.

More excellent in nothing hath brought forth,
More sacred, wonderful, or of more worth:
His Verse divinely fram'd, aloud resound
Natures deep mysteries by him out found,
As if not of an humane off-spring born:

Is by some called into question. Who (as they say) affecting divine honour, withdrew himself privately from his Companions, and leapt in at the mouth thereof, but was revealed by his brazen shooes, which the fire had thrown up again. For it is impossible to be approached, by reason of the violent wind, the suffocating smoak, and consuming fervour. But hear we *Virgils* description.

———— horrifici ———— tonat Ætna ruinis:
Interdumque atram prorumpit ad æthera nubem
Turbine fumantem piceo, & cadente favilla,
Attollitque globos flammarum, & sidera lambit,
Interdum scopulos avulsaque viscera montis
Erigit eructans, liquefactaque saxa sub auras
Cum gemitu glomerat, fundoque ex æstuat imo,
Fama est Enceladi semiustum fulmine corpus
Urgeri mole hac ingentemque insuper Ætnam
Impositam, ruptis flammam expirare caminis,
Et sessum quoties moveat latus, intremere omnem
Murmure Trinacriam, & cœlum subtexere fumo.
Æn. l.

Ætna here thunders with an horrid noise,
Sometimes black clouds evaporeth to skies,
Fuming with pitchy curles, and sparkling fires:
Tosseth up globes of flames, to Stars aspires.
Now belching rocks, the mountains entrails torn,
And groaning burles out liquid stones, thence born
Thorow th' air in showres, and from the bottom gloes.
Enceladus, with lightning struck, (same goes)
This mass o're-whelms: who under Ætna laid,
Expireth flames, by broken vents convey'd.
As often as he turns his weary sides,
All Sicil quakes; and smoak, days beauty hides.

But leave we Fables with their Allegories, and come to the true reason; given (if fully) by *Lucretius*.

————Primum totius subcava montis
Est natura, fere silicum, subsulta cavernis,
Omnibus est porro in speluncis ventus & aer.
Ventus enim fit ubi est agitando percitus aer.
Hic ubi percaluit, calefecitque omnia circum,
Saxa furens qua contingit terramque & ab ollis
Excussit calidum flammis velocibus ignem:
Tollit se, ac rectis ita faucibus ejicit alte,
Funditque ardorem longe, longeque favillam
Differt, & crassa volvit caligine fumum;
Extruditque simul mirando pondere saxa:
Ne dubites quin hæc animali turbida sit vis:
Præterea magna ex parte mare montis ad ejus
Radices frangit fluctus, a fluitique resorbet,
Et hoc usque mari speluncæ montis ad altas
Perveniunt subter fauces, hac ire fatendum est,
Atque efflare foras: ideoque extollere flammas,
Saxaque subjectare, & arenæ tollere nimbos.
Lib. 6.

Hollow the mountain is throughout, alone
Supported well-nigh with huge caves of stone,
No cave but is with wind and air repleat;
For agitated air doth wind beget.
Which heats the imprisoning rocks, when hot it grows;
The earth chaft by his fury: and from those
Strides forth fire and swift flame: it self on high
It mounts, and out at upright jaws doth flie:
And fire sheds a far off, far off dead coals
Transports: and fumes in misty darkness roles.
Ejecting stones withal of wondrous size;
All which from strength of struggling winds arise.
Besides, against the Mount ains roots the Main
Breaks her swollen waves, and swallows them again.
From whence unto the summit of the ascent
The undermining caves have their extent:
Through which the billows breath & flames out-thrust
With forced stones, and darkning showres of dust.

Besides,

LIB. IV.   Ætna. Messena.

Besides, *Ætna* is full of Sulphur and Bitumen, apt to be kindled, and so is all *Sicilia*, the principal reason that it is so fertile. This Mountain hath flamed in times past so abundantly, that by reason of the smoak and air involved with burning sand, the Inhabitants hereabout could not see one another (if we may give credit to *Cicero*) for two days together. The extraordinary eruption thereof hath been reputed ominous. For so it did after the death of *Cæsar*; when not only the Cities thereabout were damnified thereby, but divers in *Calabria*. And in the year of the World 3982. hard before the servile Wars in *Sicilia*, wherein threescore and ten thousand Slaves were slain by the Prætors, it raged so violently, that *Africa* was thereof an astonished Witness.

Hereabouts inhabited the *Cyclops*, and here *Acis* hastes to the Sea.

The Rival of thy ardor, Polypheme,
Flying from savage rage, into a stream
Resolv'd did both ease his foe, and joy,
O Galatea, his joy'd waves with thine.

Æmulus ille tuo quondam Polypheme calori,
Dum fugit agrestem violenti pectoris iram,
In tenues liquefactus aquas evasit & hostem,
Et tibi victricem, Galatea, immiscuit undam.
Sil. Ital. 13.

North-ward of *Ætna*, lesser Hills do arise in the neck one of another, all along the Sea-coast, fruitful to their tops: whereupon stand Castles and Towns, of such an height and steepness, as you would hardly think that they were to be ascended. Upon the nine and twentieth of *June*, betimes in the morning, entring the Streights, between *Sicilia* and *Calabria*, we turned on the left hand into the Haven of *Messena*. *Messena* (now *Messina* the Noble) was at the first called *Zanele*, of the crookedness of the place, which signifieth a Cycle, built by the Pirates of *Catania*, for the better execution of their robberies: when *Anaxilas*, Tyrant of the opposite *Rhegium*, drew to him the *Messeni* of *Peloponesus*, to displant the *Zaneli*. So the *Rhegians* having overthrown them by Sea, and the *Messenians* by Land, and entred their City, they were enforced to flie unto their Temples and Altars, when *Anaxilas* would have put them to the sword, but *Manticlus* and *Gorgus*, Captains of the *Messenians*, dissuaded him from being so cruel unto a *Greek* people, who originally were of their blood and alliance: whereupon they raised them from the Altars; and plighting faith unto one another, inhabited it together. So it came to be called *Messina*. This befell in the nine and twentieth Olympiad. But in the time of *Dionysius* the elder it was razed by the *Carthaginian Himilcus*, and that with such hatred, as he left not so much as the ruines. About the beginning of the first Punick Wars, the *Mamertini*, a people of *Campania*, sent hither their Colonies, who possest the place, and rebuilt the City, which was called for a long time after, rather *Mamertinum*: as the excellent Wines that grow hereabout are called by *Martial*.

If cups of old Mamertian Wine they fill,
Give it you may what name soe're you will.

Amphora Nestorea tibi Mamertina senecta,
Si detur, quodvis nomen habere potest.
Lib. 3. *Ep.* 1. 17.

The *Romans* made it their refuge in the *Sicilian* Wars against the *Carthaginians*, with whom it stood and fell, as did the whole Islands. It is seated on the West side and South-end (which is the bottom of a Bay) having behind it high Hills, whereof it ascendeth a part, strongly walled, and fortified about with Bulwarks, greater or less, according to the places necessity. Upon the West-side, and high mounted above it, stands a strong Citadel, which commandeth the whole City, manned by a Garrison of *Spaniards*. South-West of it a Fortress is mounted on the top of a higher Hill. And on the top of another towards the South, is the Castle of *Gonsage*; both without the Walls. The City is garnished with beautiful Buildings, both publick and private. *Venus*, *Neptune*, *Castor* and *Pollux*, had here their Temples, whose ruines are now the foundation of Christian Churches. Divers ancient Statues are yet to be seen. Throughout the City there are Fountains of fresh water: and towards the North-end, the ruines of an old Aquæduct. In that end which turns to the East, about the bottom of the Bay, where the City is slender, and free from concourse of people, stands the Viceroy's Palace, of no mean building, environed with delightful Gardens and Orchards, to which the Arsenal adjoyneth. This end of the City points upon *Calabria*, and extendeth almost to the Sea; where the Land in a narrow slip running on the North, and then returning West towards the rest of the City in form of a Cycle, doth make a large and admirable Haven. Now on the midst of this Cycle of Land, there standeth an

high

high Lanthorn, which by light in the night directeth such Ships as are to enter these dangerous streights: North of which there are certain late built dry stations for Gallies; and not far beyond the Lanthorn, where it beginneth to turn, is a very strong Castle (built by *Philip* the Second) and guarded by *Spaniards*. The rest of that Cycle is incloted between two Walls, to the very point which is fortified with a Bulwark; between which and the City, the Haven which opens to the North, hath a spacious entrance. Here live they in all abundance and delicacy, having more than enough of Food, and Fruits of all kinds; excellent Wines, and Snow in the Summer to qualifie the heat thereof, at a contemptible rate. The better sort are *Spanish* in attire; and the meanest Artificers Wife is cloathed in silk: whereof an infinite quantity is made by the Worm, and a part thereof wrought into Stuffs (but rudely) by the Workman. Eight thousand Bails of raw Silk are yearly made in that Island, and five thousand thereof fetcht from thence (for, as hath been said before, they will not trouble themselves to transport it) at the publick Mart here kept, which lasteth all *August*, by the Gallies of *Naples, Ostia, Ligorn*, and *Genoua*; during which time they are quitted from Customs. The Gentlemen put their monies into the common Table (for which the City stands bound) and receive it again upon their Bills, according to their uses. For they dare not venture to keep it in their houses, so ordinarily broken open by Thieves (as are the Shops and Ware-houses) for all their cross-bar'd Windows, Iron Doors, Locks, Bolts, and Bars on the inside; wherein, and in their private revenges, no night doth pass without murder. Every evening they solace themselves along the Marine (a place left throughout between the City-wall and the Haven) the men on Horse-back, and the Women in large Carosses, being drawn with the slowest procession. There is to be seen the pride and beauties of the City. There have they their Play-houses, where the parts of Women are acted by Women, and too naturally passionated; which they forbear not to frequent upon *Sundays*. The Duke of *Ossuna*, their new Viceroy, was here daily expected; for whom a sumptuous landing place was made, and that but to continue for a day.

The Phare of *Messina* (for so these streights are now called, the Lanthorn that stands on the point of *Pelorus*) is ten miles long, and against *Messina* but a mile and a half over. Insomuch that when *Himileus* took the City, a number saved their lives (although it ran with an impetuous Current) by swimming into *Italy*. On the Coast of *Sicily* is *Charybdis*.

———— Lævam implacata Charybdis,
Obsidet, atque imo barathri ter gurgite vastos
Sorbet in abruptum fluctus, rursusque sub auras
Erigit alternos, & sydera verberat unda.
Virg Æn. l. 3.

Gulphy Charybdis doth the left side keep,
And thrice sucks to the bottom of her deep
The toiling floods; as often lifts on high
Alternate waves, and beats the approached skie.

Once, as they fable, a ravenous Woman, struck with Lightning by *Jupiter*, and thrown into the Sea, for stealing of *Hercules* Oxen; who still retaining her former nature, devoureth all that comes near her. This Whirle-pit is said to have thrown up her Wracks near *Tauromenia*; which is between it and *Catania*. Then sure, by much more outragious than now, and more dangerous to the Sailer, by reason of their unskilfulness. As now, during our passage, so heretofore, it was smooth and appeased whilst calm weather lasted; but when the winds begin to ruffle (especially from the South) it forthwith runs round with violent eddies: so that many Vessels by the means thereof do miscarry. Right against this *Charybdis* stands that former Lanthorn on the neck of the Haven, whereof *Scaliger* speaketh in the person of *Messina*.

Indomitæ sedeo spectatrix tuta Charybdis,
Ostendisque aliis lumine grata viam.
Mortales si sic faciant, meliore truentur
Numine; nunc homini vera Charybdis homo.
J. C. Scal.

Unsafe Charybdis safely I survay:
And others shew with friendly light the way.
More would heaven smile on earth, did mortals so:
Man is to man Charybdis, his worst foe.

The stream thorow this streight runneth towards the *Ionian* Sea, whereof a part setteth into the Haven, which turning about, and meeting with the rest, makes so violent an encounter, that Ships (if the wind be not good) are glad to prevent the danger, by coming to an Anchor.

Almost right against *Messina* stands *Rhegium* in *Italy*; a Garrison Town, retaining his

LIB. IV.   Rhegium. Scylla.   193

his ancient name, which signifieth Broken; in memory of the division of this Island from the Continent.

By force, and with vast breaches torn, this place,
(Such power hath time to alter through long space)
Of old ('tis said) asunder brake; before
Both but one land: Seas throng'd between, and bore
Sicil from Italy; and making spoil
Of fields and towns, thorow narrow streights now toil.

Hæc loca vi quondam, & vasta convulsa ruinas
(Tantum ævi longinqua valet mutare vetustas)
Dissiluisse ferunt: cum protinus utraque tellus
Una foret: venit medio vi Pontus, & undis
Hesperium Siculo latus abscindit, arvaq; & urbes
Littore diductas angusto interluit æstu.
               Virg. Æn. l. 3.

Separated by Earth-quakes, or (which is most likely) by the continual assaults of the *Tyrrhene* and *Ionian* Sea: the Land being but low, and the water so shallow, that a Ship may anchor in the deepest. Some think it to have been cut by the labour of man; but the crookedness of the Bays and unequal bredth, do confute that conjecture.

Now having stayed three days at *Messina*; on the first of *July* I departed, accompanied by two *Spaniards* of the Garrison of *Rhegium*, in another Felluca that belonged to the City. Having crossed the *Phare*, and rowed along the *Calabrian* shore for the space of five miles towards the *Tyrrhene* Sea, we were encountred by so strong a stream, that much ado we had to hale the Boat against it. At length the Rope brake, and in an instant we were carried a great way off: when they might have fought her in the bottom of the Sea, if she had not met with her succour. That night we came unto *Scylla*, which is not past twelve miles distant from *Messina*: seated in the midst of a Bay, upon the neck of a narrow Mountain which thrusts it self into the Sea; having at the uppermost end a steep high Rock whereon there standeth a Castle. This is the Rock so celebrated by the Poets: whose unaccessible height is so hyperbolically described by *Homer*, and was so obnoxious to the Mariner.

But Scylla lurking in dark caves, displays
Her face, and Ships to crushing rocks betrays.
A Virgin to the twist divinely fram'd,
Her nether parts with shape of Monster sham'd,
Deform'd with womb of Wolves and Dolphins tails.

At Scyllam cæcis cohibet spelunca latebris
Ora exertantem & naves in saxa trahentem.
Prima hominis facies, & pulchro pectore virgo
Pube tenus: postrema immani corpore pistrix,
Delphinum caudas utero commissa luporum.
       Virg. Æn. l. 3.

She was feigned to be the Daughter of *Phorcus*, begotten on the Nymph *Cretheide*; being *Cyrces* Rival in the love of *Glaucus*. By whom preferred, the envious Witch infected this place with Weeds and Inchantments: when *Scylla* entring hereinto to bathe, was transformed into that monstrous resemblance. But she was revenged of her affected *Ulysses*:

Who hemm'd about with barking Monsters wrackt
Dulichian Ships, and in her swallowing flood
To Sea-dogs gave his fearful men for food.

———— aut quam fama secuta est
Candida succinctam latrantibus inguina monstris
Dulichias vexasse rates, & gurgite in alto
Ah timidos nautas, canibus lacerasse marinis.
       Virg. Ecl. 8.

and after that was turned into a stone. And no doubt, but the Fable was fitted to the place; there being divers little sharp Rocks at the foot of the greater (the Dogs that so bark with the noise that is made by the repercussed waters) frequented by Lamprons, and greater fishes that devoured the bodies of the drowned. But *Scylla* is now without danger, the Current at this day not setting upon it. And wonder I do at this Proverbial Verse,

Who shuns Charybdis upon Scylla falls.   Incidit in Scyllam qui vult vitare Charybdim.

when these are twelve miles distant from each other. I rather conjecture that within these streights there have been divers *Charybdis's* occasioned by the recoyling streams. As one there is between the South-end of this Bay of *Scylla*, and the opposite point of *Sicily* (whereon standeth the ancient *Pharus*:) there the justling waves make a violent eddy: which, when the winds are rough, doth more than threaten destruction to the ingaged Ships, as I have heard of the *Sicilians*: when seeking perhaps heretofore to avoid the then more impetuous turning, they have been driven by the weather upon the not far distant *Scylla*. By the Marine in *Messina* there is a Fountain of white Marble, where stands the Statue of *Neptune* holding *Scylla* and *Charybdis* in chains; with these under-written Verses.

The Æolian Islands. Auphage.

Impia nodosis cohibetur Scylla catenis;
Pergite secure per freta nostra rates,
Capta est prædatrix Siculique infamia ponti,
Nec fremit in mediis sæva Charybdis aquis.

*Fast-binding fetters wicked Scylla hold,
Sail safely thorow our streights, brave Ships behold,
Th' infamous thief that kept these Seas is tane,
And fell Charybdis rageth now in vain.*

West of *Sicilia* in the *Tyrrhene* Sea, but South, and within sight of this place, are the *Æolian* Islands, so called of

Æolus Hipporades charus immortalibus diis.
Hom. Od. l. 10.

*Æolus Hipporades
Dear t' immortal Deities.*

for such was his piety, he being Lord of them. He taught at first the use of the Sail; and by observing of the fire and smoak that ascended from those Islands, (for heretofore they all of them flamed) prognosticated of storms to come; and therefore was called the Soveraign of the Winds. Of there were seven (but now are eleven) almost of an equal magnitude. Yet *Liparia* is the greatest (being ten miles in circuit) as also the most famous, to which the other were subject: fruitful, and abounding with Bitumen, Sulphur, and Allum, having also hot Baths much frequented by the diseased. In the year 1544. it was depopulated by the *Turk*: but *Charles* the Fifth replanted it with *Spaniards*, and fortified the place. The fire here went out about an Age agone, having (as is to be supposed) consumed the matter that fed it. *Vulcano* and *Strombolo* (of which we will only speak) do now only burn. *Vulcano* receiveth that name from his nature, consecrated formerly to *Vulcan*, and called his mansion. It is said but first to have appeared above water, about the time that *Scipio Africanus* died. A barren Island, stony and un-inhabited. It had three Tunnels whereat it evapoured fire; but now hath but one, out of which it smoketh continually, and casts out stones with a horrible roaring. In the year of our Lord 1444. on the fifth of *February*, it flamed so abundantly, and flung forth fire and stones with such an hideous noise, that not only the Islands, but also *Sicilia* trembled thereat. Perhaps the last blaze; for now flame it doth not, but retaineth the rest of his terrors. Now *Strombolo*, called formerly *Strongyle*, of the rotundity thereof (for all is no other than a high round Mountain) doth burn almost continually at the top of a Beacon, and exceeding clearly: so that by night it is to be discerned a wonderful way. These places (and such like) are commonly affirmed by the *Roman* Catholicks to be the Jaws of Hell: and that within, the damned Souls are tormented. It was told me at *Naples* by a Country-man of ours, and an old Pensioner of the Popes, who was a Youth in the days of King *Henry*, that it was then generally bruited throughout *England*, that Mr. *Gresham* a Merchant setting sail from *Palermo*, (where there then dwelt one *Anthonio* called the Rich, who at one time had two Kingdoms mortgaged unto him by the King of *Spain*, being crossed by contrary winds, was constrained to anchor under the lee of this Island: now about mid-day, when for certain hours it accustomedly forbeareth to flame; he ascended the Mountain, with sight of the Sailers; and approaching as near the vent as they durst; amongst other noises they heard a voice cry aloud, dispatch, dispatch, the rich *Anthonio* is a coming. Terrified herewith they descended, and anon the Mountain again evaporated fire. But from so dismal a place they made all the haste that they could: when the winds still thwarting their course, and desiring much to know more of this matter, they returned to *Palermo*. And forthwith inquiring of *Anthonio*, it was told them that he was dead; and computing the time, did find it to agree with the very instant that the voice was heard by them. *Gresham* reported this at his return to the King: and the Mariners being called before him, confirmed by oath the narration. In *Gresham* himself, as this Gentleman said (for I no otherwise report it) it wrought so deep an impression, that he gave over all traffick; distributing his goods, a part to his Kinsfolks, and the rest to good uses, retaining only a competency for himself: and so spent the rest of his life in a solitary devotion.

All the day following we stayed at *Scylla*, the winds not favouring us. My *Spanish* Comrades were very harsh to me, (for in these parts they detest the *English*, and think us not Christians) but when upon their demand I told them that I was no *Lutheran*, they exceeded on the other side in their courtesie. One of them had been in the Voyage of eighty eight; and would say that it was not we, but the winds that overthrew them. On the third of *July* we departed, and landed that night at *Auphage*. Hereabout (as throughout this part of *Calabria*) are great store of Tarantula's, a Serpent peculiar to this Country; and taking that name from the City of *Tarentum*. Some hold

LIB. IV. *Auphage. Caftilion. Paula.* 195

hold them to be of the kind of Spiders others of Efts: but they are greater than the one, and less than the other, and (if that were a Tarantula which I have seen) not greatly resembling either. For the head of this was small, the legs slender and knotty, the body light, the tail spiny, and the colour dun, intermixed with spots of a sullied white. They lurk in Sinks and Privies, and abroad in slimy filth between furrows; for which cause the Country-people do reap in Boots. The sting is deadly, and the contrary operations thereof most miraculous. For some so stung, are still oppressed with a leaden sleep; others are vexed with continual waking, some fling up and down, and others are extremely lazy. He sweats, a second vomits, a third runs mad. Some weep continually, and some laugh continually, and that is the most usual. Insomuch, that it is an ordinary saying to a man that is extraordinary merry, that he hath been stung by a Tarantula. Hereupon not a few have thought, that there are as many kinds of Tarantula's, as several affections in the affected. But as over-liberal cups do not work with all in one manner; but according to each mans nature and constitution; some weep, some laugh, some are tongue-ty'd, some are all tongue, some sleep, some leap over tables, some kiss, and some quarrel: even so it falls out with those that are bitten. The merry, the mad, and otherwise actively disposed, are cured by Musick; at least it is the cause, in that it incites them to dance indefatigably; for by labour and sweat the poyson is expelled. And Musick also by a certain high excellency hath been found by experience to stir in the sad and drowsie so strange an alacrity, that they have wearied the spectators with continual dancing. In the mean time the pain hath asswaged, the infection being driven from the heart, and the mind released of her sufferance. If the Musick intermit, the malady renews; but again continued, and it vanisheth. And objects of wonder have wrought the same effects in the franticks. A Bishop of this Country passing in the high-way, and cloathed in red, one bit by a Tarantula, hooting thereat, fell a dancing about him. The offended Bishop commanded that he should be kept back, and made haste away. But the people did instantly intreat him to have compassion on the poor distressed Wretch, who would forthwith die unless he stood still, and were suffered to continue in that exercise. So shame or importunity inforced him to stay, until by dancing certain hours together the afflicted person became perfectly cured. The fourth of *July* we rowed against the wind, and could reach no further than *Caftilion*: where the high-wrought Seas detained us this day following. Our churlish Host, because we sent for such things to the Town whereof he had none, made us also fetch our water from thence, it being a mile off, though he had in his house a plentiful Fountain. And I think there are not that profess Christ a more uncivil people than the vulgar *Calabrians*. Over Land there is hot travelling without assuring pillage, and hardly to be avoided murder; although all that you have about you (and that they know it) be we not worth a Dollar. Wherefore the common passage is by Sea, in this manner as we passed now. Along the shore there are many of these Ostaries: but most of the Towns are a good way removed, and mounted on Hills, with no easie accesses. Divers small Forts adjoyn to the Sea, and Watch-towers throughout. For the *Turks* not seldom make incursions by night, lurking in the day time about those un-inhabited Islands. Under these Forts we nightly haled up our Boat, and slept in our cloaths on the sand. And our fare was little better than our lodging: Tunny, Onions, Cucumbers, and Melons being our ordinary Viands. Not but that we might have had better, but the Souldiers were thrifty, and I was loth to exceed them. For there being but only one house at a place, they sold every thing not according to the worth, but to the necessity of the buyer. But Mulberries we might gather, and eat of free-cost; dangerously unwholesom, if not pulled from the Trees before Sun-rising. Of them there are here every where an infinite number; insomuch, that more silk is made in *Calabria*, than besides in all *Italy*. And from the leaves of those that grow higher on the Mountains (for the *Apennine* stretcheth along the midst of this Country) they gather plenty of Manna, the best of all other, which falls thereon like a dew in the night time. Here a certain *Calabrian*, hearing that I was an *English*-man, came to me, and would needs perswade me that I had insight in Magick; for that Earl *Bothel* was my Country-man, who lives at *Naples*, and is in those parts famous for suspected Necromancy. He told me that he had treasure hidden in his house; the quantity and quality shewn him by a Boy, upon the Conjuration of a Knight of *Malta*, and offered to share it between us, if I could help him unto it. But I answered, that in *England* we were at at defiance with the Devil; and that he would do nothing for us.

On the sixth of *July* we landed by noon before *Paula*, and ascended the Town

S 2   high

high mounted on a Mountain. Here was St. *Francis* born, from whom the Order of the *Minims* is derived. A mile above there is a Monastery consecrated unto him: where one of his teeth, which cureth the tootchach (if you will believe them) is to be seen, with a Rib of his, his Beard, his Habit, and Sandals. They say, at *Messina*, that being denied passage by a Fisher-man, he swam over the *Phare* in his Gown, (having first petitioned Heaven) and for that was canonized. The next day we touched at *Belvidere*; then at *Liseare*, whereof *Carolus Spinola* is Prince, whose elder Brother was taken by the *Turks*. The consonancy of the names, or treachery of the people, have authorized the report that *Iscarios* was here born. In the cool of the Evening we rowed to *Paleneda*. *July* the 8. we crossed the Bay of *Salern*, of that ancient City so named, seated in the bottom thereof; honoured with a Prince and a famous University, but how blessed in the temper?

Quæ Boreæ gelidas furias contemnit Ovantis,	She doth the chill rage of the North despise:
Torva procellosi despicit arma Noti.	And blustring winds that from the South arise.
Medorum & sylvis fœcundas provocat auras:	For pleasant air with Media she contends,
Fundit & à biferis Indica dona jugis.	From his twice-bearing Indian fruits descends.
Protinus Autumnus Veris cum tempore certat,	Rich Autumn striveth with the fragrant Spring:
Et Ver cum Autumni tempore certat idem.	
Hunc accessit Hyems, vernantibus uda capillis;	The Spring with Autumn. Winter wondering.
Et peperit mirans, & sibi poma legit.	With flowry locks and pregnancy unknown,
Tota mari fruitur; terræ dominatur amatæ;	Doth bear and gather Apples of his own.
Et cœli mutat jura; quid ergo? Dea.	Safe Seat, a loved soil commands: Heavens free
J. C. Scal.	Appointment alters. What? a Goddess she.

That night we arrived at a little Village some twelve miles beyond, where we lodged, as the night before, in a little Chappel. The next morning betimes we reached the Cape; from

Alta procellosò speculatur vertice Pallas.   *Whose stormy crown far off high Pallas sees.*
Senec. Epist. 77.

her Temple there being said to have been erected by *Ulysses*; and formerly called the Promontory of *Minerva*. Here also stood a renowned *Athenæum*, flourishing in the several excellencies of Learning and Eloquence. Insomuch, as from hence grew the Fable of the *Syrens*, (seigned to have inhabited here about) who so inchanted with the sweetness of their Songs and deepness of their Science: of both, thus boasting to *Ulysses*:

Huc age profectus, gloriose Ulysses, ingens gloria Græ-corum,	Hither thy Ship, (of Greeks) to glory steer;
Navem siste, ut nostram vocem audias.	That our songs may delight thee, anchor here.
Non enim unquam aliquis huc præternavigavit nave nigra,	Never yet man in sable Bark sail'd by,
Priusquam nostram suavem ab ore vocem audiret,	That gave not ear to our sweet melody;
Sed hic delectatus abiit, & plura doctus.	And parted pleas'd, his knowledge bettered far:
Scimus enim tibi omnia quæcunque in Troja lata	We know what Greeks and Trojans in Troys War
Græci, Trojanique, deorum voluntate passi:	Sustained by the doom of Gods; and all
Scimus etiam quæcunque fiunt in terra multipascua.	That dust upon the food-full Earth befall.
Hom. Od. l. 12.	

the same attributes being given unto them which were given to the Muses. But after that these Students had abused their gifts to the colouring of wrongs, the corruption of manners, and subversion of good government; the *Syrens* were feigned to have been transformed into Monsters, and with their melody and blandishments, to have enticed the Passenger to his ruine, and such as came hither; consuming their Patrimonies, and poysoning their virtues with riot and effeminacy. This Promontory is beautifully enriched with Wines and Fruits: of whose pregnancy the City, that now stands on the extent thereof, may seem to be named.

Majores Massam dixerunt nomine, namque	By th' Ancients Massa call'd, for that the ground
Affluit omnigena commoditate solum.	Doth here with all commodities abound.
Cunctorum hic etiam collecta est massa bonorum,	Besides a Mass of all good thou dost hold:
Ut meritò hoc Massæ nomen habere putes,	So that of merit Mass a nam'd of old.
Paul. Partarell.	

We passed between this Cape and *Capræ*, an Island distant three miles from the same, small and rocky, having no Haven nor convenient station. But the air is there mild, even during the Winter; being defended from the bitter North by the *Surrentine* Moun-

LIB. IV. *Capræ. Naples.*

Mountains, and by the West-wind, to which it lies open, refreshed in the Summer: possessing on all sides the pleasure of the Sea, and the delicate Prospects of *Vesuvium*, *Naples*, *Cuma*, and the adjoyning Islands. The *Theleboans* did first inhabit it, so called of *Thelon*, the Father of *Oebalus*.

Nor shall our Verse thee Oebalus forget,	Nec tu carminibus nostris indictus abibis,
Whom the Nymph Sabethis to Thalon bore :	Oebale, quem generasse Thelon Sabethide Nymph
Thelon then old the Crown of Capra wore,	Fertur Theleboum Capreas cum regna teneret,
And Theleboans rul'd——	Jam senior———
	Virg. Æn. l. 7.

who were originally of *Samus*. But when *Augustus Cæsar* came into these parts, it was inhabited by *Grecians*. And because an old lapless Tree did flourish afresh upon his landing in the Island, he would needs have it of the *Neapolitans*, in exchange for *Ænaria*; which from thenceforth he variously beautified, and honoured with his retirements. But *Tyberius* made *Capræ*, by his cruelty and lusts, both infamous and unhappy; who hither withdrawing from the affairs of the Common-wealth, (for that the Island was unaccessible on all sides by reason of the upright clifts, except only at one place, no man being suffered to land but upon especial admittance) hence sent his Mandates of death. In the mean time making it a very stews of incredible beastliness, which modesty will not suffer to relate. Insomuch, that *Capræ* was stiled the Island of secret lusts, and he *Capreneus*. His usual Companions were Magicians and Sooth-sayers; whereof the Satyr, speaking of *Sejanus*,

The Princes Tutor glorying to be nam'd,	———Tutor haberi
Sitting in caves of Capræ with defam'd	Principis angusta Caprearum in rupe sedentis
Chaldeans———	Cum grege Chaldæo ———
	Juv. Sat. 10.

The principal of these was *Thrasyllus*; whom *Tyberius* intending on a time to thrust down from a cliff as they walked together, in that he had failed in a former prediction, and perceiving by his looks that he was troubled in his mind, demanded the cause. Who replied that by his Art he foresaw some hardly to be avoided danger to be near him: whereat *Tyberius* amazed, altered his purpose. A few years before his death, the *Pharus* there standing, and spoken of by *Pampinius*,

(Pharus on Theleboan rocks sweet light	Theleboumque domus trepidis ubi dulcia nautis,
Sad Sailers (Moon-light) shows in erring night.)	Lumina noctivagæ tollit Pharus æmula Lunæ.
	Stat. l. 3. Silv.

was thrown down by an Earth-quake. Unto this Island they used to confine offenders, a custom that continues to this day. Amongst other Grots here is one that hath an entrance very obscure, but leads into a lightsom Cave, exceeding pleasant, by reason of the water dropping down from on high. About the shore there are divers ruines, sufficient witnesses of the *Roman* Magnificency. Here is a little City (whereof there is a Bishop) of the name of the Island, having a strong Fortress; so seated, that by one alone it may be defended. And *Anacapræ*, a Town erected on a higher Rock, mounted by a narrow, steep, and difficult passage: yet the Inhabitants by use, and with burdens on their backs, ascended it with case. Besides these, towards the North are sundry stragling habitations. The Inhabitants are generally Fisher-men and Ship-wrights, being much imployed about the Navy at *Naples*. In regard whereof they made a Petition, that such as were banished and confined unto this Island, might not stay in *Anacapræ* by night, left they should force or corrupt their Wives in their absence. They are exempted from all payments, permitted to wear Arms, yet live in great poverty, and are often at Sea surprised by *Turks*, who lead them into servitude.

On the right hand we left *Surrentum*, so called of the *Syrens*, which doth require a more large description than our brevity will permit: destroyed by *Pial Bassa* in the year 1558. when drawing near unto *Naples*, we threw all the bread we had into the Sea, twenty Ducats being forfeited for every Loaf brought thither; for that they will have the better utterance for their own. About noon, having run all that morning before the wind, we arrived at *Naples*.

Of the time when the City was built, divers Authors do differ, not to be reconciled by reason of the antiquity. Some say, an hundred seventy years after the destruction of *Troy*, others but twenty, and others say otherwise: No less disagree they concerning the Builder; whereof the *Neapolitan* Poet,

D..eris extructa à dulci Syrene ; Phaleri
Diceris, & fœlix imperiantis honor.
Diceris, & Veneris gratiſſimus hortus, & aeris
Alcidis campus d cceris eſſe novus.
Diceris, & flavæ Cereris mitiſſima tellus ;
D ceris intonſi vinea pulchra Dei.
Non mirum ; ipſa urbes ſuperas dulcedine cunctas,
Imperio, forma, robore, fruge, mero.
Aagerianus

Built by *ſweet Syren* ; ſaid to be built by
Stern Phaleris, his Empires happy glory.
Call'd the rare Hort-yard of fair *Cyprades*,
Call'd the new field of valiant *Hercules*;
Call'd the fat ſoil of *Ceres* crown'd with corn ;
Call'd the rich Vine-yard of the God urſhorn.
No marvel ; for no *City* like to thine,
For ſweetneſs, Empire, beauty, ſtrength, corn, wine.

But that it was firſt built by the Inhabitants of *Cuma* is the moſt approved; and called *Parthenope* (a name moſt frequently given it by the Poets) of the *Syren Parthenope* ; who was here intombed under a little Hill not far from the Haven, called the Mountain, divinely honoured by the *Neapolitans* ; and whence Oracles were ſaid to be given ; demoliſhed after by an Earth-quake.

Exere ſemitutos ſubitò de pulvere vultus,
Parthenope, crinemque afflaro Monte ſepulti
Pone ſuper tumulos, & magni funus alumni.
Statius l. 5. Silv.

Parthenope, from earth thy looks half-bare
Forthwith advance, th' incloſing mountains torn ;
And on thy ſons ſad hearſe ſpread thy fore'd hair.

Now when the City began exceedingly to flouriſh, to the neglect and threatned deſolation of *Cuma*, the *Cumans* razed it to the earth ; for which being puniſhed with a plague, they were admoniſhed by an Oracle to rebuild it, and to offer ſacrifice yearly at the Tomb of the *Syren*. Of that new edification it was called *Neapolis*: but *Strabo* ſaith, of the new Inhabitants, who were *Athenians*, and others of the *Greek* Nation. This City is not only the Metropolis of *Campania*, but Queen of the *Picentines*, *Hirpines, Lucanians, Brutians, Calabrians, Salentines, Peucetians, Samnites, Veſtinians, Ferentanians*, and *Daunians*. Her Throne is anſwerable to her Dignity ; placed under a ſmiling Heaven, in a rich and flouriſhing ſoil. Bounded on the South-Eaſt ſide with a Bay of the *Tyrrhene* Sea, unacquainted with tempeſts, along which ſhe ſtretcheth ; and is back'd by Mountains ennobled for their generous Wines : whereof aſcending a part, ſhe enjoyeth the delicate proſpects of *Veſuvium, Surennum, Capre, Miſenus, Porchita*, and *Enaria*. Her beauty is inferiour unto neither. The private Buildings being graceful, and the publick ſtately ; adorned with Statues, the work of excellent Workmen ; and ſundry preſerved Antiquities.

———— Hic Gralis penitus defecta metallis
Saxa, quod Eoæ reſpergit vena Syenes,
Synade quod mœſta Phrygiæ ſudere ſecures
Per Cybeles lugentis agros, ubi marmore picto
Candida purpureo diſtinguitur area gyro.
Hic & Amyclei cæſum de monte Lycurgi
Quod viret, & molles imitatur tupibus herbas,
Hic Nomadum lucent flaventia ſaxa ; Thaſoſque,
Et Chios, & gaudens fluctuſ ſpectare Cariſtos.
Statius Silv. l. 2.

Here ſtones there are by curious Grecians wrought,
That in Syenes ſpeckled Quarries lay :
That Phrygian Tools here hew at Jad Synads
In woful Cybels fields, where purple veins
The pure white Marble beautifully ſtains.
The green, from hills cut near Amyclis Towers,
(Lycurgus ſoil) reſembling rocks and flowers.
Here Thaſian, Chian, Nomads yellow, theſe
Cariſtos mates, that joys to gaze on Seas.

As for her ſtrength, the hand of Art hath joyned with Nature to make her invincible. For, beſides the being almoſt environed with the Sea, and Mountains not to be tranſcended without much difficulty and diſadvantage ; ſhe is ſtrongly walled, and further ſtrengthened with three ſtrong Caſtles. The one, and that impregnable, ſtandeth aloft, and behind it, on the top of Mount *Hermus*, or of *Eraſmus*, (ſo called of a little Chappel there dedicated unto him.) begun by *Charles* the Second in the year 1289. and finiſhed by *Robert* his Succeſſor : where the Tower of *Bel-fort* ſtood, erected 119 years before by the *Normans*. This is a defence to the adjoyning Country ; a ſafeguard and curb to the City ; for it over-looketh it all, and hath both of Sea and Land a large ſurvey and no narrow command. *Charles* the Fifth pulling down the old, did ſtrongly rebuild it, according to the modern fortification ; cutting a way about it out of the Rock for the conveyance of Horſe-men. The Gate thereof doth preſent this Inſcription.

IMPERATORIS CAROLI V. AUG. CÆSARIS JUSSU, AC PETRI TOLEDÆ
VILLÆ FRANCHÆ MARCHIONIS JUSTISS. PRO REGIS AUPICIIS, PYR-
RHUS ALOISIUS SERINA VALENTINUS, D. JOHANNIS EQUES, CÆSA-
REUSQUE MILITUM PRO SUO BELLICIS IN REB. EXPERIMENTO,
F. CURAVIT. M. D. XXXVIII.

LIB. IV. Naples.

In the year 1587. and in the Winter feafon, it was fet on fire by Lightning; which taking hold of the powder, blew up all that was about it, and fhook the whole City: whereof much no queftion had fuffered, had it not been kept fo near the top of the Caftle. The houfe of *Don Garfia* of *Toledo*, the Governour thereof, was fhaken to the ground; whom I mention the rather, for that he was commonly called the fortunate Knight. On a time in a tempeft a wave threw him over-board, and another caft him into another Galley, and fo faved him. Then alfo the day before this accident happned, he was removed with his family, but *Philip* the Second both repaired and enlarged it. The Souldiers have goodly Orchards about it, to the increafe of their entertainment. A pleafant place, and pleafantly they live there; arriving at the extremity of old age through the excellency of the Air. Within the City, near the Sea, and aloft, there ftandeth another, called, The new Caftle, built by *Charles* Duke of *Anjou*, King of *Naples*, by the Popes donation and by conqueft, to defend the City and underlying Haven from Maritime invafions. This Caftle, *Alphonfus* the Firft having expulfed the *French-men*, greatly enlarged; fo that at this day it may ftand in comparifon with the principal Fortreffes of *Italy*; furnifhed by *Charles* the Fifth and *Philip* the Second, with all Military provifion, wherein there lieth a ftrong Garrifon. In the midft of this Caftle ftands a Royal Palace, adorned bravely both without and within; the Seat of the Viceroy. The third Caftle ftands at the South-Eaft corner of the City, upon a Rock that thrufteth like an arm into the Sea; and is joyned by the labour of man to the Continent. It was call'd *Megaris*, either of *Megara*, the Wife of *Hercules*, or of the *Megarians* which there inhabited; and *Myagra*, of the hopelefs fortunes of the imprifoned, there being from thence no hope of efcape. Called alfo the Caftle of *Lucullus*, either for that he made it firft an Ifland, or for the Fifh-ftoves by him hewn out of the Rock, and built; which yet are manifeft by their ruines. Whereof a late Traveller;

We Megaris, with Oyfters ftor'd, paft by,	Oftriferam Megarim forcitam nomen ab ove
Nam'd of an Egg; of old Lucullus joy,	Legimus, ut perhibent Luculli divitis olim
And manfion free from the Icarian fury,	Gaudia, & Icario Villam folamen ab æftu.
A cave yet extant, with a living fpring,	Extat adhuc rupes intus cava, fonfque perenni
The bearded Barbels fitly harbouring.	Dulcis aqua, ftatio barbatis commoda multis.

It is now called *Caftelo del Ovo*, in regard of the form of the Rock, built by *William* the Third, and named for a long time the Caftle of the *Normans*. Enlarged by *Charles* the Firft; repaired by the two Kings *Robert* and *Alphonfus*; and augmented, and ftrongly fortified by *Philip* the Second; teftified by this their ingraven Infcription:

PHILIPPUS II. HISPANIARUM REX
PONTEM A CONTINENTI AD LUCULLIANAS ARCES
OLIM AUSTRI FLUCTIBUS CONQUASSATUM,
NUNC SAXIS OBICIBUS RESTAURAVIT
FIRMUMQUE REDDIDIT.
D. JOANNE ZUNICA PROREGE. A. D. M. D. XCV.

To let pafs the *Arfenal* belonging to the Navy, not unfurnifhed of neceffaries, fpeak we now of the *Mole*; that from the South-winds defendeth the Haven; (yet is the whole Bay an excellent Road) a work of great charge and no fmall admiration. This ftretcheth into the Sea five hundred paces, firft, towards the South-Eaft, and then to the North-Eaft; lined on the fides, and paved under foot with great fquare ftone. In the midft whereof ftands a Marble Fountain. It was begun by *Charles* the fecond, enlarged by *Alphonfus* the Firft, but abfolutely finifhed by the Emperour *Charles* the Fifth, and *Philip* his Succeffor. The concourfe of fundry Nations to this Haven doth add an over-abundance to their native plenty; *Apulia* fends them Almonds, Oyl, Honey, Cattel, and Cheefe; *Calabria* (befides moft of the fore-named) Silk, Manna, Figs, Sugar, excellent Wines, Minerals, and matter for the building of Ships; *Sicilia* relieveth them with Corn, if at any time their own foil prove unfruitful, enriching them further-more with her fore-mentioned productions; *Africa* furnifheth them with Skins, *Spain* with Cloth and Gold; *Elba* with Steel and Iron, and we with our Countries Commodities, fo that nothing is wanting. A City dedicated from the firft foundation to delight and retirement: whereunto the *Grecians* (the Founders) were wholly addicted. Hither repaired the *Romans*, when either oppreffed with the affairs of the World, or with misfortunes, age, or infirmities; to recreate their fpirits, and poffefs a longed-for tranquillity. Whereunto *Pampinius* inviting his Wife,

I ftrive

Has ego te fedes (nam nec mihi barbara Thrace,
Nec Libye natale folum) transferre laboro,
Quas & mollis hyems, & frigida temperat æstas,
Quas imbelle fretum torpentibus alluit undis.
Pax fecura locis & defidis ocia vitæ ;
Et nunquam turbata quies, fomnique peracti,
Nulla foro rabies, aut ftrictæ jurgia legis,
Norum jura viris——

Silvar. l. 3.

*I strive, dear Sweet, (for Lybia nor wild Thrace
Gave birth to me) to draw thee to this place.
This, where warm Winters, and cool Summers rain:
Wash with calm waves of the still-quiet Main.
Here vacant Life, here Peace, here Empire keeps
Never disturbed rest, unbroken sleeps.
No noise of Courts, nor wrangling strifes of Laws,
Old usage is their rule——*

And *Virgil,*

Illo Virgilium me tempore dulcis alebat
Parthenope, studiis florentem ignobilis oti.
Georg. l. 4.

*Me Virgil sweet Parthenope then nourisht,
Who in the studies of retir'd life flourisht.*

But now the only Regal City of *Italy* ; her Royal Court is compleatly furnished with Princes and Commanders ; her Tribunals are pestered with clamorous Advocates and litigious Clients ; her streets with Citizens and Foreigners, in pursuit of their delights and profits ; whose ears are daily inured to the sound of the Drum and Fife, as their eyes to the bounding of Steeds and glistering of Armours. So that she seemeth at this day to afford you all things but her formerly vacancy. But first the receptacle of Philosophy, then of the Muses, and lastly, of the Souldiery.

Parthenope varii statuit discrimina mundi,
Quæ tria diverso tempore facta dedit.
Aurea Pythagoras communis commoda vitæ,
Et docuit Sophiæ Graecia magna procos.
Altera succedens studiorum mollior ætas,
Admisit Musas debiliore sono.
Tertia vulnifici quæsivit præmia ferri,
Atque equitum potuit sola tenere decus.
Sic ex privata & serva regia: superfum:
Roma, quod es fueram, quæ modo sum quod eras.

J. C. Scal.

*Distinguishing times changes, three of worth,
At several times Parthenope brought forth.
Pythagoras to such as wisdom soughts,
The fruits of civil life in Great Greece taught.
The next, less weighty, yet with happy wit,
The softer sounding Muses did admit.
The third devoted unto Wars pursuit,
Of honour'd Knighthood held the sole repute.
Obscure, a servant ; now I rule a Queen:
Rome, was what thou art ; and what thou hast been.*

This City was first a Common-wealth of the *Athenians* ; after a partaker of the *Roman* Priviledges ; then successively subject to the Oriental Empire. Count *Roger* the *Norman* did make it a Regal City, by joyning thereunto *Apulia* and *Sicilia* on this side the *Phare* (for so was *Calabria* then called) the first King of *Naples* : crowned in the year 1125. by *Anacletus* the Antipope ; as also of *Sicilia*, the Island whereof we have spoken before. These two Kingdoms suffering as it were one fortune, until the expulsion of the *French-men* out of the last named. But the Kingdom of *Naples* continued in a direct line in the House of *Anjou*, until *Joan* the First, the Niece unto King *Robert*, was deposed by *Urban* the Sixth, because she had defended the cause of *Clement* the Seventh : which *Urban* gave it unto *Charles* the Prince of *Durace*, descended of the Brother of the foresaid *Robert*. Possessed after by his two Children, *Ladislaus*, who was also King of *Hungaria*, (as was his Father) and another *Joan* ; but not without Wars and Rebellions. For *Joan* the First adopted *Lodowick* the Duke of *Anjou* (the second Son to the King of *France*) her Heir, by the assent of *Clement* the Seventh. And although he was slain in battel by *Charles* of *Durace*, yet *Lodowick* his Son was crowned by the said *Clement*, in vain contending, for the possession with *Ladislaus*, and Queen *Joan* the Second. But his Son *Lodowick* was called in by *Martin* the Fifth, and invested with the Royalty. Who deprived Queen *Joan*, for that she refused to aid him against *Dracehius* a Rebel to the Papacy. Whereupon the Queen adopted *Alphonsus* King of *Arragon* her Heir, provided that he should assist her against *Lodowick* her Enemy. But when he came unto *Naples*, finding all the Affairs of State to be governed by her, he attempted to commit her to Prison ; which she avoided by flight, and in revenge thereof revoked the former adoption ; adopting her former Enemy *Lodowick* in his stead. *Lodowick* dead, the Queen adopted *Renatus* his Brother, and died not long after. When *Ferdinand* the base Son of *Alphonsus*, pretending that the Kingdom was lapsed to the Church, entred *Naples* by force, and was confirmed in the Government thereof by *Eugenius*. So lost it was by the *French*, and possessed by the *Arragonians*, until after the flight of King *Frederick*, the *French* and *Spaniards* divided it between them, under the conduct of *Lewis*

Urban and this Clement were Popes at one time: but the latter was left out of the Catalogue of Popes, being held for a Schismatick. He kept his Court in Avignion.

the

the Twelfth, and *Ferdinand* firnamed the Catholick. But the *French* were foon after driven out by the *Spaniards*, who poffeffed the whole, and therein do continue to this day, not without the grudge of the other, and fecret repining of the Papacy, affirming that it belongeth to the Church, together with *Sicilia*. But they have not the will to contend with fo fait a friend, neither have they the power. Befides, who knows not that the one of them could not fo well fubfift without the other. The *Germans*, in acknowledgment of their tenure of the Papacy, gave the Pope yearly eight and forty thoufand Ducats, together with a white Horfe. The money, though remitted by *Julius* the Second unto *Ferdinand* the Catholick, yet at this day is paid together with the white Hackney. The *Spaniards* govern this Kingdom by a Viceroy; yet to be directed when occafion fhall ferve, by the Council appointed for *Italy*. The Viceroy being now Duke of *Lemos*.

The fo many innovations that have hapned to this unhappy Kingdom have proceeded partly from the over-much power and factions of the Nobility; but chiefly in that the Election of their Kings depended on the Popes, who depofed and crowned according to their fpleens and affections: whereunto the fhortnefs of their lives and often contention of the Papacy (the affifted approving, and the refifted depriving) may be added. But the *Spaniard* hath fecured his Eftate by the prevention of thefe difturbances, taking all power and greatnefs, more than titular, from the Nobility; fuppreffing the popular, and indeed the whole Country, by the foreign Souldiery garritoned amongft them, who may obey perhaps with as much love, as Galley-flaves obey thofe that have deprived them of their fortunes and liberty. The King doth keep in this Kingdom a Regiment of four thoufand *Spaniards*, befides fixteen hundred in the maritime Towns and Fortreffes. A thoufand great Horfe are inrolled, and four hundred and fifty light Horfe-men. The Battalion confifts of two hundred thoufand, five hundred threefcore and thirteen: thefe are not in pay but in time of fervice, and then raifed in part, according to occafion. For every hundred fires are charged with five Foot-men; and there are four millions, eleven thoufand four hundred fifty and four fires in this Kingdom. Thefe are named by certain in every Town deputed for the fame: but fo, that if they be not well liked by their Captains, they make choice of others in their ftead. The Captains and Officers in time of Peace have their ftanding Penfions. Their ftrength at Sea confifteth of feven and thirty Gallies. But what doth the King receive from this Kingdom more than trouble and title? For although the Revenue and Donatives: now made a Revenue) with impofitions, amount yearly to two millions, and fifty thoufand Ducats; yet defalk one million, and thirty thoufand thereof given ordinarily away in penfions and other largeffes: the reft fufficeth not by much to maintain the Garrifons, Gallies, Horfe-men, and remainder of the Souldiery.

This Country, for the better Government, is divided into thirteen Provinces, wherein are a thoufand five hundred threefcore and three Cities and Towns, (twenty of them the Seats of Archbifhops, and an hundred and feven of Bifhops) thofe along the Coafts of principal ftrength: and although it be a Peninfula, yet are there few Havens throughout, and not many fafe ftations. The Towns and Cities are fubject unto Nobles of fundry Titles, (fuch as are not, have their Captains) who as they increafe in number, decreafe in authority: for that many of them have been bought by men of bafe conditions; and many of the ancient have exhaufted their Patrimonies. Befides, no Office is alotted them, nor Command, whereby they might attain to eftimation: every Officer is countenanced againft them; all their faults lookt into; Juftice executed upon them with rigour; their Vaffals (in whofe love and obedience their Potency did formerly confift) now alienated from them, and being backt in their contentions are grown neglected of them. To conclude, they have loft their ftings; and defperate of their liberty nourifh in their breafts an hatred which they dare not exprefs, much lefs put into action, having no likelihood of foreign affiftance; all the Princes of *Italy* being either in perfect amity with the *Spaniard*, or awed by his greatnefs. As for the *French*, their memory is defervedly hateful unto them. The body of the Nobility confifts of fourteen Princes, five and twenty Dukes, thirty Marqueffes, fifty four Earls, and four thoufand Barons. For default of Heirs Male, their Principalities revert to the King, who fells them moft commonly to men of mean birth and meaner fpirits, who are hated of the honourable: whereby a defired envy and difcord is foftered amongft them. Moft of thefe do live moft part of the year in the City, where they have five Seats for their five Affemblies of *Capua*, *Nido*, *Moatana*, *Spente*, and *Laffente*.

The

202 *Naples. Labulla.* LIB. IV.

The chief Officers in the Kingdom under the Viceroy, are the high Constable, Chief Justice, Admiral, Great Chamberlain, Secretary, Mareshal, and Chancellor. The more severe that these are to the Naturals, the greater their repute with the *Spaniard*, who enrich themselves by extorting from the other, and give a pregnant proof of the many calamities which are incident unto all Kingdoms that are governed by Deputies. Nor is the King a little abused by their avarice, and that not only in the Souldiery, of whom there be fewer by an unreasonable number than are inrolled and paid for. The Taxes that are imposed upon Silks, as well wrought as unwrought, hath so inhanced the price, that the foreign Merchant neglecteth to trade; to the great impoverishment of the Citizens, whose especial Commodity doth consist, in working, and quick sale thereof. And what Rates are imposed upon Victuals and Wines, may be gathered by this, that Custom of Herbs spent yearly in *Naples* amounteth to 4000 *l.* of our money. And of Wines they have such a quantity, that 12000 Butts are every season transported out of this Kingdom.

Naples is the pleasantest of Cities, if not the most beautiful; the building all of free-stone, the streets are broad and paved with Brick, vaulted underneath for the conveyance of the sullage, and served with water by Fountains and Conduits. Her Palaces are fair; but her Temples stately, and gorgeously furnished; whereof, adding Chappels and Monasteries within her Walls and without, (for the Suburbs do equal the City in magnitude) she containeth three thousand. It is supposed that there are in her three hundred thousand men, besides women and children. Their habit is generally *Spanish*: the Gentry delight much in great Horses, whereupon they prance continually thorow the streets. The number of Carosses is incredible that are kept in this City, as of the Segges not unlike to Horse-litters, but carried by men. These wait for Fares in the corners of streets, as Water-men do at our Wharfes; where those that will not foot it in the heat, are born (if they please unseen) about the City. None do wear Weapons, without especial admittance, but the Souldiery. Their Women are beholding to Nature for much beauty, or to cunning Art, for a nott to be discerned imposture; howsoever they excel in favour, which Art can have no hand in. They are elegantly clothed; and silk is a work-day wear for the Wife of the meanest Artificer. They are not altogether so strictly guarded as in other places of *Italy*; perhaps less tempted, in regard of the number of allowed Curtizans, there being of them in the City about thirty thousand.

Before we go to *Putzole*, let us travel a little without the North-side of the City, and turn with the Land as far as *Vesuvium*. Not to speak of the admirable Orchards (though here every where so common as not to be admired) nor of the pleasant and profitable soil; we will first observe the ample Fountain of *Labulla*, there rising first, but supposed to proceed, by concealed passages, from the root of *Vesuvium*. It is called *Labulla*, in that the waters do boil as it were; and *Labiolo*, in that they throw themselves into the mouth of an Aquæduct; wherein under earth conveyed for the space of two miles, they divide asunder.

Parte alia qua perspicuo delabitur alveo
Irriguis Sebethus aquis, & gurgite leni
Prata secat, liquidísque terit sola roscida lymphis.
Gab. Alti.

Th' one way Sebethus through seen chanel glides,
And with mild streams the dewy soil divides.

Turning to the South thorow certain Marishes, and running under Saint *Magdalens* Bridge into the Sea; thereupon called *Fiume de la Magdalena*. The other part continueth her progress towards the City, called particularly *Formello*; but generally *Labulla*, as before the division. Whereof the *Neapolitan*;

Sed quò me rapis heu raucum puríssima Nympha,
Nympha Labulla, urbem fonte perenne rigans,
Illabens subiter vicatim mœnia circum,
Perque domos largo flumine, perque vias,
Atria aquis, domus omnis aquis, urbs omnis abundat
Nilis, & centum fontibus unda venit,
Præbet ubique libens, sitienti pocula lympha
Splendidior vitro, dulcior ambrosia.
Donat. Franc.

Ah whither Nymp force you faint me! *Labulla,*
Watring the Town from Springs that ne're decay.
Through houses, by high-ways, with streams profound
Under streets gliding, walls imbracing round:
Courts, dwellings, all the City serving so
With waters, that through hundred chanels flow;
With grateful cups to thirsty lips each where
Present, Ambrosia less sweet, glass less clear.

So that the whole City doth stand as it were upon Rivulets, whereby it is not only served, but purged. The former Poet thus sings of the loves of the divided streams

Care-

Care-free Sebethus (had not false love sung
His gentle breast) thus to the river sung:
Come to the Willows, to the Vines cool shade,
Come, neat Labulla, to our songs, lov'd Maid
Labulla, come. Here Garlands, sweet composures
Of Violets have I for thee in maunds of Osiers.

Cantabat vacuus curis Sebethus ad amnem,
Si vacuus fineret perfidiosus amor:
Ipsa veni ad salices, & opacæ umbracula vitis,
Ipsa veni ad nostros culta Labulla modos.
Culta Labulla veni, sunt hic tibi serra parata,
Nexa simul calathis, juncta simul violis.

The far end of this Valley is confined by *Vesuvium*, four miles removed, and East of the City; from whence the Sun is first seen to arise, as it that were his Bed-chamber. This Mountain had a double top; that towards the North doth end in a Plain: The other towards the South aspireth more high, which when hid in Clouds prognosticates Rain to the *Neapolitans*. In the top there is a large deep hollow, without danger to be descended into, in form of an Amphitheatre; in the midst a Pit which leads into the entrails of the earth, from whence the Mountain in times past did breathe forth terrible flames; the mouth whereof is almost choaked with broken Rocks and Trees that are fallen thereon. Next to this the matter thrown up is ruddy, light, and soft; more removed, black, and ponderous; the uttermost brow that declineth like the seats in a Theatre, flourishing with Trees and excellent Pasturage. The midst of the Hill is shaded with Chesnut-trees and others, bearing sundry fruits. The lower parts admirably clothed with Vines, that afford the best *Greek* Wines in the World: which hath given to the Mountain the name of *de Somma*, in regard of their excellency: affording to the owners the yearly revenue 300000 Ducats. They clarifie it with the white of Eggs, to suppress the fuming, adding Sulphur thereunto, or Salt, or Allum. So now it hath lost the name of *Vesuvium*, with the cause why it was given, which signifieth a Spark, as *Vesevus* a Conflagration. It flamed with the greatest horrour in the hill, or as some say, in the third year of the Emperour *Titus*; where, besides Beasts, Fishes, and Fowl, it destroyed two adjoyning Cities, *Herculanum* and *Pompeia*, with the people sitting in the Theatre. *Pliny* the natural Historian, then Admiral to the *Roman* Navy, was suffocated with the smoak thereof.

Then the remote Affrick suffered the dire heat
Of twofold rage, with showres of dust replete:
Scorcht Ægypt, Memphis, Nilus felt, amaz'd,
The woful tempest in Campania rais'd
Not Asia, Syria, nor the Towers that stand
In Neptunes surges, Cyprus, Crete (Joves land)
The scattered Cyclads, nor the Muses seat
Minerva's town, that vast plague scap'd. Such heat,
Such vapors break forth from full jaws: then shawra
When Earth-born, horrible Otmedon
Hot, vomits ire, beneath Vesuvium's Throne.

——— Sensit procul Africa tellus
Tunc ex pulvereis gemina incendia nimbis,
Sensit & Ægyptus, Memphisque, & Nilus atrocem
Tempestatem illam Campano è littore missam
Nec caruisse ferunt, Asiam, Syriamq; tremenda,
Peste, nec extantes Neptuni è fluctibus arces,
Cypruinque Cretamque & Cycladas ordine nullo
Per pontum sparsas; nec doctam Palladis urbem:
Tantus inexhaustis erupit faucibus ardor,
Ac vapor; Otomedon vomeret cum servidus iram
Terrigena horribilis Vesuvina mole sepultus.

Hier. Borgius.

Dion affirms in a manner as much. But *Bodin*, the Censurer of all Historians, doth deride it. Notwithstanding *Cassiodorus* writes as great matters of a later conflagration, whereupon *Theodoricus* (first King of the *Goths* in *Italy*) did remit his Tribute to the damnified *Campanians*. *Marcellinus* writes, that the ashes thereof, transported in the Air, obscured all *Europe*: and that the *Constantinopolitans* being wonderfully affrighted therewith, (insomuch that the Emperour *Leo* forsook the City) in Memorial of the same did yearly celebrate the 12. of *November*. It also burnt in the 16. year of *Constantine* the Fourth, and at such time as *Bellisarius* took *Naples*, and groaned, but ejected no cinders: and again when the *Saracens* invaded *Africa*. *Platina* writes that it flamed in the year 685. prognosticating the death of *Benedict* the Second, with ensuing Slaughters, Rapines, and Deaths of Princes. During the Papacy of two other *Benedicts*, the eighth and the ninth, it is said to have done the like. The latter, the last; which was in the year 1024. yet often since it hath been wonderfully feared. And although it hath made sundry dreadful devastations, yet the fruitful ashes thrown about doth seem to repair the fore-going losses, with a quick and marvellous fertility. At the foot of the Hill there are divers vents, out of which exceeding cold winds do continually issue, such as by Ventiducts from the vast Caves above *Padua*, they let into their rooms at their pleasure, to qualifie the heat of the Summer. *Spartacus* the Fencer, and Ring-leader of the fugitive Bond-slaves, no less a terrour unto *Rome* than *Hannibal*, did make this Mountain the seat of his War. Where besieged by *Clodius*, he he by a strange Stratagem, with bonds made of Vines, descended into the bottom of the hollow Hill, (being long before it first begun to flame) and finding out a private passage, issued suddenly upon the unsuspected *Romans*; seized on their Tents, and pursuing his Victory, over-ran all *Campania*.

A while after we went to see the Antiquities of *Puzole*, with the places adjoyn-

A. *The Grot of Pausilype.*
B. *Virgils Sepulchre.*
C. *The Lake of Agnano.*
D. *The Court of Vulcan.*
E. *The Amphitheatre.*
F. *The Pere of Puzzole.*
G. *Cicero's Academy.*
H. *Mount Gaurus.*

I. *The new Mountain.*
K. *The Lake of Lucrine.*
L. *Port Julius.*
M. *The Lake Avernus.*
N. *The Baths of Tritula.*
O. *Ruines of Diana's Temple.*
P. *A Castle built by Charles the Fifth.*
Q. *Mercato di Sabbato.*

R. *The dead Sea.*
S. *The Theatre.*
T. *Vatian Villa.*
V. *The Lake of Acherusia.*
X. *Arco felices.*
Y. *Licola.*
Z. *Mergellino.*

ing; where the wonderful Secrets of Nature are epitomized, and Art had congested together her incredible performances: whose ruines do yet affirm that Prodigality and Luxury are no new crimes, and that we do but re-do old vices. Hard without the City the way is crossed with *Pausilype*: the name doth signifie a releaser from cares; for that the Wine (wherewithall this Mountain is richly furnished) is an approved remedy for these consuming infirmities. Here *Horace*, in the person of *Teucer* exiled:

———— O fortes pejoraque passi
Mecum sæpe viri, nunc vino pellite curas:
Cras ingens iterabimus æquor.
    Horat. l. 1. Od. 7.

Stout Mates that oft with me have born a share
In harsher haps, with wine now drown your care;
To morrow will we to vast Seas repair.

and again,

Siccis omnia nam dura Deus proposuit, neque
Mordaces aliter diffugiunt follicitudines.
Quis post vina gravem militiam aut pauperiem crepet?
    Hor. 1. Od. 18.

*All things are difficult to the dry: nor can
Care otherwise be chas't from pensive man,
Who, wine-whet, of wars toils, or want complains?*

For which cause *Bacchus* was called *Liber*. But what need we, in this drinking Age, that exhortation of *Seneca*; which is, sometimes to divide an hair with the Drunkard, by the example of *Solon* and *Archesilaus*; and that the mind is now and then a little to be cherished, and set free from an over-sad sobriety? And for that cause was Wine given.

LIB. IV. *Pausilype.*

O Menelah, the gods for ever blest,   O Menelae dii vinum fecere beati,
Made wine t'expel grief from the troubled breast. Ut curas animi pellat mortalibus acres.
                                                                        H. in.

But (quoth he) rarely to be used liberally; lest thereby an evil habit be attained. This Mountain doth stretch from North-east to South-west, in form of a prostrated Pyramis; and although flat on the top, on each side steeply declining: South-eastward bordering with the Sea, and North-westward with the Country. I will not now speak of the delicate Wine which it yieldeth, neat and fragrant, of a more pleasing gust, and far less heavy than those of *Vesuvium*; nor of those Orchards both great and many, replenished with all sorts of almost to be named Fruit-trees, especially with Oranges and Lemons, which at once do delight three senses; nor how grateful the soil is (though stony) to the Tiller. The Grot of *Pausilype* (a work of wonder) doth hasten our description: which passes under the Mountain for the space of six hundred paces (some say of a Mile) affording a delightful passage to such as pass between *Naples* and *Putzole*, or that part of *Italy*, receiving so much light from the ends and tunnel in the middle (which letteth in the day from the high Mountain) as is sufficient for direction. Throughout hewn out of the living Rock, paved under foot; and being so broad that three Carts with ease may pass each by other. On the left hand, and in the midst, there is a little Chappel, where a Lamp doth continually burn before the adored Image of our Lady, who is said to safeguard that place from all out-rages; which is the easilier believed, because seldom any do there miscarry. This Vault, as the like is said to be begun by the *Cimerii*, a people that inhabited hereabout in the time of the *Trojan* wars; though placed by *Homer* beyond the *Scythian Bosphorus*; where the air is thick and dark, deprived of the Sun (there faintly shining) by the lofty bordering Mountains. Hereupon came the Proverb of *Cimmerian* darkness; where *Ovid* placeth the Palace of *Somnus*.

A Cave there is neer the Cimmerians, deep   Est prope Cimmerios longo spelunca recessu,
In hollow hill, the mansion of dull sleep;   Mons cavus, ignavi domus & penetralia somni.
Never by Phœbus seen: from earth a night   Quo nunquam radiis oriens mediusve cadensve
Thereof dim clouds ascends, and doubtful light. Phœbus adire potest; nebulæ caligine mistæ
                                                  Exhalantur humo, dubiæque crepuscula lucis.
                                                                Met. l. 11.

Those here were so called, in that they dwelt in Caves, living by theft, and not stirring abroad in the day time. They offered Sacrifice to the *Manes*, before they begun to cut these darksom habitations, and from their most retired parts gave Oracles (or rather sold them) to such as enquired. The god of dreams is therefore aptly feigned to reside amongst these dreamers, who are said to have been all put to the Sword by a certain King that was deluded by their Prophecies. The *Grecians* that inhabited this Country after them converted the *Cimmerian* Caves into Stoves, Baths, Passages, and such uses, amplified by the succeeding *Romans*, who exceeded all others in prodigious and expensive performances. Some do attribute the cutting through of this passage unto one *Bassus*, others (but falsly) to *Lucullus*, and others to *Cocceius*; but not that *Cocceius* that was Grand-father unto *Nerva*. Whereof, I know not what Poet:

Who durst with Steel the mountains womb invade? Viscera quis ferro est ausus perrumpere montis?
Who through the living rock a passage made?   Cautibus in duris quis patefecit iter?
Cocceius, truth declares, perform'd the same,   Cocceium verum est saxum montemque cavâsse;
Lucullus now surrender thy stoln fame.   Vanaque jam cessit fama, Luculle, tua.

Others there are that report that *Virgil* effected it by art magick and *Virgils* Grot it is called by many:) but whoever heard that *Virgil* was a Magician? *Seneca* tormented in this then horrid passage, doth call it a long dark dungeon: and further saith, that if it had light, the same would prove but unprofitable, by reason of the raised dust which thickned the air, and fell down again. And *Petronius*, that they used to pass through it with their bodies declining. Yet *Strabo*, that lived before either, hath written that it received light from the top, and was of that height and largeness, that two Carts might pass each by other. But the height, belike, was afterward choaked with Earth-quakes, and the passage with rubbidge. And in process of time it afforded no passage, but enforced they were to clamber over the mountain; until *Alphonsus* the first did cleanse, enlarge, and by cutting the jaws more high, did enlighten it. But *Peter* of *Toledo*, Vice-roy of this Kingdom, bestowed thereon that perfection which now it retaineth.

T   Before

Before you enter this Grot, upon the right hand aloft in the upright rock, in a Concave, there are certain small Pillars, if I forget not, sustaining an Urn; which was told me to be the Sepulchre of *Virgil*; but erroneously: For that standeth above, right over the entrace, in form of a little Oratory, which the Ivy and Myrtle do clothe with their natural Tapestry; and, which is to be wondred at, (if it grow, as they say, of it self) a Laurel thrusteth out her branches at the top of the ruined Cupulo, to honour him dead that merited it living. In the midst of the Monument stood the Urn that contained his ashes, supported by nine Pillars, whereon was ingraven this Distich:

Mantua me genuit, Calabri rapuere, tenet nunc   *Of fields, farms, fights I sung : life Mantua gave,*
Parthenope ; cecini pascua, rura, duces.   *Calabria death, Parthenope a grave.*

Seen by *Peter* of *Stephano*, (who was alive within these forty years) as himself reporteth. But one doth affirm (though contradicted by others) that the *Neapolitans* did give that Urn to the *Mantuans*, upon their importunate suit. Others, that their Regular Priests did convey it to their adjoining Covent; and from thence to have been born away by the Cardinal of *Mantua*, who dying in *Genoa* in his return there left it. But if either were true, no doubt but some memorials would have remained of so coveted a possession; especially by the *Mantuans*, who held themselves so honoured in his birth, that they stamp'd their Coin with his Figure. But rather it should seem that through time and negligence those Reliques are perished.

Quod scissus tumulus, quod fracta sit urna ; quid   *What though the Tomb be torn, th' Urn broke? the place*
inde ?   *The Poets name abundantly will grace.*
Sat celebris locus nomine vatis erit.
In antiq. manum.

He was born at *Andes*, a little Hamlet by *Mantua* : he lived 52 years, and died at *Brundusium*, the 22. of *September*, in the 1co Olympiad; having retired himself into *Calabria* to perfect his Æneads. He willed that his bones should be buried at *Naples*, where he had long lived: (which was performed by *Augustus* and *Mæcenas*, made his heirs by his Testament) even in those Groves where he had composed his Eclogs, and Georgicks. Purchased they were after by *Silvius Italicus*; who religiously celebrated his Birth-day, and frequented this Monument with a great devotion, as it had been a Temple. Nor less was it adorned by *Statius Pompinius*.

——— & genitale sequutus   *Following the fertile shore, where the fair guest*
Littus ubi Ausonio se condidit hospita portu   *Parthenope in Ausonian Port doth rest;*
Parthenope, tenues ignaro pollice chordas   *My ruder hands to strike the strings presume;*
Pulso, Maroneique sedens in margine Templi   *Sitting by Maro's Temple, I assume*
Sumo animum & magni tumulis adcanto magistri.   *Courage, and sing to my great Masters Tomb.*
l. 4. Solu.

It is fabled that the Ghost of *Virgil* hath been seen hereabout; whereof a Poet of these later times,

Anna etiam, ut fama est vatis placidissima sæpe   *True is it that this gentle Ghost hath been*
Inter adoratum cernitur umbra nemus ?   *Amongst these fragrant Groves so often seen?*
Fœlices oculi, fortunatissima sylva,   *O happy eyes, woods fortunate !*
Et quidquid sancto nascitur in nemore !   *What e're within your sacred confines grow !*
M. Am. Flam.

Having passed through the aforesaid Grot to our no small astonishment, we followed the way of *Puzzole* through a level so clothed with Fruit-Trees, and undergrowing Grain, as if it had been but one entire Orchard. After a while we turned on the right hand a little to the Lake of *Agnano*, three Miles well nigh in circuit; round, and included within high Mountains. The water thereof is sweet at the top, and salt underneath, by reason of some Mineral, so deep in the midst, that the Inhabitants say, that it hath no bottom. In the Spring of the year whole heaps of Serpents involved together do fall thereinto from the Crannies of the high Rocks, and are never more seen again. Whereupon it taketh that name, *quasi aqua Anguium*. Nothing liveth in it but Frogs; the occasion that it is so frequented by Fowl in the Summer. The Habitations hereabout are abandoned as unwholsom:

yet

LIB. IV. S. Germans Stove. Charons Cave.

yet is that inconveniency liberally recompenced by the infinite quantity of Lime that is there watered, to the not to be believed benefit of the owners; the nature of the water being such, as in eight and forty hours it prepareth it. Within the compass of the Mountains, and near to the Lake is the natural Stove of St. German.

A. *The entrance of the Gr:t of Paufilipe toward Naples.*
B. *The Castle of Mermus.*
C. *Castello Novo.*
D. *Castello dell Ovo.*
E. *The Mountain Vesuvium.*

Well call'd a Stove that water wants; mear heat
Of air insulphur'd makes the Patient sweat.
Before't a Lake, where Frogs and Snakes abound,
Which Beasts avoid, no Fish is therein found.
Who enters under this small roof, as snow
Warm'd by the Suns reflex, resolveth so.
It chears the spirits, clears the stomachs glut :
Warms water, (into any vessel put;)
Which weak Consumptions cures, the bowels heals,
And Ulcers dries that flattering skin conceals ;
Here German Capuas Prelate, thee distrest
Pascasius found, and helpt to aboads more blest.

Absque liquore domus bene sudatoria dicta ;
Nam solo patiens aëre sudat homo,
Ante domum lacus est ranis plenusque colubris,
Nec fera nec pisces inveniantur ibi.
Ingreditur si quis parvæ testudinis umbram,
More nivis tactæ corpora sola madent.
Evacuat Chymos, leve corpus reddit in ipso ;
Quovis opposita est vase tepescit aqua,
Hæc aqua languentes restaurat & illia sanat ;
Ulcera desiccat sub cute si qua latent.
Hic te Germanus Capuæ caput ædesrepertum,
Ad sacra, Pascasi, pascua te retulit.

Alcadinus.

The tale is (and St. *Gregory*, if those Dialogues be his, the teller) how St. *German*, when Bishop of *Capua*, advised by his Physicians to repair unto the Stove of the Serpents (for so was this place then called) for the cure of his infirmity, here found the soul of *Pascasius* tormented with heat; who had been an upright man, and full of piety. Whereat affrighted, and demanding the cause; he answered, that it was for taking part with *Laurentius* against *Symacus* in their contention for the Papacy; desiring him for to pray unto God for him, and if that at his return he found him not there, he might be assured that his Prayers had prevailed. Which within a few days after he found to be so; and so the place took the name of St. *German*. This stands on the South-side of the Lake. But now speak we of that mortal Cave on the East, in the foot of the bordering Mountain, and entring the same not above three fathom. The mouth of it is large enough for two to enter at once; but the roof declineth by little and little unto the uttermost point thereof. Whatsoever hath life, being thrust into the far end, doth die in an instant. Yet entred it may be a good way with safety: neither heat nor cold will oppress you, nor is there any damp or vapour to be discerned, being perspicuous to the bottom, and the sole thereof dusty. We made tryal with a Dog, which we no sooner had thrust in, but without crying, or otherwise strugling than if shot to the heart, his tongue hung out, and his eyes setled in

A *The Lake of Agnano.*   B *Charons Cave.*   C *St. Germans Stove.*

his head, to our no small amazement. Forthwith we draw him out stark dead, and to our seeming without shew of life, we threw him into the Lake; when anon he recovered, and swimming to the shore, ran crying away as fast as he could, to the not far distant *Osteria*; where they get no small part of their living by shewing this place unto Foreigners. And it is a sport to see how the Dogs thereabout will steal away, and scud to the tops of the Mountains at the approach of a Stranger. The French King *Charles* the Eighth of that name, who held the Kingdom of *Naples* for a while, made tryal thereof with an Ass, which immediately died. The like befell to a fool-hardy Souldier. *Peter* of *Toledo* caused two offenders to be thrust thereinto, and both expired in a moment. Nor found those three Gallants any better success, who tempted God with their desperate entrance; whereof *Scipio Mazella* doth report himself to be an eye-witness. This was not unknown to *Pliny*, who called it the Cave of *Charon*. The cause of so deadly an effect is said to proceed from the fervent vapours ascending by invisible pores, so thin, so dry and subtile, as not to be discerned; yet thickned by the cold that enters at the mouth of the Cave, convert into moisture, which hangs far within on the roof like to drops of Quick-Silver; and such esteemed to be by a number. *Corona Pighius*, desirous to inform himself in the mysteries thereof, ventured so far in, as to touch one of those far-off shining drops, and shewed it to his Companions, who entred also, and stayed therein about a minute of an hour; sensibly perceiving the heat to arise from their feet to their thighs, till they did sweat at the brows, without the endamaging of their senses, who return'd, to the wonder of the Guide, that thought they had preserved themselves by enchantments. By this their experiment it appears that the air is most deadly near to the pores where it first ascended; especially to such Creatures as hold their heads downward, exhaling at their nostrils the dry and excessive hot vapours. Thrust a Torch near the bottom, and it will forthwith go out; yet advanced higher, re-inflames, which approves the former assertion.

From hence we passed to the Court of *Vulcan*; aloft, and near to the ancient *Puteoli*, but distant a mile and better from the new. These Mountains were called *Leucogei* by the *Greeks*, in regard of their whiteness: and *Phlegrean* Fields, for that *Hercules* here overthrew the barbarous people, who were called *Giants* for their inhumanity and insolencies; assisted with Lightning from Heaven:

Fumat adhuc volvens vesana incendia tellus,
Et misto ardentes sulphure ructat aquas.
Portacel.

Th' Earth with imbowell'd flames, yet fuming glows;
And water with fier'd Sulphur mixt, up throws:

where

LIB. IV. The Court of Vulcan.

whereupon grew the Fable of their warring with the gods. But hear we *Petronius* describing it;

A place deep sunk in yawning cliffs, 'twixt great	Eſt locus excifo penitus emerfus hiatu,
Dicarchea and Parthenope, replete	Parthenopen inter magnæq; Dicarchidos arva,
With black Cocytus waves: for winds that ſtrain	Cocyti perfufus aqua, nam fpiritus extra
To ruſh forth there, a deadly heat contain.	Qui furit effulus functo fpargitur æſtu.
The earth fruits in Autumn bears not, nor glad field	Non hæc Autumno tellus vitem, aut alit herbas
Once puts on green, or ſprowting branches yield	Cefpite lætus ager : non verna perſona cantu;
Their vernal ſongs. But Chaos and ragg'd ſtone	Mollita difcordi ſtrepitu virgulta loquuntur,
Smircht'd with black Pumice, there rejoyce, o're grown	Sed Chaos & nigro iquallentia Pumice faxa
With mournful Cyprefs. Dis his head here raiſes,	Gaudens ferali circum-tumulata Cypreſſo.
Covered with aſhes, and with funeral blazes.	Has inter ſedes Ditis pater extulit ora
	Buſtorum flammis, & cana ſparſa favilla.
	Petr. Arbit. Satyris.

A naked level it is, in form of an oval, twelve hundred forty and ſix foot long, a thouſand broad, and environed with high-cliff Hills that fume on each ſide, and have

their ſulphurous favour tranſported by the winds to places far diſtant. You would think, and no doubt, think truly, that the hungry fire had made this Valley with continual feeding; which breaks out in a number of places. And ſtrange it ſeemeth to a ſtranger, that men dare walk up and down with ſo great a ſecurity; the earth as hot as ſufferable, being hollow underneath; where the fire and water make a horrible rumbling conjoining together, as if one were fuel to the other; here and there bubling up, as if in a Cauldron over a Furnace; and ſprowting aloft into the air, at ſuch time as the Sea is inraged in Tempeſts. In ſome place of the colour of Water which is mingled with Soot, in others as if with Lime, according to the complexion of the ſeveral Minerals. The flames do many times ſhift places, abandoning the old, and making new eruptions (the mouths of the vents environed with yellow Cinders) ariſing with ſo ſtrong a vapour, that ſtones thrown in are forthwith ejected. Yet for all theſe terrors, it is hourly trod upon both by men and horſes, and reſorted unto by the diſeaſed, in *May, June,* and *July,* who receive the fume at their mouths, ears, noſtrils, and ſuch other parts of their bodies as are ill affected, which heateth, but hurteth not; that being only ſovereign that evaporateth from Brimſtone. It molliſieth the Sinews, ſharpneth the Sight, aſſwageth the pains of the Head and Stomach, makes the barren pregnant, cures violent Feavers, Itches, Ulcers, &c. From *January* to *October* the Husbandmen hereabout do ſtir their gleab at ſuch

time

time as much smoke doth arise, and that they know that it proceedeth from Sulphur, which doth add to the soil a marvelous fertility. From hence they exact yearly three thousand pounds weight, whereof the Bishop of *Putzole* hath the tithe. Another kind of Sulphur is gotten here, not taken from the fire, but found in the earth, of especial use for the dying of hair, and familiarly experimented by women. White Salt, Armoniack is here found also, which belongeth to the aforesaid Bishop. At the foot of this Fountain that regardeth the East, are Minerals of Alom, and the best of the world; whereof, one part was given to the Hospitals of St. *Martha*, and the Annunciation; and the other belonged to a private Lord. But lest the Papacy should be thereby damnified, (for they make of Alom a principal Revenue) the Pope, on pain of his heavy curse, did prohibit the labourers. Afterward *Pius* the Fourth brought out the owner of the one half for the yearly rent of twelve thousand Ducates, and *Gregory* the Thirteenth by the payment of five and twenty thousand, extinguished that annuity; the Masters of the Hospitals having in the mean time abjured their interest in the other. In the top of the Mountain are certain little veins of a white matter like Salt, much used by Skinners; whereof a water is made, that forthwith putteth out all characters that are written in paper. The flower of Brass is here found every where, excellent and transparent, with white Nitre. This place is said by the Roman Catholicks to be disquieted with Devils; and that the fire underneath is a part of Purgatory, where departed Souls have a temporal punishment. The Friers that dwell hard by in the Monastery of St. *January* report that they often do hear fearful shrieks and groanings. They tell also a late story of a certain youth of *Apulia*, a Student in *Naples*; who desperate in his fortunes, advised with the Devil, and was perswaded by him to make him a deed of gift of himself, and to write it with his own blood; with doing whereof he should in short time recover his losses. Believing the deluder, according to appointment he came unto this place with that execrable writing: when affrighted with the multitudes of Devils that appeared unto him, he fled unto the aforesaid Monastery, and acquainted the Prior with all that had hapned. He communicated it to the Bishop (now or late living) who informed the Pope thereof; by whose command he was cast into Prison, and after condemned to the Gallies. Possible it is that this may be true; but *Damianus* the reporter of that which followeth (though a Cardinal) might have had the Whetstone, if he had not alledged his Author, who telleth of a number of hideous Birds which accustomed to arise from hence on a sudden in the evening of the Sabbath, and to be seen until the dawning of the day, stalking on the tops of the Hills, stretching out their wings, and pruning their feathers, never observed to feed, nor to be taken by the art of the Fowler; when upon the croaking of the Raven that chaced them they threw themselves into these filthy waters: said to be damned souls tormented all the week long, and suffered to refresh themselves on the Sabbath, in honour of our Saviours resurrection. This he reports from the mouth of the Arch-Bishop *Umbertus*. But if this be Hell, what a desperate end made that unhappy *German*, who not long since slipt into these Furnaces? or what had his poor Horse committed, that fell in with him, that he should be damned, at least retained in Purgatory: the matter that doth nourish these subterranean fires, is Sulphur and Bitumen. But there it is fed by the latter, where the flame doth mix with the water, which is not by water to be extinguished: approved by the composition of those *ignes admirabiles*.

From hence descending a little, we came to the ruines of a magnificent Amphitheatre, environing, in an oval, a Court an hundred threescore and twelve feet long, and fourscore and eight over, thrown down by an earth-quake not many ages since, which here happen not seldom, by the violence of inflamed and suppressed vapours. Dedicated it was to *Vulcan*, and not without cause, he seeming in these parts to have such a sovereignty. An Amphitheatre consists of two joined Theatres, and is thereof so called; containing no Stage, and consecrated commonly unto *Mars*, in that spectacles only of blood and death were there exhibited to the people, as sword-playings, combatings with wild beasts, compelling of the condemned to personate Tragedies, and acts but feigned to perform in earnest. Sword-players (who were first introduced by *Junius Brutus*, in the funeral of his Father) first begun with staves, and then with swords, to shew their arts and courages. But in latter times they entred the lists naked; their skill in defence not so much regarded or praised, as the undaunted giving or receiving of wounds, and life unfearfully parted with. The wearied or vanquished were supplyed by others; and he bare the Palm away, to whom none succeeded. Whereof *Martial*, of *Hermes*:

Hermes

LIB. IV. *The Amphitheatre.* 211

Hermes terror of his own,	Hermes turba sui tremorque ludi
Hermes whom Ælius fears alone,	Hermes quem timet Ælius, sed unum,
Hermes who Avolaus over-throws,	Hermes cui cadit Avolaus sed uni,
Hermes who conquers without blows,	Hermes vincere, nec ferire doctus:
Hermes to whom succeeded none.	Hermes suppositicius sibi ipsi.
	L. 5. Epig. 25.

When maimed, when old (sometimes for their valour) they were manumitted, and then no more to expose their persons to such hazard. *Nero*, that enemy of mankind, exposed four hundred Senators, and six hundred Knights, in those disgraceful combatings. And *Domitian*, that other Monster, produced women to under-go the like in the night.

Th'unskilful sex, not fit for broils,	Stat sexus rudis insciusque ferri,
In bloody fights too man-like toils:	Et pugnas capit improbus viriles,
You, at Tanais, would have thought,	Credas ad Tanaim, ferumque Phasin,
Or Phasis, Amazons had fought.	Thermodontiacas calere turmas.
	Stat. Silv. 6. l. 1.

And to combate with beasts; whereof that gross flatterer:

'Tis not enough that Mars whom war delights,	Belliger invictis quod Mars tibi fævit in armis,
Draws wounding steel; for Cæsar Venus fights.	Non satis est Cæsar, sævit & ipsa Venus.
The Lion slain in vast Nemean Vales,	Prostratum Nemees & vasta in valle leonem,
(Alcides noble labour) Fame retails,	Nobile & Herculeum fama canebat opus.
Peace gray Belief: since Cæsars great command,	Prisca fides taceat: nam post tua munera, Cæsar,
We see this acted by a womans band.	Hæc jam fœminea vidimus acta manu.
	Mart. Spect. Epig. 6.

Histories not only affirm that the Emperour *Commodus* did play the Gladiator, but his Statue in this fashion is yet to be seen at *Rome*, in the Palace of *Fernese*. Those that

were condemned to fight with wild beasts were produced in the mornings; the horror whereof was such, that women were prohibited to behold them: where the killers in the end were killed, and no way left to avoid destruction. A memorable accident is reported by *Seneca*, (at which himself was present) of a Lion that took knowledge of one who had been in times past his Keeper; and not only forbore him himself, but defended him from the fury of others. It should seem to be that Bond-slave *Androclus* (for the times do agree) who is mentioned by *Appian*. Some for hire,

and

The Amphitheatre. Puteoli. LIB. IV.

and some in bravery undertook to encounter with such beasts, who either perished, or made way by victory unto safety. An hundred Lions were often at once let forth into the Court of the Amphitheatre, and often beasts were set against beasts, a less savage spectacle. But O wicked delight of these barbarous Tyrants, worthy to suffer what they inflicted! who caused miserable wretches to make Histories of Fables, and put in act imaginary miseries. They being most praised of the dry-eyed beholders, that exposed themselves unto death without terrour; either by taking it from the weapon of another, or by falling on their own, as the Fable required. Nor mattered it who had the part to survive, he being but reserved for another days slaughter. And sometimes they erred in the story, to make the Catastrophe more horrid, as in that of *Orpheus*; who although said to have been cut in pieces by the *Ciconian* wives, was represented to be torn in pieces with a Bear. The matter thus described by *Martial*:

Quidquid in Orphæo Rhodope spectasse theatro
Dicitur, exhibuit, Cæsar, arena tibi
Repserunt scopuli mirandaque silva cucurrit,
Quale fuisse nemus creditur Hesperidum,
Affuit immixtum pecudum genus omne ferarum;
Et supra Vatem multa pependit avis.
Ipse sed ingrato jacuit laceratus ab Urso.
Hæc tamen ut res est facta, ita ficta alia est.

Spect. Ep. 21.

What Rhodope in Orpheus vale did see,
That, Cæsar, the sad sand presents to thee.
Rocks crept, Woods ran, to the admiring view;
Such as in fair Hesperian Orchards grew:
Beasts tame, and savage, in vast Deserts bred,
Throng thither: Birds hung o're the Poets head;
But he by an ungrateful Bear lay slain,
Yet this was done; the other they did sain.

The floor of the Amphitheatre was covered with sand, to drink up the blood that was shed thereon. *Augustus Cæsar* did redress the disorders of this in *Putzole*, committed in the confused placing of themselves; assigning particular Rooms to every degree according to their dignities. But when the *Romans* here shewed their greatest bravery, when *Nero* entertained the *Armenian Tyridates*, who from the uppermost round did wound two Bulls at one throw, to the wonder of the beholders; *Theodorick*, King of *Goths*, did utterly abolish these execrable pastimes. For what could be more inhumane, than to give the condemned life, that they might take it from each other by mutual slaughter? a shame it was to groan at the receit of a wound, to pull back their throats from the steel; or to behold their blood with other eyes than if it had been the blood of an enemy. The reliques of this is now over-grown with Bryars and Thorns, standing upon arched Concaves, yet almost intire, having several divisions, wherein, I suppose, they kept the wild beasts, and those that were to be devoured by them; from thence exhibited to the spectacle. Under the earth here are a number of Vaults, with such perplexed passages, that hardly can he get out that enters without a line or conductor; whereupon it is called the *Labyrinth*. In which are a world of Bats that hide themselves from the hated day; and will put out your lights with fluttering about if not the better guarded. Some say, that this was made to retain water for the use of the beholders; why not rather for the use aforesaid? Descending from hence by the ruines of the old *Colony*, we came unto *Putzole* (eight miles distant from *Naples*) and called formerly *Puteoli*.

That name it took, under *Hannibal*, of the many Pits there digged; or of the smell of the waters arising from Mines of Brimstone and Alom. Called it was more anciently *Dicarchia*, which signifieth a just government; being a *Greek Colony*, and built by the *Samians*, at such time as *Tarquinius Superbus* ruled in *Rome*. A Port Town, and Mart it was of the *Cumans*; amplified by the *Roman* Emperors in such sort, as called Little *Rome*, by *Cicero*. Whose Walls, Havens, Temples, Academy, Theatre, Baths, Statues, &c. (some of them yet shewing their foundations) sufficiently declare the *Roman* magnificency; possessing a part of the Mountain as well as the Shore, and supposed to contain four miles in circumference. *Neptune* was of this City the Patron: the ruines of whole Temple are yet to be seen, hard behind the Duke of *Toledo*'s Orchard, where we refreshed our selves during the heat of the day. A place of surpassing delight, in which are many excellent Statues, recovered from the decays of antiquity, and every where Fountains of fresh water, adorned with Nymphs and Satyrs: where the artificial Rocks, Shells, Moss, and Tophas, seem to excel even that which they imitate. This was made by the afore-mentioned *Peter* of *Toledo*, at such time as *Putzole* was abandoned by the Inhabitants, by reason of fearful Earth-quakes, and the horrible conflagrations of the New Mountain; building on the other side of the way, a fair Palace, thereby to animate

LIB. IV.   *Putcoli.*   213

made the people to return. For over the entrance stands this ingraven Inscription:

PETRUS TOLETUS MARCHIO VILLÆ FRANCHÆ, CAROL. IV. IMP. IN REGNO NEAP. VICARIUS. UT PUTEOLANOS OB REGENTEM ACRI CONFLAGRATIONEM PALANTES, AD PRISTINAS SEDES REVOCARET. HORTOS, PORTUS ET PONTES MARMOREOS, EX SPOLIIS QUÆ GARSA FILIUS, PARTA VICTORIA AFRICANA REPORTAVERAT, OTIO GENIOQUE DICAVIT: AC ANTIQUORUM RESTAURATO PURGATOQUE DUCTU, AQUAS SITIENTIBUS CIVIBUS SUA IMPENSA RESTITUIT. AN. A PARTU VIRG. M. D. XL.

the *Neapolitans* following his example. So that now the Town is well stored with Buildings; seated for the most part on a little Promontory that stretcheth into the Bay. In the midst whereof is a fair Temple of Marble, of *Corinthian* structure; having withstood the waste of time, the fury of the Foe, (which to this City hath been often fatal) and injury of Earth-quakes. The stones are so artificially laid, that you would think it consisted but of one. It was built by *Lucius Calphurnius*, and dedicated to *Augustus*, as appeareth by these extant characters:

        L. CALPHURNIUS. L. F. TEMPLUM
        AUGUSTO, CUM ORNAMENTIS, D. D.

the name of the Architector adjoined:

        L. COCCIEUS. L.
        C. POSTUM I. L.
        AUCTUS. ARCHITECTUS.

But now re-dedicated to St. *Proculus*. The Giants bones here shewn unto Foreigners, must not be unspoken of; confirming what hath been formerly spoken.

Learn thou, whom Giants bones astonish, why	Huc quicunque venis stupefactus ad ossa Gigantum?
They in Hetruscan soyl interred lye.	Disce cur Hetrusco sint tumulata solo.
Then when Alcides did Iberians foil,	Tempore quo domitis jam Victor agebat Iberis
And brought from thence their Oxen, a brave spoil,	Alcides, captum longa per arva pecus,
He from Dicharchean Hills, with club and bow,	Colle Dicarchææ clavaque arcuque Typhones
The wicked Typhons chas't, Gods, and mans foe.	Expulsit; & cessat noxia turba Deo.
To Hydruntum part, to Thuscan fled the rest,	Hydruntum petiit pars, & pars altera Thuscos:
The conquered terrour was in both suppresst.	Interiit victus terror utroque loco.
Their huge corps good Posterity kept here,	Hinc bona Posteritas immania corpora servat,
To witness to the world that once such were.	Et tales mundo testificatur avos.
	Pomp. Latus.

At the foot of the Hill whereon the City is mounted, the ruined Peer doth present a remarkable object; which extending towards the West made heretofore a safe and excellent Haven. Arched like a Bridge, that the flowing in of the Sea might preserve the profundity thereof from being choked with rubbidge and earth born down with the fall of Torrents. The work it was of the *Grecians*; much assisted in the building by the admirable nature of the sand hereabout, by reason of the under-burning fire, and perhaps partaking of the bituminous matter; becoming as hard and durable as the solid Rock, when mixed with lime, and placed under the water.

Dicarchean dust transported, solid grows	———— Dicharchææ translatus pulvis arenæ,
In water plac'd: whose hardned mass contains	Intratis solidatur aquis! durataque massa
Huge Structures seated on the liquid plains,	Sustinet advectos peregrino in gurgite campos.
	Sidon. pollin.

As yet is here every where to be seen, by the huge Foundations demolished above, and entire underneath; encouraging men thereby to build so far into the Sea, as they anciently did round about this Bay. The Emperour *Constantine* is said to have transported certain Ship-ladings of this Sand unto *Constantinople*. The body of this

                                                                                         mass

mass consisteth of Brick, but was covered heretofore with Marble, which afforded a delightful walk on the top. What should I speak of the Emperours that repaired it, (whose names are yet retained in stone) or of the Arch erected thereon, since the whole is utterly defaced? Yet rather by Earthquakes, than the violence of the Sea; whereof thirteen great Piles now only remain, which appear like so many square Towers in the water; the Arches thrown down that conjoined them. To this *Caligula* joined his Bridge (a prodigal, and not to be exemplified vanity) which stretched over the Bay unto *Baiæ*, three Miles and a half distant: sustained by Ships (drawn hither from all parts of his Empire) placed in two ranks, made stable with innumerable Anchors, and crossed with a broad High-way of earth. Which he did, as it is said, in imitation of *Xerxes*, who built the like over the less broad *Hellespont*: others say, that it was to terrifie the *Germans* and *Britans*, by the performance of such wonders; with whom he was to begin a War. But indeed he was incited thereunto to fulfil the prediction of *Thrasyllus* the great Astrologer, who told *Tiberius*, inquiring who should be his Successor, and desiring to confer the Empire upon his own Nephew, that *Caligula* was no more likely to be Emperour, than to ride on Horseback over the Bay of *Baiæ*. Upon this Bridge *Caligula* passed to and fro, for two days together; having before sacrificed to *Neptune* and *Envy*. The first day gallantly mounted, wearing an Oaken Garland upon his head, and a Cloak of Gold on his shoulders; the next, in the Habit of a Charioter, drawn by two Steeds of a famous breed; carrying before him *Darius*, a noble Youth, that was left in Hostage by the *Parthians*, attended upon by the *Prætorian* Souldiers, and followed by his principal Favourites and Friends in Waggons of the *British* fashion. When calling many from the shore, he caused them all to be tumbled from the Bridge for his cruel pastime; and those to be beat off with Oars and Staves that endeavoured their own safety. Such were the monstrous follies, and barbarous delights of this Monster. Much more we might write of *Putzole*: but we pursue our first intention, which is only to note what is principally note-worthy. We will therefore depart with this salutation:

Salve urbs deliciæ, quondam curisque levamen,
Grataque Romulidis post sera bella quies.
Stant ubi nunc etiam mirabilis Amphitheatri
Saxa, columnæ, arcus, diruta templa, viæ,
Impositæ pelago moles testantur honores:
Et tua quæ fuerit gloria, quale decus:
    Fran. Vivini.

Hail erst delightful City; cares release,
To Romans (fierce war past) a Port of peace.
Amphitheatre, Temples now laid low,
Ways, Arches, Columns, yet their ruines show.
Huge Piles fixt in the soyling seas declare
Thy old renown, how glorious once and fair.

Taking here a Felucco we rowed along the bottom of the Bay; first passing by *Cicero's* Villa, even at this day so called, where yet do remain the ruines of his Academy, erected in imitation of that at *Athens* (the pleasure whereof he commendeth in his Writings;) which he adorned with a School, a Grove, an open Walk, a Gallery, and a Library. After his proscription and death, this Villa became the possession of *Antistius Vetus* a follower of *Cæsars*: where *Tyro*, *Cicero's* Free-man, lived till he was an hundred years old, and in three Books composed the life of his Patron. Now long after his death divers Fountains of hot water sprung out of the earth, held Soveraign for the eye-sight; celebrated by *Tullius Laura*, (so called for his excellency in poesie) another of his Free-men, in this Epigram.

Quo tua Romanæ vindex clarissima linguæ,
Silva loco melius surgere justa viret?
Atque Academiæ celebratam nomine Villam,
Nunc reparat cultu sub meliore Vetus:
Hic etiam apparent Lymphæ, non ante repertæ,
Sanguida quæ infuso lumine rore levant;
Ni mirum locus ipse sui Ciceronis honori
Hoc cedit hæc fontes rum patefecit ope:
Ut quoniam totum legitur sine fine per orbem,
Sint plures oculis quæ medeantur aquæ.

Of Roman speech thou fam'd Restorer, where
Could thy Groves, bid to grow, thrive so as here!
Thy Villa nam'd an Academie, doth boast
By *Vetus* now repair'd with greater cost:
Here also springs, unfound before, arise:
Whose dropt-in water comforts feeble eyes.
No marvel though this place doth thus produce,
For *Tullies* sake, streams of such soveraign use;
That being thorow the whole world read, they might
More waters yield to cure decaying sight.

Here the Emperour *Adrian* was buried; *Antonius* erecting a Temple in the place of his Sepulchre. The ruines do shew that the Buildings were ample: amongst the rest, the foundation of that (as supposed) Academy is yet to be seen, in form
of

of a Cirque, three hundred and seventy foot long, and so called. Now all is overgrown with Briars; and Sheep and Goats are pastured where the Muses had once their habitation. It was seated close to the water; insomuch as *Cicero* accustomed to feed the Fishes out of his Windows, and to take them for his pleasure with an Angle. But now the Sea hath forsaken it, forced by Earth-quakes to retire, and content it self with more narrow bounders; having in times past possessed the present possessions of the Dukes of *Toledo*, whereof a part interposeth it and the Villa. The foresaid Fountains, called *Cicero's* Baths, are to be seen in a Grot at the foot of a Rock, of a marvellous nature and virtue. For they ebb and flow, according to the quality of the Sea, filling with fuming waters the place of their receptacle. Which when overswelling a part thereof proceeds to the Sea, and another part retires to their Fountains. They assswage the pains of the bowels, and aches of the body, but are good especially for the eyes; declaring thereby that they participate of Copperas.

West of this stands the eminent *Gaurus*; a stony and desolate Mountain. In which there are divers obscure Caverns, choaked almost with earth, where many have consumed much fruitless industry in the searching for treasure. Hither come such from sundry parts as boast themselves to be skilful in Magick; but have returned with no other profit, than to know the vanity of that knowledge. The common people, bewitched with the like perswasions, to digg and delve with undefatigable toil; and oft do meet, instead of hoped for Gold, with the reward of their avarice, buried in mines, or drowned by Springs, or stenched with vapour; so they practise the like also about *Forum Vulcani*. Here they dream of certain Rings of Gold, shining richly with Carbuncles, and they have been seen, but are guarded by Spirits and Goblins. Many are animated by the story of *Collenucius*, who writes, that *Robert Norman* did dig up much treasure hereabout, by the labour of the captivated *Saracens*. But, which is more to be laught at, the seeming wise, religious, and learned, do travel in that quest.

Proceeding, we rowed over the yet remaining foundations of ample Buildings; a part of them the ruines of Port *Julius*:

Or name the Port, the bars to Lucrine set	*An memorem portus, Lucrinoque addita clauſtra,*
And angry Sea that with loud tumults fret :	*Atque indignatum magnis ſtridoribus æquor,*
Where Julian waves resound their fore't recess,	*Julia qua ponto longe ſonat unda refuſo,*
And Tyrrhene floods into Avernus press :	*Tyrrhenuſque fretis immittitur æſtus Avernis.*
	Virg. Geor. l. 2.

built by *Julius Cæsar* (and therefore so named) at the Senates appointment: For that those who hired the fishing of that Lake adjoining, were damnified much by the violent breaking in of the Seas; whereof a part he excluded by these crooked moles, and left a narrow space for the Fishes to enter. Thus *Servius*; But *Suetonius* doth give the honour thereof to *Augustus*; effected by the labour of twenty thousand manumitted Servants; who gave it that name, of the name of the Family whereof he was descended by the Mother.

Here landed we: And here once was the famous Lake of *Lucrinus*; separated then from the Sea by a Bank of eight furlongs long, and so broad as afforded convenient way for a Chariot. The labour, as supposed, of *Hercules*.

Herculean way commends, in surges rear'd,	——— *Medioque in gurgite ponti*
When Amphitrides drove th' Iberian herd,	*Herculeum commendat iter, quâ diſſilit æquor*
And thronging Seas repulst.	*Amphitryoniades armenti victor Iberi.*
	Sil. Ital. 12.

But when so broken down, as hardly affording a passage, it was repaired by *Agrippa*. So *Strabo* reporteth, but makes no mention of the aforesaid Port *Julius*.

He tells how Lucrine was Cocytus nam'd:	*Aſt hic Lucrino manſiſſe vocabula quondam*
	Cocyri memorat ——— *Idem.*

Lucrinus it seems to have been called of the gain that was made by the Fishes therein taken. But the Oysters hereof had the principal reputation; whereof *Martial*,

Old wench, than Swans more sweet to me by far,	*Puella ſenior, dulcior mihi cygnis,*
More soft than Phalentine Galesus lamb.	*Agna Galeſi mollior Phalentini,*
More delicate than Lucrine Oysters are.	*Concha Lucrini delicatior ſtagni.*
	l. 5. Ep. 38.

Perhaps

Perhaps he therefore giveth to the Lake the name of Lascivious:

Dum nos blanda tenent lascivi stagna Lucrini,
Et qua pumiceis fontibus antra calent.
l. Epigr. 13.

*We haunt lascivious Lucrines pleasant Lake,
And Caves, which heat from Pumice Fountains take.*

if not for being frequented by Women in their evening solaces. But believe who that will, the story of the Dolphine frequenting this Lake, reported by *Pliny* upon the testimony of *Mecænas*, *Flavianus*, and *Flavius Alsius*, who inserted it in their Chronicles, said to have hapned not long before this time, in the Reign of *Augustus*. This Dolphin, they say, was enamoured on a Boy, a poor mans Son of *Baiæ*, who went to School daily to *Puteoli*. He about Noon accustomed to repair unto the water side, and to call upon the Dolphine by the name of *Simo*, and feeding him with bread, so allured him unto him, that in a short time he could no sooner call *Simo*, but the Dolphin would approach, and offer his back to be ascended, clapping close his sharp back-fins, and so conveyed him to *Puteoli*, and back again. *Appian* doth witness as much, and *Solinus*: that it became so ordinary a spectacle, that no body admired it. But it was more strange; the Boy being dead, and the Dolphin keeping his accustomed haunts, and still missing of him, pined away with sorrow, and was found dead on the shore, whom they laid in his Sepulchre. *Pausanias* doth report himself to have been an eye-witness almost of the like. And *Pliny* speaks of another about *Hippo*, when *Flavianus* was Proconsul of *Africa*, that would play with such as bathed in the Sea, suffering himself to be handled, and got up upon. But the hard measure that the Townsmen received from those that came to behold that spectacle caused them to kill him. *Jassus*, one City, doth afford two examples of their love unto Boys. The one casting himself on shore after him whom he loved, and so died, (*Alexander* the Great making the Boy Priest unto *Neptune*, supposing him to be affected of the Sea-god.) The other having often carried a Boy called *Hermias*, and on a time overtaken with a Tempest, insomuch as the Boy perished; the Dolphin brought the dead body to land; and would never again retire to Sea, but thrusting ashore there died for company. If these be true, why may we not credit the story of *Arion* the Musician (for Dolphins are said to be singularly delighted with Musick) related by *Herodotus* and others? But because I think it a Fable, I will rather chuse the report of a Poet, who when environed with Swords by the treacherous Mariners:

———Mortem non deprecor, inquit,
Sed liceat sumpta pauca referre lyra.
Dant veniam ridentq; moranti, capit ille coronam.
Quæ possit crines, Phœbe, decere tuos.
Induit & Tyrio distinctam muricæ pallam:
Reddidit icta suos pollice chorda sonos,
Flebilibus numeris veluti canentia dura,
Traiectus penna tempora cantat olor.
Protinus in medias ornatus dissilit undas,
Spargitur impulsa cærula puppis aqua.
Inde (fide majus) tergo delphina recurvo
Se memorant oneri supposuisse novo,
Ille sedet Citharamq; tenet, pretiumq; vehendi
Cantat, & æquoreas carmine mulcet aquas.
Ovid Fast l.2.

———Not life (quoth he) crave I:
But leave to touch my Harp before I dye.
They give consent, and laugh at his delay,
A Crown that might become the King of day
He puts on, and a fair Robe rarely wrought
With Tyrian Purple. The strings speak his thought;
He (like a dying Swan shot through by some
Hard heart) sings his own Epicedium.
And then cloth'd as he was, he leaps into .
The more safe Sea; whose blue brine upward flow.
When (past belief) a Dolphin sets him on
His crooked back; a burden erst unknown.
There set, he harps and sings; with that price pays
For Portage; and rude Seas calms with his lays.

Theophrastus also doth mention their loves unto men; and that they abhor not our company, experience doth teach us; who seem as it were to attend on Ships, and converse with the Sailers. This famous Lake extended formerly to *Avernus*, and so unto the aforesaid *Gaurus*, but is now no other than a little sedgy plash, choaked up by the horrible and astonishing eruption of the new Mountain; whereon as oft as I think, I am easie to credit whatsoever is wonderful.

For who here knows not, or who elsewhere will believe, that a Mountain should arise (partly out of the Lake, and partly out of the Sea) in one day and a night, unto such an height, as to contend in altitude with the high Mountains adjoining, in the year of our Lord 1538. and on the nine and twentieth of *September*; when for certain days foregoing the Country hereabout was so vexed with perpetual Earth-quakes, as no one house was left so entire, as not to expect an immediate

The New Mountain.

diate ruine; after that the Sea had retired two hundred paces from the shore (leaving abundance of fish, and Springs of fresh water rising in the bottom) this Mountain visibly ascended about the second hour of the night, with an hideous roaring, horribly vomiting stones, and such store of Cinders as over-whelmed all the Buildings hereabout, and the salubrious Baths of *Tripergula* for so many Ages celebrated; consumed the Vines to ashes, killing Birds and Beasts; the fearful Inhabitants of *Putzole* flying through the dark with their Wives and Children; naked, defiled, crying out, and detesting their Calamities. Manifold mischiefs have they suffered by the barbarous; yet none like this which Nature inflicted. But hear we it described by *Borgius*.

What gloomy fumes days glorious eye obscure!	Quis fumus turpat niger ora nitentia Solis!
The pitchy Lake effus'd through sulphury Caves,	Sulphureis tenebrosa palus effusa cavernis
Higher than Ætna's fire throws flaming waves:	Fluctuat Ætnæis eructans altius ignes.
Hath Phlegeton broke into Avernus with groans	Nunquid Avernales Phlegeton prorupit in undas, Terribiles fluctus, & saxa sonantia torquens?
Whirling the horrid floods, and rumbling stones?	Baianæ reboant undæ, simul agmen aquarum
The Baian waves resound: fresh streams ascend,	Dulce fluit celeri fugiens contraria cursu.
And several ways their speedy currents bend.	Excidit è tremula Miseni buccina dextra,
Misenus lets his Trumpet fall, scarce heard,	Rauca sonant, metuit rursus Prochyta ægra ruinâs,
Sick Prochyta a second ruine fear'd.	Ernea visceribus fumantis murmura terræ
Loud roarings from earths smoaking womb arise,	Terrificis complent piceas mugitibus auras,
And fill with fearful groans the darkned skies.	Tristis ab occasu facies, & torva minatur:
A sad sour face doth menace from the West;	Unde lues Latias infecit tetrior urbes,
Whence sharper plagues the Latian Towns infest.	Tum quæ saxa furens ingentia sæpe sub altum
Then furious winds to skies huge stones eject,	Spiritus emittit cœlum, ceu Circinus, orbem
Which like a compass turn'd about, erect	Amphitheatraleos struxere ad multa repente
A round Amphitheatre, floods of stone	Millia saxosus revomente voragine fluctus.
From belching gulf in millions straight forth thrown.	

Nor can what they then suffered be ever forgotten, having such a testimony still in view as is this strange Mountain; advancing his top a mile above his basis. The stones hereof are so light and pory, that they will not sink when thrown into the water. The cause of this accident is ascribed unto the neighbourhood of the Sea, and hollowness of the soil, whereby easily ingendred exhalations, being hurried about with a most violent motion, do inflame that dry and bituminous matter; casting it upward, and making way for their fiery expirations. To those also is the retiring of the Sea to be attributed, which strugling to break forth, doth rarifie, and so raise the earth, which thereby also as it were made thirsty sucks the water through crannies into her spongy, and hot entrails; increasing the vapours, not decreasing the fire by reason of the bitumen. Perhaps *Delos* and *Rhodes*, unseen in the first Ages, were made apparent by such means: howsoever, divers of the *Æolides* were without peradventure; all of them having flamed, and being now more in number than observed by the Ancients. This new Mountain, when newly raised, had a number of issues, at some of them smoaking, and sometimes flaming; at others disgorging Rivulets of hot waters, keeping within a terrible rumblings; and many miserably perished that ventured to descend into the hollowness above. But that hollow on the top is at this present an Orchard; and the Mountain throughout is bereft of his terrours.

Leaving this Mountain on the right hand, and turning about the brow of a Hill that lay on the left, we came to the Lake *Avernus*.

O're which no fowl unstruck with hasty death	Quam super haud ullæ poterant impune volantes,
Can stretch her strengthless wings; so dire a breth	Tendere iter pennis, talis sese halitus atris
Mounts high heaven from black jaws. The Greeks the same	Faucibus effundens supera ad convexa ferebat,
Avernus call; express'd in the name.	Unde locum Graii dixerunt nomine Avernum.
	Virg. Æn. l. 6.

circular in form, and environed with Mountains, save there where it seems to have joined with the Lake of *Lucrinus*; shadowed heretofore with over-grown woods, a main occasion of those pestilent vapours. For they being cut down by *Agrippa*, the place became frequently inhabited on every side; and proved both healthful, and delightful. This was supposed the entrance into Hell by ignorant Antiquity: where they offered infernal Sacrifice to *Pluto*, and the *Manes*, here said to give answers.

V   For

A. *The Lake Avernus.*   B. *The Cave, called vulgarly Sibyls.*   C. *The ruines of Apollo's Temple.*

For which purpose *Homer* brought hither his *Ulysses*, and *Virgil* his *Æneas*:

Quatuor hic primum nigrantes terga juvencos
Constituit, frontique infergit vina sacerdos.
Et summa carpens media inter cornua setas,
Ignibus imponit sacris libamina, prima
Voce vocant Hecaten, cœloqsEreboq,potentem.
Supponunt alii cultros, tepidumque cruorem
Suscipiunt pateris: ipse atri velleris agnam
Æneas matri Eumenidum magnæque sorori
Ense ferit, sterilemque tibi Proserpina vaccam:
Tum Stygio Regi nocturnas inchoat aras,
Et solida imponit taurorum viscera flammis,
Pingue superq; oleum fundens ardentibus extis:
Ecce autem primi, sub lumina solis & ortus,
Sub pedibus mugire solum, & juga cœpta moveri
Sylvarum, visæque canes ululare per umbram
Adventante Dea ——

Æn. l. 6.

Four black-back'd steers he ordains: on their curl'd skulls
The Priest sheds wine from turn'd-up cups; then pulls
Hair from between their large horns, and the same
Gave (a prime offering) to the sacred flame:
Invoking Hecate, great Heaven and Hell:
Others warm streams receive in bowls that fell
From wounds: A black fleec'd Lamb Æneas to
The Furies Mother and her Sisters slew:
A barren Cow, Proserpina, to thee;
To Stygian King night Altars then rears he:
Whole steers laid on, which hungry fire devours;
And fat oyl on the burning entrails pours.
When lo, about the prime of day the ground
Groan'd under foot, hills quak'd with all trees crown'd;
And dogs howl'd in sad shades at the approach
Of the pale Goddess ——

And feigned they were to have descended into Hell at this place; for that here those Caves were by which the infernal spirits, by the power of magick evoked, were imagined to ascend. As the Devil deluded those times, so do divers these, who affirm that Christ from hence made his triumphant Resurrection. Whereof *Eustatius*, speaking of the Baths of *Tripergula*:

Est locus Australis quo portam Christus Averni
Fregit, & eduxit mortuos inde suos.
Hac domus est triplex, hic jure Tripergula dicta.

Southward a place there is, where Christ our head
Broke ope Avernus gate, thence brought his dead;
Th' house triple-form'd, Tripergula well call'd.

And another,

There

LIB. IV.   *Avernus.*

There Chrift Avernus fad Gates broke in two,   Eſt locus effregit quo portas Chriſtus Averni,
And Holy Fathers thence victorious drew;   Et ſanctos traxit lucidus inde patres.
                                                  Alcadinus.

leading them to the top of an high adjoining Mountain, which at this day beareth his name. A tale, as it ſhould ſeem, not only credited by the vulgar. Here *Hannibal* did alſo ſacrifice to the Infernals, as is recorded by *Livy.* *Cicero* avoucheth this out of an old Poet,

Hard by, Avernus Lake, in ſhades obſcure,   Inde in vicina noſtra Averni lacus,
Where Ghoſts are rais'd at th'ever-open door   Unde animæ excitantur obſcura umbra, aperto oſtio
Of Acharon profound———   Alti Acherontis———

whereby it ſhould ſeem, that *Acheron* alſo was the name of *Avernus,* becauſe *Acheruſia,* a Lake near *Cuma,* did flow hereinto thorow concealed paſſages. *Avernus* was alſo once called *Styx,* according to *Silius,*

He ſhews Avernus, now for pleaſant fam'd   Ille olim populis dictum Styga nomine verſo,
The Stygian Lake in former ages nam'd.   Stagna inter celebrem nunc initia monſtrat Avernum.
Then dreadful in rough Woods, and Caves obſcure,   Tum triſte nemore, atque umbris nigrantibus horrens
Air tainting (bane to Birds) with breath impure.   Et formidatur volucri, lethale vomebat
And ſacred throughout every Stygian Town,   Suffuſo virus cœlo, Stygiaſque per urbes,
In their Religion bare a dire renown,   Religione ſacer ſævum retinebat honorem.

The obſcurity of the place perhaps did authorize that conjecture, that the *Cimmerians* here inhabited, of whom we have formerly ſpoken. The water of the Lake looketh black; ſo thought heretofore to have done, by reaſon of the unmeaſurable profundity. But later times have found out a bottom, and that it exceedeth not two hundred fifty and three fathoms. No leaf, nor whatſoever falleth thereon, is forthwith ever after to be ſeen. The water is not to be drunk of, in regard of the ill ſmelling, and unwholſom Minerals whereof it participates. Former ages did abſtain from the uſe thereof, for that defiled with humane blood, here wickedly ſhed in their devilliſh ſacrifices: and that *Styx* was ſuppoſed to flow from thence. Fiſh it produceth but thoſe ſmall and black; not ſerving for ſuſtenance, and therefore not fiſh'd for. In the days of King *Robert* an incredible number lay dead on the ſhore, ſtinking in ſuch ſort as no ravenous creature would taſte of them; proceeding, as was thought, by the veins of Brimſtone, that then violently burſt thereinto, and infected the waters. The Sea was accuſtomed, when urged with ſtorms, to flow in thorow the Lake of *Lucrinus,* driving Fiſhes in with it; but now not only that paſſage, but a part of *Avernus* it ſelf is choked by the new Mountain. When the Woods about it were cut down by *Agrippa,* an Image was found (ſuppoſed to be the Image of *Calipſis*) that ſweat as if endued with life. And no marvel though the Devil were troubled with the diſſolution of ſuch impious cuſtoms: though the name were ſuited to the nature, yet the Lake retaineth the one, having changed the other; for Fowl do now ordinarily frequent it.

On the North-weſt ſide are the ruins of a goodly building; ſome imagine it to have been the Temple of *Pluto,* others of *Apollo,* but the more induſtrious in Antiquities, that it was only a *Bannia*; perhaps conjectured by the Fountains of hot water adjoining, called by the Country people the Bath of *Seaſſubudello*; of ſovereign virtue for ſundry diſeaſes. On the other ſide of the Lake opens as to the admired Grot, with a ruined Frontiſpiece, but affording a large and high-roofed paſſage into the Mountain, cut out of the firm Rock, and now cleanſed of the rubbidge that poſſeſſed it, againſt the late repair hither of the Vice-roy. We entred with Torches: The far end doth ſhew that here in times paſt it ended not; but, more than by conjecture, to have extended unto *Baiæ.* And divers ſay, that it was here rammed up, for that many greedy people, in hope to find treaſure, adventured too far in, and were ſuffocated with vapours, not noyſom thereunto when curiouſly kept by the *Romans.* After we had gone an hundred and fifty yards forward, turning on the right hand we paſt thorow a narrow Entry which led into a Room about fourteen foot long, eight broad, and thirteen high; giving yet aſſurance that it had been richly guilded, and adorned with Azure, and Moſaick workmanſhip. At the upper end there is a little bench cut out of the Rock, in form of a
                                            V 2   bed;

bed; whereon our guide would needs make us believe that *Sibyl* lay, and from hence gave her Oracles, or purpose to save a labour in conducting us to *Cuma*. Yet is this generally mis-called the Grot of *Sibyl*, for what habitation could a place so dark and sultry have afforded? Within this Room a low square Door gives passage to another, wherein there is water; a witness that it was a bath, and made for that purpose; confirmed by another on the other side, which for brevity I pass over.

Before we depart from *Avernus*, fit it is that we speak of the audacious project of *Nero*, who attempted to have made a Navigable Foss between this and the *Ostia*, an hundred and threescore miles long, and of that breadth that two great Gallies might pass by each other, along the craggy Shore, and thorow opposite Mountains (a tract destitute of waters, save only in the Marishes of *Pompina*) to sail by the Sea, and not in the Sea. A work of intolerable labour. But he that desired to effect incredible things commanded that no Malefactor should suffer, but that all the Prisoners throughout the whole Empire should be conveyed hither, and imployed herein. *Severus* and *Celeris* were the over-seers of the work, and the contrivers, men of wit and impudency to attempt by Art what Nature had prohibited. They began to dig thorow the adjoining Mountains, which yet retain the impression. A lasting Monument of over-weening hopes, and frantick prodigality; the Inhabitants at this day do call it *Licola*.

But now we will lead you to the ruines of *Cuma*, that was the most ancient City of *Italy*, built by the *Grecians* of *Chaleis*, a City of *Eubœa*; who seeking an habitation planted themselves in *Ænaria*, an Island hard by, and after removed to this place, being then un-inhabited. The Generals. *Hipocles*, *Cumeus*, and *Megasthenis* of *Chalcis*, agreeing between themselves, that the one should have it, and the other should name it. So the *Chalcians* built, and possessed it, but named it *Cuma*. Others say, that it was so named of the waves of the Sea, or of repose (for the name doth signifie the same) then having ended their long navigations, or rather of a woman being great with child, whom they there found sleeping, which they took as a lucky sign of succeeding fecundity, approved by the sequel. For in process of time they sent forth divers Colonies, the Erectors and Lords of *Puteoli*, *Paliopolis*, and *Naples*; and were Sovereigns of the adjoining *Campania*, governing their flourishing Commonwealth with the wise and honest *Pythagorean* discipline. Hither *Virgil* bringeth his *Æneas*,

Et tandem Euboicis Cumarum allabitur oris. *Æn. l. 6.*	*Who toucht at length Eubæan Cuman shore*

which shewed it to have been e're the Wars of *Troy*, if his testimony be of credit. Before the Kings were expulsed *Rome*, it was governed by Tyrants, (not so called for their cruelty and oppression, as they are at this day, but for their absolute authority) of whom *Aristodemus* was not the least famous, and in the end the most infamous. Afterwards they were oppressed by the *Campanians*, but the *Romans* in the end both subjugated them, and their oppressors. And as the rest of *Campania* grew populous, and greatly affected through the *Roman* luxury, so *Cuma* decreased both in people and repute, becoming a place of retirement for men of mean and obscure condition, whereof *Juvenal*, upon the departure from *Rome* of his poor friend *Vmbritius*:

Quamvis digressu veteris confusus amici, Laudo tamen vacuis quod sedem figere cumis Destinet, atque unum civem donare Sibyllæ; Janua Baiarum est, & gratum littus amœni Secessus. *Sat. 3.*	*Griev'd at my friends remove, him yet I praise That will in quiet Cuma end his days, And give one Citizen to Sibyl more; Of Baia's is the gate and gratefull shore Of sweet retirement.*

It surveyeth the *Tyrrhene* Sea, being mounted upon a not easily approached Promontory, whose skirts are beaten with the unquiet surges; strongly walled in later times, and fortified with Bulwarks, in such fort, as *Totila*, and *Tela*, two Kings of the *Goths*, did make it the receptacle of their treasure. But now left desolate, there is nothing to be seen but a confusion of ruines, pieces of Walls, broken down Aquæducts, defaced Temples, foundations of Theatres to be admired, Caves, &c. But hear we the *Neapolitan Sannizzarius*.

Here

LIB. IV.   *Cumea. Sibylla Cumea.*

Here where the walls of famous Cuma bore
Aloft; the chief pride of the Tyrrhene shore,
Frequented by the tawny Traveller,
To view thy Tripods, Delius, from afar;
Whose Ports the wondering Sailers did invite
To seek the proofs of Dedalus his flight: [friend?]
(Who would have thought it then when Fates did
Now high woods harbour to th' wild beasts do lend.
That Cave the Shepherds flock doth nightly fold,
Which Sibyls Mysteries contain'd of old.
And Birds and Serpents do inhabit where
The sacred Fathers erst assembled were.
That Porch full of noble Imaginary,
Oppressed with their own weight, prostrate lie.
Fanes, once with Trophies fill'd, are now laid low.
And grass on the distracted gods doth grow.
So many adornments, rare works, sepulchres,
And pious urns, one ruine now inters.

Hic tibi Cumeæ surgebant inclyta fama
Mœnia, Tyrrheni gloria prima maris.
Longinquis quo sæpe hospes properabat ab oris,
Visurus Tripodas, Delie magne, tuas.
Et vagus antiquos intrabat navita portus,
Quærens Dædalæ conscia signa fugæ.
Credere quis quondam potuit dum fata mane-
  bant?
Nunc sylva agrestes occulit alta feras.
Atque ubi fatidicæ latuere arcana Sibyllæ,
Nunc claudit saturas vespere pastor oves.
Quæque prius sanctos cogebat Curia patres,
Serpentum sacta est, alituumque domus,
Plenaque tot passim generosis atria ceris,
Ipsa sua tandem subruta mole jacet.
Calcanturque olim sacris onerata Trophæis
Limina, distractos & tegit herba Deos.
Tot decora, artificumque manus, tot nota sepul-
  chra,
Totque pios cineres, una ruina premit.

On the East-side of the winding Hill a Cave there is with a Marble Frontispiece, (whereunto Nature had made an access) hewn out of the Rock, extending under the ruined Walls, and admirably spacious. Here had that famous Sibyl her being, called *Cimmeris*, of a Town hard by, where she was born, and *Cumea* of this place where she prophesied: yet others affirm that it was *Erythræa*, who removing hither was called *Cumea*; and flourished both before, and after the *Trojan* Wars; with whom *Æneas* consulted. The manner of her prophesying thus *Virgil* describeth,

There shall you see the frantick Prophetess,
Sing Destinies within a Caves recess,
And words commit to leaves: What Verse soe're
So writ, she sets in order, and leaves there.
They firmly keep the place to each assign'd.
But she, when the doors open, and rude wind
In rushing whisks the light leaves to and fro,
Nor cares to catch, nor them to re-bestow
In their first form; To seek unsought-for Fate
They thence depart; and Sibyls mansion hate.

Insaniam vatem aspicies, quæ rupe sublima
Fata canit, foliisque notas & nomina mandat,
Quæcunque in foliis descripsit carmina Virgo,
Digerit in numerum, atque antro seclusa relinquit
Illa manent immota locis, neque ab ordine cedunt.
Verùm eadem, verso tenui cum cardine ventus
Impulit, & teneras turbavit janua frondes,
Nunquam deinde cavo volitantia prendere saxo,
Nec revocare situs, aut jungere carmina curat;
Inconsulti abeunt, sedemque odère Sibyllæ.
  Æn. l. 3.

Neither did she only give answers in that order, but sometimes by signs, and sometimes by speeches; as appears by what followeth.

The Prophetess intreat that willingly
She sing, and her Oraculous tongue untie,

Quin adeas vatem, precibusque Oracula poscas
Ipsa canat, vocemque volens, atque ora resolvat.
  Idem.

And again,

Ambiguously she sings, the Cave resounds,
Truth folding in dark phrase ———

Horrendas canit ambages, antroque remugit,
Obscuris vera involvens ———
  Æn. l. 6.

It is reported of these *Sibyls*, (for many of them there were, and that was a general name unto them all) that they understood not themselves what they had said, nor remembred it, delivering their Oracles in rude and unpolished Verse, obscurely and perplexedly, being uttered out of a phrantick fury when possessed by the Spirit. Which when *Virgils Sibyl* perceived to come upon her,

Time serves, said she, now ask and know thy Fates:
The God, behold the God! Before the gates;
This saying, her looks change, the white disstants
The red, red white; hair stands on end, brest pants,
Her heart with fury swells; she shews more great:
Nor speaks with humane voice, now when replent
With the inspiring power ———

——— Poscere fata
Tempus, ait: Deus, ecce Deus! levi talia fanti
Ante fores, subitò non vultus, non color unus,
Non compæ mansere comæ; sed pectus anhelum
Et rabie fera corda tument, majorque videtur;
Nec mortale sonans, afflata est numine quando
Jam propiore Dei.
  Idem.

And when *Æneas* had ended his Orisons,

At Phœbi nondum patiens immanis in antro
Bacchatur vates, magnum si pectore possit
Excussisse Deum ; tanto magis ille fatigat
Os rabidum, fera corda domans, fingitque premendo.

Yet brooking Phœbus ill, about flings she,
Distraught, her brest strives from his power to free.
The more her forward tongue he forces ; tames
Her sturdy heart ; and both to his will frames.

Such turbulent extasies proceeded, without question, from a diabolical possession. But surely a peaceable and better spirit did inspire them with those heavenly Divinations of our Saviour ; of whom, if we will give credit unto those eight Books now extant under their names, they speak more fully and perspicuously than many of the sacred Prophets. For whereas *Esay* saith ; Behold, a Virgin shall conceive, and bear a Son ; one of them is made to say,

────── Mariæ de Virginis alvo
Exorta est nova lux, &c.
Sibyl. Orat. l. 8.

────── *From Maries Virgins womb*
A new light is up-sprung ──────

both naming him, and the place of his birth, with an History as it were of his Life, his Death, and Resurrection. Whereby it doth give cause of strong conjecture, that these Books had had much inserted into them after the event, (whereof some of the Fathers are suspected) the History besides being orderly related, though written by divers, and in divers Ages. So that the whole being to be misdoubted, in that falsified in part, or the true from the untrue not distinguishable, we are rather to believe those that have the testimony of time for their approbation. As that Prophecy of our Saviour by this of *Cumæa*, borrowed from her by *Virgil* (as he confesseth) though perhaps not applied by him where it was meant, but left at random to be construed by event, and mix'd with his fictions.

Jam nova progenies cœlo dimittitur alto :
Tu modò nascenti puero quo ferrea primum
Desinet, & toto surget gens aurea mundo,
Casta fave Lucina ; tuus jam regnat Apollo, &c.
Te duce si qua manent sceleris vestigia nostri,
Irrita perpetua solvent formidine terras.
Ille Deûm viram accipiet, Divisque videbit
Permixtos heroas, & ipse videbitur illis.
Pacatumque reget patriis virtutibus orbem.
At tibi prima puer nullo munuscula cultu,
Errantes hederas passim cum baccare tellus,
Mistaque ridenti Colocasia fundet Acantho.
Ipsæ lacte domum referent distenta capellæ
Ubera ; nec magnos metuent armenta leones.
Ipsa tibi blandos fundent cunabula flores.
Occidet & serpens & fallax herba veneni, &c.
Aggredere, ô magnos, aderit jam tempus honores,
Chara Deûm soboles, magnum Jovis incrementum,
Aspice convexo nutantem pondere mundum !
Terrasque tractusque maris, cœlumque profundum !
Aspice venturo lætentur ut omnia sæclo, &c.

Ecl. 4.

Now a new Progeny from heaven to earth
Descends, Lucina favour this Childs birth,
In whom the Iron-age ends, forthwith shall follow
A golden race, now reigneth thy Apollo, &c.
Now shall our crimes, wh. se steps do still appear,
Be raz'd ; and th' earth delivered from long fear.
He life-of gods shall lead, shall Heroes see
With gods commixt ; and seen of them shall be :
And with his Fathers power th' appeas'd world guide.
Free earth her native presents shall provide
For thee, sweet Boy : wild Ivy, Baccaris,
Smiling Acanthus, broad Colocasis ;
Goats to their homes shall their full Udders bear ;
Nor shall our herds the raging Lions fear.
Thy Cradle shall sprout flowers ; the Serpents seed
Shall be destroy'd, and the false poysonous weed, &c.
Dear issue of the gods, great Joves increase,
Produce these times of wonder, worth, and peace.
Lo how the world, surcharg'd with weight doth reel !
Which Sea and Land, and profound Heaven do feel !
Lo how all joy in this wish'd time approach ! &c.

In the midst of this roomy Grot there are three Cisterns hewn out of the floot, wherein it is said that she washed her self, and after covered with a Stole retired into the innermost part of the Cave ; where seated aloft on a Temple, she divulged her Oracles. This is she that foretold of the destruction of *Troy*, and withal of the invention of *Homer :* who hath inserted sundry of her Verses into his Poems ; and said to be she that sung the *Roman* Destinies. But I cannot believe that this was that *Sibylla*, (although she be called long-lived) that brought those three Books to sell unto *Tarquinius Superbus :* yet of *Cumæ* she was, for divers *Sibyls* there were of this place, all Priests to *Apollo* (who here was served only by Virgins) in his not far distant Temple : but rather she whom they called *Amalthæa*, although it be to be imagined that her Books contained also the prophecies of the former, by many of the self-same Verses found at *Erythræa*. An old unknown Woman demanded for those Books the value of 300 Angels. The King thinking that she doted, both denied to give her that price, and derided her: when forthwith she burnt 3 ; and returning, ask'd as much for the other 6. But *Tarquinius* scoft at her much more than before ; whereupon she burnt other three, and yet required the same sum for the remainder. Insomuch as the King being moved with her constancy (and advised thereunto by the Augures) gave her the price of the nine for

the

LIB. IV.   *Sibylla Cumea. Arco Felice.*   223

A. *Ruines of Cuma.*   B. *Arco Felice.*   C. *The Tyrrhene Sea.*

the three; she admonishing him that he should keep them carefully; and so departing was never seen after. Others say, that these Books were brought to *Tarquinius Priscus*, and that she lived in the fiftieth Olympiad. These were kept in *Jupiters* Temple adjoyning to the Capitol, in a Chest of stone; whereof first 2, then 10, and lastly, 15 Priests (their Interpreters) had the keeping; and a crime unpardonable it was for others to look on them. Never undertook they any great enterprise, nor great calamity befel them, which they endeavoured to remove, but those 15 repaired to these Books of *Sibyls*, as to an Oracle, and present remedy for all disasters. But those bought by *Tarquinius* were burnt with the Capitol, in the 173 Olympiad; *C. Norbanus* and *P. Scipio* then Consuls. When the Capitol being restored by *Sylla* the Dictator, and *Jupiters* Temple by *Q. Catulus*, Embassadors were sent by the Senate to *Erythræa*, and to other Cities of *Italy*, *Greece*, and *Asia*, to make a collection of the Verses of the *Sibyls*, but especially of hers of *Erythræa*; who returned with a 1000, but those lame and unperfect: which the 15 had in charge to reform and supply, according to their wisdoms. And although they belonged unto divers *Sibyls*, yet they were called *Cumean*. *Tyberius Cæsar* made a second search through the World, and caused them again to be refined. Those continued at *Rome* until the days of *Honorius* and *Theodosius* the younger; and then were burned by the Traitor *Stilico*. Whereof *Rutilius Claudius Numantianus*:

Nor was't enough to rob with Getick powers,	Nec tantum Geticis grassatur proditor armis,
But first with fire he Sibyls Fates devours.	Ante Sibyllinæ fata cremavit opis.

But *Amianus Marcellinus* reports that they were burnt by *Julian* the Apostata.
Although *Cuma* be high mounted on a Rock, yet stands it but low in regard of the more lofty Hills, which on the North-side environ it with a Wall, being only separated by a little Valley. Thorow these Nature hath left a passage conjoyned by Art with a goodly Arch, called *Arco Felice* by the Country-people. Whereon once stood that famous Temple of *Apollo*, remembred by *Virgil*:

Æneas to the Towers resorts, which high	At pius Æneas arces quibus altus Apollo
Apollo guards, and the vast Cave hard by	Præsidet, horrendæque procul secreta Sibyllæ,
Of reverend Sibyl. Dædalus (fame sings)	Antrum immane petit, &c.
From Minos ventring with auspicious wings	Dædalus, ut fama est, fugiens Minoia regna,
Through untrac'd airy ways to take his flight	Præpetibus pennis ausus se credere cœlo
Towards the cold North, on Chalcian Tower did light:	Insuetum per iter gelidas enavit ad Arctos,
There builds a Fane (now footing earth, and free)	Chalcidicaque levis tandem super astitit arce;
And, Phœbus, consecrates his wings to thee.	Redditus hic primum terris, tibi (Phœbe) sacravit
	Remigium alarum, posuitque immania templa.
	Æn. l. 6.

Yet by some said to have stood below. The Image of *Apollo* erected in this Temple

was

was said to weep for forty days together, at such time as the *Romans* made War against the *Achaians*, assisting *Aristonicus*, who had intruded into the possession of *Attalus*, (base Son unto his Brother) who dying, gave his Kingdom unto the people of *Rome*: Whereat the Sooth-sayers amazed, held it fit to throw the Statue into the Sea. But the *Cumeans* perswaded the contrary, alledging that it had done the like in their Wars with *Antiochus*, and after with *Persius*, both which succeeded fortunately to *Rome*; whereupon oblations and gifts were sent thither by the Senate. So the Sooth-sayers changed their opinions, and declaring that the weeping of *Apollo* was auspicious to the *Romans*, because *Cuma* was a *Greek* Colony; and that these tears did pretend confusion to the people whom it favoured; and within a while after, they heard news that *Aristonicus* was taken. Not far off there is a large Cave, called by the people *la Grotta di Piedro di Pace*, which they say led under ground from thence to *Avernus*. A report, in my opinion, of credit. For *Strabo* doth make mention of the same, and that it was digged by *Coccius*; others say, by the *Cimmerians*, through which this *Sibyl* passed to *Avernus* to offer Sacrifice to the Infernals. Whereby that seeming contradiction may be reconciled; which is, that they shew the place of her habitation both at *Avernus* and *Cuma*. But this passage is now stopt up, for the self-same cause that the other was, which leads from thence unto *Baiæ*, by us formerly mentioned. The Plain that lies between these Hills and the City is repleat with ruines: where are to be seen the foundations of Temples, Theatres, &c. Under which, no doubt but many admirable Antiquities have their sepulture. Approved by that trial made by *Alphonsus Fimentellus* the Viceroy, in the year 1606. who desirous to find out some antick Statues to send into *Spain*; and hearing that the Husbandmen hereabout turned up with their Ploughs many fragments of Arms and Images, got leave of *Ottavio* Cardinal of *Aquaviva*, and Archbishop of *Naples* (to whose Church this soil doth belong) to make further search. When having removed but the upper earth, it was their chance to light on an entire Temple, although crushed together: the Walls and Pavement of polished Marble, circled with a great *Corinthian* Wreath, with Pillars, and Epistols of like workmanship, together with a number of defaced Figures excellently wrought: the work as well of the *Grecians*, as *Latines*. There they also found the Statue of *Neptune*, his beard of a blue colour; of *Saturn* or *Priapus* (for he held in his hand the Haft of a Sycle;) of *Vesta*, with the top of her hair wond round in a Fillet; of naked *Castor*, having a Hat on his head, his Chin a little covered with doune; of *Apollo*, with long disheveled hair, at whose feet stood a Swan; of *Hercules*, with a Club, crowned with a Wreath; of *Æsculapius*, or perhaps of *Romulus*; the Colossus of *Augustus Cæsar* exquisitely formed; of *Venus* naked, and surpassing beautiful; two Images in Consular Habits; *Pallas*, the work of an admirable Workman; the armed Statue of an Emperour, with a Sphynx ingraven on his bosom; the Image of a Youth head-bound with a sacred Fillet, clothed only in a shirt girt to him with a painted Zone: Other Women there were in feminine Habits, &c. This should seem to have been built by *Agrippa*, and dedicated to *Augustus*, by these here found Characters:

LARES AUGUS.
AGRIPPÆ.

And

POTESTATIS D.
AGRIPPA.

Some think it to have been a Palace; but whatsoever, it testifieth an admirable Building.

Wide of *Cuma*, and towards the Promontory of *Misenus*, stands the Lake of *Colusius*, stored with filthy waters; yet profitable for the preparing of Lime. Called heretofore *Acherusia* and *Acheron*, which is as much to say as, of Sorrow. *Avernus* and this are said to have recourse unto each other by subterrane passages. Whereof *Silius Italicus*

Hinc vicina palus fama est Acherontis ad undas
Pandere iter, cæcas stagnante voragine fauces
Lavat, & horrendo, aperit telluris hiatus,
Interdumque novo perturbat lumine manes.

'Tis fam'd the neighbour-lake hence flows un-spide
To *Acheron*, and boiling, openeth wide
The earths blind Cave, and dreadful jaws extends,
Which mihous'd souls with uncouth light offends,

Servius writes, that *Avernus* doth spring from *Acherusia*. The Heathen would not taste
of

LIB. IV.   *Vatias Villa. Tritole.*

of it, for that (in regard of the heat thereof) they thought that it arose from the infernal *Phlegeton.* The Poets fable, that *Hercules* here ascending from Hell, took from his head the Poppy Garland that he wore, and placed it on the Banks, in memorial of his return; since when the Poppy hath been black that hereabout groweth.

Not far from this, the Mannor-house of *Servilius Vatias* presented our eyes with her ruines; who was Consul with *Aprius Claudius* 674 years after the building of the City. He over-threw the Pirats in *Cicilia,* and triumphed for the same, having taken *Caricus, Olympus, Phaselides, Isaurus,* and retaining the name of the latter. Who in the end calling off all publick employments retired to this place. Of which, and of him, thus *Seneca* to *Lucilius*; there I persevered the longer, invited by the pleasant shore, which windeth about between *Cuma* and the Mansion of *Servilius Vatias*; enclosed on the one side with the Sea, and on the other with the Lake, affording as it were a straight passage, being thickned with a late tempest. For that water, as we know, so provoked, doth often overflow, and unites those Sands which a long calm disunites, by reason of their siccity. As my manner is, I began to look about me, to see if I could find out any thing that might profit; and bent mine eyes upon the house which sometimes belonged unto *Vatias.* In this that rich Prætor (for nothing famous but for his retirement) grew old, and for that only was accounted happy. For as often as the friendship of *Asinius Gallus,* or the hatred of *Sejanus,* and in the end his love, had destroyed any, (for to have offended him, and to have loved him, was equally dangerous) men would say, *O Vatias, thou only knowest how to live!* yet knew not he how to live, but how to conceal himself. Great is the difference betwixt leading the life vacantly, and leading it slothfully. I never past by this house of *Vatias,* but I said, *Here Vatias lay buried.* Of the house it self I can write nothing certainly; I only knew it by the out-side, and as it exposeth it self to the view of the passenger. Two Caves there are of excellent workmanship, both made by Art, and both alike spacious; the one never receiveth the Sun, and the other retaineth it until Sun set. A little Brook there runneth divided by Art thorow a Grove of Plantanes, devoured by the Sea and *Acherusia,* sufficient for the nourishing of Fish, although daily taken. When the Sea is composed they spare them, but take them when enraged with storms. The chiefest commodity of this place is, in that it hath *Baiæ* beyond the walls; enjoying the delights thereof, and sequestred from the incumbrances. This praise I can give it, that it is to be dwelt in all the year long: for it lieth open to the West-winds, and so receiveth them, that it retaineth them from *Baiæ.* Not un-advisedly therefore did *Vatias* make election of this place, where now grown old he might bestow his idleness. But the place doth not greatly tend unto tranquillity, it is the mind commendeth all things.

Now remaineth it that we treat of *Tritolæ, Baiæ, Baulis,* and the Promontory of *Misenus,* with their confines, wherein we will proceed in order as they lie, and not as confusedly seen by us. And to begin with the North-west end of the South-west side of the Bay of *Putzole*; near to the place where we left our Boat when we went to *Avernus*: The crooked land here maketh a little Bay, and after a while riseth bolt upright, upon whose top, and towards *Avernus,* the Mansions of *Marius, Pompey,* and *Cæsar,* are said to have stood; gathered perhaps out of that place of *Seneca,* where he saith, those to whom at first the fortune of the people of *Rome* transferred the publick riches, *Caius Marius, Cneus Pompeyus,* and *Cæsar,* built them houses in the region of *Baiæ,* but seated them on the tops of the Mountains. This appeared more war-like, to behold from above the under-lying Country. Consider what situation they chose, in what places, what buildings they erected, and thou wilt find them to be rather Fortresses than Palaces: Thus *Seneca.* But *Pompey's Villa* only stood here. Nothing hath this place note-worthy (for time hath deprived the ruines of their History) but certain wet and dry Baths: the former in a Cave at the foot of the Rock, now not preserved, called heretofore the Baths of *Diana.* We mounted a pair of high stairs, on the out-side of the Rock, and cut out of the Rock, to the other; where certain Rooms are built for the benefit of the diseased. This Sudatory is entred by a long narrow passage hewn into the Rock, into which we were fain to go backward or stooping, by reason of the vapour, and so excessive hot, that it forthwith bathed us in our own sweat. But hear we it described by a late Traveller:

The dry-Bath high rear'd on a Mountains side	In primis celso sita Sudatoria monte,
Thrusts forth three arms, which sulphury Fountains hide	In tria divisus specus est ceu brachia, quorum
In their extream extents; where smoakie night	Sulphureos extrema tenent fumantia fontes,
Still state retains, preserv'd from Phœbus sight.	Solis inaccessus radiis sub rupe cavara:
Long is the entrance: ashes white and hot	Ingressu via longa patet, cinis impedit albus
Pester the way in midst of the dry Grot.	Atq; calens mediæ prodientes agmine fossæ

Thy

Ingrediendo cave tollas caput, arduus unde	Thy head advance not, lest fumes it involve,
Fumus agit, totoque fluunt de corpore rivi;	And all thy body into streams resolve;
Visceribusque trahens animam, vapor æstuat intus,	And vapours inly burning soul exhale
Si submissus eas, & cautè lumina serves,	From entrails. Those that stooping go prevail,
(Nam sine luminibus nulli est intrare potestas)	And lights keep in; (no entrance without light:)
Victor eris, nimium sed non tentare sinistram	But let no dire desire thy steps incite
Dira tibi mens sit, necet intus perfidus aer,	To tread the left; there treacherous Air assaults
Prosuit & nulli tacitas quæsisse latebras.	Faint life; no good there's in those silent Vaults.

Called this was formerly *Frictolæ*, of the rubbing of their bodies; and now by corruption *Tritolæ*, or, as others say, for that it cureth the Tertian Fever. There be who say, that it was called of old *Trifolus*, and do ascribe the *Trifoline* Wine to this Mountain. It cureth the French Pox, and Fluxes of the head. Men and women have several times allotted them to enter, who sweating here half an hour become prone unto venery, insomuch that Christian Widows and Virgins were admonished by St. *Jerome* to avoid the place. Both above and below these Baths were adorned with Images (whereof some fragments do remain in some of them, which together with adjoining inscriptions, expressed and declared their several virtues.) Defaced (as they say) one night by the Physitians of *Salern*, as an impeachment to their profit; they were punished for the same by the Sea, being drowned in their return.

Beyond this, where the Sea doth make a semicircled Bay, stood the principal part of

A. *The Castle built by Charles the Fifth.* C. *Ruines of the Temple of Venus.*
B. *Ruines of Diana's Temple.* D. *The Baia of Baius.*

the City of *Baiæ* (for both *Tritolæ* and *Banli* belonged thereunto) not the least part thereof stretching into the Sea, the rest possessing the shore, with the sides and tops of the adjoining Hills. It was called *Baiæ* of *Baius* the companion of *Ulysses* here interred, so write they: a place so endued by Nature, and so adorned by Art, that the *Lyrick* Poet doth celebrate it as of pleasure incomparable:

Nullus in orbe locus Baiis prælucet amœnis. *Hor.* No place on earth surpasseth pleasant *Baiæ*.

And the *Epigrammatist*,

Littus beatæ Veneris aureum Baiæ; The golden shore of blessed *Venus*, *Baiæ*;
Baiæ superbæ dona naturæ; The prodigal largess of proud Nature, *Baiæ*,
Ut mille laudem Flacce versibus Baias, Though in a thousand verses I praise *Baiæ*,
Laudabo dignè non satis tamen Baias. Yet should not I deservedly praise *Baiæ*.
Mart. l. 11. Ep. 8 t.

LIB. IV.   *Baiæ.*

I wonder why *Josephus* doth call it a little City; when it is said to have extended five miles in length, and in some places two (though in some lets) in Latitude, presenting the shape of a finger. Nor was it undeservedly admired by King *Aristobulus*. A declaration of the magnificency and riches of the *Romans*; but too much of their luxury; beautified with ample Temples, multitudes of *Bannias*, Imperial places, and the adjoining Mannor-houses of the principal *Romans*; whither they made their recourse in the time of peace, and cessation from employments. They forced the Sea to retire, and afford a foundation for their sumptuous Buildings. Scoft at in a certain old man by the *Lyrick*:

Thou Marble pus'ft to cut, thy end so near,	Tu secanda marmora loca sub ipsum funus, & se-
And thoughtless of thy Tomb, dost houses rear;	pulchri
Enforcing Baiæ to usurp the bound	Immemor struis domos:
Of muttering Seas; not pleas'd with the dry ground.	Marisq; Baiis obstrepentis urget submovere littora
	Parum locuples continente ripa. *Hor.l.2.Od.18.*

Egyptian Canopus, mentioned before, was a School of virtue, compared to the voluptuous liberty of this City. The Inn (faith *Seneca*) and receptacle for Vices; where luxury taketh the reins, and is (as is a priviledged place) there far more licentious, &c. What a sight it is to see drunkards reeling along the shoar; the banquetings of such as are rowed on the water, the Lakes reckoning their continual canzonets, and the like: which lasciviousness, as if there lawless, not only sins in, but publisheth? The mind is to be hardned, and removed far from the sorcery of enticing pleasures. One Winter only here enfeebled *Hannibal*; and the delights of *Campania* did what the Snow and the *Alps* could not do; victorious in arms, yet by vices vanquished, &c. Thinkest thou that *Cato* would ever have dwelt at *Mica*, to have numbred the by-sailing Harlots, and to behold so many divers fashioned Boats, be-painted with diversity of colours, the Lake strewed over with Roses; and to have heard the night-noises of singers? &c. Who so is a man had rather be wakened with Trumpets than effeminate harmony. But long enough have we contended with *Baiæ*, though with vices we can never sufficiently. Thus he; Wherefore no marvel though *Venus* had here her Temple, when the people were so devoted unto her, and the place it self such an enemy to chastity:

Lavina, as chaft as th' ancient Sabines were,	Casta, nec antiquis cedens Lavina Sabinis,
(Thought then her Stoick husband more severe)	Et quamvis retrico tristior ipsa viro;
Whilst now Averne, now Lucrine she frequents,	Dum modo Lucrino, modo se permittit Averno;
Oft bathes in Baian Baths; at length affents,	Et dum Baianis sæpe fovetur aquis;
To lust; her husband leaves,in strange fires burns,	Incidit in flammas, juvenemque secuta relicto
Penelope came, an Helena returns.	Conjuge, Penelope venit, abit Helena,
	Mart.l.Ep.63.

And *Ovid*:

Need I name Baiæ hem'd with sails? Boats rowing	Quid referam Baias prætextaque littora velis,
Along the shore, and springs from Brimstone flowing?	Et quæ de calido sulphure fumat aquam?
Ah, cries some one, and his fell torment shews,	Huc aliquis vulnus referens in pectore dixit;
These waters cure not as the rumour grows.	Non hac, ut fama est, unda salubris erat.
	Art. Aman. l.1.

And it should seem that the Baths there had that same undeservedly; whereof *Horace*,

Antonius Musa saith, that Baiæ be	——— nam mihi Baias
Not for my health: yet take they offence at me,	Musa supervacuas Antonius, & tamen illis
That in cold water bathe, the weather cold.	Me facit invisum gelida cum perluor unda:
	Epist.15.l.1.

And though the Physicians hereabout of this time, (but such only as have not read *Galens* method, and kill men without punishment) when they are ignorant in the disease, or to seek in the cure, send their Patients to these Baths; yet never was it known that they profited any. They rather tending to pleasure and wantoning: whereof *Pontanus* the *Neapolitan*:

You wanton Baiæ shun, Marinus,	Salaces refugis Marine Baias,
And fountains too libidinous,	Et fontes nimium libidinosos,
What marvel; Lust doth Age undo:	Quid mirum! senibus nocet libido,
O Tomacel, doth wine so too?	At non, O Tomacelle, vina prosunt ?
Falernian liquor old age chears:	Et prodest senibus liquor Falernus;
And liberal draughts of Thyons tears;	Et profunt latices Thyoniani;

Takes

An non & senibus Marine somnus,
Et prodest requie; soporque prodest,
Eaiis somniculosius quid ipsis?
Quid Thermæ, nisi molle, lene, mite,
Rorante Cyathos merumque poscunt?

Takes ease in age, and sleeps content?
Than Baiæ what more somnolent?
What crave the Baths but solace, souls
Discharg'd from cares, and flowing bowels?

And it may be that other Baths, and new-famed Fountains, are more especially frequented to cherish the diseases of the mind, than to cure those of the body. Should we give them an undeserved Title, or make them say more than the truth, if we produced them thus speaking, as the aforesaid Author did the other?

Nostrum si titulum puella nescis;
Hic est: Prægravida recede alvo,
Quæ venis vacua: hoc habet tabella, &c.

Wench, dost thou not our title know!
'Tis this: Come empty, from hence go
Full-belly'd: this contains our table, &c.

The rest I suppress, in that offensively immodest. But I should dwell too long on this place, should I speak of the *Ambubaiæ*, certain infamous women, so called for conversing about *Baiæ*, incredibly impudent, or other their particular luxuries. But behold an egregious example, that pronounceth the works of mens hands as frail as the Work-men. *Baiæ* not much inferiour unto *Rome* in magnificency, equal in beauty, and superiour in healthful situation, hath now scarce one stone left above another, demolished by War, and devoured by Water. For it should seem that the *Lombards* and *Saracens* in the destruction hereof had not only a hand; but that the extruded Sea hath again regained his usurped limits: made apparent by the paved Streets, and traces of foundations to be seen under water. The shore is all over-grown with bushes and Myrtles, the Vaults and thrown down walls inhabited by Serpents: and what is more, the air heretofore so salubrious, is now become infectious and unhealthsom. A number of Caves there are all along the bases of the Cliff; many of them were employed for Fishponds, whereinto they let in, and excluded the Sea at their pleasure: in which they greatly delighted; framed and maintained with excessive expences. But especially they delighted in Lampreys, partly for their bellies, and partly for that they were easily kept in their Stews, as not so tender, and longer liv'd than any other. For some of them have been known to have lived threescore years, and some upward. Besides, their familiarity with men was to be admired; having particular names, and coming to the hand, when so called upon. Whereof *Martial*, speaking of *Domitians* Fish-pools which were here in *Baiæ*:

Piscator fuge, ne nocens recedas,
Sacris piscibus hæ natantur undæ,
Qui norunt dominum, manumque lambunt,
Illam qua nihil est in orbe majus
Quid, quod nomen habent; & ad magistri
Vocem quisque sui venit citatus?
l.4. Epig. 30.

Angler, preserve thy innocence, forbear;
For they are sacred Fishes that swim here:
Who know their Soveraign, and will lick his hand,
Than which what greater in the worlds command?
What, that they have names, and when they called are,
Unto their Masters several call repair?

For which they have been of divers incredibly affected: insomuch as *Crassus* bewailed the death of one, no less than the loss of a Son; and built a Sepulchre for it. *Caius Hirtius* who had a Mannor-house also in *Baiæ*, was the first that invented these Stews for Lampreys; who received for the houses which were about this Fish pond two thousand Sestertians; all which he spent in food for his Fishes. He it was that lent *Cæsar* the Dictator, six hundred Lampreys to furnish his Feasts in the time of his Triumphs, to be paid again in kind, in number, and by weight: for he would neither sell them, nor exchange them for other Commodities. The Tyrants of those times (not, as *Augustus*, free from this savage pastime) took a delight to throw the condemned into these Ponds to be devoured by them; because they would see them torn in pieces in an instant. The Oysters also of *Baiæ* were exceedingly commended:

Ostrea Baianis certantia, quæ Medulorum
Dulcibus in stagnis refluit maris æstus opimus.
Accipe dilecte Theon, memorabile munus.
Auson. 38.

Oysters compar'd with those of Baiæ, fed
By tyding Seas in pits of the fresh Lake
Of Meduli, a rare gift, lov'd Theon take.

Sergius Oratus was the first that made pits for them about his house here; more for profit, than to indulge his gluttony. For by such devices he purchased much riches. He also devised the hanging Bannias, and Pools to bathe in, on the tops of Houses.

At

At the foot of the Hill that windeth towards *Tritula*, stood the Palace of *Piso*; whereunto *Nero* frequented often, and casting off state and attendance, accustomed to bathe and banquet. Here those of *Piso's* conspiracy would have executed their purpose; but he refused to give his consent, that his table should be defiled with slaughter, and the gods of hospitality provoked. Of this nothing remaineth but certain Caves and entrances hewn out of the Rock. More within the Bay, on the bending shore, stand the ruines of a goodly Building, called at this day *Truglium*. It seemeth to have been a Bannia, by the vents in the Walls for the smoak to evaporate, and by the Pipes which on either side conveyed rain-water into the ample Lavers, and other proofs which these reliques rementstrate. Yet some will have it to have been the Fane of *Venus*, for she in *Baiæ* had her Temple. But whether so or no, the Walls of a magnificent Temple here yet look aloft, seated more high, and almost against the midst of the Bay; not only known to have been consecrated to misplaced *Diana*, by that testimony of *Propertius*,

Thee, *Cynthia*, in the midst of *Baiæ* plac'd	Ecquid te mediis cessantem Cynthia Baiis
Where ways along th' *Herculean* shore are trac'd:	Qua jacet Herculeis semita littoribus.

but by the figures of Dogs, of Harts, and Barbels here ingraven, which were sacred unto her.

Now upon the high Hill opposing *Tritola*, and confining the other end of the Bay, there is a strong Castle, erected by *Philip* the Second, to protect the under-lying Sea, and places adjoyning, from the thefts and wastes of the *Turkish* Rovers; manned by threescore Souldiers; where the Mannor-house of *Julius Cæsar* stood, as is to be collected out of *Tacitus*.

Between this and *Misenus* lies *Bauli*, called first *Boaula*, as much to say, as an Oxstall; of *Gerions* Oxen, which *Hercules* brought hither in triumph out of *Spain*, where he had a Temple consecrated unto him.

———— *Boalia* this age	———— Corrupta Boalia Baulos
Corruptly *Bauli* calls————	Nuncupat hæc ætas ————

for the better sounding of the word. Here *Hortensius* the Orator had his Villa, (the ruines whereof are now buried in earth, & covered with water) who greatly delighted in his fish-stews, and was nick-named *Triton* by *Tully*; for the fishes herein would come to his hand when so called; who wept for the death of a Lamprey, and to a friend that begged two Barbels of him, (called *Mulli* in Latine) replied, that he had rather give him two Mules for his Litter. This was afterward possessed by *Antonia* the Mother of *Drusus Nero*, who hung a Jewel in the Gills of a Lamprey which she loved. A place famous for the Tragedy of *Agrippina*, here feasted by her dissembling Son, and invited by him unto *Baiæ*, to celebrate the sive days continually festival of *Minerva*; when by the way, (being by night to come, the better to cloak it) in a Galley devised by *Anicetus* Captain of the Navy at *Misenus*, by Art made loose in the bottom, The should have been, as if accidentally, drowned. But she apt to distrust, as inured to like practices, or having had some notice thereof given, caused her self to be carried in a Chair unto *Baiæ*, where by *Nero's* artificially passionate entertainment, discharged of her fears, she returned by Galley (the Sea calm, and the night starry, as detesting to cloak such a villany) with only two of her own retinue: *Crepirius Gallus* that stood not far from the stern, and *Aceronia* her Woman who lay at the feet. When with great joy relating the repentance of her Son and her recovered favour, the Watch-word was given, and the heavy covering of the place falling down as was ordered, prest *Gallus* to death: but that over the Women being stronger than the rest, though shrinking, saved them, the Vessel thereby kept alto from parting asunder; so that they were fain to sink the Galley at the side by little and little. *Aceronia* crying, that she was the Princes Mother, was slain with Poles and Oars; coming to her end by the craft which she used for her safety: *Agrippina* with silence swimming to the shore, having only received one wound on the shoulder, was succoured by small Barks, and conveyed to her house which bordered on *Lucrinus*. When casting in her mind the unlook'd for honour done her, succeeding such bitterness of hatred, the fabrick of the Galley so to dissolve, neither shaken with storms, nor crushed by rocks; the death of *Aceronia* assuming her name, and lastly, the wound she had received; she held it the

best

best course to no take notice of the treachery; sending *Agerinus* to tell her Son of the danger which she had escaped by the goodness of the gods, and by his good fortunes. But he knowing her craft, and fearing that she should presently practise a revenge, sent *Anicetus* a Captain of the Navy, and a Centurion of Sea-souldiers to dispatch her; who breaking into her house, and finding her a-bed, it is said that she presented her belly to the Sword of the Centurion; bidding him to strike it that had brought forth such a Monster; and so with many wounds perished. *Nero* standing by when she was cut up, (therein no less savage than in murdering) surveying every part of her, said to the by-standers, *That he thought he had not had so beautiful a Mother*. The same night she was burned with base Funerals, and whilst *Nero* reigned, unburied. But shortly after enclosed here at *Bauli* by her houshold-servants in a simple Sepulchre, called the Sepulchre of *Agrippina* at this day, which we entred: being placed on the side of the rising ground, partly hewn into the Rock, and now having a difficult entry. The roof and sides are figured with Sphinxes and Griffons: but sullied greatly with the smoak of Torches and Lights, born in by such as do enter.

Not far beyond, the Land pointed into the Sea, and there hollowing a little by the industry of *Agrippa*, at *Cæsars* appointment, and called the Port of *Agrippa*. Another Navy they kept at *Ravenna*, both serving aptly for employment; in that from either the one or the other they might make a swift cut, if occasion required, without compassing of Countries, to any part of their Empires within *Hercules* Pillars. *Volusius Proculus* was Admiral of this in the time of *Nero*, and *Pliny* the natural Historian, in the Reign of *Titus*. Divers stones hereabout do bear the names of Ships, and naval Commanders, with such like Antiquity. At the mouth hereof are yet to be seen certain ruinous Piles. The innermost part, now a filthy Lake, is vulgarly called the dead Sea.

On the far side of this, and stretching further into the Sea, the Mountain of *Misenus* riseth aloft,

Misenum Æoliden, quo non præstantior alter,
Ære ciere viros, Martemque accendere cantu.
Virg Æn. l. 6.

*Æolian Misen, others passing far,
With brass stern fight to excite and kindle war.*

Æneas his Trumpeter, and drowned hard by, by the envy (as they fable) of *Triton*,

At pius Æneas ingenti mole sepulchrum
Imposuit, suaque arma viro, remumque tubamque
Monte sub aerio, qui nunc Misenus ab illo
Dicitur, æternumque tenet per secula nomen.
Idem.

*But good Æneas a huge Tomb did rear,
His arms, his ore, and trumpet placing there
Under aerial mountain of his name
Misenus call'd, to his eternal fame.*

Called *Arius* before; or having that Epithete given it, in that, partly by Nature, and partly by Art, it is almost hollow throughout. This Promontory is of all other the most famous for the clemency of the Air, the City here once standing, the Mannor-houses adjoyning, the *Roman* Navy, antick Monuments, Fish-pools, Grots, Baths, and other admirable Buildings; surveying all the Sea-coasts unto the Promontory of *Minerva*, (if measured with the winding shore, 34 miles distant) all which shewed in the time of the *Roman* Monarchy like to one entire City. Whereof now (*Naples* excepted) there is little to be seen that hath escaped the fury of fire, of water, or Earth-quakes. Here *Caius Marius* had a Villa, with a place more sumptuous and fine than befitted such a Souldier, after purchased by *Cornelia*, and after that by *Lucullus*, in which *Tiberius Cæsar* departed this life (prevented by extremity of sickness) in his way unto *Capræ*. The Vault of *Traconaria* (signifying a passage for water) is near unto this. A part of the same (as conjectured by some) which was digged by *Nero*, reaching unto *Avernus* to receive all the hot waters of the Baths of *Baiæ*; being covered over head, and on each side cloystered. But this should rather seem to be made for their receipt of the rain that descended from the Promontory, as appears by the conveyances. It is about twenty foot high, the fallen down roof obscures both the length and bredth. The middle space is contained between two Walls, 18 foot broad, and 200 long. In either side of it a passage there is by four doors into four ample Vaults, the arched roofs being joyned with Walls in the middle. The ruines of the City lye below this: amongst which are the remains of a Theatre, in form of an half Amphitheatie. These Theatres were dedicated to *Venus*, as the Amphitheatres to *Mars*; those presenting delights of a more gentle nature.

LIB. IV.   *Misenus.   Mercato di Sabbato.*   231
Where loves imagined are daily sung;   Illic assiduè ficti cantantur amores.
                                                          Ovid. Remed. Amoris.

yet more anciently to *Bacchus*; rather from the seeing than hearing assuming that name, of their there presented Dancings, Pageants, and diversity of Spectacles. *Marcus Valerius Massala*, and *Cassius Longinius*, were the first among the *Romans* that adventured to erect a Theatre, although Plays were devised many Ages before.

First Romulus these careful plays devis'd,   Primus sollicitos fecisti Romule ludos,
When Roman Widowers Sabine Maids surpriz'd.   Quum juvit viduos rapta Sabina viros.
No Veil the Marble Theatre o're-spred,   Tunc neque marmoreo pendebant vela Theatro,
Nor Stage with liquid Saffron then look'd red.   Nec fuerant liquido pulpita rubra croco.
But Bowre of boughs, which neighbouring Woods impart, Illic quas tulerant nemorosa palaria frondes
There rudely framed stood; the Scene lack'd Art.   Simpliciter positæ; Scena sine arte fuit.
On seats of turfs the Auditors sit down,   In gradibus sedit populus de cespite factis
And levy Wreaths their dangling tresses crown.   Qualibet hirsutas fronde tegente comas.
                                                          Ovid. Art. Am. l. 1.

But how sumptuous they grew from so rude a beginning, the Theatre built by *Marcus Scaurus* doth declare, exceeding all other Fabricks whatsoever. It had three Stages one above another, supported with three hundred and sixty Pillars of Marble. The lowest Stage was of Marble; the front of the middle, of glass; the uppermost of boards gilt curiously over. Three thousand Statues of Brass stood between the Columns; and the semicircle was ample enough to contain fourscore thousand persons. The Furniture of Hangings, Pictures, and Apparel, was answerable to the Magnificency of the Building; and all this done by a private man. The parts of the Theatre were four; the front of the Stage, the Stage whereon they acted; the place where the Musicians played, (in which the Poets also, and Orators pronounced their compositions) and that where the Chorus danced and sung; about which sate the Senators. The Spectators sate one above another round about the round, distinguished according to their quality. The face of the Scene was made so as to turn of a sudden; 'and to present new Pictures and places, according to the argument then handled. But herein the invention of *Curio* surpassed; whose two great Theatres, framed of Wood, hung upon two Hooks, which upheld the whole Frame. In the forenoon they were placed back unto back, and Plays exhibited therein; in the afternoon turned about in a trice they affronted each other, and towards the later end of the day joyning them together, made of both one goodly Amphitheatre, (the people never removing from their seats) where Fencers at sharp succeeded the Actors. Thus bore he the *Romans* between Heaven and Earth upon the trust of the two Hooks: a bold invention, and as bold an adventure. *Nero* in person oft acted in publick Theatres, although Players were silenced by him in the beginning of his Reign, as before his time by *Tiberius*, and after by *Trajan*.

A little removed there are certain Salt-pits, and beyond towards *Cumæ* we came to a Cistern, not undeservedly called *Piscina mirabilis*. This was entred at two doors in the opposite corners (whereof one now is ramm'd up) and is descended into by forty stone-steps. The Vault is five hundred foot in length, and in bredth two hundred and twenty; the Roof sustained by four rows of Pillars, twelve in a row, wherein are divers Tunnels whereat they draw up water, now yielding a sufficient light to the same. Without, it appeareth but as a rising Bank; the Walls within consisting of Brick, and plaistered over with a composition, as they say, of floor, the white of Eggs, stone beaten into powder, hard as Marble, and not to be soked thorow by water. The making of this some impute to *Lucullus*, by reason of the neighbourhood of his mansion; but more probably we may do it to *Agrippa* for the benefit of the Navy, into which water was conducted from the River *Serinus*. Those that are called *Cemum Camerelle* (into which also we entred) of the multitude of Vaults for the preserving of water, I rather think to have belonged to *Lucullus*; mentioned by *Varro*, *Tacitus*, and *Pliny*.

Between *Misenus* and *Baiæ* there lyeth a long Plain, called by some the *Elysian* field, but more commonly *Mereati di Sabbato*, environed with ruines; heretofore a Cirque; so called of the running about of the Obelisks that stood along in the middle, with Horses and Chariots. *Tarquinius Priscus* built the first amongst the *Romans*, between the two Hills *Palatinus* and *Aventine*, named *Maximus*; enlarged and magnificently adorned by *Cæsar Augustus*, *Trajan*, and *Heliogabalus*. It contained
                                X 2   in

in length three hundred seventy and five paces, in bredth an hundred and five and twenty; square at one end, and circular at the other; the round and sides compassed with a Rivulet of ten foot broad, and of equal depth; without which were the Walls, containing three Galleries one above another, and built with Seats like an Amphitheatre, where places were assigned to each several calling; large enough to receive two hundred and threescore thousand Spectators. Entred it was at twelve Ports. At the square end the Horses under certain Arches had their stand, kept back by a Barrier drawn up upon the sign given. In the midst of the Cirque stood an Hieroglyphical Obelisk, brought by *Augustus* out of *Egypt* from the City of the Sun, there erected by *Semnesertus*, an hundred five and twenty foot and nine inches high. On each side of this stood three less, gilt afterwards over, for the other six Planets, all in a row like the lists in a Tilt-yard. They used to strew the floor with the powder of white stone. *Nero* caused it to be sprinkled with a green Mineral, found in the Mines of Gold and Brass; *Caligula* with the same, but mixed with Vermillion: *Heliogabalus* with the filings of gold and silver, and sorry he was that he could not with Amber: Although the Cirques were generally consecrated unto *Neptune*, yet it seemeth that the Sun had a special interest in this; not only in regard of his Obelisk, but of the twelve Games there exhibited in his honour, signified by the twelve gates, and perhaps having reference to the twelve Signs, as the seven times circling the List with their Chariots, had to the seven Planets, and days of them named. That Hieroglyphical Obelisk now standing at *Rome* in the Lateran, stood in the same Cirque, erected by *Constantius*, and by him brought from *Alexandria* in a Galley of three hundred Oars, being there left by *Constantine* the Great, who had taken it from *Egyptian Thebes*, (where *Ramnestes* had set it in a Temple to the honour of the Sun) with purpose to have conveyed it unto *Constantinople*. They adorned these places with the Images of their gods and spoils of their enemies. Before the beginning of the race, they carried their Idols about in a solemn Procession. Wherefore amorous *Ovid*, sitting in the Cirque by his Mistress,

Sed jam pompa venit, linguis animisque favete:	*The pomp now comes, hearts praise, nor be tongues dumb:*
Tempus adest plausus, aurea pompa venit.	*Time fits applause; the golden pomp doth come.*
Prima loco fertur sparsis victoria pennis.	*Lo, Victory with displaid wings leads the way;*
Huc ades atque meus, fac Dea, vincit amor.	*Come hither, Goddess, give our love the day.*
Plaudite Neptuno, nimium qui creditis undis:	*Serve Neptune they who too much trust to Seas;*
Nil mihi cum pelago, me mea terra tenet.	*With waves we trade not; me my soil doth please.*
Pax juvat, & medea pace repertus amor.	
Auguribus Phœbus, Phœbe venantibus adsit:	*Souldier applaud thy Mars, we Wars detest;*
Artifices in te verte Minerva manus.	*Peace love, and Love that in mild Peace thrives best,*
Agricolæ Cereri, teneroque assurgite Baccho:	*Augurs Apollo, Hunters Phœbe aid:*
Pollucem pugiles, Castora placet eques.	*Artificers applaud the brain-born Maid.*
Nos tibi blanda Venus, pueroque potentibus armis	*Ceres and Bacchus Country-swains adore;*
	Champions please Pollux; Horse-men Castor more:
Plaudimus, inceptis annue diva meis.	*To thee kind Venus, and thy Boy that arms*
Ovid. Amor. l. 3. Eleg. 1.	*All hearts (assist me) I give my applause.*

The place then cleared by the Prætor, chosen for that purpose, the Chariotters started their Horses upon a sign given, clothed in colours differing from each other:

Si viridi prasinove faves, qui coccina sumis;	*If blue or green you side with, and wear red;*
Ne fias istinc transfuga forte vide.	*Look lest they say, you from your party fled.*
Mart. l. 14. Epig. 31.	

those of their Faction wearing the same, which grew to so hot a contention in the Reign of *Justinian* between the Green and the Blue, that 40000 were slain at *Constantinople* in the quarrel. Seven times they drove about the list, as is manifest by *Propertius*.

Aut prius infecto deposcit præmia cursu,	*Or prize demands before the race be done;*
Septima quam metam triverit ante rota.	*E're wheels seven times about the list have run.*

and he reputed the most skilful, that could drive nearest to the ends of the List without danger: whereof *Ovid*, reproving a Chariotter,

Ne miserum, metam spaciofo ciruit orbe;	*Ah! from the list too far his wide wheels stray:*
Tende precor valida lora sinistra manu.	*A stronger hand upon the left reins lay.*
Am. 3. Eleg. 2.	

A

A Napkin was the reward of the Victor; as the hanging out thereof a signal to begin. Which grew into a custom upon Nero's throwing his Napkin out at the window staying long at dinner, and importuned by the people to make haste; who often played the Chariotter himself. And so had this pastime bewitched the principal Romans, that divers consumed their patrimonies therein; declared by Juvenals invective against one,

Who spent his wealth in mangers, nor doth prise	Qui bona donavit præsepibus, & caret omni
What Parents left, whilst on swift wings he flies.	Majorum censu, dum pervolat axe citato.
	Sat. 1.

And to conclude with the same Poets Satyrical description of these races.

Mean while Circensian shews do celebrate	Interea Megalesiacæ spectacula mappæ
Ideau races. In triumphant state	Ideum solemne colunt, similisque triumpho,
The horsthief Prætor sits. In truth I may	Prædo caballorum Prætor sedet, ac mihi pace
With favour of the too great Vulgar say,	Immensæ nimiæque licet si dicere plebis;
To day the Cirque all Rome contains, the cry	Totam hodie Romam circus capit, & fragor aurem
Assures me of the Green-coats victory:	Percutit, eventum viridis quo colligo panni:
Lose be, the City mourns in like dismay,	Nam si deficeret, mæstam, attonitamque videres
As when at Cannæ Consuls lost the day.	Hanc urbem, veluti Cannatum pulvere victiis
This better the bold-betting Tomb befits	Consulibus; spectent juvenes quos clamor & audax
To see, who close to his trim Mistress sits.	Sponsio, quos cultæ decet assedisse duellæ.
	Juv. Sat. 11.

The catching and killing of Beasts by the hands of men, which were of a more fearful nature, was also presented in the Cirque; thus expressed by *Vopiscus* in the life of the Emperour *Probus*: A liberal hunting he bestowed in the Cirque, to be carried all away by the people. The manner of the spectacle was; Great trees by the roots pull'd up by the Souldiers were fastned to pieces of timber, in many places conjoined; which when covered with earth, the whole Cirque did appear as a flourishing wood, into which were thrust 1000 Ostridges, 1000 Stags, 1000 Boars, 1000 Bucks, Goats, Sheep, wild beasts, and other Creatures that live upon grass, as many as could be found out and preserved. Then suffering the people to enter, they caught, and carried away whatsoever they could. From the West end of this Cirque we descended a little amongst certain ruines, where divers Urns are yet to be seen in the concaves of old walls, containing the ashes of the *Romans*. Leaving the forsaken Promontory that shewed nothing but desolation, we retired to our Boat, and crossed the Bay unto the shore of *Putzole*, to a place where the sand is so hot (notwithstanding washed with every Billow) that like it was to have scalded our hands, though suddenly pull'd forth again. From hence we rowed to *Nesis*, a little Island, and but little removed from the point of *Pausilype*; once fabled to have been a Nymph, and beloved of the mountain.

And thee, fair Nesis thrall, Pausilype,	Te quoque formosæ captum Nesidis amore,
With ireful plaints he calls upon from Sea.	Pausilype irato compellat ab æquore quæstu.
	Sannazarius.

Another speaking of the Wine of *Pausilype*,

Lo here Pausilypes tears shed when he mourn'd,	En tibi Pausilypis lacrymæ quas fudit ad undas,
Whilst flying Nesis to a Rock was turn'd.	Dum fugiens Nesis vertitur in scopulum.
	Rota.

And *Pontanus* describing the Nymphs, declares the condition of the place;

Amongst the Lotis by the shore unspide,	Illum Nisa tenet deserti ad littoris algam,
Him Nesis clips, black-kneed, red-cheek'd, gray-eyde.	Nigra genu, croceisque genis, & lumine glauco.

It containeth no more than a mile and a half in circuit; now the possession of the Duke of *Amalphus*, and honoured with his house; heretofore with the house of *Lucullus*, the place made healthful by the cutting down of the Woods, which was formerly otherwise. Of which a certain Traveller,

Next Nesis stands with Sperage stor'd, e're while	Post hanc asparagis plenam Nesida videmus;
Part of Pausilype, but now an Isle.	Pars hæc Pausilypes quondam, maris insula nunc est.

Multis ibi servat furtiva cuniculus antra,
Antra Typhonæos quondam spirantia fumos,
Et circa Eumenidum nebuloso tristia luco.

There Caves in secret Burrows Conies hold:
Caves that expir'd Typhonean fumes of old,
And flames within the Furies gloomy Groves.

It hath a round Tower in the midst over-looking those Coasts, with a little Port turning toward the South, making besides a safe station for Ships between it and the Mountain.

So we past along the side of *Pausilype*, clothed with Natures most rich and beautiful Tapestry; the frequented shore affording diversity of solaces; besides other edifices, bearing the impressions of sundry ancient Structures. Amongst the rest, that now called *Copinus*, a Grot descended into by degrees from the house that stood above it: once belonging unto *Pollio Vibius*, and left unto *Augustus Cæsar* by his will. This cruelly luxurious *Pollio* accustomed his Lampreys, kept in this stew, to feed upon mans flesh; into which he threw his condemned Slaves. Upon a time having invited *Augustus* to Supper, a Boy breaking a Crystal Glass, and for that mischance being to be devoured by Fishes, besought *Augustus* that he would not suffer him to dye so wretched a death. Then the Emperour commanded, that they should let him alone; and withal, that all the Crystals which were in the House should be fetched; which he caused to be broken, and thrown into the Fish-pool. Thus was the friend of *Cæsar* to be chastised, and well he exercised his authority. We will not speak of the roots of Hills here hollowed by *Lucullus*; for which called gowned *Xerxes* by *Tubero* the Stoick; but proceed unto the house of *Jacobus Sannazarius* that excellent Poet, given him by King *Frederick*, and called *Mergellina*, which by his last Testament he converted into a Monastery, having there built a Temple to the birth of the Virgin. And herein his Sepulchre is to be seen, of a fair white Marble, with his Figure cut to the life: from whose mouth the Bees do seem as it were to suck Honey. On the one side is the Statue of *Apollo*, and on the other of *Minerva*, though called by the names of *David* and *Judith*. He is beholding to Cardinal *Bembus* for this there engraven Epitaph.

Da sacro cineri flores; Hic ille Maroni,
Sincerus Musa proximus, ut tumulo.
Vix.an. 72. Obiit An.Dom.1530.

Strew Flowers; Here lies Sincerus in Earths womb;
His Muse, as next to Maro's, so his Tomb.

Living, this other he made of himself,

Actius hic situs est, cinceres gaudera sepulti,
Jam vaga post obitus umbra dolore vacat.

Actius here lies, interred ashes joy;
Our soul by deaths, now freed from all annoy.

who writ it poetically, and not in contempt of Religion, justified by his divine Poem; in the same manner he hath named himself *Actius Sincerus Sannazarius*. This is not far removed from the way which passeth through the Mountain, where we met our Caross; and so returned into the City.

Now upon departing from *Naples*, I was perswaded not to venture over land, by reason of the insalubrious season (the Dog-Star then raging) proving often mortal to the stranger, but especially after a rain; insomuch, that lately of four and twenty *French*-men, but four got alive unto *Florence*. So that I agreed with a *Genoese* to carry me in his Felucca to *Neptune*. But staying too long my Companion, (an *English*-man that dwelt at *Ligorn*) put the Boat from shoar, which we were fain to follow in another. Crossing the mouth of the Bay of *Putzole*, the Seas grew suddenly rough, and we out of hope of safety, when by a *French* Fisherman we were succoured, and in his Bark transported to *Prochita*, where the other Felucca stayed for us.

This Island containeth but seven miles in circuit; fourteen Miles from *Naples*, eight from *Putzole*, and two from *Inarime*, from whence it is said to have slid, and therefore so called. It lyeth in a low level; yet *Virgil*,

Tum sonitu Prochita alta tremit.
Æn. l. 9.

High Prochita then trembled at the sound.

rather giving it that Epithete of what it was when a mountain of *Inarime*, separated, as the Poets do feign, by *Typhous*:

Ut nisu ingenti partes de monte revulsas
Ænaream Prochitamque ipsis immiserit astris,
Ac totum subito cœlum tremefecerit ictu.
Sannaz.

The Mountain with huge strength asunder torn,
Ænaria he, and Prochita did throw
To Stars; Heaven trembled at the sudden blow.

others

LIB. IV.   Prochita. Inarime. Linternum.

others will have it so called of *Æneas* his Kinſ-woman there buried. Fruitful it is in Grain and Fruits, abounding with Conies, Hares, and Pheſants. The environing Seas are ſtored with Fiſh; and the ſhore with freſh Fountains. To this add we *Pontanus* his deſcription, making a Nymph of her:

By him goes *Prochita* his ſpouſe, for face	Hunc juxta conjux Prochitela incedit, & ore
And geſture prais'd: n'bom painted garments grace	Et geſtu ſpectanda, & picta tegmine palla,
With ratling cochles bem'd, her zone enlaid	Nexilibus cochleis limbus ſonat, horrida echinis
With Urchins rough, her breaſts green ſea weeds ſhade.	Zona riger, viridiſque ſinus frondeſcit in alga.
	P.mais.

A little Iſland almoſt adjoining to the Weſt of this, called the Park; where formerly they accuſtomed to hunt, but now turned into tillage. The Town regardeth the Promontory of *Miſenus*, ſeated on a neck of the Rock, and defended with a Caſtle. Divers ſtragling houſes there be throughout the Iſland. *John de Prochita*, a renowned Citizen of *Salern*, was once Lord of this place, from whence he produced his original, who deprived *Charles* of the Dominion of *Sicilia*, and was Author of that bloody Even-ſong, as formerly declared. Provoked thereunto, in that *Charles* had diſpoſſeſſed him of *Prochita*; or rather for abuſing his Wife, as is reported by others; whom the *Aragonians*, that roſe by the fall of the *French*, made Governour of *Valentia*.

The weather continuing ſtormy, we ſtayed here the day following, and ſo had the leiſure to ſurvey the near neighbouring *Ænaria*, called alſo *Arime*, and *Inarime*; an Iſland eighteen miles about, and no more, though meaſured with the ſhore; which thruſteth out many beautiful Promontories. In the midſt of the Iſland ſtands the high Mountain *Epomeus*, upon whoſe top St. *Nicholas* hath a Temple, befriended with a Fountain of freſh water: The want whereof is here greatly miſſed, there being but twelve in the whole Iſland, whereas there be of hot and medicinable ſprings (beſides Sudatories) five and twenty. For the earth is full of ſubterrene Fires, which have heretofore evaporated ſtones, and raiſed moſt of theſe Mountains; therefore was it feigned to cover *Tiphous*:

———the painful priſon Inarime	———durumque cubile
By *Joves* commaundment on *Typhous* thrown?	Inarime Jovis imperiis impoſta Typhœo.
	Virg. l. 9.

for what ſignifieth that name *Typhous*, but ſuppreſſed Whirle-winds, and impetuous inflammations? Though this Iſle was not called *Arime*, and *Pithecouſa* (for both-ſignifie one thing) of the men here feigned to have been Metamorphoſed into Apes; yet why not of their crafty and beſtial diſpoſitions? And little better are they at this day; either retaining the ſavage Cuſtoms of their Progenitors, or having their blood dryed up with over-much fire, being prone to injuries, violence and ſlaughters. But *Pliny* ſaith, that it took the name of *Inarime* of the making of earthen Pots, as *Ænaria* of the ſtation of *Æneas* his Navy. Now called it is *Iſchia*, which ſignifieth ſtrong, in regard of the ſtrength of the Town (ſome ſay, of the form expreſſing a huckle-bone) regarding *Prochita*. Seated it is on a high craggy Rock, environed in times paſt with the Sea, though now joined to the reſt by a long paſſage of ſtone; with making (according as the wind doth ſit) on each ſide a Harbour. The Rock is almoſt ſeven furlongs about, affording but a ſteep and difficult aſcent, and that made by mans labour. The Town is ſtrengthened with Iron Gates, and guarded by *Italians*. The Marqueſs of *Vaſto* is Governour of the Caſtle and Town. There are in the Iſland eight Villages. The Inhabitants be for the moſt part poor, yet is the earth in many places not niggardly in her productions. Much more might be ſaid of this Iſland; but I now grow weary of this labour.

The next day the wind blowing favourably, we ſailed cloſe under *Cuma*; and croſſed a little beyond the mouth of *Vulturnus*; a River that riſeth in the Country of the *Samnites*, and gliding by *Capua* (but three miles diſtant from the ruines of the old) here falleth into the Sea; where ſtood a City (now to be ſeen) of that name. Between this and *Cuma*, but a little removed from the ſhore, ſtand the ruines of *Linternum*, ennobled by the Sepulchre of *Scipio Africanus*; who grieved at the ungrateful accuſations of the *Romans*, abandoned the unkind City; and retiring hither here ended his days, as a man of private condition. By this there is a Lake of that name, and nearer the ſhore a Tower, at this day called *Torre della Patria*.

A

Sinuessa. Liris.

A little proceeding, *Sinuessa* shewed us her reliques, so named of the crooked shore, but more anciently *Sinope*; and then a *Greek* Colony. Hither the Emperour *Claudius* repaired, in hope to recover his health through the temperance of the air, and virtue of the waters; but contrarily here met with the Mushroms that poisoned him. At these Baths *Tigellinus*, a beastly Boy; and a vicious old man, in chief credit with *Nero* for his luxury and cruelty, received the message of his death (then dallying with his Concubines:) which with a fearful and slow hand, in the end he accomplished. These waters are said to cure Women of their barrenness; and men of their madness, but men rather here lose their wits with too much sensuality; as women that defect by the forfeiture of their virtues; sickness being but a pretence for their gadding; of old jested at by the *Epigrammatist*.

Dicet & hystericam se forsitan altera Mœcha
In sinuessano velle federe lacu.
Quanto tu melius, &c.
*Mart.l.11.ep.*8.

Another drab to cure the Mother-fits, saith
She must go bathe in *Sinuessan* Bath:
Much plainer thou, who when thou goest to do
Such foul deeds, *Paula*, tell'st thy husband true.

Not far beyond the River *Liris* hath his Waters dis-seasoned with the Sea; who fetcheth his birth from the *Apennine*, and giveth a limit to the West of *Campania*; a beholder, and an umpier of many bloody conflicts, and oft insidious to the Traveller. *Halipsrnassus* reports, that he left his course (as that of *Vulturnus*) and ran back to his Fountain, at such time as *Aristodemus* was Tyrant of *Cuma*. There standeth a Tower at the mouth of the River bearing this Inscription:

Hanc quandam terram vastavit gens Agarepa
Scandens hunc fluvium, fieri ne postea possit.
Princeps hanc turrim Pandulphus condidit Heros,
Ut sic structori decus, & memorabile nomen.

This soil once spoil'd by *Saracens*, that past
The yielding River, to resist like waste,
Pandulphus that heroick Prince did raise
This Tower; which still renowns the builders praise.

built in the days of Pope *John* the eighth. The Lobsters of this River are commended by *Athenæus*; whereof when *Apicius* had tasted (who lived in the days of *Tiberius*) a man of great substance, and devoted only to luxury and his belly, he seated himself at *Minturnum* (a City which stood a little up the stream) that he might at all times, and more liberally feed on them. And having heard that far greater were taken upon the Coast of *Africa*, he sailed thither of pupose to make proof. But finding it otherwise, (for the *African* Fisher-men fore-knowing of his coming, whilst yet a Shipboard, had presented him with the greatest) without so much as going ashore, he returned into *Italy*. This was that *Apicius* that wrote whole Volumes of Cookery; whose luxury and end are expressed in this Epigram:

Dederas Apici bis tricenties ventri,
Sed adhuc supererat centies tibi laxum.
Hoc tu gravatus, ne famem & sitim ferres,
Summa venenum potione duxisti.
Nil est Apici, tibi gulo ut factum.
*Mart.l.3.Ep.*22.

Three thousand pounds upon his belly spent
Apicius; left five hundred to prevent
Hunger and thirst (a fear that near thee went:)
This, after that, thou didst in poison put:
Therein *Apicius* the great greedy gut.

Of the Shrimps of this River, thus speaks the same Author:

Cæruleus nos Liris amat quem silva Maricæ
Protegit; hinc squillæ maxima turba fumus.
l. 13. ep. 83.

Blue *Liris* loves us, whom *Maricas* wood
Shields from the Sun; of small shrimps a great brood.

Marica was the Wife of *Faunus*, adored in this wood, standing near the Sea by the *Minturnians*. For *Minturnum* (as hath been said) stood but a little above. It sheweth, among other ruines of sumptuous buildings, the ruines of an Aquaduct, a Theatre, an Amphitheatre, &c. In the Marishes hard by *Caius Marius*, overthrown by *Sylla*, concealed himself, when the austerity of his aspect did terrifie the Souldier that was sent to kill him; and so escaped into *Africa*.

Between this River and *Tybur*, lyeth *Latium* (of whom the *Latines*) bounded on the North with the Country of the *Sabines*; taking that name, as most Authors affirm, of *Saturnus* here hiding of himself from the pursuit of *Jupiter*; whereof a Christian Poet scoffingly:

Hither

LIB. IV.   *Liris. Latium. Formiæ.*   237

Hither, a God, I flie; the aged hide,
Depriv'd of rule by Sons outragious pride.
Here let me lurk exil'd; and to your fame,
The Land Iſle Latium, people Latines name.

Sum Deus, advenio fugiens; præbete latebras
Occultare ſenem, nati ſeritate tyranni
Delectum folio: placet hic fugitivus & exul
Ut lateam, genti atque loquo Latium dabo no-
men.   Prudent.

But rather ſo called, for that no Country of *Italy* lies ſo broad and open to the view, as doth this between the Sea and the Mountains. We croſſed the Bay of *Formiæ*, in the bottom whereof now ſtandeth a Caſtle, with a Town called *Mola*; where erſt *Formiæ* built by the *Læonians* ſtood, the recreation and delight of the *Romans*, as appeareth by many notable ruines. A little above, *Cicero* had a Villa; ſlain by *Herennius*, as his Servants bore him from thence towards the Sea in a Litter; whom he had formerly defended, when accuſed for the murder of his Father. Of *Formiæ* I cannot chuſe but inſert this (though long) commendation of *Martial*, ſince it alſo toucheth the places ſpoken, and to be ſpoken of:

O temperate Formiæ, O ſweet ſhore!
Set by Apollinar before
All Seats; when tir'd with grave affairs,
At once he quits both Rome and Cares.
Thy chaſte wives Tybur, Tuſculum,
The pleaſant vacant Algidum,
Preneſte, Antium, leß priz'd are:
Dardan Cajeta, Circe fair,
Marica, Liris, Salmacis
In Lucrine bath'd, not lik't like this,
Here mild winds breathe on Thetis face,
Not dull, but lively ſmooth; quick pace
The active air to ſwollen ſails lends:
Such, Ladies, when faint heat offends,
(So cool) with purple plumes do raiſe,
Nor for ſinn'd prey the line far ſtrays;
But fiſh it tugs from window high
Thrown; whom clear waves betray to th' eye,
When Æolus rage Nereus feels,
Storms ſlighting, they from Trencher feed
Pikes, Turbots, which ſecure Ponds breed.
The Lamprey ſwims to his Lords invites,
The Beadle the known Mullet cites,
Th' old Barbels bid i' appear do come.
When theſe joys ſhall we enjoy, O Rome!
What days in City-toils loſe we,
At Formiæ to be ſpent care-free?
O happy Hindes, this happineſs
Prepar'd for your Lords you poſſeſs!

O temperate dulce Formiæ littus,
Vos, cum ſeveri fugit oppidum Martis,
Et inquietas feſſus exuit curas,
Apollinatis omnibus locis præſert.
Non ille ſanctæ dulce Tybur uxoris,
Nec Tuſculanos Algidoſque ſeceſſus,
Præneſte nec ſic, Antiumve miratur,
Non blanda Circe, Dardaniſve Cajeta
Deſiderantur, nec Marica, nec Liris,
Nec in Lucrina lota Sarinacis vena.
Hic ſumma leni ſtringitur Thetis vento;
Nec languet æquor; viva ſed quies ponti,
Pictam phaſelon adjuvante ſert aura,
Sicut puellæ non amantis æſtatem
Multa ſalubre purpura venit frigus.
Nec ſeta longo quærit in mari prædam,
Sed à cubiculo, lectulaque jactaram
Spectatus altæ lineam trahit piſcis.
Si quando Nereus ſentit Æoli regnum,
Ridens procella tuta de ſua menſa,
Piſcina rhombum paſcit & lupos vernas,
Natat ad magiſtrum delicata muræna.
Nomenclator mugilem ſcitat notum,
Et adeſſe juſſi prodeunt ſenes Mulli.
Frui ſed iſtis quando Roma permittis?
Quot Formianos imputet dies annus,
Negotiis rebus urbis hærenti!
O vinitores, viliciquæ felices,
Dominis parantur iſta, ſerviunt vobis.

Mart. l. 10. *Epiſt.* 30.

Thorow this *Via Appia* paſſeth, of which we ſhall ſpeak hereafter. Not far from *Mola* ſtands *Cajeta*, retaining the ancient name, where, long before night, we arrived.

Cajeta ſtands on the Weſtern point of the Bay of *Mola*, and of the crookedneſs thereof was ſo called by the *Laconians* that built it, although *Virgil*;

Thou dying gav'ſt our ſhore a living name:
Æneas nurſe Cajeta. Now thy fame,
And aſhes in great Italy (if grace
That any give) retain an honour'd place.

Tu quoque littoribus noſtris Æneia nutrix
Æternam moriens famam Cajeta dediſti,
Et nunc ſervat honos ſedem tuus, oſſaque no-
men,
Heſperia in magna (ſi qua eſt ea gloria) ſignat:
Æn. l. 7.

Others will have it ſo called of the burning here of *Æneas*'s his Navy by the *Trojan* Women, tired with their tedious Navigations. It hath one only acceſs to it by Land, the reſt environed by the *Tyrrhene* Sea and the aforeſaid Bay, which encroaching upon the North-ſide, lies within the Land like an ample Lake; the Weſt-ſhore bordered almoſt with continued buildings. But the City and Caſtle lye under a high Hill, which

which thrusteth into the Sea, and is also included within the same Wall, yet hath little building thereupon; crowned with the Mausoleum of *Lucius Munatius Plancus*; though vulgarly and ignorantly called, The Tower of *Orlando*. The building is round of form, and without consists of square stone, lined within with white Marble, and receiving light only from the door. In the sides there are four Concaves where Statues have stood. The top of the Monument is adorned with Spires and Trophies; and the front presenteth this Inscription:

L. MUNATIUS L. F. L. N. L. PRON. PLANCUS. COS. CENS.
IMP. ITER. VII. ViR. EPULUM. TRIUMP. EX. CÆ-
TIS. ÆDEM. SATURNI, FECIT. DE MANUB. A-
GROS, DIVISIT. IN. ITALIA. BENEVENTI,
IN GALLIA, COLONIAS DEDUXIT;
LUDUNUM, ET RAURICAM.

The Mountain and Castle are guarded by *Spaniards*, who will not easily permit a Stranger to survey them. No sooner shall you enter the Castle, but a Coffin covered with black, set on high, presents it self to your view, with this under-written Epitaph:

Francia me dio, Iaume,	*France gave me light,*
Espannam es fuerzoy ventura,	*Spain power and might;*
Roma medio la muerte,	*Death, danted Rome,*
Caeta la sepoltura.	*Cajet a Tomb.*

containing the body of *Charles* of *Bourbon*, General of the Army of *Charles* the Fifth, and slain in the sack of *Rome*. Name we only the Trophy of *Sempronius Atracinus*, which stood without the City; pulled down to build the Front of a Temple; and the Sepulchre of *Vitruvius*, feigned to have been *Cicero's* by the *Cajetanians*: Whereupon *Alphonsus* hasting thither, caused the Monument to be freed from the over-growing Bushes, but when by the Inscription he found it to belong to the other, he said, that the *Cajetanians* had received Oyl, but not Wisdom from *Minerva*. Many ruines there are hereabout, that yet accuse the foregoing Ages of Vanity and Riot; amongst the rest those of the Palace of *Faustina* (where for the night following we took up our Lodging) in which she lived so voluptuously. Of whom *Julius Capitolinus*: Many conjecture that *Commodus* was born in adultery; considering *Faustina's* behaviour at *Cajeta*: who dishonoured her self with the familiarity of Mariners and Fencers. Whereof with *Marcus Antonius* was told, and perswaded either to kill or divorce her, he replied, *If I put away my Wife, I must restore her her Dowry*.

The next day we put again to Sea, rowing along a pleasant shore. We past by the Lake of *Fundi*, that hath a Town of that name at the furthest end, erected out of the decays of the old, sackt not long ago by the Pirate *Barbarossa*. This is the Maritime limit of the *Neapolitan* Kingdom. *Terracina* a City belonging to the Papacy, appeared to us next; so called of *Trachina*, in that seated on a cliffy Hill; and *Anxur*, of the Temple here dedicated to *Jupiter, Anxurus*, which is beardless. Of this *Horace* in his Journal:

———— atque sublimus	*And rock-built Anxur rais'd on high,*
Impositum saxis late candentibus Anxur.	*Whose brightness greets the distant eye.*
Sat. 5. *l.* 1.	

First built by the *Spartans*; who flying the severity of *Lycurgus* his Laws, here planted themselves, then a Colony of the *Volscians*, and after of the *Romans*. Near this,

———— gelidusque per imas	*Cold Ufens therow low Vallies seeks his way,*
Quærit inter valles atque in mare volvitur Ufens.	*And tribute to the Tyrrhene Sea doth pay.*
Æn. l. 7.	

Three miles below stood the City of *Feronia*, so called of

———— Viridi gaudens Feronia luco.	*Feronia (joyning in green Groves)*
Idem.	

a God-

LIB. IV. *Circæan Promontory.* 239

a Goddefs greatly adored. It is feigned, that when her adjoyning Grove was accidentally fet on fire, the Inhabitants going about to remove her Image, it fuddenly reflourifhed. Multitudes of people frequented her yearly Solemnities; where fuch as were infpired with her fury did walk upon burning coals without damage.

And now we are come to the *Circæan* Promontory:

once being an Ifland; the Marifhes not then dryed up, that divided it from the Continent. The habitation of *Circe*, who expulfed out of *Sarmatia* (where fhe had tyrannically reigned after the death of her impoyfoned Husband) here made her abode. Of this place and her, thus *Virgil*:

Next on *Circæan Coafts* they plough the floods;	Proxima Circææ raduntur littora terræ,
Where Sols rich Daughter daily chants in *Woods*	Dives inacceffos ubi Solis filia lucos
Not to b' approacht, and when Stars light affume	Affiduo refonat cantu, tectifque fuperbis
Sweet Cedar-torches her proud Roofs perfume;	Urit odoratam nocturno in lumine cedrum,
Who webs divinely weaves. Hence groans refound,	Arguto tenues percurrens pectine telas.
Chac'd Lions roar (difdaining to be bound)	Hinc exauditi gemitus, iræque Leonum
In nights whilft calm. The briftled Bore and Bear	Vincla recufantum & fera fub nocte rudentem,
Inraved rage; and monftrous Wolves howl there;	Setigerique fues, atque in præfepibus urfi
Whofe forms the Goddefs fell, by virtue ftrange	Sævire, ac formæ magnorum ululare luporum.
Of herbs, from manly did to beftial change.	Quos hominum ex facie, Dea fæva potentibus herbis
	Induerat Circe in vultus & terga ferarum.
	Æn. l. 7.

The Mountain was called *Æ&a*, of the horrors and calamities of the place. The Fable was fitted to the place, in that producing a number of Herbs and Plants of different virtues. *Circe* fignifieth no other than the Suns circumvolution, whofe heat and directer beams do quicken whatfoever is vegetable. She is faid to have been prone unto love, in that heat and moifture are the Parents of venerious defires; being alfo feigned to have been begotten by *Sol* on *Perfeis*, the Daughter of the *Ocean*, and therefore an allurer unto intemperancy; whereby fhe transformed *Ulyffes* his Mates into Beafts; (for no better are the fenfual) whom he by fprinkling them with Moly (which is temperance) an Herb hardly to be found by Mortals, reftored again unto their manly proportions. The Mountain mounteth on high, and aloft on the Eaft-fide bears the ruines of an old City called formerly *Circe*. Below it ftands the New, named St. *Felice*; and nearer the fhore a ruine, the fuppofed Tomb of *Elpenor*; one, and the worft of *Ulyffes* his Mates, who though reftored from the fhape of a Swine, betook him again to his cups, and broke his neck in his drunkennefs, here buried by him. Near this *Amafeenus* falls into the Sea;and raifeth his head from the not far diftant hills of *Setinus*; of no obscure fame for their celebrated Wines. The Marishes of *Pontania* do bound the North-side of this Promontory; on the West it hath a calm Bay, and with his Southern Basis repulseth the importunate waves, the noise whereof gave invention to the fabulous roaring of Lions, &c. Certain deep Caves there are on this side, and by Frigots to be rowed into, wherein the *Turkish* Pirates not seldom do lurk in the day time. The Mountain is set about with Watch-towers. The Goddesses detesting each other, were honoured in this place: called by an ancient Inscription here found, the Promontory of *Venus*; and in the old City *Minerva* had her Altar. *Tarquinius* here planted a Roman Colony; and to this place *Augustus* confined *Lepidus* for ever.

From hence we came to *Neptune*, where they set me ashore, and proceeded on their Voyage. The Country between this and the River *Liris* is no other than a low Marish; only here and there certain Hills look aloft, as is declared before, yet producing in divers places the most excellent of Vines, which grow up by Trees, as those of *Cæcubum*, *Fundi*, and *Setinum*. It was first drained by *Cornelius Cethegus*, and after by *Cæsar*, called formerly *Pontina*, in that ferried over in sundry places, and now *Ansente Palude*. Of this *Lucan*.

Et qua Pontinas via dividit uda paludes.   *The wet way that Pontinus sens divides.*
Lucan. l. 3.

meaning the *Appian* way, extending from *Rome* by divers circuits unto *Brundusium*: which entring the Marishes at *Forum Apii*, hard by the Hills of *Setinus*, crosses to *Terracina*; and so leading to *Formiæ*, passeth over *Liris* at *Minturna*. This was so called of *Appius Claudius*, who built it on the sides of square stone, there higher than in the middle for the benefit of foot-men; paved within with flint; and broad enough for two Carriages to pass with ease by each other. At every miles end stood a little Pillar, and every where places were made for the easier mounting on Horse-back. Adorned it was on each side with Houses and Mausoleums, which now here and there do shew their half-drowned reliques.

Neptune doth possess the sole of that ancient *Antium*; so called, for that it was the first City that stood on this shore; once the chief seat of the *Volscians*, and then powerful in shipping, although destitute of a Haven. Insomuch as when taken from them by the *Romans*, they fixed the beaks of their Ships in the *Forum* at *Rome* (called thereupon *Rostra*) where they made their Orations to the people. It stands upon a Rock, and was much frequented by the principal *Romans* for their solace, and in their retirements from the encumbrances of the City, so that it might contend with the best for magnificent Builings. In it *Fortune* had her celebrated Temple, the Patroness of the City; as speaks this invocation:

O Diva, gratum quæ regis Antium,   *Sov'reign of Antium not ingrate;*
Præsens vel imo tollere de gradu   *O Goddess, that mans mean estate*
Mortale corpus, vel superbos   *Hast power to raise, and triumphs proud*
Verrere funeribus triumphos.   *In mournful funerals to shroud.*
Hor. l. 1. Od. 35.

The steepness of the Rock gives a natural strength to the City; fortified besides with two Castles, surveying the Sea, and commanding the shore. The Buildings are old, the Inhabitants none of the civillest, subject it is to the Papacy.

About one of the clock next morning, I departed with a guide of the Town. We entred a great Wood, in the time of Paganism sacred unto *Jupiter*. Having rid thorow it before the Sun was yet an hour high, we mounted the more eminent soil, which gave us the full view of the large under-lying level. We passed then thorow a Champaign Country, rich in wines and grain, seated with variety of objects, until the parched earth resisting an immoderate and unwholsom heat, enforced us to house our selves in an Inn some fifteen miles distant from *Rome*, unto which we rid in the cool of the evening. Having stayed here four days (as long as I durst) secured by the faith and care of Mr. *Nicholas Fitz-Herbert*, who accompanied me in the surveying of all the Antiquities and Glories of that City, I departed to *Siena*, and having seen *Florence*, *Bolonia*, and *Ferrara*, imbarked on the *Po*, and so returned unto *Venice*.

Finis Libri quarti & ultimi.

www.ingramcontent.com/pod-product-compliance
Lightning Source LLC
Chambersburg PA
CBHW020803230426
43666CB00007B/838